complete **baking**

martha day

complete **baking**

with over 400 recipes for pies, tarts, buns,
muffins, breads, cookies and cakes

Published by World Publications Group, Inc.
140 Laurel Street
East Bridgewater, MA 02333
www.wrldpub.net

Produced by Anness Publishing Ltd
Hermes House
88–89 Blackfriars Road
London SE1 8HA
tel. 020 7401 2077; fax 020 7633 9499

www.annesspublishing.com

If you like the images in this book and would like to investigate using them for publishing, promotions or advertising, please visit our website www.practicalpictures.com for more information.

Publisher: Joanna Lorenz
Project Editor: Felicity Forster
Text: Carole Clements
Designer: Sheila Volpe
Photography, Styling: Amanda Heywood
Food Styling: Elizabeth Wolf-Cohen, Carla Capalbo,
steps by Cara Hobday, Teresa Goldfinch, Nicola Fowler
Additional Recipes: Carla Capalbo and Laura Washburn,
Frances Cleary, Norma MacMillan
Illustrations: Anna Koska
Index: Dawn Butcher
Editorial Reader: Marion Wilson

ISBN-10: 1-57215-584-1
ISBN-13: 978-1-57215-584-8

Printed and bound in China

ETHICAL TRADING POLICY

Because of our ongoing ecological investment programme, you, as our customer, can have the pleasure and reassurance of knowing that a tree is being cultivated on your behalf to naturally replace the materials used to make the book you are holding. For further information about this scheme, go to www.annesspublishing.com/trees

PUBLISHER'S NOTE

Although the advice and information in this book are believed to be accurate and true at the time of going to press, neither the authors nor the publisher can accept any legal responsibility or liability for any errors or omissions that may be made nor for any inaccuracies nor for any harm or injury that comes about from following instructions or advice in this book.

Previously published as *The Practical Encyclopedia of Baking*

NOTES

Bracketed terms are intended for American readers.
For all recipes, quantities are given in both metric and imperial measures and, where appropriate, in standard cups and spoons. Follow one set, but not a mixture, because they are not interchangeable.
Standard spoon and cup measures are level. 1 tsp = 5ml, 1 tbsp = 15ml, 1 cup = 250ml/8fl oz.
Australian standard tablespoons are 20ml. Australian readers should use 3 tsp in place of 1 tbsp for measuring small quantities of gelatine, flour, salt, etc.
American pints are 16fl oz/2 cups. American readers should use 20fl oz/2.5 cups in place of 1 pint when measuring liquids.
Medium (US large) eggs are used unless otherwise stated.

CONTENTS

INTRODUCTION

Nothing equals the satisfaction of home baking. No commercial cake mix or shop-bought biscuit can match one that is made from the best fresh ingredients with all the added enjoyment that baking at home provides – the enticing aromas that fill the house and stimulate appetites, the delicious straight-from-the-oven flavour, as well as the pride of having created such wonderful goodies yourself.

This book is filled with familiar favourites as well as many other lesser known recipes. Explore the wealth of biscuits, buns, tea breads, yeast breads, pies, tarts, and cakes within these pages. Even if you are a novice baker, the easy-to-follow and clear step-by-step photographs will help you achieve good results. For the more experienced home baker, this book will provide some new recipes to add to your repertoire.

Baking is an exact science and needs to be approached in an ordered way. First read through the recipe from beginning to end. Set out all the required ingredients before you begin. Medium eggs are assumed unless specified otherwise, and they should be at room temperature for best results. Sift the flour after you have measured it, and incorporate other dry ingredients as specified in the individual recipes. If you sift the flour from a fair height, it will have more chance to aerate and lighten.

When a recipe calls for folding one ingredient into another, it should be done in a way that incorporates as much air as possible into the mixture. Use either a large metal spoon or a long rubber or plastic scraper. Gently plunge the spoon or scraper deep into the centre of the mixture and, scooping up a large amount of the mixture, fold it over. Turn the bowl slightly so each scoop folds over another part of the mixture.

No two ovens are alike. Buy a reliable oven thermometer and test the temperature of your oven. When possible bake in the centre of the oven where the heat is more likely to be constant. If using a fan-assisted oven, follow the manufacturer's guidelines for baking. Good quality baking tins can improve your results, as they conduct heat more efficiently.

Practice, patience and enthusiasm are the keys to confident and successful baking. The recipes that follow will inspire you to start sifting flour, breaking eggs and stirring up all sorts of delectable homemade treats – all guaranteed to bring great satisfaction to both the baker and those lucky enough to enjoy the results.

INGREDIENTS, EQUIPMENT & TECHNIQUES

KEEPING YOUR KITCHEN STOCKED
WITH THE RIGHT INGREDIENTS
AND EQUIPMENT, AS WELL AS
MASTERING THESE BASIC
TECHNIQUES, WILL ENSURE
BAKING SUCCESS EVERY TIME.

BAKING INGREDIENTS

This guide highlights a few of the most essential items that every baker should keep in their store cupboard and fridge.

BUTTER AND MARGARINE

Butter gives the best flavour for baking and should be used whenever possible, especially when there is a high fat content, as in shortbread.

Butter needs to be at room temperature before being used. It is usually either melted or diced before being worked into the other ingredients to make a batter. This is then beaten by hand or in an electric mixer. For some bread recipes, the butter is kneaded into the dough after the initial rising, since larger quantities of butter can inhibit the action of the yeast.

For a low-fat alternative to butter, try polyunsaturated margarine instead. Low-fat spreads are ideal for spreading on breads and tea breads, but are unfortunately not suitable for baking because they have a high water content.

EGGS

Eggs are a staple ingredient in most baking recipes. They should be stored and used at room temperature, so if you keep them in the fridge, remove the number you want at least 30 minutes before making a recipe.

Above: Properly fed hens lay the best and tastiest eggs.

Above: There are many different types of flour, each with different properties, so make sure you select the one that is best for your recipe.

FLOURS

Mass-produced, highly refined flours are fine for most baking purposes, but for the very best results choose organic stone-ground flours because they will add flavour as well as texture to your baking.

Strong flour

Made from hard wheat which contains a high proportion of gluten, this flour is the one to use for bread-making.

Soft flour

This flour, sometimes called sponge flour, contains less gluten than plain flour and is ideal for light cakes and biscuits.

Wholemeal flour

Because this flour contains the complete wheat kernel, it gives a coarser texture and a good wholesome flavour to bread.

Rye flour

This dark-coloured flour has a low gluten content and gives a dense loaf with a good flavour. It is best mixed with strong wheat flour to give a lighter loaf.

SWEETENERS

Sugars

Most baking recipes call for sugar. Granulated sugar is the best sweetener to use for the creaming method because the crystals dissolve easily and quickly when creamed with the fat. Granulated sugar can also be used for rubbed-in mixtures and when the sugar is heated with the fat or liquid until it dissolves.

Demerara sugar can be used when the sugar is dissolved over heat before being added to the dry ingredients. Soft light and dark brown sugars are used when a richer flavour and colour are called for.

Raw sugar is unrefined sugar which is uncoloured and pure – it also has more flavour than refined sugars, and contains some minerals.

Fruit juice

Concentrated fruit juices are very useful for baking. They have no added sweeteners or preservatives and can be diluted as required. Use them in their concentrated form for baking or for sweetening fillings.

Pear and apple spread

This is a very concentrated fruit juice spread with no added sugar. It has a

Above: Fruits add natural sweetness to baked goods.

sweet-sour taste and can be used as a spread or blended with fruit juice and added to baking recipes as a sweetener.

Dried fruits

These are a traditional addition to cakes and tea breads and there is a very wide range available, including more unusual varieties such as peach, pineapple, banana, mango and pawpaw. The natural sugars add sweetness to baked goods and keep them moist, making it possible to use less fat.

Chop and add dried fruits to breads by hand rather than putting them in an electric mixer or food processor, as the blades will blend the fruit and spoil the appearance and flavour of the loaf.

Honey

Good honey has a strong flavour so you can use less of it than the equivalent amount of sugar. It also contains traces of minerals and vitamins.

Malt extract

This is a sugary by-product of barley. It has a strong flavour and is good to use in bread, cakes and tea breads as it adds a moistness of its own.

Molasses

This is the residue left after the first stage of refining sugar cane. It has a strong, smoky and slightly bitter taste which gives a good flavour to cakes and bakes. Black treacle can often be used as a substitute for molasses.

MILK

Tea breads, sweet breads and cakes are often made with milk, whereas savoury loaves tend to be made using water. Breads made with milk are softer both in the crumb and the crust than those using water.

There are many low-fat alternatives to milk: skimmed milk and semi-skimmed milk have a much lower fat content than milk, and they don't taste as rich as whole milk.

HERBS AND SPICES

Chopped fresh herbs add a great deal of interest to baking. They add flavour to breads, scones and soda breads. In the absence of fresh herbs, dried herbs can be used; less is needed but the flavour is generally not as good.

Spices can add either strong or subtle flavours depending on the amount and variety used. The most commonly used sweet spices for baking are cinnamon, nutmeg, cloves and ginger, and the savoury spices are cumin, fennel, caraway and anise. Mace, pepper and coriander seeds can be used for both sweet and savoury bakes. Spices can be added with the flour or kneaded in with other ingredients.

SALT

Many baking recipes add salt at the beginning, stirring or sifting it into the flour. Salt is one of the few essential ingredients in bread-making, both for flavour and for the effect it has on the yeast and dough.

Above: Check that your store-cupboard supplies are kept fresh and plentiful, and stock up on the ingredients you use most often.

BAKING EQUIPMENT

Baking sheet
Choose a large, heavy baking sheet that will not warp at high temperatures.

Cake boards
Silver cake boards are perfect for presenting finished cakes. They come in a variety of shapes and sizes, in circles, squares and rectangles.

Cake tester
A simple implement that, when inserted into a cooked cake, will come out clean if the cake is ready.

Cook's knife
This has a heavy, wide blade and is ideal for chopping.

Deep round cake tin
A deep tin is useful for baking fruit cakes.

Electric whisk
Perfect for whisking egg whites and incorporating air into light mixtures.

Honey twirl
For spooning honey without making a mess!

Icing smoother
This will give a wonderfully uniform finish to fondant-covered cakes.

Juicer
Used for squeezing the juice from citrus fruits.

Loaf tin
Available in various sizes and used for making loaf-shaped breads and tea breads.

Measuring jug
Absolutely essential for measuring any kind of liquid accurately.

Measuring spoons
Standard measuring spoons are essential for measuring small quantities.

Mixing bowls
A set of different-sized mixing bowls is essential in any kitchen for whisking and mixing.

Non-stick baking paper
For lining tins and baking sheets to ensure that cakes, meringues and biscuits do not stick.

Nylon sieve
Suitable for most baking purposes, and particularly for sieving foods that react adversely with metal.

Palette knives
These are used for loosening pies, tarts and breads from baking sheets and for smoothing icing over cakes.

Pastry brush
Useful for brushing excess flour from pastry and brushing glazes over pastries, breads and tarts.

Pastry cutters
A variety of shapes and sizes of cutter is useful when stamping out pastry, biscuit and scone doughs.

Plastic chopping board
Use this as a smooth, flat surface for cutting or rolling ingredients.

Plastic scrapers
These can be used to create all sorts of "combing" patterns in butter icing.

Rectangular cake tin
For making tray cakes and other bakes served cut into slices.

Ring mould
Perfect for making angel cakes and other ring-shaped cakes.

Rolling pin
Use a heavy rolling pin for rolling out dough, marzipan and fondant.

Sable paint brushes
These are expensive, but are well worth the extra cost when painting fine details on to cakes.

Serrated knives
Sharp knives are essential for cutting fruit and vegetables, and those with a serrated edge will allow you to cut cakes without them breaking into pieces.

Square cake tin
Used for making square cakes or cakes served cut into smaller squares.

Vegetable knife
A useful knife for preparing fruit and vegetables for your bakes.

Weighing scales
These are essential for accuracy when weighing ingredients for baking.

Wooden cocktail sticks
These can be used to make designs on cakes, or to support pieces of cake to make a particular shape. Always remove them before serving.

Wooden spoons
Essential for mixing ingredients for baking and for creaming mixtures. These are available in a wide variety of sizes.

Above: To be able to bake efficiently and with pleasure, you need good equipment. That is not to say that you should invest in an extensive and expensive collection of tins, tools and gadgets, but a basic range is essential. In addition, buy the best equipment you can afford, adding more as your budget allows. Well-made equipment lasts and is a sound investment; inexpensive tins are likely to dent or break.

BAKING TECHNIQUES

Baking your own muffins and breads is easy and satisfying, even if you're a beginner. Just follow the recipes and the tips, hints, and step-by-step techniques and you'll get perfect results every time.

1 ▲ For liquids measured in jugs: Use a glass or clear plastic measuring jug. Put the jug on a flat surface and pour in the liquid. Bend down and check that the liquid is exactly level with the marking on the jug, as specified in the recipe.

2 ▲ For measuring dry ingredients in a spoon: Fill the spoon with the ingredient. Level the surface even with the rim of the spoon, using the straight edge of a knife.

3 ▲ For liquids measured in spoons: Pour the liquid into the measuring spoon, to the brim, and then pour it into the mixing bowl.

4 ▲ For measuring flour in a cup or spoon: Scoop the flour from the canister in the measuring cup or spoon. Hold it over the canister and level the surface.

5 ▲ For measuring butter: Cut with a sharp knife and weigh, or cut off the specified amount following the markings on the wrapping paper.

6 ▲ For rectangular and square cake tins: Fold the paper and crease it with your fingernail to fit snugly into the corners of the tin. Then press the bottom paper lining into place.

7 ▲ To line muffin tins: Use paper cases of the required size. Or grease and flour the tins.

Making Scones

Scone dough may be rolled out and cut into shapes for baking in the oven or cooking on a griddle. To ensure light, well risen scones, do not handle the dough too much and do not roll it out too thinly.

Drop scones are made from a batter that has the consistency of thick cream. The batter is dropped in spoonfuls on to a hot griddle or frying pan.

1 Sift the dry ingredients into a bowl (flour, baking powder with or without bicarbonate of soda, salt, sugar, ground spices, etc).

2 ▲ Add the fat (butter, margarine, vegetable fat, etc). With a pastry blender or two knives used scissor-fashion, cut the fat into the dry ingredients until the mixture resembles fine crumbs, or rub in the fat with your fingertips.

3 ▲ Add the liquid ingredients (milk, cream, buttermilk, eggs). Stir with a fork until the dry ingredients are thoroughly moistened and will come together in a ball of fairly soft dough in the centre of the bowl.

Date Oven Scones
Sift 8 oz (225 g) self-raising flour with a pinch of salt and rub in 2 oz (55 g) butter. Add 2 oz (55 g) chopped dates. Mix to a soft dough with ¼ pint (150 ml) milk. Roll out and cut 2 in (5 cm) rounds. Glaze with egg or milk. Bake at 450°F/230°C/Gas 8 for 8–10 minutes or until risen and golden brown. *Makes about 12.*

4 ▲ Turn the dough on to a lightly floured surface. Knead it very lightly, folding and pressing, to mix evenly – about 30 seconds. Roll or pat out the dough to ¾ in (2 cm) thickness.

6 ▲ **For griddle scones:** If using a well-seasoned cast iron griddle, there is no need to grease it. Heat it slowly and evenly. Put scone triangles or rounds on the hot griddle and cook for 4–5 minutes on each side or until golden brown and cooked through.

5 ▲ **For oven-baked scones:** With a floured, sharp-edged cutter, cut out rounds or other shapes. Or cut diamond shapes or triangles with a floured knife. Arrange on an ungreased baking sheet, not touching. Brush the tops with beaten egg, milk or cream if the recipe specifies. Bake until risen and golden brown.

Cutting tips
● Be sure the cutter or knife is sharp so that the edges of the scone shapes are not compressed; this would inhibit rising.
● Cut the shapes close together so that you won't have to reroll the dough more than once.
● If necessary, a short, sturdy drinking glass can be pressed into service as a cutter. Flour the rim well and do not press too hard.

MAKING TEABREADS AND MUFFINS

These sorts of bread are very quick and easy to make. The raising agent reacts quickly with moisture and heat to make the breads and muffins rise, without the need for a rising (or proving) period before baking.

The raising agent is usually bicarbonate of soda or baking powder, which is a mixture of bicarbonate of soda and an acid salt such as cream of tartar. Many recipes use self-raising flour which conveniently includes a raising agent. Remember that the raising agent will start to work as soon as it comes into contact with liquid, so don't mix the dry and liquid ingredients until just before you are ready to fill the tin or tins and bake.

1 ▲ **For muffins:** Combine the dry ingredients in a bowl. It is a good idea to sift the flour with the raising agent, salt and any spices to mix them evenly. Add the liquid ingredients and stir just until the dry ingredients are moistened; the mixture will not be smooth. Do not overmix attempting to remove all the lumps. If you do, the muffins will be tough and will have air holes in them.

2 ▲ Divide the mixture evenly among the greased muffin tins or deep bun tins lined with paper cases, filling them about two-thirds full. Bake until golden brown and a wooden skewer inserted in the centre comes out clean. To prevent soggy bottoms, remove the muffins immediately from the tins to a wire rack. Cool, and serve warm or at room temperature.

Crunchy Muesli Muffins
Make the mixture from 5 oz (145 g) plain flour, 2½ teaspoons baking powder, 2 tablespoons caster sugar, 8 fl oz (240 ml) milk, 2 oz (55 g) melted butter or corn oil, and 1 egg, adding 7 oz (200 g) toasted oat cereal with raisins to the dry ingredients. Pour into muffin tins or deep bun tins. Bake in a 200°C/400°F/Gas 6 oven for 20 minutes or until golden brown. *Makes 10*.

3 ▲ **For fruit and/or nut teabreads:** Method 1: Stir together all the liquid ingredients. Add the dry ingredients and beat just until smoothly blended. Method 2: Beat the butter with the sugar until the mixture is light and fluffy. Beat in the eggs followed by the other liquid ingredients. Stir in the dry ingredients. Pour the mixture into a prepared tin (typically a loaf tin). Bake until a wooden skewer inserted in the centre comes out clean. If the bread is browning too quickly, cover the top with foil.

4 ▲ Cool in the tin for 5 minutes, then turn out on to a wire rack to cool completely. A lengthways crack on the surface is characteristic of teabreads. For easier slicing, wrap the bread in greaseproof paper and overwrap in foil, then store overnight at room temperature.

MAKING SIMPLE MERINGUE

There are two types of this egg white and sugar foam: a soft meringue used as an insulating topping for pies and baked Alaska and a firm meringue that can be shaped into containers for luscious fillings.

Take care when separating the egg whites and yolks because even the smallest trace of yolk will prevent the whites from being whisked to their maximum volume. All equipment must be scrupulously clean and free of grease.

1 ▲ Put the egg whites in a large, scrupulously clean and grease-free bowl. With a whisk or electric mixer, whisk the whites until they are foamy. If not using a copper bowl, add a pinch of cream of tartar.

2 ▲ Continue whisking until the whites hold soft peaks when you lift the whisk or beaters (the tips of the peaks will flop over).

Meringue Nests
Make a firm meringue using 2 egg whites and 4 oz (115 g) caster sugar. Scoop large spoonfuls of meringue on to a baking sheet lined with baking parchment. Slightly hollow out the centre of each with the back of the spoon, to make a nest shape. Alternatively, put the meringue into a piping bag fitted with a ½ in (1.5 cm) plain nozzle and pipe the nest shapes. Sprinkle lightly with a little extra sugar. Dry in a 200°F/100°C/Gas low oven for 3–4 hours or until crisp and firm but not brown. Leave to cool. To serve, fill with sweetened whipped cream and fresh fruit. *Makes 4–6.*

3 ▲ **For a soft meringue:** Sprinkle the sugar over the whites, whisking constantly. Continue whisking for about 1 minute or until the meringue is glossy and holds stiff peaks when you lift the whisk or beaters. The meringue is now ready to be spread on a pie filling or used for baked Alaska.

Sweetened whipped cream
This is used as a topping and filling for many hot and cold desserts. Whip ½ pint (300 ml) chilled whipping or double cream until it starts to thicken. Add 2 tablespoons sifted icing sugar and continue whipping until the cream holds a soft peak on the beaters. If liked, the cream may be flavoured with ½ teaspoon vanilla or almond essence or 2 teaspoons brandy or liqueur, added with the sugar.

4 ▲ **For a firm meringue:** Add a little of the sugar (about 1½ teaspoons for each egg white). Continue whisking until the meringue is glossy and will hold stiff peaks.

5 ▲ Add the remaining sugar to the bowl, with any flavouring the recipe specifies. With a rubber spatula, fold the sugar into the meringue as lightly as possible by cutting down with the spatula to the bottom of the bowl and then turning the mixture over. The meringue is now ready to be shaped into containers or gâteau layers.

MAKING SHORTCRUST PASTRY

A meltingly short, crumbly pastry sets off any filling to perfection, whether sweet or savoury. The pastry dough can be made with half butter or margarine and half white vegetable fat or with all one kind of fat.

FOR A 9 IN (23 CM) PASTRY CASE

8 oz (225 g) plain flour

¼ teaspoon salt

4 oz (115 g) fat, chilled and diced

3–4 tablespoons iced water

1 ▲ Sift the flour and salt into a bowl. Add the fat. Rub it into the flour with your fingertips until the mixture is crumb-like.

2 ▲ Sprinkle 3 tablespoons water over the mixture. With a fork, toss gently to mix and moisten it.

Pastry making tips

● It helps if the fat is cold and firm, particularly if making the dough in a food processor. Cold fat has less chance of warming and softening too much when it is being rubbed into the flour, resulting in an oily pastry. Use block margarine rather than the soft tub-type.

● When rubbing the fat into the flour, if it begins to soften and feel oily, put the bowl in the refrigerator to chill for 20–30 minutes. Then continue making the dough.

● Liquids used should be ice-cold so that they will not soften or melt the fat.

● Take care when adding the water: start with the smaller amount (added all at once, not in a dribble), and add more only if the mixture will not come together into a dough. Too much water will result in tough pastry.

● When gathering the mixture together into a ball of dough, handle it as little as possible: over-worked pastry will be tough.

● To avoid shrinkage, refrigerate the pastry dough before rolling out and baking. This 'resting time' will allow any elasticity developed during mixing to relax.

4 ▲ Press the dough into a ball. If it is too dry to form a dough, add the remaining water.

7 ▲ **To make pastry in a food processor:** Combine the flour, salt and cubed fat in the work bowl. Process, turning the machine on and off, just until the mixture is crumbly. Add the iced water and process again briefly – just until the dough starts to pull away from the sides of the bowl. It should still look crumbly. Remove the dough from the processor and gather it into a ball. Wrap and refrigerate.

5 ▲ Wrap the ball of dough with cling film or greaseproof paper and refrigerate it for at least 30 minutes.

Shortcrust pastry variations

● For *Nut Shortcrust:* Add 1 oz (30 g) finely chopped walnuts or pecan nuts to the flour mixture.

● For *Rich Shortcrust:* Use 8 oz (225 g) flour and 6 oz (170 g) fat (preferably all butter), plus 1 tablespoon caster sugar if making a sweet pie. Bind with 1 egg yolk and 2–3 tablespoons water.

● For a *Two-crust Pie*, increase the proportions for these pastries by 50%, thus the amounts needed for basic shortcrust pastry are: 12 oz (340 g) flour, ½ teaspoon salt, 6 oz (170 g) fat, 5–6 tablespoons water. For Nut Shortcrust, as above with 2 oz (55 g) nuts. For Rich Shortcrust, as above but using 9 oz (260 g) fat, 4–5 tablespoons water and 1 egg yolk.

Making French Flan Pastry

The pastry for tarts, flans and quiches is made with butter or margarine, giving a rich and crumbly result. The more fat used, the richer the pastry will be – almost like a biscuit dough – and the harder to roll out. If you have difficulty rolling it, you can press it into the tin instead, or roll it out between sheets of cling film. Flan pastry, like shortcrust, can be made by hand or in a food processor. Tips for making, handling and using shortcrust pastry apply equally to French flan pastry.

For a 9 in (23 cm) flan case
7 oz (200 g) plain flour
½ teaspoon salt
4 oz (115 g) butter or margarine, chilled
1 egg yolk
¼ teaspoon lemon juice
2–3 tablespoons iced water

1 ▲ Sift the flour and salt into a bowl. Add the butter or margarine. Rub into the flour until the mixture resembles fine crumbs.

2 ▲ In a small bowl, mix the egg yolk, lemon juice and 2 tablespoons water. Add to the flour mixture. With a fork, toss gently to mix and moisten.

3 ▲ Press the dough into a rough ball. If it is too dry to come together, add the remaining water. Turn on to the work surface or a pastry board.

4 ▲ With the heel of your hand, push small portions of dough away from you, smearing them on the surface.

Flan pastry variations

● For *Sweet Flan Pastry:* Reduce the amount of salt to ¼ teaspoon; add 1 tablespoon caster sugar with the flour.

● For *Rich Flan Pastry:* Use 7 oz (200 g) flour, ½ teaspoon salt, 5 oz (145 g) butter, 2 egg yolks, and 1–2 tablespoons water.

● For *Rich Sweet Flan Pastry:* Make rich flan pastry, adding 3 tablespoons caster sugar with the flour and, if liked, ½ teaspoon vanilla essence with the egg yolks.

5 ▲ Continue mixing the dough in this way until it feels pliable and can be peeled easily off the surface.

6 ▲ Press the dough into a smooth ball. Wrap in cling film and chill for at least 30 minutes.

ROLLING OUT AND LINING A TIN

A neat pastry case that doesn't distort or shrink in baking is the desired result. The key to success is handling the dough gently. Use the method here for lining a round pie or tart tin that is about 2 in (5 cm) deep.

Remove the chilled dough from the refrigerator and allow it to soften slightly at room temperature. Unwrap and put it on a lightly floured surface. Flatten the dough into a neat, round disc. Lightly flour the rolling pin.

Rolling out and lining tips
- Reflour the surface and rolling pin if the dough starts to stick.
- Should the dough tear, patch with a piece of moistened dough.
- When rolling out and lining the pie or tart tin, do not stretch the dough. It will only shrink back during baking, spoiling the shape of the pastry case.
- Once or twice during rolling out, gently push in the edges of the dough with your cupped palms, to keep the circular shape.
- A pastry scraper will help lift the dough from the work surface, to wrap it around the rolling pin.
- Tins made from heat-resistant glass or dull-finish metal such as heavyweight aluminium will give a crisp crust.
- When finishing the edge, be sure to hook the dough over the rim all the way round or to press the dough firmly to the rim. This will prevent the dough pulling away should it start to shrink.
- If covering a pie dish, roll the dough to a round or oval 2 in (5 cm) larger than the dish. Cut a 1 in (2.5 cm) strip from the outside and lay this on the moistened rim of the dish. Brush the strip with water and lay the sheet of dough on top. Press edges to seal, then trim even with the rim. Knock up the edge with a knife.

1 ▲ Using even pressure, start rolling out the dough, working from the centre to the edge each time and easing the pressure slightly as you reach the edge.

2 ▲ Lift up the dough and give it a quarter turn from time to time during the rolling. This will prevent the dough sticking to the surface, and will help keep the thickness even.

3 ▲ Continue rolling out until the dough circle is about 2 in (5 cm) larger all round than the tin. The dough will be about ⅛ in (3 mm) thick.

4 ▲ Set the rolling pin on the dough, near one side of the circle. Fold the outside edge of dough over the pin, then roll the pin over the dough to wrap the dough round it. Do this gently and loosely.

5 ▲ Hold the pin over the tin and gently unroll the dough so it drapes into the tin, centring it as much as possible.

6 ▲ With your fingertips, lift and ease the dough into the tin, gently pressing it over the bottom and up the side. Turn excess dough over the rim and trim it with a knife or scissors, depending on the edge to be made.

LINING A FLAN TIN OR RING

A flan tin is shallow, with no rim. Its straight sides (smooth or fluted) give a tart or flan the traditional shape. The most useful tins have removable bases, making it very easy to turn out a tart. Flan rings are straight-sided metal rings that are set on a baking sheet.

In addition to flan tins and rings, there are porcelain quiche dishes and small, individual tartlet tins, both plain and fluted.

Pecan Nut Tartlets

Line six 4 in (10 cm) tartlet tins with flan pastry. Place 1 oz (30 g) pecan nut halves in each. In a bowl, beat 3 eggs to mix. Add 1 oz (30 g) melted butter, 10 oz (300 g) golden syrup and ½ teaspoon vanilla essence. Sift together 4 oz (115 g) caster sugar and 1 tablespoon plain flour. Add to the egg mixture and stir until evenly blended. Fill the tartlet cases and leave until the nuts rise to the surface. Bake in a 350°F/180°C/Gas 4 oven for 35–40 minutes or until a knife inserted near the centre comes out clean. Cool in the tins for 15 minutes, then turn on to a wire rack.

1 ▲ Remove the chilled dough from the refrigerator and let it soften slightly at room temperature. Roll out to a circle about 2 in (5 cm) larger all round than the tin or ring. It will be about ⅛ in (3 mm) thick.

3 ▲ With your fingertips, ease the dough into the tin or ring, gently pressing it smoothly over the bottom, without stretching it.

5 ▲ Roll the rolling pin over the top of the tin or ring to cut off excess dough. Smooth the cut edge and press it against the side of the tin or ring, if necessary, to keep it in place.

2 ▲ Roll up the dough round the rolling pin, then unroll it over the tin or ring, draping it gently.

4 ▲ Fold the overhanging dough down inside the tin or ring, to thicken the side of the pastry case. Smooth and press the side of the case against the side of the tin or ring.

6 ▲ For tartlet tins: Arrange them close together and unroll the dough over them, draping it loosely. Roll the rolling pin over the top to cut off excess pastry. Press into the bottom and sides of the tins.

FINISHING THE EDGE

1 ▲ **For a forked edge:** Trim the dough even with the rim and press it flat. Firmly and evenly press the prongs of a fork all round the edge. If the fork sticks, dip it in flour.

2 ▲ **For a crimped edge:** Trim the dough to leave an overhang of about ½ in (1.5 cm) all round. Fold the extra dough under. Put the knuckle or tip of the index finger of one of your hands inside the edge, pointing directly out. With the thumb and index finger of your other hand, pinch the dough edge around your index finger into a 'V' shape. Continue all round the edge.

3 ▲ **For a ruffled edge:** Trim the dough to leave an overhang of about ½ in (1.5 cm) all round. Fold the extra dough under. Hold the thumb and index finger of one of your hands about 1 in (2.5 cm) apart, inside the edge, pointing directly out. With the index finger of your other hand, gently pull the dough between them, to the end of the rim. Continue all the way round the edge.

Apple and Cherry Crumble Pie
Mix together 12 oz (340 g) peeled, cored and sliced Granny Smith apples, 10 oz (300 g) stoned cherries and 4 oz (115 g) soft light brown sugar. Put into a 9 in (23 cm) pastry case. For the topping, combine 4 oz (115 g) plain flour, 4 oz (115 g) soft light brown sugar and 1 teaspoon ground cinnamon. Rub in 3 oz (85 g) butter until the mixture resembles coarse crumbs. Sprinkle over the fruit. Bake in a 375°F/190°C/Gas 5 oven for about 45 minutes or until golden. *Serves 6.*

4 ▲ **For a cutout edge:** Trim the dough even with the rim and press it flat on the rim. With a small pastry cutter, cut out decorative shapes from the dough trimmings. Moisten the edge of the pastry case and press the cutouts in place, overlapping them slightly if you like.

5 ▲ **For a ribbon edge:** Trim the dough even with the rim and press it flat on the rim. Cut long strips about ¾ in (2 cm) wide from the dough trimmings. Moisten the edge and press one end of a strip on to it. Twist the strip gently and press it on to the edge again. Continue all the way round the edge.

BAKING BLIND

Baked custard and cream fillings can make pastry soggy, so the cases for these flans and tarts are often given an initial baking before the filling is added and the final baking is done. Such pre-baking is referred to as baking 'blind'. The technique is also used for pastry cases that are to be filled with an uncooked or precooked mixture.

The purpose of using weights is to prevent the bottom of the pastry case from rising too much and becoming distorted, thus keeping its neat shape.

Fresh Strawberry Flan
Make the case using sweet flan pastry or rich sweet flan pastry. Bake it blind fully, then cool. Beat 14 oz (400 g) full-fat soft cheese with 1 ¾ oz (50 g) caster sugar, 1 egg yolk and 4 tablespoons whipping cream until smooth. Fold in 1 stiffly whisked egg white. Pour into the case and spread evenly. Bake at 350°F/180°C/Gas 4 for 15–20 minutes or until the filling is softly set; it will set further as it cools. When cool, arrange halved strawberries on top in concentric circles. Melt 5oz (145 g) redcurrant jelly and brush over the berries to glaze them. Leave the flan to cool before serving. *Serves* 6.

1 ▲ Set the pie or flan tin, or flan ring, on a sheet of greaseproof paper or foil. Draw or mark around its base. Cut out a circle about 3 in (7.5 cm) larger all round than the drawn or marked one.

3 ▲ Lay the circle of greaseproof paper or foil in the pastry case and press it smoothly over the bottom and up the side.

5 ▲ **For partially baked pastry:** Bake the case in a 400°F/200°C/Gas 6 oven for 15–20 minutes or until it is slightly dry and set. Remove the paper or foil and beans. The pastry is now ready to be filled and baked further.

2 ▲ Roll out the pastry dough and use to line the tin or ring set on a baking sheet. Prick the bottom of the pastry case all over with a fork.

4 ▲ Put enough dried beans or baking beans in the case to cover the bottom thickly.

6 ▲ **For fully baked pastry:** After baking for 15 minutes, remove the paper or foil and beans. Prick the bottom again with a fork. Return to the oven and bake for 5–10 minutes or until golden brown. Cool completely before adding the filling.

MAKING A TWO-CRUST PIE

Two succulent pastry layers enveloping a sweet filling – what could be nicer? Use the same method for making small pies, such as mince pices.

American-style Apple Pie
Combine 2 lb (900 g) peeled, cored and thinly sliced Granny Smith apples, 1 tablespoon plain flour, 3½ oz (100 g) caster sugar and ¾ teaspoon mixed spice. Toss to coat the fruit evenly with the sugar and flour. Use to fill the two-crust pie. Bake in a 375°F/190°C/ Gas 5 oven for about 45 minutes or until the pastry is golden brown and the fruit is tender (test with a skewer through a slit in the top crust). Cool on a rack.

1 ▲ Roll out half of the pastry dough on a floured surface and line a pie tin that is about 2 in (5 cm) deep. Trim the dough even with the rim.

2 ▲ Put in the filling. Brush the edge of the pastry case evenly with water to moisten it.

3 ▲ Roll out a second piece of dough to a circle that is about 1 in (2.5 cm) larger all round than the tin. Roll it up around the rolling pin and unroll over the pie. Press the edges together.

4 ▲ Trim the edge of the lid to leave a ½ in (1.5 cm) overhang. Cut slits or a design in the centre. These will act as steam vents during baking.

5 ▲ Fold the overhang of the lid under the edge of the case. Press the two together gently and evenly to seal. Finish the edge as wished.

6 ▲ Brush the top of the pie with milk or cream for a shiny finish. Or brush with 1 egg yolk mixed with 1 teaspoon water for a glazed golden brown finish. Or brush with water and then sprinkle with caster sugar or cinnamon and sugar for a sugary crust.

7 ▲ If you like, cut out decorative shapes from the dough trimmings, rolled out as thinly as possible. Moisten the cutouts with a little water and press them on to the top. Glaze the decorations before baking.

MAKING A LATTICE TOP

A woven pastry lattice is a very attractive finish for a pie. Prepare shortcrust for a two-crust pie.

Roll out half of the pastry dough and line the pie tin. Trim the dough to leave a ½ in (1.5 cm) overhang all round. Put in the filling. Roll out the second piece of dough into a circle that is about 2 in (5 cm) larger all round than the pie tin.

Apricot Lattice Pie
Toss together 2¼ lb (1 kg) peeled, stoned and thinly sliced apricots, 2 tablespoons plain flour and 3½ oz (100 g) sugar. Fill the pastry case and make a lattice top. Glaze with milk and bake in a 375°F/190°C/Gas 5 oven for about 45 minutes or until the pastry is golden and the filling is bubbling. Cool on a wire rack.

1 ▲ With the help of a ruler, cut neat straight strips of dough that are about ½ in (1.5 cm) wide, using a knife or fluted pastry wheel.

3 ▲ Fold back every other strip from the centre. Lay another strip across the centre, on the flat strips, at right angles to them. Lay the folded strips flat again.

5 ▲ Continue folding the strips in this way until half of the lattice is completed. Repeat on the other half of the pie.

2 ▲ **For a square woven lattice:** Lay half of the strips across the pie filling, keeping them neatly parallel and spacing them evenly.

4 ▲ Now fold back those strips that were not folded the first time. Lay another strip across those that are flat now, spacing this new strip evenly from the centre strip.

6 ▲ Trim the ends of the strips even with the rim of the pie tin. Moisten the edge of the pastry case and press the strips gently to it to seal. Finish the edge.

7 ▲ **For a diamond lattice:** Weave as above, laying the intersecting strips diagonally instead of at right angles. Or lay half the strips over the filling and the remaining strips on top.

MAKING A BISCUIT CASE

A biscuit case is one of the simplest bases to make, and the variations in flavouring are almost endless. Crumbs from any dry biscuit can be used, both sweet and savoury. You can also use breadcrumbs and cake crumbs. Most biscuit cases are sweet, to hold sweet fillings, but there are also unsweetened biscuit cases for savoury cheesecakes.

MAKES AN 8–9 IN (20–23 CM) CASE

8 oz (225 g) biscuits (see below), crushed

4 oz (115 g) butter, melted

3–4 tablespoons caster sugar (optional)

Biscuit case flavourings
- Use digestive biscuits. Sweeten with sugar to taste, if liked. Add 1 teaspoon ground cinnamon or ginger or mixed spice or ½ teaspoon grated nutmeg.
- Use digestive biscuits and sweeten with sugar to taste, if liked. Add 1 teaspoon grated lemon zest or 2 teaspoons grated orange zest.
- Use 7 oz (200 g) digestive biscuits and 1½ oz (45 g) ground or finely chopped nuts (almonds, hazelnuts, pecan nuts or walnuts).
- Use ginger nuts, shortbread, almond butter biscuits, amaretti biscuits or crisp almond macaroons. No sugar is needed.
- Use water biscuits or other cheese biscuits, without adding sugar, for a savoury filling.

Crushing the biscuits
To make fine crumbs, break the biscuits into small pieces. Put them, a small batch at a time, in a heavy plastic bag and roll over them with a rolling pin. Or grind them finely in a blender or food processor.

1 ▲ Combine the biscuits, melted butter and sugar, plus other flavourings, if using. Stir well to mix.

2 ▲ Turn the biscuit mixture into a buttered 8 in (20 cm) springform cake tin or 9 in (23 cm) tart tin. Spread it over the bottom and up the side.

3 ▲ With the back of a large spoon or your fingers, press the biscuit mixture firmly against the tin, to pack the crumbs into a solid crust.

4 ▲ According to the recipe, refrigerate the case to set it, usually at least 1 hour. Or bake the case in a 350°F/180°C/Gas 4 oven for 8–10 minutes; cool before filling.

Easy Chocolate Tart
Prepare the biscuit case using ginger biscuits and pressing it into a 9 in (23 cm) tin. Bake and cool. Melt 6 oz (170 g) plain chocolate with 4 tablespoons milk; cool. Whip ¾ pint (450 ml) double or whipping cream until thick. Fold into the cooled chocolate. Spread evenly in the case. Cover and refrigerate until firm. Just before serving, garnish with chocolate curls or grated chocolate. *Serves 6.*

Making Choux Pastry

Unlike other pastries, where the fat is rubbed into the flour, with choux pastry the butter is melted with water and then the flour is added, followed by eggs. The result is more of a paste than a pastry. It is easy to make, but care must be taken in measuring the ingredients.

For 18 profiteroles or 12 eclairs

4 oz (115 g) butter, cut into small pieces

8 fl oz (240 ml) water

2 teaspoons caster sugar (optional)

¼ teaspoon salt

5 oz (145 g) plain flour

4 eggs, beaten to mix

1 ▲ Combine the butter, water, sugar, if using, and salt in a large heavy-based saucepan. Bring to the boil over moderately high heat, stirring occasionally.

2 ▲ As soon as the mixture is boiling, remove the pan from the heat. Add the flour all at once and beat vigorously with a wooden spoon to mix the flour into the liquid.

3 ▲ Return the pan to moderate heat and cook, stirring, until the mixture will form a ball, pulling away from the side of the pan. This will take about 1 minute. Remove from the heat again and allow to cool for 3–5 minutes.

4 ▲ Add a little of the beaten egg and beat well with the spoon or an electric mixer to incorporate. Add a little more egg and beat in well. Continue beating in the eggs until the mixture becomes a smooth, shiny paste thick enough to hold its shape.

Shaping choux pastry

• For *large puffs:* Use two large spoons dipped in water. Drop the paste in 2–2½ in (5–6 cm) wide blobs on the paper-lined baking sheet, leaving 1½ in (4 cm) between each. Neaten the blobs as much as possible. Alternatively, for well-shaped puffs, pipe the paste using a piping bag fitted with a ¾ in (2 cm) plain nozzle.

• For *profiteroles:* Use two small spoons or a piping bag fitted with a ½ in (1.5 cm) nozzle and shape 1 in (2.5 cm) blobs.

• For *éclairs:* Use a piping bag fitted with a ¾ in (2 cm) nozzle. Pipe strips 4–5 in (10–12 cm) long.

• For *a ring:* draw a 12 in (30 cm) circle on the paper. Spoon the paste in large blobs on the circle to make a ring. Or pipe two rings round the circle and a third on top.

Baking times for choux pastry
Bake large puffs and éclairs 30–35 minutes, profiteroles 20–25 minutes, rings 40–45 minutes.

5 ▲ While still warm, shape large choux puffs, éclairs, profiteroles or large rings on a baking sheet lined with baking parchment.

6 ▲ Glaze with 1 egg beaten with 1 teaspoon cold water. Put into a 425°F/ 220°C/Gas 7 oven, then reduce the heat to 400°F/200°C/Gas 6. Bake until puffed and golden brown.

MAKING CAKES BY THE CREAMING METHOD

The Victoria sandwich, with its tender crumb and rich, moist flavour, is always popular. It is delicious enough to be served plain, with just a dusting of sugar, or it can be filled and iced.

To make cakes by the creaming method, the fat and sugar are 'creamed' – or beaten – together before the eggs and dry ingredients are added. The fat (usually butter or margarine) should be soft enough to be beaten, so if necessary remove it from the refrigerator and leave it at room temperature for at least 30 minutes. For best results, the eggs should be at room temperature.

Mocha Victoria Sponge
Make the mixture using 6 oz (170 g) each butter or margarine, caster sugar and self-raising flour and 3 eggs. Divide between two bowls. To one add 1 tablespoon strong black coffee; to the other add 1 tablespoon cocoa powder mixed to a paste with 1–2 tablespoons boiling water. Place alternate spoonfuls of each flavour, side by side, in 2 greased and bottom-lined 7 in (18 cm) round sandwich tins. Lightly smooth the top. Bake at 350°F/180°C/Gas 4 for 25–30 minutes. Turn out on to a wire rack and leave to cool. Sandwich the cakes together with coffee buttercream. Cover the top, or top and sides, with buttercream.

1 ▲ Sift the flour with the salt, raising agent(s) and any other dry ingredients, such as spices or cocoa powder. Set aside.

3 ▲ Add the sugar to the creamed fat gradually. With the mixer at medium-high speed, beat it into the fat until the mixture is pale and very fluffy. The sugar should be completely incorporated. This will take 4–5 minutes. During this process, air will be beaten into the mixture, which will help the cake to rise.

5 ▲ Add the dry ingredients to the mixture, beating at low speed just until smoothly combined. Or fold in with a large metal spoon.

2 ▲ Put the fat in a large, deep bowl and beat with an electric mixer at medium speed, or a wooden spoon, until the texture is soft and pliable.

4 ▲ Add the eggs or egg yolks, one at a time, beating well after each addition (about 45 seconds). Scrape the bowl often so all the ingredients are evenly combined. When adding the eggs, the mixture may begin to curdle, especially if the eggs are cold. If this happens, add 1 tablespoon of the measured flour.

6 ▲ If the recipe calls for any liquid, add it in small portions alternately with portions of the dry ingredients.

7 ▲ If the recipe specifies, whisk egg whites separately until frothy, add sugar and continue whisking until stiff peaks form. Fold into the mixture.

8 ▲ Pour the mixture into a cake tin or tins, prepared according to the recipe, and bake as specified.

9 ▲ To test creamed-method cakes, insert a metal skewer or wooden cocktail stick into the centre; it should come out clean.

Making American Frosting

This fluffy white frosting has an attractive gloss and a texture like meringue. It is a delicious filling and icing for sanwich cakes.

Makes enough to fill and ice a 9 in (23 cm) sandwich cake

10 oz (300 g) sugar
¼ teaspoon cream of tartar
2 egg whites
4 tablespoons cold water
1 tablespoon liquid glucose
2 teaspoons vanilla essence

1 ▲ Combine the sugar, cream of tartar, egg whites, water and glucose in a large heatproof bowl or the top of a double saucepan. Stir just to mix.

2 ▲ Set the bowl over a saucepan of boiling water. The base of the bowl should not touch the water.

Frosting variations

For *Orange Frosting*: Use orange juice instead of water and add 1 teaspoon grated orange zest. Reduce the vanilla to ½ teaspoon.

For *Lemon Frosting*: Use 2 tablespoons each lemon juice and water and add ½ teaspoon grated lemon zest. Reduce the vanilla to ½ teaspoon.

3 ▲ Beat with a hand-held electric mixer at high speed for about 7 minutes or until the frosting is thick and white and will form stiff peaks.

4 ▲ Remove from the heat. Add the vanilla and continue beating for about 3 minutes or until the frosting has cooled slightly. Use immediately.

MAKING CAKES BY THE ALL-IN-ONE METHOD

Many cakes are made by an easy all-in-one method where all the ingredients are combined in a bowl and beaten thoroughly. The mixture can also be made in a food processor, but take care not to over-process. A refinement on the all-in-one method is to separate the eggs and make the mixture with the yolks. The whites are whisked separately and then folded in.

1 ▲ Sift the dry ingredients (flour, salt, raising agent, spices and so on) into a bowl.

2 ▲ Add the liquid ingredients (eggs, melted or soft fat, milk, fruit juices and so on) and beat until smooth, with an electric mixer for speed. Pour into the prepared tins and bake as specified in the recipe.

MAKING SIMPLE BUTTERCREAM

Quick to make and easy to spread, buttercream is ideal for all kinds of cakes, from simple ones to gâteaux. The basic buttercream can be varied with many other flavours, and it can be tinted with food colouring, too.

MAKES ENOUGH TO COVER THE TOP AND SIDE OF A 7–8 IN (17–20 CM) CAKE

4 oz (115 g) butter, preferably unsalted, at room temperature

8 oz (225 g) icing sugar, sifted

1 teaspoon vanilla essence

about 2 teaspoons milk

1 ▲ Put the butter in a deep mixing bowl and beat it with an electric mixer at medium speed, or a wooden spoon, until it is soft and pliable.

2 ▲ Gradually add the icing sugar and beat at medium-high speed. Continue beating until the mixture is pale and fluffy.

Buttercream variations
- For *Orange or Lemon Buttercream*, grate the zest from 1 small orange or ½ lemon; squeeze the juice. Beat in the zest with the sugar; use the juice instead of the vanilla and milk.
- For *Chocolate Buttercream*, add 4 tablespoons cocoa powder, beating it in with the sugar. Increase the milk to 3–4 tablespoons.

- For *Mocha Buttercream*: Warm the milk and dissolve 1 teaspoon instant coffee powder in it; cool and use to make chocolate buttercream, adding more milk if needed.
- For *Coffee Buttercream*, warm the milk and dissolve 1 tablespoon of instant coffee powder in it; cool before adding to the buttercream.

3 ▲ Add the vanilla essence and 1 tablespoon milk. Beat until smooth and of a spreading consistency. If it is too thick, beat in more milk. If too thin, beat in more sugar.

MAKING CAKES BY THE MELTING METHOD

Cakes made by the melting method are wonderfully moist and keep quite well. Ingredients such as sugar, syrup (treacle, honey, golden syrup) and fat are warmed together until melted and smoothly combined before being added to the dry ingredients.

1 ▲ Sift the dry ingredients (such as flour, raising agent, salt, ground spices) into a large bowl.

2 ▲ Put the sugar and/or syrup and fat in a saucepan with any other ingredients specified in the recipe. Warm over a low heat, stirring occasionally, until the fat has melted and sugar dissolved. The mixture should not boil.

3 ▲ If recipe instructs, warm fruit in the syrup mixture. Remove from the heat and leave to cool slightly (if too hot, it will not combine well with dry ingredients).

4 ▲ Make a well in the centre of the dry ingredients and pour in the cooled melted mixture. Add beaten eggs and any other liquid ingredients (milk, water, etc) and beat to a smooth, thick batter.

Fruit Cake
Sift 8 oz (225 g) self-raising flour, a pinch of salt and 1 teaspoon mixed spice. Melt together 4 oz (115 g) butter or margarine, 4 oz (115 g) soft light brown sugar, ¼ pint (150 ml) water and the grated zest and juice of 1 orange. When smooth, add 4 oz (115 g) each sultanas, currants and raisins and simmer gently for about 10 minutes, stirring occasionally. Cool. Add the fruit mixture to the dry ingredients. Add 2 oz (55 g) each chopped glacé cherries and chopped mixed peel, 1 tablespoon orange marmalade and 2 beaten eggs. Mix thoroughly. Pour into a greased and lined 8 in (20 cm) round cake tin. Bake at 325°F/170°C/Gas 3 for 1½ hours or until firm and golden; a skewer inserted in the centre should come out clean. Cool in the tin for 30 minutes before turning out on to a wire rack.

5 ▲ If called for in the recipe, stir in fruit and/or nuts (if these have not been warmed in the syrup). Turn the cake mixture into a lined tin and bake according to the recipe.

Maturing for flavour
Melting-method cakes taste best if they are allowed to 'mature' before serving. After the cake has cooled completely, wrap it in greaseproof paper and then overwrap in foil. Keep it in a cool place for 1–2 days before cutting into slices.

Making a Classic Whisked Sponge

The classic whisked sponge contains no fat and no raising agents – just eggs, sugar and flour. The light, airy texture of the finished cake depends on the large quantity of air beaten into the mixture.

Sometimes the eggs are separated for a whisked sponge and sometimes the cake is enriched with butter. American angel food cake uses egg whites only.

A whisked sponge can be simply dusted with icing or caster sugar, filled with sweetened whipped cream, a fruit jam or fresh fruit, or used to make a Swiss roll.

If you use a table-top electric mixer to beat the eggs and sugar, or if using separated eggs, there is no need to set the bowl over a pan of simmering water.

Whisked Sponge
Make the mixture using 4 whole eggs, 5 oz (145 g) caster sugar and 4 oz (115 g) plain flour. Pour into a greased, bottom-lined and floured 9 in (23 cm) round cake tin. Bake in a 350°F/180°C/Gas 4 oven for 25–30 minutes. Cool in the tin for 10 minutes, then turn out on to a wire rack and cool completely. Before serving, peel off the lining paper. Dust the top lightly with sifted icing sugar.

1 ▲ In a heatproof bowl, combine the eggs (at room temperature) and sugar. Set the bowl over a saucepan of simmering water; the base of the bowl should not touch the water.

3 ▲ Lift out the beaters; the mixture on the beaters should trail back on to the surface of the remaining mixture in the bowl to make a ribbon that holds it shape.

5 ▲ Sift the flour and fold it into the mixture, cutting in to the bottom of the bowl with a rubber spatula or large metal spoon and turning the mixture over, working gently yet thoroughly to retain the volume of the whisked egg and sugar mixture.

2 ▲ Beat with a hand-held electric mixer at medium-high speed, or a rotary beater or whisk, until the mixture is very thick and pale – about 10 minutes.

4 ▲ Remove the bowl from over the pan of water and continue beating for 2–3 minutes or until the mixture is cool.

6 ▲ Pour the mixture into the prepared tin or tins and bake as directed in the recipe. To test a whisked sponge, press the centre lightly with your fingertip: the cake should spring back.

MAKING A SWISS ROLL

A rolled sponge reveals an attractive spiral of filling when it is sliced. The filling could be sweetened whipped cream, ice cream, fruit jam or buttercream.

   The whisked sponge mixture can be made using whole or separated eggs, as preferred.

   Line the tin with greaseproof paper or baking parchment, grease the paper and dust with flour.

1 ▲ Pour the mixture into the prepared tin and spread it evenly into the corners with a palette knife. Bake as specified in the recipe.

2 ▲ Spread a tea towel flat and lay a sheet of baking parchment on top. Sprinkle the paper evenly, as specified, with caster or icing sugar, cocoa or a sugar and spice mixture. Invert the cake on to the paper.

Chocolate Ice Cream Roll
Make the sponge mixture using 4 eggs, separated, 4 oz (115 g) caster sugar and 4 oz (115 g) plain flour sifted with 3 tablespoons cocoa powder. Pour into a prepared 15 × 10 in (37.5 × 25 cm) Swiss roll tin. Bake in a 375°F/190°C/Gas 5 oven for about 15 minutes. Turn out, roll up and cool. When cold, unroll the cake and spread with 1 pint (600 ml) softened vanilla or chocolate ice cream. Roll up the cake again, wrap in foil and freeze until firm. About 30 minutes be-fore serving, transfer the cake to the refrigerator. Sprinkle with caster or icing sugar before serving. If you like, serve with warm bittersweet chocolate sauce. *Serves 8.*

3 ▲ Carefully peel off the lining paper from the cake. If necessary, trim off any crisp edges from the side of the cake.

4 ▲ Carefully roll up the cake, with the paper inside, starting from a short side. Wrap the towel round the cake roll and leave to cool on a wire rack.

5 ▲ Remove the towel and unroll the cake. Lift off the paper. Spread the chosen filling over the cake.

6 ▲ Roll up the cake again, using the paper to help move it forward. Sprinkle with sugar or ice the cake, as the recipe specifies.

PREPARING CAKE TINS

Instructions vary from recipe to recipe for preparing cake tins. Some are simply greased, some are greased and floured, some are lined with baking parchment or greased greaseproof paper. The preparation required depends on the type of cake mixture and the length of the baking time. Proper preparation aids turning out.

Flavourful coatings
Some cake recipes specify that the greased tin be coated with sugar, cocoa powder or ground nuts. Follow the method for flouring.

1 ▲ **To grease a tin:** Use butter, margarine, or a mild or flavourless oil. If using butter or margarine, hold a small piece in a paper towel (or use your fingers), and rub it all over the bottom and up the side of the tin to make a thin, even coating. If using oil, brush it on with a pastry brush.

2 ▲ **To flour a tin:** Put a small scoopful of flour in the centre of the greased tin. Tip and rotate the tin so that the flour spreads and coats all over the bottom and up the side. Turn the tin over and shake out excess flour, tapping the base of the tin to dislodge any pockets of flour.

3 ▲ **To line the bottom of a tin:** Set the tin on the sheet of paper and draw round the base. Cut out this circle, square or rectangle, cutting just inside the drawn line. Press the paper smoothly on to the bottom of the tin.

4 ▲ **To line the sides of a tin** (for rich mixtures and fruit cakes): Cut a strip of paper long enough to wrap round the outside of the tin and overlap by 1½ in (4 cm). The strip should be wide enough to extend 1 in (2.5 cm) above the rim of the tin.

5 ▲ Fold the strip lengthways at the 1 in (2.5 cm) point and crease firmly. With scissors, snip at regular intervals along the 1 in (2.5 cm) fold, from the edge to the crease. Line the side of the tin, with the snipped part of the strip on the bottom.

6 ▲ For square and rectangular cake tins, fold the paper and crease it with your fingernail to fit snugly into the corners of the tin. Then press the bottom paper lining into place.

7 ▲ If the recipe specifies, grease the paper before you put it in the tin. If the tin is to be floured, do this after the paper is in place.

8 ▲ **To line bun and muffin tins:** Use paper liners of the required size. Or grease and flour the tins.

9 ▲ **To line a Swiss roll tin:** Cut a rectangle of paper 2 in (5 cm) larger all round than the tin. Grease the bottom of the tin lightly to prevent the paper from slipping.

10 ▲ Lay the paper evenly in the tin. With a table knife, press the paper into the angle all round the bottom of the tin, creasing the paper firmly but not cutting it.

11 ▲ With scissors, snip the paper in the corners, from top to bottom, so it will fit neatly into them. Grease the paper according to recipe instructions, unless using baking parchment.

USING SEPARATED EGGS FOR A WHISKED SPONGE

This version of whisked sponge is easier to make than the classic one that uses whole eggs, but the results are no less light and delicious. There is no need to set the bowl over a pan of simmering water for whisking, although if you are using a balloon whisk rather than an electric mixer or rotary beater you may want to do so to speed up the thickening of the egg yolk and sugar mixture and to increase its volume. Bowls and beaters used with egg whites must be scrupulously clean.

1 ▲ Separate the eggs, taking care that there is no trace of yolk with the whites. Put the yolks and whites in separate large bowls.

2 ▲ Add most of the sugar to the yolks. With a hand-held or table-top electric mixer, whisk at medium-high speed until the mixture is very thick and pale. Lift out the beaters: the mixture on the beaters should trail back on to the surface of the remaining mixture in the bowl to make a ribbon that holds its shape.

3 ▲ Whisk the egg whites until they form soft peaks (if not using a copper bowl, add a pinch of cream of tartar once the whites are frothy). Add the remaining sugar and continue whisking until the whites will form stiff peaks.

4 ▲ With a rubber spatula, fold the sifted flour into the egg yolk mixture, then fold in the whisked egg whites. Fold gently but thoroughly. Pour the mixture into the prepared tin and bake as instructed.

A Genoese sponge
This whisked sponge, made with whole or separated eggs, is more rich and trickier to make, as melted butter is folded in just before pouring into the tin.

MAKING YEAST DOUGH

Making bread is a very enjoyable and satisfying culinary experience – with no other preparation do you have such 'hands-on' contact. And from the kneading through to the shaping of the risen (or proven) dough, you are working with a living organism, yeast, not a chemical raising agent. You can use either fresh yeast or dried yeast, which is available in an easy-blend variety too.

Everyday White Bread
Sift 1½ lb (700 g) strong plain flour into a large bowl with 1½ teaspoons salt and 1 tablespoon caster sugar. Stir in 2 teaspoons easy-blend dried yeast. Make a well in the centre and add ¾ pint (450 ml) mixed warm water and milk and 1 oz (30 g) melted and cooled butter. Mix to a soft dough, adding more flour or liquid if necessary, then knead until smooth and elastic. Leave to rise until doubled in bulk. Knock back the dough to deflate. Divide it in half and shape each piece into a loaf, tucking the ends under. Put in 2 greased 8½ × 4½ in (21 × 11 cm) loaf tins. Leave in a warm place to rise for 30–45 minutes. Glaze the tops of the loaves with 1 egg beaten with 1 tablespoon milk. Bake in a 450°F/230°C/Gas 8 oven for 30–35 minutes. *Makes 2 loaves.*

1 ▲ If using ordinary dried yeast, put it in a small bowl, add some of the warm liquid (105–110°F/40–43°C) called for in the recipe and whisk with a fork until dissolved. Add a little sugar if the recipe specifies.

3 ▲ Using your fingers or a spoon, gradually draw the flour into the liquids. Mix until all the flour is incorporated and the dough pulls away from the sides of the bowl. If the dough feels too soft and wet, work in a little more flour. If it doesn't come together, add a little more liquid.

5 ▲ Shape the dough into a ball. Put it in a lightly greased bowl and turn the dough to grease all over. Cover the bowl with a towel or cling film. Set it aside in a warm, draught-free place (about 80°F/27°C).

2 ▲ Sift the flour into a large warm bowl (with other dry ingredients such as salt). Make a well in the centre and add the yeast mixture plus any other liquid ingredients.

4 ▲ Turn the dough on to a lightly floured surface. Fold the dough over on to itself towards you and then press it down away from you with the heels of your hands. Rotate the dough slightly and fold and press it again. Knead until the dough looks satiny and feels elastic, about 10 minutes.

6 ▲ Leave to rise until about doubled in bulk, 1–1½ hours. To test if it is sufficiently risen, press a finger about 1 in (2.5 cm) into the dough and withdraw it quickly; the indentation should remain.

7 ▲ Gently punch the centre of the dough with your fist to deflate it and fold the edges to the centre. Turn the dough on to a lightly floured surface and knead it again for 2–3 minutes. If instructed, shape the dough into a ball again and rise a second time.

8 ▲ Shape the dough into loaves, rolls or other shapes as instructed. Put into prepared tins or on to baking sheets. Cover and leave to rise in a warm place for ¾–1 hour. If the recipe instructs, glaze the loaves or rolls.

9 ▲ Bake in the centre of a heated oven until well risen and golden brown. To test, tip the loaf out of the tin and tap the base with your knuckle. If it sounds hollow, like a drum, it is fully cooked. Immediately transfer to a wire rack for cooling.

SHAPING ROLLS

A basket of freshly baked bread rolls, in decorative shapes, is a delightful accompaniment for soups or salads. After shaping, arrange the rolls on a baking sheet, leaving space around each roll for spreading, and leave to rise for 30 minutes before baking.

Working with yeast

Easy-blend (or fast-action) is the most readily available dried yeast. Unlike ordinary dried yeast, there is no need to mix it with liquid. Just combine it with the flour and other dry ingredients and then add the warm liquids.

If using fresh yeast, allow ½ oz (15 g) to each 1 tablespoon dried. Crumble it into a small bowl, add warm liquid and mash with a fork until blended.

If you are in any doubt about the freshness of ordinary dried or fresh yeast, set the mixture aside in a warm place; after 10 minutes or so it should be foamy. If it isn't, discard it.

1 ▲ For Parker House rolls: Roll out the risen dough to ¼ in (5 mm) thickness and cut out 2½–3 in (6–7 cm) rounds using a floured cutter. Brush the rounds with melted butter. Fold them in half, slightly off-centre so the top overlaps the bottom. Press the folded edge firmly. Arrange the rolls on a greased baking sheet.

2 ▲ For crescent rolls: Roll out the risen dough to a large round ¼ in (5 mm) thick. Brush with melted butter. With a sharp knife, cut into wedges that are 2½–3 in (6–7 cm) at their wide end. Roll up each wedge, from the wide end. Set the rolls on a greased baking sheet, placing the points underneath.

3 ◄ For bowknot rolls: Divide the risen dough into pieces. Roll each with your palms on a lightly floured surface to make ropes that are about ½ in (1.5 cm) thick. Divide the ropes into 9 in (27 cm) lengths. Tie each rope loosely into a knot, tucking the ends under. Arrange the rolls on a greased baking sheet.

Making Pizza Dough

The range of toppings for a pizza is virtually limitless. Although you can buy pizza bases, it's very easy to make your own at home, and takes much less time than you would expect.

Makes a 14 in (35 cm) pizza base

2 teaspoons dried yeast
6fl oz (180 ml) warm water
11½ oz (315 g) strong plain flour
1 teaspoon salt
1½ tablespoons olive oil

Tomato and Mozzarella Pizza
Spread ½ pint (300 ml) tomato-garlic sauce over the pizza base, not quite to the edges. Scatter 4oz (115 g) grated mozzarella cheese evenly over the sauce (plus thinly sliced pepperoni or salami if you like). Sprinkle over freshly grated Parmesan cheese and then add a drizzle of olive oil. Bake in a 475°F/240°C/Gas 9 oven for 15–20 minutes.

Food processor pizza dough
Combine the flour, salt, yeast mixture and olive oil in the processor container. Process briefly, then add the rest of the warm water. Work until the dough begins to form a ball. Process 3–4 minutes to knead the dough, then knead it by hand for 2–3 minutes.

1 ▲ Put the yeast in a small bowl, add 4 tablespoons of the water and soak for 1 minute. Whisk lightly with a fork until dissolved.

3 ▲ Using your fingers, gradually draw the flour into the liquids. Continue mixing until all the flour is incorporated and the dough will just hold together.

5 ▲ Cover the bowl with cling film. Set aside in a warm place to rise about 1 hour until doubled in bulk. Turn the dough on to the lightly floured surface again. Gently knock back to deflate it, then knead lightly until smooth.

2 ▲ Sift the flour and salt into a large warm bowl. Make a well in the centre and add the yeast mixture, olive oil and remaining warm water.

4 ▲ Turn the dough on to a lightly floured surface. Knead it until it is smooth and silky, about 5 minutes. Shape the dough into a ball. Put it in an oiled bowl and rotate to coat the surface evenly with oil.

6 ▲ Roll out the dough into a round or square about ¼ in (5 mm) thick. Transfer it to a lightly oiled metal pizza tin or baking sheet. Add the topping as specified in the recipe. Bake until the pizza crust is puffy and well browned. Serve hot.

Making Focaccia and Bread Sticks

Italian flatbreads, such as focaccia, and bread sticks can be topped with herbs and seeds for tasty accompaniments or starters. Personalize them with combinations of your favourite ingredients for unusual snacks, or split and fill flatbreads with ham or cheese for an Italian-style sandwich.

This basic dough can be used for other recipes, such as pizza. The dough may be frozen before it is baked, and thawed before filling.

1 ▲ For focaccia: Warm a mixing bowl by swirling some hot water in it. Drain. Place the yeast in the bowl, and pour on the warm water. Stir in the sugar, mix with a fork, and allow to stand until the yeast has dissolved and starts to foam, 5–10 minutes.

Working with yeast
Easy-blend (or fast-action) is the most readily available dried yeast. Unlike ordinary dried yeast, there is no need to mix it with liquid. Just combine it with the flour and other dry ingredients and then add the warm liquids.

If using fresh yeast, allow ½ oz (15 g) to each 1 tablespoon dried. Crumble it into a small bowl, add warm liquid and mash with a fork until blended.

If you are in any doubt about the freshness of ordinary dried or fresh yeast, set the mixture aside in a warm place; after 10 minutes or so it should be foamy.

2 ▲ Use a wooden spoon to mix in the salt and about one-third of the flour. Mix in another third of the flour, stirring with the spoon until the dough forms a mass and begins to pull away from the sides of the bowl.

3 ▲ Sprinkle some of the remaining flour onto a smooth work surface. Remove the dough from the bowl and begin to knead it, working in the remaining flour a little at a time. Knead for 8–10 minutes. By the end the dough should be elastic and smooth. Form it into a ball.

4 Lightly oil a mixing bowl. Place the dough in the bowl. Stretch a damp dish towel or clear film across the top of the bowl, and leave it to stand in a warm place until the dough has doubled in volume, about 40–50 minutes or more, depending on the type of yeast used. To test whether the dough has risen enough, poke two fingers into the dough. If the indentations remain, the dough is ready to use.

5 ▲ Punch the dough down with your fist to release the air. Knead for 1–2 minutes.

6 ▲ Brush a tin with oil. Press the dough into the tin with your fingers to a layer 2 cm/1 inch thick. Cover and leave to rise for 30 minutes. Preheat the oven. Make indentations all over the focaccia with your fingers. Brush with oil, add filling and bake until pale golden brown.

7 ▲ For bread sticks: There's no need for the first rising. Divide dough into walnut-size pieces and roll out on a floured surface with your hands, into thin sausage shapes. Transfer to a greased baking tray, cover and leave in a warm place for 10–15 minutes. Bake until crisp.

BISCUITS
& BARS

KEEP THE BISCUIT TIN FILLED WITH
THIS WONDERFUL ARRAY OF
BISCUITS AND BARS – SOME SOFT
AND CHEWY, SOME CRUNCHY AND
NUTTY, SOME RICH AND SINFUL,
AND SOME PLAIN AND WHOLESOME.
ALL ARE IRRESISTIBLE.

Farmhouse Biscuits

Makes 18

4 oz (115 g) butter or margarine, at room temperature

3¹/₂ oz (100 g) light brown sugar

2¹/₂ oz (70 g) crunchy peanut butter

1 egg

2 oz (55 g) plain flour

¹/₂ tsp baking powder

¹/₂ tsp ground cinnamon

¹/₈ tsp salt

6 oz (170 g) muesli

2 oz (55 g) raisins

2 oz (55 g) chopped walnuts

1 Preheat a 350°F/180°C/Gas 4 oven. Grease a baking sheet.

2 With an electric mixer, cream the butter or margarine and sugar until light and fluffy. Beat in the peanut butter. Beat in the egg.

3 ▲ Sift the flour, baking powder, cinnamon and salt over the peanut butter mixture and stir to blend. Stir in the muesli, raisins and walnuts. Taste the mixture to see if it needs more sugar, as muesli varies.

4 ▲ Drop rounded tablespoonfuls of the mixture onto the prepared baking sheet about 1 in (2.5 cm) apart. Press gently with the back of a spoon to spread each mound into a circle.

5 Bake until lightly coloured, about 15 minutes. With a metal spatula, transfer to a rack to cool. Store in an airtight container.

Crunchy Oatmeal Biscuits

MAKES 14

6 oz (170 g) butter or margarine, at room temperature

6 oz (170 g) caster sugar

1 egg yolk

6 oz (170 g) plain flour

1 tsp bicarbonate of soda

¹/₂ tsp salt

2 oz (55 g) rolled oats

2 oz (55 g) small crunchy nugget cereal

~ VARIATION ~

For Nutty Oatmeal Biscuits, substitute an equal quantity of chopped walnuts or pecans for the cereal, and prepare as described.

1 ▲ With an electric mixer, cream the butter or margarine and sugar together until light and fluffy. Mix in the egg yolk.

2 Sift over the flour, bicarbonate of soda and salt, then stir into the butter mixture. Add the oats and cereal and stir to blend. Refrigerate for at least 20 minutes.

3 Preheat a 375°F/190°C/Gas 5 oven. Grease a baking sheet.

4 ▲ Roll the mixture into balls. Place them on the sheet and flatten with the bottom of a floured glass.

5 Bake until golden, 10–12 minutes. With a metal spatula, transfer to a rack to cool completely. Store in an airtight container.

Farmhouse Biscuits (top), Crunchy Oatmeal Biscuits

Oaty Coconut Biscuits

MAKES 48

6 oz (170 g) quick-cooking oats

3 oz (85 g) desiccated coconut

8 oz (225 g) butter or margarine, at room temperature

4 oz (115 g) caster sugar + 2 tbsp

2 oz (55 g) dark brown sugar

2 eggs

4 tbsp milk

1¹/₂ tsp vanilla essence

4 oz (115 g) plain flour

¹/₂ tsp bicarbonate of soda

¹/₂ tsp salt

1 tsp ground cinnamon

1 Preheat a 400°F/200°C/Gas 6 oven. Lightly grease 2 baking sheets.

2 ▲ Spread the oats and coconut on an ungreased baking sheet. Bake until golden brown, 8–10 minutes, stirring occasionally.

3 With an electric mixer, cream the butter or margarine and both sugars until light and fluffy. Beat in the eggs, 1 at a time, then the milk and vanilla. Sift over the dry ingredients and fold in. Stir in the oats and coconut.

4 ▼ Drop spoonfuls of the mixture 1–2 in (2.5–5 cm) apart on the prepared sheets and flatten with the bottom of a greased glass dipped in sugar. Bake until golden, 8–10 minutes. Transfer to a rack to cool.

Crunchy Jumbles

MAKES 36

4 oz (115 g) butter or margarine, at room temperature

8 oz (225 g) caster sugar

1 egg

1 tsp vanilla essence

5 oz (140 g) plain flour

¹/₂ tsp bicarbonate of soda

¹/₈ tsp salt

2 oz (55 g) crisped rice cereal

6 oz (170 g) chocolate chips

~ VARIATION ~

For even crunchier biscuits, add 2 oz (55 g) walnuts, coarsely chopped, with the cereal and chocolate chips.

---

1 Preheat a 350°F/180°C/Gas 4 oven. Lightly grease 2 baking sheets.

2 ▲ With an electric mixer, cream the butter or margarine and sugar until light and fluffy. Beat in the egg and vanilla. Sift over the flour, bicarbonate of soda and salt and fold in carefully.

3 ▼ Add the cereal and chocolate chips. Stir to mix thoroughly.

4 Drop spoonfuls of the mixture 1–2 in (2.5–5 cm) apart on the sheets. Bake until golden, 10–12 minutes. Transfer to a rack to cool.

Oaty Coconut Biscuits (top), Crunchy Jumbles

Ginger Biscuits

Makes 36

8 oz (225 g) caster sugar
3½ oz (100 g) light brown sugar
4 oz (115 g) butter, at room temperature
4 oz (115 g) margarine, at room temperature
1 egg
3 fl oz (85 ml) black treacle
9 oz (250 g) plain flour
2 tsp ground ginger
½ tsp grated nutmeg
1 tsp ground cinnamon
2 tsp bicarbonate of soda
½ tsp salt

1 Preheat a 325°F/170°C/Gas 3 oven. Line 2–3 baking sheets with greaseproof paper and grease lightly.

2 ▲ With an electric mixer, cream half of the caster sugar, the brown sugar, butter and margarine until light and fluffy. Add the egg and continue beating to blend well. Add the treacle.

3 ▲ Sift the flour, spices and bicarbonate of soda 3 times, then stir into the butter mixture. Refrigerate for 30 minutes.

4 ▲ Place the remaining sugar in a shallow dish. Roll tablespoonfuls of the biscuit mixture into balls, then roll the balls in the sugar to coat.

5 Place the balls 2 in (5 cm) apart on the prepared sheets and flatten slightly. Bake until golden around the edges but soft in the middle, 12–15 minutes. Let stand for 5 minutes before transferring to a rack to cool.

~ VARIATION ~

To make Gingerbread Men, increase the amount of flour by 1 oz (30 g). Roll out the mixture and cut out shapes with a special cutter. Decorate with icing, if wished.

Orange Biscuits

MAKES 30

4 oz (115 g) butter, at room temperature
7 oz (200 g) sugar
2 egg yolks
1 tablespoon fresh orange juice
grated rind of 1 large orange
7 oz (200 g) plain flour
1 tablespoon cornflour
¹/₂ teaspoon salt
1 teaspoon baking powder

1 ▲ With an electric mixer, cream the butter and sugar until light and fluffy. Add the yolks, orange juice and rind, and continue beating to blend. Set aside.

2 In another bowl, sift together the flour, cornflour, salt and baking powder. Add to the butter mixture and stir until it forms a dough.

4 Preheat the oven to 375°F/190°C/ Gas 5. Grease 2 baking sheets.

6 ▼ Press down with a fork to flatten. Bake until golden brown, 8–10 minutes. With a metal palette knife transfer to a rack to cool.

3 ▲ Wrap the dough in greaseproof paper and refrigerate for 2 hours.

5 ▲ Roll spoonfuls of the dough into balls and place 1–2 in (2.5–5 cm) apart on the prepared sheets.

Cinnamon-Coated Cookies

MAKES 30

4 oz (115 g) butter, at room temperature
12 oz (350 g) caster sugar
1 tsp vanilla essence
2 eggs
2 fl oz (65 ml) milk
14 oz (400 g) plain flour
1 tsp bicarbonate of soda
2 oz (55 g) finely chopped walnuts
FOR THE COATING
5 tbsp sugar
2 tbsp ground cinnamon

1 Preheat a 375°F/190°C/Gas 5 oven. Grease 2 baking sheets.

2 With an electric mixer, cream the butter until light. Add the sugar and vanilla and continue mixing until fluffy. Beat in the eggs, then the milk.

3 ▲ Sift the flour and bicarbonate of soda over the butter mixture and stir to blend. Stir in the nuts. Refrigerate for 15 minutes.

4 ▲ For the coating, mix the sugar and cinnamon. Roll tablespoonfuls of the mixture into walnut-size balls. Roll the balls in the sugar mixture. You may need to work in batches.

5 Place 2 in (5 cm) apart on the prepared sheets and flatten slightly. Bake until golden, about 10 minutes. Transfer to a rack to cool.

Chewy Chocolate Biscuits

MAKES 18

4 egg whites
10 oz (285 g) icing sugar
4 oz (115 g) cocoa powder
2 tbsp plain flour
1 tsp instant coffee
1 tbsp water
4 oz (115 g) finely chopped walnuts

1 Preheat a 350°F/180°C/Gas 4 oven. Line 2 baking sheets with greaseproof paper and grease the paper.

~ **VARIATION** ~

If wished, add 3 oz (85 g) chocolate chips to the mixture with the nuts.

2 With an electric mixer, beat the egg whites until frothy.

3 ▼ Sift the sugar, cocoa, flour and coffee into the whites. Add the water and continue beating on low speed to blend, then on high for a few minutes until the mixture thickens. With a rubber spatula, fold in the walnuts.

4 ▲ Place generous spoonfuls of the mixture 1 in (2.5 cm) apart on the prepared sheets. Bake until firm and cracked on top but soft on the inside, 12–15 minutes. With a metal spatula, transfer to a rack to cool.

Cinnamon-Coated Cookies (top), Chewy Chocolate Biscuits

Chocolate Pretzels

MAKES 28

5 oz (140 g) plain flour
1/8 teaspoon salt
3/4 oz (25 g) unsweetened cocoa powder
4 oz (115 g) butter, at room temperature
4 1/2 oz (125 g) sugar
1 egg
1 egg white, lightly beaten, for glazing
sugar crystals, for sprinkling

1 Sift together the flour, salt and cocoa powder. Set aside. Grease 2 baking sheets.

2 ▲ With an electric mixer, cream the butter until light. Add the sugar and continue beating until light and fluffy. Beat in the egg. Add the dry ingredients and stir to blend. Gather the dough into a ball, wrap in clear film, and refrigerate for 1 hour or freeze for 30 minutes.

3 ▲ Roll the dough into 28 small balls. Refrigerate the balls until needed. Preheat the oven to 375°F/ 190°C/Gas 5.

4 ▲ Roll each ball into a rope about 10 in (25 cm) long. With each rope, form a loop with the two ends facing you. Twist the ends and fold back on to the circle, pressing in to make a pretzel shape. Place on the sheets.

5 ▲ Brush the pretzels with the egg white. Sprinkle sugar crystals over the tops and bake until firm, 10–12 minutes. Transfer to a rack to cool.

Cream Cheese Spirals

MAKES 32

8 oz (225 g) butter, at room temperature

8 oz (225 g) cream cheese

2 tsp caster sugar

8 oz (225 g) plain flour

1 egg white beaten with 1 tbsp water, for glazing

caster sugar, for sprinkling

FOR THE FILLING

4 oz (115 g) finely chopped walnuts

4 oz (115 g) light brown sugar

1 tsp ground cinnamon

1 With an electric mixer, cream the butter, cream cheese and sugar until soft. Sift over the flour and mix until combined. Gather into a ball and divide in half. Flatten each half, wrap in greaseproof paper and refrigerate for at least 30 minutes.

2 Meanwhile, make the filling. Mix together the chopped walnuts, the brown sugar and the cinnamon and set aside.

3 Preheat a 375°F/190°C/Gas 5 oven. Grease 2 baking sheets.

4 ▲ Working with one half of the mixture at a time, roll out thinly into a circle about 11 in (28 cm) in diameter. Trim the edges with a knife, using a dinner plate as a guide.

5 ▼ Brush the surface with the egg white glaze and then sprinkle evenly with half the filling.

6 Cut the circle into quarters, and each quarter into 4 sections, to form 16 triangles.

7 ▲ Starting from the base of the triangles, roll up to form spirals.

8 Place on the sheets and brush with the remaining glaze. Sprinkle with caster sugar. Bake until golden, 15–20 minutes. Cool on a rack.

Vanilla Crescents

MAKES 36

6 oz (175 g) unblanched almonds

4 oz (115 g) plain flour

pinch of salt

8 oz (225 g) unsalted butter

4 oz (115 g) granulated sugar

1 teaspoon vanilla essence

icing sugar for dusting

1 Grind the almonds with a few tablespoons of the flour in a food processor, blender or nut grinder.

2 Sift the remaining flour with the salt into a bowl. Set aside.

3 With an electric mixer, cream together the butter and sugar until light and fluffy.

4 ▼ Add the almonds, vanilla essence and the flour mixture. Stir to mix well. Gather the dough into a ball, wrap in greaseproof paper, and chill for at least 30 minutes.

5 Preheat the oven to 325°F/170°C/ Gas 3. Lightly grease two baking sheets.

6 ▲ Break off walnut-size pieces of dough and roll into small cylinders about ¹/₂ in (1 cm) in diameter. Bend into small crescents and place on the prepared baking sheets.

7 Bake for about 20 minutes until dry but not brown. Transfer to a wire rack to cool only slightly. Set the rack over a baking sheet and dust with an even layer of icing sugar. Leave to cool completely.

Walnut Crescents

MAKES 72

4 oz (115 g) walnuts

8 oz (225 g) unsalted butter

4 oz (115 g) granulated sugar

¹/₂ teaspoon vanilla extract

8 oz (225 g) flour

¹/₄ teaspoon salt

confectioners' sugar for dusting

1 Preheat the oven to 350°F/ 180°C/Gas 4.

2 Grind the walnuts in a food processor, blender or nut grinder until they are almost a paste. Transfer to a bowl.

3 Add the butter to the walnuts and mix with a wooden spoon until blended. Add the granulated sugar and vanilla and stir to blend.

4 ▼ Sift the flour and salt into the walnut mixture. Work into a dough.

5 Shape the dough into small cylinders about 1¹/₂ in (4 cm) long. Bend into crescents and place evenly spaced on an ungreased baking sheet.

6 ▲ Bake until lightly browned, about 15 minutes. Transfer to a rack to cool only slightly. Set the rack over a baking sheet and dust lightly with confectioners' sugar.

Vanilla Crescents (top), Walnut Crescents

Pecan Puffs

MAKES 24

4 oz (115 g) unsalted butter
2 tablespoons granulated sugar
pinch of salt
1 teaspoon vanilla essence
4 oz (115 g) pecans
4 oz (115 g) plain flour, sifted
icing sugar for dusting

1 Preheat the oven to 300°F/150°C/ Gas 2. Grease two baking sheets.

2 ▲ Cream the butter and sugar until light and fluffy. Stir in the salt and vanilla essence.

3 Grind the nuts in a food processor, blender or nut grinder. Stir several times to prevent nuts becoming oily. If necessary, grind in batches.

4 ▲ Push the ground nuts through a sieve set over a bowl to aerate them. Pieces too large to go through the sieve can be ground again.

5 ▲ Stir the nuts and flour into the butter mixture to make a firm, springy dough.

6 Roll the dough into marble-size balls between the palms of your hands. Place on the prepared baking sheets and bake for 45 minutes.

7 ▲ While the puffs are still hot, roll them in icing sugar. Leave to cool completely, then roll once more in icing sugar.

Pecan Tassies

MAKES 24

4 oz (115 g) cream cheese
4 oz (115 g) butter
4 oz (115 g) plain flour
FOR THE FILLING
2 eggs
4 oz (115 g) dark brown sugar
1 teaspoon vanilla essence
pinch of salt
2 tablespoons butter, melted
4 oz (115 g) pecans

1 Place a baking sheet in the oven and preheat to 350°F/180°C/Gas 4. Grease 24 mini-muffin tins.

2 Chop the cream cheese and butter into cubes. Put them in a mixing bowl. Sift over half the flour and mix. Add the remaining flour and continue mixing to form a dough.

3 ▲ Roll out the dough thinly. With a floured fluted pastry cutter, stamp out 24 2½ in/7 cm rounds. Line the tins with the rounds and chill.

~ **VARIATION** ~

To make Jam Tassies, fill the cream cheese pastry shells with raspberry or blackberry jam, or other fruit jams. Bake as described.

4 To make the filling, lightly whisk the eggs in a bowl. Gradually whisk in the brown sugar, and add the vanilla essence, salt and butter. Set aside until required.

5 ▼ Reserve 24 undamaged pecan halves and chop the rest coarsely with a sharp knife.

6 ▲ Place a spoonful of chopped nuts in each muffin tin and cover with the filling. Set a pecan half on the top of each.

7 Bake on the hot baking sheet for about 20 minutes, until puffed and set. Transfer to a wire rack to cool. Serve at room temperature.

Lady Fingers

MAKES 18

3¹/₂ oz (90 g) plain flour

pinch of salt

4 eggs, separated

4 oz (115 g) granulated sugar

¹/₂ teaspoon vanilla essence

icing sugar for sprinkling

1 Preheat the oven to 300°F/150°C/ Gas 2. Grease 2 baking sheets, then coat lightly with flour, and shake off the excess.

2 Sift the flour and salt together twice in a bowl.

~ COOK'S TIP ~

To make the biscuits all the same length, mark parallel lines 4 in (10 cm) apart on the greased baking sheets.

---

3 With an electric mixer beat the egg yolks with half of the sugar until thick enough to leave a ribbon trail when the beaters are lifted.

4 ▲ In another bowl, beat the egg whites until stiff. Beat in the remaining sugar until glossy.

5 Sift the flour over the yolks and spoon a large dollop of egg whites over the flour. Carefully fold in with a large metal spoon, adding the vanilla essence. Gently fold in the remaining whites.

6 ▲ Spoon the mixture into a piping bag fitted with a large plain nozzle. Pipe 4 in (10 cm) long lines on the prepared baking sheets about 1 in (2.5 cm) apart. Sift over a layer of icing sugar. Turn the sheet upside down to dislodge any excess sugar.

7 Bake for about 20 minutes until crusty on the outside but soft in the centre. Cool slightly on the baking sheets before transferring to a wire rack to cool completely.

Walnut Cookies

MAKES 60

4 oz (115 g) butter or margarine

6 oz (175 g) caster sugar

4 oz (115 g) plain flour

2 teaspoons vanilla essence

4 oz (115 g) walnuts, finely chopped

~ VARIATION ~

To make Almond Cookies, use an equal amount of finely chopped unblanched almonds instead of walnuts. Replace half the vanilla with ¹/₂ teaspoon almond essence.

---

1 Preheat the oven to 300°F/150°C/ Gas 2. Grease 2 baking sheets.

2 ▲ With an electric mixer, cream the butter or margarine until soft. Add 2 oz (50 g) of the sugar and continue beating until light and fluffy. Stir in the flour, vanilla essence and walnuts.

3 Drop teaspoonfuls of the batter 1–2 in (2.5–5 cm) apart on the prepared baking sheets and flatten slightly. Bake for about 25 minutes.

4 ▼ Transfer to a wire rack set over a baking sheet and sprinkle with the remaining sugar.

Lady Fingers (top), Walnut Cookies

Italian Almond Biscotti

MAKES 48

7 oz (200 g) whole unblanched almonds
7½ oz (215 g) plain flour
3½ oz (100 g) sugar
⅛ teaspoon salt
⅛ teaspoon saffron powder
½ teaspoon bicarbonate of soda
2 eggs
1 egg white, lightly beaten

~ COOK'S TIP ~

Serve biscotti after a meal, for dunking in glasses of sweet white wine, such as an Italian *Vin Santo* or a French *Muscat de Beaumes-de-Venise*.

1 Preheat a 375°F/190°C/Gas 5 oven. Grease and flour 2 baking sheets.

2 ▲ Spread the almonds in a baking tray and bake until lightly browned, about 15 minutes. When cool, grind 2 oz (55 g) of the almonds in a food processor, blender, or coffee grinder until pulverized. Coarsely chop the remaining almonds in 2 or 3 pieces each. Set aside.

3 ▲ Combine the flour, sugar, salt, saffron, bicarbonate of soda and ground almonds in a bowl and mix to blend. Make a well in the centre and add the eggs. Stir to form a rough dough. Transfer to a floured surface and knead until well blended. Knead in the chopped almonds.

4 ▲ Divide the dough into 3 equal parts. Roll into logs about 1 in (2.5 cm) in diameter. Place on one of the prepared sheets, brush with the egg white and bake for 20 minutes. Remove from the oven.

5 ▲ With a very sharp knife, cut into each log at an angle making ½ in (1 cm) slices. Return the slices on the baking sheets to a 275°F/140°C/ Gas 1 oven and bake for 25 minutes more. Transfer to a rack to cool.

Christmas Cookies

MAKES 30

6 oz (170 g) unsalted butter, at room
   temperature

10 oz (285 g) caster sugar

1 egg

1 egg yolk

1 tsp vanilla essence

grated rind of 1 lemon

¹/₄ tsp salt

10 oz (285 g) plain flour

FOR DECORATING (OPTIONAL)

coloured icing and small decorations

1 Preheat a 350°F/180°C/Gas 4 oven.

2 ▲ With an electric mixer, cream
the butter until soft. Add the sugar
gradually and continue beating until
light and fluffy.

3 ▲ Using a wooden spoon, slowly
mix in the whole egg and the egg yolk.
Add the vanilla, lemon rind and salt.
Stir to mix well.

4 Add the flour and stir until
blended. Gather the mixture into a
ball, wrap in greaseproof paper, and
refrigerate for at least 30 minutes.

5 ▼ On a floured surface, roll out the
mixture about ¹/₈ in (3 mm) thick.

6 ▲ Stamp out shapes or rounds with
biscuit cutters.

7 Bake until lightly coloured, about 8
minutes. Transfer to a rack and let
cool completely before icing and
decorating, if wished.

Toasted Oat Meringues

MAKES 12

2 oz (55 g) rolled oats
2 egg whites
1/8 tsp salt
1 1/2 tsp cornflour
6 oz (170 g) caster sugar

1 Preheat a 275°F/140°C/Gas 1 oven. Spread the oats on a baking sheet and toast in the oven until golden, about 10 minutes. Lower the heat to 250°F/130°C/Gas 1/2. Grease and flour a baking sheet.

~ VARIATION ~

Add 1/2 teaspoon ground cinnamon with the oats, and fold in gently.

---

2 ▼ With an electric mixer, beat the egg whites and salt until they start to form soft peaks.

3 Sift over the cornflour and continue beating until the whites hold stiff peaks. Add half the sugar and whisk until glossy.

4 ▲ Add the remaining sugar and fold in, then fold in the oats.

5 Gently spoon the mixture onto the prepared sheet and bake for 2 hours.

6 When done, turn off the oven. Lift the meringues from the sheet, turn over, and set in another place on the sheet to prevent sticking. Leave in the oven as it cools down.

Meringues

MAKES 24

4 egg whites
1/8 tsp salt
10 oz (285 g) caster sugar
1/2 tsp vanilla or almond essence (optional)
8 fl oz (250 ml) whipped cream (optional)

1 Preheat a 225°F/110°C/Gas 1/4 oven. Grease and flour 2 large baking sheets.

2 With an electric mixer, beat the egg whites and salt in a very clean metal bowl on low speed. When they start to form soft peaks, add half the sugar and continue beating until the mixture holds stiff peaks.

3 ▲ With a large metal spoon, fold in the remaining sugar and vanilla or almond essence, if using.

4 ▼ Pipe the meringue mixture or gently spoon it on the prepared sheet.

5 Bake for 2 hours. Turn off the oven. Loosen the meringues, invert, and set in another place on the sheets to prevent sticking. Leave in the oven as it cools. Serve sandwiched with whipped cream, if wished.

Toasted Oat Meringues (top), *Meringues*

Traditional Sugar Biscuits

MAKES 36

12 oz (350 g) plain flour

1 tsp bicarbonate of soda

2 tsp baking powder

¼ tsp grated nutmeg

4 oz (115 g) butter or margarine, at room temperature

8 oz (225 g) caster sugar

½ tsp vanilla essence

1 egg

4 fl oz (125 ml) milk

coloured or demerara sugar, for sprinkling

1 Sift the flour, bicarbonate of soda, baking powder and nutmeg into a small bowl. Set aside.

2 ▲ With an electric mixer, cream the butter or margarine, caster sugar and vanilla together until the mixture is light and fluffy. Add the egg and beat to mix well.

3 ▲ Add the flour mixture alternately with the milk, stirring with a wooden spoon to make a soft dough. Wrap the dough in cling film and refrigerate at least 30 minutes, or overnight.

4 ▲ Preheat a 350°F/180°C/Gas 4 oven. Roll out the dough on a lightly floured surface to ⅛ in (3 mm) thickness. Cut into rounds or other shapes with biscuit cutters.

5 ▲ Transfer the biscuits to ungreased baking trays. Sprinkle each one with coloured or demerara sugar.

6 Bake until golden brown, for about 10–12 minutes. With a slotted spatula, transfer the biscuits to a wire rack and let cool.

Chocolate Chip Nut Biscuits

MAKES 36

4 oz (115 g) plain flour

1 tsp baking powder

¼ tsp salt

3 oz (85 g) butter or margarine, at room temperature

4 oz (115 g) caster sugar

1¾ oz (50 g) light brown sugar

1 egg

1 tsp vanilla essence

4½ oz (130 g) chocolate chips

2 oz (55 g) hazelnuts, chopped

1 ▲ Preheat a 350°F/180°C/Gas 4 oven. Grease 2–3 baking trays.

2 Sift the flour, baking powder and salt into a small bowl. Set aside.

3 ▲ With an electric mixer, cream the butter or margarine and sugars together. Beat in the egg and vanilla.

4 Add the flour mixture and beat well with the mixer on low speed.

5 ▼ Stir in the chocolate chips and half of the hazelnuts using a wooden spoon.

6 Drop teaspoonfuls of the mixture onto the prepared baking trays, to form ¾ in (2 cm) mounds. Space the biscuits 1–2 in (2–5 cm) apart.

7 ▲ Flatten each biscuit lightly with a wet fork. Sprinkle the remaining hazelnuts on top of the biscuits and press lightly into the surface.

8 Bake until golden brown, about 10–12 minutes. With a slotted spatula, transfer the biscuits to a wire rack and let cool.

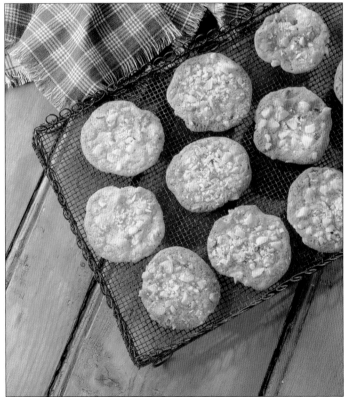

Chocolate Macaroons

MAKES 24

2 oz (55 g) plain chocolate
6 oz (170 g) blanched almonds
8 oz (225 g) caster sugar
2 egg whites
1/2 tsp vanilla essence
1/4 tsp almond essence
icing sugar, for dusting

1 Preheat a 300°F/150°C/Gas 2 oven. Line 2 baking sheets with greaseproof paper and grease the paper.

2 ▼ Melt the chocolate in the top of a double boiler, or in a heatproof bowl set over a pan of hot water.

3 ▲ Grind the almonds finely in a food processor, blender or grinder. Transfer to a mixing bowl.

4 ▲ In a mixing bowl, whisk the egg whites until they form soft peaks. Fold in the sugar, vanilla and almond essence, ground almonds and cooled melted chocolate. Refrigerate for 15 minutes.

5 ▲ Use a teaspoon and your hands to shape the mixture into walnut-size balls. Place on the sheets and flatten slightly. Brush each ball with a little water and sift over a thin layer of icing sugar. Bake until just firm, about 20–25 minutes. With a metal spatula, transfer to a rack to cool.

> ### ~ VARIATION ~
>
> For Chocolate Pine Nut Macaroons, spread 3 oz (85 g) pine nuts in a shallow dish. Press the chocolate macaroon balls into the nuts to cover one side and bake as described, nut-side up.

Coconut Macaroons

MAKES 24

1 1/2 oz (45 g) plain flour
1/8 tsp salt
8 oz (225 g) desiccated coconut
5 1/2 fl oz (170 ml) sweetened condensed milk
1 tsp vanilla essence

1 Preheat a 350°F/180°C/Gas 4 oven. Grease 2 baking sheets.

2 Sift the flour and salt into a bowl. Stir in the coconut.

3 ▲ Pour in the milk. Add the vanilla and stir from the centre to make a very thick mixture.

4 ▼ Drop heaped tablespoonfuls of mixture 1 in (2.5 cm) apart on the sheets. Bake until golden brown, about 20 minutes. Cool on a rack.

Chocolate Macaroons (top), Coconut Macaroons

Almond Tiles

MAKES 40

2 oz (55 g) blanched almonds
4 oz (115 g) sugar
1³/₄ oz (50 g) unsalted butter
2 egg whites
1¹/₂ oz (45 g) plain flour
¹/₂ teaspoon vanilla essence
4 oz (115 g) slivered almonds

1 Grind the blanched almonds with 2 tablespoons of the sugar in a food processor, blender or nut grinder. If necessary, grind in batches.

2 Preheat the oven to 425°F/220°C/ Gas 7. Grease 2 baking sheets.

3 ▲ Put the butter in a large bowl and mix in the remaining sugar, using a metal spoon. With an electric mixer, cream them together until light and fluffy.

4 Add the egg whites and stir until blended. Sift over the flour and fold in with a metal spoon. Fold in the ground almonds and vanilla essence.

5 ▲ Working in small batches, drop tablespoonfuls of the mixture 3 in (7.5 cm) apart on one of the prepared sheets. With the back of a spoon, spread out into thin, almost transparent circles about 6 cm (2¹/₂ in) in diameter. Sprinkle each circle with some of the slivered almonds.

6 Bake until the outer edges have browned slightly, about 4 minutes.

7 ▲ Remove from the oven. With a metal spatula, quickly drape the biscuits over a rolling pin to form a curved shape. Transfer to a rack when firm. If the biscuits harden too quickly to shape, reheat briefly. Repeat the baking and shaping process until the mixture is used up. Store in an airtight container.

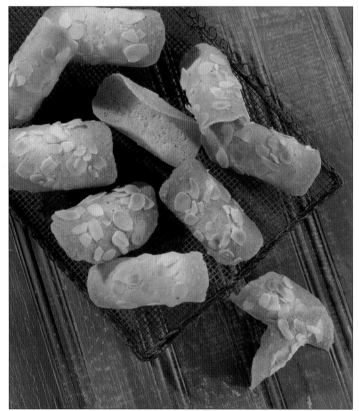

Florentines

MAKES 36

1¹/₂ oz (45 g) butter
4 fl oz (125 ml) whipping cream
4¹/₂ oz (125 g) sugar
4¹/₂ oz (125 g) flaked almonds
2 oz (55 g) orange or mixed peel, finely chopped
1¹/₂ oz (45 g) glacé cherries, chopped
2¹/₂ oz (70 g) plain flour, sifted
8 oz (225 g) plain chocolate
1 teaspoon vegetable oil

1 Preheat the oven to 350°F/180°C/ Gas 4. Grease 2 baking sheets.

2 ▲ Melt the butter, cream and sugar together and slowly bring to the boil. Take off the heat and stir in the almonds, orange or mixed peel, cherries and flour until blended.

3 Drop teaspoonfuls of the batter 1–2 in (2.5–5 cm) apart on the prepared sheets and flatten with a fork.

4 Bake until the cookies brown at the edges, about 10 minutes. Remove from the oven and correct the shape by quickly pushing in any thin uneven edges with a knife or a round biscuit cutter. Work fast or they will cool and harden while still on the sheets. If necessary, return to the oven for a few moments to soften. While still hot, use a metal palette knife to transfer the florentines to a clean, flat surface.

5 Melt the chocolate in the top of a double boiler or in a heatproof bowl set over a pan of hot water. Add the oil and stir to blend.

6 ▲ With a metal palette knife, spread the smooth underside of the cooled florentines with a thin coating of the melted chocolate.

7 ▼ When the chocolate is about to set, draw a serrated knife across the surface with a slight sawing motion to make wavy lines. Store in an airtight container in a cool place.

Nut Lace Wafers

MAKES 18

2¹/₂ oz (70 g) whole blanched almonds

2 oz (55 g) butter

1¹/₂ oz (45 g) plain flour

3¹/₂ oz (100 g) sugar

1 fl oz (30 ml) double cream

¹/₂ teaspoon vanilla essence

1 Preheat the oven to 375°F/190°C/ Gas 5. Grease 1–2 baking sheets.

2 With a sharp knife, chop the almonds as fine as possible. Alternatively, use a food processor, blender, or coffee grinder to chop the nuts very fine.

3 ▼ Melt the butter in a saucepan over low heat. Remove from the heat and stir in the remaining ingredients and the almonds.

4 Drop teaspoonfuls 2¹/₂ in (6 cm) apart on the prepared sheets. Bake until golden, about 5 minutes. Cool on the baking sheets briefly, just until the wafers are stiff enough to remove.

5 ▲ With a metal palette knife, transfer to a rack to cool completely.

~ **VARIATION** ~
Add 2 oz (55 g) finely chopped orange peel to the mixture.

Oatmeal Lace Rounds

MAKES 36

5¹/₂ oz (150 g) butter or margarine

4¹/₂ oz (125 g) quick-cooking porridge oats

5³/₄ oz (165 g) dark brown sugar

5¹/₄ oz (150 g) caster sugar

1¹/₂ oz (45 g) plain flour

¹/₄ teaspoon salt

1 egg, lightly beaten

1 teaspoon vanilla essence

2¹/₂ oz (70 g) pecans or walnuts, finely chopped

1 Preheat the oven to 350°F/180°C/ Gas 4. Grease 2 baking sheets.

2 Melt the butter in a saucepan over low heat. Set aside.

3 In a mixing bowl, combine the oats, brown sugar, caster sugar, flour and salt.

4 ▲ Make a well in the centre and add the butter or margarine, egg and vanilla.

5 ▼ Mix until blended, then stir in the chopped nuts.

6 Drop rounded teaspoonfuls of the mixture about 2 in (5 cm) apart on the prepared sheets. Bake until lightly browned on the edges and bubbling, 5–8 minutes. Let cool on the sheet for 2 minutes, then transfer to a rack to cool completely.

Nut Lace Wafers (top), Oatmeal Lace Rounds

Raspberry Sandwich Biscuits

MAKES 32

6 oz (170 g) blanched almonds
6 oz (170 g) plain flour
6 oz (170 g) butter, at room temperature
4 oz (115 g) caster sugar
grated rind of 1 lemon
1 tsp vanilla essence
1 egg white
1/8 tsp salt
1 oz (30 g) flaked almonds
8 fl oz (250 ml) raspberry jam
1 tbsp fresh lemon juice

1 Place the blanched almonds and 3 tablespoons of the flour in a food processor, blender or coffee grinder and process until finely ground. Set aside.

2 With an electric mixer, cream the butter and sugar together until light and fluffy. Stir in the lemon rind and vanilla. Add the ground almonds and remaining flour and mix well until combined. Gather into a ball, wrap in greaseproof paper, and refrigerate for at least 1 hour.

3 Preheat a 325°F/170°C/Gas 3 oven. Line 2 baking sheets with greaseproof paper.

4 Divide the biscuit mixture into 4 equal parts. Working with one section at a time, roll out to a thickness of 1/8 in (3 mm) on a lightly floured surface. With a 2 1/2 in (6 cm) fluted pastry cutter, stamp out circles. Gather the scraps, roll out and stamp out more circles. Repeat with the remaining sections.

5 ▲ Using a 3/4 in (2 cm) piping nozzle or pastry cutter, stamp out the centres from half the circles. Place the rings and circles 1 in (2.5 cm) apart on the prepared sheets.

6 ▲ Whisk the egg white with the salt until just frothy. Chop the flaked almonds. Brush only the biscuit rings with the egg white, then sprinkle over the almonds. Bake until very lightly browned, 12–15 minutes. Let cool for a few minutes on the sheets before transferring to a rack.

7 ▲ In a saucepan, melt the jam with the lemon juice until it comes to a simmer. Brush the jam over the biscuit circles and sandwich together with the rings. Store in an airtight container with sheets of greaseproof paper between the layers.

Brandysnaps

MAKES 18

2 oz (55 g) butter, at room temperature
5 oz (140 g) caster sugar
1 rounded tbsp golden syrup
1¹/₂ oz (45 g) plain flour
¹/₂ tsp ground ginger
FOR THE FILLING
8 fl oz (250 ml) whipping cream
2 tbsp brandy

1 With an electric mixer, cream together the butter and sugar until light and fluffy, then beat in the golden syrup. Sift over the flour and ginger and mix together.

2 ▲ Transfer the mixture to a work surface and knead until smooth. Cover and refrigerate for 30 minutes.

3 Preheat a 375°F/190°C/Gas 5 oven. Grease a baking sheet.

4 ▲ Working in batches of 4, form the mixture into walnut-size balls. Place far apart on the sheet and flatten slightly. Bake until golden and bubbling, about 10 minutes.

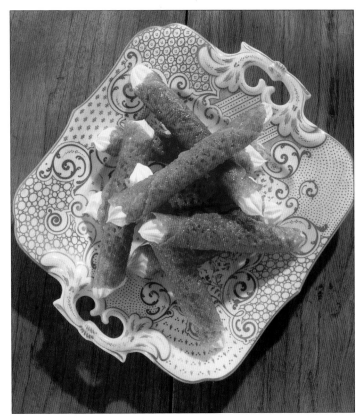

5 ▼ Remove from the oven and let cool a few moments. Working quickly, slide a metal spatula under each one, turn over, and wrap around the handle of a wooden spoon (have 4 spoons ready). If they firm up too quickly, reheat for a few seconds to soften. When firm, slide the snaps off and place on a rack to cool.

6 ▲ When all the brandy snaps are cool, prepare the filling. Whip the cream and brandy until soft peaks form. Fill a piping bag with the brandy cream. Pipe into each end of the brandy snaps just before serving.

Spicy Pepper Biscuits

MAKES 48

7 oz (200 g) plain flour

2 oz (55 g) cornflour

2 tsp baking powder

½ tsp ground cardamom

½ tsp ground cinnamon

½ tsp grated nutmeg

½ tsp ground ginger

½ tsp ground allspice

½ tsp salt

½ tsp freshly ground black pepper

8 oz (225 g) butter or margarine, at room temperature

3½ oz (100 g) light brown sugar

½ tsp vanilla essence

1 tsp finely grated lemon rind

2 fl oz (65 ml) whipping cream

3 oz (85 g) finely ground almonds

2 tbsp icing sugar

1 Preheat a 350°F/180°C/Gas 4 oven.

2 Sift the flour, cornflour, baking powder, spices, salt and pepper into a bowl. Set aside.

3 With an electric mixer, cream the butter or margarine and brown sugar together until light and fluffy. Beat in the vanilla and lemon rind.

4 ▲ With the mixer on low speed, add the flour mixture alternately with the cream, beginning and ending with flour. Stir in the ground almonds.

5 ▲ Shape the dough into ¾ in (2 cm) balls. Place them on ungreased baking trays about 1 in (2.5 cm) apart. Bake until the biscuits are golden brown underneath, 15–20 minutes.

6 Let the biscuits cool on the baking trays about 1 minute before transferring them to a wire rack to cool completely. Before serving, sprinkle them lightly with icing sugar.

Chocolate and Coconut Slices

MAKES 24

6 oz (175 g) digestive biscuits, crushed

2 oz (55 g) caster sugar

⅛ tsp salt

4 oz (115 g) butter or margarine, melted

3 oz (85 g) desiccated coconut

9 oz (260 g) plain chocolate chips

8 fl oz (250 ml) sweetened condensed milk

4 oz (115 g) chopped walnuts

1 Preheat a 350°F/180°C/Gas 4 oven.

2 ▼ In a bowl, combine the crushed biscuits, sugar, salt and butter or margarine. Press the mixture evenly over the bottom of an ungreased 13 × 9 in (33 × 23 cm) baking dish.

3 ▲ Sprinkle the coconut over the biscuit base, then scatter over the chocolate chips. Pour the condensed milk evenly over the chocolate. Sprinkle the walnuts on top.

4 Bake 30 minutes. Unmould onto a wire rack and let cool, preferably overnight. When cooled, cut into slices.

Spicy Pepper Biscuits (top), Chocolate and Coconut Slices

Shortbread

MAKES 8

5¹/₂ oz (150 g) unsalted butter, at room
   temperature

3¹/₂ oz (100 g) caster sugar

6¹/₄ oz (180 g) plain flour

2 oz (55 g) rice flour

¹/₄ teaspoon baking powder

¹/₈ teaspoon salt

1 Preheat the oven to 325°F/170°C/
Gas 3. Grease a shallow 8 in (20 cm)
cake tin, preferably with a removable
bottom.

2 With an electric mixer, cream the
butter and sugar together until light
and fluffy. Sift over the flours, baking
powder and salt and mix well.

3 ▲ Press the dough neatly into the
prepared tin, smoothing the surface
with the back of a spoon.

4 Prick all over with a fork, then
score into 8 equal wedges.

5 ▲ Bake until golden, 40–45
minutes. Leave in the tin until cool
enough to handle, then turn out and
recut the wedges while still hot. Store
in an airtight container.

Flapjacks

MAKES 8

2 oz (55 g) butter

1 rounded tablespoon golden syrup

2³/₄ oz (80 g) dark brown sugar

3¹/₂ oz (100 g) quick-cooking porridge oats

¹/₈ teaspoon salt

1 ▲ Preheat a 350°F/180°C/Gas 4
oven. Line an 8 in (20 cm) cake tin
with greaseproof paper and grease.

2 ▼ Place the butter, golden syrup
and sugar in a saucepan over a low
heat. Cook, stirring, until melted and
combined.

~ VARIATION ~

If wished, add 1 teaspoon ground
ginger to the melted butter.

3 ▲ Remove from the heat and add
the oats and salt. Stir to blend.

4 Spoon into the prepared tin and
smooth the surface. Place in the
centre of the oven and bake until
golden brown, 20–25 minutes. Leave
in the tin until cool enough to handle,
then turn out and cut into wedges
while still hot.

Shortbread (top), Flapjacks

Chocolate Delights

MAKES 50

1 oz (30 g) plain chocolate
1 oz (30 g) bitter cooking chocolate
8 oz (225 g) plain flour
¹/₂ tsp salt
8 oz (225 g) unsalted butter, at room temperature
8 oz (225 g) caster sugar
2 eggs
1 tsp vanilla essence
4 oz (115 g) finely chopped walnuts

1 Melt the chocolates in the top of a double boiler, or in a heatproof bowl set over a pan of gently simmering water. Set aside.

2 ▼ In a small bowl, sift together the flour and salt. Set aside.

3 With an electric mixer, cream the butter until soft. Add the sugar and continue beating until the mixture is light and fluffy.

4 Mix the eggs and vanilla, then gradually stir into the butter mixture.

5 ▲ Stir in the chocolate, then the flour. Stir in the nuts.

6 ▲ Divide the mixture into 4 equal parts, and roll each into 2 in (5 cm) diameter logs. Wrap tightly in foil and refrigerate or freeze until firm.

7 Preheat a 375°F/190°C/Gas 5 oven. Grease 2 baking sheets.

8 With a sharp knife, cut the logs into ¹/₄ in (5mm) slices. Place the rounds on the prepared sheets and bake until lightly coloured, about 10 minutes. Transfer to a rack to cool.

~ VARIATION ~

For two-tone biscuits, melt only half the chocolate. Combine all the ingredients, except the chocolate, as above. Divide the mixture in half. Add the chocolate to one half. Roll out the plain mixture to a flat sheet. Roll out the chocolate mixture, place on top of the plain one and roll up. Wrap, slice and bake as described.

Cinnamon Treats

MAKES 50

9 oz (250 g) plain flour
1/2 tsp salt
2 tsp ground cinnamon
8 oz (225 g) unsalted butter, at room temperature
8 oz (225 g) caster sugar
2 eggs
1 tsp vanilla essence

1 In a bowl, sift together the flour, salt and cinnamon. Set aside.

2 ▲ With an electric mixer, cream the butter until soft. Add the sugar and continue beating until the mixture is light and fluffy.

3 Beat the eggs and vanilla, then gradually stir into the butter mixture.

4 ▲ Stir in the dry ingredients.

5 ▲ Divide the mixture into 4 equal parts, then roll each into 2 in (5 cm) diameter logs. Wrap tightly in foil and refrigerate or freeze until firm.

6 Preheat a 375°F/190°C/Gas 5 oven. Grease 2 baking sheets.

7 ▼ With a sharp knife, cut the logs into 1/4 in (5 mm) slices. Place the rounds on the prepared sheets and bake until lightly coloured, about 10 minutes. With a metal spatula, transfer to a rack to cool.

Coffee Ice Cream Sandwiches

MAKES 8

4 oz (115 g) butter or margarine, at room temperature
2 oz (55 g) caster sugar
4 oz (115 g) plain flour
2 tbsp instant coffee
icing sugar, for sprinkling
16 fl oz (450 ml) coffee ice cream
2 tbsp cocoa powder, for sprinkling

1 Lightly grease 2–3 baking trays.

2 With an electric mixer or wooden spoon, beat the butter or margarine until soft. Beat in the caster sugar.

3 ▲ Add the flour and coffee and mix by hand to form an evenly blended dough. Wrap in a plastic bag and refrigerate at least 1 hour.

4 Lightly sprinkle the work surface with icing sugar. Knead the dough on the sugared surface for a few minutes to soften it slightly.

5 ▼ Using a rolling pin dusted with icing sugar, roll out the dough to ⅛ in (3 mm) thickness. With a 2½ in (6 cm) fluted pastry cutter, cut out 16 rounds. Transfer the rounds to the prepared baking trays. Refrigerate for at least 30 minutes.

6 Preheat a 300°F/150°C/Gas 2 oven. Bake the biscuits until they are lightly golden, about 30 minutes. Let them cool and firm up before removing them from the trays to a wire rack to cool completely.

7 Remove the ice cream from the freezer and let soften 10 minutes at room temperature.

8 ▲ With a metal spatula, spread the ice cream evenly on the flat side of eight of the biscuits, leaving the edges clear. Top with the remaining biscuits, flat-side down.

9 Arrange the ice cream sandwiches on a baking tray. Cover and freeze at least 1 hour, longer if a firmer sandwich is desired. Sift the cocoa powder over the tops before serving.

Hazelnut Squares

MAKES 9

2 oz (55 g) plain chocolate
2½ oz (70 g) butter or margarine
8 oz (225 g) caster sugar
2 oz (55 g) plain flour
½ tsp baking powder
2 eggs, beaten
½ tsp vanilla essence
4 oz (115 g) skinned hazelnuts, roughly chopped

1 Preheat the oven to 350°F/180°C/ Gas 4. Grease an 8 in (20 cm) square baking tin.

2 ▲ In a heatproof bowl set over a pan of barely simmering water, or in a double boiler, melt the chocolate and butter or margarine. Remove the bowl from the heat.

3 ▲ Add the sugar, flour, baking powder, eggs, vanilla and half the hazelnuts to the melted mixture and stir well with a wooden spoon.

4 ▼ Pour the mixture into the prepared tin. Bake 10 minutes, then sprinkle the reserved hazelnuts over the top. Return to the oven and continue baking until firm to the touch, about 25 minutes.

5 ▲ Let cool in the tin, set on a wire rack, for 10 minutes, then unmould onto the rack and let cool completely. Cut into squares for serving.

Peanut Butter Biscuits

MAKES 24

5 oz (140 g) plain flour
$^1/_2$ teaspoon bicarbonate of soda
$^1/_2$ teaspoon salt
4 oz (115 g) butter, at room temperature
5$^3/_4$ oz (165 g) light brown sugar
1 egg
1 teaspoon vanilla essence
9$^1/_2$ oz (265 g) crunchy peanut butter

1 Sift together the flour, bicarbonate of soda and salt and set aside.

2 With an electric mixer, cream the butter and sugar together until light and fluffy.

3 In another bowl, mix the egg and vanilla, then gradually beat into the butter mixture.

4 ▲ Stir in the peanut butter and blend thoroughly. Stir in the dry ingredients. Refrigerate for at least 30 minutes, or until firm.

5 Preheat the oven to 350°F/180°C/ Gas 4. Grease 2 baking sheets.

6 Spoon out rounded teaspoonfuls of the dough and roll into balls.

7 ▲ Place the balls on the prepared sheets and press flat with a fork into circles about 2$^1/_2$ in (6 cm) in diameter, making a criss-cross pattern. Bake until lightly coloured, 12–15 minutes. Transfer to a rack to cool.

> **~ VARIATION ~**
>
> Add 3 oz (85 g) peanuts, coarsely chopped, with the peanut butter.

Chocolate Chip Cookies

MAKES 24

4 oz (115 g) butter or margarine, at room temperature
1$^3/_4$ oz (50 g) caster sugar
3$^3/_4$ oz (110 g) dark brown sugar
1 egg
$^1/_2$ teaspoon vanilla essence
6 oz (170 g) plain flour
$^1/_2$ teaspoon bicarbonate of soda
$^1/_8$ teaspoon salt
6 oz (170 g) chocolate chips
2 oz (55 g) walnuts, chopped

1 Preheat the oven to 350°F/180°C/ Gas 4. Grease 2 large baking sheets.

2 ▼ With an electric mixer, cream the butter or margarine and two sugars together until light and fluffy.

3 In another bowl, mix the egg and vanilla, then gradually beat into the butter mixture. Sift over the flour, bicarbonate of soda and salt and stir.

4 ▲ Add the chocolate chips and walnuts, and mix to combine well.

5 Place heaped teaspoonfuls of the dough 2 in (5 cm) apart on the prepared sheets. Bake until lightly coloured, 10–15 minutes. Transfer to a rack to cool.

Peanut Butter Biscuits (top), Chocolate Chip Cookies

Apple-sauce Biscuits

MAKES 36

3½oz (90g) sugar

2oz (50g) butter or vegetable fat,
  at room temperature

6fl oz (175ml) thick apple sauce

⅛ teaspoon grated lemon rind

4oz (115g) flour

½ teaspoon baking powder

¼ teaspoon bicarbonate of soda

¼ teaspoon salt

½ teaspoon ground cinnamon

½ cup chopped walnuts

~ COOK'S TIP ~
If the apple sauce is runny, put
it in a strainer over a bowl and
let it drain for 10 minutes.

1 Preheat oven to 190°C/375°F/Gas 5.

2 In a medium bowl, beat together
the sugar and butter or vegetable fat
until well mixed. Beat in the apple
sauce and lemon rind.

3 ▲ Sift the flour, baking powder,
bicarbonate of soda, salt and
cinnamon into the mixture, and stir to
blend. Fold in the chopped walnuts.

4 ▲ Drop teaspoonfuls of the dough
on a lightly greased baking sheet,
spacing them about 2 in (5 cm) apart.

5 Bake the biscuits in the centre of
the oven until they are golden brown,
8–10 minutes. Transfer the biscuits to
a wire rack to cool.

Toffee Bars

MAKES 32

1lb (450g) soft light brown sugar,
  firmly packed

1lb (450g) butter or margarine,
  at room temperature

2 egg yolks

1½ teaspoons vanilla essence

1lb (450g) plain or wholemeal flour

½ teaspoon salt

4oz (115g) milk chocolate, broken
  in pieces

4oz (115g) chopped walnuts or pecans

1 Preheat the oven to 180°C/350°F/
Gas 4.

2 Beat together the sugar and butter
or margarine until light and fluffy.
Beat in the egg yolks and vanilla. Stir
in the flour and salt.

3 ▼ Spread the dough in a greased
13 × 9 × 2 in (33 × 23 × 5 cm)
baking tin. Bake until lightly browned,
25–30 minutes. The texture will be soft.

4 ▲ Remove from the oven and
immediately place the chocolate
pieces on the hot biscuit base. Let
stand until the chocolate softens,
then spread it evenly with a spatula.
Sprinkle with the nuts.

5 While still warm, cut into bars
about 2 × 1½ in (5 × 4 cm).

Apple-sauce Biscuits (top), Toffee Bars

Chocolate Chip Brownies

MAKES 24

4 oz (115 g) plain chocolate
4 oz (115 g) butter
3 eggs
7 oz (200 g) sugar
$^1/_2$ teaspoon vanilla essence
pinch of salt
5 oz (140 g) plain flour
6 oz (170 g) chocolate chips

1 ▼ Preheat a 350°F/180°C/Gas 4 oven. Line a 13 × 9 in (33 × 23 cm) tin with greaseproof paper and grease.

2 ▲ Melt the chocolate and butter in the top of a double boiler, or in a heatproof bowl set over a pan of gently simmering water.

3 ▲ Beat together the eggs, sugar, vanilla and salt. Stir in the chocolate mixture. Sift over the flour and fold in. Add the chocolate chips.

4 ▲ Pour the mixture into the prepared tin and spread evenly. Bake until just set, about 30 minutes. Do not overbake; the brownies should be slightly moist inside. Cool in the pan.

5 To turn out, run a knife all around the edge and invert onto a baking sheet. Remove the paper. Place another sheet on top and invert again so the brownies are right-side up. Cut into squares for serving.

Marbled Brownies

MAKES 24

8 oz (225 g) plain chocolate
3 oz (85 g) butter
4 eggs
10^1/$_2$ oz (300 g) sugar
5 oz (140 g) plain flour
^{1}/$_2$ teaspoon salt
1 teaspoon baking powder
2 teaspoons vanilla essence
4 oz (115 g) walnuts, chopped
FOR THE PLAIN MIXTURE
2 oz (55 g) butter, at room temperature
6 oz (170 g) cream cheese
3^1/$_2$ oz (100 g) sugar
2 eggs
1 oz (30 g) plain flour
1 teaspoon vanilla essence

1 Preheat a 350°F/180°C/Gas 4 oven. Line a 13 × 9 in (33 × 23 cm) tin with greaseproof paper and grease.

2 Melt the chocolate and butter over very low heat, stirring constantly. Set aside to cool.

3 Meanwhile, beat the eggs until light and fluffy. Gradually add the sugar and continue beating until blended. Sift over the flour, salt and baking powder and fold to combine.

4 ▲ Stir in the cooled chocolate mixture. Add the vanilla and walnuts. Measure and set aside 16 fl oz (450 ml) of the chocolate mixture.

5 ▲ For the plain mixture, cream the butter and cream cheese with an electric mixer.

6 Add the sugar and continue beating until blended. Beat in the eggs, flour and vanilla.

7 Spread the unmeasured chocolate mixture in the tin. Pour over the plain mixture. Drop spoonfuls of the reserved chocolate mixture on top.

8 ▲ With a metal palette knife, swirl the mixtures to marble. Do not blend completely. Bake until just set, 35–40 minutes. Turn out when cool and cut into squares for serving.

Nutty Chocolate Squares

MAKES 16

2 eggs
2 tsp vanilla essence
1/8 tsp salt
6 oz (170 g) pecan nuts, coarsely chopped
2 oz (55 g) plain flour
2 oz (55 g) caster sugar
4 fl oz (125 ml) golden syrup
3 oz (85 g) plain chocolate, finely chopped
1 1/2 oz (45 g) butter
16 pecan halves, for decorating

1 Preheat a 325°F/170°C/Gas 3 oven. Line the bottom and sides of an 8 in (20 cm) square baking tin with greaseproof paper and grease lightly.

2 ▼ Whisk together the eggs, vanilla and salt. In another bowl, mix together the pecans and flour. Set both aside.

3 In a saucepan, bring the sugar and golden syrup to a boil. Remove from the heat and stir in the chocolate and butter and blend thoroughly with a wooden spoon.

4 ▲ Mix in the beaten eggs, then fold in the pecan mixture.

5 Pour the mixture into the prepared tin and bake until set, about 35 minutes. Cool in the tin for 10 minutes before unmoulding. Cut into 2 in (5 cm) squares and press pecan halves into the tops while warm. Cool completely on a rack.

Raisin Brownies

MAKES 16

4 oz (115 g) butter or margarine
2 oz (55 g) cocoa powder
2 eggs
8 oz (225 g) caster sugar
1 tsp vanilla essence
1 1/2 oz (45 g) plain flour
3 oz (85 g) chopped walnuts
3 oz (85 g) raisins

1 Preheat the oven to 350°F/ 180°C/Gas 4. Line the bottom and sides of an 8 in (20 cm) square baking tin with greaseproof paper and grease the paper.

2 ▼ Gently melt the butter or margarine in a small saucepan. Remove from the heat and stir in the cocoa powder.

3 With an electric mixer, beat the eggs, sugar and vanilla together until light. Add the cocoa mixture and stir to blend.

4 ▲ Sift the flour over the cocoa mixture and gently fold in. Add the walnuts and raisins and scrape the mixture into the prepared tin.

5 Bake in the centre of the oven for 30 minutes. Do not overbake. Leave in the tin to cool before cutting into 2 in (5 cm) squares and removing. The brownies should be soft and moist.

Nutty Chocolate Squares (top), Raisin Brownies

Chocolate Walnut Bars

MAKES 24

2 oz (55 g) walnuts
2¼ oz (60 g) caster sugar
3¾ oz (110 g) plain flour, sifted
3 oz (85 g) cold unsalted butter, cut into pieces
FOR THE TOPPING
1 oz (30 g) unsalted butter
3 fl oz (85 ml) water
1 oz (30 g) unsweetened cocoa powder
3½ oz (100 g) caster sugar
1 teaspoon vanilla essence
⅛ teaspoon salt
2 eggs
icing sugar, for dusting

1 Preheat a 350°F/180°C/Gas 4 oven. Grease the bottom and sides of an 8 in (20 cm) square baking tin.

2 ▼ Grind the walnuts with a few tablespoons of the sugar in a food processor, blender or coffee grinder.

3 In a bowl, combine the ground walnuts, remaining sugar and flour. With your fingertips, rub in the butter until the mixture resembles coarse breadcrumbs. Alternatively, process all the ingredients in a food processor until the mixture resembles coarse breadcrumbs.

4 ▲ Pat the walnut mixture into the bottom of the prepared tin in an even layer. Bake for 25 minutes.

5 ▲ Meanwhile, for the topping, melt the butter with the water. Whisk in the cocoa and sugar. Remove from the heat, stir in the vanilla and salt and let cool for 5 minutes. Whisk in the eggs until blended.

6 ▲ Pour the topping over the crust when baked.

7 Return to the oven and bake until set, about 20 minutes. Set the tin on a rack to cool. Cut into 2½ × 1 in (6 × 2.5 cm) bars and dust with icing sugar. Store in the refrigerator.

Pecan Squares

MAKES 36

8 oz (225 g) plain flour
pinch of salt
4 oz (115 g) granulated sugar
8 oz (225 g) cold butter or margarine, chopped
1 egg
finely grated rind of 1 lemon
FOR THE TOPPING
6 oz (175 g) butter
3 oz (75 g) honey
2 oz (50 g) granulated sugar
4 oz (115 g) dark brown sugar
5 tablespoons whipping cream
1 lb (450 g) pecan halves

1 Preheat the oven to 375°F/190°C/ Gas 5. Lightly grease a 15$^{1}/_{2}$ × 10$^{1}/_{2}$ × 1 in (37 × 27 × 2.5 cm) Swiss roll tin.

2 ▲ Sift the flour and salt into a mixing bowl. Stir in the sugar. Cut and rub in the butter or margarine until the mixture resembles coarse crumbs. Add the egg and lemon rind and blend with a fork until the mixture just holds together.

3 ▼ Spoon the mixture into the prepared tin. With floured fingertips, press into an even layer. Prick the pastry all over with a fork and chill for 10 minutes.

4 Bake the pastry crust for 15 minutes. Remove the tin from the oven, but keep the oven on while making the topping.

5 ▲ To make the topping, melt the butter, honey and both sugars. Bring to the boil. Boil, without stirring, for 2 minutes. Off the heat, stir in the cream and pecans. Pour over the crust, return to the oven and bake for 25 minutes. Leave to cool.

6 When cool, run a knife around the edge. Invert on to a baking sheet, place another sheet on top and invert again. Dip a sharp knife into very hot water and cut into squares for serving.

Figgy Bars

Makes 48

12 oz (350 g) dried figs
3 eggs
6 oz (170 g) caster sugar
3 oz (85 g) plain flour
1 tsp baking powder
¹/₂ tsp ground cinnamon
¹/₄ tsp ground cloves
¹/₄ tsp grated nutmeg
¹/₄ tsp salt
3 oz (85 g) finely chopped walnuts
2 tbsp brandy or cognac
icing sugar, for dusting

1 Preheat a 325°F/170°C/Gas 3 oven.

2 Line a 12 × 8 × 1¹/₂ in (30 × 20 × 3 cm) tin with greaseproof paper and grease the paper.

3 ▲ With a sharp knife, chop the figs roughly. Set aside.

4 In a bowl, whisk the eggs and sugar until well blended. In another bowl, sift together the dry ingredients, then fold into the egg mixture in several batches.

5 ▼ Stir in the figs, walnuts and brandy or cognac.

6 Scrape the mixture into the prepared tin and bake until the top is firm and brown, 35–40 minutes. It should still be soft underneath.

7 Let cool in the tin for 5 minutes, then unmould and transfer to a sheet of greaseproof paper lightly sprinkled with icing sugar. Cut into bars.

Lemon Bars

Makes 36

2 oz (55 g) icing sugar
6 oz (170 g) plain flour
¹/₂ tsp salt
6 oz (170 g) butter, cut in small pieces
For the topping
4 eggs
12 oz (350 g) caster sugar
grated rind of 1 lemon
4 fl oz (125 ml) fresh lemon juice
6 fl oz (175 ml) whipping cream
icing sugar, for dusting

1 Preheat a 325°F/170°C/Gas 3 oven.

2 Grease a 13 × 9 in (33 × 23 cm) baking tin.

3 Sift the sugar, flour and salt into a bowl. With a pastry blender, cut in the butter until the mixture resembles coarse breadcrumbs.

4 ▲ Press the mixture into the bottom of the prepared tin. Bake until golden brown, about 20 minutes.

5 Meanwhile, for the topping, whisk the eggs and sugar together until blended. Add the lemon rind and juice and mix well.

6 ▲ Lightly whip the cream and fold into the egg mixture. Pour over the still warm base, return to the oven, and bake until set, about 40 minutes.

7 Cool completely before cutting into bars. Dust with icing sugar.

Figgy Bars (top), Lemon Bars

Apricot Specials

MAKES 12

3¹/₂ oz (100 g) light brown sugar
3 oz (85 g) plain flour
3 oz (85 g) cold unsalted butter, cut in pieces

FOR THE TOPPING

5 oz (140 g) dried apricots
8 fl oz (250 ml) water
grated rind of 1 lemon
2¹/₂ oz (75 g) caster sugar
2 tsp cornflour
2 oz (55 g) chopped walnuts

1 Preheat a 350°F/180°C/Gas 4 oven.

2 ▲ In a bowl, combine the brown sugar and flour. With a pastry blender, cut in the butter until the mixture resembles coarse breadcrumbs.

3 ▲ Transfer to an 8 in (20 cm) square baking tin and press level. Bake for 15 minutes. Remove from the oven but leave the oven on.

4 Meanwhile, for the topping, combine the apricots and water in a saucepan and simmer until soft, about 10 minutes. Strain the liquid and reserve. Chop the apricots.

5 ▲ Return the apricots to the saucepan and add the lemon rind, caster sugar, cornflour, and 4 tablespoons of the soaking liquid. Cook for 1 minute.

6 ▲ Cool slightly before spreading the topping over the base. Sprinkle over the walnuts and continue baking for 20 minutes more. Let cool in the tin before cutting into bars.

Almond-Topped Squares

MAKES 18

3 oz (75 g) butter
2 oz (50 g) granulated sugar
1 egg yolk
grated rind and juice of 1/2 lemon
1/2 teaspoon vanilla essence
2 tablespoons whipping cream
4 oz (115 g) plain flour
FOR THE TOPPING
8 oz (225 g) granulated sugar
3 oz (75 g) sliced almonds
4 egg whites
1/2 teaspoon ground ginger
1/2 teaspoon ground cinnamon

1 ▲ Preheat the oven to 375°F/
190°C/Gas 5. Line a 13 × 9 in (33 ×
23 cm) Swiss roll tin with greaseproof
paper and grease the paper.

2 Cream the butter and sugar. Beat
in the egg yolk, lemon rind and juice,
vanilla essence and cream.

3 ▲ Gradually stir in the flour.
Gather into a ball of dough.

4 With lightly floured fingers, press
the dough into the prepared tin. Bake
for 15 minutes. Remove from the
oven but leave the oven on.

5 ▲ To make the topping, combine
all the ingredients in a heavy
saucepan. Cook, stirring until the
mixture comes to the boil.

6 Continue boiling until just golden,
about 1 minute. Pour over the dough,
spreading evenly.

7 ▲ Return to the oven and bake
for about 45 minutes. Remove and
score into bars or squares. Cool
completely before cutting into
squares and serving.

Spiced Raisin Bars

MAKES 30

3¾ oz (110 g) plain flour

1½ teaspoons baking powder

1 teaspoon ground cinnamon

½ teaspoon grated nutmeg

¼ teaspoon ground cloves

¼ teaspoon ground allspice

7½ oz (215 g) raisins

4 oz (115 g) butter or margarine, at room temperature

3½ oz (100 g) sugar

2 eggs

5¾ oz (165 g) molasses

2 oz (55 g) walnuts, chopped

1 Preheat a 350°F/180°C/Gas 4 oven. Line a 13 × 9 in (33 × 23 cm) tin with greaseproof paper and grease.

2 Sift together the flour, baking powder and spices.

3 ▲ Place the raisins in another bowl and toss with a few tablespoons of the flour mixture.

4 ▲ With an electric mixer, cream the butter or margarine and sugar together until light and fluffy. Beat in the eggs, 1 at a time, then the molasses. Stir in the flour mixture, raisins and walnuts.

5 Spread evenly in the tin. Bake until just set, 15–18 minutes. Let cool in the tin before cutting into bars.

Toffee Meringue Bars

MAKES 12

2 oz (55 g) butter

7½ oz (215 g) dark brown sugar

1 egg

½ teaspoon vanilla essence

2½ oz (70 g) plain flour

½ teaspoon salt

¼ teaspoon grated nutmeg

FOR THE TOPPING

1 egg white

⅛ teaspoon salt

1 tablespoon golden syrup

3½ oz (100 g) caster sugar

2 oz (55 g) walnuts, finely chopped

1 ▲ Combine the butter and brown sugar in a saucepan and heat until bubbling. Set aside to cool.

2 Preheat the oven to 350°F/180°C/ Gas 4. Line the bottom and sides of an 8 in (20 cm) square cake tin with greaseproof paper and grease.

3 Beat the egg and vanilla into cooled sugar mixture. Sift over the flour, salt and nutmeg and fold in. Spread in the bottom of the tin.

4 ▲ For the topping, beat the egg white with the salt until it holds soft peaks. Beat in the golden syrup, then the sugar and continue beating until the mixture holds stiff peaks. Fold in the nuts and spread on top. Bake for 30 minutes. Cut into bars when cool.

Spiced Raisin Bars (top), Toffee Meringue Bars

Strawberry Shortcake

SERVES 6

1 lb (450 g) strawberries, hulled and halved or quartered, depending on size

3 tbsp icing sugar

8 fl oz (250 ml) whipping cream

mint leaves, for garnishing

FOR THE SHORTCAKE

8 oz (225 g) plain flour

3 oz (85 g) caster sugar

1 tbsp baking powder

½ tsp salt

8 fl oz (250 ml) whipping cream

1   Preheat a 400°F/200°C/Gas 6 oven. Lightly grease a baking tray.

2 ▲ For the shortcake, sift the flour into a mixing bowl. Add 2 oz (55 g) of the caster sugar, the baking powder and salt. Stir well.

3 ▲ Gradually add the cream, tossing lightly with a fork until the mixture forms clumps.

4 ▲ Gather the clumps together, but do not knead the dough. Shape the dough into a 6 in (15 cm) log. Cut into 6 slices and place them on the prepared baking tray.

5 ▲ Sprinkle with the remaining 1 oz (30 g) caster sugar. Bake until light golden brown, about 15 minutes. Let cool on a wire rack.

6 ▲ Meanwhile, combine one-quarter of the strawberries with the icing sugar. Mash with a fork. Stir in the remaining strawberries. Let stand 1 hour at room temperature.

7 ▲ In a bowl, whip the cream until soft peaks form.

8 ▲ To serve, slice each shortcake in half horizontally using a serrated knife. Put the bottom halves on individual dessert plates. Top each half with some of the whipped cream. Divide the strawberries among the 6 shortcakes. Replace the tops and garnish with mint. Serve with the remaining whipped cream.

~ COOK'S TIP ~

For best results when whipping cream, refrigerate the bowl and beaters until thoroughly chilled. If using an electric mixer, increase speed gradually, and turn the bowl while beating to incorporate as much air as possible.

BUNS & TEA BREADS

EASY TO MAKE AND SATISFYING TO
EAT, THESE BUNS AND TEA BREADS
WILL FILL THE HOUSE WITH
MOUTHWATERING SCENTS AND LURE
YOUR FAMILY AND FRIENDS TO
LINGER OVER BREAKFAST, COFFEE OR
TEA — AND THEY ARE GREAT FOR
SNACKS OR LUNCH.

Raisin Bran Buns

MAKES 15

2 oz (55 g) butter or margarine
1½ oz (45 g) plain flour
2 oz (55 g) wholewheat flour
1½ tsp bicarbonate of soda
⅛ tsp salt
1 tsp ground cinnamon
1 oz (30 g) bran
3 oz (85 g) raisins
2½ oz (65 g) dark brown sugar
2 oz (55 g) caster sugar
1 egg
8 fl oz (250 ml) buttermilk
juice of ½ lemon

1 Preheat a 400°F/200°C/Gas 6 oven. Grease 15 bun-tray cups.

2 ▲ Place the butter or margarine in a saucepan and melt over gentle heat. Set aside.

3 In a mixing bowl, sift together the flours, bicarbonate of soda, salt and cinnamon.

4 ▲ Add the bran, raisins and sugars and stir until blended.

5 In another bowl, mix together the egg, buttermilk, lemon juice and melted butter.

6 ▲ Add the buttermilk mixture to the dry ingredients and stir lightly and quickly just until moistened; do not mix until smooth.

7 ▲ Spoon the mixture into the prepared bun tray, filling the cups almost to the top. Half-fill any empty cups with water.

8 Bake until golden, 15–20 minutes. Serve warm or at room temperature.

Raspberry Crumble Buns

MAKES 12

6 oz (170 g) plain flour
2 oz (55 g) caster sugar
1³/₄ oz (50 g) light brown sugar
2 tsp baking powder
¹/₈ tsp salt
1 tsp ground cinnamon
4 oz (115 g) butter, melted
1 egg
4 fl oz (125 ml) milk
5 oz (140 g) fresh raspberries
grated rind of 1 lemon

FOR THE CRUMBLE TOPPING

1 oz (30 g) finely chopped pecan nuts or walnuts
2 oz (55 g) dark brown sugar
3 tbsp plain flour
1 tsp ground cinnamon
3 tbsp butter, melted

1 Preheat a 350°F/180°C/Gas 4 oven. Lightly grease a 12-cup bun tray or use paper cases.

2 Sift the flour into a bowl. Add the sugars, baking powder, salt and cinnamon and stir to blend.

3 ▲ Make a well in the centre. Place the butter, egg and milk in the well and mix until just combined. Stir in the raspberries and lemon rind. Spoon the mixture into the prepared bun tray, filling the cups almost to the top.

4 ▼ For the crumble topping, mix the nuts, dark brown sugar, flour and cinnamon in a bowl. Add the melted butter and stir to blend.

5 ▲ Spoon some of the crumble over each bun. Bake until browned, about 25 minutes. Transfer to a rack to cool slightly. Serve warm.

Carrot Buns

MAKES 12

6 oz (170 g) margarine, at room
temperature

3¹/₂ oz (100 g) dark brown sugar

1 egg, at room temperature

1 tbsp water

8 oz (225 g) carrots, grated

5 oz (140 g) plain flour

1 tsp baking powder

¹/₂ tsp bicarbonate of soda

1 tsp ground cinnamon

¹/₄ tsp grated nutmeg

¹/₂ tsp salt

1 Preheat a 350°F/180°C/Gas 4 oven.
Grease a 12-cup bun tray or use paper
cases.

2 With an electric mixer, cream the
margarine and sugar until light and
fluffy. Beat in the egg and water.

3 ▲ Stir in the carrots.

4 Sift over the flour, baking powder,
bicarbonate of soda, cinnamon,
nutmeg and salt. Stir to blend.

5 ▼ Spoon the mixture into the
prepared bun tray, filling the cups
almost to the top. Bake until the tops
spring back when touched lightly,
about 35 minutes. Let stand 10
minutes before transferring to a rack.

Dried Cherry Buns

MAKES 16

8 fl oz (250 ml) plain yoghurt

6 oz (170 g) dried cherries

4 oz (115 g) butter, at room temperature

6 oz (170 g) caster sugar

2 eggs, at room temperature

1 tsp vanilla essence

7 oz (200 g) plain flour

2 tsp baking powder

1 tsp bicarbonate of soda

¹/₈ tsp salt

1 In a mixing bowl, combine the
yoghurt and cherries. Cover and let
stand for 30 minutes.

2 Preheat a 350°F/180°C/Gas 4 oven.
Grease 16 bun-tray cups or use paper
cases.

3 With an electric mixer, cream the
butter and sugar together until light
and fluffy.

4 ▼ Add the eggs, 1 at a time,
beating well after each addition. Add
the vanilla and the cherry mixture and
stir to blend. Set aside.

5 ▲ In another bowl, sift together
the flour, baking powder, bicarbonate
soda and salt. Fold into the cherry
mixture in 3 batches.

6 Fill the prepared cups two-thirds
full. For even baking, half-fill any
empty cups with water. Bake until the
tops spring back when touched
lightly, about 20 minutes. Transfer to
a rack to cool.

Carrot Buns (top), Dried Cherry Buns

Blueberry Muffins

MAKES 12

6¼ oz (180 g) plain flour

2¼ oz (60 g) sugar

2 teaspoons baking powder

¼ teaspoon salt

2 eggs

2 oz (55 g) butter, melted

6 fl oz (175 ml) milk

1 teaspoon vanilla essence

1 teaspoon grated lemon rind

6 oz (170 g) fresh blueberries

1   Preheat a 400°F/200°C/Gas 6 oven.

2 ▼   Grease a 12-cup muffin tin or use paper cases.

3 ▲ Sift the flour, sugar, baking powder and salt into a bowl.

4   In another bowl, whisk the eggs until blended. Add the melted butter, milk, vanilla and lemon rind and stir to combine.

5   Make a well in the dry ingredients and pour in the egg mixture. With a large metal spoon, stir just until the flour is moistened, not until smooth.

6 ▲   Fold in the blueberries.

7 ▲   Spoon the batter into the cups, leaving room for the muffins to rise.

8   Bake until the tops spring back when touched lightly, 20–25 minutes. Let cool in the pan for 5 minutes before turning out.

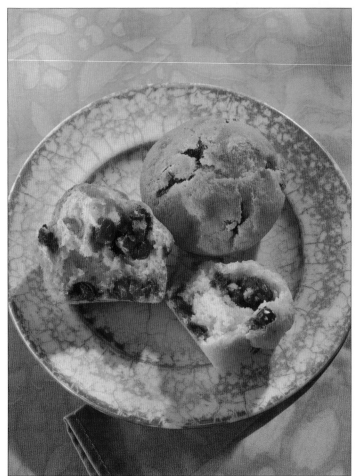

Apple and Cranberry Muffins

MAKES 12

2 oz (55 g) butter or margarine
1 egg
3¹/₂ oz (100 g) sugar
grated rind of 1 large orange
4 fl oz (125 ml) freshly squeezed orange juice
5 oz (140 g) plain flour
1 teaspoon baking powder
¹/₂ teaspoon bicarbonate of soda
1 teaspoon ground cinnamon
¹/₂ teaspoon grated nutmeg
¹/₂ teaspoon ground allspice
¹/₄ teaspoon ground ginger
¹/₄ teaspoon salt
1–2 dessert apples
6 oz (170 g) cranberries
2 oz (55 g) walnuts, chopped
icing sugar, for dusting (optional)

1 Preheat the oven to 350°F/180°C/Gas 4. Grease a 12-cup muffin tin or use paper cases.

2 Melt the butter or margarine over gentle heat. Set aside to cool.

3 ▲ Place the egg in a mixing bowl and whisk lightly. Add the melted butter or margarine and whisk to combine.

4 Add the sugar, orange rind and juice. Whisk to blend, then set aside.

5 In a large bowl, sift together the flour, baking powder, bicarbonate of soda, cinnamon, nutmeg, allspice, ginger and salt. Set aside.

6 ▲ Quarter, core and peel the apples. With a sharp knife, chop coarsely.

7 Make a well in the dry ingredients and pour in the egg mixture. With a spoon, stir until just blended.

8 ▲ Add the apples, cranberries and walnuts and stir to blend.

9 Fill the cups three-quarters full and bake until the tops spring back when touched lightly, 25–30 minutes. Transfer to a rack to cool. Dust with icing sugar, if desired.

Chocolate Chip Muffins

MAKES 10

4 oz (115 g) butter or margarine, at room temperature
2¹/₂ oz (70 g) caster sugar
1 oz (30 g) dark brown sugar
2 eggs, at room temperature
7¹/₂ oz (215 g) plain flour
1 teaspoon baking powder
4 fl oz (125 ml) milk
6 oz (170 g) plain chocolate chips

1 Preheat the oven to 375°F/190°C/Gas 5. Grease 10 muffin cups or use paper cases.

2 ▼ With an electric mixer, cream the butter until soft. Add both sugars and beat until light and fluffy. Beat in the eggs, 1 at a time.

3 Sift together the flour and baking powder, twice. Fold into the butter mixture, alternating with the milk.

4 ▲ Divide half the mixture between the muffin cups. Sprinkle several chocolate chips on top, then cover with a spoonful of the batter. To ensure even baking, half-fill any empty cups with water.

5 Bake until lightly coloured, about 25 minutes. Let stand 5 minutes before turning out.

Chocolate Walnut Muffins

MAKES 12

6 oz (170 g) unsalted butter
5 oz (140 g) plain chocolate
7 oz (200 g) caster sugar
2 oz (55 g) dark brown sugar
4 eggs
1 teaspoon vanilla essence
¹/₄ teaspoon almond essence
3³/₄ oz (110 g) plain flour
1 tablespoon unsweetened cocoa powder
4 oz (115 g) walnuts, chopped

1 Preheat the oven to 350°F/180°C/Gas 4. Grease a 12-cup muffin pan or use paper cases.

2 ▼ Melt the butter with the chocolate in the top of a double boiler or in a heatproof bowl set over a pan of hot water. Transfer to a large mixing bowl.

3 Stir both the sugars into the chocolate mixture. Mix in the eggs, 1 at a time, then add the vanilla and almond essences.

4 Sift over the flour and cocoa.

5 ▲ Fold in and stir in the walnuts.

6 Fill the prepared cups almost to the top and bake until a skewer inserted in the centre barely comes out clean, 30–35 minutes. Let stand 5 minutes before turning out onto a rack to cool completely.

Chocolate Chip Muffins (top), Chocolate Walnut Muffins

Oat and Raisin Muffins

MAKES 12

3 oz (85 g) rolled oats

8 fl oz (250 ml) buttermilk

4 oz (120 g) butter, at room temperature

3½ oz (100 g) dark brown sugar

1 egg, at room temperature

4 oz (120 g) flour

1 teaspoon baking powder

½ teaspoon bicarbonate of soda

¼ teaspoon salt

1 oz (30 g) raisins

1 ▲ In a bowl, combine the oats and buttermilk and let soak for 1 hour.

3 ▲ Preheat the oven to 400°F/200°C/Gas 6. With an electric mixer, cream the butter and sugar until light and fluffy. Beat in the egg.

4 In another bowl, sift the flour, baking powder, bicarbonate of soda and salt. Stir into the butter mixture, alternating with the oat mixture. Fold in the raisins. Do not overmix.

```
~ COOK'S TIP ~

If buttermilk is not available, add
1 teaspoon lemon juice or vinegar
to milk. Let the mixture stand
for a few minutes to curdle.
```

2 ▲ Lightly grease a 12-cup muffin tin or use paper cases.

5 Fill the prepared cups two-thirds full. Bake until a skewer inserted in the centre comes out clean, 20–25 minutes. Transfer to a rack to cool.

Pumpkin Muffins

MAKES 14

4 oz (120 g) butter or margarine, at room temperature

5 oz (150 g) dark brown sugar

4 tablespoons molasses

1 egg, at room temperature, beaten

8 oz (225 g) cooked or canned pumpkin

8 oz (225 g) flour

¼ teaspoon salt

1 teaspoon bicarbonate of soda

1½ teaspoons ground cinnamon

1 teaspoon grated nutmeg

1 oz (30 g) currants or raisins

1 Preheat the oven to 400°F/200°C/Gas 6. Grease 14 muffin cups or use paper cases.

2 With an electric mixer, cream the butter or margarine until soft. Add the sugar and molasses and beat until light and fluffy.

3 ▲ Add the egg and pumpkin and stir until well blended.

4 Sift over the flour, salt, bicarbonate of soda, cinnamon and nutmeg. Fold just enough to blend; do not overmix.

5 ▼ Fold in the currants or raisins.

6 Spoon the mixture into the prepared muffin cups, filling them three-quarters full.

7 Bake until the tops spring back when touched lightly, 12–15 minutes. Serve warm or cold.

Oat and Raisin Muffins (top), Pumpkin Muffins

Prune Muffins

MAKES 12

1 egg
8 fl oz (250 ml) milk
4 fl oz (125 ml) vegetable oil
1 3/4 oz (50 g) caster sugar
1 oz (30 g) dark brown sugar
10 oz (285 g) plain flour
2 teaspoons baking powder
1/2 teaspoon salt
1/4 teaspoon grated nutmeg
4 oz (115 g) cooked stoned prunes, chopped

1   Preheat a 400°F/200°C/Gas 6 oven. Grease a 12-cup muffin tin.

2   Break the egg into a mixing bowl and beat with a fork. Beat in the milk and oil.

3 ▼   Stir in the sugars. Set aside.

4   Sift the flour, baking powder, salt and nutmeg into a mixing bowl. Make a well in the centre, pour in the egg mixture and stir until moistened. Do not overmix; the batter should be slightly lumpy.

5 ▲   Fold in the prunes.

6   Fill the prepared cups two-thirds full. Bake until golden brown, about 20 minutes. Let stand 10 minutes before turning out. Serve warm or at room temperature.

Yogurt and Honey Muffins

MAKES 12

2 oz (55 g) butter
5 tablespoons clear honey
8 fl oz (250 ml) plain yogurt
1 large egg, at room temperature
grated rind of 1 lemon
2 fl oz (65 ml) lemon juice
5 oz (140 g) plain flour
6 oz (170 g) wholemeal flour
1 1/2 teaspoons bicarbonate of soda
1/8 teaspoon grated nutmeg

~ VARIATION ~

For Walnut Yogurt Honey Muffins, add 2 oz (55 g) chopped walnuts, folded in with the flour. This makes a more substantial muffin.

1   Preheat a 375°F/190°C/Gas 5 oven. Grease a 12-cup muffin tin or use paper cases.

2   In a saucepan, melt the butter and honey. Remove from the heat and set aside to cool slightly.

3 ▲   In a bowl, whisk together the yogurt, egg, lemon rind and juice. Add the butter and honey mixture. Set aside.

4 ▲   In another bowl, sift together the dry ingredients.

5   Fold the dry ingredients into the yogurt mixture to blend.

6   Fill the prepared cups two-thirds full. Bake until the tops spring back when touched lightly, 20–25 minutes. Let cool in the tin for 5 minutes before turning out. Serve warm or at room temperature.

Prune Muffins (top), Yogurt and Honey Muffins

Banana Muffins

MAKES 10

9 oz (250 g) plain flour
1 teaspoon baking powder
1 teaspoon bicarbonate of soda
1/4 teaspoon salt
1/2 teaspoon ground cinnamon
1/4 teaspoon grated nutmeg
3 large ripe bananas
1 egg
2 1/2 oz (70 g) dark brown sugar
2 fl oz (50 ml) vegetable oil
1 oz (30 g) raisins

1 ▼ Preheat the oven to 375°F/190°C/Gas 5. Lightly grease or line 10 deep muffin tins with paper cases.

2 Sift together the flour, baking powder, bicarbonate of soda, salt, cinnamon and nutmeg. Set aside.

3 ▲ With an electric mixer, beat the peeled bananas at moderate speed until mashed.

4 ▲ Beat in the egg, sugar and oil.

5 Add the dry ingredients and beat in gradually, on low speed. Mix just until blended. With a wooden spoon, stir in the raisins.

6 Fill the prepared cups two-thirds full. For even baking, half-fill any empty cups with water.

7 ▲ Bake until the tops spring back when touched lightly, 20–25 minutes. Transfer to a rack to cool.

Maple Pecan Muffins

MAKES 20

6 oz (170 g) pecans
12 oz (340 g) flour
1 teaspoon baking powder
1 teaspoon bicarbonate of soda
1/4 teaspoon salt
1/4 teaspoon ground cinnamon
3 1/2 oz (100 g) caster sugar
2 1/2 oz (70 g) light brown sugar
3 tablespoons maple syrup
5 oz (150 g) butter, at room temperature
3 eggs, at room temperature
1/2 pint (300 ml) buttermilk
60 pecan halves, for decorating

1   Preheat the oven to 350°F/180°C/
Gas 4. Lightly grease 24 deep muffin
tins or use paper cases.

2 ▲   Spread the pecans on a baking
sheet and toast in the oven for 5
minutes. When cool, chop coarsely
and set aside.

~ VARIATION ~

For Pecan Spice Muffins,
substitute an equal quantity of
golden syrup for the maple syrup.
Increase the cinnamon to
1/2 teaspoon, and add 1 teaspoon
ground ginger and 1/2 teaspoon
grated nutmeg, sifted with the
dry ingredients.

3   In a bowl, sift together the flour,
baking powder, bicarbonate of soda,
salt and cinnamon. Set aside.

4 ▲   In a large mixing bowl, combine
the caster sugar, light brown sugar,
maple syrup and butter. Beat with an
electric mixer until light and fluffy.

5   Add the eggs, 1 at a time, beating
to incorporate thoroughly after each
addition.

6 ▲   Pour half the buttermilk and
half the dry ingredients into the butter
mixture, then stir until blended.
Repeat with the remaining buttermilk
and dry ingredients.

7   Fold in the chopped pecans. Fill
the prepared cups two-thirds full. Top
with the pecan halves. For even
baking, half-fill any empty cups with
water.

8   Bake until puffed up and golden,
20–25 minutes. Let stand 5 minutes
before unmoulding.

Banana and Pecan Muffins

MAKES 8

5 oz (150 g) plain flour

1½ teaspoons baking powder

2 oz (55 g) butter or margarine,
   at room temperature

5 oz (150 g) caster sugar

1 egg

1 teaspoon vanilla essence

3 medium bananas, mashed

2 oz (55 g) pecans, chopped

5 tablespoons milk

1 Preheat the oven to 375°F/190°C/
Gas 5. Lightly grease 8 deep muffin tins.

2 Sift the flour and baking powder
into a small bowl. Set aside.

3 ▲ With an electric mixer, cream
the butter or margarine and sugar
together. Add the egg and vanilla and
beat until fluffy. Mix in the banana.

4 ▼ Add the pecans. With the mixer
on low speed, beat in the flour
mixture alternately with the milk.

5 Spoon the mixture into the
prepared muffin cups, filling them
two-thirds full. Bake until golden
brown and a skewer inserted into the
centre of a muffin comes out clean,
20–25 minutes.

6 Let cool in the tin on a wire rack
for 10 minutes. To loosen, run a knife
gently around each muffin and
unmould on to the wire rack. Let cool
10 minutes longer before serving.

~ VARIATION ~

Use an equal quantity of walnuts
instead of the pecans.

Blueberry and Cinnamon Muffins

MAKES 8

4 oz (120 g) plain flour

1 tablespoon baking powder

pinch of salt

2½ oz (70 g) light brown sugar

1 egg

6 fl oz (175 ml) milk

3 tablespoons vegetable oil

2 teaspoons ground cinnamon

4 oz (120 g) fresh or thawed frozen
   blueberries

1 Preheat the oven to 375°F/190°C/
Gas 5. Lightly grease 8 deep muffin tins.

2 With an electric mixer, beat
the first 8 ingredients together
until smooth.

3 ▲ Fold in the blueberries.

4 ▲ Spoon the mixture into the
muffin cups, filling them two-thirds
full. Bake until a skewer inserted in
the centre of a muffin comes out
clean, about 25 minutes.

5 Let cool in the tins on a wire rack
for 10 minutes, then unmould the
muffins on to the wire rack and allow
to cool completely.

Banana and Pecan Muffins (top), Blueberry and Cinnamon Muffins

Raspberry Muffins

MAKES 10–12

4 oz (120 g) self-raising flour
4 oz (120 g) wholemeal self-raising flour
3 tablespoons caster sugar
½ teaspoon salt
2 eggs, beaten
7 fl oz (200 ml) milk
2 oz (55 g) butter, melted
6 oz (170 g) raspberries, fresh or frozen (defrosted for less than 30 minutes)

1 ▼ Preheat the oven to 375°F/ 190°C/Gas 5. Lightly grease the muffin tins, or use paper cases. Sift the dry ingredients together, then tip back in the wholewheat flakes from the sieve.

2 ▲ Beat the eggs, milk and butter with the dry ingredients to give a thick batter. Add the raspberries.

3 ▲ Stir in the raspberries gently. (If you are using frozen raspberries, work quickly as the cold berries make the mixture solidify.) If you mix too much the raspberries begin to disintegrate and colour the dough. Spoon the mixture into the tins or paper cases.

4 Bake the muffins for 30 minutes, until well risen and just firm. Serve warm or cool.

Cherry Marmalade Muffins

MAKES 12

8 oz (225 g) self-raising flour
1 teaspoon mixed spice
3 oz (85 g) caster sugar
4 oz (120 g) glacé cherries, quartered
2 tablespoons orange marmalade
¼ pint (150 ml) skimmed milk
2 oz (55 g) soft sunflower margarine
marmalade, to brush

1 ▲ Preheat the oven to 400°F/200°C/Gas 6. Lightly grease 12 deep muffin tins with oil.

2 ▲ Sift together the flour and spice then stir in the sugar and cherries.

3 Mix the marmalade with the milk and beat into the dry ingredients with the margarine. Spoon into the greased tins. Bake for 20–25 minutes, until golden brown and firm.

4 ▼ Turn out on to a wire rack and brush the tops with warmed marmalade. Serve warm or cold.

~ VARIATION ~

To make Honey, Nut and Lemon Muffins, substitute 2 tablespoons clear honey for the orange marmalade, and the juice and finely grated rind of a lemon, and 2 oz (55 g) toasted, chopped hazelnuts, instead of the glacé cherries.

Blackberry and Almond Muffins

MAKES 12

11 oz (300 g) plain flour
2 oz (50 g) light brown sugar
4 teaspoons baking powder
pinch of salt
2¼ oz (60 g) chopped blanched almonds
3½ oz (100 g) fresh blackberries
2 eggs
7 fl oz (200 ml) milk
4 tablespoons melted butter, plus a little more to grease cups, if using
1 tablespoon sloe gin
1 tablespoon rosewater

1 ▼ Mix the flour, sugar, baking powder and salt in a bowl and stir in the almonds and blackberries, mixing them well to coat with the flour mixture. Preheat the oven to 400°F/200°C/Gas 6.

2 ▲ In another bowl, mix the eggs with the milk, then gradually add the butter, sloe gin and rosewater. Make a well in the centre of the bowl of dry ingredients and add the egg and milk mixture. Stir well.

3 Lightly grease 12 deep muffin tins. Spoon in the mixture and bake for 20–25 minutes or until browned. Turn out the muffins on to a wire rack to cool. Serve with butter.

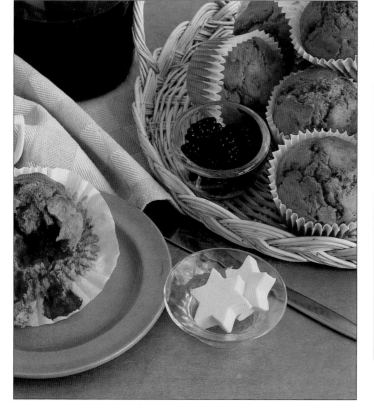

> ~ COOK'S TIP ~
>
> Other berries can be substituted for the blackberries, such as elderberries or blueberries.

> ~ VARIATION ~
>
> For Blackberry and Apple Muffins, substitute 2 dessert apples, peeled, cored and diced for the almonds. Add 1 teaspoon ground coriander to the flour mixture, and instead of the sloe gin and rosewater, substitute 2 tablespoons of Crème de Mûre.

Bacon and Cornmeal Muffins

MAKES 14

8 bacon rashers
2 oz (55 g) butter
2 oz (55 g) margarine
4 oz (120 g) plain flour
1 tablespoon baking powder
1 teaspoon sugar
1/4 teaspoon salt
8 oz (225 g) cornmeal
4 fl oz (125 ml) milk
2 eggs

1 Preheat the oven to 400°F/200°C/ Gas 6. Lightly grease 14 deep muffin tins or use paper cases.

2 ▲ Fry the bacon until crisp. Drain on kitchen paper, then chop into small pieces. Set aside.

3 Gently melt the butter and margarine and set aside.

4 ▲ Sift the flour, baking powder, sugar, and salt into a large mixing bowl. Stir in the cornmeal, then make a well in the centre.

5 In a saucepan, heat the milk to lukewarm. In a small bowl, lightly whisk the eggs, then add to the milk. Stir in the melted fats.

6 ▼ Pour the milk mixture into the centre of the well and stir until smooth and well blended.

7 ▲ Stir the bacon into the mixture, then spoon the mixture into the prepared cups, filling them half-full. Bake until risen and lightly coloured, about 20 minutes. Serve hot or warm.

Cheese Muffins

MAKES 9

2 oz (55 g) butter

7 oz (200 g) plain flour

2 teaspoons baking powder

2 tablespoons sugar

1/4 teaspoon salt

1 teaspoon paprika

2 eggs

4 fl oz (125 ml) milk

1 teaspoon dried thyme

2 oz (55 g) mature Cheddar cheese, cut into 1/2 in (1 cm) dice

1   Preheat the oven to 375°F/190°C/ Gas 5. Thickly grease 9 deep muffin tins or use paper cases.

2   Melt the butter and set aside.

3 ▼   In a mixing bowl, sift together the flour, baking powder, sugar, salt and paprika.

4 ▲   In another bowl, combine the eggs, milk, melted butter and thyme, and whisk to blend.

5   Add the milk mixture to the dry ingredients and stir just until moistened; do not mix until smooth.

6 ▲   Place a heaped spoonful of batter into the prepared cups. Drop a few pieces of cheese over each, then top with another spoonful of batter. For even baking, half-fill any empty muffin cups with water.

7 ▲   Bake until puffed and golden, about 25 minutes. Let stand 5 minutes before unmoulding on to a rack. Serve warm or at room temperature.

Sweet Potato Scones

MAKES ABOUT 24

5oz (150g) plain flour
4 teaspoons baking powder
1 teaspoon salt
1 tablespoon soft light brown sugar
2fl oz (50ml) mashed cooked sweet potatoes
¼ pint (150ml) milk
2oz (50g) butter or margarine, melted

1 Preheat the oven to 230°C/450°F/ Gas 8.

2 ▲ Sift the flour, baking powder and salt into a bowl. Add the sugar and stir to mix.

3 ▲ In a separate bowl, combine the sweet potatoes with the milk and melted butter or margarine. Mix well until evenly blended.

4 ▼ Stir the dry ingredients into the sweet potato mixture to make a dough. Turn on to a lightly floured surface and knead lightly, just to mix, for 1–2 minutes.

5 ▲ Roll or pat out the dough to ½ in (1 cm) thickness. Stamp out rounds with a 1½ in (4 cm) biscuit cutter.

6 Arrange the rounds on a greased baking sheet. Bake until puffed and lightly golden, about 15 minutes. Serve the scones warm.

Buttermilk Scones

MAKES 15

7 oz (200 g) plain flour

1 teaspoon salt

1 teaspoon baking powder

1/2 teaspoon bicarbonate of soda

4 tablespoons cold butter or margarine

6 fl oz (175 ml) buttermilk

1   Preheat the oven to 425°F/220°C/ Gas 7. Grease a baking sheet.

2   Sift the dry ingredients into a bowl. Rub in the butter or margarine with your fingertips until the mixture resembles breadcrumbs.

3 ▼   Gradually pour in the buttermilk, stirring with a fork to form a soft dough.

4 ▲   Roll out the dough until about 1/2 in (1 cm) thick. Stamp out rounds with a 2-inch (5 cm) biscuit cutter.

5   Place on the prepared baking sheet and bake until golden, 12–15 minutes. Serve warm or at room temperature.

Traditional Sweet Scones

MAKES 8

6 oz (170 g) flour

2 tablespoons sugar

3 teaspoons baking powder

1/8 teaspoon salt

5 tablespoons cold butter, cut in pieces

4 fl oz (125 ml) milk

~ VARIATION ~

To make a delicious and speedy dessert, split the scones in half while still warm. Butter one half, top with lightly sugared fresh strawberries, raspberries or blueberries, and sandwich with the other half. Serve at once with dollops of whipped cream.

1   Preheat the oven to 425°F/220°C/ Gas 7. Grease a baking sheet.

2 ▲   Sift the flour, sugar, baking powder, and salt into a bowl.

3   Cut in the butter with a pastry blender until the mixture resembles coarse crumbs.

4   Pour in the milk and stir with a fork to form a soft dough.

5 ▲   Roll out the dough about 1/4 in (1/2 cm) thick. Stamp out rounds using a 2 1/2 in (6 cm) biscuit cutter.

6   Place on the prepared sheet and bake until golden, about 12 minutes. Serve hot or warm, with butter and jam, to accompany tea or coffee.

Buttermilk Scones (top), Traditional Sweet Scones

Wholemeal Scones

MAKES 16

6 oz (170 g) cold butter
12 oz (350 g) wholemeal flour
5 oz (140 g) plain flour
2 tablespoons sugar
¹/₂ teaspoon salt
2¹/₂ teaspoons bicarbonate of soda
2 eggs
6 fl oz (175 ml) buttermilk
1¹/₄ oz (35 g) raisins

1   Preheat the oven to 400°F/200°C/Gas 6. Grease and flour a large baking sheet.

2 ▲   Cut the butter into small pieces.

3   Combine the dry ingredients in a bowl. Add the butter and rub in with your fingertips until the mixture resembles coarse breadcrumbs. Set aside.

4   In another bowl, whisk together the eggs and buttermilk. Set aside 2 tablespoons for glazing.

5   Stir the remaining egg mixture into the dry ingredients until it just holds together. Stir in the raisins.

6   Roll out the dough about ³/₄ in (2 cm) thick. Stamp out circles with a biscuit cutter. Place on the prepared sheet and brush with the glaze.

7   Bake until golden, 12–15 minutes. Allow to cool slightly before serving. Split in two with a fork while still warm and spread with butter and jam, if wished.

Orange and Raisin Scones

MAKES 16

10 oz (285 g) plain flour
1¹/₂ teaspoons baking powder
2¹/₄ oz (60 g) sugar
¹/₂ teaspoon salt
2¹/₂ oz (70 g) butter, diced
2¹/₂ oz (70 g) margarine, diced
grated rind of 1 large orange
2 oz (55 g) raisins
4 fl oz (125 ml) buttermilk
milk, for glazing

1   Preheat the oven to 425°F/220°C/ Gas 7. Grease and flour a large baking sheet.

2   Combine the dry ingredients in a large bowl. Add the butter and margarine and rub in with your fingertips until the mixture resembles coarse breadcrumbs.

3 ▲   Add the orange rind and raisins.

4   Gradually stir in the buttermilk to form a soft dough.

5 ▲   Roll out the dough about ³/₄ in (2 cm) thick. Stamp out circles with a biscuit cutter.

6 ▲   Place on the prepared sheet and brush the tops with milk.

7   Bake until golden, 12–15 minutes. Serve hot or warm, with butter, or whipped or clotted cream, and jam.

~ COOK'S TIP ~

For light tender scones, handle the dough as little as possible. If you wish, split the scones when cool and toast them under a preheated grill. Butter them while still hot.

Wholemeal Scones (top), Orange and Raisin Scones

Sunflower Sultana Scones

MAKES 10–12

8 oz (225 g) self-raising flour

1 teaspoon baking powder

1 oz (30 g) soft sunflower margarine

2 tablespoons caster sugar

2 oz (55 g) sultanas

2 tablespoons sunflower seeds

5 oz (150 g) natural yogurt

about 2–3 tablespoons skimmed milk

1   Preheat the oven to 450°F/230°C/
Gas 8. Lightly oil a baking sheet. Sift
the flour and baking powder into a
bowl and rub in the margarine evenly.

2   Stir in the sugar, sultanas and half
the sunflower seeds, then mix in the
yogurt, with just enough milk to make
a fairly soft, but not sticky dough.

3 ▼   Roll out on a lightly floured
surface to about ¾ in (2 cm)
thickness. Cut into 2½ in (6 cm)
flower shapes or rounds with a biscuit
cutter and lift on to the baking sheet.

4 ▲   Brush with milk and sprinkle
with the reserved sunflower seeds,
then bake for 10–12 minutes, until
well risen and golden brown.

5   Cool the scones on a wire rack.
Serve split and spread with butter
and jam.

Prune and Peel Rock Buns

MAKES 12

8 oz (225 g) plain flour

2 teaspoons baking powder

3 oz (85 g) demerara sugar

2 oz (55 g) chopped ready-to-eat dried
prunes

2 oz (55 g) chopped mixed peel

finely grated rind of 1 lemon

2 fl oz (50 ml) sunflower oil

5 tablespoons skimmed milk

~ VARIATION ~

For Spicy Rock Buns, substitute
2 oz (50 g) currants for the ready-
to-eat dried prunes, 2 oz (50 g)
raisins for the mixed peel, and add
1 teaspoon mixed spice,
¼ teaspoon ground ginger, and
¼ teaspoon ground cinnamon.

1 ▼   Preheat the oven to 400°F/
200°C/Gas 6. Lightly oil a large
baking sheet. Sift together the flour
and baking powder, then stir in the
sugar, prunes, peel and lemon rind.

3 ▲   Spoon into rocky heaps on the
baking sheet and bake for 20 minutes,
until golden. Cool on a wire rack.

2   Mix the oil and milk, then stir into
the mixture, to make a dough which
just binds together.

Sunflower Sultana Scones (top), Prune and Peel Rock Buns

Cheese and Marjoram Scones

MAKES 18

4 oz (120 g) wholemeal flour

4 oz (120 g) self-raising flour

pinch of salt

1 1/2 oz (45 g) butter

1/4 teaspoon dry mustard

2 teaspoons dried marjoram

2–3 oz (55–85 g) Cheddar cheese, finely grated

4 fl oz (125 ml) milk, or as required

1 teaspoon sunflower oil

2 oz (50 g) pecan or walnuts, chopped

1 ▼   Sift the two kinds of flour into a bowl and add the salt. Cut the butter into small pieces, and rub into the flour until the mixture resembles fine breadcrumbs.

2 ▲   Add the mustard, marjoram and grated cheese, and mix in sufficient milk to make a soft dough. Knead the dough lightly.

3   Preheat the oven to 425°F/220°C/ Gas 7. Roll out the dough on a floured surface to about a 3/4 in (2 cm) thickness and cut out about 18 scones using a 2 in (5 cm) square cutter. Grease two baking sheets with a little sunflower oil, and place the scones on the trays.

4   Brush the scones with a little milk and sprinkle the chopped pecans or walnuts over the top. Bake for 12 minutes. Serve warm.

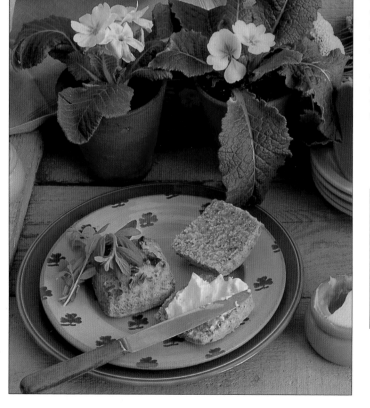

~ VARIATION ~

For Mixed Herb and Mustard Scones, use 2 tablespoons chopped fresh parsley or chives instead of the dried marjoram and 1 teaspoon Dijon mustard instead of the dry mustard. Substitute 2 oz (50 g) chopped pistachio nuts for the pecans or walnuts.

Cheese and Chive Scones

MAKES 9

4 oz (120 g) self-raising flour
5 oz (150 g) self-raising wholemeal flour
1/2 teaspoon salt
3 oz (85 g) feta cheese
1 tablespoon snipped fresh chives
1/4 pint (150 ml) skimmed milk, plus extra for glazing
1/4 teaspoon cayenne pepper

1 ▲ Pre-heat the oven to 400°F/ 200°C/Gas 6. Sift the flours and salt into a mixing bowl, adding any bran left over from the flour in the sieve.

2 ▲ Crumble the feta cheese and rub into the dry ingredients. Stir in the chives, then add the milk and mix to a soft dough.

3 ▼ Turn out the dough on to a floured surface and lightly knead until smooth. Roll out to 3/4 in (2 cm) thick and stamp out nine scones with a 2 1/2 in (6 cm) biscuit cutter.

4 ▲ Transfer the scones to a non-stick baking sheet. Brush with skimmed milk, then sprinkle over the cayenne pepper. Bake in the oven for 15 minutes, or until golden brown. Serve warm or cold.

Dill and Potato Cakes

MAKES 10

8 oz (225 g) self-raising flour
3 tablespoons butter, softened
pinch of salt
1 tablespoon finely chopped fresh dill
6 oz (170 g) mashed potato, freshly made
2–3 tablespoons milk, as required

1 ▼ Preheat the oven to 450°F/ 230°C/Gas 8. Sift the flour into a bowl, and add the butter, salt and dill. Mix in the mashed potato and enough milk to make a soft, pliable dough.

2 ▲ Roll out the dough on a well-floured surface until it is fairly thin. Cut into neat rounds using a 3 in (7.5 cm) cutter.

3 ▲ Grease a baking sheet, place the cakes on it, and bake for 20–25 minutes until risen and golden.

```
~ VARIATION ~
For Cheese and Herb Potato
Cakes, stir in about 2 oz (55 g)
crumbled blue cheese, and
substitute 1 tablespoon snipped
fresh chives for the dill. Mix in
3 tablespoons soured cream
instead of the butter.
```

Parmesan Popovers

MAKES 6

2 oz (55 g) freshly grated Parmesan cheese
4 oz (120 g) plain flour
¼ teaspoon salt
2 eggs
4 fl oz (125 ml) milk
1 tablespoon melted butter or margarine

1 ▼ Preheat the oven to 450°F/ 230°C/Gas 8. Grease six deep bun or tartlet tins. Sprinkle each tin with 1 tablespoon of the grated Parmesan. Alternatively, you can use ramekins; heat them on a baking sheet in the oven, then grease and sprinkle with Parmesan just before filling.

2 Sift the flour and salt into a small bowl. Set aside.

3 ▲ In a mixing bowl, beat together the eggs, milk, and butter or margarine. Add the flour mixture and stir until smoothly blended.

4 ▼ Divide the mixture evenly among the tins, filling each one about half full. Bake for 15 minutes, then sprinkle the tops of the popovers with the remaining grated Parmesan cheese. Reduce the heat to 350°F/ 180°C/Gas 4 and continue baking until the popovers are firm and golden brown, 20–25 minutes.

5 ▲ Remove the popovers from the oven. To unmould, run a thin knife around the inside of each tin to loosen the popovers. Gently ease out, then transfer to a wire rack to cool.

Herb Popovers

MAKES 12

3 eggs
8 fl oz (250 ml) milk
1 oz (30 g) butter, melted
3 oz (85 g) plain flour
¹/₈ tsp salt
1 small sprig each mixed fresh herbs, such as chives, tarragon, dill and parsley

1   Preheat a 425°F/220°C/Gas 7 oven. Grease 12 small ramekins or individual baking cups.

2   With an electric mixer, beat the eggs until blended. Beat in the milk and melted butter.

3   Sift together the flour and salt, then beat into the egg mixture to combine thoroughly.

4 ▼   Strip the herb leaves from the stems and chop finely. Mix together and measure out 2 tablespoons. Stir the herbs into the batter.

5 ▲   Fill the prepared cups half-full.

6   Bake until golden, 25–30 minutes. Do not open the oven door during baking time or the popovers may collapse. For drier popovers, pierce each one with a knife after the 30 minute baking time and bake for 5 minutes more. Serve hot.

Cheese Popovers

MAKES 12

3 eggs
8 fl oz (250 ml) milk
1 oz (30 g) butter, melted
3 oz (85 g) plain flour
¹/₄ tsp salt
¹/₄ tsp paprika
1 oz (30 g) freshly grated Parmesan cheese

~ VARIATION ~

For traditional Yorkshire Pudding, omit the cheese and paprika, and use 4–6 tablespoons of beef dripping to replace the butter. Put them into the oven in time to serve warm as an accompaniment for roast beef.

1   Preheat a 425°F/220°C/Gas 7 oven. Grease 12 small ramekins.

2 ▲   With an electric mixer, beat the eggs until blended. Beat in the milk and melted butter.

3 ▲   Sift together the flour, salt and paprika, then beat into the egg mixture. Add the cheese and stir.

4   Fill the prepared cups half-full and bake until golden, 25–30 minutes. Do not open the oven door or the popovers may collapse. For drier popovers, pierce each one with a knife after the 30 minute baking time and bake for 5 minutes more. Serve hot.

Herb Popovers (top), Cheese Popovers

Orange and Honey Tea Bread

MAKES 1 LOAF

13½ oz (385 g) plain flour
2½ teaspoons baking powder
½ teaspoon bicarbonate of soda
½ teaspoon salt
1 oz (30 g) margarine
8 fl oz (250 ml) clear honey
1 egg, at room temperature, lightly beaten
1½ tablespoons grated orange rind
6 fl oz (175 ml) freshly squeezed orange juice
4 oz (115 g) walnuts, chopped

1   Preheat a 325°F/170°C/Gas 3 oven.

2   Sift together the flour, baking powder, bicarbonate of soda and salt.

3   Line the bottom and sides of a 9 × 5 in (23 × 13 cm) loaf tin with greaseproof paper and grease.

4 ▲ With an electric mixer, cream the margarine until soft. Stir in the honey until blended, then stir in the egg. Add the orange rind and stir to combine thoroughly.

5 ▲ Fold the flour mixture into the honey and egg mixture in 3 batches, alternating with the orange juice. Stir in the walnuts.

6   Pour into the tin and bake until a skewer inserted in the centre comes out clean, 60–70 minutes. Let stand 10 minutes before turning out onto a rack to cool.

Apple Loaf

MAKES 1 LOAF

1 egg
8 fl oz (250 ml) bottled or homemade apple sauce
2 oz (55 g) butter or margarine, melted
3¾ oz (110 g) dark brown sugar
1¾ oz (50 g) caster sugar
10 oz (285 g) plain flour
2 teaspoons baking powder
½ teaspoon bicarbonate of soda
½ teaspoon salt
1 teaspoon ground cinnamon
½ teaspoon grated nutmeg
2½ oz (70 g) currants or raisins
2 oz (55 g) pecans or walnuts, chopped

1   Preheat a 350°F/180°C/Gas 4 oven. Line a 9 × 5 in (23 × 13 cm) loaf tin with greaseproof paper and grease.

2 ▲ Break the egg into a bowl and beat lightly. Stir in the apple sauce, butter or margarine and both sugars. Set aside.

3   In another bowl, sift together the flour, baking powder, bicarbonate of soda, salt, cinnamon and nutmeg. Fold dry ingredients into the apple sauce mixture in 3 batches.

4 ▼ Stir in the currants or raisins, and nuts.

5   Pour into the prepared tin and bake until a skewer inserted in the centre comes out clean, about 1 hour. Let stand 10 minutes. Turn out onto a rack and cool completely.

Orange and Honey Tea Bread (top), Apple Loaf

Malt Loaf

MAKES 1 LOAF

¼ pint (150 ml) warm skimmed milk
1 teaspoon (5 ml) dried yeast
pinch of caster sugar
12 oz (350 g) plain flour
½ teaspoon (1.5 ml) salt
2 tablespoons (30 ml) light muscovado sugar
6 oz (175 g) sultanas
1 tablespoons (15 ml) sunflower oil
3 tablespoons (45 ml) malt extract
FOR THE GLAZE
2 tablespoons (30 ml) caster sugar
2 tablespoons (30 ml) water

~ COOK'S TIP ~

This is a rich and sticky loaf. If it lasts long enough to go stale, try toasting it for a delicious tea-time treat.

~ VARIATION ~

To make buns, divide the dough into 10 pieces, shape into rounds, leave to rise, then bake for about 15–20 minutes. Brush with the glaze while still hot.

1 ▲ Place the warm milk in a bowl. Sprinkle the yeast on top and add the sugar. Leave for 30 minutes until frothy. Stir the flour and salt into a mixing bowl, stir in the muscovado sugar and sultanas, and make a well.

2 ▲ Add the yeast mixture with the oil and malt extract. Gradually incorporate the flour and mix to a soft dough, adding a little extra milk if necessary.

3 ▲ Turn on to a floured surface and knead for about 5 minutes until smooth and elastic. Grease a 1 lb (450 g) loaf tin.

4 ▲ Shape the dough and place it in the prepared loaf tin. Cover with a damp dish towel and leave in a warm place for about 1–2 hours until the dough is well risen. Preheat the oven to 190°C/375°F/Gas 5.

5 ▲ Bake the loaf for 30–35 minutes, or until it sounds hollow when it is tapped underneath.

6 ▲ Meanwhile, prepare the glaze by dissolving the sugar in the water in a small pan. Bring to the boil, stirring, then lower the heat and simmer for 1 minute. Place the loaf on a wire rack and brush with the glaze while still hot. Leave the loaf to cool before serving.

Lemon and Walnut Tea Bread

MAKES 1 LOAF

4 oz (115 g) butter or margarine, at room temperature

3¹/₂ oz (100 g) sugar

2 eggs, at room temperature, separated

grated rind of 2 lemons

2 tablespoons lemon juice

7¹/₂ oz (215 g) plain flour

2 teaspoons baking powder

4 fl oz (125 ml) milk

2 oz (55 g) walnuts, chopped

¹/₈ teaspoon salt

1 Preheat a 350°F/180°C/Gas 4 oven. Line a 9 × 5 in (23 × 13 cm) loaf tin with greaseproof paper and grease.

2 With an electric mixer, cream the butter or margarine with the sugar until light and fluffy.

3 ▲ Beat in the egg yolks.

4 Add the lemon rind and juice and stir until blended. Set aside.

5 ▲ In another bowl, sift together the flour and baking powder, 3 times. Fold into the butter mixture in 3 batches, alternating with the milk. Fold in the walnuts. Set aside.

6 ▲ Beat the egg whites and salt until stiff peaks form. Fold a large dollop of the egg whites into the walnut mixture to lighten it. Fold in the remaining egg whites carefully until just blended.

7 ▲ Pour the batter into the prepared tin and bake until a skewer inserted in the centre of the loaf comes out clean, 45–50 minutes. Let stand 5 minutes before turning out onto a rack to cool completely.

Banana Bread

MAKES 1 LOAF

7 oz (200 g) plain flour
2¼ teaspoons baking powder
½ teaspoon salt
¾ teaspoon ground cinnamon (optional)
4 tablespoons wheat germ
2½ oz (75 g) butter or margarine, at room temperature
4 oz (115 g) caster sugar
¾ teaspoon grated lemon zest
3 ripe bananas, mashed
2 eggs, beaten to mix

1 Preheat a 350°F/180°C/Gas 4 oven. Grease and flour an 8½ × 4½ in (21 × 11 cm) loaf tin.

2 ▲ Sift the flour, baking powder, salt and cinnamon, if using, into a bowl. Stir in the wheat germ.

3 ▲ In another bowl, combine the butter or margarine with the sugar and lemon zest. Beat until the mixture is light and fluffy.

4 ▲ Add the mashed bananas and eggs and mix well.

5 Add the dry ingredients and blend quickly and evenly.

~ **VARIATION** ~

For Banana Walnut Bread, add 2–3 oz (55–85 g) finely chopped walnuts with the dry ingredients.

6 ▼ Spoon into the prepared loaf tin. Bake for 50–60 minutes or until a wooden skewer inserted in the centre comes out clean.

7 Cool in the pan for about 5 minutes, then turn out on to a wire rack to cool completely.

Pineapple and Apricot Cake

SERVES 10–12

6 oz (170 g) unsalted butter

5 oz (150 g) caster sugar

3 eggs, beaten

few drops of vanilla essence

8 oz (225 g) plain flour, sifted

1/2 teaspoon salt

1 1/2 teaspoons baking powder

8 oz (225 g) ready-to-eat dried apricots, chopped

4 oz (120 g) each chopped crystallized ginger and crystallized pineapple

grated rind and juice of 1/2 orange

grated rind and juice of 1/2 lemon

a little milk

1 ▲ Preheat the oven to 350°F/180°C/Gas 4. Double line an 8 in (20 cm) round or 7 in (18 cm) square cake tin. Cream the butter and sugar together until light and fluffy.

2 Gradually beat the eggs into the creamed mixture with the vanilla essence, beating well after each addition. Sift together the flour, salt and baking powder, and add a little with the last of the egg, then fold in the rest.

3 ▲ Fold in the fruit, crystallized fruit and fruit rinds gently, then add sufficient fruit juice and milk to give a fairly soft dropping consistency.

4 ▲ Spoon into the prepared tin and smooth the top with a wet spoon. Bake for 20 minutes, then reduce the heat to 325°F/160°C/Gas 3 for a further 1 1/2 –2 hours, or until firm to the touch and a skewer comes out of the centre clean. Leave the cake to cool in the tin, turn out and wrap in fresh paper before storing in an airtight tin.

~ COOK'S TIP ~

This is not a long-keeping cake, but it does freeze, well-wrapped in greaseproof paper and then foil.

Date and Nut Malt Loaf

1 Sift the flours and salt into a large bowl, adding any bran from the sieve. Stir in the sugar and yeast.

2 ▲ Mix the butter or margarine with the treacle and malt extract. Stir over a low heat until melted. Leave to cool, then combine with the milk.

3 Stir the liquid into the dry ingredients and knead for 15 minutes until the dough is elastic. (If you have a dough blade on your food processor, follow the manufacturer's instructions for timings.)

4 ▲ Knead in the fruits and nuts. Transfer the dough to an oiled bowl, cover with clear film, and leave in a warm place for about 1½ hours, until the dough has doubled in size.

5 ▲ Grease two 1 lb (450 g) loaf tins. Knock back the dough and knead lightly. Divide in half, form into loaves and place in the tins. Cover and leave in a warm place for about 30 minutes, until risen. Meanwhile, preheat the oven to 190°C/375°F/Gas 5.

6 Bake for 35–40 minutes, until well risen and sounding hollow when tapped underneath. Cool on a wire rack. Brush with honey while warm.

MAKES 2 LOAVES

11 oz (300 g) strong plain flour
10 oz (275 g) strong plain wholemeal flour
1 teaspoon (5 ml) salt
3 oz (75 g) soft brown sugar
1 teaspoon (15 ml) easy-blend dried yeast
2oz (50 g) butter or margarine
1 tablespoon (15 ml) black treacle
4 tablespoons (60 ml) malt extract
scant 8fl oz (250 ml) tepid milk
4oz (115 g) chopped dates
3oz (75 g) sultanas
3oz (75 g) raisins
2oz (50 g) chopped nuts
2 tablespoons (30 ml) clear honey, to glaze

~ COOK'S TIP ~

This moist loaf is perfect for packed lunches.

Banana Orange Loaf

For the best banana flavour and a really good, moist texture, make sure the bananas are very ripe for this cake.

MAKES 1 LOAF

2 tablespoons (30 ml) sunflower oil
3½ oz (90 g) wholemeal plain flour
3½ oz (90 g) plain flour
1 teaspoon (5 ml) baking powder
1 teaspoon (5 ml) ground mixed spice
3 tablespoons (45 ml) flaked hazelnuts, toasted
2 large ripe bananas
1 egg
2 tablespoons (30 ml) clear honey
finely grated rind and juice of 1 small orange
4 orange slices, halved
2 teaspoons (10 ml) icing sugar

1 Preheat the oven to 180°C/350°F/ Gas 4.

2 ▲ Brush a 1¾ pint (1 litre) loaf tin with sunflower oil and line the base with non-stick baking paper.

3 ▲ Sift the flours with the baking powder and spice, adding any bran that is caught in the sieve. Stir in the toasted hazelnuts.

4 ▲ Peel and mash the bananas. Beat together with the egg, oil, honey and the orange rind and juice. Stir evenly into the dry ingredients.

5 Spoon into the prepared tin and smooth the top. Bake for 40–45 minutes, or until firm and golden brown. Turn out and cool on a wire rack. Sprinkle the orange slices with the icing sugar and grill until golden brown. Use to decorate the cake.

> **~ COOK'S TIP ~**
> If you plan to keep the loaf for more than two or three days, omit the orange slices, brush with honey and sprinkle with flaked hazelnuts.

Apple, Apricot and Walnut Loaf

Serve warm and store what is left in an airtight tin.

1 ▲ Preheat the oven to 180°C/ 350°F/Gas 4. Line and grease a 2lb (900 g) loaf tin.

2 ▲ Sift the flour, baking powder and salt into a large mixing bowl, then tip the bran remaining in the sieve into the mixture. Add the margarine, sugar, eggs, orange rind and juice. Stir, then beat with a hand-held electric beater until smooth.

3 ▲ Stir in the walnuts and apricots. Peel, quarter, and core the apple, chop it roughly and add it to the mixture. Stir, then spoon into the prepared tin and level the top.

MAKES 1 LOAF

8 oz (225 g) plain wholemeal flour
1 teaspoon (5 ml) baking powder
pinch of salt
4 oz (115 g) sunflower margarine
6 oz (175 g) soft light brown sugar
2 size 2 eggs, lightly beaten
grated rind and juice of 1 orange
2 oz (50 g) chopped walnuts
2 oz (50 g) ready-to-eat dried apricots, chopped
1 large cooking apple

4 Bake for 1 hour, or until a skewer inserted into the centre comes out clean. Cool in the tin for 5 minutes, then turn the loaf out on to a wire rack and peel off the lining paper.

Banana and Ginger Tea Bread

Serve this tea bread in slices with low-fat spread. The stem ginger adds an interesting flavour.

MAKES 1 LOAF

6 oz (175 g) self-raising flour
1 teaspoon (5 ml) baking powder
1½ oz (40 g) soft margarine
2 oz (50 g) dark muscovado sugar
2 oz (50 g) drained stem ginger, chopped
4 tablespoons (60 ml) skimmed milk
2 ripe bananas, mashed

1 ▲ Preheat the oven to 180°C/ 350°F/Gas 4. Grease and line a 1 lb (450 g) loaf tin. Sift the flour and baking powder into a mixing bowl.

2 ▲ Rub in the margarine until the mixture resembles breadcrumbs.

3 ▲ Stir in the sugar. Add the ginger, milk and bananas and mix.

4 ▲ Spoon into the prepared tin and bake for 40–45 minutes, or until an inserted skewer comes out clean. Run a palette knife around the edges to loosen, then turn the tea bread on to a wire rack and leave to cool.

Pear and Sultana Tea Bread

This is an ideal tea bread to make when pears are plentiful – an excellent use for windfalls.

MAKES 1 LOAF

1 oz (25 g) rolled oats
2 oz (50 g) light muscovado sugar
2 tablespoons (30 ml) pear or apple juice
2 tablespoons (30 ml) sunflower oil
1 large or 2 small pears
4 oz (115 g) self-raising flour
4 oz (115 g) sultanas
½ teaspoon (2.5 ml) baking powder
2 teaspoons (10 ml) mixed spice
1 egg

1 ▲ Preheat the oven to 180°C/350°F/Gas 4. Grease and line a 1 lb (450 g) loaf tin with baking paper. Mix the oats with the sugar, pour over the pear or apple juice and oil, mix well and leave for 15 minutes.

4 ▲ Transfer the tea bread on to a wire rack and peel off the lining paper. Leave to cool completely.

~ COOK'S TIP ~

Health food shops sell concentrated pear and apple juice, ready for diluting as required.

2 ▲ Quarter, core and coarsely grate the pears. Add the fruit to the oat mixture with the flour, sultanas, baking powder, mixed spice and egg, then mix together thoroughly.

3 ▲ Spoon the mixture into the prepared loaf tin and level the top. Bake for 50–60 minutes or until a skewer inserted into the centre comes out clean.

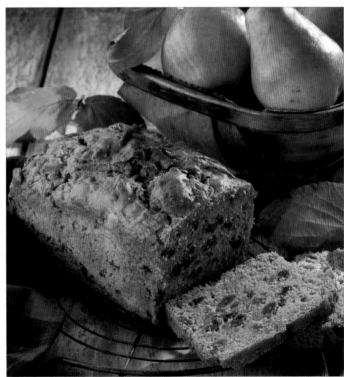

Cardamom and Saffron Tealoaf

An aromatic sweet bread ideal for afternoon tea or lightly toasted for breakfast. Using the sachets of fast-action or easy-blend yeasts make tealoaf-making so simple.

MAKES 1 LOAF

good pinch of saffron strands

1¼ pints (750 ml) lukewarm milk

1 oz (30 g) butter

32 oz (900 g) strong plain flour

2 teaspoons fast-action yeast

1½ oz (30 g) caster sugar

6 cardamom pods, split open and seeds extracted

4 oz (115 g) raisins

2 tablespoons clear honey, plus extra for brushing

1 egg, beaten

~ COOK'S TIP ~

Slice this loaf when cold and spread with butter. It is also good lightly toasted.

1 ▲ Crush the saffron into a cup containing a little of the warm milk and leave to infuse for 5 minutes.

2 Rub the butter into the flour, then mix in the yeast, sugar and cardamom seeds (these may need rubbing to separate them). Stir in the raisins.

3 ▲ Beat the remaining milk with the honey and egg, then mix this into the flour with the saffron milk and strands, stirring well until a firm dough is formed. You may not need all the milk; it depends on the flour.

4 ▲ Turn out the dough and knead it on a lightly floured board for about 5 minutes until smooth.

5 Return the dough to the mixing bowl, cover with oiled clear film and leave in a warm place until doubled in size. This could take between 1–3 hours. Grease a 2 lb (1 kg) loaf tin. Turn the dough out on to a floured board again, punch it down, knead for 3 minutes, then shape it into a fat roll and fit it into the greased loaf tin.

6 Cover with a sheet of lightly oiled clear film and stand in a warm place until the dough begins to rise again. Preheat the oven to 200°C/400°F/ Gas 6. Bake the loaf for 25 minutes until golden brown and firm on top. Turn out of the tin and as it cools, brush the top with honey.

Bilberry Tea Bread

MAKES 8 PIECES

2 oz (55 g) butter or margarine, at room temperature
6 oz (170 g) caster sugar
1 egg, at room temperature
4 fl oz (125 ml) milk
8 oz (225 g) plain flour
2 tsp baking powder
1/2 tsp salt
10 oz (285 g) fresh bilberries, or blueberries
FOR THE TOPPING
4 oz (115 g) sugar
1 1/2 oz (45 g) plain flour
1/2 tsp ground cinnamon
2 oz (55 g) butter, cut in pieces

1   Preheat a 375°F/190°C/Gas 5 oven. Grease a 9 in (23 cm) baking dish.

2   With an electric mixer, cream the butter or margarine with the sugar until light and fluffy. Add the egg, beat to combine, then mix in the milk until blended.

3 ▼   Sift over the flour, baking powder and salt and stir just enough to blend the ingredients.

4 ▲   Add the berries and stir.

5   Transfer to the baking dish.

6 ▲   For the topping, place the sugar, flour, cinnamon and butter in a mixing bowl. Cut in with a pastry blender until the mixture resembles coarse breadcrumbs.

7 ▲   Sprinkle the topping over the mixture in the baking dish.

8   Bake until a skewer inserted in the centre comes out clean, about 45 minutes. Serve warm or cold.

Glazed Banana Spice Loaf

Makes 1 loaf

1 large ripe banana
4 oz (115 g) butter, at room temperature
5^1/$_2$ oz (150 g) caster sugar
2 eggs, at room temperature
7^1/$_2$ oz (215 g) plain flour
1 teaspoon salt
1 teaspoon bicarbonate of soda
^{1}/$_2$ teaspoon grated nutmeg
^{1}/$_4$ teaspoon ground allspice
^{1}/$_4$ teaspoon ground cloves
6 fl oz (175 ml) soured cream
1 teaspoon vanilla essence
For the glaze
4 oz (115 g) icing sugar
1–2 tablespoons lemon juice

1 Preheat a 350°F/180°C/Gas 4 oven. Line an 8^1/$_2$ × 4^1/$_2$ in (21.5 × 11.5 cm) loaf tin with greaseproof and grease.

2 ▼ With a fork, mash the banana in a bowl. Set aside.

3 With an electric mixer, cream the butter and sugar until light and fluffy. Add the eggs, 1 at a time, beating to blend well after each addition.

4 Sift together the flour, salt, bicarbonate of soda, nutmeg, allspice and cloves. Add to the butter mixture and stir to combine well.

5 ▲ Add the soured cream, banana, and vanilla and mix just enough to blend. Pour into the prepared tin.

6 ▲ Bake until the top springs back when touched lightly, 45–50 minutes. Let cool in the pan for 10 minutes. Turn out onto a wire rack to cool.

7 ▲ For the glaze, combine the icing sugar and lemon juice, then stir until smooth.

8 To glaze, place the cooled loaf on a rack set over a baking sheet. Pour the glaze over the top of the loaf and allow to set.

Chocolate Chip Walnut Loaf

MAKES 1 LOAF

3¹/₂ oz (100 g) caster sugar
3¹/₂ oz (100 g) flour
1 teaspoon baking powder
4 tablespoons cornflour
4¹/₂ oz (130 g) butter, at room temperature
2 eggs, at room temperature
1 teaspoon vanilla extract
2 tablespoons currants or raisins
1 oz (30 g) walnuts, finely chopped
grated rind of ¹/₂ lemon
3 tablespoons plain chocolate chips
icing sugar, for dusting

1 Preheat the oven to 350°F/180°C/ Gas 4. Grease and line an 8¹/₂ × 4¹/₂ in (22 × 12 cm) loaf tin.

2 ▲ Sprinkle 1¹/₂ tablespoons of the caster sugar into the pan and tilt to distribute the sugar in an even layer over the bottom and sides. Shake out any excess.

~ VARIATION ~

For the best results, the eggs should be at room temperature. If they are too cold when folded into the creamed butter mixture, they may separate. If this happens, add a spoonful of the flour to help stabilize the mixture.

3 ▼ Sift together the flour, baking powder and cornflour into a mixing bowl, 3 times. Set aside.

4 With an electric mixer, cream the butter until soft. Add the remaining sugar and continue beating until light and fluffy. Add the eggs, 1 at a time, beating to incorporate thoroughly after each addition.

5 Gently fold the dry ingredients into the butter mixture, in 3 batches; do not overmix.

6 ▲ Fold in the vanilla, currants or raisins, walnuts, lemon rind, and chocolate chips until just blended.

7 Pour the mixture into the prepared tin and bake until a cake tester inserted in the centre comes out clean, 45–50 minutes. Let cool in the tin for 5 minutes before transferring to a rack to cool completely. Dust over an even layer of icing sugar before serving.

Fruity Tea Bread

MAKES 1 LOAF

8 oz (225 g) plain flour

4 oz (115 g) caster sugar

1 tbsp baking powder

1/2 tsp salt

grated rind of 1 large orange

5 1/2 fl oz (170 ml) fresh orange juice

2 eggs, lightly beaten

3 oz (85 g) butter or margarine, melted

4 oz (115 g) fresh cranberries, or bilberries

2 oz (55 g) chopped walnuts

1 Preheat a 350°F/180°C/Gas 4 oven. Line a 9 × 5 in (23 × 13 cm) loaf tin with greaseproof paper and grease.

2 Sift the flour, sugar, baking powder and salt into a mixing bowl.

3 ▼ Stir in the orange rind.

4 ▲ Make a well in the centre and add the orange juice, eggs and melted butter or margarine. Stir from the centre until the ingredients are blended; do not overmix.

5 ▲ Add the berries and walnuts and stir until blended.

6 Transfer the mixture to the prepared tin and bake until a skewer inserted in the centre comes out clean, 45–50 minutes.

7 ▲ Let cool in the tin for 10 minutes before transferring to a rack to cool completely. Serve thinly sliced, toasted or plain, with butter or cream cheese and jam.

Dried Fruit Loaf

MAKES 1 LOAF

1 lb (450 g) mixed dried fruit, such as currants, raisins, chopped dried apricots and dried cherries
10 fl oz (300 ml) cold strong tea
7 oz (200 g) dark brown sugar
grated rind and juice of 1 small orange
grated rind and juice of 1 lemon
1 egg, lightly beaten
7 oz (200 g) plain flour
1 tbsp baking powder
1/8 tsp salt

1 ▲ In a bowl, mix the dried fruit with the tea and soak overnight.

2 Preheat a 350°F/180°C/Gas 4 oven. Line the bottom and sides of a 9 × 5 in (23 × 13 cm) loaf tin with greaseproof paper and grease the paper.

3 ▲ Strain the fruit, reserving the liquid. In a bowl, combine the brown sugar, grated orange and lemon rind, and fruit.

4 ▼ Pour the orange and lemon juice into a measuring jug; if the quantity is less than 8 fl oz (250 ml), top up with the soaking liquid.

5 Stir the citrus juices and egg into the dried fruit mixture.

6 In another bowl, sift together the flour, baking powder and salt. Stir into the fruit mixture until blended.

7 Transfer to the prepared tin and bake until a skewer inserted in the centre comes out clean, about 1 1/4 hours. Let stand 10 minutes before unmoulding.

Mango Tea Bread

MAKES 2 LOAVES

10 oz (285 g) plain flour
2 teaspoons bicarbonate of soda
2 teaspoons ground cinnamon
1/2 teaspoon salt
4 oz (115 g) margarine, at room temperature
3 eggs, at room temperature
10 1/2 oz (300 g) sugar
4 fl oz (125 ml) vegetable oil
1 large ripe mango, peeled and chopped
3 1/4 oz (90 g) desiccated coconut
2 1/2 oz (70 g) raisins

1 Preheat the oven to 350°F/180°C/ Gas 4. Line the bottom and sides of 2 9 × 5 in (23 × 13 cm) loaf tins with greaseproof paper and grease.

2 Sift together the flour, bicarbonate of soda, cinnamon and salt. Set aside.

3 With an electric mixer, cream the margarine until soft.

4 ▼ Beat in the eggs and sugar until light and fluffy. Beat in the oil.

5 Fold the dry ingredients into the creamed ingredients in 3 batches.

6 Fold in the mangoes, two-thirds of the coconut and the raisins.

7 ▲ Spoon the batter into the pans.

8 Sprinkle over the remaining coconut. Bake until a skewer inserted in the centre comes out clean, 50–60 minutes. Let stand for 10 minutes before turning out onto a rack to cool completely.

Courgette Tea Bread

MAKES 1 LOAF

2 oz (55 g) butter
3 eggs
8 fl oz (250 ml) vegetable oil
10 1/2 oz (300 g) sugar
2 medium unpeeled courgettes, grated
10 oz (285 g) plain flour
2 teaspoons bicarbonate of soda
1 teaspoon baking powder
1 teaspoon salt
1 teaspoon ground cinnamon
1 teaspoon grated nutmeg
1/4 teaspoon ground cloves
4 oz (115 g) walnuts, chopped

1 Preheat the oven to 350°F/180°C/ Gas 4.

2 Line the bottom and sides of a 9 × 5 in (23 × 13 cm) loaf tin with greaseproof paper and grease.

3 ▲ In a saucepan, melt the butter over low heat. Set aside.

4 With an electric mixer, beat the eggs and oil together until thick. Beat in the sugar. Stir in the melted butter and courgettes. Set aside.

5 ▲ In another bowl, sift all the dry ingredients together 3 times. Carefully fold into the courgette mixture. Fold in the walnuts.

6 Pour into the tin and bake until a skewer inserted in the centre comes out clean, 60–70 minutes. Let stand 10 minutes before turning out onto wire rack to cool completely.

Mango Tea Bread (top), Courgette Tea Bread

PIES & TARTS

HERE IS EVERY SORT OF FILLING –
FROM ORCHARD FRUITS TO AUTUMN
NUTS, TANGY CITRUS TO LUSCIOUS
CHOCOLATE – FOR THE MOST
MEMORABLE PIES AND TARTS. SOME
ARE PLAIN AND SOME ARE FANCY,
BUT ALL ARE DELICIOUS.

Traditional Apple Pie

SERVES 8

about 2 lb (900 g) tart eating apples,
    such as Granny Smith, peeled, cored
    and sliced

1 tbsp fresh lemon juice

1 tsp vanilla essence

4 oz (115 g) caster sugar

½ tsp ground cinnamon

1½ oz (45 g) butter or margarine

1 egg yolk

2 tsp whipping cream

FOR THE PASTRY

8 oz (225 g) plain flour

1 tsp salt

6 oz (170 g) lard or vegetable fat

4–5 tbsp iced water

1 tbsp quick-cooking tapioca

1 Preheat a 450°F/230°C/Gas 8 oven.

2 For the pastry, sift the flour and salt
into a bowl. Using a pastry blender,
cut in the fat until the mixture
resembles coarse breadcrumbs.

3 ▲ Sprinkle in the water, 1
tablespoon at a time, tossing lightly
with your fingertips or with a fork
until the pastry forms a ball.

4 ▲ Divide the pastry in half and
shape each half into a ball. On a
lightly floured surface, roll out one of
the balls to a circle about 12 in
(30 cm) in diameter.

5 ▲ Use it to line a 9 in (23 cm) pie
tin, easing the dough in and being
careful not to stretch it. Trim off the
excess pastry and use the trimmings
for decorating. Sprinkle the tapioca
over the bottom of the pie shell.

6 ▲ Roll out the remaining pastry to
⅛ in (3 mm) thickness. With a sharp
knife, cut out 8 large leaf-shapes. Cut
the trimmings into small leaf shapes.
Score the leaves with the back of the
knife to mark veins.

7 ▲ In a bowl, toss the apples with
the lemon juice, vanilla, sugar and
cinnamon. Fill the pastry case with
the apple mixture and dot with the
butter or margarine.

8 ▲ Arrange the large pastry leaves
in a decorative pattern on top.
Decorate the edge with small leaves.

9 ▲ Mix together the egg yolk and
cream and brush over the leaves to
glaze them.

10 Bake 10 minutes, then reduce the
heat to 350°F/180°C/Gas 4 and
continue baking until the pastry is
golden brown, 35–45 minutes. Let the
pie cool in the tin, set on a wire rack.

Apple and Cranberry Lattice Pie

SERVES 8

grated rind of 1 orange
3 tablespoons fresh orange juice
2 large, tart cooking apples
6 oz (170 g) cranberries
2½ oz (70 g) raisins
1 oz (30 g) walnuts, chopped
7½ oz (215 g) caster sugar
4 oz (115 g) dark brown sugar
2 tablespoons plain flour
FOR THE CRUST
10 oz (285 g) plain flour
½ teaspoon salt
3 oz (85 g) cold butter, cut into pieces
3 oz (85 g) cold vegetable fat or lard, cut into pieces
2–4 fl oz (65–125 ml) iced water

1 ▼ For the crust, sift the flour and salt into a bowl. Add the butter and fat and rub in with your fingertips until the mixture resembles coarse breadcrumbs. With a fork, stir in just enough water to bind the dough. Gather into 2 equal balls, wrap in cling film, and refrigerate for at least 20 minutes.

2 ▲ Put the orange rind and juice into a mixing bowl. Peel and core the apples and grate into the bowl. Stir in the cranberries, raisins, walnuts, all except 1 tablespoon of the caster sugar, the brown sugar and flour.

3 Place a baking sheet in the oven and preheat to 400°F/200°C/Gas 6.

4 On a lightly floured surface, roll out 1 ball of dough about ⅛ in (3mm) thick. Transfer to a 9 in (23 cm) pie plate and trim. Spoon the cranberry and apple mixture into the shell.

5 ▲ Roll out the remaining dough to a circle about 11 in (28 cm) in diameter. With a serrated pastry wheel, cut the dough into 10 strips, ¾ in (2 cm) wide. Place 5 strips horizontally across the top of the tart at 1 in (2.5 cm) intervals. Weave in 5 vertical strips and trim. Sprinkle the top with the remaining sugar.

6 Bake the pie for 20 minutes. Reduce the heat to 350°F/180°C/Gas 4 and bake for about 15 minutes more, until the crust is golden and the filling is bubbling.

Rhubarb and Cherry Pie

SERVES 8

1 lb (450 g) rhubarb, cut into 1 in (2.5 cm) pieces

1 lb (450 g) canned stoned tart red or black cherries, drained

10 oz (285 g) caster sugar

1 oz (30 g) quick-cooking tapioca

FOR THE PASTRY

10 oz (285 g) plain flour

1 tsp salt

3 oz (85 g) cold butter, cut in pieces

2 oz (55 g) cold vegetable fat or lard, cut in pieces

2–4 fl oz (65–125 ml) iced water

milk, for glazing

1 ▲ For the pastry, sift the flour and salt into a bowl. Add the butter and fat to the dry ingredients and cut in with a pastry blender until the mixture resembles coarse breadcrumbs.

2 With a fork, stir in just enough water to bind the pastry. Gather into 2 balls, 1 slightly larger than the other. Wrap the pastry in greaseproof paper and refrigerate for at least 20 minutes.

3 Preheat a baking sheet in the centre of a 400°F/200°C/Gas 6 oven.

4 On a lightly floured surface, roll out the larger pastry ball to a thickness of about ⅛ in (3 mm).

5 ▼ Roll the pastry around the rolling pin and transfer to a 9 in (23 cm) pie dish. Trim the edge to leave a ½ in (1 cm) overhang.

6 Refrigerate the pastry case while making the filling.

7 In a mixing bowl, combine the rhubarb, cherries, sugar and tapioca and spoon into the pie shell.

8 ▲ Roll out the remaining pastry and cut out leaf shapes.

9 Transfer the pastry lid to the pie and trim to leave a ¾ in (2 cm) overhang. Fold the top edge under the bottom and flute. Roll small balls from the scraps. Mark veins in the pastry leaves and place on top with the balls.

10 Glaze the top and bake until golden, 40–50 minutes.

Rhubarb Pie

1 ▲ For the pastry, sift the flour, salt, and sugar into a bowl. Using a pastry blender or two knives, cut the butter or fat into the dry ingredients as quickly as possible until the mixture resembles coarse breadcrumbs.

2 Sprinkle with the iced water and mix until the dough holds together. If the dough is too crumbly, add a little more water, 1 tablespoon at a time.

~ COOK'S TIP ~

Be sure to cut off and discard the green rhubarb leaves from the pink stalks as they are toxic and not edible.

3 ▲ Gather the dough into a ball, flatten into a disc, wrap in grease-proof paper, and chill for at least 20 minutes.

4 ▲ Roll out the dough between two sheets of greaseproof paper to a thickness of about ⅛ in (3 mm). Use to line a 9 in (23 cm) pie dish. Trim all round, leaving a ½ in (1 cm) overhang. Fold the overhang under the edge and flute. Refrigerate the pie shell and dough trimmings for 30 minutes.

5 ▲ For the filling, place the rhubarb in a bowl and sprinkle with the cornflour. Toss to coat.

6 Preheat oven to 220°C/425°F/Gas 7.

7 In a small bowl, beat the egg with the sugar. Mix in the orange rind.

8 ▲ Stir the sugar mixture into the rhubarb and mix well. Spoon the fruit into the pie shell.

9 ▲ Roll out the dough trimmings. Stamp out decorative shapes with a biscuit cutter or cut shapes with a small knife, using a template made out of card as a guide, if wished.

10 Arrange the shapes on top of the pie. Brush the trimmings and the rim of the pie with cream.

11 Bake for 30 minutes. Reduce the heat to 160°C/325°F/Gas 3 and continue baking until the pastry is golden brown and the rhubarb is tender, about 15–20 minutes more.

Plum Pie

SERVES 8

2 lb (900 g) red or purple plums

grated rind of 1 lemon

1 tbsp fresh lemon juice

4–6 oz (115–170 g) caster sugar

3 tbsp quick-cooking tapioca

1/8 tsp salt

1/2 tsp ground cinnamon

1/4 tsp grated nutmeg

FOR THE PASTRY

10 oz (285 g) plain flour

1 tsp salt

3 oz (85 g) cold butter, cut in pieces

2 oz (55 g) cold vegetable fat or lard, cut in pieces

2–4 fl oz (65–125 ml) iced water

milk, for glazing

1 ▼ For the pastry, sift the flour and salt into a bowl. Add the butter and fat and cut in with a pastry blender until the mixture resembles coarse breadcrumbs.

2 Stir in just enough water to bind the pastry. Gather into 2 balls, 1 slightly larger than the other. Wrap and refrigerate for 20 minutes.

3 Preheat a baking sheet in the centre of a 425°F/220°C/Gas 7 oven.

4 On a lightly floured surface, roll out the larger pastry ball to about 1/8 in (3 mm) thick. Transfer to a 9 in (23 cm) pie dish and trim the edge.

5 ▲ Halve the plums, discard the stones, and cut into large pieces. Mix all the filling ingredients together (if the plums are very tart, use extra sugar). Transfer to the pastry case.

6 ▲ Roll out the remaining pastry and place on a baking tray lined with greaseproof paper. With a cutter, stamp out 4 hearts. Transfer the pastry lid to the pie using the paper.

7 Trim to leave a 3/4 in (2 cm) overhang. Fold the top edge under the bottom and pinch to seal. Arrange the hearts on top. Brush with the milk. Bake for 15 minutes. Reduce the heat to 350°F/180°C/Gas 4 and bake 30–35 minutes more. If the crust browns too quickly, protect with a sheet of foil.

Lattice Berry Pie

SERVES 8

1 lb (450 g) berries, such as bilberries, blueberries, blackcurrants etc
4 oz (115 g) caster sugar
3 tbsp cornflour
2 tbsp fresh lemon juice
1 oz (30 g) butter, diced
FOR THE PASTRY
10 oz (285 g) plain flour
3/4 tsp salt
4 oz (115 g) cold butter, cut in pieces
1 1/2 oz (45 g) cold vegetable fat or lard, cut in pieces
5–6 tbsp iced water
1 egg beaten with 1 tbsp water, for glazing

1 For the pastry, sift the flour and salt into a bowl. Add the butter and fat and cut in with a pastry blender until the mixture resembles coarse breadcrumbs. With a fork, stir in just enough water to bind the pastry. Form into 2 balls, wrap in greaseproof paper, and refrigerate for 20 minutes.

2 On a lightly floured surface, roll out one ball about 1/8 in (3 mm) thick. Transfer to a 9 in (23 cm) pie dish and trim to leave a 1/2 in (1 cm) overhang. Brush the bottom with egg glaze.

3 ▲ Mix all the filling ingredients together, except the butter (reserve a few berries for decoration). Spoon into the pastry case and dot with the butter. Brush the egg glaze around the rim of the pastry case.

4 Preheat a baking sheet in the centre of a 425°F/220°C/Gas 7 oven.

5 ▼ Roll out the remaining pastry on a baking tray lined with grease-proof paper. With a serrated pastry wheel, cut out 24 thin pastry strips. Roll out the scraps and cut out leaf shapes. Mark veins in the leaves with the point of a knife.

6 ▲ Weave the strips in a close lattice, then transfer to the pie using the paper. Press the edges to seal and trim. Arrange the pastry leaves around the rim. Brush with egg glaze.

7 Bake for 10 minutes. Reduce the heat to 350°F/180°C/Gas 4 and bake until the pastry is golden, 40–45 minutes more. Decorate with berries.

Cherry Pie

SERVES 8

2 lb (900 g) fresh Morello cherries,
stoned, or 2 × 1 lb (450 g) cans or
jars, drained and stoned

2½ oz (70 g) caster sugar

1 oz (30 g) plain flour

1½ tbsp fresh lemon juice

¼ tsp almond essence

1 oz (30 g) butter or margarine

FOR THE PASTRY

8 oz (225 g) plain flour

1 tsp salt

6 oz (175 g) lard or vegetable fat

4–5 tbsp iced water

1 For the pastry, sift the flour and salt
into a mixing bowl. Using a pastry
blender, cut in the fat until the mixture
resembles coarse breadcrumbs.

2 ▲ Sprinkle in the water, 1
tablespoon at a time, tossing lightly
with your fingertips or a fork until the
pastry forms a ball.

3 Divide the pastry in half and shape
each half into a ball. On a lightly
floured surface, roll out one of the
balls to a circle about 12 in (30 cm) in
diameter.

4 ▲ Use it to line a 9 in (23 cm) pie
tin, easing the pastry in and being
careful not to stretch it. With scissors,
trim off excess pastry, leaving a ½ in
(1 cm) overhang around the pie rim.

5 ▲ Roll out the remaining pastry to
⅛ in (3 mm) thickness. Cut out 11
strips ½ in (1 cm) wide.

6 ▲ In a mixing bowl, combine the
cherries, sugar, flour, lemon juice and
almond essence. Spoon the mixture
into the pastry case and dot with the
butter or margarine.

7 ▲ To make the lattice, place 5 of
the pastry strips evenly across the
filling. Fold every other strip back.
Lay the first strip across in the
opposite direction. Continue in this
pattern, folding back every other strip
each time you add a cross strip.

8 ▲ Trim the ends of the lattice
strips even with the case overhang.
Press together so that the edge rests on
the pie-tin rim. With your thumbs,
flute the edge. Refrigerate 15 minutes.

9 Preheat a 425°F/220°C/Gas 7 oven.

10 Bake the pie 30 minutes, covering
the edge of the pastry case with foil, if
necessary, to prevent over-browning.
Let cool, in the tin, on a wire rack.

Peach Leaf Pie

SERVES 8

2 lb 8 oz (1.2 kg) ripe peaches
juice of 1 lemon
3^1/$_2$ oz (100 g) sugar
3 tablespoons cornflour
^{1}/$_4$ teaspoon grated nutmeg
^{1}/$_2$ teaspoon ground cinnamon
1 oz (30 g) butter, diced
FOR THE CRUST
10 oz (285 g) plain flour
^{3}/$_4$ teaspoon salt
4 oz (115 g) cold butter, cut into pieces
2^1/$_4$ oz (60 g) cold vegetable fat or lard, cut into pieces
5–6 tablespoons iced water
1 egg beaten with 1 tablespoon water, for glazing

1 For the pastry, sift the flour and salt into a bowl. Add the butter and fat and rub in with your fingertips until the mixture resembles coarse breadcrumbs.

2 ▲ With a fork, stir in just enough water to bind the dough. Gather into 2 balls, one slightly larger than the other. Wrap in clear film and refrigerate for at least 20 minutes.

3 Place a baking sheet in the oven and preheat to 425°F/220°C/Gas 7.

4 ▲ Drop a few peaches at a time into boiling water for 20 seconds, then transfer to a bowl of cold water. When cool, peel off the skins.

5 Slice the peaches and combine with the lemon juice, sugar, cornstarch and spices. Set aside.

6 ▲ On a lightly floured surface, roll out the larger dough ball about ^{1}/$_8$ in (3 mm) thick. Transfer to a 9 in (23 cm) pie tin and trim. Refrigerate.

7 ▲ Roll out the remaining dough ^{1}/$_4$ in (5 mm) thick. Cut out leaf shapes 3 in (8 cm) long, using a template if needed. Mark veins with a knife. With the scraps, roll a few balls.

8 ▲ Brush the bottom of the pastry shell with egg glaze. Add the peaches, piling them higher in the centre. Dot with the butter.

9 ▲ To assemble, start from the outside edge and cover the peaches with a ring of leaves. Place a second ring of leaves above, staggering the positions. Continue with rows of leaves until covered. Place the balls in the centre. Brush with glaze.

10 Bake for 10 minutes. Lower the heat to 350°F/180°C/Gas 4 and bake for 35–40 minutes more.

~ COOK'S TIP ~

Baking the pie on a preheated baking sheet helps to make the bottom crust crisp. The moisture from the filling keeps the bottom crust more humid than the top, but this baking method helps to compensate for the top crust being better exposed to the heat source.

Blueberry Pie

SERVES 6–8

basic or rich shortcrust for a two-crust
   pie (page 222, shortcrust variations)

1¼ lb (575 g) blueberries

5½ oz (160 g) caster sugar

3 tablespoons plain flour

1 teaspoon grated orange zest

¼ teaspoon grated nutmeg

2 tablespoons orange juice

1 teaspoon lemon juice

1 Preheat a 375°F/190°C/Gas 5 oven.

2 ▲ Roll out half of the pastry and
use to line a 9 in (23 cm) pie tin that is
about 2 in (5 cm) deep.

3 ▲ Combine the blueberries, 5 oz
(145 g) of the sugar, the flour, orange
zest and nutmeg in a bowl. Toss the
mixture gently to coat the fruit evenly
with the dry ingredients.

4 ▼ Pour the blueberry mixture into
the pastry case and spread it evenly.
Sprinkle over the citrus juices.

5 ▲ Roll out the remaining pastry
and cover the pie. Cut out small
decorative shapes or cut 2–3 slits for
steam vents. Finish the edge.

6 ▲ Brush the top lightly with water
and sprinkle evenly with the
remaining caster sugar.

7 Bake for about 45 minutes or until
the pastry is golden brown. Serve
warm or at room temperature.

Walnut and Pear Lattice Pie

SERVES 6–8

nut shortcrust for a two-crust pie (page 222, pastry variations), using walnuts

2 lb (900 g) pears, peeled, cored and thinly sliced

2 oz (55 g) caster sugar

1 oz (30 g) plain flour

½ teaspoon grated lemon zest

1 oz (30 g) raisins or sultanas

1 oz (30 g) walnuts, chopped

½ teaspoon ground cinnamon

2 oz (55 g) icing sugar

1 tablespoon lemon juice

about 2 teaspoons cold water

1 Preheat a 375°F/190°C/Gas 5 oven.

2 Roll out half of the pastry dough and use to line a 9 in (23 cm) tin that is about 2 in (5 cm) deep.

3 ▲ Combine the pears, caster sugar, flour and lemon zest in a bowl. Toss gently until the fruit is evenly coated with the dry ingredients. Mix in the raisins, nuts and cinnamon.

~ COOK'S TIP ~

For a simple cutout lattice top, roll out the dough for the top into a circle. Using a small pastry cutter, cut out shapes in a pattern, spacing them evenly and not too close together.

4 ▲ Put the pear filling into the pastry case and spread it evenly.

5 Roll out the remaining pastry dough and use to make a lattice top.

6 Bake for 55 minutes or until the pastry is golden brown.

7 Combine the icing sugar, lemon juice and water in a bowl and stir until smoothly blended.

8 ▼ Remove the pie from the oven. Drizzle the icing sugar glaze evenly over the top of the pie, on pastry and filling. Leave the pie to cool, set on a wire rack, before serving.

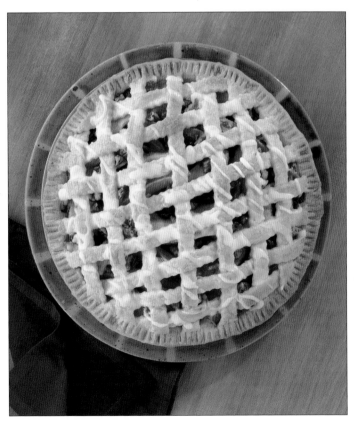

Mince Pies

MAKES 36

6 oz (170 g) finely chopped blanched
  almonds

5 oz (140 g) dried apricots, finely chopped

6 oz (170 g) raisins

5 oz (140 g) currants

5 oz (140 g) glacé cherries, chopped

5 oz (140 g) cut mixed peel, chopped

4 oz (115 g) finely chopped beef suet

grated rind and juice of 2 lemons

grated rind and juice of 1 orange

7 oz (200 g) dark brown sugar

4 cooking apples, peeled, cored and
  chopped

2 tsp ground cinnamon

1 tsp grated nutmeg

1/2 tsp ground cloves

8 fl oz (250 ml) brandy

8 oz (225 g) cream cheese

2 tbsp caster sugar

icing sugar, for dusting (optional)

FOR THE PASTRY

15 oz (420 g) plain flour

5 oz (140 g) icing sugar

12 oz (350 g) cold butter, cut in pieces

grated rind and juice of 1 orange

milk, for glazing

1 Mix the nuts, dried and preserved fruit, suet, citrus rind and juice, brown sugar, apples and spices.

2 ▲ Stir in the brandy. Cover and leave in a cool place for 2 days.

3 For the pastry, sift the flour and icing sugar into a bowl. Cut in the butter until the mixture resembles coarse breadcrumbs.

4 ▲ Add the orange rind. Stir in just enough orange juice to bind. Gather into a ball, wrap in greaseproof paper, and refrigerate for at least 20 minutes.

5 Preheat a 425°F/220°C/Gas 7 oven. Grease 2–3 bun trays. Beat together the cream cheese and sugar.

6 ▲ Roll out the pastry 1/4 in (5 mm) thick. With a fluted pastry cutter, stamp out 36 3 in (8 cm) rounds.

~ COOK'S TIP ~

The mincemeat mixture may be packed into sterilized jars and sealed. It will keep refrigerated for several months. Add a few tablespoonfuls to give apple pies a lift, or make small mincemeat-filled parcels using filo pastry.

7 ▲ Transfer the rounds to the bun tray. Fill halfway with mincemeat. Top with a teaspoonful of the cream cheese mixture.

8 ▲ Roll out the remaining pastry and stamp out 36 2 in (5 cm) rounds with a fluted cutter. Brush the edges of the pies with milk, then set the rounds on top. Cut a small steam vent in the top of each pie.

9 ▲ Brush lightly with milk. Bake until golden, 15–20 minutes. Let cool for 10 minutes before unmoulding. Dust with icing sugar, if wished.

Pear and Apple Crumble Pie

SERVES 8

3 firm pears
4 cooking apples
6 oz (170 g) caster sugar
2 tbsp cornflour
⅛ tsp salt
grated rind of 1 lemon
2 tbsp fresh lemon juice
3 oz (85 g) raisins
3 oz (85 g) plain flour
1 tsp ground cinnamon
3 oz (85 g) cold butter, cut in pieces
FOR THE PASTRY
5 oz (140 g) plain flour
½ tsp salt
2½ oz (70 g) cold vegetable fat or lard, cut in pieces
2 tbsp iced water

1 For the pastry, combine the flour and salt in a bowl. Add the fat and cut in with a pastry blender until the mixture resembles coarse breadcrumbs. Stir in just enough water to bind the pastry. Gather into a ball and transfer to a lightly floured surface. Roll out ⅛ in (3 mm) thick.

2 ▲ Transfer to a shallow 9 in (23 cm) pie dish and trim to leave a ½ in (1 cm) overhang. Fold the overhang under for double thickness. Flute the edge. Refrigerate.

3 Preheat a baking sheet in the centre of a 450°F/230°C/Gas 8 oven.

4 ▲ Peel and core the pears. Slice them into a bowl. Peel, core and slice the apples. Add to the pears. Stir in one-third of the sugar, the cornflour, salt and lemon rind. Add the lemon juice and raisins and stir to blend.

5 For the crumble topping, combine the remaining sugar, flour, cinnamon, and butter in a bowl. Blend with your fingertips until the mixture resembles coarse breadcrumbs. Set aside.

6 ▲ Spoon the fruit filling into the pastry case. Sprinkle the crumbs lightly and evenly over the top.

7 Bake for 10 minutes, then reduce the heat to 350°F/180°C/Gas 4. Cover the top of the pie loosely with a sheet of foil and continue baking until browned, 35–40 minutes more.

Open Apple Pie

SERVES 8

3 lb (1.4 kg) sweet-tart firm eating or cooking apples
1³/4 oz (50 g) sugar
2 teaspoons ground cinnamon
grated rind and juice of 1 lemon
1 oz (30 g) butter, diced
2–3 tablespoons honey
FOR THE CRUST
10 oz (285 g) plain flour
¹/2 teaspoon salt
4 oz (115 g) cold butter, cut into pieces
2¹/4 oz (60 g) cold vegetable fat or lard, cut into pieces
5–6 tablespoons iced water

1 For the crust, sift the flour and salt into a bowl. Add the butter and fat and rub in with your fingertips until the mixture resembles coarse breadcrumbs.

2 ▲ With a fork, stir in just enough water to bind the dough. Gather into a ball, wrap in clear film, and refrigerate for at least 20 minutes.

3 Place a baking sheet in the centre of the oven and preheat to 400°F/200°C/Gas 6.

4 ▼ Peel, core, and slice the apples. Combine the sugar and cinnamon in a bowl. Add the apples, lemon rind and juice and stir.

5 On a lightly floured surface, roll out the dough to a circle about 12 in (30 cm) in diameter. Transfer to a 9 in (23 cm) diameter deep pie dish; leave the dough hanging over the edge. Fill with the apple slices.

6 ▲ Fold in the edges and crimp loosely for a decorative border. Dot the apples with diced butter.

7 Bake on the hot sheet until the pastry is golden and the apples are tender, about 45 minutes.

8 Melt the honey in a saucepan and brush over the apples to glaze. Serve warm or at room temperature.

Brethren's Cider Pie

SERVES 6

6oz (175g) plain flour

¼ teaspoon salt

2 teaspoons sugar

4oz (115g) cold butter or margarine

2fl oz (50ml) or more iced water

FOR THE FILLING

1 pint (600ml) unfiltered apple juice

½oz (15g) butter

8fl oz (250ml) maple syrup

2fl oz (50ml) water

¼ teaspoon salt

2 eggs, at room temperature, separated

1 teaspoon grated nutmeg

3 ▲ Meanwhile, place the apple juice in a heavy pan. Boil until only 6fl oz (175ml) remains. Leave to cool.

4 ▲ Roll out the dough between two sheets of greaseproof paper to a thickness of about ⅛ in (3 mm). Use to line a 9 in (23 cm) pie dish.

1 ▲ For the pastry, sift the flour, salt, and sugar into a bowl. Using a pastry blender or two knives, cut the butter or margarine into the dry ingredients as quickly as possible until the mixture resembles coarse breadcrumbs.

2 Sprinkle the iced water over the flour mixture. Combine with a fork until the dough holds together. If the dough is too crumbly, add a little more water, 1 tablespoon at a time. Gather the dough into a ball and flatten into a disk. Wrap in greaseproof paper and refrigerate for at least 20 minutes.

5 ▲ Trim the edge, leaving a ½ in (1 cm) overhang. Fold the overhang under to form the edge. Using a fork, press the edge to the rim of the dish and press up from under with your fingers at intervals for a ruffle effect. Refrigerate for 20 minutes.

6 Preheat a 180°C/350°F/Gas 4 oven.

7 ▲ For the filling, add the butter, maple syrup, water and salt to the juice and simmer gently for 5–6 minutes. Remove the pan from the heat and leave to cool slightly. Beat the egg yolks and whisk them into the pan.

8 ▲ In a large bowl, beat the egg whites until they form stiff peaks. Add the juice mixture and fold gently together until evenly blended.

9 ▲ Pour into the prepared pastry case. Dust with the grated nutmeg.

10 Bake until the pastry is golden brown and the filling is well set, 30–35 minutes. Serve warm.

Caramelized Upside-Down Pear Pie

SERVES 8

5–6 firm, ripe pears
6 oz (170 g) sugar
4 oz (115 g) unsalted butter
whipped cream, for serving
FOR THE PASTRY
4 oz (115 g) plain flour
1/4 teaspoon salt
4 1/2 oz (125 g) cold butter, cut into pieces
1 1/2 oz (45 g) cold vegetable fat, cut into pieces
4 tablespoons iced water

1 ▲ For the pastry, combine the flour and salt in a bowl. Add the butter and vegetable fat and cut in with a pastry blender until the mixture resembles coarse crumbs. With a fork, stir in enough iced water to bind the dough. Gather into a ball, wrap in clear film and refrigerate for at least 20 minutes. Preheat the oven to 400°F/200°C/Gas 6.

~ VARIATION ~

For Caramelized Upside-Down Apple Pie, replace the pears with 8–9 firm, tart apples. There may seem to be too many apples, but they shrink slightly as they cook.

2 ▲ Quarter, peel and core the pears. Place in a bowl and toss with a few tablespoons of the sugar.

3 ▲ In a 10 1/2 in (27 cm) ovenproof frying pan, melt the butter over moderately high heat. Add the remaining sugar. When it starts to colour, arrange the pears evenly around the edge and in the centre.

4 ▲ Continue cooking, uncovered, until caramelized, about 20 minutes.

5 ▲ Let the fruit cool. Roll out a circle of dough slightly larger than the diameter of the pan. Place the dough on top of the pears, tucking it around the edges. Transfer the pan to the oven and bake for 15 minutes, then reduce the heat to 350°F/180°C/Gas 4. Bake until golden, about 15 minutes more.

6 ▲ Let the pie cool in the pan for about 3–4 minutes. Run a knife around the edge of the pan to loosen the pie, ensuring that the knife reaches down to the bottom of the pan. Invert a plate on top and, protecting your hands with oven gloves, hold plate and pan firmly, and turn them both over quickly.

7 Lift off the pan. If any pears stick to the pan, remove them gently with a metal spatula and replace them carefully on the pie. Serve warm, with the whipped cream passed separately.

Lemon Meringue Pie

SERVES 8

grated rind and juice of 1 large lemon
8 fl oz (250 ml) plus 1 tbsp cold water
4 oz (115 g) plus 6 tbsp caster sugar
1 oz (30 g) butter
3 tbsp cornflour
3 eggs, separated
1/8 tsp salt
1/8 tsp cream of tartar
FOR THE PASTRY
5 oz (140 g) plain flour
1/2 tsp salt
2 1/2 oz (70 g) cold vegetable fat or lard, cut in pieces
2 tbsp iced water

1 For the pastry, sift the flour and salt into a bowl. Add the fat and cut in with a pastry blender until the mixture resembles coarse breadcrumbs. With a fork, stir in just enough water to bind the mixture. Gather the pastry into a ball.

2 ▲ On a lightly floured surface, roll out the pastry about 1/8 in (3 mm) thick. Transfer to a 9 in (23 cm) pie dish and trim the edge to leave a 1/2 in (2 cm) overhang.

3 ▲ Fold the overhang under and crimp the edge. Refrigerate the pastry case for at least 20 minutes.

4 Preheat a 400°F/200°C/Gas 6 oven.

5 ▲ Prick the case all over with a fork. Line with crumpled greaseproof paper and fill with baking beans. Bake for 12 minutes. Remove the paper and beans and continue baking until golden, 6–8 minutes more.

6 In a saucepan, combine the lemon rind and juice, 8 fl oz (250 ml) of the water, 4 oz (115 g) of the sugar, and butter. Bring the mixture to a boil.

7 Meanwhile, in a mixing bowl, dissolve the cornflour in the remaining water. Add the egg yolks.

8 ▲ Add the egg yolks to the lemon mixture and return to the boil, whisking continuously until the mixture thickens, about 5 minutes.

9 Cover the surface with greaseproof paper and let cool.

10 ▲ For the meringue, using an electric mixer beat the egg whites with the salt and cream of tartar until they hold stiff peaks. Add the remaining sugar and beat until glossy.

11 ▲ Spoon the lemon mixture into the pastry case and level. Spoon the meringue on top, smoothing it up to the pastry rim to seal. Bake until golden, 12–15 minutes.

Lime Meringue Pie

SERVES 8

3 egg yolks

12 fl oz (350 ml) sweetened condensed milk

finely grated rind and juice of 4 limes

7 egg whites

⅛ tsp salt

squeeze of fresh lemon juice

4 oz (115 g) sugar

½ tsp vanilla essence

FOR THE PASTRY

5½ oz (165 g) plain flour

½ tsp salt

4 oz (115 g) lard or vegetable fat

2–3 tbsp iced water

1 Preheat a 425°F/220°C/Gas 7 oven.

3 ▲ On a lightly floured surface, roll out the pastry. Use it to line a 9 in (23 cm) pie tin, easing in the pastry. Make a fluted edge.

4 Using a fork, prick the bottom and sides of the pastry case all over. Bake until lightly browned, 10–15 minutes. Let cool, in the tin, on a wire rack. Reduce oven temperature to 350°F/180°C/Gas 4.

2 ▲ For the pastry, sift the flour and salt into a mixing bowl. Using a pastry blender or 2 knives, cut in the fat until the mixture resembles coarse breadcrumbs. Sprinkle in the water, 1 tablespoon at a time, tossing lightly with a fork until the mixture forms a ball.

> **~ COOK'S TIP ~**
>
> When beating egg whites with an electric mixer, start slowly, and increase speed after they become frothy. Turn the bowl constantly.

5 ▲ With an electric mixer on high speed, beat the yolks and condensed milk. Stir in the lime rind and juice.

6 ▲ In another clean bowl, beat 3 of the egg whites until stiff. Fold into the lime mixture.

7 ▲ Spread the lime filling in the pastry case. Bake 10 minutes.

8 ▲ Meanwhile, beat the remaining egg whites with the salt and lemon juice until soft peaks form. Beat in the sugar, 1 tablespoon at a time, until stiff peaks form. Add the vanilla.

9 ▲ Remove the pie from the oven. Using a metal spatula, spread the meringue over the lime filling, making a swirled design and covering the surface completely.

10 Bake until the meringue is lightly browned and the pastry is golden brown, about 12 minutes longer. Let cool, in the tin, on a wire rack.

Glacé Fruit Pie

SERVES 10

1 tablespoon rum
2 oz (55 g) mixed glacé fruit, chopped
16 fl oz (450 ml) milk
4 teaspoons gelatin
3¹/₂ oz (100 g) sugar
¹/₂ teaspoon salt
3 eggs, separated
8 fl oz (250 ml) whipping cream
chocolate curls, for decorating
FOR THE CRUST
6 oz (170 g) digestive biscuits, crushed
2¹/₂ oz (70 g) butter, melted
1 tablespoon sugar

1 For the crust, mix the crushed digestive biscuits, butter and sugar. Press evenly and firmly over the bottom and side of a 9 in (23 cm) pie plate. Refrigerate until firm.

2 ▲ In a bowl, stir together the rum and glacé fruit. Set aside.

3 Pour 4 fl oz (125 ml) of the milk into a small bowl. Sprinkle over the gelatin and let stand 5 minutes to soften.

4 ▲ In the top of a double boiler, combine 1³/₄ oz (50 g) of the sugar, the remaining milk and salt. Stir in the gelatin mixture. Cook over hot water, stirring, until gelatin dissolves.

5 Whisk in the egg yolks and cook, stirring, until thick enough to coat a spoon. Do not boil. Pour the custard over the glacé fruit mixture. Set in a bowl of ice water to cool.

6 Whip the cream lightly. Set aside.

7 With an electric mixer, beat the egg whites until they hold soft peaks. Add the remaining sugar and beat just enough to blend. Fold in a large dollop of the egg whites into the cooled gelatin mixture. Pour into the remaining egg whites and carefully fold together. Fold in the cream.

8 ▲ Pour into the pie shell and chill until firm. Decorate the top with chocolate curls.

Pumpkin Pie

SERVES 8

1 lb (450 g) cooked or canned pumpkin
8 fl oz (250 ml) whipping cream
2 eggs
4 oz (115 g) dark brown sugar
4 tablespoons golden syrup
1 1/2 teaspoons ground cinnamon
1 teaspoon ground ginger
1/4 teaspoon ground cloves
1/2 teaspoon salt
FOR THE PASTRY
6 oz (170 g) plain flour
1/2 teaspoon salt
3 oz (85 g) cold butter, cut into pieces
1 1/2 oz (45 g) cold vegetable fat, cut into pieces
3–4 tablespoons iced water

1 For the pastry, sift the flour and salt into a bowl. Cut in the butter and fat until it resembles coarse crumbs. Bind with iced water. Wrap in clear film and refrigerate for 20 minutes.

2 Roll out the dough and line a 9 in (23 cm) pie tin. Trim off the overhang. Roll out the trimmings and cut out leaf shapes. Wet the rim of the pastry case with a brush dipped in water.

3 ▲ Place the dough leaves around the rim of the pastry case. Chill for about 20 minutes. Preheat the oven to 400°F/200°C/Gas 6.

4 ▲ Line the pastry case with greaseproof paper. Fill with baking beans and bake for 12 minutes. Remove paper and beans and bake until golden, 6–8 minutes more. Reduce the heat to 375°F/190°C/Gas 5.

5 ▼ Beat together the pumpkin, cream, eggs, sugar, golden syrup, spices and salt. Pour into the pastry case and bake until set, 40 minutes.

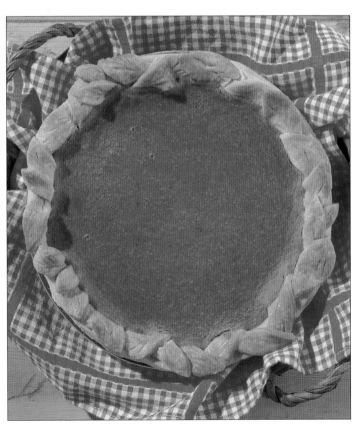

Chess Pie

SERVES 8

2 eggs
3 tablespoons whipping cream
4 oz (115 g) dark brown sugar
2 tablespoons granulated sugar
2 tablespoons plain flour
1 tablespoon whisky
1¹/₂ oz (45 g) butter, melted
2 oz (55 g) chopped walnuts
3 oz (85 g) stoned dates
whipped cream, for serving
FOR THE PASTRY
3 oz (85 g) cold butter
1¹/₂ oz (45 g) cold vegetable fat
6 oz (170 g) plain flour
¹/₂ teaspoon salt
3–4 tablespoons iced water

1 ▲ For the pastry, cut the butter and fat into small pieces.

2 Sift the flour and salt into a bowl. With a pastry blender, cut in the butter and fat until the mixture resembles coarse crumbs. Stir in just enough water to bind. Gather into a ball, wrap in greaseproof paper and refrigerate for at least 20 minutes.

3 Place a baking sheet in the oven and preheat it to 375°F/190°C/Gas 5.

4 Roll out the dough thinly and line a 9 in (23 cm) pie tin. Trim the edge. Roll out the trimmings, cut thin strips and plait them. Brush the edge of the pastry case with water and fit the pastry plaits around the rim.

5 ▲ In a mixing bowl, whisk together the eggs and cream.

6 Add both sugars and beat until well combined. Sift over 1 tablespoon of the flour and stir in. Add the whisky, the melted butter and the walnuts. Stir to combine.

7 ▲ Mix the dates with the remaining tablespoon of flour and stir into the walnut mixture.

8 Pour into the pastry case and bake until the pastry is golden and the filling puffed up, about 35 minutes. Serve at room temperature, with whipped cream, if liked.

Shoofly Pie

SERVES 8

4 oz (115 g) plain flour
4 oz (115 g) dark brown sugar
$^1/_4$ teaspoon each salt, ground ginger, cinnamon, mace and grated nutmeg
3 oz (85 g) cold butter, cut into pieces
2 eggs
4 fl oz (125 ml) molasses
4 fl oz (125 ml) boiling water
$^1/_2$ teaspoon bicarbonate of soda
FOR THE PASTRY
4 oz (115 g) cream cheese, at room temperature, cut into pieces
4 oz (115 g) cold butter, at room temperature, cut into pieces
4 oz (115 g) plain flour

1 For the pastry, put the cream cheese and butter in a mixing bowl. Sift over the flour.

2 ▲ Cut in with a pastry blender until the dough just holds together. Wrap in clear film and refrigerate for at least 30 minutes.

3 Put a baking sheet in the centre of the oven and preheat the oven to 375°F/190°C/Gas 5.

4 In a bowl, mix the flour, sugar, salt and spices. Rub in the butter with your fingertips until the mixture resembles coarse crumbs. Set aside.

5 On a lightly floured surface, roll out the dough and line a 9 in (23 cm) pie tin. Trim the overhanging pastry and flute the rim.

6 ▲ Spoon a third of the crumbed mixture into the pastry case.

7 ▲ To complete the filling, whisk the eggs with the molasses in a large bowl until combined.

8 Pour the boiling water into a small bowl. Stir in the bicarbonate of soda; the mixture will foam. Immediately whisk into the egg mixture. Pour carefully into the pastry case and sprinkle the remaining crumbed mixture evenly over the top.

9 Stand on the hot baking sheet and bake until browned, about 35 minutes. Leave to cool to room temperature, then serve.

Rich Chocolate Pie

SERVES 8

3 oz (85 g) plain chocolate

2 oz (55 g) butter or margarine

3 tbsp golden syrup

3 eggs, beaten

5 oz (140 g) caster sugar

1 tsp vanilla essence

4 oz (115 g) milk chocolate

16 fl oz (500 ml) whipping cream

FOR THE PASTRY

5½ oz (165 g) plain flour

½ tsp salt

4 oz (115 g) lard or vegetable fat

2–3 tbsp iced water

1 Preheat a 425°F/220°C/Gas 7 oven.

2 For the pastry, sift the flour and salt into a mixing bowl. Using a pastry blender, cut in the fat until the mixture resembles coarse breadcrumbs. Sprinkle in the water, 1 tablespoon at a time. Toss lightly with a fork until the pastry forms a ball.

3 On a lightly floured surface, roll out the pastry. Use to line an 8 or 9 in (20 or 23 cm) pie tin, easing in the pastry and being careful not to stretch it. Make a fluted edge.

4 Using a fork, prick the bottom and sides of the pastry case all over. Bake until lightly browned, 10–15 minutes. Let cool, in the tin, on a wire rack.

5 ▲ In a heatproof bowl set over a pan of simmering water, or in a double boiler, melt the plain chocolate, the butter or margarine and golden syrup. Remove the bowl from the heat and stir in the eggs, sugar and vanilla.

6 Reduce the oven temperature to 350°F/180°C/Gas 4. Pour the chocolate mixture into the case. Bake until the filling is set, 35–40 minutes. Let cool in the tin, set on a rack.

7 ▲ For the decoration, use the heat of your hands to soften the chocolate bar slightly. Draw the blade of a swivel-headed vegetable peeler along the side of the chocolate bar to shave off short, wide curls. Chill the chocolate curls until needed.

8 Before serving, lightly whip the cream until soft peaks form. Using a rubber spatula, spread the cream over the surface of the chocolate filling. Decorate with the chocolate curls.

Chocolate Chiffon Pie

SERVES 8

7 oz (200 g) plain chocolate
8 fl oz (250 ml) milk
1 tablespoon gelatin
3¹/₂ oz (100 g) sugar
2 extra-large eggs, separated
1 teaspoon vanilla essence
12 fl oz (350 ml) whipping cream
¹/₈ teaspoon salt
whipped cream and chocolate curls, for decorating

FOR THE CRUST

7 oz (200 g) digestive biscuits, crushed
3 oz (85 g) butter, melted

1 Place a baking sheet in the oven and preheat to 350°F/180°C/ Gas 4.

2 For the crust, mix the crushed digestive biscuits and butter in a bowl. Press evenly over the bottom and side of a 9 in (23 cm) pie plate. Bake for 8 minutes. Let cool.

3 Chop the chocolate, then grate in a food processor or blender. Set aside.

4 Place the milk in the top of a double boiler. Sprinkle over the gelatin. Let stand 5 minutes to soften.

5 ▲ Set the top of a double boiler over hot water. Add 1¹/₂ oz (45 g) sugar, the chocolate and the egg yolks. Stir until dissolved. Add the vanilla essence.

6 ▲ Set the top of the double boiler in a bowl of ice and stir until the mixture reaches room temperature. Remove from the ice and set aside.

7 Whip the cream lightly. Set aside. With an electric mixer, beat the egg whites and salt until they hold soft peaks. Add the remaining sugar and beat only enough to blend.

8 Fold a dollop of egg whites into the chocolate mixture, then pour back into the whites and fold in.

9 ▲ Fold in the whipped cream and pour into the pie shell. Put in the freezer until just set, about 5 minutes. If the centre sinks, fill with any remaining mixture. Refrigerate for 3–4 hours. Decorate with whipped cream and chocolate curls. Serve cold.

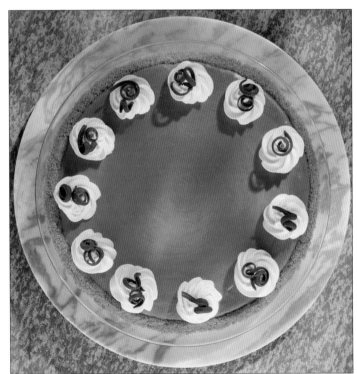

Black Bottom Pie

SERVES 8

2 teaspoons gelatin
3 tablespoons cold water
2 eggs, separated
5 oz (140 g) caster sugar
1/2 oz (15 g) cornflour
1/2 teaspoon salt
16 fl oz (450 ml) milk
2 oz (55 g) plain chocolate, finely chopped
2 tablespoons rum
1/4 teaspoon cream of tartar
chocolate curls, for decorating
FOR THE CRUST
6 oz (170 g) gingersnaps, crushed
2 1/2 oz (70 g) butter, melted

1 Preheat a 350°F/180°C/Gas 4 oven.

2 For the crust, mix the crushed gingersnaps and melted butter.

3 ▲ Press the mixture evenly over the bottom and side of a 9 in (23 cm) pie plate. Bake for 6 minutes.

4 Sprinkle the gelatin over the water and let stand to soften.

5 Beat the egg yolks in a large mixing bowl and set aside.

6 In a saucepan, combine half the sugar, the cornflour and salt. Gradually stir in the milk. Boil for 1 minute, stirring constantly.

7 ▲ Whisk the hot milk mixture into the yolks, then pour all back into the saucepan and return to the boil, whisking. Cook for 1 minute, still whisking. Remove from the heat.

8 ▲ Measure out 8 oz (225 g) of the hot custard mixture and pour into a bowl. Add the chopped chocolate to the custard mixture, and stir until melted. Stir in half the rum and pour into the pie shell.

9 ▲ Whisk the softened gelatin into the plain custard until it has dissolved, then stir in the remaining rum. Set the pan in cold water until it reaches room temperature.

10 ▲ With an electric mixer, beat the egg whites and cream of tartar until they hold stiff peaks. Add the remaining sugar gradually, beating or whisking thoroughly at each addition.

11 ▲ Fold the custard into the egg whites, then spoon over the chocolate mixture in the pie shell. Refrigerate until set, about 2 hours.

12 Decorate the top with chocolate curls. Keep the pie refrigerated until ready to serve.

~ COOK'S TIP ~

To make chocolate curls, melt 8 oz (225 g) plain chocolate over hot water, stir in 1 tablespoon of vegetable fat and mould in a small foil-lined loaf tin. For large curls, soften the bar between your hands and scrape off curls from the wide side with a vegetable peeler; for small curls, grate from the narrow side using a box grater.

Brown Sugar Pie

SERVES 8

6oz (175g) plain flour
½ teaspoon salt
2 teaspoons granulated sugar
3oz (75g) cold butter
2fl oz (50ml) or more iced water
FOR THE FILLING
1oz (25g) plain flour, sifted
8oz (225g) soft light brown sugar
½ teaspoon vanilla essence
12fl oz (350ml) whipping cream
1½oz (40g) butter, cut in tiny pieces
⅛ teaspoon grated nutmeg

1 Sift the flour, salt, and sugar into a bowl. Using a pastry blender or two knives, cut in the butter until it resembles coarse breadcrumbs.

2 ▲ Sprinkle with the water and mix until the dough holds together. If it is too crumbly, add more water, 1 tablespoon at a time. Gather into a ball and flatten. Wrap in greaseproof paper and refrigerate for 20 minutes.

3 Roll out the dough about ⅛ in (3 mm) thick and line a 9 in (23 cm) pie dish. Trim the edge, leaving a ½ in (1 cm) overhang. Fold it under and flute the edge. Refrigerate for 30 minutes.

4 Preheat a 220°C/425°F/Gas 7 oven.

5 Line the pastry case with a piece of greaseproof paper that is 2 in (5 cm) larger all around than the diameter of the pan. Fill the case with dried beans. Bake until the pastry has just set, 8–10 minutes. Remove from the oven and lift out the paper and beans. Prick the bottom of the pastry case all over with a fork. Return to the oven and bake for 5 minutes more. Let the pastry case cool slightly before filling. Turn the oven down to 190°C/375°F/Gas 5.

6 ▲ In a small bowl, mix together the flour and sugar using a fork. Spread this mixture in an even layer on the bottom of the pastry case.

7 ▲ Stir the vanilla into the cream. Pour the flavoured cream over the flour and sugar mixture and gently swirl with a fork to mix. Dot with the butter. Sprinkle the nutmeg on top.

8 Cover the edge of the pie with foil strips to prevent overbrowning. Set on a baking sheet and bake until the filling is golden brown and firm to the touch, about 45 minutes. Serve the pie at room temperature.

Creamy Banana Pie

SERVES 6

7 oz (200 g) ginger biscuits, finely crushed

2½ oz (70 g) butter or margarine, melted

½ tsp grated nutmeg or ground cinnamon

6 oz (175 g) ripe bananas, mashed

12 oz (350 g) cream cheese, at room temperature

2 fl oz (65 ml) thick plain yogurt or soured cream

3 tbsp dark rum or 1 tsp vanilla essence

FOR THE TOPPING

8 fl oz (250 ml) whipping cream

3–4 bananas

1 Preheat a 375°F/190°C/Gas 5 oven.

2 ▲ In a mixing bowl, combine the crushed biscuits, butter or margarine and spice. Mix thoroughly with a wooden spoon.

3 ▲ Press the biscuit mixture into a 9 in (23 cm) pie dish, building up thick sides with a neat edge. Bake 5 minutes. Let cool, in the dish.

4 ▼ With an electric mixer, beat the mashed bananas with the cream cheese. Fold in the yogurt or soured cream and rum or vanilla. Spread the filling in the biscuit base. Refrigerate at least 4 hours or overnight.

5 ▲ For the topping, whip the cream until soft peaks form. Spread on the pie filling. Slice the bananas and arrange on top in a decorative pattern.

Georgia Peanut Butter Pie

SERVES 8

4oz (115g) fine digestive crumbs

2oz (50g) soft light brown sugar,
    firmly packed

3oz (75g) butter or margarine, melted

whipped cream or ice cream,
    for serving

FOR THE FILLING

3 egg yolks

3½oz (90g) granulated sugar

2oz (50g) soft light brown sugar,
    firmly packed

2oz (50g) cornflour

⅛ teaspoon salt

1 pint (600ml) evaporated milk

1oz (25g) unsalted butter or margarine

1½ teaspoons vanilla essence

4oz (115g) chunky peanut butter,
    preferably made from freshly ground
    peanuts

3oz (75g) icing sugar

1 Preheat a 180°C/350°F/Gas 4 oven.

2 ▲ Combine the crumbs, sugar, and butter or margarine in a bowl and blend well. Spread the mixture in a well-greased 9 in (23 cm) pie dish, pressing evenly over the bottom and sides with your fingertips.

3 Bake the crumb crust for 10 minutes. Remove from the oven and leave to cool. Leave the oven on.

4 ▲ For the filling, combine the egg yolks, granulated and brown sugars, cornflour and salt in a heavy saucepan.

5 Slowly whisk in the milk. Cook over a medium heat, stirring constantly, until the mixture thickens, about 8–10 minutes. Reduce the heat to very low and cook until very thick, 3–4 minutes more.

6 ▲ Beat in the butter or margarine. Stir in the vanilla. Remove from the heat. Cover the surface closely with clear film and leave to cool.

~ VARIATIONS ~

If preferred, use an equal amount of finely crushed ginger biscuits in place of digestives for the crumb crust. Or make the pie with a ready-made biscuit crust.

7 ▲ In a small bowl, combine the peanut butter with the icing sugar, working with your fingers to blend the ingredients to the consistency of fine crumbs.

8 ▲ Sprinkle all but 3 tablespoons of the peanut butter crumbs evenly over the bottom of the crumb crust.

9 ▲ Pour in the filling, spreading it in an even layer. Sprinkle with the remaining crumbs. Bake for 15 minutes.

10 Let the pie cool for 1 hour. Serve with whipped cream or ice cream.

Lime Tart

SERVES 8

3 large egg yolks

1 × 14 oz (400 g) can sweetened condensed milk

1 tbsp grated lime rind

4 fl oz (125 ml) fresh lime juice

green food colouring (optional)

4 fl oz (125 ml) whipping cream

FOR THE BASE

4 oz (115 g) digestive biscuits, crushed

2¹/₂ oz (70 g) butter or margarine, melted

1 Preheat a 350°F/180°C/Gas 4 oven.

2 ▲ For the base, place the crushed biscuits in a bowl and add the butter or margarine. Mix to combine.

~ VARIATION ~

Use lemons instead of limes, with yellow food colouring.

3 Press the mixture evenly over the bottom and sides of a 9 in (23 cm) pie dish. Bake for 8 minutes. Let cool.

4 ▲ Beat the yolks until thick. Beat in the milk, lime rind and juice and colouring, if using. Pour into the pastry case and refrigerate until set, about 4 hours. To serve, whip the cream. Pipe a lattice pattern on top.

Fruit Tartlets

MAKES 8

6 fl oz (175 ml) red currant jelly

1 tbsp fresh lemon juice

6 fl oz (175 ml) whipping cream

1¹/₂ lb (700 g) fresh fruit, such as
strawberries, raspberries, kiwi fruit,
peaches, grapes or currants, peeled
and sliced as necessary

FOR THE PASTRY

5 oz (140 g) cold butter, cut in pieces

2¹/₂ oz (65 g) dark brown sugar

3 tbsp cocoa powder

7 oz (200 g) plain flour

1 egg white

1 For the pastry, combine the butter, brown sugar and cocoa over low heat. When the butter is melted, remove from the heat and sift over the flour. Stir, then add just enough egg white to bind the mixture. Gather into a ball, wrap in greaseproof paper, and refrigerate for 30 minutes.

2 ▲ Grease 8 3 in (8 cm) tartlet tins. Roll out the pastry between 2 sheets of greaseproof paper. Stamp out 8 4 in (10 cm) rounds with a fluted cutter.

3 Line the tartlet tins. Prick the bottoms. Refrigerate for 15 minutes. Preheat a 350°F/180°C/Gas 4 oven.

4 Bake until firm, 20–25 minutes. Cool, then remove from the tins.

5 ▲ Melt the jelly with the lemon juice. Brush a thin layer in the bottom of the tartlets. Whip the cream and spread a thin layer in the tartlet cases. Arrange the fruit on top. Brush with the glaze and serve.

Lime Tart (top), Fruit Tartlets

Chocolate Lemon Tart

SERVES 8–10

8¾ oz (240 g) caster sugar

6 eggs

grated rind of 2 lemons

5½ fl oz (170 ml) fresh lemon juice

5½ fl oz (170 ml) whipping cream

chocolate curls, for decorating

FOR THE CRUST

6¼ oz (180 g) plain flour

2 tablespoons unsweetened cocoa powder

1 oz (30 g) icing sugar

½ teaspoon salt

4 oz (115 g) butter or margarine

1 tablespoon water

1 ▲ Grease a 10 in (25 cm) tart tin.

2 For the crust, sift the flour, cocoa powder, icing sugar and salt into a bowl. Set aside.

3 ▲ Melt the butter and water over a low heat. Pour over the flour mixture and stir with a wooden spoon until the dough is smooth and the flour has absorbed all the liquid.

4 Press the dough evenly over the base and side of the prepared tart tin. Refrigerate the tart shell while preparing the filling.

5 Preheat a baking sheet in a 375°F/190°C/Gas 5 oven.

6 ▲ Whisk the sugar and eggs until the sugar is dissolved. Add the lemon rind and juice and mix well. Add the cream. Taste the mixture and add more lemon juice or sugar if needed. It should taste tart but also sweet.

7 Pour the filling into the tart shell and bake on the hot sheet until the filling is set, 20–25 minutes. Cool on a rack. When cool, decorate with the chocolate curls.

Lemon Almond Tart

SERVES 8

5¹/₂ oz (150 g) whole blanched almonds
3¹/₂ oz (100 g) sugar
2 eggs
grated rind and juice of 1¹/₂ lemons
4 oz (115 g) butter, melted
strips of lemon rind, for decorating
FOR THE CRUST
6¹/₄ oz (180 g) plain flour
1 tablespoon sugar
¹/₂ teaspoon salt
¹/₂ teaspoon baking powder
3 oz (85 g) cold unsalted butter, cut into pieces
3–4 tablespoons whipping cream

1 For the crust, sift the flour, sugar, salt and baking powder into a bowl. Add the butter and rub in with your fingertips until the mixture resembles coarse breadcrumbs.

2 ▲ With a fork, stir in just enough cream to bind the dough.

3 Gather into a ball and transfer to a lightly floured surface. Roll out the dough about ¹/₈ in (3 mm) thick and carefully transfer to a 9 in (23 cm) tart tin. Trim and prick the base all over with a fork. Refrigerate for at least 20 minutes.

4 Preheat a baking sheet in a 400°F/200°C/Gas 6 oven.

5 Line the tart shell with crumpled greaseproof paper and fill with dried beans. Bake for 12 minutes. Remove the paper and beans and continue baking until golden, 6–8 minutes more. Reduce the oven temperature to 350°F/180°C/Gas 4.

6 ▲ Grind the almonds finely with 1 tablespoon of the sugar in a food processor, blender, or coffee grinder.

7 ▲ Set a mixing bowl over a pan of hot water. Add the eggs and the remaining sugar, and beat with an electric mixer until the mixture is thick enough to leave a ribbon trail when the beaters are lifted.

8 Stir in the lemon rind and juice, butter and ground almonds.

9 Pour into the prebaked shell. Bake until the filling is golden and set, about 35 minutes. Decorate with lemon rind.

Orange Tart

SERVES 8

7 oz (200 g) sugar

8 fl oz (250 ml) fresh orange juice, strained

2 large navel oranges

5¹/₂ oz (150 g) whole blanched almonds

2 oz (55 g) butter

1 egg

1 tablespoon plain flour

3 tablespoons apricot jam

FOR THE CRUST

7¹/₂ oz (215 g) plain flour

¹/₂ teaspoon salt

2 oz (55 g) cold butter, cut into pieces

1¹/₂ oz (45 g) cold margarine, cut into pieces

3–4 tablespoons iced water

1 For the crust, sift the flour and salt into a bowl. Add the butter and margarine and rub in with your fingertips until the mixture resembles coarse breadcrumbs. Stir in just enough water to bind the dough. Gather into a ball, wrap in clear film, and refrigerate for at least 20 minutes.

2 On a lightly floured surface, roll out the dough ¹/₄ in (5 mm) thick and transfer to an 8 in (20 cm) tart tin. Trim off the overhang. Refrigerate until needed.

3 In a saucepan, combine 5¹/₂ oz (150 g) of the sugar and the orange juice and boil until thick and syrupy, about 10 minutes.

4 ▲ Cut the oranges into ¹/₄ in (5 mm) slices. Do not peel. Add to the syrup. Simmer gently for 10 minutes, or until glazed. Transfer to a rack to dry. When cool, cut in half. Reserve the syrup. Place a baking sheet in the oven and heat to 400°F/200°C/Gas 6.

5 Grind the almonds finely in a food processor, blender or coffee grinder. With an electric mixer, cream the butter and remaining sugar until light and fluffy. Beat in the egg and 2 tablespoons of the orange syrup. Stir in the almonds and flour.

6 Melt the jam over low heat, then brush over the tart shell. Pour in the almond mixture. Bake until set, about 20 minutes. Let cool.

7 ▲ Arrange overlapping orange slices on top. Boil the remaining syrup until thick. Brush on top to glaze.

Rich Orange Cheesecake

SERVES 8

1½ lb (700 g) full-fat soft cheese, at room temperature

7 oz (200 g) caster sugar

2 tablespoons plain flour

3 eggs

4 oz (115 g) butter, melted

1 teaspoon vanilla essence

1 tablespoon grated orange zest

8 in (20 cm) biscuit case, made with digestive biscuits and orange zest, chilled

4 sweet oranges, peeled and segmented

squeeze of lemon juice

1–2 tablespoons orange liqueur (optional)

4 ▲ Pour the filling into the biscuit case. Set the springform tin on a baking sheet.

5 Bake for 1–1¼ hours or until the filling is gently set (it will continue to firm up as it cools). If the top browns too quickly, cover with foil. Turn off the oven and open the door.

6 Leave the cheesecake to cool in the oven. When it is cold, cover and refrigerate overnight.

7 Mix together the orange segments, lemon juice and liqueur, if using. Serve with the cheesecake.

~ VARIATIONS ~

For Lemon Cheesecake, use 1½ teaspoons lemon zest instead of orange in the filling. For a lighter cheesecake, use a mixture of ricotta or curd cheese and full-fat soft cheese, worked in a food processor until smooth.

1 Preheat a 300°F/150°C/Gas 2 oven.

2 ▲ Combine the soft cheese, sugar and flour in a bowl. Beat until the mixture is light and fluffy.

3 ▲ Add the eggs, butter, vanilla essence and orange zest and beat until smoothly blended.

Blueberry-Hazelnut Cheesecake

SERVES 6–8

12oz (350g) blueberries
1 tablespoon honey
3oz (75g) granulated sugar
1 teaspoon plus 1 tablespoon fresh lemon juice
6oz (175g) cream cheese, at room temperature
1 egg
1 teaspoon hazelnut liqueur (optional)
4fl oz (120ml) whipping cream

FOR THE BASE

5¾oz (170g) ground hazelnuts
3oz (75g) plain flour
⅛ teaspoon salt
2oz (50g) butter, at room temperature
5½oz (65g) soft light brown sugar, firmly packed
1 egg yolk

1 ▲ For the base, put the hazelnuts in a large bowl. Sift in the flour and salt, and stir to mix. Set aside.

~ COOK'S TIP ~

The cheesecake can be prepared a day in advance, but add the fruit shortly before serving. Instead of covering the top completely, leave spaces to make a design, if wished.

2 Beat the butter with the brown sugar until light and fluffy. Beat in the egg yolk. Gradually fold in the nut mixture, in three batches.

3 ▲ Press the mixture into a greased 9 in (23 cm) pie dish, spreading it evenly against the sides. Form a rim around the top edge that is slightly thicker than the sides. Cover and refrigerate for at least 30 minutes.

4 Preheat a 180°C/350°F/Gas 4 oven.

5 ▲ Meanwhile, for the topping, combine the blueberries, honey, 1 tablespoon of the granulated sugar, and 1 teaspoon lemon juice in a heavy saucepan. Cook the mixture over a low heat, stirring occasionally, until the berries have given off some liquid but still retain their shape, 5–7 minutes. Remove from the heat and set aside.

6 Place the base in the oven and bake 15 minutes. Remove and leave to cool while making the filling.

7 ▲ Beat together the cream cheese and remaining granulated sugar until light and fluffy. Add the egg, remaining lemon juice, the liqueur, if using, and the cream and beat until thoroughly incorporated.

8 ▲ Pour the cheese mixture into the base and spread evenly. Bake until just set, 20–25 minutes.

9 Let the cheesecake cool completely on a wire rack, then cover and refrigerate for at least 1 hour.

10 Spread the blueberry mixture evenly over the top of the cheesecake. Serve the cheesecake at a cool room temperature.

Chocolate Cheesecake Tart

SERVES 8

12 oz (350 g) cream cheese
4 tbsp whipping cream
8 oz (225 g) caster sugar
2 oz (55 g) cocoa powder
¹/₂ tsp ground cinnamon
3 eggs
whipped cream, for decorating
chocolate curls, for decorating
FOR THE BASE
3 oz (85 g) digestive biscuits, crushed
1¹/₂ oz (45 g) crushed amaretti biscuits (if unavailable, use extra crushed digestive biscuits)
3 oz (85 g) butter, melted

1 Preheat a baking sheet in the centre of a 350°F/180°C/Gas 4 oven.

2 For the base, mix the crushed biscuits and butter in a bowl.

3 ▲ With a spoon, press the mixture over the bottom and sides of a 9 in (23 cm) pie dish. Bake for 8 minutes. Let cool. Keep the oven on.

4 With an electric mixer, beat the cheese and cream together until smooth. Beat in the sugar, cocoa and cinnamon until blended.

5 ▼ Add the eggs, 1 at a time, beating just enough to blend.

6 Pour into the biscuit base and bake on the hot sheet for 25–30 minutes. The filling will sink down as it cools. Decorate with whipped cream and chocolate curls.

Frozen Strawberry Tart

SERVES 8

8 oz (225 g) cream cheese
8 fl oz (250 ml) soured cream
1 lb 4 oz (575 g) frozen strawberries, thawed and sliced
FOR THE BASE
4 oz (115 g) digestive biscuits, crushed
1 tbsp caster sugar
2¹/₂ oz (70 g) butter, melted

~ VARIATION ~

For Frozen Raspberry Tart, use raspberries in place of the strawberries and prepare the same way, or try other frozen fruit.

1 ▲ For the base, mix together the biscuits, sugar and butter.

2 Press the mixture evenly and firmly over the bottom and sides of a 9 in (23 cm) pie dish. Freeze until firm.

3 ▼ Blend together the cream cheese and soured cream. Reserve 6 tablespoons of the strawberries. Add the rest to the cream cheese mixture.

4 Pour the filling into the biscuit base and freeze 6–8 hours until firm. To serve, spoon some of the reserved berries and juice on top.

Chocolate Cheesecake Pie (top), Frozen Strawberry Tart

Kiwi Ricotta Cheese Tart

SERVES 8

3 oz (75 g) blanched almonds, ground
3¹/₂ oz (130 g) sugar
2 lb (900 g) ricotta cheese
8 fl oz (250 ml) whipping cream
1 egg and 3 egg yolks
1 tablespoon plain flour
pinch of salt
2 tablespoons rum
grated rind of 1 lemon
2¹/₂ tablespoons lemon juice
2 tablespoons honey
5 kiwi fruit
FOR THE PASTRY
5 oz (150 g) plain flour
1 tablespoon sugar
¹/₂ teaspoon salt
¹/₂ teaspoon baking powder
6 tablespoons butter
1 egg yolk
3–4 tablespoons whipping cream

1 For the pastry, mix together the flour, sugar, salt and baking powder in a large bowl. Cut the butter into cubes and gradually rub it into the pastry mixture. Mix in the egg yolk and cream. Stir in just enough to bind the pastry.

2 ▲ Transfer to a lightly floured surface, flatten slightly, wrap and refrigerate for 30 minutes. Preheat the oven to 425°F/220°C/Gas 7.

3 ▲ On a lightly floured surface, roll out the dough to a ¹/₈ in (3 mm) thickness. Transfer to a 9 in (23 cm) springform tin. Crimp the edge.

4 ▲ Prick the pastry with a fork. Line with greaseproof paper and fill with dried beans. Bake for 10 minutes. Remove the paper and beans and bake for 6–8 minutes more until golden. Leave to cool. Reduce the temperature to 350°F/180°C/Gas 4.

5 ▲ Mix the almonds with 1 tablespoon of the sugar in a food processor or blender.

6 Beat the ricotta until creamy. Add the cream, egg, yolks, remaining sugar, flour, salt, rum, lemon rind and 2 tablespoons of lemon juice. Combine.

7 ▲ Stir in the ground almonds until well blended.

8 Pour into a pastry case and bake for 1 hour. Chill, loosely covered for 2–3 hours. Unmould and put on a plate.

9 Combine the honey and remaining lemon juice for the glaze.

10 ▲ Peel the kiwis. Halve them lengthwise, then slice. Arrange the slices in rows across the top of the tart. Just before serving, brush with the honey glaze.

Raspberry Tart

SERVES 8

4 egg yolks
2¹/₂ oz (70 g) caster sugar
3 tbsp plain flour
10 fl oz (300 ml) milk
¹/₈ tsp salt
¹/₂ tsp vanilla essence
1 lb (450 g) fresh raspberries
5 tbsp red currant jelly
1 tbsp fresh orange juice
FOR THE PASTRY
6¹/₂ oz (190 g) plain flour
¹/₂ tsp baking powder
¹/₄ tsp salt
1 tbsp sugar
grated rind of ¹/₂ orange
3 oz (85 g) cold butter, cut in pieces
1 egg yolk
3–4 tbsp whipping cream

1 For the pastry, sift the flour, baking powder and salt into a bowl. Stir in the sugar and orange rind. Add the butter and cut in with a pastry blender until the mixture resembles coarse breadcrumbs. Stir in the egg yolk and just enough cream to bind the dough. Gather into a ball, wrap in greaseproof paper and refrigerate.

2 For the custard filling, beat the egg yolks and sugar until thick and lemon coloured. Gradually stir in the flour.

3 In a saucepan, bring the milk and salt just to the boil, then remove from the heat. Whisk into the egg yolk mixture, return to the pan and continue whisking over moderately high heat until just bubbling. Cook for 3 minutes to thicken. Transfer immediately to a bowl. Add the vanilla and stir to blend.

4 ▲ Cover with greaseproof paper to prevent a skin from forming.

5 ▲ Preheat a 400°F/200°C/Gas 6 oven. On a floured surface, roll out the pastry ¹/₈ in (3 mm) thick, transfer to a 10 in (25 cm) pie dish and trim. Prick the bottom with a fork and line with crumpled greaseproof paper. Fill with baking beans and bake for 15 minutes. Remove the paper and beans. Continue baking until golden, 6–8 minutes more. Let cool.

6 ▲ Spread an even layer of the pastry cream filling in the pastry case and arrange the raspberries on top. Melt the jelly and orange juice in a pan and brush on top to glaze.

Treacle Tart

SERVES 4–6

6 fl oz (175 ml) golden syrup
3 oz (85 g) fresh white breadcrumbs
grated rind of 1 lemon
2 tbsp fresh lemon juice
FOR THE PASTRY
6 oz (170 g) plain flour
$^1/_2$ tsp salt
3 oz (85 g) cold butter, cut in pieces
$1^1/_2$ oz (45 g) cold margarine, cut in pieces
3–4 tbsp iced water

1 For the pastry, combine the flour and salt in a bowl. Add the butter and margarine and cut in with a pastry blender until the mixture resembles coarse breadcrumbs.

2 ▲ With a fork, stir in just enough water to bind the pastry. Gather into a ball, wrap in greaseproof paper, and refrigerate for at least 20 minutes.

3 On a lightly floured surface, roll out the pastry to a thickness of $^1/_8$ in (3 mm). Transfer to an 8 in (20 cm) pie dish and trim off the overhang. Refrigerate for at least 20 minutes. Reserve the trimmings for the lattice top.

4 Preheat a baking sheet at the top of a 400°F/200°C/Gas 6 oven.

5 In a saucepan, warm the syrup until thin and runny.

6 ▲ Remove from the heat and stir in the breadcrumbs and lemon rind. Let sit for 10 minutes so the bread can absorb the syrup. Add more breadcrumbs if the mixture is thin. Stir in the lemon juice and spread evenly in the pastry case.

7 Roll our the pastry trimmings and cut into 10–12 thin strips.

8 ▼ Lay half the strips on the filling, then lay the remaining strips at an angle over them to form a lattice.

9 Place on the hot sheet and bake for 10 minutes. Lower the heat to 375°F/190°C/Gas 5. Bake until golden, about 15 minutes more. Serve warm or cold.

Coconut Cream Tart

SERVES 8

5 oz (140 g) desiccated coconut
5 oz (140 g) caster sugar
4 tbsp cornflour
1/8 tsp salt
1 pt (625 ml) milk
2 fl oz (65 ml) whipping cream
2 egg yolks
1 oz (30 g) unsalted butter
2 tsp vanilla essence
FOR THE PASTRY
5 oz (140 g) plain flour
1/4 tsp salt
1 1/2 oz (45 g) cold butter, cut in pieces
1 oz (30 g) cold vegetable fat or lard
2–3 tbsp iced water

1 For the pastry, sift the flour and salt into a bowl. Add the butter and fat and cut in with a pastry blender until the mixture resembles coarse breadcrumbs.

2 ▲ With a fork, stir in just enough water to bind the pastry. Gather into a ball, wrap in greaseproof paper and refrigerate for 20 minutes.

3 Preheat a 425°F/220°C/Gas 7 oven. Roll out the pastry 1/8 in (3 mm) thick. Line a 9 in (23 cm) pie dish. Trim and flute the edges. Prick the bottom. Line with crumpled greaseproof and fill with baking beans. Bake 10–12 minutes. Remove paper and beans, reduce heat to 350°F/180°C/Gas 4 and bake until brown, 10–15 minutes.

4 ▲ Spread 2 oz (55 g) of the coconut on a baking sheet and toast in the oven until golden, 6–8 minutes, stirring often. Set aside for decorating.

5 Put the sugar, cornflour and salt in a saucepan. In a bowl, whisk the milk, cream and egg yolks. Add the egg mixture to the saucepan.

6 ▼ Cook over a low heat, stirring, until the mixture comes to the boil. Boil for 1 minute, then remove from the heat. Add the butter, vanilla and remaining coconut.

7 Pour into the prebaked pastry case. When cool, sprinkle toasted coconut in a ring in the centre.

Brandy Alexander Tart

SERVES 8

4 fl oz (125 ml) cold water
1 tablespoon powdered gelatine
4 oz (115 g) sugar
3 eggs, separated
4 tablespoons brandy
4 tablespoons crème de cacao
pinch of salt
10 fl oz (300 ml) whipping cream
chocolate curls, for decorating
FOR THE BISCUIT CRUST
8 oz (225 g) digestive biscuits, crumbed
2½ oz (70 g) butter, melted
1 tablespoon sugar

1 Preheat the oven to 375°F/190°C/ Gas 5.

2 For the crust, mix the biscuit crumbs with the butter and sugar in a bowl.

3 ▲ Press the crumbs evenly on to the bottom and sides of a 9 in (23 cm) tart tin. Bake until just brown, about 10 minutes. Cool on a rack.

4 Place the water in the top of a double boiler set over hot water. Sprinkle over the powdered gelatine and leave to stand for 5 minutes to soften. Add half the sugar and the egg yolks. Whisk constantly over a very low heat until the gelatine dissolves and the mixture has thickened slightly. Do not allow the mixture to boil.

5 ▲ Remove from the heat and stir in the brandy and crème de cacao.

6 Set the pan over iced water and stir occasionally until it cools and thickens; it should not set firmly.

7 With an electric mixer, beat the egg whites and salt until they hold stiff peaks. Beat in the remaining sugar. Spoon a dollop of whites into the yolk mixture and fold in to lighten.

8 ▼ Pour the egg yolk mixture over the remaining whites and fold together.

9 Whip the cream until soft peaks form, then gently fold into the filling. Spoon into the baked biscuit case and chill until set, 3–4 hours. Decorate the top with chocolate curls before serving.

Velvety Mocha Tart

SERVES 8

2 tsp instant espresso coffee

2 tbsp hot water

12 fl oz (350 ml) whipping cream

6 oz (170 g) plain chocolate

1 oz (30 g) bitter cooking chocolate

4 fl oz (125 ml) whipped cream, for decorating

chocolate-covered coffee beans, for decorating

FOR THE BASE

5 oz (140 g) chocolate wafers, crushed

2 tbsp caster sugar

2¹/₂ oz (70 g) butter, melted

1 ▲ For the base, mix the crushed chocolate wafers and sugar together, then stir in the melted butter.

2 Press the mixture evenly over the bottom and sides of a 9 in (23 cm) pie dish. Refrigerate until firm.

3 In a bowl, dissolve the coffee in the water and set aside.

4 Pour the cream into a mixing bowl. Set the bowl in hot water to warm the cream, bringing it closer to the temperature of the chocolate.

5 Melt both the chocolates in the top of a double boiler, or in a heatproof bowl set over a pan of hot water. Remove from the heat when nearly melted and stir to continue melting. Set the bottom of the pan in cool water to reduce the temperature. Be careful not to splash any water on the chocolate or it will become grainy.

6 ▲ With an electric mixer, whip the cream until it is lightly fluffy. Add the dissolved coffee and whip until the cream just holds its shape.

7 ▲ When the chocolate is at room temperature, fold it gently into the cream with a large metal spoon.

8 Pour into the chilled biscuit base and refrigerate until firm. To serve, pipe a ring of whipped cream rosettes around the edge, then place a chocolate-covered coffee bean in the centre of each rosette.

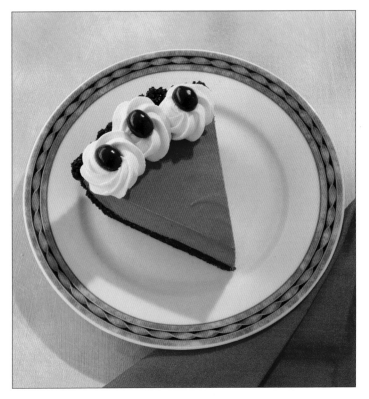

Chocolate Pear Tart

SERVES 8

4 oz (115 g) plain chocolate, grated
3 large firm, ripe pears
1 egg
1 egg yolk
4 fl oz (125 ml) single cream
1/2 tsp vanilla essence
3 tbsp caster sugar
FOR THE PASTRY
5 oz (140 g) plain flour
1/8 tsp salt
2 tbsp sugar
4 oz (115 g) cold unsalted butter, cut into pieces
1 egg yolk
1 tbsp fresh lemon juice

1 For the pastry, sift the flour and salt into a bowl. Add the sugar and butter. Cut in with a pastry blender until the mixture resembles coarse breadcrumbs. Stir in the egg yolk and lemon juice until the mixture forms a ball. Wrap in greaseproof paper, and refrigerate for at least 20 minutes.

2 Preheat a baking sheet in the centre of a 400°F/200°C/Gas 6 oven.

3 On a lightly floured surface, roll out the pastry 1/8 in (3 mm) thick. Transfer to a 10 in (25 cm) tart dish and trim.

4 ▲ Sprinkle the bottom of the case with the grated chocolate.

5 ▲ Peel, halve and core the pears. Cut in thin slices crosswise, then fan them out slightly.

6 Transfer the pear halves to the tart with the help of a metal spatula and arrange on top of the chocolate like the spokes of a wheel.

7 ▼ Whisk together the egg and egg yolk, cream and vanilla. Ladle over the pears, then sprinkle with sugar.

8 Bake for 10 minutes. Reduce the heat to 350°F/180°C/Gas 4 and cook until the custard is set and the pears begin to caramelize, about 20 minutes more. Serve warm.

Maple Walnut Tart

SERVES 8

3 eggs

1/8 tsp salt

2 oz (55 g) caster sugar

2 oz (55 g) butter or margarine, melted

8 fl oz (250 ml) pure maple syrup

4 oz (115 g) chopped walnuts

whipped cream, for decorating

FOR THE PASTRY

2 1/2 oz (70 g) plain flour

2 1/2 oz (70 g) wholewheat flour

1/8 tsp salt

2 oz (55 g) cold butter, cut in pieces

1 1/2 oz (45 g) cold vegetable fat or lard, cut in pieces

1 egg yolk

2–3 tbsp iced water

1 ▼ For the pastry, mix the flours and salt in a bowl. Add the butter and fat and cut in with a pastry blender until the mixture resembles coarse breadcrumbs. With a fork, stir in the egg yolk and just enough water to bind the pastry. Form into a ball.

2 Wrap in greaseproof paper and refrigerate for 20 minutes.

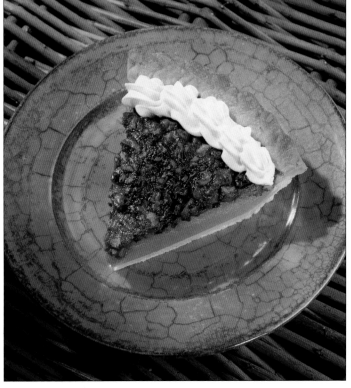

3 Preheat a 425°F/220°C/Gas 7 oven.

4 On a lightly floured surface, roll out the pastry about 1/8 in (3 mm) thick and transfer to a 9 in (23 cm) pie dish. Trim the edge. To decorate, roll out the trimmings. With a small heart-shaped cutter, stamp out enough hearts to go around the rim of the pie. Brush the edge with water, then arrange the pastry hearts all around.

5 ▲ Prick the bottom with a fork. Line with crumpled greaseproof paper and fill with baking beans. Bake for 10 minutes. Remove the paper and beans and continue baking until golden brown, 3–6 minutes more.

6 In a bowl, whisk the eggs, salt and sugar together. Stir in the butter and maple syrup.

7 ▲ Set the pastry case on a baking sheet. Pour in the filling, then sprinkle the nuts over the top.

8 Bake until just set, for about 35 minutes. Cool on a rack. Decorate with whipped cream, if wished.

Pecan Tart

SERVES 8

3 eggs
1/8 tsp salt
7 oz (200 g) dark brown sugar
4 fl oz (125 ml) golden syrup
2 tbsp fresh lemon juice
3 oz (85 g) butter, melted
5 oz (140 g) chopped pecan nuts
2 oz (55 g) pecan halves
FOR THE PASTRY
6 oz (170 g) plain flour
1 tbsp caster sugar
1 tsp baking powder
1/2 tsp salt
3 oz (85 g) cold unsalted butter, cut in pieces
1 egg yolk
3–4 tbsp whipping cream

1 For the pastry, sift the flour, sugar, baking powder and salt into a bowl. Add the butter and cut in with a pastry blender until the mixture resembles coarse breadcrumbs.

2 ▼ In a bowl, beat together the egg yolk and cream until blended.

~ COOK'S TIP ~

Serve this tart warm, accompanied by ice cream or whipped cream, if wished.

3 ▲ Pour the cream mixture into the flour mixture and stir with a fork.

4 Gather the pastry into a ball. On a lightly floured surface, roll out 1/8 in (3 mm) thick and transfer to a 9 in (23 cm) pie dish. Trim the overhang and flute the edge with your fingers. Refrigerate for at least 20 minutes.

5 Preheat a baking sheet in the middle of a 400°F/200°C/Gas 6 oven.

6 In a bowl, lightly whisk the eggs and salt. Add the sugar, syrup, lemon juice and butter. Mix well and stir in the chopped nuts.

7 ▲ Pour into the pastry case and arrange the pecan halves in concentric circles on top.

8 Bake for 10 minutes. Reduce the heat to 325°F/170°C/Gas 3 and continue baking for 25 minutes.

Peach Tart with Almond Cream

SERVES 8–10

4 large ripe peaches
4 oz (115 g) blanched almonds
2 tbsp plain flour
3½ oz (100 g) unsalted butter, at room temperature
4 oz (115 g) plus 2 tbsp caster sugar
1 egg
1 egg yolk
½ tsp vanilla essence, or 2 tsp rum
FOR THE PASTRY
6½ oz (190 g) plain flour
¾ tsp salt
3½ oz (100 g) cold unsalted butter, cut in pieces
1 egg yolk
2½–3 tbsp iced water

1 ▲ For the pastry, sift the flour and salt into a bowl.

2 Add the butter and cut in with a pastry blender until the mixture resembles coarse breadcrumbs. Stir in the egg yolk and just enough water to bind the pastry. Gather into a ball, wrap in greaseproof paper, and refrigerate for at least 20 minutes.

3 Preheat a baking sheet in the centre of a 400°F/200°C/Gas 6 oven.

4 ▲ On a floured surface, roll out the pastry ⅛ in (3mm) thick. Transfer to a 10 in (25 cm) pie dish. Trim the edge, prick the bottom and refrigerate.

5 ▲ Score the bottoms of the peaches. Drop the peaches, 1 at a time, into boiling water. Boil for 20 seconds, then dip in cold water. Peel off the skins using a sharp knife.

6 ▲ Grind the almonds finely with the flour in a food processor, blender or grinder. With an electric mixer, cream the butter and 4 oz (115 g) of the sugar until light and fluffy. Gradually beat in the egg and yolk. Stir in the almonds and vanilla or rum. Spread in the pastry case.

7 ▲ Halve the peaches and remove the stones. Cut crosswise in thin slices and arrange on top of the almond cream like the spokes of a wheel; keep the slices of each peach-half together. Fan out by pressing down gently at a slight angle.

8 ▲ Bake until the pastry begins to brown, 10–15 minutes. Lower the heat to 350°F/180°C/Gas 4 and continue baking until the almond cream sets, about 15 minutes more. Ten minutes before the end of the cooking time, sprinkle with the remaining 2 tablespoons of sugar.

~ VARIATION ~

For a Nectarine and Apricot Tart with Almond Cream, replace the peaches with nectarines, prepared and arranged the same way. Peel and chop 3 fresh apricots. Fill the spaces between the fanned-out nectarines with 1 tablespoon of chopped apricots. Bake as above.

Almond Syrup Tart

SERVES 6

3 oz (85 g) fresh white breadcrumbs

8 oz (225 g) golden syrup

finely grated zest of ½ lemon

2 teaspoons lemon juice

9 in (23 cm) pastry case, made with basic, nut or rich shortcrust pastry

1 oz (30 g) flaked almonds

1 Preheat a 200°C/400°F/Gas 6 oven.

2 ▲ In a mixing bowl, combine the breadcrumbs with the golden syrup and the lemon zest and juice.

3 Spoon into the pastry case and spread out evenly.

4 ▲ Sprinkle the flaked almonds evenly over the top.

5 ▼ Brush the pastry with milk to glaze, if you like. Bake for 25–30 minutes or until the pastry and filling are golden brown.

6 Remove to a wire rack to cool. Serve warm or cold, with cream, custard or ice cream.

~ VARIATIONS ~

For Walnut Syrup Tart, replace the almonds with chopped walnuts. For Ginger Syrup Tart, mix 1 teaspoon ground ginger with the breadcrumbs before adding the syrup and lemon zest and juice. Omit the nuts if liked. For Coconut Syrup Tart, replace 1 oz (30 g) of the breadcrumbs with 1½ oz (45 g) desiccated coconut.

Apple Maple Dumplings

SERVES 8

18oz (475g) plain flour
2 teaspoons salt
12oz (350g) vegetable fat
2–8fl oz (50–250ml) iced water
8 firm eating apples
1 egg white
4½oz (130g) sugar
3 tablespoons whipping cream
½ teaspoon vanilla essence
8fl oz (250ml) maple syrup
whipped cream, for serving

1 Sift the flour and salt into a large bowl. Using a pastry blender or two knives, cut in the fat until the mixture resembles coarse breadcrumbs. Sprinkle with 6fl oz (175ml) water and mix until the dough holds together. If it is too crumbly, add a little more water. Gather into a ball. Wrap in greaseproof paper and refrigerate for at least 20 minutes.

2 Preheat a 220°C/425°F/Gas 7 oven.

3 Peel the apples. Remove the cores, without cutting through the base.

4 ▲ Roll out the dough thinly. Cut squares almost large enough to enclose the apples. Brush the squares with egg white. Set an apple in the centre of each square of dough.

5 Combine the sugar, cream and vanilla in a small bowl. Spoon some into the hollow in each apple.

6 ▼ Pull the points of the dough squares up around the apples and moisten the edges where they overlap. Mould the dough round the apples, pleating the top. Do not cover the centre hollows. Crimp the edges tightly to seal.

7 Set the apples in a large greased baking dish, at least ¾ in (2 cm) apart. Bake for 30 minutes. Lower the oven temperature to 180°C/350°F/Gas 4 and continue baking until the pastry is golden brown and the apples are tender, about 20 minutes more.

8 Transfer the dumplings to a serving dish. Mix the maple syrup with the juices in the baking dish and drizzle over the dumplings.

9 Serve the dumplings hot with whipped cream.

Apple Strudel

SERVES 10–12

3 oz (85 g) raisins
2 tbsp brandy
5 eating apples, such as Granny Smith or Cox's
3 large cooking apples
3¹/₂ oz (100 g) dark brown sugar
1 tsp ground cinnamon
grated rind and juice of 1 lemon
1 oz (30 g) dry breadcrumbs
2 oz (55 g) chopped pecans or walnuts
12 sheets frozen filo pastry, thawed
6 oz (170 g) butter, melted
icing sugar, for dusting

1 Soak the raisins in the brandy for at least 15 minutes.

2 ▼ Peel, core and thinly slice the apples. In a bowl, combine the sugar, cinnamon and lemon rind. Stir in the apples and half the breadcrumbs.

3 Add the raisins, nuts and lemon juice and stir until blended.

4 Preheat a 375°F/190°C/Gas 5 oven. Grease 2 baking sheets.

5 ▲ Carefully unfold the filo sheets. Keep the unused sheets covered with greaseproof paper. Lift off 1 sheet, place on a clean surface and brush with melted butter. Lay a second sheet on top and brush with butter. Continue until you have a stack of 6 buttered sheets.

6 Sprinkle a few tablespoons of breadcrumbs over the last sheet and spoon half the apple mixture at the bottom edge of the strip.

7 ▲ Starting at the apple-filled end, roll up the pastry, as for a Swiss roll. Place on a baking sheet, seam-side down, and carefully fold under the ends to seal. Repeat the procedure to make a second strudel. Brush both with butter.

8 Bake the strudels for 45 minutes. Let cool slightly. Using a small sieve, dust with a fine layer of icing sugar. Serve warm.

Cherry Strudel

SERVES 8

2¹/₂ oz (70 g) fresh breadcrumbs
6 oz (170 g) butter, melted
7 oz (200 g) sugar
1 tablespoon ground cinnamon
1 teaspoon grated lemon rind
1 lb (450 g) sour cherries, stoned
8 sheets filo pastry
icing sugar, for dusting

1 In a frying pan, lightly fry the fresh breadcrumbs in 2¹/₂ oz (70 g) of the melted butter until golden. Set aside to cool.

2 ▲ In a large mixing bowl, toss together the sugar, cinnamon and lemon rind.

3 Stir in the cherries.

4 Preheat the oven to 375°F/190°C/ Gas 5. Grease a baking sheet.

5 Carefully unfold the filo sheets. Keep the unused sheets covered with damp kitchen paper. Lift off one sheet, place on a flat surface lined with parchment paper. Brush the pastry with melted butter. Sprinkle about an eighth of the breadcrumbs evenly over the surface.

6 ▲ Lay a second sheet of filo on top, brush with butter and sprinkle with crumbs. Continue until you have a stack of 8 buttered, crumbed sheets.

7 Spoon the cherry mixture at the bottom edge of the strip. Starting at the cherry-filled end, roll up the dough as for a Swiss roll. Use the paper to help flip the strudel onto the baking sheet, seam-side down.

8 ▼ Carefully fold under the ends to seal in the fruit. Brush the top with any remaining butter.

9 Bake the strudel for 45 minutes. Let cool slightly. Using a small sieve, dust with a fine layer of icing sugar.

Chicken-Mushroom Pie

SERVES 6

½oz (15g) dried porcini mushrooms
2oz (50g) butter
½oz (15g) flour
8fl oz (250ml) hot chicken stock
2fl oz (50ml) whipping cream or milk
salt and pepper
1 onion, roughly chopped
2 carrots, sliced
2 celery sticks, roughly chopped
2oz (50g) fresh mushrooms, quartered
1lb (450g) cooked chicken meat, cubed
2oz (50g) shelled fresh or frozen peas
beaten egg, for glazing
FOR THE CRUST
8oz (225g) plain flour
¼ teaspoon salt
4oz (115g) cold butter, cut in pieces
3oz (75g) vegetable fat
4–8 tablespoons iced water

1 ▲ For the crust, sift the flour and salt into a bowl. With a pastry blender or two knives, cut in the butter and fat until the mixture resembles coarse breadcrumbs. Sprinkle with 6 tablespoons iced water and mix until the dough holds together. If the dough is too crumbly, add a little more water, 1 tablespoon at a time. Gather the dough into a ball and flatten into a disk. Wrap in greaseproof paper and refrigerate for at least 30 minutes.

2 Place the porcini mushrooms in a small bowl. Add hot water to cover and soak until soft, about 30 minutes. Lift out of the water with a slotted spoon to leave any grit behind and drain. Discard the soaking water.

3 Preheat a 190°C/375°F/Gas 5 oven.

4 ▲ Melt 1oz (25g) of the butter in a heavy saucepan. Whisk in the flour and cook until bubbling, whisking constantly. Add the stock and cook over a moderate heat, whisking, until the mixture boils. Cook for 2–3 minutes more. Whisk in the cream or milk. Season with salt and pepper. Set aside.

5 ▲ Heat the remaining butter in a large non-stick frying pan until foamy. Add the onion and carrots and cook until softened, about 5 minutes. Add the celery and fresh mushrooms and cook for 5 minutes more. Stir in the chicken, peas, and drained porcini mushrooms.

6 Add the chicken mixture to the cream sauce and stir to mix. Taste for seasoning. Transfer to a 2.8 litre (3¾ pint) rectangular pie dish.

7 ▲ Roll out the dough to about ⅛ in (3 mm) thickness. Cut out a rectangle about 1 in (2.5 cm) larger all round than the dish. Lay the rectangle of dough over the filling. Make a decorative edge, crimping the dough by pushing the index finger of one hand between the thumb and index finger of the other.

8 Cut several vents to allow steam to escape. Brush with the egg glaze.

9 ▲ Press together the dough trimmings, then roll out again. Cut into strips and lay them over the top. Glaze again. If desired, roll small balls of dough and set them in the "windows" in the lattice.

10 Bake until the pastry top is browned, about 30 minutes. Serve the pie hot from the dish.

Ricotta and Basil Tart

SERVES 8–10

2 oz (55 g) basil leaves
1 oz (30 g) flat-leaf parsley
4 fl oz (125 ml) extra-virgin olive oil
salt and pepper
2 eggs
1 egg yolk
1 lb 12 oz (800 g) ricotta cheese
3¹/₂ oz (100 g) black olives, stoned
2¹/₄ oz (60 g) Parmesan cheese, freshly grated
FOR THE CRUST
6¹/₂ oz (180 g) plain flour
¹/₂ teaspoon salt
3 oz (85 g) cold butter, cut into pieces
1¹/₂ oz (45 g) cold margarine, cut into pieces
3–4 tablespoon iced water

1 ▲ For the crust, combine the flour and salt in a bowl. Add the butter and margarine.

2 Rub in with your fingertips until the mixture resembles coarse breadcrumbs. With a fork, stir in just enough water to bind the dough. Gather into a ball, wrap in clear film, and refrigerate for at least 20 minutes.

3 Preheat a baking sheet in a 375°F/190°C/Gas 5 oven.

4 Roll out the dough ¹/₈ in (3 mm) thick and transfer to a 10 in (25 cm) tart tin. Prick the base with a fork and line with greaseproof paper. Fill with dried beans and bake for 12 minutes. Remove the paper and beans and bake until golden, 3–5 minutes more. Lower the heat to 350°F/180°C/Gas 4.

5 ▲ In a food processor, combine the basil, parsley and olive oil. Season well with salt and pepper and process until finely chopped.

6 In a bowl, whisk the eggs and yolk to blend. Gently fold in the ricotta.

7 ▲ Fold in the basil mixture and olives until well combined. Stir in the Parmesan and adjust the seasoning.

8 Pour into the prebaked shell and bake until set, 30–35 minutes.

Onion and Anchovy Tart

SERVES 8

4 tablespoons olive oil
2 lb (900 g) onions, sliced
1 teaspoon dried thyme
salt and pepper
2–3 tomatoes, sliced
24 small black olives, stoned
1 × 2 oz (55 g) can anchovy fillets, drained and sliced
6 sun-dried tomatoes, cut into slivers
FOR THE CRUST
6¼ oz (180 g) plain flour
½ teaspoon salt
4 oz (115 g) cold butter, cut into pieces
1 egg yolk
2–3 tablespoons iced water

3 ▲ Heat the oil in a frying pan. Add the onions, thyme and seasoning. Cook over low heat, covered, for 25 minutes. Uncover and continue cooking until soft. Let cool. Preheat the oven to 400°F/200°C/Gas 6.

4 ▼ Spoon the onions into the tart shell and top with the tomato slices. Arrange the olives in rows. Make a lattice pattern, alternating lines of anchovies and sun-dried tomatoes. Bake until golden, 20–25 minutes.

1 ▲ For the crust, sift the flour and salt into a bowl. Rub in the butter with your fingertips until the mixture resembles coarse breadcrumbs. Stir in the yolk and enough water to bind.

2 ▲ Roll out the dough to a thickness of about ⅛ in (3 mm). Transfer to a 9 in (23 cm) tart tin and trim the edge. Chill in the refrigerator until needed.

Asparagus, Sweetcorn and Red Pepper Quiche

SERVES 6

8 oz (225 g) fresh asparagus, woody stalks removed

1 oz (30 g) butter or margarine

1 small onion, finely chopped

1 red pepper, seeded and finely chopped

4 oz (115 g) drained canned sweetcorn, or frozen sweetcorn, thawed

2 eggs

8 fl oz (250 ml) single cream

2 oz (55 g) Cheddar cheese, grated

salt and pepper

FOR THE PASTRY

6½ oz (190 g) plain flour

½ tsp salt

4 oz (115 g) lard or vegetable fat

2–3 tbsp iced water

1 Preheat a 400°F/200°C/Gas 6 oven.

2 For the pastry, sift the flour and salt into a mixing bowl. Using a pastry blender or 2 knives, cut in the fat until the mixture resembles coarse breadcrumbs. Sprinkle in the water, 1 tablespoon at a time, tossing lightly with your fingertips or a fork until the dough forms a ball.

3 ▲ On a lightly floured surface, roll out the dough. Use it to line a 10 in (25 cm) quiche dish or loose-bottomed tart tin, easing the pastry in and being careful not to stretch it. Trim off excess pastry.

4 ▲ Line the pastry case with greaseproof paper and weigh it down with pastry weights or dried beans. Bake 10 minutes. Remove the paper and weight or beans and bake until the pastry is set and beige in colour, about 5 minutes longer. Let cool.

5 Trim the stem ends of 8 of the asparagus spears to make them 4 in (10 cm) in length. Set aside.

6 ▲ Finely chop the asparagus trimmings and any remaining spears. Place in the bottom of the case.

7 ▲ Melt the butter or margarine in a frying pan. Add the onion and red pepper and cook until softened, about 5 minutes. Stir in the sweetcorn and cook 2 minutes longer.

8 Spoon the sweetcorn mixture over the chopped asparagus.

9 ▲ In a small bowl, beat the eggs with the cream. Stir in the cheese and salt and pepper to taste. Pour into the pastry case.

10 ▲ Arrange the reserved asparagus spears like the spokes of a wheel on top of the filling.

11 Bake until the filling is set, about 25–30 minutes.

~ VARIATION ~

To make individual tarts, roll out the pastry and use to line a 12-cup bun tray. For the filling, cut off and reserve the asparagus tips and chop the tender part of the stalks. Mix the asparagus and the cooked vegetables into the egg mixture with the cheese. Spoon the filling into the pastry cases and bake as directed, decreasing baking time by about 8–10 minutes.

Cheesy Tomato Quiche

SERVES 6–8

10 medium tomatoes
1 × 2 oz (55 g) can anchovy fillets, drained and finely chopped
4 fl oz (125 ml) whipping cream
7 oz (200 g) mature Cheddar cheese, grated
1 oz (30 g) wholemeal breadcrumbs
1/2 teaspoon dried thyme
salt and pepper
FOR THE CRUST
71/2 oz (215 g) plain flour
4 oz (115 g) cold butter, cut into pieces
1 egg yolk
2–3 tablespoons iced water

1 Preheat the oven to 400°F/200°C/Gas 6.

2 For the crust, sift the flour into a bowl. Rub in the butter with your fingertips until the mixture resembles coarse breadcrumbs.

3 ▲ With a fork, stir in the egg yolk and enough water to bind the dough.

4 Roll out the dough about 1/8 in (3 mm) thick and transfer to a 9 in (23 cm) tart tin. Refrigerate until needed.

5 ▲ Score the bottoms of the tomatoes. Plunge in boiling water for 1 minute. Remove and peel off the skin with a knife. Cut in quarters and remove the seeds with a spoon.

6 ▲ In a bowl, mix the anchovies and cream. Stir in the cheese.

7 Sprinkle the breadcrumbs in the tart. Arrange the tomatoes on top. Season with thyme, salt and pepper.

8 ▲ Spoon the cheese mixture on top. Bake until golden, 25–30 minutes. Serve warm.

Quiche Lorraine

SERVES 6

8 oz (225 g) smoked streaky bacon
  rashers, chopped

9 in (23 cm) flan case, partially baked
  blind

3 eggs

2 egg yolks

12 fl oz (360 ml) whipping cream

4 fl oz (120 ml) milk

salt and pepper

1 Preheat a 200°C/400°F/Gas 6 oven.

2 ▲ Fry the bacon in a frying pan
until it is crisp and golden brown.
Drain the bacon on paper towels.

3 ▲ Scatter the bacon in the
partially baked flan case.

4 In a bowl, whisk together the eggs,
egg yolks, cream and milk. Season
with salt and pepper.

5 ▼ Pour the egg mixture into the
flan case.

6 Bake for 35–40 minutes or until
the filling is set and golden brown
and the pastry is golden. Serve warm
or at room temperature.

~ VARIATIONS ~

Add 3 oz (85 g) grated Gruyère
cheese with the bacon. Replace the
bacon with diced cooked ham, if
desired. For a vegetarian quiche,
omit the bacon. Slice 1 lb (450 g)
courgettes and fry in a little oil
until lightly browned on both sides.
Drain on paper towels, then arrange
in the flan case. Scatter 2 oz (55 g)
grated cheese on top. Make the egg
mixture with 4 eggs, 8 fl oz
(240 ml) cream, 4 tablespoons milk,
1/8 teaspoon grated nutmeg, salt
and pepper.

Pizza

MAKES 2

1 lb 2 oz (500 g) plain flour
1 tsp salt
2 tsp active dry yeast
10 fl oz (300 ml) lukewarm water
2–4 fl oz (65–125 ml) extra-virgin olive oil
tomato sauce, grated cheese, olives and herbs, for topping

1 Combine the flour and salt in a large mixing bowl. Make a well in the centre and add the yeast, water and 2 tablespoons of the olive oil. Leave for 15 minutes to dissolve the yeast.

2 With your hands, stir until the dough just holds together. Transfer to a floured surface and knead until smooth and elastic. Avoid adding too much flour while kneading.

3 ▲ Brush the inside of a clean bowl with 1 tablespoon of the oil. Place the dough in the bowl and roll around to coat with the oil. Cover with a plastic bag and leave to rise in a warm place until more than doubled in volume, about 45 minutes.

4 Divide the dough into 2 balls. Preheat a 400°F/200°C/Gas 6 oven.

5 ▲ Roll each ball into a 10 in (25 cm) circle. Flip the circles over and onto your palm. Set each circle on the work surface and rotate, stretching the dough as you turn, until it is about 12 in (30 cm) in diameter.

6 ▲ Brush 2 pizza pans with oil. Place the dough circles in the pans and neaten the edges. Brush with oil.

7 ▲ Cover with the toppings and bake until golden, 10–12 minutes.

Onion, Olive and Anchovy Pizza

SERVES 4

6 tbsp olive oil

1 lb (450 g) onions, thinly sliced

3 garlic cloves, crushed

1 bay leaf

2 tsp dried thyme

salt and pepper

2 cans anchovy fillets, drained and
  blotted dry on kitchen paper

12 olives, mixed black and green

FOR THE PIZZA DOUGH

4 oz (115 g) wholewheat flour

3 oz (85 g) plain flour

1¼ tsp active dry yeast

⅛ tsp sugar

5 fl oz (150 ml) tepid water

2 tbsp olive oil

½ tsp salt

1 For the pizza dough, in a food
processor combine the flours, yeast
and sugar. With the motor running,
pour in the tepid water. Turn the
motor off. Add the oil and salt.
Process until a ball of dough is formed.

2 Put the dough in an oiled bowl and
turn it to coat with oil. Cover and let
rise until doubled in size.

3 ▲ Heat 3 tablespoons of the oil in
a frying pan. Add the onions, garlic
and herbs. Cook over a low heat until
the onions are very soft and the
moisture has evaporated, about 45
minutes. Season with salt and pepper.

4 Preheat the oven to the highest
setting. Oil a 13 × 9 in (33 × 23 cm)
baking tray.

5 ▼ Transfer the risen dough onto a
lightly floured surface. Punch down
the dough and knead it briefly. Roll it
out into a rectangle to fit the baking
tray. Lay the dough on the tray and
press it up the edges of the tray.

6 Brush the dough with 1 tablespoon
olive oil. Discard the bay leaf, and
spoon the onion mixture onto the
dough. Spread it out evenly, leaving a
½ in (1 cm) border around the edge.

7 ▲ Arrange the anchovies and
olives on top of the onions. Drizzle the
remaining 2 tablespoons olive oil over
the top.

8 Bake the pizza until the edges are
puffed and browned, 15–20 minutes.

Broccoli and Goat Cheese Pizza

SERVES 2–3

8 oz (225 g) broccoli florets
2 tbsp cornmeal, or polenta
4 fl oz (125 ml) fresh tomatoes, skinned, cooked and sieved
6 cherry tomatoes, halved
12 black olives, stoned
4 oz (115 g) goat cheese, cut into pieces
1½ oz (45 g) Parmesan cheese, grated
1 tbsp olive oil
FOR THE PIZZA DOUGH
8–9 oz (225–250 g) plain flour
1 package active dry yeast (¼ oz/7.5 g)
⅛ tsp sugar
5 fl oz (150 ml) tepid water
2 tbsp olive oil
½ tsp salt

1 For the pizza dough, combine 3 oz (85 g) of the flour, the yeast and sugar in a food processor. With the motor running, pour in the water. Turn the motor off. Add the oil, 5 oz (140 g) of the remaining flour and the salt.

2 ▲ Process until a ball of dough is formed, adding more water, 1 teaspoon at a time, if the dough is too dry, or the remaining flour, 1 tablespoon at a time, if it is too wet.

3 ▲ Put the dough in an oiled bowl and turn it so the ball of dough is oiled all over. Cover the bowl and let the dough rise in a warm place until doubled in size, about 1 hour.

4 ▲ Meanwhile, cook the broccoli florets in boiling salted water or steam them until just tender, about 5 minutes. Drain well and set aside.

5 Preheat the oven to the highest setting. Oil a 12 in (30 cm) round pizza pan and sprinkle with the cornmeal.

6 When the dough has risen, turn out onto a lightly floured surface. Punch down the dough to deflate it, and knead it briefly.

> ~ COOK'S TIP~
>
> If it is more convenient, the pizza dough can be used as soon as it is made, without any rising.

7 ▲ Roll out the dough to a 12 in (30 cm) round. Lay the dough on the pizza pan and press it down evenly.

8 ▲ Spread the tomato sauce evenly onto the pizza base, leaving a rim of dough uncovered around the edge about ½ in (1 cm) wide.

9 ▲ Arrange the broccoli florets, tomatoes, and olives on the tomato sauce and sprinkle with the cheeses. Drizzle the olive oil over the top.

10 Bake until the cheese melts and the edge of the pizza base is puffed and browned, 10–15 minutes.

CAKES & GATEAUX

AS DELICIOUS AS THEY ARE
BEAUTIFUL, THESE CAKES AND
GÂTEAUX ARE PERFECT TO SERVE
AT TEATIME OR FOR DESSERT.
DELIGHTFUL PARTY CAKES MAKE
SPECIAL OCCASIONS MEMORABLE.

Apple Ring Cake

SERVES 12

7 eating apples, such as Cox's or Granny
  Smith

12 fl oz (350 ml) vegetable oil

1 lb (450 g) caster sugar

3 eggs

15 oz (420 g) plain flour

1 tsp salt

1 tsp bicarbonate of soda

1 tsp ground cinnamon

1 tsp vanilla essence

4 oz (115 g) chopped walnuts

6 oz (170 g) raisins

icing sugar, for dusting

1 Preheat a 350°F/180°C/Gas 4 oven.
Grease a 9 in (23 cm) ring mould.

2 ▲ Quarter, peel, core and slice the
apples into a bowl. Set aside.

3 With an electric mixer, beat the
oil and sugar together until blended.
Add the eggs and continue beating
until the mixture is creamy.

4 Sift together the flour, salt,
bicarbonate of soda and cinnamon.

5 ▼ Fold the flour mixture into the
egg mixture with the vanilla. Stir in
the apples, walnuts and raisins.

6 Pour into the tin and bake until
the cake springs back when touched
lightly, about 1¼ hours. Let stand for
15 minutes, then unmould and
transfer to a cooling rack. Dust with
a layer of icing sugar before serving.

Orange Cake

SERVES 6

6 oz (170 g) plain flour

1½ tsp baking powder

⅛ tsp salt

4 oz (115 g) butter or margarine

4 oz (115 g) caster sugar

grated rind of 1 large orange

2 eggs, at room temperature

2 tbsp milk

FOR THE SYRUP AND DECORATION

4 oz (115 g) caster sugar

8 fl oz (250 ml) fresh orange juice,
  strained

3 orange slices, for decorating

1 Preheat the oven to 350°F/
180°C/Gas 4. Line an 8 in (20 cm)
cake tin with greaseproof paper and
grease the paper.

2 ▲ Sift the flour, salt and baking
powder onto greaseproof paper.

3 With an electric mixer, cream the
butter or margarine until soft. Add the
sugar and orange rind and continue
beating until light and fluffy. Beat in
the eggs, 1 at a time. Fold in the flour
in 3 batches, then add the milk.

4 Spoon into the tin and bake until
the cake pulls away from the sides,
about 30 minutes. Remove from the
oven but leave in the tin.

5 Meanwhile, for the syrup, dissolve
the sugar in the orange juice over a
low heat. Add the orange slices and
simmer for 10 minutes. Remove and
drain. Let the syrup cool.

6 ▲ Prick the cake all over with a
fine skewer. Pour the syrup over the
hot cake. It may seem at first that
there is too much syrup for the cake to
absorb, but it will soak it all up.
Unmould when completely cooled
and decorate with small triangles of
the orange slices arranged on top.

Apple Ring Cake (top), Orange Cake

Angel Cake

SERVES 12–14

4¹/₂ oz (125 g) sifted plain flour
2 tablespoons cornflour
10¹/₂ oz (300 g) caster sugar
10–11 oz (285–310 g) egg whites (about 10–11 eggs)
1¹/₄ teaspoons cream of tartar
¹/₄ teaspoon salt
1 teaspoon vanilla essence
¹/₄ teaspoon almond essence
icing sugar, for dusting

1 Preheat the oven to 325°F/170°C/ Gas 3.

2 ▼ Sift the flours before measuring, then sift them 4 times with 3¹/₂ oz (100 g) of the sugar.

3 With an electric mixer, beat the egg whites until foamy. Sift over the cream of tartar and salt and continue to beat until the whites hold soft peaks when the beaters are lifted.

4 ▲ Add the remaining sugar in 3 batches, beating well after each addition. Stir in the vanilla and almond essences.

5 ▲ Add the flour mixture, in 2 batches, and fold in with a large metal spoon after each addition.

6 Transfer to an ungreased 10 in (25 cm) tube tin and bake until just browned on top, about 1 hour.

7 ▲ Turn the tin upside down onto a cake rack and let cool for 1 hour. If the cake does not turn out, run a knife around the edge to loosen it. Invert on a serving plate.

8 When cool, lay a star-shaped template on top of the cake, sift over icing sugar and remove template.

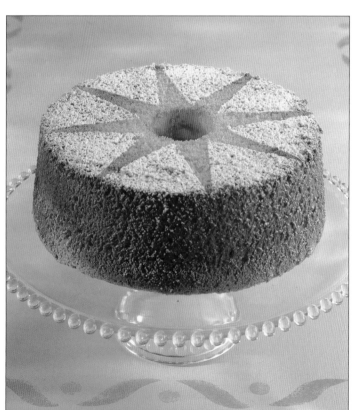

Marbled Ring Cake

SERVES 16

4 oz (115 g) plain chocolate
12 oz (350 g) plain flour
1 tsp baking powder
1 lb (450 g) butter, at room temperature
1 lb 10 oz (740 g) caster sugar
1 tbsp vanilla essence
10 eggs, at room temperature
icing sugar, for dusting

1 ▲ Preheat a 350°F/180°C/Gas 4 oven. Line a 10 × 4 in (25 × 10 cm) ring mould with greaseproof paper and grease the paper. Dust with flour.

3 In a bowl, sift together the flour and baking powder. In another bowl, cream the butter, sugar and vanilla with an electric mixer until light and fluffy. Add the eggs, 2 at a time, then gradually incorporate the flour mixture on low speed.

2 ▲ Melt the chocolate in the top of a double boiler, or in a heatproof bowl set over a pan of hot water. Stir occasionally. Set aside.

4 ▲ Spoon half of the mixture into the prepared tin.

5 ▲ Stir the chocolate into the remaining mixture, then spoon into the tin. With a metal spatula, swirl the mixtures for a marbled effect.

6 Bake until a skewer inserted in the centre comes out clean, about 1 hour 45 minutes. Cover with foil halfway through baking. Let stand for 15 minutes, then unmould and transfer to a cooling rack. To serve, dust with icing sugar.

Carrot Cake

1 lb (450 g) caster sugar
8 fl oz (250 ml) vegetable oil
4 eggs
about 8 oz (225 g) carrots, finely grated
8 oz (225 g) plain flour
1½ tsp bicarbonate of soda
1½ tsp baking powder
1 tsp ground allspice
1 tsp ground cinnamon

For the icing

8 oz (225 g) icing sugar
8 oz (225 g) cream cheese, at room temperature
2 oz (55 g) butter or margarine, at room temperature
2 tsp vanilla essence
6 oz (175 g) chopped walnuts or pecans

1 Preheat a 375°F/190°C/Gas 5 oven.

2 Butter and flour 2 × 9 in (23 cm) round cake tins.

3 ▲ In a mixing bowl, combine the caster sugar, vegetable oil, eggs, and carrots. Beat for 2 minutes.

4 Sift the dry ingredients into another bowl. Add in 4 equal batches to the carrot mixture, mixing well after each addition.

5 ▲ Divide the cake mixture evenly between the prepared cake tins. Bake until a skewer inserted in the centre of the cake comes out clean, 35–45 minutes.

6 Let cool in the tins on wire racks for 10 minutes, then unmould the cakes from the tins onto the wire racks and let cool completely.

7 For the icing, combine everything but the nuts in a bowl and beat until smooth.

8 ▲ To assemble, set 1 cake layer on a serving plate and spread with one-third of the icing. Place the second cake layer on top. Spread the remaining icing all over the top and sides of the cake, swirling it to make a decorative finish. Sprinkle the nuts around the top edge.

Madeira Cake

SERVES 12

8 oz (225 g) plain flour

1 tsp baking powder

8 oz (225 g) butter or margarine, at room temperature

8 oz (225 g) caster sugar

grated rind of 1 lemon

1 tsp vanilla essence

4 eggs

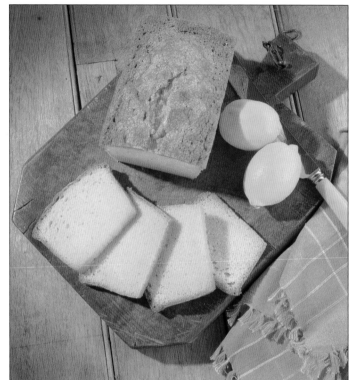

1 Preheat a 325°F/170°C/Gas 3 oven. Grease a 9 × 5 in (23 × 13 cm) loaf tin.

2 Sift the flour and baking powder into a small bowl. Set aside.

3 ▲ With an electric mixer, cream the butter or margarine, adding the sugar 2 tablespoons at a time, until light and fluffy. Stir in the lemon rind and vanilla.

4 ▲ Add the eggs one at a time, beating for 1 minute after each addition.

5 ▼ Add the flour mixture and stir until just combined.

6 ▲ Pour the cake mixture into the tin and tap lightly. Bake until a metal skewer inserted in the centre comes out clean, about 1¼ hours.

7 Let cool in the tin on a wire rack for 10 minutes, then unmould the cake from the tin onto the wire rack and let cool completely.

Lemon Yogurt Ring

SERVES 12

8 oz (225 g) butter, at room temperature
10¹/₂ oz (300 g) caster sugar
4 eggs, at room temperature, separated
2 teaspoons grated lemon rind
3 fl oz (85 ml) lemon juice
8 fl oz (250 ml) plain yogurt
10 oz (285 g) plain flour
2 teaspoons baking powder
1 teaspoon bicarbonate of soda
¹/₂ teaspoon salt
FOR THE GLAZE
4 oz (115 g) icing sugar
2 tablespoons lemon juice
3–4 tablespoons plain yogurt

1 Preheat a 350°F/180°C/Gas 4 oven. Grease a 4²/₃ pt (3 litre) bundt or fluted tube tin and dust with flour.

2 With an electric mixer, cream the butter and caster sugar until light and fluffy. Add the egg yolks, 1 at a time, beating well after each addition.

3 ▲ Add the lemon rind, juice and yogurt and stir to blend.

4 Sift together the flour, baking powder and bicarbonate of soda. In another bowl, beat the egg whites and salt until they hold stiff peaks.

5 ▲ Fold the dry ingredients into the butter mixture, then fold in a dollop of egg whites. Fold in the remaining whites until blended.

6 Pour into the tin and bake until a skewer inserted in the centre comes out clean, about 50 minutes. Let stand 15 minutes, then turn out and cool on a rack.

7 For the glaze, sift the icing sugar into a bowl. Stir in the lemon juice and just enough yogurt to make a smooth glaze.

8 ▲ Set the cooled cake on the rack over a sheet of greaseproof paper or a baking sheet. Pour over the glaze and let it drip down the sides. Allow the glaze to set before serving.

Banana Lemon Layer Cake

SERVES 8–10

9oz (250g) flour
1¼ teaspoons baking powder
½ teaspoon salt
4oz (115g) butter, at room temperature
7oz (200g) granulated sugar
4oz (115g) soft light brown sugar, firmly packed
2 eggs
½ teaspoon grated lemon rind
3 medium very ripe bananas, mashed
1 teaspoon vanilla essence
2fl oz (50 ml) milk
3oz (75g) chopped walnuts
FOR THE FROSTING
4oz (115g) butter, at room temperature
18oz (475g) icing sugar
¼ teaspoon grated lemon rind
3–5 tablespoons fresh lemon juice

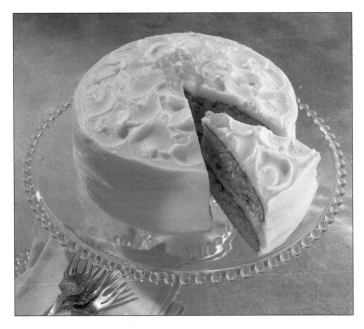

1 Preheat the oven to 180°C/350°F/ Gas 4. Grease two 9 in (23 cm) round cake tins, and line the bottoms with disks of buttered greaseproof paper.

2 Sift the flour with the baking powder and salt.

3 ▲ In a large mixing bowl, cream the butter with the sugars until light and fluffy. Beat in the eggs, one at a time. Stir in the lemon rind.

4 ▲ In a small bowl, mix the bananas with the vanilla and milk. Add the banana mixture and the dry ingredients to the butter mixture alternately in two or three batches and stir until just blended. Fold in the nuts.

5 Divide the batter between the cake tins and spread it out evenly. Bake until a skewer inserted in the centre comes out clean, 30–35 minutes. Leave to stand for 5 minutes before unmoulding on to a wire rack. Peel off the greaseproof paper.

6 For the frosting, cream the butter until smooth, then gradually beat in the sugar. Stir in the lemon rind and enough juice to make a spreadable consistency.

7 ▼ Set one of the cake layers on a serving plate. Cover with about one-third of the frosting. Top with the second cake layer. Spread the remaining frosting evenly over the top and sides of the cake.

Light Fruit Cake

MAKES 2 LOAVES

8 oz (225 g) prunes
8 oz (225 g) dates
8 oz (225 g) currants
8 oz (225 g) sultanas
8 fl oz (250 ml) dry white wine
8 fl oz (250 ml) rum
12 oz (350 g) plain flour
2 tsp baking powder
1 tsp ground cinnamon
1/2 tsp grated nutmeg
8 oz (225 g) butter, at room temperature
8 oz (225 g) caster sugar
4 eggs, at room temperature, lightly beaten
1 tsp vanilla essence

1 Stone the prunes and dates and chop finely. Place in a bowl with the currants and sultanas.

2 ▲ Stir in the wine and rum and let stand, covered, for 48 hours. Stir occasionally.

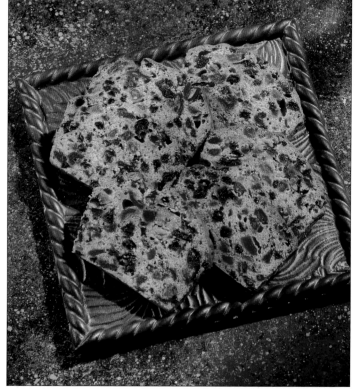

3 Preheat a 300°F/150°C/Gas 2 oven with a tray of hot water in the bottom. Line 2 9 × 5 in (23 × 13 cm) tins with greaseproof paper and grease.

4 Sift together the flour, baking powder, cinnamon, and nutmeg.

5 ▲ With an electric mixer, cream the butter and sugar together until light and fluffy.

6 Gradually add the eggs and vanilla. Fold in the flour mixture in 3 batches. Fold in the dried fruit mixture and its soaking liquid.

7 ▲ Divide the mixture between the tins and bake until a skewer inserted in the centre comes out clean, about 1 1/2 hours.

8 Let stand 20 minutes, then unmould and transfer to a cooling rack. Wrap in foil and store in an airtight container. If possible, leave for at least 1 week before serving to allow the flavours to mellow.

Rich Fruit Cake

SERVES 12

5 oz (140 g) currants
6 oz (170 g) raisins
2 oz (55 g) sultanas
2 oz (55 g) glacé cherries, halved
3 tbsp sweet sherry
6 oz (170 g) butter
7 oz (200 g) dark brown sugar
2 size 1 eggs, at room temperature
7 oz (200 g) plain flour
2 tsp baking powder
2 tsp each ground ginger, allspice, and cinnamon
1 tbsp golden syrup
1 tbsp milk
2 oz (55 g) cut mixed peel
4 oz (115 g) chopped walnuts

FOR THE DECORATION

8 oz (225 g) caster sugar
4 fl oz (125 ml) water
1 lemon, thinly sliced
1/2 orange, thinly sliced
4 fl oz (125 ml) orange marmalade
glacé cherries

1 One day before preparing, combine the currants, raisins, sultanas and cherries in a bowl. Stir in the sherry. Cover and let stand overnight to soak.

2 Preheat a 300°F/150°C/Gas 2 oven. Line a 9 × 3 in (23 × 8 cm) spring-form tin with greaseproof paper and grease. Place a tray of hot water on the bottom of the oven.

3 With an electric mixer, cream the butter and sugar until light and fluffy. Beat in the eggs, 1 at a time.

4 ▲ Sift the flour, baking powder and spices together 3 times. Fold into the butter mixture in 3 batches. Fold in the syrup, milk, dried fruit and liquid, mixed peel and nuts.

5 ▲ Spoon into the tin, spreading out so there is a slight depression in the centre of the mixture.

6 Bake until a skewer inserted in the centre comes out clean, 2¹/₂–3 hours. Cover with foil when the top is golden to prevent over-browning. Cool in the tin on a rack.

7 ▲ For the decoration, combine the sugar and water in a saucepan and bring to the boil. Add the lemon and orange slices and cook until crystallized, about 20 minutes. Work in batches, if necessary. Remove the fruit with a slotted spoon. Pour the remaining syrup over the cake and let cool. Melt the marmalade over low heat, then brush over the top of the cake. Decorate with the crystallized citrus slices and cherries.

Ginger Cake with Spiced Whipped Cream

SERVES 9

6 oz (170 g) plain flour
2 tsp baking powder
½ tsp salt
2 tsp ground ginger
2 tsp ground cinnamon
1 tsp ground cloves
¼ tsp grated nutmeg
2 eggs
8 oz (225 g) caster sugar
8 fl oz (250 ml) whipping cream
1 tsp vanilla essence
icing sugar, for sprinkling
FOR THE SPICED WHIPPED CREAM
6 fl oz (175 ml) whipping cream
1 tsp icing sugar
¼ tsp ground cinnamon
¼ tsp ground ginger
⅛ tsp grated nutmeg

1 Preheat a 350°F/180°C/Gas 4 oven. Grease a 9 in (23 cm) square baking tin.

2 Sift the flour, baking powder, salt and spices into a bowl. Set aside.

3 ▲ With an electric mixer, beat the eggs on high speed until very thick, about 5 minutes. Gradually beat in the caster sugar.

4 ▲ With the mixer on low speed, beat in the flour mixture alternately with the cream, beginning and ending with the flour. Stir in the vanilla.

5 ▲ Pour the cake mixture into the tin and bake until the top springs back when touched lightly, 35–40 minutes. Let cool in the tin on a wire rack for 10 minutes.

6 ▲ Meanwhile, to make the spiced whipped cream, combine the ingredients in a bowl and whip until the cream will hold soft peaks.

7 Sprinkle icing sugar over the hot cake, cut in 9 squares, and serve with spiced whipped cream.

Rich Sticky Gingerbread

MAKES AN 8 IN (20 CM) SQUARE CAKE

8 oz (225 g) plain flour
pinch of salt
1 teaspoon bicarbonate of soda
2 teaspoons ground ginger
1 teaspoon mixed spice
4 oz (115 g) butter or margarine
4 oz (115 g) golden syrup
4 oz (115 g) black treacle
2 oz (55 g) soft dark brown sugar
2 eggs, beaten
4 fl oz (120 ml) milk
4 oz (115 g) sultanas or chopped stem ginger (optional)

FOR THE ICING (OPTIONAL)

4 oz (115 g) icing sugar
about 4 teaspoons water

1 ▲ Preheat a 350°F/180°C/Gas 4 oven. Grease and line an 8 in (20 cm) square cake tin.

2 ▲ Sift the flour, salt, bicarbonate of soda and spices into a bowl.

3 Put the butter or margarine, golden syrup, treacle and brown sugar in a saucepan and warm over a gentle heat, stirring occasionally, until the fat has melted and the mixture is smooth. Remove from the heat and leave to cool slightly.

4 ▼ Make a well in the centre of the dry ingredients and add the melted mixture, the beaten eggs and milk. Beat with a wooden spoon until the mixture is smooth. Add the sultanas or ginger, if using.

5 Turn the cake mixture into the prepared tin. Bake for about 1 hour. To test if the gingerbread is done, press it lightly in the centre; it should spring back. Allow to cool in the tin for 5 minutes before turning out on to a wire rack to cool completely.

6 ▲ If icing the gingerbread, sift the icing sugar into a bowl and add 3 teaspoons of the water. Stir to mix, then add more water 1 teaspoon at a time until the icing is smooth and has a pouring consistency. Pour the icing over the gingerbread and leave to set before serving.

Walnut Layer Cake

SERVES 8

8oz (225g) plain flour

1 tablespoon baking powder

½ teaspoon salt

4oz (115g) butter or margarine,
   at room temperature

7oz (200g) granulated sugar

2 eggs

1 teaspoon grated orange rind

1 teaspoon vanilla essence

4oz (115g) ground walnuts

6fl oz (175ml) milk

black walnut halves, for decoration

FOR THE FROSTING

4oz (115g) butter

6oz (175g) soft light brown sugar,
   firmly packed

3 tablespoons maple syrup

2fl oz (50ml) milk

6–8oz (175–225g) icing sugar, sifted

1 ▲ Grease two 8 × 2 in (20 × 5 cm) cake tins and line the bottom of each with a disk of buttered greaseproof paper. Preheat the oven to 190°C/ 375°F/Gas 5.

2 Sift together the flour, baking powder and salt.

~ VARIATION ~

If black walnuts are not available, substitute ordinary walnuts, or use pecans instead.

3 ▲ Beat the butter or margarine to soften, then gradually beat in the granulated sugar until light and fluffy. Beat in the eggs, one at a time. Add the orange rind and vanilla and beat to mix well.

4 ▲ Stir in the ground walnuts. Add the flour alternately with the milk, stirring only enough to blend after each addition.

5 ▲ Divide the mixture between the prepared cake tins. Bake until a skewer inserted in the centre comes out clean, about 25 minutes. Cool in the cake tins for 5 minutes before unmoulding on to a wire rack.

6 ▲ For the frosting, melt the butter in a medium saucepan. Add the brown sugar and maple syrup and boil for 2 minutes, stirring constantly.

7 ▲ Add the milk. Bring back to the boil and stir in 1oz (25g) of the icing sugar. Remove from the heat and allow to cool until lukewarm. Gradually beat in the remaining icing sugar. Set the pan in a bowl of iced water and stir until the frosting is thick enough to spread.

8 ▲ Spread some of the frosting on one of the cake layers. Set the other layer on top. Spread the remaining frosting over the top and sides of the cake. Decorate with walnut halves.

Coffee-Iced Ring

SERVES 16

10 oz (285 g) plain flour
1 tbsp baking powder
1 tsp salt
12 oz (350 g) caster sugar
4 fl oz (125 ml) vegetable oil
7 eggs, at room temperature, separated
6 fl oz (175 ml) cold water
2 tsp vanilla essence
2 tsp grated lemon rind
¹/₂ tsp cream of tartar
FOR THE ICING
5¹/₂ oz (165 g) unsalted butter, at room temperature
1 lb 4 oz (575 g) icing sugar
4 tsp instant coffee dissolved in 4 tbsp hot water

1 Preheat a 325°F/170°C/Gas 3 oven.

2 ▼ Sift the flour, baking powder and salt into a bowl. Stir in 8 oz (225 g) of the sugar. Make a well in the centre and add in the following order: oil, egg yolks, water, vanilla and lemon rind. Beat with a whisk or metal spoon until smooth.

3 With an electric mixer, beat the egg whites with the cream of tartar until they hold soft peaks. Add the remaining 4 oz (115 g) of sugar and beat until they hold stiff peaks.

4 ▲ Pour the flour mixture over the whites in 3 batches, folding well after each addition.

5 Transfer the mixture to a 10 × 4 in (25 × 10 cm) ring mould and bake until the top springs back when touched lightly, about 1 hour.

6 ▲ When baked, remove from the oven and immediately hang the cake upside-down over the neck of a funnel or a narrow bottle. Let cool. To remove the cake, run a knife around the inside to loosen, then turn the tin over and tap the sides sharply. Invert the cake onto a serving plate.

7 For the icing, beat together the butter and icing sugar with an electric mixer until smooth. Add the coffee and beat until fluffy. With a metal spatula, spread over the sides and top of the cake.

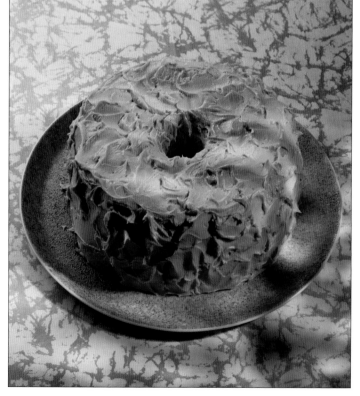

Forgotten Gâteau

SERVES 6

6 egg whites, at room temperature

$^1/_2$ teaspoon cream of tartar

$^1/_8$ teaspoon salt

$10^1/_2$ oz (300 g) caster sugar

1 teaspoon vanilla essence

6 fl oz (175 ml) whipping cream

FOR THE SAUCE

12 oz (350 g) fresh or thawed frozen
  raspberries

2–3 tablespoons icing sugar

1 Preheat a 450°F/230°C/Gas 8 oven.
Grease a $2^1/_3$ pt (1.5 litre) ring mould.

2 ▲ With an electric mixer, beat the
egg whites, cream of tartar and salt
until they hold soft peaks. Gradually
add the sugar and beat until glossy and
stiff. Fold in the vanilla.

3 ▲ Spoon into the prepared mould
and smooth the top level.

4 Place in the oven, then turn the
oven off. Leave overnight; do not
open the oven door at any time.

5 ▼ To serve, gently loosen the edge
with a sharp knife and turn out onto a
serving plate. Whip the cream until
firm. Spread it over the top and upper
sides of the meringue and decorate
with any meringue crumbs.

6 ▲ For the sauce, purée the fruit,
then strain. Sweeten to taste.

~ COOK'S TIP ~

This recipe is not suitable for fan
assisted and solid fuel ovens.

Nut and Apple Gâteau

SERVES 8

4 oz (115 g) pecan nuts or walnuts
2 oz (55 g) plain flour
2 tsp baking powder
1/4 tsp salt
2 large cooking apples
3 eggs
8 oz (225 g) caster sugar
1 tsp vanilla essence
6 fl oz (175 ml) whipping cream

1 Preheat a 325°F/170°C/Gas 3 oven. Line 2 9 in (23 cm) cake tins with greaseproof paper and grease the paper. Spread the nuts on a baking sheet and bake for 10 minutes.

2 Finely chop the nuts. Reserve 1½ tablespoons and place the rest in a mixing bowl. Sift over the flour, baking powder and salt and stir.

3 ▲ Quarter, core and peel the apples. Cut into 1/8 in (3 mm) dice, then stir into the nut-flour mixture.

4 ▲ With an electric mixer, beat the eggs until frothy. Gradually add the sugar and vanilla and beat until a ribbon forms, about 8 minutes. Gently fold in the flour mixture.

5 Pour into the tins and level the tops. Bake until a skewer inserted in the centre comes out clean, about 35 minutes. Let stand 10 minutes.

6 ▲ To loosen, run a knife around the inside edge of each layer. Let cool.

7 ▲ Whip the cream until firm. Spread half over the cake. Top with the second cake. Pipe whipped cream rosettes on top and sprinkle over the reserved nuts before serving.

Almond Cake

SERVES 4–6

8 oz (225 g) blanched whole almonds, plus more for decorating
1 oz (30 g) butter
3 oz (85 g) icing sugar
3 eggs
¹/₂ tsp almond essence
1 oz (30 g) plain flour
3 egg whites
1 tbsp caster sugar

1 ▲ Preheat a 325°F/170°C/Gas 3 oven. Line a 9 in (23 cm) round cake tin with greaseproof paper and grease.

2 ▲ Spread the almonds in a baking tray and toast for 10 minutes. Cool, then coarsely chop 8 oz (225 g).

3 Melt the butter and set aside.

4 Preheat a 400°F/200°C/Gas 6 oven.

5 Grind the chopped almonds with half the icing sugar in a food processor, blender or grinder. Transfer to a mixing bowl.

6 ▲ Add the whole eggs and remaining icing sugar. With an electric mixer, beat until the mixture forms a ribbon when the beaters are lifted. Mix in the butter and almond essence. Sift over the flour and fold in gently.

7 With an electric mixer, beat the egg whites until they hold soft peaks. Add the caster sugar and beat until stiff and glossy.

8 ▲ Fold the whites into the almond mixture in 4 batches.

9 Spoon the mixture into the prepared tin and bake in the centre of the oven until golden brown, about 15–20 minutes. Decorate the top with the remaining toasted whole almonds. Serve warm.

Walnut Coffee Gâteau

SERVES 8–10

5 oz (140 g) walnuts
5¹/₂ oz (150 g) sugar
5 eggs, separated
2 oz (55 g) dry breadcrumbs
1 tablespoon unsweetened cocoa powder
1 tablespoon instant coffee
2 tablespoons rum or lemon juice
¹/₈ teaspoon salt
6 tablespoons redcurrant jelly
chopped walnuts, for decorating
FOR THE FROSTING
8 oz (225 g) plain chocolate
1¹/₄ pt (750 ml) whipping cream

3 ▲ Grind the nuts with 3 tablespoons of the sugar in a food processor, blender, or coffee grinder.

4 With an electric mixer, beat the egg yolks and remaining sugar until thick and lemon-coloured.

1 ▲ For the frosting, combine the chocolate and cream in the top of a double boiler, or in a heatproof bowl set over simmering water. Stir until the chocolate melts. Let cool, then cover and refrigerate overnight or until the mixture is firm.

2 Preheat the oven to 350°F/180°C/ Gas 4. Line a 9 × 2 in (23 × 5 cm) cake tin with greaseproof paper and grease.

5 ▲ Fold in the walnuts. Stir in the breadcrumbs, cocoa, coffee and rum or lemon juice.

6 ▲ In another bowl, beat the egg whites with the salt until they hold stiff peaks. Fold carefully into the walnut mixture with a rubber scraper.

7 Pour the meringue batter into the prepared tin and bake until the top of the cake springs back when touched lightly, about 45 minutes. Let the cake stand for 5 minutes, then turn out and cool on a rack.

8 ▲ When cool, slice the cake in half horizontally.

9 With an electric mixer, beat the chocolate frosting mixture on low speed until it becomes lighter, about 30 seconds. Do not overbeat or it may become grainy.

10 ▲ Warm the jelly in a saucepan until melted, then brush over the cut cake layer. Spread with some of the chocolate frosting, then sandwich with the remaining cake layer. Brush the top of the cake with jelly, then cover the side and top with the remaining chocolate frosting. Make a starburst pattern by pressing gently with a table knife in lines radiating from the centre. Sprinkle the chopped walnuts around the edge.

Coconut Cake

<u>SERVES 10</u>

6 oz (175 g) icing sugar
4 oz (115 g) plain flour
12 fl oz (375 ml) egg whites (about 12)
1½ tsp cream of tartar
8 oz (225 g) caster sugar
¼ tsp salt
2 tsp almond essence
3½ oz (100 g) desiccated coconut

<u>FOR THE ICING</u>

2 egg whites
4 oz (115 g) caster sugar
¼ tsp salt
2 tbsp cold water
2 tsp almond essence
7 oz (200 g) desiccated coconut, toasted

1 ▲ Preheat a 350°F/180°C/Gas 4 oven. Sift the icing sugar and flour into a bowl. Set aside.

2 With an electric mixer, beat the egg whites with the cream of tartar on medium speed until very thick. Turn the mixer to high speed and beat in the caster sugar, 2 tablespoons at a time, reserving 2 tablespoons.

3 ▲ Continue beating until stiff and glossy. Swiftly beat in the reserved 2 tablespoons of sugar, with the salt and almond essence.

4 ▲ One heaped teaspoon at a time, sprinkle the flour mixture over the meringue, quickly folding until just combined. Fold in the desiccated coconut in 2 batches.

5 ▲ Transfer the cake mixture to an ungreased 10 in (25 cm) non-stick tube tin, and cut gently through the mixture with a metal spatula. Bake until the top of the cake springs back when touched lightly, 30–35 minutes.

6 ▲ As soon as the cake is done, turn the tin upside down and suspend its funnel over the neck of a funnel or bottle. Let cool, about 1 hour.

7 ▲ For the icing, combine the egg whites, sugar, salt and water in a heatproof bowl. Beat with an electric mixer until blended. Set the bowl over a pan of boiling water and continue beating on medium speed until the icing is stiff, about 3 minutes. Remove the pan from the heat and stir in the almond essence.

8 ▲ Unmould the cake onto a serving plate. Spread the icing gently over the top and sides of the cake. Sprinkle with the toasted coconut.

Lemon Coconut Layer Cake

SERVES 8–10

6 oz (175 g) plain flour
¹/4 teaspoon salt
7 eggs
12 oz (350 g) caster sugar
1 tablespoon grated orange rind
grated rind of 1¹/2 lemons
juice of 1 lemon
2¹/2 oz (65 g) desiccated coconut
1 tablespoon cornflour
4 fl oz (120 ml) water
1¹/2 oz (40 g) butter
FOR THE ICING
3 oz (75 g) unsalted butter
6 oz (175 g) icing sugar
grated rind of 1¹/2 lemon
2 tablespoons lemon juice
7 oz (200 g) desiccated coconut

1 Preheat the oven to 350°F/180°C/ Gas 4. Line three 8 in (20 cm) cake tins with greaseproof paper and grease. In a bowl, sift together the flour and salt and set aside.

2 ▲ Place six of the eggs in a large heatproof bowl set over hot water. With an electric mixer, beat until frothy. Gradually beat in 8 oz (225 g) caster sugar until the mixture doubles in volume and leaves a ribbon trail when the beaters are lifted, about 10 minutes.

3 ▲ Remove the bowl from the hot water. Fold in the orange rind, half the grated lemon rind and 1 tablespoon of the lemon juice until blended. Fold in the coconut.

4 Sift over the flour mixture in three batches, gently folding in thoroughly after each addition.

5 ▲ Divide the mixture between the prepared tins.

6 Bake until the cakes pull away from the sides of the tins, 20–25 minutes. Leave to stand for 5 minutes, then turn out to cool on a rack.

7 In a bowl, blend the cornflour with a little cold water to dissolve. Whisk in the remaining egg until just blended. Set aside.

8 ▲ In a saucepan, combine the remaining lemon rind and juice, the water, remaining sugar and butter.

9 Over a medium heat, bring the mixture to the boil. Whisk in the eggs and cornflour mixture, and return to the boil. Whisk continuously until thick, about 5 minutes. Remove from the heat and pour into a bowl. Cover with clear film and set aside to cool.

10 ▲ For the icing, cream the butter and icing sugar until smooth. Stir in the lemon rind and enough lemon juice to obtain a thick, spreadable consistency.

11 Sandwich the three cake layers with the lemon custard mixture. Spread the icing over the top and sides. Cover the cake with the coconut, pressing it in gently.

Coconut Lime Gâteau

SERVES 8 OR MORE

8 oz (225 g) plain flour

2½ teaspoons baking powder

¼ teaspoon salt

8 oz (225 g) butter, at room temperature

8 oz (225 g) caster sugar

grated zest of 2 limes

4 eggs

4 tablespoons fresh lime juice (from about 2 limes)

3 oz (85 g) desiccated coconut

1 recipe quantity American frosting (page 239)

1 Preheat a 350°F/180°C/Gas 4 oven. Grease two 9 in (23 cm) sandwich tins and line the bottoms with greased greaseproof paper.

2 Sift together the flour, baking powder and salt.

3 In a large bowl, beat the butter until it is soft and pliable. Add the sugar and lime zest and beat until the mixture is pale and fluffy. Beat in the eggs, one at a time.

4 ▲ Using a wooden spoon fold in the sifted dry ingredients in small portions, alternating with the lime juice. When the mixture is smooth, stir in two-thirds of the coconut.

5 ▲ Divide the mixture between the prepared tins and spread it evenly to the sides. Bake for 30–35 minutes (test with a skewer).

6 ▲ Remove the cakes from the oven and set them, in their tins, on a wire rack. Cool for 10 minutes. Then turn out and peel off the lining paper. Cool completely on the rack.

7 ▲ Spread the remaining coconut in another cake tin. Bake until golden brown, stirring occasionally. Watch carefully so that the coconut does not get too dark. Cool.

8 ▲ Put one of the cakes, base up, on a serving plate. Spread a layer of frosting evenly over the cake.

9 ▲ Set the second layer on top, base down. Spread the remaining frosting all over the top and round the sides of the cake.

10 ▲ Scatter the toasted coconut over the top of the cake and leave to set before serving.

Cranberry Upside-Down Cake

12–14 oz (350–400 g) fresh cranberries
2 oz (55 g) butter
5 oz (140 g) sugar
FOR THE CAKE MIXTURE
2¹/₂ oz (70 g) plain flour
1 teaspoon baking powder
3 eggs
4 oz (115 g) sugar
grated rind of 1 orange
1¹/₂ oz (45 g) butter, melted

1 Preheat the oven to 350°F/180°C/ Gas 4. Place a baking sheet on the middle shelf of the oven.

2 Wash the cranberries and pat dry. Thickly smear the butter on the bottom and sides of a 9 × 2 in (23 × 5 cm) round cake tin. Add the sugar and swirl the tin to coat evenly.

3 ▲ Add the cranberries and spread in an even layer over the bottom of the tin.

4 For the cake mixture, sift the flour and baking powder twice. Set aside.

5 ▲ Combine the eggs, sugar and orange rind in a heatproof bowl set over a pan of hot but not boiling water. With an electric mixer, beat until the eggs leave a ribbon trail when the beaters are lifted.

6 Add the flour mixture in 3 batches, folding in well after each addition. Gently fold in the melted butter, then pour over the cranberries.

7 Bake for 40 minutes. Leave to cool for 5 minutes, then run a knife around the inside edge to loosen.

8 ▲ While the cake is still warm, invert a plate on top of the tin. Protecting your hands with oven gloves, hold plate and tin firmly and turn them both over quickly. Lift off the tin carefully.

Pineapple Upside-Down Cake

SERVES 8

4 oz (115 g) butter
7 oz (200 g) dark brown sugar
16 oz (450 g) canned pineapple slices, drained
4 eggs, separated
grated rind of 1 lemon
¹/₈ tsp salt
4 oz (115 g) caster sugar
3 oz (85 g) plain flour
1 tsp baking powder

1 Preheat a 350°F/180°C/Gas 4 oven.

2 Melt the butter in a 10 in (25 cm) ovenproof cast-iron frying pan. Remove 1 tablespoon of the melted butter and set aside.

3 ▲ Add the brown sugar to the pan and stir until blended. Place the drained pineapple slices on top in one layer. Set aside.

~ **VARIATION** ~

For Dried Apricot Upside-Down Cake, replace the pineapple slices with 8 oz (225 g) of dried apricots. If they need softening, simmer the apricots in about 4 fl oz (125 ml) orange juice until plump and soft. Drain the apricots and discard any remaining cooking liquid.

4 In a bowl, whisk together the egg yolks, reserved butter and lemon rind until well blended. Set aside.

5 ▼ With an electric mixer, beat the egg whites with the salt until stiff. Fold in the caster sugar, 2 tablespoons at a time. Fold in the egg yolk mixture.

6 Sift the flour and baking powder together. Carefully fold into the egg mixture in 3 batches.

7 ▲ Pour the mixture over the pineapple and smooth level.

8 Bake until a skewer inserted in the centre comes out clean, about 30 minutes.

9 While still hot, place a serving plate on top of the pan, bottom-side up. Holding them tightly together with oven gloves, quickly flip over. Serve hot or cold.

Spice Cake with Cream Cheese Frosting

SERVES 10–12

10 fl oz (300 ml) milk
2 tablespoons golden syrup
2 teaspoons vanilla essence
3 oz (85 g) walnuts, chopped
6 oz (170 g) butter, at room temperature
10^1/2 oz (300 g) sugar
1 egg, at room temperature
3 egg yolks, at room temperature
10 oz (285 g) plain flour
1 tablespoon baking powder
1 teaspoon grated nutmeg
1 teaspoon ground cinnamon
^{1}/2 teaspoon ground cloves
^{1}/4 teaspoon ground ginger
^{1}/4 teaspoon ground allspice
FOR THE FROSTING
6 oz (170 g) cream cheese
1 oz (30 g) unsalted butter
70 oz (200 g) icing sugar
2 tablespoons finely chopped stem ginger
2 tablespoons syrup from stem ginger
stem ginger pieces, for decorating

1 Preheat a 350°F/180°C/Gas 4 oven. Line 3 8 in (20 cm) cake tins with greaseproof paper and grease. In a bowl, combine the milk, golden syrup, vanilla and walnuts.

2 ▼ With an electric mixer, cream the butter and sugar until light and fluffy. Beat in the egg and egg yolks. Add the milk mixture and stir well.

3 Sift together the flour, baking powder and spices 3 times.

4 ▲ Add the flour mixture in 4 batches, and fold in carefully after each addition.

5 Divide the cake mixture between the tins. Bake until the cakes spring back when touched lightly, about 25 minutes. Let stand 5 minutes, then turn out and cool on a rack.

6 ▼ For the frosting, combine all the ingredients and beat with an electric mixer. Spread the frosting between the layers and over the top. Decorate with pieces of stem ginger.

Soured Cream Crumble Cake

SERVES 12–14

4 oz (115 g) butter, at room
  temperature

4 1/2 oz (125 g) caster sugar

3 eggs, at room temperature

7 1/2 oz (215 g) plain flour

1 teaspoon bicarbonate of soda

1 teaspoon baking powder

8 fl oz (250 ml) soured cream

FOR THE TOPPING

8 oz (225 g) dark brown sugar

2 teaspoons ground cinnamon

4 oz (115 g) walnuts, finely chopped

2 oz (55 g) cold butter, cut into pieces

1 Preheat a 350°F/180°C/Gas 4 oven.
Line the bottom of a 9 in (23 cm)
square cake tin with greaseproof paper
and grease.

2 ▲ For the topping, place the
brown sugar, cinnamon and walnuts
in a bowl. Mix with your fingertips,
then add the butter and continue
working with your fingertips until the
mixture resembles breadcrumbs.

3 To make the cake, cream the butter
with an electric mixer until soft. Add
the sugar and continue beating until
the mixture is light and fluffy.

4 Add the eggs, 1 at a time, beating
well after each addition.

5 In another bowl, sift the flour,
bicarbonate of soda and baking
powder together 3 times.

6 ▲ Fold the dry ingredients into
the butter mixture in 3 batches,
alternating with the soured cream.
Fold until blended after each addition.

7 ▲ Pour half of the batter into the
prepared tin and sprinkle over half of
the walnut crumb topping mixture.

8 Pour the remaining batter on top
and sprinkle over the remaining
walnut crumb mixture.

9 Bake until browned, 60–70 minutes.
Let stand 5 minutes, then turn out
and cool on a rack.

Carrot Cake with Maple Butter Icing

SERVES 12

1 lb (450 g) carrots, peeled
6 oz (170 g) plain flour
2 tsp baking powder
½ tsp bicarbonate of soda
1 tsp salt
2 tsp ground cinnamon
4 eggs
2 tsp vanilla essence
4 oz (115 g) dark brown sugar
2 oz (55 g) caster sugar
10 fl oz (300 ml) sunflower oil
4 oz (115 g) finely chopped walnuts
3 oz (85 g) raisins
walnut halves, for decorating (optional)
FOR THE ICING
3 oz (85 g) unsalted butter, at room temperature
12 oz (350 g) icing sugar
2 fl oz (65 ml) maple syrup

1 Preheat a 350°F/180°C/Gas 4 oven. Line an 11 × 8 in (28 × 20 cm) tin with greaseproof paper and grease.

2 ▲ Grate the carrots and set aside.

3 Sift the flour, baking powder, bicarbonate of soda, salt and cinnamon into a bowl. Set aside.

4 With an electric mixer, beat the eggs until blended. Add the vanilla, sugars and oil; beat to incorporate. Add the dry ingredients, in 3 batches, folding in well after each addition.

5 ▲ Add the carrots, walnuts and raisins and fold in thoroughly.

6 Pour the mixture into the prepared tin and bake until the cake springs back when touched lightly, 40–45 minutes. Let stand 10 minutes, then unmould and transfer to a rack.

7 ▼ For the icing, cream the butter with half the icing sugar until soft. Add the syrup, then beat in the remaining sugar until blended.

8 Spread the icing over the top of the cake. Using the tip of a palette knife, make decorative ridges in the icing. Cut into squares. Decorate with walnut halves, if wished.

Peach Torte

SERVES 8

4 oz (115 g) plain flour
1 teaspoon baking powder
pinch of salt
4 oz (115 g) unsalted butter, at room temperature
6 oz (170 g) sugar
2 eggs, at room temperature
6–7 peaches
sugar and lemon juice, for sprinkling
whipped cream, for serving (optional)

1 Preheat the oven to 350°F/180°C/ Gas 4. Grease a 10 in (25 cm) spring-form tin.

2 ▲ Sift together the flour, baking powder and salt. Set aside.

3 With an electric mixer, cream the butter and sugar until light and fluffy. Beat in the eggs, then fold in the dry ingredients until blended.

4 ▲ Spoon the mixture into the tin and smooth it to make an even layer over the bottom.

5 ▼ To skin the peaches, drop several at a time into a pan of gently boiling water. Boil for 10 seconds, then remove with a slotted spoon. Peel off the skin with the aid of a sharp knife. Cut the peaches in half and discard the stones.

6 ▲ Arrange the peach halves on top of the mixture. Sprinkle lightly with sugar and lemon juice.

7 Bake until golden brown and set, 50–60 minutes. Serve warm, with whipped cream, if liked.

Plum Crumble Cake

SERVES 8–10

5 oz (140 g) butter or margarine, at room temperature

5 oz (140 g) caster sugar

4 eggs, at room temperature

1½ tsp vanilla essence

5 oz (140 g) plain flour

1 tsp baking powder

1½ lb (700 g) red plums, halved and stoned

FOR THE TOPPING

4 oz (115 g) plain flour

4½ oz (130 g) light brown sugar

1½ tsp ground cinnamon

3 oz (85 g) butter, cut in pieces

1 Preheat a 350°F/180°C/Gas 4 oven.

2 For the topping, combine the flour, light brown sugar and cinnamon in a bowl. Add the butter and work the mixture lightly with your fingertips until it resembles coarse breadcrumbs. Set aside.

3 ▲ Line a 10 × 2 in (25 × 5 cm) tin with greaseproof paper and grease.

4 Cream the butter and sugar until light and fluffy.

5 ▲ Beat in the eggs, 1 at a time. Stir in the vanilla.

6 In a bowl, sift together the flour and baking powder, then fold into the butter mixture in 3 batches.

7 ▲ Pour the mixture into the tin. Arrange the plums on top.

8 ▲ Sprinkle the topping over the plums in an even layer.

9 Bake until a skewer inserted in the centre comes out clean, about 45 minutes. Let cool in the tin.

10 To serve, run a knife around the inside edge and invert onto a plate. Invert again onto a serving plate so the topping is right-side up.

~ VARIATION ~

This cake can also be made with the same quantity of apricots, peeled if preferred, or stoned cherries, or use a mixture of fruit, such as red or yellow plums, greengages and apricots.

Yule Log Cake

SERVES 8 OR MORE

| 4 eggs, separated |
| 5 oz (145 g) caster sugar |
| 1 teaspoon vanilla essence |
| pinch of cream of tartar (if needed) |
| 4 oz (115 g) plain flour, sifted |
| 8 fl oz (240 ml) whipping cream |
| 10 oz (300 g) plain or bittersweet chocolate, chopped |
| 2 tablespoons rum or Cognac |

1 Preheat a 375°F/190°C/Gas 5 oven. Grease, line and flour a 16 × 11 in (40 × 28 cm) Swiss roll tin.

2 Put the egg yolks in a large bowl. Reserve 2 tablespoons sugar; add the remainder to the egg yolks. Whisk until pale and thick. Add the vanilla.

3 In another bowl, scrupulously clean and grease-free, whisk the egg whites (with the cream of tartar if not using a copper bowl) until they will hold soft peaks. Add the reserved sugar and continue whisking until the whites are glossy and will hold stiff peaks.

4 Gently fold half the flour into the egg yolk mixture. Add one-quarter of the egg whites and fold in to lighten the mixture. Fold in the remaining flour, then the remaining egg whites.

5 ▲ Spread the mixture in the prepared tin. Bake for 15 minutes.

6 Turn on to paper sprinkled with caster sugar. Roll up and cool.

7 Bring the cream to the boil in a small saucepan. Put the chocolate in a bowl, add the cream and stir until the chocolate has melted.

8 ▲ Beat the chocolate mixture until it is fluffy and has thickened to a spreading consistency. Spoon one-third of the chocolate mixture into another bowl. Mix in rum or Cognac.

9 Unroll the cake. Spread the rum and chocolate mixture evenly over the surface. Roll up the cake again.

10 Cut off about one-quarter of the cake, at an angle. Place it against the side of the larger piece of cake, to resemble a branch from a tree trunk.

11 ▼ Spread the remaining chocolate mixture all over the cake. Mark with the prongs of a fork to resemble bark. Before serving, add small Christmas decorations and sprigs of holly if liked, and dust with a little icing sugar 'snow'.

Orange and Walnut Swiss Roll

SERVES 8

4 eggs, separated

4 oz (115 g) caster sugar

4 oz (115 g) very finely chopped walnuts

1/8 tsp cream of tartar

1/8 tsp salt

icing sugar, for dusting

FOR THE FILLING

10 fl oz (300 ml) whipping cream

1 tbsp caster sugar

grated rind of 1 orange

1 tbsp orange liqueur, such as Grand
  Marnier

1 Preheat a 350°F/180°C/Gas 4 oven.
Line a 12 × 9½ in (30 × 24 cm) Swiss
roll tin with greaseproof paper and
grease the paper.

2 With an electric mixer, beat the
egg yolks and sugar until thick.

3 ▲ Stir in the walnuts.

4 In another bowl, beat the egg
whites with the cream of tartar and
salt until they hold stiff peaks. Fold
gently but thoroughly into the
walnut mixture.

5 Pour the mixture into the prepared
tin and spread level with a spatula.
Bake for 15 minutes.

6 Run a knife along the inside edge to
loosen, then invert the cake onto a
sheet of greaseproof paper dusted with
icing sugar.

7 ▲ Peel off the baking paper. Roll
up the cake while it is still warm with
the help of the sugared paper. Set
aside to cool.

8 For the filling, whip the cream
until it holds soft peaks. Stir together
the caster sugar and orange rind, then
fold into the whipped cream. Add the
liqueur.

9 ▲ Gently unroll the cake. Spread
the inside with a layer of orange
whipped cream, then re-roll. Keep
refrigerated until ready to serve. Dust
the top with icing sugar just before
serving.

Chocolate Swiss Roll

SERVES 10

8 oz (225 g) plain chocolate
3 tbsp water
2 tbsp rum, brandy or strong coffee
7 eggs, separated
6 oz (170 g) caster sugar
1/8 tsp salt
12 fl oz (350 ml) whipping cream
icing sugar, for dusting

1 Preheat a 350°F/180°C/Gas 4 oven. Line a 15 × 13 in (38 × 33 cm) Swiss roll tin with greaseproof paper and grease the paper.

2 ▲ Combine the chocolate, water and rum or other flavouring in the top of a double boiler, or in a heatproof bowl set over hot water. Heat until melted. Set aside.

3 With an electric mixer, beat the egg yolks and sugar until thick.

4 ▲ Stir in the melted chocolate.

5 In another bowl, beat the egg whites and salt until they hold stiff peaks. Fold a large dollop of egg whites into the yolk mixture to lighten it, then carefully fold in the rest of the whites.

6 ▼ Pour the mixture into the pan; smooth evenly with a metal spatula.

7 Bake for 15 minutes. Remove from the oven, cover with greaseproof paper and a damp cloth. Let stand for 1–2 hours.

8 With an electric mixer, whip the cream until stiff. Set aside.

9 Run a knife along the inside edge to loosen, then invert the cake onto a sheet of greaseproof paper that has been dusted with icing sugar.

10 Peel off the baking paper. Spread with an even layer of whipped cream, then roll up the cake with the help of the sugared paper.

11 Refrigerate for several hours. Before serving, dust with an even layer of icing sugar.

Traditional Chocolate Cake

Serves 10

4 oz (115 g) plain chocolate

9 fl oz (275 ml) milk

7 oz (200 g) light brown sugar

1 egg yolk

9 oz (260 g) plain flour

1 tsp bicarbonate of soda

½ tsp salt

5 oz (140 g) butter or margarine, at room
  temperature

9 oz (260 g) caster sugar

3 eggs

1 tsp vanilla essence

For the icing

8 oz (225 g) plain chocolate

¼ tsp salt

6 fl oz (175 ml) soured cream

1 Preheat a 350°F/180°C/Gas 4 oven.
Line 2 × 8–9 in (20–23 cm) round
cake tins with greaseproof paper.

2 ▲ In a heatproof bowl set over a
pan of simmering water, or in a double
boiler, combine the chocolate, one-
third of the milk, the brown sugar and
egg yolk. Cook, stirring, until smooth
and thickened. Let cool.

3 ▲ Sift the flour, bicarbonate of
soda and salt into a bowl. Set aside.

4 ▲ With an electric mixer, cream
the butter or margarine with the caster
sugar until light and fluffy. Beat in the
whole eggs, one at a time. Mix in the
vanilla.

5 On low speed, beat the flour
mixture into the butter mixture
alternately with the remaining milk,
beginning and ending with flour.

6 ▲ Pour in the chocolate mixture
and mix until just combined.

7 Divide the cake mixture evenly
between the cake tins. Bake until a
skewer inserted in the centre comes
out clean, 35–40 minutes.

8 Let cool in the tins on wire racks
for 10 minutes, then unmould the
cakes from the tins onto the wire racks
and let cool completely.

9 ▲ For the icing, melt the
chocolate in a heatproof bowl set over
a pan of hot, not boiling, water, or in
the top of a double boiler. Remove the
bowl from the heat and stir in the salt
and soured cream. Let cool slightly.

10 ▲ Set 1 cake layer on a serving
plate and spread with one-third of the
icing. Place the second cake layer on
top. Spread the remaining icing all
over the top and sides of the cake,
swirling it to make a decorative finish.

Chocolate Frosted Layer Cake

SERVES 8

8 oz (225 g) butter or margarine, at room temperature
10¹/₂ oz (300 g) sugar
4 eggs, at room temperature, separated
2 teaspoons vanilla essence
13¹/₂ oz (385 g) plain flour
2 teaspoons baking powder
¹/₈ teaspoon salt
8 fl oz (250 ml) milk
FOR THE FROSTING
5 oz (140 g) plain chocolate
4 fl oz (125 ml) soured cream
¹/₈ teaspoon salt

1 Preheat a 350°F/180°C/Gas 4 oven. Line 2 8 in (20 cm) round cake tins with greaseproof paper and grease. Dust the tins with flour and shake to evenly distribute. Tap to dislodge excess flour.

2 With an electric mixer, cream the butter or margarine until soft. Gradually add the sugar and continue beating until light and fluffy.

3 ▲ Lightly beat the egg yolks, then mix into the creamed butter and sugar with the vanilla.

4 Sift the flour with the baking powder 3 times. Set aside.

5 In another bowl, beat the egg whites with the salt until they hold stiff peaks. Set aside.

6 ▲ Gently fold the dry ingredients into the butter mixture in 3 batches, alternating with the milk.

7 Add a large dollop of the whites and fold in to lighten the mixture. Carefully fold in the remaining whites until just blended.

8 Divide the batter between the tins and bake until the cakes pull away from the sides of the tins, for about 30 minutes. Let stand 5 minutes. Turn out and cool on a rack.

9 ▲ For the frosting, melt the chocolate in the top of a double boiler or a bowl set over hot water. When cool, stir in the soured cream and salt.

10 Sandwich the layers with frosting, then spread on the top and side.

Devil's Food Cake with Orange Frosting

SERVES 8–10

2 oz (55 g) unsweetened cocoa powder

6 fl oz (175 ml) boiling water

6 oz (170 g) butter, at room temperature

12 oz (350 g) dark brown sugar

3 eggs, at room temperature

10 oz (285 g) plain flour

1½ teaspoons bicarbonate of soda

¼ teaspoon baking powder

4 fl oz (125 ml) soured cream

orange rind strips, for decoration

FOR THE FROSTING

10½ oz (300 g) caster sugar

2 egg whites

4 tablespoons frozen orange juice concentrate

1 tablespoon lemon juice

grated rind of 1 orange

1 Preheat a 350°F/180°C/Gas 4 oven. Line 2 9 in (23 cm) cake tins with greaseproof paper and grease. In a bowl, mix the cocoa and water until smooth. Set aside.

2 With an electric mixer, cream the butter and sugar until light and fluffy. Add the eggs, 1 at a time, beating well after each addition.

3 ▲ When the cocoa mixture is lukewarm, add to the butter mixture.

4 ▼ Sift together the flour, soda and baking powder twice. Fold into the cocoa mixture in 3 batches, alternating with the soured cream.

5 Pour into the tins and bake until the cakes pull away from the sides of the tins, 30–35 minutes. Let stand for 15 minutes. Turn out onto a rack.

6 Thinly slice the orange rind strips. Blanch in boiling water for 1 minute.

7 ▲ For the frosting, place all the ingredients in the top of a double boiler or in a bowl set over hot water. With an electric mixer, beat until the mixture holds soft peaks. Continue beating off the heat until thick enough to spread.

8 Sandwich the cake layers with frosting, then spread over the top and side. Arrange the blanched orange rind strips on top of the cake.

Best-Ever Chocolate Sandwich

SERVES 12–14

4 oz (115 g) unsalted butter
4 oz (115 g) plain flour
2 oz (55 g) cocoa powder
1 tsp baking powder
1/8 tsp salt
6 eggs
8 oz (225 g) caster sugar
2 tsp vanilla essence
FOR THE ICING
8 oz (225 g) plain chocolate, chopped
3 oz (85 g) unsalted butter
3 eggs, separated
8 fl oz (250 ml) whipping cream
3 tbsp caster sugar

1 Preheat a 350°F/180°C/Gas 4 oven. Line 3 8 × 1 1/2 in (20 × 3 cm) round tins with greaseproof paper and grease.

2 ▲ Dust evenly with flour and spread with a brush. Set aside.

~ VARIATION ~

For a simpler icing, combine 8 fl oz (250 ml) whipping cream with 8 oz (225 g) finely chopped plain chocolate in a saucepan. Stir over a low heat until the chocolate has melted. Cool and whisk to spreading consistency.

---

3 ▲ Melt the butter over a low heat. With a spoon, skim off any foam that rises to the surface. Set aside.

4 ▲ Sift the flour, cocoa, baking powder and salt together 3 times and set aside.

5 Place the eggs and sugar in a large heatproof bowl set over a pan of hot water. With an electric mixer, beat until the mixture doubles in volume and is thick enough to leave a ribbon trail when the beaters are lifted, about 10 minutes. Add the vanilla.

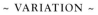

6 ▲ Sift over the dry ingredients in 3 batches, folding in carefully after each addition. Fold in the butter.

7 Divide the mixture between the tins and bake until the cakes pull away from the sides of the tin, about 25 minutes. Transfer to a rack.

8 For the icing, melt the chopped chocolate in the top of a double boiler, or in a heatproof bowl set over hot water.

9 ▲ Off the heat, stir in the butter and egg yolks. Return to a low heat and stir until thick. Remove from the heat and set aside.

10 Whip the cream until firm; set aside. In another bowl, beat the egg whites until stiff. Add the sugar and beat until glossy.

11 Fold the cream into the chocolate mixture, then carefully fold in the egg whites. Refrigerate for 20 minutes to thicken the icing.

12 ▲ Sandwich the cake layers with icing, stacking them carefully. Spread the remaining icing evenly over the top and sides of the cake.

Mississippi Mud Cake

SERVES 8–10

8oz (225g) plain flour

⅛ teaspoon salt

1 teaspoon baking powder

½ pint (300ml) strong brewed coffee

2fl oz (50ml) bourbon or brandy

5oz (150g) unsweetened chocolate

½lb (225g) butter or margarine

14oz (400g) caster sugar

2 eggs, at room temperature

1½ teaspoons vanilla essence

unsweetened cocoa powder

sweetened whipped cream or ice cream,
    for serving

1 Preheat the oven to 140°C/275°F/
Gas 1.

2 Sift the flour, salt and baking
powder together.

3 ▼ Combine the coffee, bourbon or
brandy, chocolate, and butter or
margarine in the top of a double
boiler. Heat until the chocolate and
butter have melted and the mixture is
smooth, stirring occasionally.

4 ▲ Pour the chocolate mixture into
a large bowl. Using an electric mixer
on low speed, gradually beat in the
sugar. Continue beating until the
sugar has dissolved.

5 Increase the speed to medium and
add the sifted dry ingredients. Mix
well, then beat in the eggs and vanilla
until thoroughly blended.

6 Pour the batter into a well-greased
5 pint (3 litre) ring mould that has
been dusted lightly with cocoa
powder. Bake until a skewer inserted
in the cake comes out clean, about
1 hour 20 minutes.

7 ▲ Leave to cool in the mould for
15 minutes, then unmould on to a
wire rack. Leave to cool completely.

8 When the cake is cold, dust it
lightly with cocoa powder. Serve with
sweetened whipped cream or ice
cream, if desired.

Blueberry Cake

SERVES 10

8oz (225g) plain flour
1 tablespoon baking powder
1 teaspoon salt
6oz (175g) butter or margarine, at room temperature
5oz (150g) granulated sugar
1 egg
8fl oz (250ml) milk
½ teaspoon grated lemon rind
8oz (225g) fresh or frozen blueberries, well drained
4oz (115g) icing sugar
2 tablespoons fresh lemon juice

1 Preheat a 180°C/350°F/Gas 4 oven.

2 ▲ Sift the flour with the baking powder and salt.

3 ▲ In a large bowl, beat the butter or margarine with the granulated sugar until light and fluffy. Beat in the egg and milk. Fold in the flour mixture, mixing well until evenly blended to a batter. Mix in the lemon rind.

4 ▼ Spread half the batter in a greased 13 × 9 × 2 in (33 × 23 × 5 cm) ovenproof dish. Sprinkle with 4oz (115g) of the berries. Top with the remaining batter and sprinkle with the rest of the berries. Bake until golden brown and a skewer inserted in the centre comes out clean, 35–45 minutes.

5 ▲ Mix the icing sugar gradually into the lemon juice to make a smooth glaze with a pourable consistency. Drizzle the glaze over the top of the warm cake and allow it to set before serving, still warm or at room temperature.

Rich Chocolate Nut Cake

SERVES 10

8 oz (225 g) butter
8 oz (225 g) plain chocolate
4 oz (115 g) cocoa powder
12 oz (350 g) caster sugar
6 eggs
3 fl oz (85 ml) brandy or cognac
8 oz (225 g) finely chopped hazelnuts
FOR THE GLAZE
2 oz (55 g) butter
5 oz (140 g) bitter cooking chocolate
2 tbsp milk
1 tsp vanilla essence

1 Preheat a 350°F/180°C/Gas 4 oven. Line a 9 × 2 in (23 × 5 cm) round tin with greaseproof paper and grease.

2 Melt the butter and chocolate together in the top of a double boiler, or in a heatproof bowl set over hot water. Set aside to cool.

3 ▼ Sift the cocoa into a bowl. Add the sugar and eggs and stir until just combined. Pour in the melted chocolate mixture and brandy.

4 Fold in three-quarters of the nuts, then pour the mixture into the prepared tin.

5 ▲ Set the tin inside a large tin and pour 1 in (2.5 cm) of hot water into the outer tin. Bake until the cake is firm to the touch, about 45 minutes. Let stand 15 minutes, then unmould and transfer to a cooling rack.

6 Wrap the cake in greaseproof paper and refrigerate for 6 hours.

7 For the glaze, combine the butter, chocolate, milk and vanilla in the top of a double boiler or in a heatproof bowl set over hot water, until melted.

8 Place a piece of greaseproof paper under the cake, then drizzle spoonfuls of glaze along the edge to drip down and coat the sides. Pour the remaining glaze on top of the cake.

9 ▲ Cover the sides of the cake with the remaining nuts, gently pressing them on with the palm of your hand.

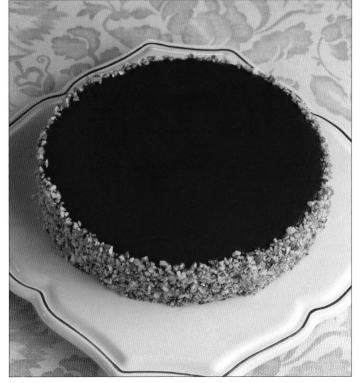

Chocolate Layer Cake

SERVES 8–10

4 oz (115 g) plain chocolate
6 oz (170 g) butter
1 lb (450 g) caster sugar
3 eggs
1 tsp vanilla essence
6 oz (170 g) plain flour
1 tsp baking powder
4 oz (115 g) chopped walnuts
FOR THE TOPPING
12 fl oz (350 ml) whipping cream
8 oz (225 g) plain chocolate
1 tbsp vegetable oil

1 Preheat a 350°F/180°C/Gas 4 oven. Line two 8 in (20 cm) cake tins, at least 1³/₄ in (4.5 cm) deep, with grease-proof paper and grease.

2 Melt the chocolate and butter together in the top of a double boiler, or in a heatproof bowl set over a saucepan of hot water.

3 ▲ Transfer to a mixing bowl and stir in the sugar. Add the eggs and vanilla and mix until well blended.

~ VARIATION ~

To make Chocolate Ice Cream Layer Cake, sandwich the cake layers with softened vanilla ice cream. Freeze before serving.

4 ▲ Sift over the flour and baking powder. Stir in the walnuts.

5 Divide the mixture between the prepared tins and spread level.

6 Bake until a skewer inserted in the centre comes out clean, for about 30 minutes. Let stand 10 minutes, then unmould and transfer to a rack.

7 When the cakes are cool, whip the cream until firm. With a long serrated knife, carefully slice each cake in half horizontally.

8 Sandwich the layers with some of the whipped cream and spread the remainder over the top and sides of the cake. Refrigerate until needed.

9 ▼ For the chocolate curls, melt the chocolate and oil in the top of a double boiler or a bowl set over hot water. Transfer to a non-porous surface. Spread to a ³/₈ in (1 cm) thick rectangle. Just before the chocolate sets, hold the blade of a straight knife at an angle to the chocolate and scrape across the surface to make curls. Place on top of the cake.

Sachertorte

SERVES 8–10

4 oz (115 g) plain chocolate
3 oz (85 g) unsalted butter, at room temperature
2 oz (55 g) sugar
4 eggs, separated
1 extra egg white
1/4 teaspoon salt
2 1/2 oz (70 g) plain flour, sifted
FOR THE TOPPING
5 tablespoons apricot jam
8 fl oz (250 ml) plus 1 tablespoon water
1/2 oz (15 g) unsalted butter
6 oz (170 g) plain chocolate
3 oz (85 g) sugar
ready-made chocolate decorating icing (optional)

1 Preheat the oven to 325°F/170°C/ Gas 3. Line a 9 × 2 in (23 × 5 cm) cake tin with greaseproof paper and grease.

2 ▲ Melt the chocolate in the top of a double boiler, or in a heatproof bowl set over hot water. Set aside.

3 With an electric mixer, cream the butter and sugar until light and fluffy. Stir in the chocolate.

4 ▲ Beat in the yolks, 1 at a time.

5 In another bowl, beat the egg whites with the salt until stiff.

6 ▲ Fold a dollop of whites into the chocolate mixture to lighten it. Fold in the remaining whites in 3 batches, alternating with the sifted flour.

7 ▲ Pour into the tin and bake until a cake tester comes out clean, about 45 minutes. Turn out onto a rack.

8 ▲ Meanwhile, melt the jam with 1 tablespoon of the water over low heat, then strain for a smooth consistency.

9 For the frosting, melt the butter and chocolate in the top of a double boiler or a bowl set over hot water.

10 ▲ In a heavy saucepan, dissolve the sugar in the remaining water over low heat. Raise the heat and boil until it reaches 225°F/107°C (thread stage) on a sugar thermometer. Immediately plunge the bottom of the pan into cold water for 1 minute. Pour into the chocolate mixture and stir to blend. Let cool for a few minutes.

11 To assemble, brush the warm jam over the cake. Starting in the centre, pour over the frosting and work outward in a circular movement. Tilt the rack to spread; use a palette knife to smooth the side of the cake. Leave to set overnight. If wished, decorate with chocolate icing.

Boston Cream Pie

SERVES 8

8oz (225g) plain flour

1 tablespoon baking powder

½ teaspoon salt

4oz (115g) butter, at room
    temperature

7oz (200g) granulated sugar

2 eggs

1 teaspoon vanilla essence

6fl oz (175ml) milk

FOR THE FILLING

8fl oz (250ml) milk

3 egg yolks

3½oz (90g) granulated sugar

1oz (25g) flour

½oz (15g) butter

1 tablespoon brandy or 1 teaspoon
    vanilla essence

FOR THE CHOCOLATE GLAZE

1oz (25g) plain chocolate

1oz (25g) butter or margarine

2oz (50g) icing sugar, plus extra
    for dusting

½ teaspoon vanilla essence

about 1 tablespoon hot water

1 Preheat the oven to 190°C/375°F/
Gas 5.

2 Grease two 8 × 2 in (20 × 5 cm)
round cake tins, and line the bottoms
with rounds of buttered greaseproof
paper.

3 Sift the flour with the baking
powder and salt.

4 Beat the butter and granulated
sugar together until light and fluffy.
Add the eggs one at a time, beating
well after each addition. Stir in the
vanilla. Add the milk and dry
ingredients alternately, mixing only
enough to blend thoroughly. Do not
over-beat the mixture.

5 Divide the cake mixture between
the prepared tins and spread it out
evenly. Bake until a skewer inserted
in the centre comes out clean, about
25 minutes.

6 Meanwhile, make the filling. Heat
the milk in a small saucepan to
boiling point. Remove from the heat.

7 ▲ In a heatproof mixing bowl,
beat the egg yolks until smooth.
Gradually add the granulated sugar
and continue beating until pale
yellow. Beat in the flour.

8 ▲ Pour the hot milk into the egg
yolk mixture in a steady stream, beating
constantly. When all the milk has
been added, place the bowl over
a pan of boiling water, or pour the
mixture into the top of a double
boiler. Heat, stirring constantly, until thickened.
Cook 2 minutes more, then remove
from the heat. Stir in the butter and
brandy or vanilla. Allow to cool.

9 ▲ When the cakes have cooled, use
a large sharp knife to slice off the
domed top to make a flat surface.
Place one cake on a serving plate and
spread on the filling in a thick layer.
Set the other cake on top, cut side
down. Smooth the edge of the filling
layer so it is flush with the sides of the
cake layers.

10 ▲ For the glaze, melt the
chocolate with the butter or
margarine in the top of a double
boiler. When smooth, remove from
the heat and beat in the sugar to
make a thick paste. Add the vanilla.
Beat in a little of the hot water. If the
glaze does not have a spreadable
consistency, add more water,
1 teaspoon at a time.

11 Spread the glaze evenly over the
top of the cake, using a palette knife.
Dust the top with icing sugar. Because
of the custard filling, refrigerate any
leftover cake.

Caramel Layer Cake

SERVES 8–10

10 oz (285 g) plain flour
1¹/₂ teaspoons baking powder
6 oz (170 g) butter, at room temperature
5¹/₂ oz (150 g) caster sugar
4 eggs, at room temperature, beaten
1 teaspoon vanilla essence
8 tablespoons milk
whipped cream, for decorating
caramel threads, for decorating (optional, see below)

FOR THE FROSTING

10¹/₂ oz (300 g) dark brown sugar
8 fl oz (250 ml) milk
1 oz (30 g) unsalted butter
3–5 tablespoons whipping cream

1 Preheat a 350°F/180°C/Gas 4 oven. Line 2 8 in (20 cm) cake tins with greaseproof paper and grease lightly.

2 ▲ Sift the flour and baking powder together 3 times. Set aside.

~ COOK'S TIP ~

To make caramel threads, combine 2¹/₂ oz (70 g) sugar and 2 fl oz (65 ml) water in a heavy saucepan. Boil until light brown. Dip the pan in cold water to halt cooking. Trail from a spoon on an oiled baking sheet.

3 With an electric mixer, cream the butter and caster sugar until light and fluffy.

4 ▲ Slowly mix in the beaten eggs. Add the vanilla. Fold in the flour mixture, alternating with the milk.

5 ▲ Divide the batter between the prepared tins and spread evenly, hollowing out the centres slightly.

6 Bake until the cakes pull away from the sides of the tin, about 30 minutes. Let stand 5 minutes, then turn out and cool on a rack.

7 ▲ For the frosting, combine the brown sugar and milk in a saucepan.

8 Bring to the boil, cover and cook for 3 minutes. Remove lid and continue to boil, without stirring, until the mixture reaches 238°F/119°C (soft ball stage) on a sugar thermometer.

9 ▲ Immediately remove the pan from the heat and add the butter, but do not stir it in. Let cool until lukewarm, then beat until the mixture is smooth and creamy.

10 Stir in enough cream to obtain a spreadable consistency. If necessary, refrigerate to thicken more.

11 ▲ Spread a layer of frosting on top of one cake. Sandwich with the second cake, then spread the top and sides with the rest of the frosting and smooth the surface.

12 To decorate, pipe whipped cream rosettes around the edge. If using, place a mound of caramel threads in the centre before serving.

Whiskey Cake

MAKES 1 LOAF

6 oz (170 g) chopped walnuts
3 oz (85 g) raisins, chopped
3 oz (85 g) currants
4 oz (115 g) plain flour
1 tsp baking powder
1/4 tsp salt
4 oz (115 g) butter
8 oz (225 g) caster sugar
3 eggs, at room temperature, separated
1 tsp grated nutmeg
1/2 tsp ground cinnamon
3 fl oz (85 ml) Irish whiskey or bourbon
icing sugar, for dusting

1 ▼ Preheat a 325°F/170°C/Gas 3 oven. Line a 9 × 5 in (23 × 13 cm) loaf tin with greaseproof paper. Grease the paper and sides of the pan.

2 ▲ Place the walnuts, raisins, and currants in a bowl. Sprinkle over 2 tablespoons of the flour, mix and set aside. Sift together the remaining flour, baking powder and salt.

3 ▲ Cream the butter and sugar until light and fluffy. Beat in the egg yolks.

4 Mix the nutmeg, cinnamon and whiskey. Fold into the butter mixture, alternating with the flour mixture.

5 ▲ In another bowl, beat the egg whites until stiff. Fold into the whiskey mixture until just blended. Fold in the walnut mixture.

6 Bake until a skewer inserted in the centre comes out clean, about 1 hour. Let cool in the pan. Dust with icing sugar over a template.

American Berry Shortcake

SERVES 8

½ pint (300 ml) whipping cream
1 oz (30 g) icing sugar, sifted
1½ lb (700 g) strawberries or mixed berries, halved or sliced if large
2 oz (55 g) caster sugar, or to taste
FOR THE SHORTCAKE
10 oz (300 g) plain flour
2 teaspoons baking powder
2½ oz (75 g) caster sugar
4 oz (115 g) butter
5 tablespoons milk
1 size-1 egg

1 Preheat a 450°F/230°C/Gas 8 oven. Grease an 8 in (20 cm) round cake tin.

2 For the shortcake, sift the flour, baking powder and sugar into a bowl. Add the butter and rub in until the mixture resembles fine crumbs. Combine the milk and egg. Add to the crumb mixture and stir just until evenly mixed to a soft dough.

3 Put the dough in the prepared tin and pat out to an even layer. Bake for 15–20 minutes or until a wooden skewer inserted in the centre comes out clean. Leave to cool slightly.

5 Put the berries in a bowl. Sprinkle with the caster sugar and toss together lightly. Cover and set aside for the berries to give up some juice.

6 ▼ Remove the cooled shortcake from the tin. With a long, serrated knife, split the shortcake horizontally into two equal layers.

4 ▲ Whip the cream until it starts to thicken. Add the icing sugar and continue whipping until the cream will hold soft peaks.

7 ▲ Put the bottom layer on a serving plate. Top with half of the berries and most of the cream. Set the second layer on top and press down gently. Spoon the remaining berries over the top layer (or serve them separately) and add the remaining cream in small, decorative dollops.

Lady Baltimore Cake

Serves 8–10

10 oz (285 g) plain flour
2¹/₂ teaspoons baking powder
¹/₂ teaspoon salt
4 eggs
12 oz (350 g) sugar
grated rind of 1 large orange
8 fl oz (250 ml) fresh orange juice
8 fl oz (250 ml) vegetable oil
18 pecan halves, for decorating
For the frosting
2 egg whites
12 oz (350 g) sugar
5 tablespoons cold water
¹/₄ teaspoon cream of tartar
1 teaspoon vanilla essence
2 oz (55 g) pecans, finely chopped
3 oz (85 g) raisins, chopped
3 dried figs, finely chopped

1 Preheat the oven to 350°F/180°C/ Gas 4. Grease 2 9 in (23 cm) round cake tins and line with greaseproof paper. Grease the paper. In a bowl, sift together the flour, baking powder and salt. Set aside.

2 ▲ With an electric mixer, beat the eggs and sugar until thick and lemon-coloured. Beat in the orange rind and juice, then the oil.

3 On low speed, beat in the flour mixture in 3 batches. Divide the cake mixture between the tins.

4 ▲ Bake until a skewer inserted in the centre comes out clean, about 30 minutes. Leave to stand for 15 minutes, then run a knife around the inside of the cakes and transfer them to racks to cool completely.

5 ▲ For the frosting, combine the egg whites, sugar, water and cream of tartar in the top of a double boiler, or in a heatproof bowl set over boiling water. With an electric mixer, beat until glossy and thick. Off the heat, add the vanilla essence and continue beating until thick. Fold in the pecans, raisins and figs.

6 Spread a layer of frosting on top of one cake. Sandwich with the second cake, then spread the top and sides with the rest of the frosting. Arrange the pecan halves on top.

Raspberry-Hazelnut Meringue Cake

SERVES 8

5 oz (140 g) hazelnuts
4 egg whites
1/8 teaspoon salt
7 oz (200 g) sugar
1/2 teaspoon vanilla essence
FOR THE FILLING
10 fl oz (300 ml) whipping cream
1 lb 8 oz (700 g) raspberries

1 Preheat a 350°F/180°C/Gas 4 oven. Line the bottom of 2 8 in (20 cm) cake tins with greaseproof paper and grease.

2 Spread the hazelnuts on a baking sheet and bake until lightly toasted, about 8 minutes. Let cool slightly.

3 ▲ Rub the hazelnuts vigorously in a clean tea towel to remove most of the skins.

4 Grind the nuts in a food processor, blender, or coffee grinder until they are the consistency of coarse sand.

5 Reduce oven to 300°F/150°C/Gas 2.

6 With an electric mixer, beat the egg whites and salt until they hold stiff peaks. Beat in 2 tablespoons of the sugar, then fold in the remaining sugar, a few tablespoons at a time, with a rubber scraper. Fold in the vanilla and the hazelnuts.

7 ▲ Divide the batter between the prepared tins and spread level.

8 Bake for 1 1/4 hours. If the meringues brown too quickly, protect with a sheet of foil. Let stand 5 minutes, then carefully run a knife around the inside edge of the tins to loosen. Turn out onto a rack to cool.

9 For the filling, whip the cream just until firm.

10 ▲ Spread half the cream in an even layer on one meringue round and top with half the raspberries.

11 Top with the other meringue round. Spread the remaining cream on top and arrange the remaining raspberries over the cream. Refrigerate for 1 hour to facilitate cutting.

Classic Cheesecake

SERVES 8

2 oz (55 g) digestive biscuits, crushed

2 lb (900 g) cream cheese, at room temperature

8³/4 oz (240 g) sugar

grated rind of 1 lemon

3 tablespoons lemon juice

1 teapoon vanilla essence

4 eggs, at room temperature

1 Preheat the oven to 325°F/170°C/Gas 3. Grease an 8 in (20 cm) springform tin. Place on a round of foil 4–5 in (10–12.5 cm) larger than the diameter of the tin. Press it up the sides to seal tightly.

2 Sprinkle the crushed biscuits in the base of the tin. Press to form an even layer.

3 With an electric mixer, beat the cream cheese until smooth. Add the sugar, lemon rind and juice, and vanilla, and beat until blended. Beat in the eggs, 1 at a time. Beat just enough to blend thoroughly.

4 ▲ Pour into the prepared tin. Set the tin in a larger baking tray and place in the oven. Pour enough hot water in the outer tray to come 1 in (2.5 cm) up the side of the tin.

5 Bake until the top of the cake is golden brown, about 1¹/2 hours. Let cool in the tin.

6 ▼ Run a knife around the edge to loosen, then remove the rim of the tin. Refrigerate for at least 4 hours before serving.

Chocolate Cheesecake

SERVES 10–12

10 oz (285 g) plain chocolate

2 lb 8 oz (1.2 kg) cream cheese, at room temperature

7 oz (200 g) sugar

2 teaspoons vanilla essence

4 eggs, at room temperature

6 fl oz (175 ml) soured cream

1 tablespoon cocoa powder

FOR THE BASE

7 oz (200 g) chocolate biscuits, crushed

3 oz (85 g) butter, melted

¹/2 teaspoon ground cinnamon

1 Preheat a 350°F/180°C/Gas 4 oven. Grease the bottom and sides of a 9 × 3 in (23 × 7.5 cm) springform tin.

2 ▲ For the base, mix the crushed biscuits with the butter and cinnamon. Press evenly onto the bottom of the tin.

3 Melt the chocolate in the top of a double boiler, or in a heatproof bowl set over hot water. Set aside.

4 Beat the cream cheese until smooth, then beat in the sugar and vanilla. Add the eggs, 1 at a time.

5 Stir the soured cream into the cocoa powder to form a paste. Add to the cream cheese mixture. Stir in the melted chocolate.

6 ▼ Pour into the crust. Bake for 1 hour. Let cool in the tin; remove rim. Refrigerate before serving.

Classic Cheesecake (top), Chocolate Cheesecake

Lemon Mousse Cheesecake

SERVES 10–12

2¹/₂ lb (1.2 kg) cream cheese, at room temperature
12 oz (350 g) caster sugar
1¹/₂ oz (45 g) plain flour
4 eggs, at room temperature, separated
4 fl oz (125 ml) fresh lemon juice
grated rind of 2 lemons
4 oz (115 g) digestive biscuits, crushed

1 Preheat a 325°F/170°C/Gas 3 oven. Line a 10 × 2 in (25 × 5 cm) round cake tin with greaseproof paper and grease the paper.

2 With an electric mixer, beat the cream cheese until smooth. Gradually add 10 oz (285 g) of the sugar, and beat until light. Beat in the flour.

3 ▲ Add the egg yolks, and lemon juice and rind, and beat until smooth and well blended.

4 In another bowl, beat the egg whites until they hold soft peaks. Add the remaining sugar and beat until stiff and glossy.

5 ▲ Add the egg whites to the cheese mixture and gently fold in.

6 Pour the mixture into the prepared tin, then place the tin in a larger baking tin. Place in the oven and pour hot water in the outer tin to come 1 in (2.5 cm) up the side.

7 Bake until golden, 60–65 minutes. Let cool in the pan on a rack. Cover and refrigerate for at least 4 hours.

8 To unmould, run a knife around the inside edge. Place a flat plate, bottom-side up, over the pan and invert onto the plate. Smooth the top with a metal spatula.

9 ▲ Sprinkle the biscuits over the top in an even layer, pressing down slightly to make a top crust.

10 To serve, cut slices with a sharp knife dipped in hot water.

Marbled Cheesecake

SERVES 10

2 oz (55 g) unsweetened cocoa powder

5 tablespoons hot water

2 lb (900 g) cream cheese, at room
temperature

7 oz (200 g) sugar

4 eggs

1 teaspoon vanilla essence

2^1/$_2$ oz (70 g) digestive biscuits, crushed

1 Preheat a 350°F/180°C/Gas 4 oven.
Line an 8 × 3 in (20 × 8 cm) cake tin
with greaseproof paper and grease.

2 Sift the cocoa powder into a bowl.
Pour over the hot water and stir to
dissolve. Set aside.

3 With an electric mixer, beat the
cheese until smooth and creamy. Add
the sugar and beat to incorporate.
Beat in the eggs, one at a time. Do not
overmix.

4 Divide the mixture evenly between
2 bowls. Stir the chocolate mixture
into one, then add the vanilla to the
remaining mixture.

5 ▲ Pour a cupful of the plain
mixture into the centre of the tin;
it will spread out into an even layer.
Slowly pour over a cupful of chocolate
mixture in the centre.

6 ▲ Repeat alternating cupfuls of
the batters in a circular pattern until
both are used up.

7 Set the tin in a larger baking tray
and pour in hot water to come 1^1/$_2$ in
(3 cm) up the sides of the cake tin.

8 Bake until the top of the cake is
golden, about 1^1/$_2$ hours. It will rise
during baking but will sink later. Let
cool in the tin on a rack.

9 To turn out, run a knife around the
inside edge. Place a flat plate, bottom-
side up, over the tin and invert onto
the plate.

10 ▼ Sprinkle the crushed biscuits
evenly over the base, gently place
another plate over them, and invert
again. Cover and refrigerate for at
least 3 hours, or overnight. To serve,
cut slices with a sharp knife dipped in
hot water.

Chocolate Fairy Cakes

MAKES 24

4 oz (115 g) good-quality plain
   chocolate, cut into small pieces

1 tablespoon water

10 oz (300 g) plain flour

1 teaspoon baking powder

½ teaspoon bicarbonate of soda

pinch of salt

10 oz (300 g) caster sugar

6 oz (170 g) butter or margarine, at room
   temperature

¼ pint (150 ml) milk

1 teaspoon vanilla essence

3 eggs

1 recipe quantity buttercream, flavoured
   to taste

1 Preheat a 350°F/180°C/Gas 4 oven.
Grease and flour 24 deep bun tins,
about 2¼ in (6.5 cm) in diameter, or
use paper cases in the tins.

2 ▲ Put the chocolate and water in a
bowl set over a pan of almost
simmering water. Heat until melted
and smooth, stirring. Remove from
the heat and leave to cool.

3 Sift the flour, baking powder,
bicarbonate of soda, salt and sugar
into a large bowl. Add the chocolate
mixture, butter, milk and vanilla
essence.

4 ▲ With an electric mixer on
medium-low speed, beat until
smoothly blended. Increase the speed
to high and beat for 2 minutes. Add
the eggs and beat for 2 minutes.

5 Divide the mixture evenly among
the prepared bun tins.

6 Bake for 20–25 minutes or until a
skewer inserted into the centre of a
cake comes out clean. Cool in the tins
for 10 minutes, then turn out to cool
completely on a wire rack.

7 ▼ Ice the top of each cake with
buttercream, swirling it into a peak in
the centre.

Chocolate Orange Sponge Drops

MAKES ABOUT 14

2 eggs

2 oz (55 g) caster sugar

½ teaspoon grated orange zest

2 oz (55 g) plain flour

4 tablespoons fine shred orange marmalade

1½ oz (45 g) plain chocolate, cut into small pieces

1 Preheat a 400°F/200°C/Gas 6 oven. Line 3 baking sheets with baking parchment.

2 ▲ Put the eggs and sugar in a large bowl and set over a pan of just simmering water. Whisk until the mixture is thick and pale.

3 ▲ Remove the bowl from the pan of water and continue whisking until the mixture is cool. Whisk in the grated orange zest.

4 Sift the flour over the whisked mixture and fold it in gently with a rubber spatula.

5 ▲ Using a dessertspoon, put spoonfuls of the mixture on the prepared baking sheets, leaving space around each spoonful to allow for spreading. The mixture will make 28–30 drops.

6 Bake for about 8 minutes or until golden. Cool for a few minutes on the baking sheets, then transfer to a wire rack to cool completely.

7 Sandwich pairs of sponge drops together with the orange marmalade.

8 ▼ Melt the chocolate in a double saucepan over simmering water until smooth. Using a small spoon, drizzle chocolate over the tops of the sponge drops, or pipe it in fine lines using a small greaseproof paper piping bag. Leave to set before serving.

Iced Fancies

MAKES 16

4 oz (115 g) butter, at room temperature
8 oz (225 g) caster sugar
2 eggs, at room temperature
6 oz (170 g) plain flour
¼ tsp salt
1½ tsp baking powder
4 fl oz (125 ml) plus 1 tbsp milk
1 tsp vanilla essence
FOR ICING AND DECORATING
2 large egg whites
14 oz (400 g) sifted icing sugar
1–2 drops glycerine
juice of 1 lemon
food colourings
hundreds and thousands, for decorating
crystallized lemon and orange slices, for decorating

1 Preheat a 375°F/190°C/Gas 5 oven.

2 ▲ Line 16 bun-tray cups with fluted paper baking cases, or grease.

~ COOK'S TIP ~

Ready-made cake decorating products are widely available, and may be used, if preferred, instead of the recipes given for icing and decorating. Coloured icing in ready-to-pipe tubes is useful.

3 With an electric mixer, cream the butter and sugar until light and fluffy. Add the eggs, 1 at a time, beating well after each addition.

4 Sift together the flour, salt and baking powder. Stir into the butter mixture, alternating with the milk. Stir in the vanilla.

5 ▲ Fill the cups half-full and bake until the tops spring back when touched lightly, about 20 minutes. Let the cakes stand in the tray for 5 minutes, then unmould and transfer to a rack to cool completely.

6 For the icing, beat the egg whites until stiff but not dry. Gradually add the sugar, glycerine and lemon juice, and continue beating for 1 minute. The consistency should be spreadable. If necessary, thin with a little water or add more sifted icing sugar.

7 ▲ Divide the icing between several bowls and tint with food colourings. Spread different coloured icings over the cooled cakes.

8 ▲ Decorate the cakes as wished, with sugar decorations such as hundreds and thousands.

9 ▲ Other decorations include crystallized orange and lemon slices. Cut into small pieces and arrange on top of the cakes. Alternatively, use other suitable sweets.

10 ▲ To make freehand iced decorations, fill paper piping bags with different colour icings. Pipe on faces, or make other designs.

Heart Cake

MAKES 1 CAKE

8 oz (225 g) butter or margarine, at room temperature
8 oz (225 g) caster sugar
4 eggs, at room temperature
6 oz (170 g) plain flour
1 tsp baking powder
1/2 tsp bicarbonate of soda
2 tbsp milk
1 tsp vanilla essence
FOR ICING AND DECORATING
3 egg whites
12 oz (350 g) caster sugar
2 tbsp cold water
2 tbsp fresh lemon juice
1/4 tsp cream of tartar
pink food colouring
3–4 oz (85–115 g) icing sugar

1 Preheat a 350°F/180°C/Gas 4 oven. Line an 8 in (20 cm) heart-shaped tin with greaseproof paper and grease.

2 ▲ With an electric mixer, cream the butter or margarine and sugar until light and fluffy. Add the eggs, 1 at a time, beating thoroughly after each addition.

3 Sift the flour, baking powder and baking soda together. Fold the dry ingredients into the butter mixture in 3 batches, alternating with the milk. Stir in the vanilla.

4 ▲ Spoon the mixture into the prepared tin and bake until a skewer inserted in the centre comes out clean, 35–40 minutes. Let the cake stand in the tin for 5 minutes, then unmould and transfer to a rack to cool completely.

5 For the icing, combine 2 of the egg whites, the caster sugar, water, lemon juice and cream of tartar in the top of a double boiler or in a bowl set over simmering water. With an electric mixer, beat until thick and holding soft peaks, about 7 minutes. Remove from the heat and continue beating until the mixture is thick enough to spread. Tint the icing with the pink food colouring.

6 ▲ Put the cake on a board, about 12 in (30 cm) square, covered in foil or in paper suitable for contact with food. Spread the icing evenly on the cake. Smooth the top and sides. Leave to set for 3–4 hours, or overnight.

7 ▲ For the paper piping bags, fold an 11 × 8 in (28 × 20 cm) sheet of greaseproof paper in half diagonally, then cut into 2 pieces along the fold mark. Roll over the short side, so that it meets the right-angled corner and forms a cone. To form the piping bag, hold the cone in place with one hand, wrap the point of the long side of the triangle around the cone, and tuck inside, folding over twice to secure. Snip a hole in the pointed end and slip in a small metal piping nozzle to extend about 1/4 in (5 mm).

8 For the piped decorations, place 1 tablespoon of the remaining egg white in a bowl and whisk until frothy. Gradually beat in enough icing sugar to make a stiff mixture suitable for piping.

9 ▲ Spoon into a paper piping bag to half-fill. Fold over the top and squeeze to pipe decorations on the top and sides of the cake.

Snake Cake

SERVES 10–12

8 oz (225 g) butter or margarine, at room temperature

grated rind and juice of 1 small orange

8 oz (225 g) sugar

4 eggs, at room temperature, separated

6 oz (170 g) plain flour

1 teaspoon baking powder

pinch of salt

FOR THE ICING AND DECORATING

1 oz (30 g) butter, at room temperature

12 oz (350 g) icing sugar

5 oz (140 g) plain chocolate

pinch of salt

4 fl oz (125 ml) soured cream

1 egg white

green and blue food colourings

1 Preheat the oven to 375°F/190°C/ Gas 5. Grease 2 8½ oz (22 cm) ring tins and dust them with flour.

2 Cream the butter or margarine, orange rind and sugar until light. Beat in the egg yolks, 1 at a time.

3 Sift the flour and baking powder. Fold into the butter mixture, alternating with the orange juice.

4 ▲ In another bowl, beat the egg whites and salt until stiff.

5 Fold a large dollop of the egg whites into the creamed butter mixture to lighten it, then gently fold in the remaining whites.

6 Divide the mixture between the prepared tins and bake until a skewer inserted in the centre comes out clean, about 25 minutes. Leave to stand for 5 minutes, then turn out on to a wire rack to cool.

7 Prepare a board, 24 × 8 in (60 × 20 cm), covered in paper suitable for contact with food, or in foil.

8 ▲ Cut the cakes into 3 even pieces. Trim to level the flat side, if necessary, and shape the head by cutting off wedges from the front. Shape the tail in the same way.

9 ▲ For the buttercream, mix the butter with 1½ oz (45 g) of the icing sugar. Use to join the cake sections and arrange on the board.

10 ▲ For the chocolate icing, melt the chocolate. Stir in the salt and soured cream. When cool, spread over the cake and smooth the surface.

11 ▲ For the decoration, beat the egg white until frothy. Add enough of the remaining icing sugar to obtain a thick mixture. Divide among several bowls and add food colourings.

12 ▲ Fill paper piping bags with icing and pipe decorations along the top of the cake.

Sun Cake

SERVES 10–12

4 oz (115 g) unsalted butter
6 eggs
8 oz (225 g) caster sugar
4 oz (115 g) plain flour
1/2 tsp salt
1 tsp vanilla essence
FOR ICING AND DECORATING
1 oz (30 g) unsalted butter, at room temperature
1 lb (450 g) sifted icing sugar
4 fl oz (125 ml) apricot jam
2 tbsp water
2 large egg whites
1–2 drops glycerine
juice of 1 lemon
yellow and orange food colourings

1 Preheat a 350°F/180°C/Gas 4 oven. Line 28 × 2 in (20 × 5 cm) round cake tins, then grease and flour.

2 In a saucepan, melt the butter over very low heat. Skim off any foam that rises to the surface, then set aside.

3 ▲ Place a heatproof bowl over a saucepan of hot water. Add the eggs and sugar. Beat with an electric mixer until the mixture doubles in volume and is thick enough to leave a ribbon trail when the beaters are lifted, 8–10 minutes.

4 Sift the flour and salt together 3 times. Sift over the egg mixture in 3 batches, folding in well after each addition. Fold in the melted butter and vanilla.

5 Divide the mixture between the tins. Level the surfaces and bake until the cakes shrink slightly from the sides of the tins, 25–30 minutes. Let stand 5 minutes, then unmould and transfer to a cooling rack.

6 Prepare a board, 16 in (40 cm) square, covered in paper suitable for contact with food, or in foil.

7 ▲ For the sunbeams, cut one of the cakes into 8 equal wedges. Cut away a rounded piece from the base of each so that they fit nearly up against the sides of the whole cake.

8 ▲ For the butter icing, mix the butter and 1 oz (30 g) of the icing sugar. Use to attach the sunbeams.

9 ▲ Melt the jam with the water and brush over the cake. Place on the board and straighten, if necessary.

10 ▲ For the icing, beat the egg whites until stiff but not dry. Gradually add 14 oz (400 g) icing sugar, the glycerine and lemon juice, and continue beating for 1 minute. If necessary, thin with water or thicken with a little more sugar. Tint with yellow food colouring and spread over the cake.

11 ▲ Divide the remaining icing in half and tint with more food colouring to obtain bright yellow and orange. Pipe decorative zigzags on the sunbeams and a face in the middle.

Jack-O'-Lantern Cake

SERVES 8–10

6 oz (170 g) plain flour

2¹/₂ teaspoons baking powder

pinch of salt

4 oz (115 g) butter, at room
   temperature

8 oz (225 g) sugar

3 egg yolks, at room temperature,
   well beaten

1 teaspoon grated lemon rind

6 fl oz (175 ml) milk

FOR THE CAKE COVERING

1 lb 4 oz–1 lb 8 oz (565–700 g) icing
   sugar

2 egg whites

2 tablespoons liquid glucose

orange and black food colourings

1 Preheat the oven to 375°F/190°C/
Gas 5. Line an 8 in (20 cm) round
cake tin with greaseproof paper
and grease.

2 Sift together the flour, baking
powder and salt. Set aside.

3 With an electric mixer, cream the
butter and sugar until light and fluffy.
Gradually beat in the egg yolks, then
add the lemon rind. Fold in the flour
mixture in 3 batches, alternating
with the milk.

4 Spoon the mixture into the
prepared tin. Bake until a skewer
inserted in the centre comes out
clean, about 35 minutes. Leave to
stand, then turn out on to a rack.

~ COOK'S TIP ~

If preferred, use ready-made
roll-out cake covering,
available at cake decorating
supply shops. Knead in food
colouring, if required.

5 For the icing, sift 1 lb 4 oz (565 g)
of the icing sugar into a bowl. Make
a well in the centre, add 1 egg white,
the glucose and orange food colouring.
Stir until a dough forms.

6 ▲ Transfer to a clean work
surface dusted with icing sugar and
knead briefly.

7 ▲ Carefully roll out the orange
cake covering to a thin sheet.

8 ▲ Place the sheet on top of the
cooled cake and smooth the sides.
Trim the excess icing and reserve.

9 ▲ From the trimmings, cut shapes
for the top. Tint the remaining cake
covering trimmings with black food
colouring. Roll out thinly and cut
shapes for the face.

10 ▲ Brush the undersides with
water and arrange the face on top of
the cake.

11 ▲ Place 1 tablespoon of the
remaining egg white in a bowl and
stir in enough icing sugar to make a
thick icing. Tint with black food
colouring, fill a paper piping bag and
complete the decoration.

Stars and Stripes Cake

SERVES 20

8 oz (225 g) butter or margarine, at room temperature
8 oz (225 g) dark brown sugar
8 oz (225 g) granulated sugar
5 eggs, at room temperature
10 oz (285 g) plain flour
2 teaspoons baking powder
1 teaspoon bicarbonate of soda
1 teaspoon ground cinnamon
1 teaspoon ground ginger
1/2 teaspoon ground allspice
1/4 teaspoon ground cloves
1/4 teaspoon salt
12 fl oz (350 ml) buttermilk
3 oz (85 g) raisins
FOR THE CAKE COVERING
1 oz (30 g) butter
2 lb 4 oz–2 lb 10 oz (1–1.3 kg) icing sugar
3 egg whites
4 tablespoons liquid glucose
red and blue food colourings

1 Preheat the oven to 350°F/180°C/ Gas 4. Line a 12 × 9 in (30 × 23 cm) baking tin with greaseproof paper and lightly grease.

2 With an electric mixer, cream the butter or margarine and sugars until light and fluffy. Gradually beat in the eggs, 1 at a time, beating well after each addition.

3 Sift together the flour, baking powder, bicarbonate of soda, spices and salt. Fold into the butter mixture in 3 batches, alternating with the buttermilk. Stir in the raisins.

4 Pour the mixture into the prepared tin and bake until the cake springs back when touched lightly, about 35 minutes. Leave to stand for 10 minutes, then turn out on to a wire rack.

5 Make buttercream for assembling the cake by mixing the butter with 1 1/2 oz (45 g) of the icing sugar.

6 ▲ When the cake is cool, cut a curved shape from the top.

7 ▲ Attach it to the bottom of the cake with the buttercream.

8 Prepare a board, about 16 × 12 in (40 × 30 cm), covered in paper suitable for contact with food, or in foil. Transfer the cake to the board.

9 For the cake covering, sift 2 lb 4 oz (1 kg) of the icing sugar into a bowl. Add 2 of the egg whites and the liquid glucose. Stir until the mixture forms a dough.

10 Cover and set aside half of the covering. On a clean work surface lightly dusted with icing sugar, roll out the remaining covering to a sheet. Carefully transfer to the cake. Smooth the sides and trim any excess from the bottom edges.

11 ▲ Tint one quarter of the remaining covering blue and tint the rest red. Roll out the blue to a thin sheet and cut out the background for the stars. Place on the cake.

12 ▲ Roll out the red covering, cut out stripes and place on the cake.

13 ▲ For the stars, mix 1 tablespoon of the egg white with just enough icing sugar to thicken. Pipe small stars on to a sheet of greaseproof paper and leave to set. When dry, peel them off and place on the blue background.

LOW-FAT CAKES & BAKES

ALL THE CAKES AND BAKES IN THIS
CHAPTER ARE LOW IN FAT, IN MANY
CASES CONTAIN LITTLE OR NO
EGGS, AND OFTEN SUGAR IS
REDUCED BY USING FRUITS TO
SWEETEN THE MIXTURE.
EVERYONE WILL LOVE THESE
BAKED GOODS – THEY'RE BURSTING
WITH FLAVOUR AND SUITED TO
ALL OCCASIONS.

Spiced Apple Cake

Grated apple and chopped dates give this cake a natural sweetness.

SERVES 8

8 oz (225 g) self-raising
  wholemeal flour

1 teaspoon (5 ml) baking powder

2 teaspoons (10 ml) ground
  cinnamon

6 oz (175 g) chopped dates

3 oz (75 g) light muscovado sugar

1 tablespoon (15 ml) pear and
  apple spread

4 fl oz (120 ml) apple juice

2 eggs

6 tablespoons (90 ml) sunflower oil

2 eating apples, cored and grated

1 tablespoon (15 ml) chopped
  walnuts

1 ▲ Preheat the oven to 180°C/
350°F/Gas 4. Grease and line a deep
round 8 in (20 cm) cake tin. Sift the
flour, baking powder and cinnamon
into a mixing bowl, then mix in the
dates and make a well in the centre.

2 ▲ Mix the sugar with the pear and
apple spread in a small bowl.
Gradually stir in the apple juice. Add
to the dry ingredients with the eggs,
oil and grated apples. Mix thoroughly.

3 ▲ Spoon the mixture into the
prepared cake tin, sprinkle liberally
with the walnuts and bake for 60–65
minutes or until a skewer inserted
into the centre of the cake comes out
clean. Transfer to a wire rack, remove
the lining paper and leave to cool.

NUTRITION NOTES
Per portion

Energy	331Kcals/13895kJ
Fat	11.41g
Saturated Fat	1.68g
Cholesterol	48.13mg
Fibre	2.5g

Spiced Date and Walnut Cake

A classic flavour combination, which makes a very easy low-fat, high-fibre cake.

1 Preheat the oven to 180°C/350°F/ Gas 4. Grease and line a 2 lb (900 g) loaf tin with greaseproof paper.

2 ▲ Sift together the flour and spice, adding back any bran from the sieve. Stir in the dates and walnuts.

3 ▲ Mix the oil, sugar and milk, then stir evenly into the dry ingredients.

4 ▲ Spoon into the prepared tin and arrange the walnut halves on top. Bake the cake for about 45–50 minutes, or until golden brown and firm. Turn out the cake, remove the lining paper and leave to cool.

SERVES 10

11 oz (300 g) wholemeal self-raising flour
2 teaspoons (10 ml) mixed spice
5 oz (150 g) chopped dates
2 oz (50 g) chopped walnuts
4 tablespoons (60 ml) sunflower oil
4 oz (115 g) dark muscovado sugar
½ pint (300 ml) skimmed milk
walnut halves, to decorate

NUTRITION NOTES
Per portion
Energy	265Kcals/1114kJ
Fat	9.27g
Saturated Fat	1.14g
Cholesterol	0.6mg
Fibre	3.51g

~ COOK'S TIP ~
Pecan nuts can be used
in place of the walnuts in
this cake.

Greek Honey and Lemon Cake

Moist and tangy, a delicious tea-time treat.

MAKES 16 SLICES

1½ oz (40 g) sunflower margarine

4 tablespoons (60 ml) clear honey

finely grated rind and juice of
  1 lemon

¼ pint (150 ml) skimmed milk

5 oz (150 g) plain flour

1½ teaspoons (7.5 ml) baking powder

½ teaspoon (2.5 ml) grated nutmeg

2 oz (50 g) semolina

2 egg whites

2 teaspoons (10 ml) sesame seeds

1 Preheat the oven to 200°C/400°F/ Gas 6. Lightly oil a 7½ in (19 cm) square deep cake tin and line the base with non-stick baking paper.

2 ▲ Gently melt the margarine and 3 tablespoons (45 ml) of the honey. Reserve 1 tablespoon (15 ml) lemon juice, then stir in the rest with the rind and milk. Transfer to a bowl.

3 ▲ Add the flour, baking powder and nutmeg, and stir through. Gradually beat the semolina into the mixture. Whisk the egg whites until soft peaks form, then fold them in.

4 ▲ Spoon into the tin and sprinkle with sesame seeds. Bake the cake for 25–30 minutes, until golden brown. Mix together the reserved honey and lemon juice and drizzle over the cake while warm. Cool in the tin, then cut into fingers to serve.

NUTRITION NOTES
Per portion

Energy	82Kcals/342kJ
Fat	2.62g
Saturated Fat	0.46g
Cholesterol	0.36mg
Fibre	0.41g

Cranberry and Apple Ring

Tangy cranberries add an unusual flavour to this low-fat cake. It is best eaten very fresh.

SERVES 8

8 oz (225 g) self-raising flour
1 teaspoon (5 ml) ground cinnamon
3 oz (75 g) light muscovado sugar
1 crisp eating apple, cored and diced
3 oz (75 g) fresh or frozen cranberries
4 tablespoons (60 ml) sunflower oil
¼ pint (150 ml) apple juice
cranberry jelly and apple slices, to decorate

1 ▲ Preheat the oven to 180°C/ 350°F/Gas 4. Lightly grease a 1¾ pint (1 litre) ring mould with oil.

2 Sift together the flour and ground cinnamon, then stir in the sugar.

3 ▲ Toss together the diced apple and cranberries. Stir into the dry ingredients, then add the oil and apple juice and beat well.

4 ▲ Spoon the mixture into the prepared ring mould and bake for about 35–40 minutes, or until the cake is firm to the touch. Turn out and leave to cool completely.

5 To serve, drizzle warmed cranberry jelly over the cake and decorate with apple slices.

NUTRITION NOTES
Per portion

Energy	202Kcals/848kJ
Fat	5.91g
Saturated Fat	0.76g
Cholesterol	0
Fibre	1.55g

~ COOK'S TIP ~

Fresh cranberries are available throughout the winter months and if you don't use them all at once, they can be frozen for up to a year.

Lemon Chiffon Cake

Lemon mousse provides a tangy filling for this light lemon sponge.

SERVES 8

2 eggs	
3 oz (75 g) caster sugar	
grated rind of 1 lemon	
2 oz (50 g) sifted plain flour	
lemon shreds, to decorate	

FOR THE FILLING

2 eggs, separated	
3 oz (75 g) caster sugar	
grated rind and juice of 1 lemon	
2 tablespoons (70 ml) water	
1 tablespoon (15 ml) gelatine	
4 fl oz (125 ml) low-fat fromage frais	

FOR THE ICING

1 tablespoon (15 ml) lemon juice	
4 oz (115 g) icing sugar, sifted	

~ COOK'S TIP ~

The mousse should be just setting when the egg whites are added. Speed up this process by placing the bowl of mousse in iced water.

NUTRITION NOTES

Per portion

Energy	202Kcals/849kJ
Fat	2.81g
Saturated Fat	0.79g
Cholesterol	96.4mg
Fibre	0.2g

1 ▲ Preheat the oven to 180°C/350°F/Gas 4. Grease and line an 8 in (20 cm) loose-bottomed cake tin. Whisk the eggs, sugar and lemon rind together until mousse-like. Gently fold in the flour, then turn the mixture into the tin.

2 ▲ Bake for 20–25 minutes until the cake springs back when lightly pressed in the centre. Turn on to a wire rack. Once cold, split the cake in half horizontally and return the lower half to the clean cake tin.

3 ▲ Make the filling. Put the egg yolks, sugar, lemon rind and juice in a bowl. Beat with a hand-held electric whisk until thick, pale and creamy.

4 ▲ Pour the water into a heatproof bowl and sprinkle the gelatine on top. Leave until spongy, then stir over simmering water until dissolved. Cool, then whisk into the yolk mixture. Fold in the fromage frais. When the mixture begins to set, whisk the egg whites to soft peaks. Fold the egg whites into the mousse.

5 ▲ Pour the lemon mousse over the sponge in the cake tin, spreading it to the edges. Set the second layer of sponge on top and chill until set.

6 ▲ Slide a palette knife dipped in hot water between the tin and the cake to loosen it. Transfer to a plate. To make icing, add enough lemon juice to the icing sugar to make a mixture thick enough to coat the back of a wooden spoon. Pour over the cake. Decorate with lemon shreds.

Strawberry Gâteau

It's hard to believe that this delicious gâteau is low in fat, but it's true, so enjoy!

SERVES 6

2 eggs

3 oz (75 g) caster sugar

grated rind of ½ orange

2 oz (50 g) plain flour

strawberry leaves, to decorate (optional)

icing sugar, for dusting

FOR THE FILLING

10 oz (275 g) low-fat soft cheese

grated rind of ½ orange

2 tablespoons (30 ml) caster sugar

4 tablespoons (60 ml) low-fat fromage frais

8 oz (225 g) strawberries, halved

1 oz (25 g) chopped almonds, toasted

~ COOK'S TIP ~
Use other soft fruits in season, such as currants, raspberries, blackberries or blueberries, or try a mixture of different berries.

NUTRITION NOTES
Per portion
Energy	213Kcals/893kJ
Fat	6.08g
Saturated Fat	1.84g
Cholesterol	70.22mg
Fibre	1.02g

1 ▲ Preheat the oven to 190°C/ 375°F/Gas 5. Grease a 12 × 8 in (30 × 20 cm) Swiss roll tin and line with non-stick baking paper.

2 ▲ In a bowl, whisk the eggs, sugar and orange rind together with a hand-held electric whisk until thick and mousse-like (when the whisk is lifted, a trail should remain on the surface of the mixture for 15 seconds).

3 ▲ Fold in the flour with a metal spoon, being careful not to knock out any air. Turn into the prepared tin. Bake for 15–20 minutes, or until the cake springs back when lightly pressed. Turn the cake on to a wire rack, remove the lining paper and leave to cool.

4 ▲ Meanwhile, make the filling. In a bowl, mix the soft cheese with the orange rind, sugar and fromage frais until smooth. Divide between two bowls. Chop half of the strawberry halves and add to one bowl of filling.

5 ▲ Cut the sponge widthways into three equal pieces and sandwich them together with the strawberry filling. Spread two-thirds of the plain filling over the sides of the cake and press on the toasted almonds.

6 ▲ Spread the rest of the filling over the top of the cake and decorate with strawberry halves, and strawberry leaves, if liked. Dust with icing sugar and transfer to a serving plate.

Tia Maria Gâteau

A feather-light coffee sponge with a creamy liqueur-flavoured filling.

SERVES 8

3 oz (75 g) plain flour
2 tablespoons (30 ml) instant coffee powder
3 eggs
4 oz (115 g) caster sugar
coffee beans, to decorate (optional)

FOR THE FILLING

6 oz (175 g) low-fat soft cheese
1 tablespoon (15 ml) clear honey
1 tablespoon (15 ml) Tia Maria liqueur
2 oz (50 g) stem ginger, roughly chopped

FOR THE ICING

8 oz (225 g) icing sugar, sifted
2 teaspoons (10 ml) coffee essence
1 tablespoon (15 ml) water
1 teaspoon (5 ml) reduced-fat cocoa powder

1 ▲ Preheat the oven to 190°C/375°F/Gas 5. Grease and line an 8 in (20 cm) deep round cake tin. Sift the flour and coffee powder together on to a sheet of greaseproof paper.

2 ▲ Whisk the eggs and sugar in a bowl with a hand-held electric whisk until thick and mousse-like (when the whisk is lifted, a trail should remain on the surface of the mixture for at least 15 seconds).

~ COOK'S TIP ~
When folding in the flour mixture in step 3, be careful not to remove the air, as it helps the cake to rise.

3 ▲ Gently fold in the flour mixture with a metal spoon. Turn the mixture into the prepared tin. Bake the sponge for 30–35 minutes or until it springs back when lightly pressed. Turn on to a wire rack to cool completely.

4 ▲ To make the filling, mix the soft cheese with the honey in a bowl. Beat until smooth, then stir in the Tia Maria and chopped stem ginger.

5 ▲ Split the cake in half horizontally and sandwich the two halves together with the Tia Maria filling.

6 Make the icing. In a bowl, mix the icing sugar and coffee essence with enough of the water to make a consistency that will coat the back of a wooden spoon. Pour three-quarters of the icing over the cake, spreading it evenly to the edges. Stir the cocoa into the remaining icing until smooth. Spoon into a piping bag fitted with a writing nozzle and pipe the mocha icing over the coffee icing. Decorate with coffee beans, if liked.

NUTRITION NOTES

Per portion

Energy	226Kcals/951kJ
Fat	3.14g
Saturated Fat	1.17g
Cholesterol	75.03mg
Fibre	0.64g

Chocolate Banana Cake

A chocolate cake that's deliciously low in fat – it is moist enough to eat without the icing if you want to cut down on calories.

SERVES 8

8 oz (225 g) self-raising flour

3 tablespoons (45 ml) fat-reduced cocoa powder

4 oz (115 g) light muscovado sugar

2 tablespoons (30 ml) malt extract

2 tablespoons (30 ml) golden syrup

2 eggs

4 tablespoons (60 ml) skimmed milk

4 tablespoons (60 ml) sunflower oil

2 large ripe bananas

FOR THE ICING

8 oz (225 g) icing

sugar, sifted

7 teaspoons (35 ml) fat-reduced cocoa powder, sifted

1–2 tablespoons (15–30 ml) warm water

NUTRITION NOTES
Per portion

Energy	411Kcals/1727kJ
Fat	8.791g
Saturated Fat	2.06g
Cholesterol	48.27mg
Fibre	2.06g

1 ▲ Preheat the oven to 160°C/ 325°F/Gas 3. Grease and line a deep round 8 in (20 cm) cake tin.

2 ▲ Sift the flour into a mixing bowl with the cocoa. Stir in the sugar.

3 ▲ Make a well in the centre and add the malt extract, golden syrup, eggs, milk and oil. Mash the bananas thoroughly and stir them into the mixture until well combined.

4 ▲ Pour the cake mixture into the prepared tin and bake for 1–1¼ hours or until the centre of the cake springs back when lightly pressed.

5 ▲ Remove the cake from the tin and leave on a wire rack to cool.

6 ▲ Reserve 2 oz (50 g) icing sugar and 1 teaspoon (5 ml) cocoa powder. Make a dark icing by beating the remaining sugar and cocoa powder with enough of the warm water to make a thick icing. Pour it over the cake and spread evenly. Make a light icing by mixing the remaining icing sugar and cocoa powder with a few drops of water. Drizzle this icing across the top of the cake.

Chocolate and Orange Angel Cake

This light-as-air sponge with its fluffy icing is virtually fat-free, yet tastes heavenly.

SERVES 10

1 oz (25 g) plain flour

½ oz (15 g) reduced-fat cocoa powder

½ oz (15 g) cornflour

pinch of salt

5 egg whites

½ teaspoon (2.5 ml) cream of tartar

4 oz (115 g) caster sugar

blanched and shredded rind of
  1 orange, to decorate

FOR THE ICING

7 oz (200 g) caster sugar

1 egg white

1 ▲ Preheat the oven to 180°C/ 350°F/Gas 4. Sift the flour, cocoa powder, cornflour and salt together three times. Beat the egg whites in a large clean, dry bowl until foamy. Add the cream of tartar, then whisk.

2 ▲ Add the caster sugar to the egg whites a spoonful at a time, whisking after each addition. Sift a third of the flour and cocoa mixture over the meringue and gently fold in. Repeat, sifting and folding in the flour and cocoa mixture two more times.

3 ▲ Spoon the mixture into a non-stick 8 in (20 cm) ring mould and level the top. Bake for 35 minutes or until springy to the touch. Turn upside down on to a wire rack and leave to cool in the tin. Carefully ease out of the tin.

4 ▲ For the icing, mix the sugar with 5 tablespoons (75 ml) cold water. Stir over a low heat until dissolved. Boil until the syrup reaches 120°C/250°F on a sugar thermometer or when a drop of the syrup makes a soft ball when dripped into cold water. Remove from the heat.

5 ▲ Whisk the egg white until stiff. Add the syrup in a thin stream, whisking all the time. Continue to whisk until the mixture is very thick.

6 ▲ Spread the icing over the top and sides of the cooled cake. Sprinkle the orange rind over the top of the cake and serve.

NUTRITION NOTES

Per portion

Energy	153Kcals/644kJ
Fat	0.27g
Saturated Fat	0.13g
Cholesterol	0
Fibre	0.25g

Eggless Christmas Cake

A deliciously clever way to create a low-calorie Christmas treat!

SERVES 12

3 oz (75 g) sultanas
3 oz (75 g) raisins
3 oz (75 g) currants
3 oz (75 g) halved glacé cherries
2 oz (50 g) cut mixed peel
8 fl oz (250 ml) apple juice
1 oz (25 g) toasted hazelnuts
2 tablespoons (30 ml) pumpkin seeds
2 pieces stem ginger in syrup, chopped
finely grated rind of 1 lemon
4 fl oz (120 ml) skimmed milk
4 fl oz (120 ml) sunflower oil
8 oz (225 g) self-raising flour
2 teaspoons (10 ml) mixed spice
3 tablespoons (45 ml) brandy or rum
apricot jam, for brushing

1 ▲ Place the sultanas, raisins, currants, halved cherries and mixed peel in a bowl and stir in the apple juice. Cover and leave to soak overnight.

2 Preheat the oven to 150°C/300°F/ Gas 2.

3 ▲ Lightly grease and line a 7 in (18 cm) square cake tin.

4 ▲ Add the hazelnuts, pumpkin seeds, ginger and lemon rind to the fruit. Stir in the milk, oil, sifted flour and spice, and the brandy or rum.

5 ▲ Spoon into the prepared tin and bake for 1½ hours, or until golden brown and firm to the touch. Turn out and cool on a wire rack. Brush with sieved apricot jam and decorate with glacé fruits, if desired.

NUTRITION NOTES
Per portion

Energy	225Kcals/946kJ
Fat	6.13g
Saturated Fat	0.89g
Cholesterol	0.2mg
Fibre	2.45g

Fruit and Nut Cake

A rich fruit cake that improves with keeping.

1 ▲ Preheat the oven to 160°C/
325°F/Gas 3. Grease and line a deep
round 8 in (20 cm) cake tin. Secure
brown paper around the outside.

2 ▲ Sift the flours into a mixing
bowl together with the mixed spice
and make a well in the centre.

3 ▲ Put the apple and apricot spread
in a small bowl. Gradually stir in the
honey and molasses. Add to the dry
ingredients with the oil, orange juice,
eggs and dried fruit and mix.

4 ▲ Turn the mixture into the
prepared tin and smooth the surface.
Arrange the almonds and cherries in
a pattern over the top. Bake for
2 hours or until a skewer comes out
clean. Transfer to a wire rack until
cold, then lift out of the tin and
remove the paper.

SERVES 12–14

6 oz (175 g) self-raising wholemeal flour	
6 oz (175 g) self-raising white flour	
2 teaspoons (10 ml) mixed spice	
1 tablespoon (15 ml) apple and apricot spread	
3 tablespoons (45 ml) clear honey	
1 tablespoon (15 ml) molasses	
6 tablespoons (90 ml) sunflower oil	
6 fl oz (175 ml) orange juice	
2 eggs, beaten	
1½ lb (675 g) mixed dried fruit	
3 tablespoons (45 ml) split almonds	
2 oz (50 g) glacé cherries, halved	

NUTRITION NOTES

Per portion

Energy	333Kcals/14000kJ
Fat	8.54g
Saturated Fat	1.12g
Cholesterol	29.62mg
Fibre	3.08g

Banana Ginger Parkin

Parkin keeps well and really improves over time. Store it in a container for up to two months.

SERVES 12

7 oz (200 g) plain flour
2 tsp (10 ml) bicarbonate of soda
2 tsp (10 ml) ground ginger
5 oz (150 g) medium oatmeal
4 tbsp (60 ml) dark muscovado sugar
3 oz (75 g) sunflower margarine
5 oz (150 g) golden syrup
1 egg, beaten
3 ripe bananas, mashed
3 oz (75 g) icing sugar

NUTRITION NOTES
Per portion
Energy	277Kcals/1163kJ
Fat	6.9g
Saturated Fat	6.9g
Cholesterol	16.4mg
Fibre	1.72g

1 Preheat the oven to 160°C/325°F/ Gas 3. Grease and line a 7 × 11 in (18 × 28 cm) cake tin.

2 ▲ Sift together the flour, bicarbonate of soda and ginger, then stir in the oatmeal. Melt the sugar, margarine and syrup in a saucepan, then stir into the flour mixture. Beat in the egg and mashed bananas.

3 ▲ Spoon into the tin and bake for about 1 hour, or until firm to the touch. Allow to cool in the tin, then turn out and cut into squares.

4 ▲ Sift the icing sugar into a bowl and stir in just enough water to make a smooth, runny icing. Drizzle the icing over each square and top with a piece of stem ginger, if desired.

~ COOK'S TIP ~
This is a nutritious, energy-giving cake that is a really good choice for packed lunches as it doesn't break up too easily.

Nectarine Amaretto Cake

Amaretto liqueur adds a hint of luxury to this fruity cake.

1 ▲ Preheat the oven to 180°C/ 350°F/Gas 4. Grease an 8 in (20 cm) round, loose-bottomed cake tin. Whisk together the egg yolks, caster sugar, lemon rind and juice in a bowl until the mixture is thick and creamy.

2 Fold in the semolina, almonds and flour until smooth.

3 ▲ Whisk the egg whites in a bowl until fairly stiff. Use a metal spoon to stir a generous spoonful of the whites into the semolina mixture, then fold in the remaining egg whites. Spoon the mixture into the cake tin.

4 Bake for 30–35 minutes until the centre of the cake springs back when pressed lightly. Remove from the oven and loosen around the edge with a palette knife. Prick the top with a skewer. Leave to cool in the tin.

5 To make the syrup, heat the sugar and water in a small pan, stirring until the sugar is dissolved. Boil without stirring for 2 minutes. Add the Amaretto liqueur and drizzle the liqueur syrup over the cake in the tin.

6 ▲ Remove the cake from the tin and transfer to a serving plate. Decorate with sliced nectarines. Brush with warm apricot glaze.

SERVES 8

3 eggs, separated
6 oz (175 g) caster sugar
grated rind and juice of 1 lemon
2 oz (50 g) semolina
1 oz (25 g) ground almonds
1 oz (25 g) plain flour
2 nectarines, halved and stoned
4 tablespoons (60 ml) apricot glaze
FOR THE SYRUP
3 oz (45 g) caster sugar
6 tablespoons (90 ml) water
2 tablespoons (30 ml) Amaretto

NUTRITION NOTES
Per portion
Energy	264Kcals/1108kJ
Fat	5.7g
Saturated Fat	0.85g
Cholesterol	72.19mg
Fibre	1.08g

Apricot and Orange Roulade

This elegant dessert is very good served with a spoonful of natural yogurt or crème fraîche.

SERVES 6

4 egg whites

4 oz (115 g) golden caster sugar

2 oz (50 g) plain flour

finely grated rind of 1 small orange

3 tablespoons (45 ml) orange juice

2 teaspoons (10 ml) icing sugar and
   shreds of orange zest, to decorate

FOR THE FILLING

4 oz (115 g) dried apricots

4 oz (115 g) orange juice

NUTRITION NOTES
Per portion
Energy	203Kcals/853kJ
Fat	10.52g
Saturated Fat	2.05g
Cholesterol	0
Fibre	2.53g

1 Preheat the oven to 200°C/400°F/
Gas 6. Grease a 9 × 13 in (23 × 33 cm)
Swiss roll tin and line it with non-
stick baking paper. Grease the paper.

2 ▲ For the roulade, place the egg
whites in a large bowl and whisk
them until they hold peaks.
Gradually add the sugar, whisking
hard between each addition.

3 Fold in the flour, orange rind and
juice. Spoon the mixture into the
prepared tin and spread it evenly.

4 Bake for about 15–18 minutes, or
until the sponge is firm and light
golden in colour. Turn out on to a
sheet of non-stick baking paper and
roll it up Swiss roll-style loosely from
one short side. Leave to cool.

5 ▲ For the filling, roughly chop the
apricots, and place them in a
saucepan with the orange juice.
Cover the tin and leave to simmer
until most of the liquid has been
absorbed. Purée the apricots.

6 ▲ Unroll the roulade and spread
with the apricot mixture. Roll up,
arrange strips of paper diagonally
across the roll, sprinkle lightly with
lines of icing sugar, remove the paper
and scatter with orange zest to serve.

~ COOK'S TIP ~
Make and bake the sponge
mixture a day in advance and
keep it, rolled with the paper,
in a cool place. Fill it with
the fruit purée 2–3 hours
before serving.

Strawberry Roulade

A creamy fruit filling is delicious in a light roulade.

1 Preheat the oven to 200°C/400°F/ Gas 6. Oil a 9 × 13 in (23 × 33 cm) Swiss roll tin and line with non-stick baking paper.

2 ▲ Place the egg whites in a large bowl and whisk until they form soft peaks. Gradually whisk in the sugar. Fold in half of the sifted flour, then fold in the rest with the orange juice.

3 Spoon the mixture into the prepared tin, spreading evenly. Bake for 15–18 minutes, or until golden brown and firm to the touch.

4 ▲ Meanwhile, spread out a sheet of non-stick baking paper and sprinkle with caster sugar. Turn out the cake on to this and remove the lining paper. Roll up the sponge loosely from one short side, with the paper inside. Cool.

5 Unroll and remove the paper. Stir the strawberries into the fromage frais and spread over the sponge. Re-roll and serve decorated with strawberries.

SERVES 6

4 egg whites
4 oz (115 g) golden caster sugar
3 oz (75 g) plain flour, sifted
2 tablespoons (30 ml) orange juice
caster sugar, for sprinkling
4 oz (115 g) strawberries, chopped
5 oz (150 g) low-fat fromage frais
strawberries, to decorate

NUTRITION NOTES
Per portion
Energy	154Kcals/646kJ
Fat	0.24g
Saturated Fat	0.01g
Cholesterol	0.25mg
Fibre	0.61g

Peach Swiss Roll

A feather-light sponge enclosing peach jam – delicious at tea time.

SERVES 6–8

3 eggs
4 oz (115 g) caster sugar, plus extra for sprinkling
3 oz (75 g) plain flour, sifted
1 tablespoon (15 ml) boiling water
6 tablespoons (90 ml) peach jam
icing sugar, for dusting (optional)

1 ▲ Preheat the oven to 200°C/ 400°F/Gas 6. Grease a 12 × 8 in (30 × 20 cm) Swiss roll tin and line with non-stick baking paper. Combine the eggs and sugar in a bowl. Beat with an electric whisk until thick and mousse-like (when the whisk is lifted, a trail should remain on the surface of the mixture for 15 seconds).

2 ▲ Carefully fold in the flour with a large metal spoon, then add the boiling water in the same way.

3 ▲ Spoon into the prepared tin, spread evenly to the edges and bake for about 10–12 minutes until the cake springs back when lightly pressed in the centre.

4 ▲ Spread a sheet of greaseproof paper on a flat surface, sprinkle it with caster sugar, then invert the cake on top. Peel off the paper.

5 ▲ Neatly trim the edges of the cake. Make a cut two-thirds of the way through the cake, about ½ in (1 cm) from the short edge nearest you.

6 ▲ Spread the cake with the peach jam and roll up quickly from the partially cut end. Hold in position for a minute, making sure the join is underneath. Cool on a wire rack. Decorate with piped glacé icing (see Cook's Tip) or dust with icing sugar before serving.

~ COOK'S TIP ~

To decorate the Swiss roll with glacé icing, make the icing with 4 oz (115 g) icing sugar and enough warm water to make a thin glacé icing. Put in a piping bag fitted with a small writing nozzle and pipe lines over the top.

NUTRITION NOTES
Per portion
Energy	178Kcals/746kJ
Fat	2.54g
Saturated Fat	0.67g
Cholesterol	82.5mg
Fibre	0.33g

Chestnut and Orange Roulade

This moist cake is ideal to serve as a dessert.

SERVES 8

3 eggs, separated

4 oz (115 g) caster sugar

8 oz (225 g) canned unsweetened chestnut purée

grated rind and juice of 1 orange

icing sugar, for dusting

FOR THE FILLING

8 oz (225 g) low-fat soft cheese

1 tablespoon (15 ml) clear honey

1 orange

1 ▲ Preheat the oven to 180°C/ 350°/Gas 4. Grease a 12 × 8 in (30 × 20 cm) Swiss roll tin and line with baking paper. Whisk the egg yolks and sugar in a bowl until thick.

2 ▲ Put the chestnut purée in a separate bowl. Whisk in the orange rind and juice, then whisk the chestnut purée into the egg mixture.

3 ▲ Whisk the egg whites in a grease-free bowl until fairly stiff. Using a metal spoon, stir a generous spoonful of the whites into the chestnut mixture to lighten it, then fold in the rest. Spoon into the prepared tin and bake for 30 minutes until firm. Cool for 5 minutes, then cover with a clean damp tea towel until completely cold.

4 ▲ Meanwhile, make the filling. Mix the soft cheese with the honey. Add the orange rind, finely grated. Peel away all the pith from the orange, cut the fruit into segments, chop roughly and set aside. Add any juice to the cheese mixture, then beat until smooth. Mix in the orange.

5 ▲ Dust a sheet of greaseproof paper thickly with icing sugar. Carefully turn the roulade out on to the paper, then peel off the lining paper. Spread the filling over the roulade and roll up like a Swiss roll. Transfer to a plate and dust with some more icing sugar.

~ COOK'S TIP ~

Do not whisk the egg whites too stiffly or it will be difficult to fold them into the mixture and they will form lumps in the roulade.

NUTRITION NOTES

Per portion

Energy	185Kcals/775kJ
Fat	4.01g
Saturated Fat	1.47g
Cholesterol	76.25mg
Fibre	1.4g

Chocolate, Date and Walnut Pudding

Proper puddings are not totally taboo when you're cutting calories or fat – this one stays within the rules! Serve hot, with yogurt or skimmed-milk custard.

SERVES 4

1 oz (25 g) chopped walnuts
1 oz (25 g) chopped dates
2 eggs
1 teaspoon (5 ml) vanilla essence
2 tablespoons (30 ml) golden caster sugar
3 tablespoons (45 ml) plain flour
1 tablespoon (15 ml) cocoa powder
2 tablespoons (30 ml) skimmed milk

NUTRITION NOTES

Per portion

Energy	169Kcals/708kJ
Fat	8.1g
Saturated Fat	1.7g
Cholesterol	96mg
Fibre	1.8g

1 ▲ Preheat the oven to 180°C/ 350°F/Gas 4. Grease a 2 pint (1.2 litre) pudding basin and place a small circle of greaseproof or non-stick baking paper in the base. Spoon in the walnuts and dates.

2 ▲ Separate the eggs and place the yolks in a bowl with the vanilla essence and sugar. Place the bowl over a pan of hot water and whisk until the mixture is thick and pale.

3 ▲ Sift the flour and cocoa into the mixture and fold them in with a metal spoon. Stir in the milk, to soften the mixture slightly. Whisk the egg whites until they hold soft peaks and fold them in.

4 ▲ Spoon the mixture into the basin and bake for 40–45 minutes, or until the pudding is well risen and firm to the touch. Run a knife around the pudding, turn it out and serve.

Feather-light Peach Pudding

On chilly days, try this hot fruit pudding with its tantalizing sponge topping.

1 ▲ Preheat the oven to 180°C/350°F/Gas 4. Drain the peaches and put into a 1¾ pint (1 litre) dish with 2 tablespoons (30 ml) of the juice.

2 ▲ Put all the remaining ingredients, except the icing sugar into a mixing bowl. Beat for 3–4 minutes, until thoroughly combined.

3 ▲ Spoon the sponge mixture over the peaches and level the top evenly. Cook in the oven for 35–40 minutes, or until springy to the touch.

4 ▲ Lightly dust the top with icing sugar before serving hot with custard.

~ COOK'S TIP ~
For a simple sauce, blend 1 teaspoon (5 ml) arrowroot with 1 tablespoon (15 ml) peach juice in a small saucepan. Stir in the remaining peach juice from the can and simmer for 1 minute.

SERVES 4

14 oz (400 g) canned peach slices
2 oz (50 g) low-fat spread
1½ oz (40 g) soft light brown sugar
1 egg, beaten
2 oz (50 g) plain wholemeal flour
2 oz (50 g) plain flour
1 teaspoon (5 ml) baking powder
½ teaspoon (2.5 ml) ground cinnamon
4 tablespoons (60 ml) skimmed milk
½ teaspoon (2.5 ml) vanilla essence
2 teaspoons (10 ml) icing sugar
low-fat ready-to-serve custard

NUTRITION NOTES
Per portion
Energy	255Kcals/1071kJ
Fat	6.78g
Saturated Fat	1.57g
Cholesterol	0
Fibre	2.65g

Snowballs

A variation on the basic meringue recipe, these snowballs are made with cornflour. They make an excellent accompaniment to ice cream.

MAKES ABOUT 20

2 egg whites
4 oz (115 g) caster sugar
1 tablespoon (15 ml) cornflour, sifted
1 teaspoon (5 ml) white wine vinegar
¼ teaspoon (1.5 ml) vanilla essence

NUTRITION NOTES

Per portion

Energy	29Kcal/124kJ
Fat	0.01g
Saturated Fat	0
Cholesterol	0
Fibre	0

1 ▲ Preheat the oven to 150°C/ 300°F/Gas 2. Line two baking sheets with non-stick baking paper. Whisk the egg whites in a large grease-free bowl until stiff, using an electric whisk.

2 ▲ Add the sugar, whisking until the meringue is very stiff. Whisk in the cornflour, vinegar and vanilla.

3 ▲ Drop teaspoonfuls of the mixture on to the baking sheets, shaping them into mounds, and bake for 30 minutes until crisp.

4 ▲ Remove from the oven and leave to cool on the baking sheet. When the snowballs are cold, remove them from the baking paper with a palette knife.

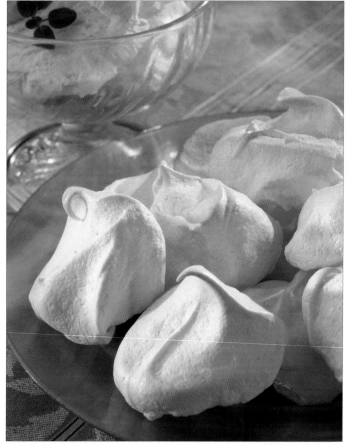

Muscovado Meringues

These light brown meringues are extremely low in fat and are delicious served on their own or sandwiched together with a fresh fruit soft cheese filling.

1 ▲ Preheat the oven to 160°C/ 325°F/Gas 3. Line two baking sheets with non-stick baking paper. Press the sugar through a metal sieve.

2 ▲ Whisk the egg whites in a clean, dry bowl, until very stiff and dry, then whisk in the sugar, about 1 tablespoon (15 ml) at a time, until the meringue is very thick and glossy.

3 ▲ Spoon small mounds of the meringue mixture on to the prepared baking sheets.

4 ▲ Sprinkle the meringues with the chopped walnuts. Bake for 30 minutes. Cool for 5 minutes on the baking sheets, then leave on a wire rack.

MAKES ABOUT 20

4 oz (115 g) light muscovado sugar	
2 egg whites	
1 teaspoon (5 ml) finely chopped walnuts	

NUTRITION NOTES
Per portion
Energy	197Kcals/826kJ
Fat	6.8g
Saturated Fat	1.4g
Cholesterol	25mg
Fibre	0.7g

Coffee Sponge Drops

These are delicious on their own, but taste even better with a filling made by mixing low-fat soft cheese with drained and chopped stem ginger.

MAKES 12

2 oz (50 g) plain flour

1 tablespoon (15 ml) instant coffee powder

2 eggs

3 oz (75 g) caster sugar

FOR THE FILLING

4 oz (115 g) low-fat soft cheese

1½ oz (40 g) chopped stem ginger

1 ▲ Preheat the oven to 190°C/375°F/Gas 5. Line two baking sheets with non-stick baking paper. Beat the soft cheese and stem ginger together. Chill until required. Sift the flour and coffee powder together.

3 ▲ Carefully add the sifted flour and coffee mixture and gently fold in with a metal spoon, being careful not to knock out any air.

2 ▲ Combine the eggs and caster sugar in a bowl. Beat with a hand-held electric whisk until thick and mousse-like. (When the whisk is lifted, a trail should remain on the surface of the mixture for at least 15 seconds.)

4 ▲ Spoon the mixture into a piping bag fitted with a ½ in (1 cm) plain nozzle. Pipe 1½ in (4 cm) rounds on the baking sheets. Bake for 12 minutes. Cool on a wire rack, then sandwich together with the filling.

~ COOK'S TIP ~

As an alternative to stem ginger in the filling, try walnuts.

NUTRITION NOTES
Per portion
Energy   69Kcals/290kJ
Fat   1.36g
Saturated Fat   0.5g
Cholesterol   33.33mg
Fibre   0.29g

Raspberry Vacherin

Meringue rounds filled with orange-flavoured fromage frais and fresh raspberries make a perfect dinner-party dessert.

SERVES 6

3 egg whites
6 oz (175 g) caster sugar
1 teaspoon (5 ml) chopped almonds
icing sugar, for dusting
raspberry leaves, to decorate (optional)

FOR THE FILLING

6 oz (175 g) low-fat soft cheese
1–2 tablespoons (15–30 ml) clear honey
1 tablespoon (15 ml) Cointreau
4 fl oz (120 ml) low-fat fromage frais
8 oz (225 g) raspberries

~ COOK'S TIP ~

When making the meringue, whisk the egg whites until they are so stiff that you can turn the bowl upside down without them falling out.

NUTRITION NOTES

Per portion	
Energy	248Kcals/1041kJ
Fat	2.22g
Saturated Fat	0.82g
Cholesterol	4mg
Fibre	1.06g

1 ▲ Preheat the oven to 140°C/ 275°F/Gas 1. Draw an 8 in (20 cm) circle on two pieces of non-stick baking paper. Turn the paper over so the marking is on the underside and use it to line two heavy baking sheets.

2 ▲ Whisk the egg whites in a grease-free bowl until very stiff, then gradually whisk in the caster sugar to make a stiff meringue mixture.

3 ▲ Spoon the mixture on to the circles on the prepared baking sheets, spreading the meringue evenly to the edges. Sprinkle one meringue round with the chopped almonds.

4 ▲ Bake for 1½–2 hours, then carefully lift the meringue rounds off the baking sheets, peel away the paper and cool on a wire rack.

5 ▲ To make the filling, cream the soft cheese with the honey and liqueur in a bowl. Fold in the fromage frais and raspberries, reserving three for decoration.

6 ▲ Place the plain meringue round on a board, spread with the filling and top with the nut-covered round. Dust with icing sugar, transfer to a serving plate and decorate with the reserved raspberries, and a sprig of raspberry leaves, if liked.

Baked Blackberry Cheesecake

This light, low-fat cheesecake is best made with wild blackberries, but cultivated ones will do; or substitute other soft fruit, such as loganberries, raspberries or blueberries.

SERVES 5

6 oz (175 g) low-fat cottage cheese
5 oz (150 g) low-fat natural yogurt
1 tablespoon (15 ml) plain wholemeal flour
1 oz (25 g) golden caster sugar
1 egg
1 egg white
finely grated rind and juice of ½ lemon
7 oz (200 g) fresh or frozen and thawed blackberries

1 ▲ Preheat the oven to 180°C/ 350°F/Gas 4. Lightly grease and line base of a 7 in (18 cm) sandwich tin.

2 ▲ Place the cottage cheese in a food processor and process until smooth. Alternatively, rub it through a sieve, to obtain a smooth mixture.

3 ▲ Add the yogurt, flour, sugar, egg and egg white and mix. Add the lemon rind, juice and blackberries, reserving a few for decoration.

4 ▲ Tip the mixture into the tin and bake for 30–35 minutes, or until it is just set. Turn off the oven and leave for a further 30 minutes.

5 ▲ Run a knife around the edge of the cheesecake, then turn it out. Remove the lining paper and place the cheesecake on a warm serving plate.

6 Decorate the cheesecake with the reserved blackberries and serve it warm.

~ COOK'S TIP ~

If you prefer to use canned blackberries, choose those canned in natural juice and drain the fruit well before adding it to the cheesecake mixture. The juice can be served with the cheesecake, but this will increase the total calories.

NUTRITION NOTES

Per portion

Energy	103Kcals/437kJ
Fat	2g
Saturated Fat	0.8g
Cholesterol	41mg
Fibre	1.6g

Mango and Amaretti Strudel

Fresh mango and crushed amaretti wrapped in wafer-thin filo pastry make a special treat that is equally delicious made with apricots or plums.

SERVES 4

1 large mango
grated rind of 1 lemon
2 amaretti biscuits
1 oz (25 g) demerara sugar
4 tablespoons (60 ml) wholemeal breadcrumbs
2 sheets filo pastry, each 19 x 11 in (48 x 28 cm)
¾ oz (20 g) soft margarine, melted
1 tablespoon (15 ml) chopped almonds
icing sugar, for dusting

1 ▲ Preheat the oven to 190°C/375°F/Gas 5. Lightly grease a large baking sheet. Halve, stone and peel the mango. Cut the flesh into cubes, then place them in a bowl, and sprinkle with grated lemon rind.

2 ▲ Crush the amaretti biscuits and mix them with the demerara sugar and the wholemeal breadcrumbs.

~ COOK'S TIP ~

The easiest way to prepare a mango is to cut horizontally through the fruit, keeping the knife blade close to the stone. Repeat on the other side of the stone and peel off the skin. Remove the remaining skin and flesh from around the stone.

NUTRITION NOTES
Per portion

Energy	239Kcals/1006kJ
Fat	8.45g
Saturated Fat	4.43g
Cholesterol	17.25mg
Fibre	3.3g

3 ▲ Lay one sheet of filo on a flat surface and brush with a quarter of the margarine. Top with the second sheet, brush with one-third of the remaining margarine, then fold both sheets over to make a rectangle 11 × 9 in (28 × 23 cm). Brush with half the remaining margarine.

4 ▲ Sprinkle the filo with the amaretti mixture, leaving a 2 in (5 cm) border on each long side. Arrange the mango cubes over the top.

5 ▲ Roll up the filo from one of the long sides. Lift the strudel on to the baking sheet with the join underneath. Brush with the remaining melted margarine and sprinkle with the chopped almonds.

6 ▲ Bake for 20–25 minutes until golden brown, then transfer to a board. Dust with the icing sugar, slice diagonally and serve warm.

Blueberry and Orange Crêpe Baskets

Impress your guests with these pretty, fruit-filled crêpes. When blueberries are out of season, replace them with other soft fruit, such as raspberries.

SERVES 6

FOR THE PANCAKES

5 oz (150 g) plain flour

pinch of salt

2 egg whites

7 fl oz (200 ml) skimmed milk

¼ pint (150 ml) orange juice

FOR THE FILLING

4 medium-size oranges

8 oz (225 g) blueberries

1 ▲ Preheat the oven to 200°C/400°F/Gas 6. To make the pancakes, sift the flour and salt into a bowl. Make a well in the centre of the flour and add the egg whites, milk and orange juice. Whisk hard, until all the liquid has been incorporated and the batter is smooth and bubbly.

2 ▲ Lightly grease a heavy or non-stick pancake pan and heat until it is very hot. Pour in just enough batter to cover the base of the pan, swirling it to cover the pan evenly.

3 ▲ Cook until the pancake has set and is golden, and then turn it to cook the other side. Remove the pancake to a sheet of absorbent kitchen paper, and then cook the remaining batter, to make a total of 6–8 pancakes.

4 ▲ Place six small ovenproof bowls or moulds on a baking sheet and arrange the pancakes over these. Bake the pancakes in the oven for about 10 minutes, until they are crisp and set into the shape of the moulds. Lift the "baskets" off the moulds.

5 ▲ For the filling, pare a thin piece of orange rind from one orange and cut it in fine strips. Blanch the strips in boiling water for 30 seconds, rinse in cold water and set aside. Cut the peel and white pith from the oranges.

6 ▲ Divide the oranges into segments, catching the juice, combine with the blueberries and warm them gently. Spoon the fruit into the baskets and scatter the shreds of rind over the top. Serve with yogurt or light crème fraîche.

~ COOK'S TIP ~

Don't fill the pancake baskets until you're ready to serve them because they will absorb the fruit juice and begin to soften.

NUTRITION NOTES

Per portion	
Energy	159Kcals/673kJ
Fat	0.5g
Saturated Fat	0.1g
Cholesterol	1mg
Fibre	3.3g

Filo and Apricot Purses

Filo pastry is very easy to use and is low in fat. Keep a packet in the freezer ready for rustling up a speedy tea-time treat.

MAKES 12

4 oz (115 g) dried apricots

3 tablespoons (45 ml) apricot compote or conserve

3 amaretti biscuits, crushed

3 sheets filo pastry

4 teaspoons (20 ml) soft margarine, melted

icing sugar, for dusting

NUTRITION NOTES

Per portion

Energy	58Kcals/245kJ
Fat	1.85g
Saturated Fat	0.4g
Cholesterol	0.12mg
Fibre	0.74g

1 ▲ Preheat the oven to 180°C/350°F/Gas 4. Grease two baking sheets. Chop the apricots, put them in a bowl and stir in the apricot compote. Add the crushed amaretti biscuits and mix well.

2 ▲ Cut the filo pastry into 24 5 in (13 cm) squares, pile the squares on top of each other and cover with a clean tea towel to prevent the pastry from drying and becoming brittle.

3 ▲ Lay one pastry square on a flat surface, brush lightly with melted margarine and lay another square diagonally on top. Brush the top square with melted margarine. Spoon a small mound of apricot mixture in the centre of the pastry, bring up the edges and pinch together in a money-bag shape. Repeat with the remaining squares to make 12 purses.

4 ▲ Arrange the purses on the prepared baking sheets and bake for 5–8 minutes until golden brown. Dust with icing sugar and serve warm.

Filo Scrunchies

Quick and easy to make, these pastries are ideal to serve at tea time. Eat them warm or they will lose their crispness.

MAKES 6

5 apricots or plums
4 sheets filo pastry
4 tbsp (20 ml) soft margarine, melted
2 oz (50 g) demerara sugar
2 tbsp (30 ml) flaked almonds
icing sugar, for dusting

1 ▲ Preheat the oven to 190°C/375°F/Gas 5. Halve the apricots or plums, remove the stones and slice the fruit. Cut the filo pastry into 12 7 in (18 cm) squares. Pile the squares on top of each other and cover with a clean tea towel.

4 ▲ Place the scrunchies on a baking sheet. Bake for 8–10 minutes until golden brown, then loosen the scrunchies from the baking sheet with a palette knife and transfer to a wire rack. Dust with icing sugar and serve at once.

NUTRITION NOTES
Per portion
Energy	132Kcals/555kJ
Fat	4.19g
Saturated Fat	0.63g
Cholesterol	0
Fibre	0.67g

2 ▲ Remove one square of filo and brush it with melted margarine. Lay a second filo square on top, then, using your fingers, mould the pastry into folds. Make five more scrunchies in the same way, working quickly so that the pastry does not dry out.

3 ▲ Arrange a few slices of fruit in the folds of each scrunchie, then sprinkle generously with the demerara sugar and flaked almonds.

Plum Filo Pockets

These attractive party parcels are high in fibre as well as being a tasty treat.

SERVES 4

4 oz (115 g) skimmed milk soft cheese

1 tablespoon (15 ml) light muscovado sugar

½ teaspoon (2.5 ml) ground cloves

8 large plums, halved and stoned

8 sheets filo pastry

sunflower oil, for brushing

icing sugar, to sprinkle

NUTRITION NOTES

Per portion	
Energy	188Kcals/790kJ
Fat	1.87g
Saturated Fat	0.27g
Cholesterol	0.29mg
Fibre	2.55g

1 ▲ Preheat the oven to 220°C/ 425°F/Gas 7. Mix together the cheese, sugar and cloves.

2 ▲ Sandwich the plum halves back together with a spoonful of the cheese mixture in each plum.

3 Spread out the pastry and cut into 16 pieces, about 9 in (23 cm) square. Brush one lightly with oil and place a second at a diagonal on top. Repeat with the remaining squares.

4 ▲ Place a plum on each pastry square, and gather the corners together. Place on a baking sheet. Bake for 15–18 minutes, until golden, then dust with icing sugar.

Glazed Apricot Sponge

Puddings can be very high in saturated fat, but this one uses the minimum of oil and no eggs.

1 ▲ Preheat the oven to 180°C/350°F/ Gas 4. Lightly oil a 1½ pint (900 ml) pudding basin. Spoon in the syrup.

2 ▲ Drain the apricots and reserve the juice. Arrange about eight halves in the basin. Purée the rest of the apricots with the juice and set aside.

3 ▲ Mix the flour, breadcrumbs, sugar and cinnamon, then beat in the oil and milk. Spoon into the basin and bake for 50–55 minutes, or until firm and golden. Turn out and serve with the puréed fruit as a sauce.

SERVES 4

2 teaspoons (10 ml) golden syrup
14½ oz (411 g) can apricot halves in fruit juice
5 oz (150 g) self-raising flour
3 oz (75 g) fresh breadcrumbs
3½ oz (90 g) light muscovado sugar
1 teaspoon (5 ml) ground cinnamon
2 tablespoons (30 ml) sunflower oil
6 fl oz (175 ml) skimmed milk

NUTRITION NOTES
Per portion
Energy   364Kcals/1530kJ
Fat   6.47g
Saturated Fat   0.89g
Cholesterol   0.88mg
Fibre   2.37g

Latticed Peaches

An elegant dessert; it certainly doesn't look low in fat, but it really is. Use canned peach halves when fresh peaches are out of season, or if you're short of time.

SERVES 6

FOR THE PASTRY

4 oz (115 g) plain flour

3 tablespoons (45 ml) butter or sunflower margarine

3 tablespoons (45 ml) low-fat natural yogurt

2 tablespoons (30 ml) orange juice

skimmed milk, for glaze

FOR THE FILLING

3 ripe peaches or nectarines

3 tablespoons (45 ml) ground almonds

2 tablespoons (30 ml) low-fat natural yogurt

finely grated rind of 1 small orange

½ teaspoon (1.5 ml) natural almond essence

FOR THE SAUCE

1 ripe peach or nectarine

3 tablespoons (45 ml) orange juice

1 ▲ For the pastry, sift the flour into a bowl and, using your fingertips, rub in the butter or margarine evenly. Stir in the yogurt and orange juice to bind the mixture into a firm dough.

2 ▲ Roll out about half the pastry thinly and use a biscuit cutter to stamp out rounds about 3 in (7.5 cm) in diameter, slightly larger than the circumference of the peaches. Place on a lightly greased baking sheet.

3 ▲ Skin the peaches or nectarines, halve and remove the stones. Mix together the almonds, yogurt, orange rind and almond essence. Spoon into each peach half and place, cut-side down, on to the pastry rounds.

4 ▲ Roll out the remaining pastry thinly and cut into thin strips. Arrange the strips over the peaches to form a lattice, brushing with milk to secure firmly. Trim off the ends.

5 ▲ Chill in the fridge for 30 minutes. Preheat the oven to 200°C/400°F/ Gas 6. Brush with milk and bake for 15–18 minutes, until golden brown.

6 ▲ For the sauce, skin the peach or nectarine and halve it to remove the stone. Place the flesh in a food processor, with the orange juice, and purée it until smooth. Serve the peaches hot, with the peach sauce spooned around.

~ COOK'S TIP ~

This dessert is best eaten fairly fresh from the oven, as the pastry can toughen slightly if left to stand. So assemble the peaches in their pastry on a baking sheet, chill in the fridge, and bake just before serving.

NUTRITION NOTES

Per portion

Energy	219Kcal/916kJ
Fat	10.8g
Saturated Fat	1.6g
Cholesterol	1mg
Fibre	2.4g

EVERYDAY BREADS

THOUGH THE PACE OF TODAY'S LIFE
LEAVES LITTLE TIME FOR BAKING,
BREADMAKING CAN BE VERY
THERAPEUTIC. THE PROCESS IS
SIMPLE YET INFINITELY VARIABLE,
AS THE LOAVES THAT FOLLOW
PROVE. ROLL UP YOUR SLEEVES AND
CREATE A TRADITION.

White Bread

MAKES 2 LOAVES

2 fl oz (65 ml) lukewarm water
1 tablespoon active dried yeast
2 tablespoons sugar
16 fl oz (450 ml) lukewarm milk
1 oz (30 g) butter or margarine, at room temperature
2 teaspoons salt
1 lb 14 oz–2 lbs (850–900 g) strong flour

1 Combine the water, dried yeast and 1 tablespoon of sugar in a measuring jug and leave to stand for 15 minutes until the mixture is frothy.

2 ▼ Pour the milk into a large bowl. Add the remaining sugar, the butter or margarine, and salt. Stir in the yeast mixture.

3 Stir in the flour, 5 oz (140 g) at a time, until a stiff dough is obtained. Alternatively, use a food processor.

4 ▲ Transfer the dough to a floured surface. To knead, push the dough away from you with the palm of your hand, then fold it towards you, and push it away again. Repeat until the dough is smooth and elastic.

5 Place the dough in a large greased bowl, cover with a plastic bag, and leave to rise in a warm place until doubled in volume, 2–3 hours.

6 Grease 2 9 × 5 in (23 × 13 cm) tins.

7 ▲ Punch down the risen dough with your fist and divide in half. Form into a loaf shape and place in the tins, seam-side down. Cover and let rise in a warm place until almost doubled in volume, about 45 minutes.

8 Preheat a 375°F/190°C/Gas 5 oven.

9 Bake until firm and brown, 45–50 minutes. Turn out and tap the bottom of a loaf: if it sounds hollow the loaf is done. If necessary, return to the oven and bake a few minutes more. Let cool on a rack.

Country Bread

MAKES 2 LOAVES

12 oz (350 g) wholewheat flour
12 oz (350 g) plain flour
5 oz (140 g) strong plain flour
4 tsp salt
2 oz (55 g) butter, at room temperature
16 fl oz (450 ml) lukewarm milk
FOR THE STARTER
1 tbsp active dry yeast
8 fl oz (250 ml) lukewarm water
5 oz (140 g) plain flour
1/4 tsp caster sugar

1 ▲ For the starter, combine the yeast, water, flour and sugar in a bowl and stir with a fork. Cover and leave in a warm place for 2–3 hours, or leave overnight in a cool place.

2 Place the flours, salt and butter in a food processor and process just until blended, 1–2 minutes.

3 Stir together the milk and starter, then slowly pour into the processor, with the motor running, until the mixture forms a dough. If necessary, add more water. Alternatively, the dough can be mixed by hand. Transfer to a floured surface and knead until smooth and elastic.

4 Place in an ungreased bowl, cover with a plastic bag, and leave to rise in a warm place until doubled in volume, about 1 1/2 hours.

5 Transfer to a floured surface and knead briefly. Return to the bowl and leave to rise until tripled in volume, about 1 1/2 hours.

6 ▲ Divide the dough in half. Cut off one-third of the dough from each half and shape into balls. Shape the larger remaining portion of each half into balls. Grease a baking sheet.

7 ▲ For each loaf, top the large ball with the small ball and press the centre with the handle of a wooden spoon to secure. Cover with a plastic bag, slash the top, and leave to rise.

8 Preheat a 400°F/200°C/Gas 6 oven. Dust the dough with flour and bake until the top is browned and the bottom sounds hollow when tapped, 45–50 minutes. Cool on a rack.

Split Tin

MAKES 1 LOAF

1¼ lb (500 g) unbleached white bread flour, plus extra for dusting
2 teaspoons (10 ml) salt
½ oz (15 g) fresh yeast
½ pint (300 ml) lukewarm water
4 tablespoons (60 ml) lukewarm milk

As its name suggests, this homely loaf is so called because of the centre split. Some bakers mould the dough in two loaves – they join together whilst proving but retain the characteristic crack after baking.

1 Lightly grease a 2 lb (900 g) loaf tin 7¼ × 4½ in (18.5 × 12 cm). Sift the flour and salt together and make a well in the centre. Mix the yeast with half the lukewarm water in a jug, then stir in the remaining water.

2 Pour the yeast mixture into the centre of the flour and using your fingers, mix in a little flour. Gradually mix in more of the flour from around the edge of the bowl to form a batter.

3 Sprinkle a little more flour from around the edge over the batter and leave in a warm place to "sponge". Bubbles will appear in the batter after about 20 minutes. Add the milk and remaining flour; mix to a firm dough.

4 ▲ Place on a lightly floured surface and knead for about 10 minutes until smooth and elastic. Place in a lightly oiled bowl, cover with lightly oiled clear film and leave to rise, in a warm place, for 1–1¼ hours, or until nearly doubled in bulk.

5 Knock back the dough and turn out on to a lightly floured surface. Shape it into a rectangle. Roll up lengthways, tuck the ends under and place seam side down in the tin. Cover and leave to rise for about 20–30 minutes, or until nearly doubled in bulk.

6 ▲ Using a sharp knife, make one deep central slash the length of the bread; dust with flour. Leave for 10–15 minutes.

7 Meanwhile, preheat the oven to 230°C/450°F/Gas 8. Bake for 15 minutes, then reduce the oven temperature to 200°C/400°F/Gas 6. Bake for 20–25 minutes more, or until the bread is golden.

Plaited Loaf

MAKES 1 LOAF

1 tablespoon active dried yeast
1 teaspoon honey
8 fl oz (250 ml) lukewarm milk
2 oz (55 g) butter, melted
15 oz (420 g) strong flour
1 teaspoon salt
1 egg, lightly beaten
1 egg yolk beaten with 1 teaspoon milk, for glazing

1 ▼ Combine the yeast, honey, milk and butter. Stir and leave for 15 minutes to dissolve.

2 In a large bowl, mix together the flour and salt. Make a well in the centre and add the yeast mixture and egg. With a wooden spoon, stir from the centre, incorporating flour with each turn, to obtain a rough dough.

3 Transfer to a floured surface and knead until smooth and elastic. Place in a clean bowl, cover and leave to rise in a warm place until doubled in volume, about 1½ hours.

4 Grease a baking sheet. Punch down the dough and divide into three equal pieces. Roll to shape each piece into a long thin strip.

5 ▲ Begin plaiting with the centre strip, tucking in the ends. Cover loosely and leave to rise in a warm place for 30 minutes.

6 ▲ Preheat the oven to 375°F/ 190°C/Gas 5 oven. Place the bread in a cool place while the oven heats. Brush with the glaze and bake until golden, for 40–45 minutes. Turn out onto a rack to cool.

Sourdough Bread

MAKES 1 LOAF

12 oz (350 g) flour
1 tablespoon salt
8 fl oz (250 ml) Sourdough Starter
4 fl oz (120 ml) lukewarm water

1 ▲ Combine the flour and salt in a large bowl. Make a well in the centre and add the starter and water. With a wooden spoon, stir from the centre, incorporating more flour with each turn, to obtain a rough dough.

2 ▲ Transfer the dough to a floured surface. To knead, push the dough away from you with the palm of your hand, then fold it towards you, and push it away again. Repeat the process until the dough has become smooth and elastic.

3 Place in a clean bowl, cover, and leave to rise in a warm place until doubled in volume, about 2 hours.

4 Lightly grease an 8 × 4 in (20 × 10 cm) bread tin.

5 ▼ Punch down the dough with your fist. Knead briefly, then form into a loaf shape and place in the tin, seam-side down. Cover with a plastic bag, and leave to rise in a warm place, for about 1¹/₂ hours.

6 Preheat the oven to 425°F/220°C/ Gas 7. Dust the top of the loaf with flour, then score lengthways. Bake for 15 minutes. Lower the heat to 375°F/ 190°C/Gas 5 and bake for about 30 minutes more, or until the bottom sounds hollow when tapped.

Sourdough Starter

MAKES 1¹/₄ PINTS (750 ML)

1 teaspoon active dried yeast
6 fl oz (175 ml) lukewarm water
2 oz (50 g) flour

~ COOK'S TIP ~

After using, feed the starter with a handful of flour and enough water to restore it to a thick batter. The starter can be refrigerated for up to 1 week, but must be brought back to room temperature before using.

1 ▲ For the starter, combine the yeast and water, stir and leave for 15 minutes to dissolve.

2 ▼ Sprinkle over the flour and whisk until it forms a batter. Cover and leave to rise in a warm place for at least 24 hours or preferably 2–4 days, before using.

Rye Bread

Rye bread is popular in northern Europe and makes an excellent base for open sandwiches.

MAKES 2 LOAVES

12 oz (350 g) wholemeal flour
8 oz (225 g) rye flour
4 oz (115 g) strong white flour
1½ teaspoons (7.5ml) salt
2 tablespoons (30 ml) caraway seeds
16 fl oz (475 ml) warm water
2 teaspoons (10 ml) dried yeast
pinch of sugar
2 tablespoons (30 ml) molasses

1 ▲ Put the flours and salt in a bowl. Set aside 1 tsp (5 ml) of the caraway seeds and add the rest to the bowl.

2 ▲ Put half the water in a jug. Sprinkle the yeast on top. Add the sugar, mix and leave for 10 minutes.

3 ▲ Make a well in the flour mixture, then add the yeast mixture with the molasses and the remaining water. Gradually incorporate the flour and mix to a soft dough, adding a little extra water, if necessary.

4 ▲ Transfer to a floured surface and knead for 5 minutes until smooth and elastic. Return to the clean bowl, cover and leave in a warm place for about 2 hours until doubled in bulk. Grease a baking sheet.

5 ▲ Turn the dough on to a floured surface and knead for 2 minutes. Divide the dough in half, then shape into two 9 in (23 cm) long oval loaves. Flatten the loaves slightly and place them on the baking sheet.

6 ▲ Brush with water and sprinkle with the remaining caraway seeds. Cover and leave in a warm place for about 40 minutes, until well risen. Preheat the oven to 200°C/400°F/ Gas 6. Bake the loaves for 30 minutes or until they sound hollow when tapped underneath. Cool on a wire rack.

~ COOK'S TIP ~

To make caraway-seed bread rolls, divide each of the two flattened loaves into eight equal portions. Place them on the baking sheet, brush with water and sprinkle with caraway seeds. Vary the topping by using poppy seeds, if you prefer.

Pecan Rye Bread

MAKES 2 LOAVES

1¹/₂ tablespoons active dried yeast
24 fl oz (700 ml) lukewarm water
1 lb 8 oz (700 g) strong flour
1 lb 2 oz (500 g) rye flour
2 tablespoons salt
1 tablespoon honey
2 teaspoons caraway seeds, (optional)
4 oz (115 g) butter, at room temperature
8 oz (225 g) pecans, chopped

1   Combine the yeast and 4 fl oz (125 ml) of the water. Stir and leave for 15 minutes to dissolve.

2   In the bowl of an electric mixer, combine the flours, salt, honey, caraway seeds and butter. With the dough hook, mix on low speed until well blended.

3   Add the yeast mixture and the remaining water and mix on medium speed until the dough forms a ball.

4 ▲   Transfer to a floured surface and knead in the pecans.

5   Return the dough to a bowl, cover with a plastic bag and leave in a warm place until doubled, about 2 hours.

6   Grease 2 8¹/₂ × 4¹/₂ in (21.5 × 11.5 cm) bread tins.

7 ▲   Punch down the risen dough.

8   Divide the dough in half and form into loaves. Place in the tins, seam side down. Dust the tops with flour.

9   Cover with plastic bags and leave to rise in a warm place until doubled in volume, about 1 hour.

10   Preheat a 375°F/190°C/Gas 5 oven.

11 ▼   Bake until the bottoms sound hollow when tapped, 45–50 minutes. Cool on racks.

Sourdough Rye Bread

MAKES 2 LOAVES

2 teaspoons active dried yeast
4 fl oz (125 ml) lukewarm water
1 oz (30 g) butter, melted
1 tablespoon salt
4 oz (115 g) wholemeal flour
14–16 oz (400–450 g) plain flour
1 egg mixed with 1 tablespoon water, for glazing

FOR THE STARTER

1 tablespoon active dried yeast
12 fl oz (350 ml) lukewarm water
3 tablespoons black treacle
2 tablespoons caraway seeds
9 oz (250 g) rye flour

1 For the starter, combine the dried yeast and water, stir and leave for 15 minutes to dissolve.

2 ▲ Stir in the black treacle, caraway seeds and rye flour. Cover and leave in a warm place for 2–3 days.

3 In a large bowl, combine the dried yeast and water, stir and leave for 10 minutes. Stir in the melted butter, salt, wholemeal flour and 14 oz (400 g) of the plain flour.

4 ▲ Make a well in the centre and pour in the starter.

5 Stir to obtain a rough dough, then transfer to a floured surface and knead until smooth and elastic. Return to the bowl, cover and leave to rise in a warm place until doubled in volume, about 2 hours.

6 Grease a large baking sheet. Knock back the dough and knead briefly. Cut the dough in half and form each half into log-shaped loaves.

7 ▼ Place the loaves on the baking sheet and score the tops with a sharp knife. Cover and leave to rise in a warm place until almost doubled, about 50 minutes.

8 Preheat the oven to 375°F/190°C/ Gas 5. Brush the loaves with the egg wash to glaze them, then bake until the bottoms sound hollow when tapped, about 50–55 minutes. If the tops brown too quickly, place a sheet of foil over the tops to protect them. Cool on a wire rack.

Buttermilk Graham Bread

SERVES 8

2 teaspoons active dried yeast

4 fl oz (120 ml) lukewarm water

8 oz (225 g) graham or wholewheat flour

12 oz (350 g) plain flour

4½ oz (130 g) cornmeal

2 teaspoons salt

2 tablespoons sugar

4 tablespoons butter, at room temperature

16 fl oz (475 ml) lukewarm buttermilk

1 beaten egg, for glazing

sesame seeds, for sprinkling

1 Combine the yeast and water, stir, and leave for 15 minutes to dissolve.

2 ▲ Mix together the two flours, cornmeal, salt and sugar in a large bowl. Make a well in the centre and pour in the yeast mixture, then add the butter and the buttermilk.

3 ▲ Stir from the centre, mixing in the flour until a rough dough is formed. If too stiff, use your hands.

4 ▲ Transfer to a floured surface and knead until smooth. Place in a clean bowl, cover, and leave in a warm place for 2–3 hours.

5 ▲ Grease 2 8 in (20 cm) square baking tins. Punch down the dough. Divide into eight pieces and roll them into balls. Place four in each tin. Cover and leave in a warm place for about 1 hour.

6 Preheat the oven to 375°F/190°C/ Gas 5. Brush with the glaze, then sprinkle over the sesame seeds. Bake for about 50 minutes, or until the bottoms sound hollow when tapped. Cool on a wire rack.

Bread Stick

A bread stick is perfect for garlic bread or sandwiches.

1 Combine the yeast and water, stir, and leave for 15 minutes to dissolve. Stir in the salt.

2 Add the flour, 4 oz (115 g) at a time. Beat in with a wooden spoon, adding just enough flour to obtain a dough. Alternatively, use an electric mixer with a dough hook attachment.

3 Transfer to a floured surface and knead until smooth and elastic.

4 Shape into a ball, place in a greased bowl, and cover with a plastic bag. Leave to rise in a warm place until doubled in volume, for 2–4 hours.

5 ▲ Transfer to a lightly floured board, halve the dough and shape into two long loaves. Place on a baking sheet sprinkled with cornmeal, and leave to rise for 5 minutes.

6 ▲ Score the tops in several places with a very sharp knife. Brush with water and place in a cold oven. Set a pan of boiling water on the bottom of the oven and set the oven to 200°C/400°F/Gas 6. Bake for about 40 minutes. Cool on a rack.

MAKES 2 LOAVES

2 teaspoons (10 ml) active dry yeast
16 fl oz (475 ml) lukewarm water
1 teaspoon (5 ml) salt
1½–2 lb (675–900 g) plain flour
cornmeal, for sprinkling

Three Grain Bread

A mixture of grains gives this close-textured bread a delightful nutty flavour. Make two smaller twists, if preferred.

Makes 1 loaf

16 fl oz (475 ml) warm water
2 teaspoons (10 ml) dried yeast
pinch of sugar
8 oz (225 g) strong white flour
1½ teaspoons (7.5 ml) salt
8 oz (225 g) malted brown flour
8 oz (225 g) rye flour
2 tablespoons (30 ml) linseed
3 oz (75 g) medium oatmeal
3 tablespoons (45 ml) sunflower seeds
2 tablespoons (30 ml) malt extract

1 ▲ Put half the water in a jug. Sprinkle the yeast on top. Add the sugar, mix and leave for 10 minutes.

2 ▲ Sift the white flour and salt into a bowl and add the other flours. Set aside 1 teaspoon (5 ml) of the linseed and add the rest to the flour mixture with the oatmeal and sunflower seeds. Add the yeast mixture to the bowl with the malt extract and the remaining water.

3 Gradually incorporate the flour.

4 ▲ Mix to a soft dough, adding extra water if necessary. Turn out on to a floured surface and knead for 5 minutes until smooth and elastic. Return to the clean bowl, cover with a damp dish towel and leave to rise for about 2 hours until doubled in bulk.

5 ▲ Grease a baking sheet. Turn the dough on to a floured surface, knead for 2 minutes, then divide in half. Roll each half into a 12 in (30 cm) sausage.

6 ▲ Twist the two sausages together, dampen the ends and press to seal. Lift the twist on to the prepared baking sheet. Brush the plait with water, sprinkle with the remaining linseed and cover loosely with a large plastic bag. Leave in a warm place until well risen. Preheat the oven to 220°C/425°F/Gas 7.

7 ▲ Bake the loaf for 10 minutes, then lower the oven temperature to 200°C/400°F/Gas 6 and cook for 20 minutes more, or until the loaf sounds hollow when it is tapped underneath. Transfer to a wire rack to cool.

Multi-Grain Bread

MAKES 2 LOAVES

1 tablespoon active dried yeast
2 fl oz (65 ml) lukewarm water
2¹/₂ oz (70 g) rolled oats (not quick cooking)
16 fl oz (450 ml) milk
2 teaspoons salt
2 fl oz (65 ml) oil
2 oz (55 g) light brown sugar
2 tablespoons honey
2 eggs, lightly beaten
1 oz (30 g) wheat germ
6 oz (170 g) soya flour
12 oz (350 g) wholemeal flour
15 oz–1 lb 1¹/₂ oz (420–490 g) strong flour

1 Combine the yeast and water, stir, and leave for 15 minutes to dissolve.

2 ▲ Place the oats in a large bowl. Scald the milk, then pour over the rolled oats.

3 Stir in the salt, oil, sugar and honey. Leave until lukewarm.

~ VARIATION ~

Different flours may be used in this recipe, such as rye, barley, buckwheat or cornmeal. Try replacing the wheat germ and the soya flour with one or two of these, using the same total amount.

4 ▲ Stir in the yeast mixture, eggs, wheat germ, soya and wholemeal flours. Gradually stir in enough strong flour to obtain a rough dough.

5 Transfer the dough to a floured surface and knead, adding flour if necessary, until smooth and elastic. Return to a clean bowl, cover and leave to rise in a warm place until doubled in volume, about 2¹/₂ hours.

6 Grease 2 8¹/₂ × 4¹/₂ in (21.5 × 11.5 cm) bread tins. Punch down the risen dough and knead briefly.

7 Divide the dough into quarters. Roll each quarter into a cylinder 1¹/₂ in (3 cm) thick. Twist together 2 cylinders and place in a tin; repeat for remaining cylinders.

8 Cover and leave to rise until doubled in size, about 1 hour.

9 Preheat a 375°F/190°C/Gas 5 oven.

10 ▲ Bake for 45–50 minutes, until the bottoms sound hollow when tapped lightly. Cool on a rack.

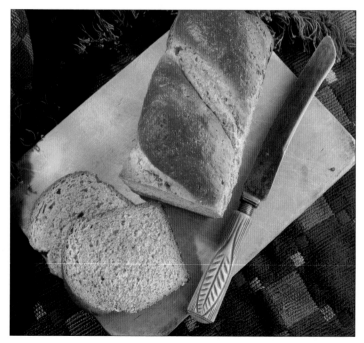

Sesame Seed Bread

MAKES 1 LOAF

2 tsp active dry yeast
10 fl oz (300 ml) lukewarm water
7 oz (200 g) plain flour
7 oz (200 g) wholewheat flour
2 tsp salt
2¹/₂ oz (70 g) toasted sesame seeds
milk, for glazing
2 tbsp sesame seeds, for sprinkling

1   Combine the yeast and 5 tbsp of the water and leave to dissolve. Mix the flours and salt in a large bowl. Make a well in the centre and pour in the yeast and water.

2 ▲   With a wooden spoon, stir from the centre, incorporating flour with each turn, to obtain a rough dough.

3 ▲   Transfer to a lightly floured surface. To knead, push the dough away from you with the palm of your hand, then fold it towards you and push away again. Repeat until smooth and elastic, then return to the bowl and cover with a plastic bag. Leave the dough in a warm place for about 1¹/₂–2 hours, until doubled in volume.

4 ▲   Grease a 9 in (23 cm) cake tin. Punch down the dough and knead in the sesame seeds. Divide the dough into 16 balls and place in the pan. Cover with a plastic bag and leave in a warm place until risen above the rim of the tin.

5 ▼   Preheat a 425°F/220°C/Gas 7 oven. Brush the loaf with milk and sprinkle with the sesame seeds. Bake for 15 minutes. Lower the heat to 375°F/190°C/Gas 5 and bake until the bottom sounds hollow when tapped, about 30 minutes more. Cool on a rack.

Granary Cob

MAKES 1 LOAF

1 lb (450 g) granary or malthouse flour
2 teaspoons (10 ml) salt
½ oz (15 g) fresh yeast
½ pint (300 ml) lukewarm water or milk and water mixed
FOR THE TOPPING
2 tablespoons (30 ml) water
½ teaspoon (2.5ml) salt
wheat flakes or cracked wheat, to sprinkle

Cob is an old word meaning "head". If you make a slash across the top of the dough, the finished loaf, known as a Danish cob, will look like a large roll. A Coburg cob has a cross cut in the top before baking.

1 Lightly flour a baking sheet. Sift the flour and salt together in a large bowl and make a well in the centre. Place in a very low oven for 5 minutes.

2 ▲ Mix the yeast with a little of the water or milk mixture then blend in the rest. Add the yeast mixture to the centre of the flour and mix to a dough.

3 Turn out on to a floured surface and knead for about 10 minutes. Place in a lightly oiled bowl, cover with lightly oiled clear film and leave to rise, in a warm place, for 1¼ hours, or until doubled in bulk.

4 ▲ Turn the dough out on to a lightly floured surface and knock back. Knead for 2–3 minutes, then roll into a plump, round ball. Place in the centre of the prepared baking sheet. Cover with an inverted bowl and leave to rise, in a warm place, for 30–45 minutes.

5 Mix the water and salt and brush over the bread. Sprinkle with wheat flakes or cracked wheat.

6 Meanwhile, preheat the oven to 230°C/450°F/Gas 8. Bake for 15 minutes, then reduce the oven temperature to 200°C/400°F/Gas 6 and bake for a further 20 minutes, or until the loaf is firm to the touch and sounds hollow when tapped on the base.

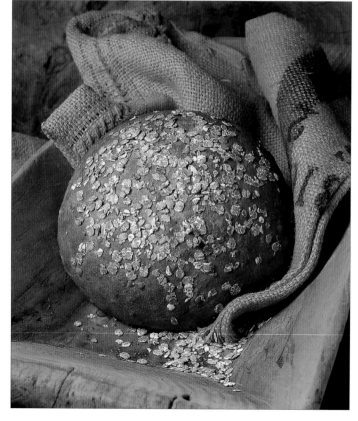

Oatmeal Bread

MAKES 2 LOAVES

16 fl oz (450 ml) milk
1 oz (30 g) butter
2 oz (55 g) dark brown sugar
2 teaspoons salt
1 tablespoon active dried yeast
2 fl oz (65 ml) lukewarm water
13¾ oz (390 g) rolled oats (not quick-cooking)
1 lb 8 oz–1 lb 14 oz (700–850 g) strong flour

1 ▲ Scald the milk. Remove from the heat and stir in the butter, brown sugar and salt. Leave until lukewarm.

2 Combine the yeast and warm water in a large bowl and leave until the yeast is dissolved and the mixture is frothy. Stir in the milk mixture.

3 ▲ Add 10 oz (285 g) of the oats and enough flour to obtain a soft dough.

4 Transfer to a floured surface and knead until smooth and elastic.

5 ▲ Place in a greased bowl, cover with a plastic bag, and leave until doubled in volume, 2–3 hours.

6 Grease a large baking sheet. Transfer the dough to a lightly floured surface and divide in half.

7 ▼ Shape into rounds. Place on the baking sheet, cover with a tea towel and leave to rise until doubled in volume, about 1 hour.

8 Preheat a 400°F/200°C/Gas 6 oven. Score the tops and sprinkle with the remaining oats. Bake until the bottoms sound hollow when tapped, 45–50 minutes. Cool on racks.

Granary Baps

These make excellent picnic fare, filled with cottage cheese, tuna, salad and mayonnaise. They are also very good served warm with soup.

MAKES 8

½ pint (300 ml) warm water
1 teaspoon (5 ml) dried yeast
pinch of sugar
1 lb (450 g) malted brown flour
1 teaspoon (5 ml) salt
1 tablespoon (15 ml) malt extract
1 tablespoon (15 ml) rolled oats

1 ▲ Put half the warm water in a jug. Sprinkle in the yeast. Add the sugar, mix and leave for 10 minutes.

2 ▲ Put the malted brown flour and salt in a mixing bowl and make a well in the centre. Add the yeast mixture with the malt extract and the remaining water. Gradually mix in the flour to make a soft dough.

3 ▲ Turn the dough on to a floured surface and knead for 5 minutes until smooth and elastic. Return to the clean bowl, cover with a damp dish towel and leave in a warm place to rise for about 2 hours until doubled in bulk.

4 ▲ Lightly grease two large baking sheets. Turn the dough on to a floured surface, knead for 2 minutes, then divide into eight pieces. Shape the pieces into balls and flatten them to make neat 4 in (10 cm) rounds.

5 ▲ Place the rounds on the baking sheets, cover loosely with a large plastic bag, and leave to stand in a warm place until well risen. Preheat the oven to 220°C/425°F/Gas 7.

6 ▲ Brush the baps with water, sprinkle with the oats and bake for about 20–25 minutes or until they sound hollow when tapped underneath. Cool on a wire rack, then serve with the filling of your choice.

~ COOK'S TIP ~

To make a large loaf, shape the dough into a round, flatten it slightly and bake for 30–40 minutes. Test by tapping the base of the loaf – if it sounds hollow, it is cooked.

Brown Soda Bread

This is very easy to make – simply mix and bake. Instead of yeast, bicarbonate of soda and cream of tartar are the raising agents. This is a great recipe for those new to bread making.

MAKES 1 LOAF

1 lb (450 g) plain flour
1 lb (450 g) wholemeal flour
2 teaspoons (10 ml) salt
1 tablespoon (15 ml) bicarbonate of soda
4 teaspoons (20 ml) cream of tartar
2 teaspoons (10 ml) caster sugar
2 oz (50 g) butter
up to 1½ pints (900 ml) buttermilk or skimmed milk
extra wholemeal flour, to sprinkle

1 Lightly grease a baking sheet. Preheat the oven to 190°C/375°F/Gas 5.

2 ▲ Sift all the dry ingredients into a large bowl, tipping any bran from the flour back into the bowl.

3 ▲ Rub the butter into the flour mixture, then add enough buttermilk or milk to make a soft dough. You may not need it all, so add cautiously.

4 ▲ Knead the dough lightly until smooth, then transfer to the baking sheet and shape to a large round about 2 in (5 cm) thick.

5 ▲ Using the floured handle of a wooden spoon, make a large cross on top of the dough. Sprinkle over a little extra wholemeal flour. Bake for 40–50 minutes until risen and firm. Leave to cool for 5 minutes before transferring to a wire rack.

Sage Soda Bread

This wonderful loaf, quite unlike bread made with yeast, has a velvety texture and a powerful sage aroma.

1 ▲ Preheat the oven to 220°C/425°F/Gas 7. Sift the dry ingredients into a mixing bowl.

2 ▲ Stir in the sage and add enough buttermilk to make a soft dough.

3 ▲ Shape the dough into a round loaf with your hands and place on a lightly oiled baking sheet.

4 ▲ Cut a deep cross in the top. Bake in the oven for about 40 minutes until the loaf is well risen and sounds hollow when tapped on the bottom. Leave to cool on a wire rack.

MAKES 1 LOAF

6 oz (175 g) wholemeal flour
4 oz (115 g) strong white flour
½ teaspoon (2.5 ml) salt
1 teaspoon (5 ml) bicarbonate of soda
2 tablespoons (30 ml) shredded fresh sage or 2 teaspoons (10 ml) dried sage
½–¾ pint (300–450 ml) cups buttermilk

~ COOK'S TIP ~

As an alternative to the sage, try using either finely chopped rosemary or thyme.

Rosemary Bread

Sliced thinly, this herb bread is delicious with soup for a light meal.

MAKES 1 LOAF

¼ oz (10 g) dried fast-action yeast

6 oz (175 g) wholemeal flour

6 oz (175 g) self-raising flour

2 teaspoons (10 ml) butter, melted, plus extra to grease bowl and tin

2 fl oz (50 ml) warm water

8 fl oz (250 ml) skimmed milk, at room temperature

1 tablespoon (15 ml) sugar

1 teaspoon (5 ml) salt

1 tablespoon (15 ml) sesame seeds

1 tablespoon (15 ml) dried chopped onion

1 tablespoon (15 ml) fresh rosemary leaves, plus extra to decorate

4 oz (115 g) cubed Cheddar cheese

coarse salt, to decorate

1 ▲ Mix the fast-action yeast with the flours in a large mixing bowl. Add the melted butter. Stir in the warm water, milk, sugar, salt, sesame seeds, onion and rosemary. Knead thoroughly until quite smooth.

2 ▲ Flatten the dough, then add the cheese cubes. Quickly knead them in until they are well combined.

3 Place the dough in a large clean bowl greased with a little butter, turning it so that it becomes lightly greased on all sides. Cover with a clean, dry cloth. Put the greased bowl and dough in a warm place for about 1½ hours, or until the dough has risen and doubled in size.

4 Grease a 9 × 5 in (23 × 13 cm) loaf tin with the remaining butter. Knock down the dough to remove some of the air, and shape it into a loaf. Put the loaf into the tin, cover with the clean cloth used earlier and leave for about 1 hour until it has doubled in size once again. Preheat the oven to 190°C/375°F/Gas 5.

5 Bake for 30 minutes. During the last 5–10 minutes of baking, cover the loaf with foil to prevent it becoming too dark in colour. Remove from the loaf tin and leave to cool on a wire rack. Decorate with rosemary leaves and coarse salt scattered on top.

Spiral Herb Bread

MAKES 2 LOAVES

2 tablespoons active dried yeast
1 pt (600 ml) lukewarm water
15 oz (420 g) strong flour
1 lb 2 oz (505 g) wholemeal flour
3 teaspoons salt
1 oz (30 g) butter
1 large bunch of parsley, finely chopped
1 bunch of spring onions, chopped
1 garlic clove, finely chopped
salt and freshly ground black pepper
1 egg, lightly beaten
milk, for glazing

1 Combine the yeast and 2 fl oz (65 ml) of the water, stir and leave for 15 minutes to dissolve.

2 Combine the flours and salt in a large bowl. Make a well in the centre and pour in the yeast mixture and the remaining water. With a wooden spoon, stir from the centre, working outwards to obtain a rough dough.

3 Transfer the dough to a floured surface and knead until smooth and elastic. Return to the bowl, cover with a plastic bag, and leave until doubled in volume, about 2 hours.

4 ▲ Meanwhile, combine the butter, parsley, spring onions and garlic in a large frying pan. Cook over low heat, stirring, until softened. Season and set aside.

5 Grease 2 9 × 5 in (23 × 13 cm) tins. When the dough has risen, cut in half and roll each half into a rectangle about 14 × 9 in (35 × 23 cm).

6 ▼ Brush both with the beaten egg. Divide the herb mixture between the two, spreading just up to the edges.

7 ▲ Roll up to enclose the filling and pinch the short ends to seal. Place in the tins, seam-side down. Cover, and leave in a warm place until the dough rises above the rim of the tins.

8 Preheat a 375°F/190°C/Gas 5 oven. Brush with milk and bake until the bottoms sound hollow when tapped, about 55 minutes. Cool on a rack.

Dill Bread

MAKES 2 LOAVES

4 teaspoons active dried yeast
16 fl oz (450 ml) lukewarm water
2 tablespoons sugar
2 lb 5¹/₂ oz (1.05 kg) strong flour
¹/₂ onion, chopped
4 tablespoons oil
1 large bunch of dill, finely chopped
2 eggs, lightly beaten
5¹/₂ oz (150 g) cottage cheese
4 teaspoons salt
milk, for glazing

1   Mix together the yeast, water and sugar in a large bowl and leave for 15 minutes to dissolve.

2 ▼ Stir in about half of the flour. Cover and leave to rise in a warm place for 45 minutes.

3 ▲ In a frying pan, cook the onion in 1 tablespoon of the oil until soft. Set aside to cool, then stir into the yeast mixture. Stir the dill, eggs, cottage cheese, salt and remaining oil into the yeast. Gradually add the remaining flour until the mixture is too stiff to stir.

4 ▲ Transfer to a floured surface and knead until smooth and elastic. Place in a bowl, cover and leave to rise until doubled in volume, 1–1¹/₂ hours.

5 ▲ Grease a large baking sheet. Cut the dough in half and shape into 2 rounds. Leave to rise in a warm place for 30 minutes.

6   Preheat a 375°F/190°C/Gas 5 oven. Score the tops, brush with the milk and bake until browned, for about 50 minutes. Cool on a rack.

Cheese Bread

MAKES 1 LOAF

1 tablespoon active dried yeast
8 fl oz (250 ml) lukewarm milk
1 oz (30 g) butter
15 oz (420 g) strong flour
2 teaspoons salt
3½ oz (100 g) mature cheddar cheese, grated

1   Combine the yeast and milk. Stir and leave for 15 minutes to dissolve.

2   Melt the butter, let cool, and add to the yeast mixture.

3   Mix the flour and salt together in a large bowl. Make a well in the centre and pour in the yeast mixture.

4   With a wooden spoon, stir from the centre, incorporating flour with each turn, to obtain a rough dough. If the dough seems too dry, add 2–3 tablespoons water.

5   Transfer to a floured surface and knead until smooth and elastic. Return to the bowl, cover and leave to rise in a warm place until doubled in volume, 2–3 hours.

6 ▲   Grease a 9 × 5 in (23 × 13 cm) bread tin. Punch down the dough with your fist. Knead in the cheese, distributing it as evenly as possible.

7 ▼   Twist the dough, form into a loaf shape and place in the tin, tucking the ends under. Leave in a warm place until the dough rises above the rim of the tin.

8 ▲   Preheat a 400°F/200°C/Gas 6 oven. Bake for 15 minutes, then lower to 375°F/190°C/Gas 5 and bake until the bottom sounds hollow when tapped, about 30 minutes more.

Sun-Dried Tomato Plait

This is a marvellous Mediterranean-flavoured bread to serve at a summer buffet or barbecue.

MAKES 1 LOAF

½ pint (300 ml) warm water
1 teaspoon (5 ml) dried yeast
pinch of sugar
8 oz (225 g) wholemeal flour
8 oz (225 g) strong white flour
1 teaspoon (5 ml) salt
¼ teaspoon (1.5 ml) freshly ground black pepper
4 oz (115 g) drained sun-dried tomatoes in oil, chopped, plus 1 tablespoon (15 ml) oil from the jar
1 oz (25 g) freshly grated Parmesan cheese
2 tablespoons (30 ml) red pesto
1 teaspoon (5 ml) coarse sea salt

1 ▲ Put half the warm water in a jug. Sprinkle the yeast on top. Add the sugar, mix and leave for 10 minutes.

2 ▲ Put the wholemeal flour in a mixing bowl. Sift in the white flour, salt and pepper. Add the yeast mixture, sun-dried tomatoes, oil, Parmesan, pesto and the remaining water. Gradually incorporate the flour and mix to a soft dough, adding a little extra water if necessary.

3 ▲ Transfer the dough to a floured surface and knead for 5 minutes until smooth and elastic. Return to the clean bowl, cover with a damp dish towel and leave in a warm place for about 2 hours until doubled in bulk. Lightly grease a baking sheet.

4 ▲ Transfer the dough on to a lightly floured surface and knead for a few minutes. Divide the dough into three equal pieces and shape each into a 12 in (30 cm) long sausage.

5 ▲ Dampen the ends of the three sausages. Press them together at one end, plait them loosely, then press them together at the other end. Place on the baking sheet, cover and leave in a warm place for 30 minutes until well risen. Preheat the oven to 220°C/425°F/Gas 7.

6 ▲ Sprinkle the plait with the coarse sea salt. Bake for 10 minutes, then lower the temperature to 200°C/400°F/Gas 6 and bake for a further 15–20 minutes, or until the loaf sounds hollow when tapped underneath. Cool on a wire rack.

~ COOK'S TIP ~

If you are unable to locate red pesto, use 2 tablespoons (30 ml) chopped fresh basil mixed with 1 tablespoon (15 ml) sun-dried tomato paste.

Parma Ham and Parmesan Bread

This nourishing bread is almost a meal in itself.

MAKES 1 LOAF

8 oz (225 g) self-raising wholemeal flour

8 oz (225 g) self-raising white flour

1 teaspoon (5 ml) baking powder

1 teaspoon (5 ml) salt

1 teaspoon (5 ml) black pepper

3 oz (75 g) Parma ham

1 oz (25 g) freshly grated Parmesan cheese

2 tablespoons (30 ml) chopped fresh parsley

3 tablespoons (45 ml) Meaux mustard

12 fl oz (350 ml) buttermilk

skimmed milk, to glaze

1 ▲ Preheat the oven to 200°C/ 400°F/Gas 6. Flour a baking sheet. Place the wholemeal flour in a bowl and sift in the white flour, baking powder and salt. Add the pepper and the ham. Set aside about 1 tablespoon (15 ml) of the grated Parmesan and stir the rest into the flour mixture with the parsley. Make a well in the centre.

2 ▲ Mix the mustard and buttermilk, pour into the flour and quickly mix to a soft dough.

3 ▲ Transfer the dough to a floured surface and knead briefly. Shape into an oval loaf, brush with milk and sprinkle with the reserved Parmesan. Place on the prepared baking sheet.

4 ▲ Bake the loaf for 25–30 minutes, or until it sounds hollow when tapped underneath. Allow to cool before serving.

Courgette Yeast Bread

The grated courgettes give extra moisture to this tasty loaf.

MAKES 1 LOAF

1 lb (450 g) courgettes, grated
2 tablespoons (30 ml) salt
2 teaspoons (10 ml) active dry yeast
½ pint (300 ml) lukewarm water
14 oz (400 g) plain flour
olive oil, for brushing

1 ▲ In a colander, alternate layers of grated courgettes and salt. Leave for 30 minutes, then squeeze out the moisture with your hands.

2 Combine the yeast with 2 fl oz (50 ml) of the lukewarm water, stir and leave for 15 minutes to dissolve the yeast.

3 ▲ Place the courgettes, yeast and flour in a bowl. Stir together and add just enough of the remaining water to obtain a rough dough.

4 Transfer to a floured surface and knead until smooth and elastic. Return the dough to the bowl, cover with a plastic bag, and leave to rise in a warm place until doubled in volume, for about 1½ hours.

5 Grease a baking sheet. Punch down the risen dough with your fist and knead into a tapered cylinder. Place on the baking sheet, cover and leave to rise in a warm place until doubled in volume, for about 45 minutes.

6 ▲ Preheat the oven to 220°C/ 425°F/Gas 7. Brush the bread with olive oil and bake for about 40–45 minutes, or until the loaf is a golden colour. Cool on a rack before serving.

Spinach and Bacon Bread

This bread is so tasty that it is a good idea to make double the quantity and freeze one of the loaves. Use smoked lean back bacon for the best possible flavour with the minimum of fat.

MAKES 2 LOAVES

¾ pint (450 ml) warm water

2 teaspoons (10 ml) dried yeast

pinch of sugar

1 tablespoon (15 ml) olive oil

1 onion, chopped

4 oz (115 g) rindless smoked bacon rashers, chopped

8 oz (225 g) chopped spinach, thawed if frozen

1½ lb (675 g) strong plain flour

1½ teaspoons (7.5 ml) salt

1½ teaspoons (7.5 ml) grated nutmeg

1 oz (25 g) grated reduced-fat Cheddar cheese

1 ▲ Put the water in a bowl. Sprinkle the yeast on top and add the sugar. Mix, and leave for 10 minutes. Grease two 9 in (23 cm) cake tins.

2 ▲ Heat the oil in a frying pan and fry the onion and bacon for 10 minutes until golden brown. If using frozen spinach, drain it thoroughly.

3 ▲ Sift the flour, salt and nutmeg into a mixing bowl and make a well in the centre. Add the yeast mixture. Tip in the fried bacon and onion (with the oil), then add the spinach. Gradually incorporate the flour mixture and mix to a soft dough.

4 ▲ Transfer the dough to a floured surface and knead for 5 minutes. Return to the clean bowl, cover with a damp dish towel and leave in a warm place to rise for about 2 hours, until doubled in bulk.

5 ▲ Transfer the dough to a floured surface, knead briefly, then divide it in half. Shape each half into a ball, flatten slightly and place in a tin, pressing the dough to the edges. Mark each loaf into eight wedges and sprinkle with the cheese. Cover loosely with a plastic bag and leave in a warm place until well risen. Preheat the oven to 200°C/400°F/Gas 6.

6 ▲ Bake the loaves for 25–30 minutes, or until they sound hollow when they are tapped underneath. Transfer to a wire rack to cool.

~ COOK'S TIP ~

If using frozen spinach, be sure to squeeze out any excess liquid or the resulting dough will be too sticky.

Walnut Bread

MAKES 1 LOAF

15 oz (420 g) wholemeal flour	
5 oz (140 g) strong flour	
2½ teaspoons salt	
18 fl oz (525 ml) lukewarm water	
1 tablespoon honey	
1 tablespoon active dried yeast	
5 oz (140 g) walnut pieces, plus more for decorating	
1 beaten egg, for glazing	

1 Combine the flours and salt in a large bowl. Make a well in the centre and add 8 fl oz (250 ml) of the water, the honey and the yeast.

2 Set aside until the yeast dissolves and the mixture is frothy.

3 Add the remaining water. With a wooden spoon, stir from the centre, incorporating flour with each turn, to obtain a smooth dough. Add more flour if the dough is too sticky and use your hands if the dough becomes too stiff to stir.

4 Transfer to a floured board and knead, adding flour if necessary, until the dough is smooth and elastic. Place in a greased bowl and roll the dough around in the bowl to coat thoroughly on all sides.

5 ▲ Cover with a plastic bag and leave in a warm place until doubled in volume, about 1½ hours.

6 ▲ Punch down the dough and knead in the walnuts evenly.

7 Grease a baking sheet. Shape into a round loaf and place on the baking sheet. Press in walnut pieces to decorate the top. Cover loosely with a damp cloth and leave to rise in a warm place until doubled, 25–30 minutes.

8 Preheat a 425°F/220°C/Gas 7 oven.

9 ▲ With a sharp knife, score the top. Brush with the glaze. Bake for 15 minutes. Lower the heat to 375°F/190°C/Gas 5 and bake until the bottom sounds hollow when tapped, about 40 minutes. Cool on a rack.

Courgette and Walnut Loaf

A moist and crunchy loaf – a real treat.

1 ▲ Preheat the oven to 180°C/ 350°F/Gas 4. Grease the base and sides of a 2 lb (900 g) loaf tin and line with greaseproof paper.

2 Beat the eggs and sugar together and gradually add the oil.

3 ▲ Sift the flour together with the baking powder, bicarbonate of soda, cinnamon and allspice.

4 ▲ Mix into the egg mixture with the rest of the ingredients, reserving 1 tablespoon (15 ml) of the seeds.

5 Spoon into the loaf tin, level off the top, and sprinkle with the reserved sunflower seeds.

6 ▲ Bake for about 1 hour or until a skewer inserted in the centre of the loaf comes out clean. Leave to cool slightly, then turn out on to a wire cooling rack.

MAKES 1 LOAF
3 eggs
3 oz (75 g) light brown sugar
2 fl oz (50 ml) sunflower oil
8 oz (225 g) wholemeal flour
1 teaspoon (5 ml) baking powder
1 teaspoon (5 ml) bicarbonate of soda
1 teaspoon (5 ml) ground cinnamon
½ teaspoon (2.5 ml) ground allspice
½ tablespoon (7.5 ml) green cardamoms, seeds removed and crushed
5 oz (150 g) coarsely grated courgette
2 oz (50 g) walnuts, chopped
2 oz (50 g) sunflower seeds

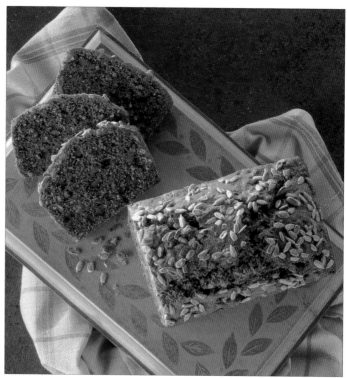

Corn Bread

MAKES 1 LOAF

4 oz (115 g) plain flour
2¹/₂ oz (75 g) caster sugar
1 tsp salt
1 tbsp baking powder
6 oz (170 g) cornmeal, or polenta
12 fl oz (350 ml) milk
2 eggs
3 oz (85 g) butter, melted
4 oz (115 g) margarine, melted

1 Preheat a 400°F/200°C/Gas 6 oven. Line a 9 × 5 in (23 × 13 cm) loaf tin with greaseproof paper and grease.

2 Sift the flour, sugar, salt and baking powder into a mixing bowl.

3 ▼ Add the cornmeal and stir to blend. Make a well in the centre.

4 ▲ Whisk together the milk, eggs, butter and margarine. Pour the mixture into the well. Stir until just blended; do not overmix.

5 Pour into the tin and bake until a skewer inserted in the centre comes out clean, about 45 minutes. Serve hot or at room temperature.

Spicy Sweetcorn Bread

MAKES 9 SQUARES

3–4 whole canned chilli peppers, drained
2 eggs
16 fl oz (450 ml) buttermilk
2 oz (55 g) butter, melted
2 oz (55 g) plain flour
1 tsp bicarbonate of soda
2 tsp salt
6 oz (170 g) cornmeal, or polenta
12 oz (350 g) canned sweetcorn or frozen sweetcorn, thawed

1 Preheat a 400°F/200°C/Gas 6 oven. Line the bottom and sides of a 9 in (23 cm) square cake tin with greaseproof paper and grease lightly.

2 ▲ With a sharp knife, finely chop the chillis and set aside.

3 ▲ In a large bowl, whisk the eggs until frothy, then whisk in the buttermilk. Add the melted butter.

4 In another large bowl, sift together the flour, bicarbonate of soda and salt. Fold into the buttermilk mixture in 3 batches, then fold in the cornmeal in 3 batches.

5 ▲ Fold in the chillis and sweetcorn.

6 Pour the mixture into the prepared tin and bake until a skewer inserted in the middle comes out clean, 25–30 minutes. Let stand for 2–3 minutes before unmoulding. Cut into squares and serve warm.

Corn Bread (top), Spicy Sweetcorn Bread

Onion Focaccia

This pizza-like flat bread is characterized by its soft dimpled surface.

MAKES 2 ROUND LOAVES

1½ lb (675 g) strong plain flour
½ teaspoon (2.5 ml) salt
½ teaspoon (2.5 ml) caster sugar
1 tablespoon (15 ml) easy-blend dried yeast
4 tablespoons (60 ml) extra virgin olive oil
¾ pint (450 ml) hand-hot water
TO FINISH
2 red onions, thinly sliced
3 tablespoons (45 ml) extra virgin olive oil
1 tablespoon (15 ml) coarse salt

1 Sift the flour, salt and sugar into a large bowl. Stir in the yeast, oil and water and mix to a dough using a round-bladed knife. (Add a little extra water if the dough is dry.)

2 ▲ Turn out on to a lightly floured surface and knead for 10 minutes until smooth and elastic. Put the dough in a clean, lightly oiled bowl and cover with clear film. Leave to rise in a warm place until doubled in bulk.

3 ▲ Place two 10 in (25 cm) metal flan rings on baking sheets. Oil the sides of the rings and the baking sheets.

4 ▲ Preheat the oven to 200°C/400°F/Gas 6. Halve the dough and roll each piece to a 10 in (25 cm) round. Press into the rings, cover with a dampened dish towel and leave for 30 minutes to rise.

5 ▲ Make deep holes, about 1 in (2.5 cm) apart, in the dough. Cover and leave for a further 20 minutes.

6 ▲ Scatter with the onions and drizzle over the oil. Sprinkle with the salt, then a little cold water, to stop a crust from forming.

7 ▲ Bake for about 25 minutes, sprinkling with water again during cooking. Cool on a wire rack.

Saffron Focaccia

A dazzling yellow bread with a distinctive flavour.

MAKES 1 ROUND LOAF

pinch of saffron threads
¼ pint (150 ml) boiling water
8 oz (225 g) plain flour
½ teaspoon (2.5 ml) salt
1 teaspoon (5 ml) easy-blend dried yeast
1 tablespoon (15 ml) olive oil
FOR THE TOPPING
2 garlic cloves, sliced
1 red onion, cut into thin wedges
rosemary sprigs
12 black olives, stoned and coarsely chopped
1 tablespoon (15 ml) olive oil

1 ▲ Infuse the saffron in the boiling water. Leave until cooled to lukewarm.

2 ▲ Place the flour, salt, yeast and olive oil in a food processor. Turn on and gradually add the saffron and its liquid until the dough forms a ball.

3 ▲ Transfer to a floured board and knead for 10–15 minutes. Place in a bowl, cover and leave to rise for about 30–40 minutes, until doubled in size.

4 ▲ Punch down the risen dough on a lightly floured surface and roll out into an oval shape, ½ in (1 cm) thick. Place on a lightly greased baking sheet and leave to rise for 20–30 minutes.

5 Preheat the oven to 200°C/400°F/ Gas 6. Press indentations in the dough.

6 ▲ Cover with the topping ingredients, brush lightly with olive oil, and bake for about 25 minutes or until the loaf sounds hollow when tapped on the bottom. Leave to cool.

Cheese and Onion Sticks

An extremely tasty bread which is very good with soups or salads. Use an extra-strong cheese to give plenty of flavour without piling on the fat.

MAKES 2 STICKS

½ pint (300 ml) warm water
1 teaspoon (5 ml) dried yeast
pinch of sugar
1 tablespoon (15 ml) sunflower oil
1 red onion, finely chopped
1 lb (450 g) strong white flour
1 teaspoon (5 ml) salt
1 teaspoon (5 ml) dry mustard
3 tablespoons (45 ml) chopped fresh herbs, such as thyme, parsley, marjoram or sage
3 oz (75 g) grated reduced-fat Cheddar cheese

~ COOK'S TIP ~

To make Onion and Coriander Sticks, omit the cheese, herbs and mustard. Add 1 tablespoon (15 ml) ground coriander and 3 tablespoons (45 ml) chopped fresh coriander instead.

1 ▲ Put the water in a jug. Sprinkle the yeast on top. Add the sugar, mix well and leave for 10 minutes.

2 ▲ Heat the oil in a frying pan and fry the onion until it is well coloured.

3 ▲ Stir the flour, salt and mustard into a mixing bowl, then add the chopped herbs. Set aside 2 tablespoons (30 ml) of the cheese. Stir the rest into the flour mixture and make a well in the centre. Add the yeast mixture with the fried onions and oil, then gradually incorporate the flour and mix to a soft dough, adding extra water if necessary.

4 ▲ Transfer the dough to a floured surface and knead for 5 minutes until smooth and elastic. Return to the clean bowl, cover with a damp dish towel and leave in a warm place to rise for 2 hours, until doubled in bulk. Lightly grease two baking sheets.

5 ▲ Transfer the dough on to a floured surface, knead briefly, then divide the mixture in half and roll each piece into a 12 in (30 cm) long stick. Place on a baking sheet and make diagonal cuts along the top.

6 ▲ Sprinkle the sticks with the reserved cheese. Cover and leave for 30 minutes until well risen. Preheat the oven to 220°C/425°F/Gas 7. Bake the sticks for 25 minutes or until they sound hollow when tapped underneath.

Saffron and Basil Breadsticks

Saffron lends its delicate flavour, as well as rich yellow colour, to these tasty breadsticks.

MAKES 32 STICKS

generous pinch of saffron strands
2 tablespoons (30 ml) hot water
1 lb (450 g) strong white flour
1 teaspoon (5 ml) salt
2 teaspoons (10 ml) easy-blend dried yeast
½ pint (300 ml) lukewarm water
3 tablespoons (45 ml) olive oil
3 tablespoons (45 ml) chopped fresh basil

1 ▲ Infuse the saffron strands in the hot water for 10 minutes.

2 ▲ Sift the flour and salt into a large mixing bowl. Stir in the yeast, then make a well in the centre of the dry ingredients. Pour in the lukewarm water and saffron liquid.

3 ▲ Add the oil and basil and mix to a soft dough.

4 ▲ Turn out and knead the dough on a lightly floured surface for about 10 minutes until smooth and elastic. Place in a greased bowl, cover with clear film and leave for about 1 hour until it has doubled in size.

5 ▲ Knock back and knead the dough on a lightly floured surface for 2–3 minutes.

6 ▲ Preheat the oven to 220°C/425°F/Gas 7. Divide the dough into 32 pieces and shape into long sticks. Place well apart on greased baking sheets, then leave for a further 15–20 minutes until they become puffy. Bake for about 15 minutes until crisp and golden. Serve warm.

~ COOK'S TIP ~
Use powdered saffron if saffron strands are not available. Turmeric is an inexpensive alternative: it imparts a lovely gold colour, but its flavour is not as delicate.

Flat Bread with Sage

This bread is perfect served hot to accompany a pasta supper.

MAKES 1 ROUND LOAF

2 teaspoons (10 ml) active dry yeast

8 fl oz (250 ml) lukewarm water

12 oz (375 g) plain flour

2 teaspoons (10 ml) salt

5 tablespoons (75 ml) extra virgin olive oil

12 fresh sage leaves, chopped

1 Combine the yeast and water, stir and leave for 15 minutes to dissolve.

2 Mix the flour and salt in a large bowl, and make a well in the centre.

3 Stir in the yeast mixture and 4 tablespoons (60 ml) of the oil. Stir gently from the centre, incorporating flour with each turn, to obtain a rough dough.

4 ▲ Transfer to a floured surface and knead until smooth and elastic. Place in a lightly oiled bowl. Cover and leave to rise in a warm place until doubled in volume, for about 2 hours.

5 ▲ Preheat the oven to 200°C/400°F/Gas 6 and place a baking sheet in the centre of the oven.

6 ▲ Punch down the dough. Knead in the sage, then roll into a 12 in (30 cm) round. Leave to rise slightly.

7 ▲ Dimple the surface all over with your finger. Drizzle the remaining oil on top. Slide a floured board under the bread, carry to the oven, and slide off on to the hot baking sheet. Bake for about 35 minutes or until golden brown. Cool on a rack.

Sweet Sesame Loaf

MAKES 1 OR 2 LOAVES

3 oz (85 g) sesame seeds
10 oz (285 g) plain flour
2¹/₂ teaspoons baking powder
1 teaspoon salt
2 oz (55 g) butter or margarine, at room temperature
4¹/₂ oz (125 g) sugar
2 eggs, at room temperature
grated rind of 1 lemon
12 fl oz (350 ml) milk

1 Preheat a 350°F/180°C/Gas 4 oven. Line a 9 × 5 in (23 × 13 cm) loaf tin with greaseproof paper and grease.

2 ▲ Reserve 2 tablespoons of the sesame seeds. Spread the rest on a baking sheet and bake until lightly toasted, about 10 minutes.

3 Sift the flour, salt and baking powder into a bowl.

4 ▲ Stir in the toasted sesame seeds and set aside.

5 With an electric mixer, cream the butter or margarine and sugar together until light and fluffy. Beat in the eggs, then stir in the lemon rind and milk.

6 ▼ Pour the milk mixture over the dry ingredients and fold in with a large metal spoon until just blended.

7 ▲ Pour into the tin and sprinkle over the reserved sesame seeds.

8 Bake until a skewer inserted in the centre comes out clean, about 1 hour. Let cool in the tin for about 10 minutes. Turn out onto a wire rack to cool completely.

Apricot Nut Loaf

MAKES 1 LOAF

4 oz (115 g) dried apricots
1 large orange
3 oz (85 g) raisins
5 oz (140 g) caster sugar
3 fl oz (85 ml) oil
2 eggs, lightly beaten
9 oz (250 g) plain flour
2 tsp baking powder
1/2 tsp salt
1 tsp bicarbonate of soda
2 oz (55 g) chopped walnuts

1 Preheat a 350°F/180°C/Gas 4 oven. Line a 9 × 5 in (23 × 13 cm) loaf tin with greaseproof paper and grease.

2 Place the apricots in a bowl, cover with lukewarm water and leave to stand for 30 minutes.

3 ▲ With a vegetable peeler, remove the orange rind, leaving the pith.

4 With a sharp knife, finely chop the orange rind strips.

5 Drain the apricots and chop coarsely. Place in a bowl with the orange rind and raisins. Set aside.

6 Squeeze the peeled orange. Measure the juice and add enough hot water to obtain 6 fl oz (175 ml) liquid.

7 ▼ Pour the orange juice mixture over the apricot mixture. Stir in the sugar, oil and eggs. Set aside.

8 In another bowl, sift together the flour, baking powder, salt and bicarbonate of soda. Fold the flour mixture into the apricot mixture in 3 batches.

9 ▲ Stir in the walnuts.

10 Spoon the mixture into the prepared tin and bake until a skewer inserted in the centre comes out clean, 55–60 minutes. If the loaf browns too quickly, protect the top with a sheet of foil. Let cool in the pan for 10 minutes before transferring to a rack to cool completely.

Apple-sauce Bread

Apples and spices such as cinnamon and nutmeg are a match made in heaven.

1 Preheat the oven to 180°C/
350°F/Gas 4. Grease and line a 9 ×
5 in (23 × 13 cm) loaf tin with
greaseproof paper.

2 ▲ Break the egg into a bowl and
beat lightly. Stir in the apple sauce,
butter or margarine, and both sugars.

3 In another bowl, sift together the
flour, baking powder, bicarbonate of
soda, salt, cinnamon and nutmeg.
Fold the dry ingredients into the
apple-sauce mixture in three batches.

4 ▲ Stir in the currants or raisins
and chopped pecans.

5 Pour into the prepared tin and
bake for about 1 hour, or until a
skewer inserted in the centre
comes out clean. Allow to stand
for 10 minutes before transferring
to a cooling rack.

MAKES 1 LOAF
1 egg
8 fl oz (250 ml) apple sauce
4 tablespoons (60 ml) butter or margarine, melted
3 oz (75 g) dark brown sugar, firmly packed
2 oz (50 g) granulated sugar
8 oz (225 g) flour
2 teaspoons (10 ml) baking powder
½ teaspoon (2.5 ml) bicarbonate of soda
½ teaspoon (2.5 ml) salt
1 teaspoon (5 ml) ground cinnamon
½ teaspoon (2.5 ml) grated nutmeg
3 oz (75 g) currants or raisins
6 oz (175 g) pecans, chopped

Banana and Cardamom Bread

The combination of banana and cardamom is delicious in this soft-textured moist loaf. It is perfect for tea time, served with butter and jam.

MAKES 1 LOAF

¼ pint (150 ml) warm water
1 teaspoon (5 ml) dried yeast
pinch of sugar
10 cardamom pods
14 oz (400 g) strong white flour
1 teaspoon (5 ml) salt
2 tablespoons (30 ml) malt extract
2 ripe bananas, mashed
1 teaspoon (5 ml) sesame seeds

1 ▲ Put the warm water in a bowl. Sprinkle the yeast on top. Add the sugar, mix and leave for 10 minutes.

2 ▲ Split the cardamom pods. Remove the seeds and chop finely.

3 ▲ Sift the flour and salt into a mixing bowl and make a well in the centre. Add the yeast mixture with the malt extract, chopped cardamom seeds and bananas.

4 ▲ Gradually incorporate the flour and mix to a soft dough, adding extra water if necessary. Turn the dough on to a floured surface and knead for about 5 minutes. Return to the clean bowl, cover with a damp dish towel and leave to rise for 2 hours, until doubled in bulk.

5 ▲ Grease a baking sheet. Turn the dough on to a floured surface, knead briefly, then divide into three and shape into a plait. Place the plait on the baking sheet and cover loosely with a plastic bag. Leave until well risen. Preheat the oven to 220°C/425°F/Gas 7.

6 ▲ Brush the plait lightly with water and sprinkle with the sesame seeds. Bake for 10 minutes, then lower the oven temperature to 200°C/400°F/Gas 6. Cook for 15 minutes more, or until the loaf sounds hollow when tapped.

~ COOK'S TIP ~

Make sure the bananas are really ripe so that they impart maximum flavour to the bread. If you prefer, place the dough in one piece in a 1 lb (450 g) loaf tin and bake for an extra 5 minutes. As well as being low in fat, bananas are a good source of potassium, therefore making an ideal nutritious, low-fat snack.

Wholewheat Banana Nut Loaf

MAKES 1 LOAF

4 oz (115 g) butter, at room temperature

4 oz (115 g) caster sugar

2 eggs, at room temperature

4 oz (115 g) plain flour

1 tsp bicarbonate of soda

¼ tsp salt

1 tsp ground cinnamon

2 oz (55 g) wholewheat flour

3 large ripe bananas

1 tsp vanilla essence

2 oz (55 g) chopped walnuts

1 Preheat a 350°F/180°C/Gas 4 oven. Line the bottom and sides of a 9 × 5 in (23 × 13 cm) loaf tin with greaseproof paper and grease the paper.

2 With an electric mixer, cream the butter and sugar together until light and fluffy.

3 ▲ Add the eggs, 1 at a time, beating well after each addition.

4 Sift the plain flour, bicarbonate of soda, salt and cinnamon over the butter mixture and stir to blend.

5 ▲ Stir in the wholewheat flour.

6 ▲ With a fork, mash the bananas to a purée, then stir into the mixture. Stir in the vanilla and nuts.

7 ▲ Pour the mixture into the prepared tin and spread level.

8 Bake for about 50–60 minutes, until a skewer inserted in the centre comes out clean. Let stand 10 minutes before transferring to a rack.

Date and Pecan Loaf

MAKES 1 LOAF

6 oz (170 g) stoned dates, chopped
6 fl oz (175 ml) boiling water
2 oz (55 g) unsalted butter, at room temperature
2 oz (55 g) dark brown sugar
2 oz (55 g) caster sugar
1 egg, at room temperature
2 tbsp brandy
5¹/₂ oz (165 g) plain flour
2 tsp baking powder
¹/₂ tsp salt
³/₄ tsp freshly grated nutmeg
3 oz (85 g) coarsely chopped pecans or walnuts

1 ▲   Place the dates in a bowl and pour over the boiling water. Set aside to cool.

2   Preheat a 350°F/180°C/Gas 4 oven. Line a 9 × 5 in (23 × 13 cm) loaf tin with greaseproof paper and grease.

3 ▲   With an electric mixer, cream the butter and sugars until light and fluffy. Beat in the egg and brandy, then set aside.

4   Sift the flour, baking powder, salt and nutmeg together, 3 times.

5 ▼   Fold the dry ingredients into the sugar mixture in 3 batches, alternating with the dates and water.

6 ▲   Fold in the nuts.

7   Pour the mixture into the prepared tin and bake for 45–50 minutes, until a skewer inserted in the centre comes out clean. Allow to cool in the tin for 10 minutes before transferring to a rack to cool completely.

Raisin Bread

MAKES 2 LOAVES

1 tablespoon active dried yeast
16 fl oz (450 ml) lukewarm milk
5 oz (140 g) raisins
2¹/₂ oz (70 g) currants
1 tablespoon sherry or brandy
¹/₂ teaspoon grated nutmeg
grated rind of 1 large orange
2¹/₄ oz (60 g) sugar
1 tablespoon salt
4 oz (115 g) butter, melted
1 lb 8 oz–1 lb 14 oz (700–850 g) strong flour
1 egg beaten with 1 tablespoon cream, for glazing

1   Stir together the yeast and 4 fl oz (125 ml) of the milk and let stand for 15 minutes to dissolve.

2 ▲   Mix the raisins, currants, sherry or brandy, nutmeg and orange rind together and set aside.

3   In another bowl, mix the remaining milk, sugar, salt and half the butter. Add the yeast mixture. With a wooden spoon, stir in half the flour, 5 oz (140 g) at a time, until blended. Add the remaining flour as needed for a stiff dough.

4   Transfer to a floured surface and knead until smooth and elastic. Place in a greased bowl, cover and leave to rise in a warm place until doubled in volume, about 2¹/₂ hours.

5   Punch down the dough, return to the bowl, cover and leave to rise in a warm place for 30 minutes.

6   Grease 2 8¹/₂ × 4¹/₂ in (21.5 × 11.5 cm) bread tins. Divide the dough in half and roll each half into a 20 × 7 in (50 × 18 cm) rectangle.

7 ▲   Brush the rectangles with the remaining melted butter. Sprinkle over the raisin mixture, then roll up tightly, tucking in the ends slightly as you roll. Place in the prepared tins, cover, and leave to rise until almost doubled in volume.

8 ▲   Preheat the oven to 400°F/ 200°C/Gas 6. Brush the loaves with the glaze. Bake for 20 minutes, then lower the temperature to 350°F/ 180°C/ Gas 4 and bake until golden, for about 25–30 minutes more. Cool on racks.

Sweet Potato and Raisin Bread

The natural sweetness of sweet potato is used in this healthy loaf.

1 ▲ Preheat the oven to 180°C/350°F/Gas 4. Grease a 9 × 5 in (23 × 13 cm) loaf tin.

2 Sift the flour, baking powder, salt, cinnamon and nutmeg into a small bowl. Set aside.

3 ▲ With an electric mixer, beat the mashed sweet potatoes with the brown sugar, butter or margarine and eggs until well mixed.

4 ▲ Add the flour mixture and the raisins. Stir with a wooden spoon until the flour is just mixed in.

5 ▲ Transfer the batter to the prepared tin. Bake for 1–1¼ hours, or until a skewer inserted in the centre comes out clean.

6 Cool in the pan on a wire rack for 15 minutes, then turn the bread on to the wire rack and cool completely.

MAKES 1 LOAF
8–10 oz (225–275 g) plain flour
2 teaspoons (10 ml) baking powder
½ teaspoon (2.5 ml) salt
1 teaspoon (5 ml) ground cinnamon
½ teaspoon (2.5 ml) grated nutmeg
1 lb (450 g) mashed cooked sweet potatoes
3 oz (75 g) light brown sugar, firmly packed
4 oz (115 g) butter or margarine, melted and cooled
3 eggs, beaten
3 oz (75 g) raisins

Sultana Bread

A lightly sweetened fruit bread that is delicious served warm. It is also excellent toasted and topped with butter.

MAKES 1 LOAF

¼ pint (150 ml) warm water
1 teaspoon (5 ml) dried yeast
1 tablespoon (15 ml) clear honey
8 oz (225 g) wholemeal flour
8 oz (225 g) strong white flour
1 teaspoon (5 ml) salt
4 oz (115 g) sultanas
2 oz (50 g) walnuts, finely chopped
6 fl oz (175 ml) warm skimmed milk, plus extra for glazing

1 ▲ Put the water in a jug. Sprinkle the yeast on top. Add a few drops of the honey to activate the yeast, mix well and leave for 10 minutes.

2 ▲ Put the flours in a mixing bowl, with the salt and sultanas. Set aside 1 tablespoon (15 ml) of the walnuts and add the rest to the bowl. Mix lightly and make a well in the centre.

3 ▲ Add the yeast and honey mixture to the flour mixture with the milk and remaining honey. Gradually incorporate the flour, mixing to a soft dough; add a little extra water if the dough feels too dry to work with.

4 ▲ Turn the dough on to a floured surface and knead for 5 minutes until smooth and elastic. Return to the clean bowl, cover with a damp dish towel and leave in a warm place to rise for about 2 hours until doubled in bulk. Grease a baking sheet.

5 ▲ Turn the dough on to a floured surface and form into a 11 in (28 cm) long sausage shape. Place on the baking sheet. Make some diagonal cuts down the length of the loaf.

6 ▲ Brush the loaf with milk, sprinkle with the reserved walnuts and leave to rise for about 40 minutes. Preheat the oven to 220°C/425°F/Gas 7. Bake for 10 minutes. Lower the temperature to 200°C/400°F/Gas 6 and bake for about 20 minutes more, or until the loaf sounds hollow when tapped.

~ COOK'S TIP ~

To make Apple and Hazelnut Bread, replace the sultanas with two chopped eating apples and use chopped toasted hazelnuts instead of the walnuts. Add 1 teaspoon (5 ml) ground cinnamon with the flour.

Plaited Prune Bread

MAKES 1 LOAF

1 tbsp active dry yeast
2 fl oz (65 ml) lukewarm water
2 fl oz (65 ml) lukewarm milk
2 oz (55 g) caster sugar
1/2 tsp salt
1 egg
2 oz (55 g) butter, at room temperature
15 oz–1 lb 2 oz (420–500 g) plain flour
1 egg beaten with 2 tsp water, for glazing

FOR THE FILLING

7 oz (200 g) cooked prunes
2 tsp grated lemon rind
1 tsp grated orange rind
1/4 tsp freshly grated nutmeg
1 1/2 oz (45 g) butter, melted
2 oz (55 g) very finely chopped walnuts
2 tbsp caster sugar

1 In a large bowl, combine the yeast and water, stir and leave for 15 minutes to dissolve.

2 Stir in the milk, sugar, salt, egg and butter. Gradually stir in 12 oz (350 g) of the flour to obtain a soft dough.

3 Transfer to a floured surface and knead in just enough flour to obtain a dough that is smooth and elastic. Put into a clean bowl, cover and leave to rise in a warm place until doubled in volume, about 1 1/2 hours.

~ VARIATION ~

For Plaited Apricot Bread, replace the prunes with the same amount of dried apricots. It is not necessary to cook them, but to soften, soak them in hot tea and discard the liquid before using.

---

4 ▲ Meanwhile, for the filling, combine the prunes, lemon and orange rinds, nutmeg, butter, walnuts and sugar and stir together to blend. Set aside.

5 Grease a large baking sheet. Punch down the dough and transfer to a lightly floured surface. Knead briefly, then roll out into a 15 × 10 in (38 × 25 cm) rectangle. Carefully transfer to the baking sheet.

6 ▲ Spread the filling in the centre.

7 ▲ With a sharp knife, cut 10 strips at an angle on either side of the filling, cutting just to the filling.

8 ▲ For a plaited pattern, fold up one end neatly, then fold over the strips from alternating sides until all the strips are folded over. Tuck excess dough underneath at the ends.

9 ▲ Cover loosely with a tea towel and leave to rise in a warm place until almost doubled in volume.

10 ▲ Preheat a 375°F/190°C/Gas 5 oven. Brush with the glaze. Bake until browned, about 30 minutes. Transfer to a rack to cool.

CLASSIC BREADS FROM AROUND THE WORLD

THIS COLLECTION FEATURES SAVOURY AND SWEET CLASSICS FROM AROUND THE WORLD, INCLUDING A GOOD SELECTION OF LESSER-KNOWN SPECIALITIES.

British Cottage Loaf

MAKES 1 LOAF

1½ lb (675 g) unbleached white bread flour

2 teaspoons (10 ml) salt

¾ oz (20 g) fresh yeast

14 fl oz (400 ml) lukewarm water

~ COOK'S TIPS ~

• To ensure a good-shaped cottage loaf the dough needs to be firm enough to support the weight of the top ball.

• Do not over-prove the dough on the second rising or the loaf may topple over.

Snipping the top and bottom sections of the dough at 2 in (5 cm) intervals not only looks good but also helps the loaf to expand in the oven.

1 Lightly grease 2 baking sheets. Sift the flour and salt into a large bowl and make a well in the centre.

2 Mix the yeast in ¼ pint (150 ml) of the water until dissolved. Pour into the flour with the remaining water and mix to a firm dough.

3 Knead on a lightly floured surface for 10 minutes until smooth and elastic. Place in a lightly oiled bowl, cover with lightly oiled clear film and leave to rise, in a warm place, for 1 hour, or until doubled in bulk.

4 ▲ Turn out on to a lightly floured surface and knock back. Knead for 2–3 minutes then divide the dough into two-thirds and one-third; shape each to a ball. Transfer to the prepared baking sheets. Cover with inverted bowls and leave to rise, in a warm place, for about 30 minutes (see Cook's Tips).

5 Gently flatten the top of the larger round of dough and cut a cross in the centre, about 1½ in (4 cm) across. Brush with a little water and place the smaller round on top.

6 ▲ Press a hole through the middle of the top ball, down into the lower part, using the thumb and first two fingers of one hand. Cover with oiled clear film and leave in a warm place for 10 minutes. Preheat the oven to 220°C/425°F/Gas 7 and place the bread on the lower shelf. It will finish expanding as the oven heats up. Bake for 35–40 minutes, or until it is golden brown and sounds hollow when tapped. Cool on a wire rack.

British Grant Loaves

This quick and easy recipe was created by Doris Grant and was included in her cookbook, published in the 1940s – the dough requires no kneading and takes only a minute to mix. The loaves should keep moist for several days.

MAKES 3 LOAVES

3 lb (1.5 kg) wholemeal bread flour
1 tablespoon (15 ml) salt
1 tablespoon (15 ml) easy-blend dried yeast
2 pints (1.2 litres) warm water
1 tablespoon (15 ml) muscovado sugar

1 Grease 3 loaf tins, 8½ × 4½ × 2½ in (21 × 12 × 6 cm) and set aside in a warm place. Sift the flour and salt in a large bowl and warm slightly to take off the chill.

2 Sprinkle the dried yeast over ¼ pint (150 ml) of the water. After a couple of minutes stir in the sugar. Leave for 10 minutes.

3 Make a well in the centre of the flour and stir in the yeast mixture and remaining water. The dough should be slippery. Mix for about 1 minute, working the sides into the middle.

4 ▲ Divide among the prepared tins, cover with oiled clear film and leave to rise, in a warm place, for 30 minutes, or until the dough has risen by about a third.

5 Meanwhile, preheat the oven to 200°C/400°F/Gas 6. Bake for 40 minutes, or until the loaves are crisp and sound hollow when tapped. Turn out on to a wire rack to cool.

British Poppy-Seeded Bloomer

MAKES 1 LOAF

1½ lb (675 g) unbleached white bread flour
2 teaspoons (10 ml) salt
½ oz (15 g) fresh yeast
15 fl oz (430 ml) water
FOR THE TOPPING
½ teaspoon (2.5 ml) salt
2 tablespoons (30 ml) water
poppy seeds, for sprinkling

This satisfying white bread, which is the British version of the chunky baton loaf found throughout Europe, is made by a slower rising method and with less yeast than usual. It produces a longer-keeping loaf with a fuller flavour. The dough takes about 8 hours to rise, so you'll need to start this bread early in the morning.

1 Lightly grease a baking sheet. Sift the flour and salt together into a large bowl and make a well in the centre.

2 ▲ Mix the yeast and ¼ pint (150 ml) of the water in a jug or bowl. Mix in the remaining water. Add to the centre of the flour. Mix, gradually incorporating the surrounding flour, until the mixture forms a firm dough.

~ COOK'S TIP ~

The traditional cracked, crusty appearance of this loaf is difficult to achieve in a domestic oven. However, you can get a similar result by spraying the oven with water before baking. If the underneath of the loaf is not very crusty at the end of baking, turn the loaf over on the baking sheet, switch off the heat and leave in the oven for a further 5–10 minutes.

3 ▲ Turn out on to a lightly floured surface and knead the dough very well, for at least 10 minutes, until smooth and elastic. Place the dough in a lightly oiled bowl, cover with lightly oiled clear film and leave to rise, at cool room temperature, about 15–18°C/60–65°F, for 5–6 hours, or until doubled in bulk.

4 Knock back the dough, turn out on to a lightly floured surface and knead it quite hard for about 5 minutes. Return the dough to the bowl, and re-cover. Leave to rise, at cool room temperature, for a further 2 hours.

5 ▲ Knock back again and repeat the thorough kneading. Leave to rest for 5 minutes, then roll out on a lightly floured surface into a rectangle 1 in (2.5 cm) thick. Roll the dough up from one long side and shape it into a square-ended thick baton shape about 13 × 5 in (33 × 13 cm).

6 ▲ Place it seam side up on a lightly floured baking sheet, cover and leave to rest for 15 minutes. Turn the loaf over and place on the greased baking sheet. Plump up by tucking the dough under the sides and ends, then cut 6 diagonal slashes on the top. Leave to rest, covered, in a warm place, for 10 minutes. Meanwhile preheat the oven to 230°C/450°F/Gas 8.

7 ▲ Mix the salt and water together and brush this glaze over the bread. Sprinkle with poppy seeds.

8 Spray the oven with water, bake the bread immediately for 20 minutes, then reduce the oven temperature to 200°C/400°F/Gas 6; bake for 25 minutes more, or until golden. Transfer to a wire rack to cool.

British Harvest Festival Sheaf

MAKES 1 LARGE LOAF

2 lb (900 g) unbleached white bread flour
1 tablespoon (15 ml) salt
½ oz (15 g) fresh yeast
5 tablespoons (75 ml) lukewarm milk
14 fl oz (400 ml) cold water
FOR THE GLAZE
1 egg
1 tablespoon (15 ml) milk

This is one of the most visually stunning breads. Celebratory loaves can be seen in various forms in churches and at some bakers throughout Britain around the September harvest.

1 Lightly grease a large baking sheet, at least 15 × 13 in (38 × 33 cm). Sift the flour and salt together into a large bowl and make a well in the centre.

2 Cream the yeast with the milk in a jug. Add to the centre of the flour with the water and mix to a stiff dough. Turn out on to a lightly floured surface and knead for about 10–15 minutes until smooth and elastic.

3 Place in a lightly oiled bowl, cover with lightly oiled clear film and leave to rise, at room temperature, for about 2 hours, or until doubled in bulk.

4 Turn the dough out on to a lightly floured surface, knock back and knead for about 1 minute. Cover and leave to rest for 10 minutes.

5 ▲ Divide the dough in two. Roll out one piece to a 14 × 10 in (35 × 25 cm) oblong. Fold loosely in half lengthways. Cut out a half mushroom shape for the sheaf (leave the folded edge uncut). Make the stalk "base" about 7 in (18 cm) long.

6 Place the dough on the baking sheet and open out. Prick with a fork and brush with water to prevent a skin from forming. Reserve 3 oz (75 g) of the trimmings for the tie. Cover and set aside. Divide the remaining dough in two and mix the rest of the trimmings with one half. Cover and set aside. Beat together the egg and milk for the glaze.

7 ▲ Roll out the remaining dough on a lightly floured surface to a rectangle, 11 × 7 in (28 × 18 cm), and cut into 30–35 thin strips 7 in (18 cm) long. Place side by side lengthways on the base, as close as possible, to represent wheat stalks. Brush with some glaze.

8 Take the larger piece of reserved dough and divide into four. Divide each piece into 25 and shape into oblong rolls to make 100 wheat ears. Make each roll pointed at one end.

9 ▲ Holding one roll at a time, snip along each side towards the centre, using scissors, to make wheat ears.

10 Preheat the oven to 220°C/425°F/Gas 7. Arrange the ears around the outer edge of the top of the mushroom shape, overlapping on to the baking sheet. Make a second row lower down, placing it between the first ears. Repeat until they are all used. Brush with glaze as you work to stop the dough from drying out.

11 ▲ Divide the smaller piece of reserved dough into 6 pieces and roll each to a 17 in (43 cm) strip. Make 2 plaits each with 3 strips. Place across the wheat stalks to make a tied bow. Brush with some glaze. Prick between the wheat ears and stalks using a sharp knife and bake the sheaf for 15 minutes.

12 Reduce the oven temperature to 180°C/350°F/Gas 4. Brush the bread with the remaining glaze and bake for a further 30–35 minutes, or until golden and firm. Leave to cool on the baking sheet.

> **~ COOK'S TIP ~**
> Harvest loaves are often baked for display, rather than for eating. If you'd like to do this, then leave the baked loaf in the oven, reduce the temperature to very low, 120°C/250°F/Gas ½, for several hours until the dough dries out.

British Lardy Cake

MAKES 1 LOAF

| 1 lb (450 g) unbleached white bread flour |
| 1 teaspoon (5 ml) salt |
| ½ oz (15 g) lard |
| 1 oz (25 g) caster sugar |
| ¾ oz (20 g) fresh yeast |
| ½ pint (300 ml) lukewarm water |

FOR THE FILLING

| 3 oz (75 g) lard |
| 3 oz (75 g) soft light brown sugar |
| 4 oz (115 g) currants, slightly warmed |
| 3 oz (75 g) sultanas, slightly warmed |
| 1 oz (25 g) mixed chopped peel |
| 1 teaspoon (5 ml) mixed spice |

FOR THE GLAZE

| 2 teaspoons (10 ml) sunflower oil |
| 1–2 tablespoons (15–30 ml) caster sugar |

This special rich fruit bread was originally made throughout many counties of England for celebrating the harvest. Using lard rather than butter or margarine makes an authentic lardy cake.

1 Grease a 10 × 8 in (25 × 20 cm) shallow roasting tin. Sift the flour and salt into a bowl and rub in the lard. Add the sugar. Make a well in the centre.

2 Cream the yeast with half of the water, then blend in the rest. Add to the flour and mix to a smooth dough.

3 Turn out on to a lightly floured surface and knead for about 10 minutes until smooth and elastic. Place in a lightly oiled bowl, cover with lightly oiled clear film and leave to rise, in a warm place, for 1 hour, or until doubled in bulk.

4 Turn the dough out on to a lightly floured surface and knock back. Knead for 2–3 minutes. Roll into a rectangle about ¼ in (5 mm) thick.

5 ▲ Using half the lard for the filling, cover the top two-thirds of the dough with flakes of lard. Sprinkle over half the sugar, half the dried fruits and peel and half the mixed spice. Fold the bottom third up and the top third down, sealing the edges with the rolling pin.

6 Turn the dough by 90 degrees. Repeat the rolling and cover with the remaining lard, fruit and peel and mixed spice. Fold, seal and turn as before. Roll out to fit the prepared tin. Cover with oiled clear film and leave to rise, in a warm place, for 30–45 minutes, until doubled in size.

7 Meanwhile, preheat the oven to 200°C/400°F/Gas 6. Brush the cake with oil and sprinkle with caster sugar.

8 ▲ Score a criss-cross pattern on top using a sharp knife, then bake for 30–40 minutes until golden. Turn out on to a wire rack to cool slightly. Serve warm, cut into slices or squares.

British Malted Currant Bread

This spiced currant bread makes a good tea or breakfast bread, sliced and spread with a generous amount of butter. It also makes superb toast.

Ingredients
2 oz (50 g) malt extract
2 tablespoons (30 ml) golden syrup
2 oz (50 g) butter
1 lb (450 g) unbleached white bread flour
1 teaspoon (5 ml) mixed spice
¾ oz (20 g) fresh yeast
6 fl oz (175 ml) lukewarm milk
6 oz (175 g) currants, slightly warmed
FOR THE GLAZE
2 tablespoons (30 ml) milk
2 tablespoons (30 ml) caster sugar

> ~ COOK'S TIP ~
> When making more than one loaf, the easiest way to prove them is to place the tins in an oiled large polythene bag.

1 ▲ Lightly grease two 1 lb (450 g) loaf tins. Place the malt extract, golden syrup and butter in a saucepan and heat gently until the butter has melted. Set aside to cool completely.

2 Sift the flour and mixed spice together into a large bowl and make a well in the centre. Cream the yeast with a little of the milk, then blend in the remaining milk. Add the yeast mixture and cooled malt mixture to the centre of the flour and blend together to form a dough.

3 Turn out the dough on to a lightly floured surface and knead for about 10 minutes until smooth and elastic. Place in a lightly oiled bowl, cover with lightly oiled clear film and leave to rise, in a warm place, for 1½–2 hours, or until doubled in bulk.

4 Turn the dough out on to a floured surface, knock back, then knead in the currants. Divide the dough in two and shape into two loaves. Place in the prepared tins. Cover with oiled clear film and leave to rise, in a warm place, for 2–3 hours, or until the dough reaches the top of the tins.

5 ▲ Meanwhile, preheat the oven to 200°C/400°F/Gas 6. Bake for 35–40 minutes or until golden. While the loaves are baking, heat the milk and sugar for the glaze in a small pan. Turn out the loaves on to a wire rack, then invert them, so that they are the right way up. Brush the glaze evenly over the loaves and leave to cool.

Welsh Bara Brith

MAKES 1 LOAF

¾ oz (20 g) fresh yeast
7 fl oz (210 ml) lukewarm milk
1 lb (450 g) unbleached white bread flour
3 oz (75 g) butter or lard
1 teaspoon (5 ml) mixed spice
½ teaspoon (2.5 ml) salt
2 oz (50 g) light brown sugar
1 egg, lightly beaten
4 oz (115 g) seedless raisins, slightly warmed
3 oz (75 g) currants, slightly warmed
1½ oz (40 g) mixed chopped peel
1–2 tablespoons (15–30 ml) clear honey, for glazing

This rich, fruity bread – the name literally means "speckled bread" – is a speciality from North Wales. The honey glaze makes a delicious topping.

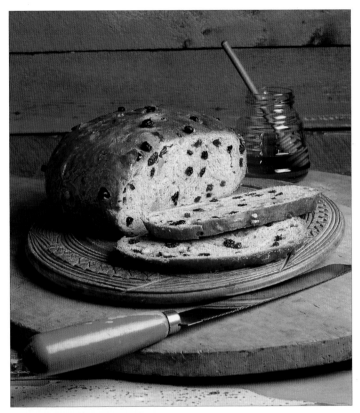

1 Grease a baking sheet. In a jug, blend the yeast with a little of the milk, then stir in the remainder. Set aside for 10 minutes.

2 ▲ Sift the flour into a large bowl and rub in the butter or lard until the mixture resembles breadcrumbs. Stir in the mixed spice, salt and sugar and make a well in the centre.

3 Add the yeast mixture and beaten egg to the centre of the flour and mix to a rough dough.

4 Turn out the dough on to a lightly floured surface and knead for about 10 minutes until smooth and elastic. Place in a lightly oiled bowl, cover with lightly oiled clear film and leave to rise, in a warm place, for 1½ hours, or until doubled in bulk.

5 ▲ Turn out the dough on to a floured surface, knock back, and knead in the dried fruits and peel. Shape into a round and place on the baking sheet. Cover with oiled clear film and leave to rise, in a warm place, for 1 hour, or until doubled in size.

6 Meanwhile, preheat the oven to 200°C/400°F/Gas 6. Bake for 30 minutes or until the bread sounds hollow when tapped on the base. If the bread starts to over-brown, cover it loosely with foil for the last 10 minutes. Transfer the bread to a wire rack, brush with honey and leave to cool.

> **~ VARIATION ~**
>
> The bara brith can be baked in a 2½–3 pint (1.5–1.75 litre) loaf tin or deep round or square cake tin, if you prefer.

Welsh Clay Pot Loaves

These breads are flavoured with chives, sage, parsley and garlic. You can use any selection of your favourite herbs. For even more flavour, try adding a little grated raw onion and grated cheese to the dough.

MAKES 2 LOAVES

4 oz (115 g) wholemeal bread flour
12 oz (350 g) unbleached white bread flour
1½ teaspoons (7.5 ml) salt
½ oz (15 g) fresh yeast
¼ pint (150 ml) lukewarm milk
4 fl oz (120 ml) lukewarm water
2 oz (50 g) butter, melted
1 tablespoon (15 ml) chopped fresh chives
1 tablespoon (15 ml) chopped fresh parsley
1 teaspoon (5 ml) chopped fresh sage
1 garlic clove, crushed
beaten egg, for glazing
fennel seeds, for sprinkling (optional)

1 ▲ Lightly grease 2 clean 5½ in (14 cm) diameter, 4½ in (12 cm) high clay flower pots. Sift the flours and salt into a bowl and make a well in the centre. Blend the yeast with a little of the milk until smooth, then stir in the remaining milk. Pour into the centre of the flour and sprinkle over a little of the flour from around the edge. Cover and leave in a warm place for 15 minutes.

2 ▲ Add the water, melted butter, herbs and garlic to the flour mixture and blend together to form a dough. Turn out on to a floured surface and knead for 10 minutes until the dough is smooth and elastic.

3 Place in a lightly oiled bowl, cover with lightly oiled clear film and leave to rise, in a warm place, for 1¼–1½ hours, or until doubled in bulk.

4 Turn the dough out on to a floured surface and knock back. Divide in two. Shape and fit into the flower pots. They should about half fill the pots. Cover with oiled clear film and leave to rise for 30–45 minutes, in a warm place, or until the dough is 1 in (2.5 cm) from the top of the pots.

5 ▲ Meanwhile, preheat the oven to 200°C/400°F/Gas 6. Brush the tops with beaten egg and sprinkle with fennel seeds, if using. Bake for 35–40 minutes or until golden. Turn out on to a wire rack to cool.

Scottish Morning Rolls

MAKES 10 ROLLS

1 lb (450 g) unbleached plain white flour, plus extra for dusting
2 teaspoons (10 ml) salt
¾ oz (20 g) fresh yeast
¼ pint (150 ml) lukewarm milk
¼ pint (150 ml) lukewarm water
2 tablespoons (30 ml) milk

These rolls are best served warm, as soon as they are baked. In Scotland they are a firm favourite for breakfast with a fried egg and bacon.

1 Grease 2 baking sheets. Sift the flour and salt into a bowl and make a well in the centre. Mix the yeast with the milk, then mix in the water. Add to the centre of the flour and mix together to form a soft dough.

2 Knead the dough lightly in the bowl, then cover with lightly oiled clear film and leave to rise, in a warm place, for 1 hour, or until doubled in bulk. Turn the dough out on to a floured surface and knock back.

3 ▲ Divide the dough into 10 equal pieces. Knead lightly and, using a rolling pin, shape each piece to a flat oval 4 × 3 in (10 × 7.5 cm) or a flat round 3½ in (9 cm).

4 Place on the baking sheets and cover with oiled clear film. Leave to rise, in a warm place, for 30 minutes.

5 ▲ Meanwhile, preheat the oven to 200°C/400°F/Gas 6. Press each roll in the centre with the three middle fingers to equalise the air bubbles and to help prevent blistering. Brush with milk and dust with flour. Bake for 15–20 minutes or until lightly browned. Dust with more flour and cool slightly. Serve warm.

Cornish Saffron Breads

Often called saffron cake, this light, delicately spiced bread contains strands of saffron and is made in a loaf tin. Whatever the name, the flavour and texture are superb.

MAKES 2 LOAVES

½ pint (300 ml) milk
½ teaspoon (2.5 ml) saffron strands
14 oz (400 g) unbleached white bread flour
1 oz (25 g) fresh yeast
2 oz (50 g) ground almonds
½ teaspoon (2.5 ml) grated nutmeg
½ teaspoon (2.5 ml) ground cinnamon
2 oz (50 g) caster sugar
½ teaspoon (2.5 ml) salt
3 oz (75 g) butter, softened
2 oz (50 g) sultanas
2 oz (50 g) currants
extra milk and sugar, to glaze

1 Grease two 2 lb (900 g) loaf tins. Heat half the milk until almost boiling.

2 ▲ Place the saffron strands in a small heatproof bowl and pour over the milk. Stir gently, then leave to infuse for 30 minutes.

3 Heat the remaining milk in the same pan until it is just lukewarm.

4 Place 2 oz (50 g) flour in a small bowl, crumble in the yeast and stir in the lukewarm milk. Mix well, then leave for about 15 minutes until the yeast starts to ferment.

5 Mix the remaining flour, ground almonds, spices, sugar and salt together in a large bowl and make a well in the centre. Add the saffron infusion, yeast mixture and softened butter to the centre of the flour and mix to a very soft dough.

6 Turn out on to a floured surface and knead the dough for 5 minutes until smooth and elastic. Place in a lightly oiled bowl, cover with oiled clear film and leave to rise, in a warm place, for 1½–2 hours, or until doubled in bulk.

7 ▲ Turn the dough out on to a lightly floured surface, knock back, and knead in the sultanas and currants. Divide in two and shape into two loaves. Place in the prepared tins. Cover with oiled clear film and leave to rise, in a warm place, for 1½ hours, or until the dough reaches the top of the tins.

8 Preheat the oven to 220°C/425°F/Gas 7. Bake the loaves for 10 minutes, then reduce the oven temperature to 190°C/375°F/Gas 5 and bake for 15–20 minutes or until golden.

9 To make the glaze, heat milk and sugar together. When the loaves are cooked, brush them with the glaze, leave in the tins for 5 minutes, then turn out on to a wire rack to cool.

French Kugelhopf

MAKES 1 LOAF

5 oz (150 g) unsalted butter, softened
12 walnut halves
1½ lb (675 g) unbleached white bread flour
1½ teaspoons (7.5 ml) salt
¾ oz (20 g) fresh yeast
10 fl oz (300 ml) milk
4 oz (115 g) smoked bacon, diced
1 onion, finely chopped
1 tablespoon (15 ml) vegetable oil
5 eggs, beaten
freshly ground black pepper

This inviting, fluted ring-shaped bread originates from Alsace, although Germany, Hungary and Austria all have their own variations of this popular recipe. Kugelhopf can be sweet or savoury; this version is richly flavoured with nuts, onion and bacon.

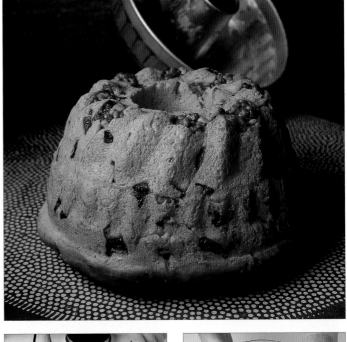

~ VARIATION ~

For a sweet kugelhopf, replace the walnuts with almonds and the bacon and onion with 4 oz (115 g) raisins and 2 oz (50 g) mixed peel. Add 2 oz (50 g) caster sugar in step 2 and omit the pepper.

1 ▲ Use 1 oz (25 g) of the butter to grease a 9 in (23 cm) kugelhopf mould. Place 8 walnut halves around the base and chop the remainder.

2 Sift the flour and salt into a bowl and season with pepper. Make a well in the centre. Cream the yeast with 3 tablespoons (45 ml) of the milk. Pour into the centre of the flour with the remaining milk. Mix in a little flour to make a thick batter. Sprinkle a little of the remaining flour over the top of the batter, cover with clear film and leave in a warm place for 20–30 minutes until the mixture bubbles.

3 ▲ Fry the bacon and onion in the oil until the onion is golden.

4 Add the eggs to the flour mixture and gradually beat in the flour, using your hand. Beat in the remaining butter to form a soft dough. Cover with oiled clear film and leave to rise, in a warm place, for 45–60 minutes, or until almost doubled in bulk. Preheat the oven to 200°C/400°F/Gas 6.

5 ▲ Knock back the dough and gently knead in the bacon, onion and nuts. Place in the mould, cover with oiled clear film and leave to rise, in a warm place, for about 1 hour.

6 Bake for 40–45 minutes, or until the loaf has browned and sounds hollow when tapped on the base. Cool in the mould for 5 minutes, then on a wire rack.

French Pain Polka

This attractive, deeply cut, crusty bread is made by using a little of the previous day's dough as a starter. However, if you do not have any you can make a starter dough, the details for which are given.

MAKES 1 LOAF
8 oz (225 g) 6–15-hours-old French baguette dough
OR FOR THE STARTER
¼ oz (10 g) fresh yeast
4 fl oz (120 ml) lukewarm water
4 oz (115 g) unbleached plain flour
FOR THE DOUGH
¼ oz (10 g) fresh yeast
scant ½ pint (300 ml) lukewarm water
1 lb (450 g) unbleached white bread flour, plus extra for dusting
1 tablespoon (15 ml) salt

> ~ COOK'S TIP ~
> The piece of previously made dough can be kept covered in the fridge for up to 2 days, or frozen for up to a month. Just let it come back to room temperature and allow it to rise for an hour before using.

1 ▲ Lightly flour a baking sheet. If you have French baguette dough, proceed to step 2. Make the starter. Mix the yeast with the water, then gradually stir in sufficient flour to form a batter. Beat vigorously, then gradually add the remaining flour and mix to a soft dough. Knead for 5 minutes. Place in a bowl, cover with oiled clear film, and leave at room temperature for 4–5 hours, or until well risen and starting to collapse.

2 In a bowl, mix the yeast for the dough with half of the water, then stir in the remainder. Add the previously made dough or starter (step 1) and knead to dissolve the dough. Gradually add the flour and salt and mix to a dough. Turn out on to a lightly floured surface and knead for 8–10 minutes until the dough is smooth and elastic.

3 Place the dough in a lightly oiled bowl, cover with lightly oiled clear film and leave to rise, in a warm place, for about 1½ hours, or until doubled in bulk.

4 Turn out the dough on to a lightly floured surface, knock back and shape into a round ball. Flatten slightly and place on the prepared baking sheet. Cover with oiled clear film and leave to rise, in a warm place, for 1 hour.

5 ▲ Dust the top of the loaf with flour and cut the top fairly deeply in a criss-cross pattern. Leave to rest for 10 minutes. Meanwhile, preheat the oven to 230°C/450°F/Gas 8.

6 Bake for 25–30 minutes, or until browned. Spray the inside of the oven with water as soon as the bread goes into the oven, and 3 times during the first 10 minutes of baking. Transfer to a wire rack to cool.

French Pain Bouillie

¼ oz (10 g) fresh yeast

2 tablespoons (30 ml) lukewarm water

1 teaspoon (5 ml) caraway seeds,
  crushed

2 teaspoons (10 ml) salt

12 oz (350 g) unbleached white
  bread flour

olive oil, for brushing

FOR THE PORRIDGE

8 oz (225 g) rye flour

¾ pint (450 ml) boiling water

1 teaspoon (5 ml) clear honey

This is an old-fashioned style of rye bread, made before sourdough starters
were used. Rye flour is mixed with boiling water like a porridge and left
overnight to ferment. The finished bread has a rich earthy flavour, with just
a hint of caraway.

3 Turn out on to a lightly floured
surface and knead for 6–8 minutes
until smooth and elastic. Return to
the bowl, cover with oiled clear film
and leave to rise, in a warm place, for
1½ hours, until doubled in bulk.

4 ▲ Turn out the dough on to a
floured surface and knock back. Cut
and roll into rectangles 15 × 4½ in
(38 × 12 cm). Fold the bottom third
up and the top third down and seal
the edges. Turn over.

5 Brush one side of each piece of folded
dough with olive oil and place side by
side in the prepared tin, oiled edges
next to each other. Cover with lightly
oiled clear film and leave to rise, in a
warm place, for 1 hour, or until the
dough reaches the top of the tin.

6 Meanwhile, preheat the oven to
220°C/425°F/Gas 7. Brush the tops of
the loaves with olive oil and, using a
sharp knife, slash with one or two
cuts. Bake for 30 minutes, then
reduce the oven temperature to
190°C/375°F/Gas 5 and bake for a
further 25–30 minutes. Turn out on
to a wire rack to cool.

> **~ COOK'S TIP ~**
> Serve thickly sliced,
> with a little butter.

1 ▲ Lightly grease a 9¼ × 5 in (23.5
× 13 cm) loaf tin. Place the rye flour
for the porridge in a large bowl. Pour
over the boiling water and leave to
stand for 5 minutes. Stir in the honey.
Cover with clear film and leave in a
warm place for about 12 hours.

2 ▲ Make the dough. Put the yeast in
a jug and blend in the water. Stir the
mixture into the porridge with the
crushed caraway seeds and salt. Add
the white flour a little at a time,
mixing first with a wooden spoon and
then with your hands, until the
mixture forms a firm dough.

French Epi

This pretty, wheat-ear shaped crusty loaf makes a good presentation bread. The recipe uses a piece of fermented French baguette dough as a starter, which improves the flavour and texture of the finished bread.

MAKES 2 LOAVES

¼ oz (7 g) fresh yeast
9 fl oz (275 ml) lukewarm water
4 oz (115 g) 6–10-hours-old French baguette dough
8 oz (225 g) unbleached white bread flour
3 oz (75 g) fine French plain flour
1 teaspoon (5 ml) salt

~ COOK'S TIP ~

You can use any amount up to 10 per cent of previously made French baguette dough for this recipe. The épi can also be shaped into a circle.

1 ▲ Sprinkle a baking sheet with flour. Mix the yeast with the water in a jug. Place the French bread dough in a large bowl and break up. Add a little of the yeast water to soften the dough. Mix in a little of the bread flour, then alternate the additions of yeast water and both flours until incorporated. Sprinkle the salt over the dough and knead in. Turn out on to a floured surface and knead for 5 minutes until smooth and elastic.

2 Place in an oiled bowl, cover with oiled clear film and leave to rise, in a warm place, for about 1 hour, or until the dough has doubled in bulk.

3 ▲ Knock back the dough with your fist, then cover the bowl again with the oiled clear film and leave to rise, in a warm place, for about 1 hour.

4 Divide the dough in half, place on a lightly floured surface and stretch each piece into a baguette.

5 Let the dough rest between rolling for a few minutes, if necessary, to avoid tearing. Pleat a floured dish towel on a baking sheet to make 2 moulds for the loaves. Place them between the pleats of the towel, cover with lightly oiled clear film and leave to rise, in a warm place, for 30 minutes.

6 ▲ Preheat the oven to 230°C/450°F/ Gas 8. Using scissors, make diagonal cuts halfway through the dough about 2 in (5 cm) apart, alternating the cuts along the loaf. Gently pull the dough in the opposite direction.

7 Place on the baking sheet and bake for 20 minutes, until golden. Spray inside the oven with water 2–3 times during the first 5 minutes of baking. Transfer to a wire rack to cool.

French Pain de Campagne Rustique

MAKES 1 LOAF

FOR THE CHEF

2 oz (50 g) wholemeal bread flour

3 tablespoons (45 ml) warm water

FOR THE 1ST REFRESHMENT

4 tablespoons (60 ml) warm water

3 oz (75 g) wholemeal bread flour

FOR THE 2ND REFRESHMENT

4 fl oz (120 ml) lukewarm water

4 oz (115 g) unbleached white
   bread flour

1 oz (25 g) wholemeal bread flour

FOR THE DOUGH

5–6 fl oz (150–175 ml) lukewarm
   water

12 oz (350 g) unbleached white
   bread flour

2 teaspoons (10 ml) salt

~ COOK'S TIPS ~

• You will need to start making
this bread about four days
before you'd like to eat it.

• To make another loaf, keep
the piece of starter dough (see
step 6) in the fridge for up to
3 days. Use dough for the 2nd
refreshment in place of the
levain in step 3, gradually mix
in the water, then the flours
and leave to rise as described.

---

1 ▲ To make the *chef*, place the flour
in a small bowl, add the water and
knead for 3–4 minutes to form a
dough. Cover with clear film and leave
the *chef* in a warm place for 2 days.

This superb country bread is made using a natural French *chef* starter to produce
a rustic flavour and texture. In France, breads like this are often made three or
four times the size of this loaf.

2 Pull off the crust and discard, then
remove 2 tablespoons (30 ml) of the
moist centre. Place in a bowl and
gradually mix in the water for the 1st
refreshment. Mix in the flour and
knead for 3–4 minutes to form a
dough or *levain*, cover with clear film
and leave in a warm place for a day.

3 ▲ Discard the crust from the *levain*
and gradually mix in the water for the
2nd refreshment. Mix in the flours a
little at a time, working well after each
addition to form a firm dough. Cover
with lightly oiled clear film and leave
to rise, in a warm place, for about
10 hours, or until doubled in bulk.

4 Lightly flour a baking sheet. For the
final stage in the preparation of the
dough, gradually mix the water into
the *levain* in the bowl, then gradually
mix in the flour, then the salt. Turn
out the dough on to a lightly floured
surface and knead for about 5 minutes
until smooth and elastic.

5 Place the dough in a large lightly
oiled bowl, cover with lightly oiled
clear film and leave to rise, in a warm
place, for 1½–2 hours, or until the
dough has almost doubled in bulk.

6 Knock back the dough and cut off
4 oz (115 g). Set aside for making the
next loaf. Shape the remaining dough
into a ball – you should have about
12 oz (350 g).

7 Line a 4 in (10 cm) high, 9 in
(23 cm) round basket or large bowl
with a dish towel and dust with flour.

8 ▲ Place the dough ball seam side
up in the prepared basket or bowl.
Cover with lightly oiled clear film and
leave to rise, in a warm place, for 2–3
hours, or until almost doubled in bulk.

9 Preheat the oven to 230°C/450°F/
Gas 8. Invert the loaf on to the
baking sheet and sprinkle with flour.

10 ▲ Slash the top of the loaf, using
a sharp knife, four times at right
angles to each other, to form a
square pattern.

11 Sprinkle with a little more flour,
if you like, then bake for 30–35
minutes, or until the loaf has
browned and sounds hollow when
tapped on the base. Transfer to a
wire rack to cool.

French Fougasse

Makes 2 loaves

| 1 lb (450 g) unbleached white bread flour |
| 1 teaspoon (5 ml) salt |
| ¾ oz (20 g) fresh yeast |
| 9 fl oz (280 ml) lukewarm water |
| 1 tablespoon (15 ml) extra virgin olive oil |

For the filling

| 2 oz (50 g) Roquefort cheese, crumbled |
| 1½ oz (40 g) walnut pieces, chopped |
| 1 oz (25 g) drained, canned anchovy fillets, soaked in milk and drained again, chopped |
| olive oil, for brushing |

~ VARIATION ~

To make a sweet fougasse, replace 1 tablespoon (15 ml) of the water with orange flower water. Include 2 oz (50 g) chopped candied orange peel and 1 oz (25 g) sugar.

A fougasse is a lattice-shaped, flattish loaf from the South of France. It can be cooked as a plain bread or flavoured with cheese, anchovies, herbs, nuts or olives. On Christmas Eve in Provence a fougasse flavoured with orange flower water is part of a table centrepiece of thirteen desserts, used to symbolize Christ and the Twelve Apostles.

2 Place the dough in an oiled bowl, cover with oiled clear film and leave to rise, in a warm place, for about 1 hour, or until doubled in bulk.

3 ▲ Turn out on to a floured surface and knock back. Divide in half and flatten one piece. Sprinkle over the cheese and walnuts and fold the dough over on itself 2–3 times to incorporate. Repeat with the other piece of dough, this time incorporating the anchovies. Shape each piece of flavoured dough into a ball.

4 Flatten each ball of dough and fold the bottom third up and the top third down, to make an oblong. Roll the cheese dough into a rectangle measuring about 11 × 6 in (28 × 15 cm). Make 4 diagonal cuts almost to the edge. Stretch the dough evenly, so that it resembles a ladder.

5 Shape the anchovy dough into an oval with a flat base, about 10 in (25 cm) long. Make 3 diagonal slits on each side towards the flat base, and pull to open the cuts. Transfer to the baking sheets, cover with oiled clear film and leave to rise, in a warm place, for about 30–45 minutes, or until nearly doubled in bulk.

6 Meanwhile, preheat the oven to 220°C/425°F/Gas 7. Brush both loaves with a little olive oil and bake for 25 minutes, or until golden. Transfer to a wire rack to cool.

1 ▲ Lightly grease 2 baking sheets. Sift the flour and salt together into a large bowl and make a well in the centre. In a measuring jug, cream the yeast with 4 tablespoons (60 ml) of the water. Pour the yeast mixture into the centre of the flour with the remaining water and the olive oil and mix to a soft dough. Turn out on to a floured surface and knead for 8–10 minutes until smooth and elastic.

French Pain aux Noix

This delicious butter- and milk-enriched wholemeal bread is filled with walnuts. It is the perfect companion for cheese.

MAKES 2 LOAVES

2 oz (50 g) butter
12 oz (350 g) wholemeal bread flour
4 oz (115 g) unbleached white bread flour
1 tablespoon (15 ml) light brown muscovado sugar
1½ teaspoons (7.5 ml) salt
¾ oz (20 g) fresh yeast
9 fl oz (275 ml) lukewarm milk
6 oz (175 g) walnut pieces

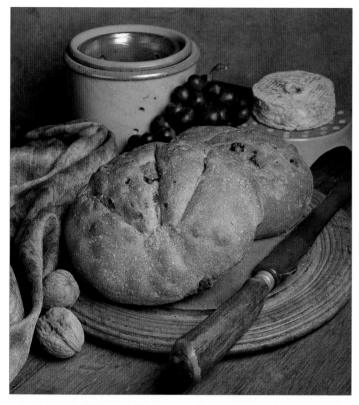

3 Knead on a lightly floured surface for 6–8 minutes. Place in a lightly oiled bowl, cover with oiled clear film and leave to rise, in a warm place, for 1 hour, or until doubled in bulk.

4 ▲ Turn out the dough on to a lightly floured surface and gently knock back. Press or roll out to flatten and then sprinkle over the nuts. Gently press the nuts into the dough, then roll it up. Return to the oiled bowl, re-cover and leave, in a warm place, for 30 minutes.

5 Turn out on to a floured surface, divide in half and shape each piece into a ball. Place on the baking sheets, cover with oiled clear film and leave to rise, in a warm place, for 45 minutes, until doubled in bulk.

6 Preheat the oven to 220°C/425°F/ Gas 7. Slash the top of each loaf 3 times. Bake for 35 minutes, or until they sound hollow when tapped. Transfer to a wire rack to cool.

1 ▲ Grease 2 baking sheets. Place the butter in a small pan and heat until melted and starting to brown, then set aside to cool. Mix the flours, sugar and salt in a bowl and make a well in the centre. Cream the yeast with half the milk. Add to the centre of the flour with the remaining milk.

2 ▲ Pour the cool melted butter through a fine strainer into the centre of the flour so that it joins the liquids already there. Using your hand, mix the liquids together in the bowl and gradually mix in small quantities of the flour to make a batter. Continue until the mixture forms a moist dough.

French Baguettes

MAKES 3 LOAVES

1¼ lb (500 g) unbleached white bread flour
4 oz (115 g) fine French plain flour
2 teaspoons (10 ml) salt
½ oz (15 g) fresh yeast
18 fl oz (550 ml) lukewarm water

Baguettes are difficult to reproduce at home as they require a very hot oven and steam. However, by using less yeast and a triple fermentation you can produce a bread with a superior taste and far better texture than mass-produced baguettes. These are best eaten on the day of baking.

1 Sift the flours and salt into a bowl. Add the yeast to the water in another bowl and stir to dissolve. Gradually beat in half the flour mixture to form a batter. Cover with clear film and leave at room temperature for 3 hours, or until nearly trebled in size and starting to collapse.

2 Add the remaining flour a little at a time, beating with your hand. Turn out on to a floured surface and knead for 8–10 minutes to form a moist dough. Place in an oiled bowl, cover with oiled clear film and leave to rise, in a warm place, for 1 hour.

3 When the dough has almost doubled in bulk, knock it back, turn out on to a floured surface and divide into 3. Shape each into a rectangle 6 × 3 in (15 × 7.5 cm).

4 Fold the bottom third up lengthways and the top third down and press down to make sure the pieces of dough are in contact. Seal the edges. Repeat two or three more times until each loaf is an oblong. Leave to rest in between folding for a few minutes, if necessary, to avoid tearing the dough.

5 ▲ Gently stretch each piece of dough lengthways into a 13–14 in (33–35 cm) long loaf. Pleat a floured dish towel on a baking sheet to make 3 moulds for the loaves. Place the breads between the pleats of the towel to help hold their shape while rising. Cover with lightly oiled clear film and leave to rise, in a warm place, for about 45–60 minutes.

6 Preheat the oven to maximum, at least 230°C/450°F/Gas 8. Roll the loaves on to a baking sheet, spaced well apart. Slash the top of each loaf several times with long diagonal slits. Bake at the top of the oven for 20–25 minutes, or until golden. Spray inside the oven with water 2–3 times during the first 5 minutes of baking. Transfer to a wire rack to cool.

~ VARIATION ~

If you make baguettes regularly you may want to purchase baguette frames to hold and bake the breads in, or long *bannetons* in which to prove this wonderful bread.

French Brioche

Rich and buttery yet light and airy, this wonderful loaf captures the essence of the classic French bread.

1 Sift the flour and salt together into a large bowl and make a well in the centre. Put the yeast in a measuring jug and stir in the milk.

2 ▲ Add the yeast mixture to the centre of the flour with the eggs and mix together to form a soft dough.

3 ▲ Using your hand, beat the dough for 4–5 minutes until smooth and elastic. Cream the butter and sugar together. Gradually add the butter mixture to the dough, ensuring it is incorporated before adding more. Beat until smooth, shiny and elastic.

MAKES 1 LOAF
12 oz (350 g) unbleached white bread flour
½ teaspoon (2.5 ml) salt
½ oz (15 g) fresh yeast
4 tablespoons (60 ml) lukewarm milk
3 eggs
6 oz (175 g) butter, softened
1 oz (25 g) caster sugar
FOR THE GLAZE
1 egg yolk
1 tablespoon (15 ml) milk

4 Cover the bowl with lightly oiled clear film and leave the dough to rise, in a warm place, for 1–2 hours or until doubled in bulk.

5 Lightly knock back the dough, then re-cover and place in the fridge for 8–10 hours or overnight.

6 Lightly grease a 2¾ pint (1.6 litre) brioche mould. Turn the dough out on to a lightly floured surface. Cut off almost a quarter and set aside. Shape the rest into a ball and place in the prepared mould. Shape the reserved dough into an elongated egg shape. Using two or three fingers, make a hole in the centre of the large ball of dough. Gently press the narrow end of the egg-shaped dough into the hole.

7 Mix together the egg yolk and milk for the glaze, and brush a little over the brioche. Cover with lightly oiled clear film and leave to rise, in a warm place, for 1½–2 hours, or until the dough nearly reaches the top of the mould.

8 Meanwhile, preheat the oven to 230°C/450°F/Gas 8. Brush the brioche with the remaining glaze and bake for 10 minutes. Reduce the oven temperature to 190°C/375°F/Gas 5 and bake for a further 20–25 minutes, or until golden. Turn out on to a wire rack to cool.

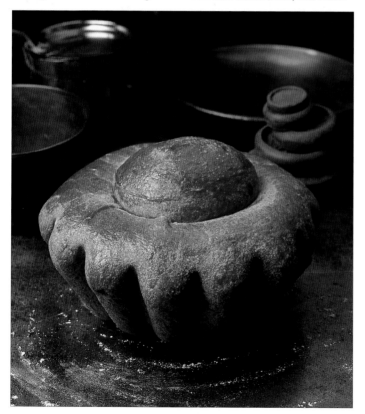

French Croissants

Makes 14 croissants

12 oz (350 g) unbleached white bread flour
4 oz (115 g) fine French plain flour
1 teaspoon (5 ml) salt
1 oz (25 g) caster sugar
½ oz (15 g) fresh yeast
scant 8 fl oz (225 ml) lukewarm milk
1 egg, lightly beaten
8 oz (225 g) butter
For the Glaze
1 egg yolk
1 tablespoon (15 ml) milk

Golden layers of flaky pastry, puffy, light and flavoured with butter is how the best croissants should be. Serve warm on the day of baking.

3 Knock back, re-cover and chill in the fridge for 1 hour. Flatten the butter into a block about ¾ in (2 cm) thick. Knock back the dough and turn out on to a floured surface. Roll out into a rough 10 in (25 cm) square, with edges thinner than the centre.

4 ▲ Place the block of butter diagonally in the centre and fold the corners of the dough over the butter like an envelope, tucking in the edges to completely enclose the butter.

7 Place the dough triangles on 2 baking sheets, cover with clear film and chill for 10 minutes.

8 ▲ To shape the croissants, place each one with the wide end at the top, hold each side and pull gently to stretch the top of the triangle a little, then roll towards the point, finishing with the pointed end tucked underneath. Curve the ends towards the pointed end to make a crescent. Place on two baking sheets, spaced well apart.

9 Mix together the egg yolk and milk for the glaze. Lightly brush a little glaze over the croissants, avoiding the cut edges of the dough. Cover the croissants loosely with lightly oiled clear film and leave to rise, in a warm place, for about 30 minutes, or until they are nearly doubled in size.

10 Meanwhile, preheat the oven to 220°C/425°F/Gas 7. Brush the croissants with the remaining glaze and bake for 15–20 minutes, or until crisp and golden. Transfer to a wire rack to cool slightly. Serve warm.

~ COOK'S TIP ~

Make sure that the block of butter and the dough are about the same temperature when combining, to ensure the best results.

---

1 ▲ Sift the flours and salt into a bowl. Stir in the sugar. Make a well in the centre. Cream the yeast with 3 tablespoons (45 ml) of the milk, then stir in the rest. Add the yeast mixture to the centre of the flour, then add the egg and gradually beat in the flour until it forms a dough.

2 Turn out on to a floured surface and knead for 3–4 minutes. Place in an oiled bowl, cover with oiled clear film and leave to rise, in a warm place, for about 45 minutes–1 hour, or until doubled in bulk.

5 ▲ Roll the dough into a rectangle about ¾ in (2 cm) thick, twice as long as it is wide. Fold the bottom third up and the top third down and seal the edges. Chill for 20 minutes.

6 Repeat the rolling, folding and chilling twice more, turning the dough by 90 degrees each time. Roll out on a floured surface into a 25 × 13 in (62 × 33 cm) rectangle; trim to leave a 24 × 12 in (60 × 30 cm) rectangle. Cut in half lengthways. Cut crossways into 14 equal triangles with 6 in (15 cm) bases.

~ VARIATION ~

To make chocolate-filled croissants, place a small square of chocolate at the wide end of each triangle before rolling up as in step 8.

French Petits Pains au Lait

MAKES 12 ROLLS

1 lb (450 g) unbleached white bread flour
2 teaspoons (10 ml) salt
1 tablespoon (15 ml) caster sugar
2 oz (50 g) butter, softened
½ oz (15 g) fresh yeast
9 fl oz (275 ml) lukewarm milk, plus 1 tablespoon (15 ml) extra milk, for glazing

~ VARIATION ~

These can also be made into long rolls. To shape, flatten each ball of dough and fold in half. Roll back and forth, using your hand to form a 5 in (13 cm) long roll, tapered at either end.

These classic French round milk rolls have a soft crust and a light, slightly sweet crumb. They won't last long!

1 Lightly grease 2 baking sheets. Sift the flour and salt together into a large bowl. Stir in the sugar. Rub the softened butter into the flour.

2 Cream the yeast with 4 tablespoons (60 ml) of the milk. Stir in the remaining milk. Pour into the flour mixture and mix to a soft dough.

3 Turn out on to a floured surface and knead for 8–10 minutes until smooth and elastic. Place in an oiled bowl, cover with oiled clear film and leave to rise, in a warm place, for 1 hour, or until doubled in bulk.

4 Turn out the dough on to a floured surface and gently knock back. Divide into 12, shape into balls and space well apart on the baking sheets.

5 ▲ Using a sharp knife, cut a cross in the top of each roll. Cover with lightly oiled clear film and leave to rise, in a warm place, for about 20 minutes, or until doubled in size.

6 Preheat the oven to 200°C/400°F/ Gas 6. Brush the rolls with milk and bake for 20–25 minutes, or until golden. Transfer to a wire rack to cool.

French Dimpled Rolls

MAKES 10 ROLLS

14 oz (400 g) unbleached white bread flour
1½ teaspoons (7.5 ml) salt
1 tablespoon (5 ml) caster sugar
½ oz (15 g) fresh yeast
4 fl oz (120 ml) lukewarm milk
6 fl oz (175 ml) lukewarm water

A French and Belgian speciality, these attractive rolls are distinguished by the split down the centre. They have a crusty finish while remaining soft and light inside – they taste lovely, too.

1 Lightly grease 2 baking sheets. Sift the flour and salt into a large bowl. Stir in the sugar and make a well in the centre.

2 Cream the yeast with the milk until dissolved, then pour into the centre of the flour mixture. Sprinkle over a little of the flour from around the edge. Leave at room temperature for 15–20 minutes, or until the mixture starts to bubble.

3 Add the water and gradually mix in the flour to form a fairly moist, soft dough. Turn out on to a lightly floured surface and knead for 8–10 minutes until smooth and elastic. Place in a lightly oiled bowl, cover with lightly oiled clear film and leave to rise, at room temperature, for about 1½ hours, or until doubled in bulk.

4 Turn out on to a floured surface and knock back. Re-cover and leave to rest for 5 minutes. Divide the dough into 10 pieces. Shape into balls by rolling under your hand, then roll until oval. Lightly flour the tops. Place spaced well apart on the baking sheets, cover with oiled clear film and leave to rise, at room temperature, for about 30 minutes, until almost doubled in size.

5 ▲ Oil the side of your hand and press the centre of each roll to make a deep split. Re-cover and leave to rest for 15 minutes. Place a roasting tin in the bottom of the oven and preheat the oven to 230°C/450°F/Gas 8. Pour 8 fl oz (250 ml) water into the tin and bake the rolls on a higher shelf for 15 minutes or until golden. Let cool.

Swiss Braid

MAKES 1 LOAF

12 oz (375 g) unbleached white bread flour

1 teaspoon (5 ml) salt

¾ oz (20 g) fresh yeast

2 tablespoons (30 ml) lukewarm water

¼ pint (150 ml) soured cream

1 egg, lightly beaten

2 oz (50 g) butter, softened

FOR THE GLAZE

1 egg yolk

1 tablespoon (15 ml) water

This plaited, attractively tapered loaf is known as zupfe in Switzerland. Often eaten at the weekend, it is has a glossy crust and a wonderfully light crumb.

1 Lightly grease a baking sheet. Sift the flour and salt together into a large bowl and make a well in the centre. Mix the yeast with the water in a jug.

2 ▲ Gently warm the soured cream in a small pan until it reaches blood heat (35–38°C). Add to the yeast mixture and mix together.

3 Add the yeast mixture and egg to the centre of the flour and mix to a dough. Beat in the softened butter.

4 ▲ Turn out on to a floured surface and knead for 5 minutes until smooth and elastic. Place in a lightly oiled bowl, cover with oiled clear film and leave to rise, in a warm place, for 1½ hours, or until doubled in size.

5 Turn out on to a floured surface and knock back. Cut in half and shape each piece of dough into a long rope about 14 in (35 cm) in length.

6 To make the braid, place the two pieces of dough on top of each other to form a cross. Starting with the bottom rope, fold the top end over and place between the two bottom ropes. Fold the remaining top rope over so that all four ropes are pointing down. Starting on the left, plait the first rope over the second, and the third over the fourth.

7 Continue plaiting to form a tapered bread. Tuck under the ends and place on the baking sheet. Cover with oiled clear film and leave to rise, in a warm place, for about 40 minutes.

8 Meanwhile, preheat the oven to 190°C/ 375°F/Gas 5. Mix the egg yolk and water for the glaze, and brush over the loaf. Bake the bread for 30–35 minutes, or until golden. Cool on a wire rack.

German Sourdough Bread

This bread includes rye, wholemeal and plain flours for a superb depth of flavour. Serve it cut in thick slices, with creamy butter or a sharp cheese.

MAKES 1 LOAF
FOR THE SOURDOUGH STARTER
3 oz (75 g) rye flour
3 fl oz (80 ml) warm water
pinch caraway seeds
FOR THE DOUGH
½ oz (15 g) fresh yeast
11 fl oz (315 ml) lukewarm water
10 oz (275 g) rye flour
5 oz (150 g) wholemeal bread flour
5 oz (150 g) unbleached white bread flour
2 teaspoons (10 ml) salt

1 ▲ Mix the rye flour, warm water and caraway for the starter together in a large bowl with your fingertips, to make a soft paste. Cover with a damp dish towel and leave in a warm place for about 36 hours. Stir after 24 hours.

2 Lightly grease a baking sheet. In a measuring jug, blend the yeast for the dough with the lukewarm water. Add to the starter and mix thoroughly.

3 ▲ Mix the rye flour, wholemeal bread flour and unbleached white bread flour for the dough with the salt in a large bowl; make a well in the centre. Pour in the yeast liquid and gradually incorporate the surrounding flour to make a smooth dough.

4 Turn out the dough on to a lightly floured surface and knead for 8–10 minutes until smooth and elastic. Place in a lightly oiled bowl, cover with lightly oiled clear film and leave to rise, in a warm place, for 1½ hours, or until nearly doubled in bulk.

5 ▲ Turn out on to a lightly floured surface, knock back and knead gently. Shape into a round and place in a floured basket or *couronne*, with the seam side up. Cover with lightly oiled clear film and leave to rise, in a warm place, for 2–3 hours.

6 Meanwhile, preheat the oven to 200°C/400°F/Gas 6. Turn out the loaf on to the baking sheet and bake for 35–40 minutes. Cool on a wire rack.

~ COOK'S TIP ~

Proving the dough in a floured basket or *couronne* gives it its characteristic patterned crust, but is not essential. Make sure that you flour the basket well, otherwise the dough may stick.

German Stollen

MAKES 1 LOAF

3 oz (75 g) sultanas
2 oz (50 g) currants
3 tablespoons (45 ml) rum
13 oz (375 g) unbleached white bread flour
½ teaspoon (2.5 ml) salt
2 oz (50 g) caster sugar
¼ teaspoon (1.5 ml) ground cardamom
½ teaspoon (2.5 ml) ground cinnamon
1½ oz (40 g) fresh yeast
4 fl oz (120 ml) lukewarm milk
2 oz (50 g) butter, melted
1 egg, lightly beaten
2 oz (50 g) mixed chopped peel
2 oz (50 g) blanched whole almonds, chopped
melted butter, for brushing
icing sugar, for dusting
FOR THE ALMOND FILLING
4 oz (115 g) ground almonds
2 oz (50 g) caster sugar
2 oz (50 g) icing sugar
½ teaspoon (2.5 ml) lemon juice
½ egg, lightly beaten

This German speciality bread, made for the Christmas season, is rich with rum-soaked fruits and is wrapped around a moist almond filling. The folded shape of the dough over the filling represents the baby Jesus wrapped in swaddling clothes.

3 ▲ Mix the yeast with the milk until creamy. Pour into the flour and mix in a little of the flour from around the edge to make a thick batter. Sprinkle some of the remaining flour over the top of the batter, then cover with clear film and leave in a warm place for 30 minutes.

4 Add the melted butter and egg and mix to a soft dough. Turn out the dough on to a floured surface and knead for 8–10 minutes until smooth and elastic. Place in an oiled bowl, cover with lightly oiled clear film and leave to rise, in a warm place, for 2–3 hours, until doubled in bulk.

1 ▲ Grease a baking sheet. Preheat the oven to 180°C/350°F/Gas 4. Put the sultanas and currants in a heatproof bowl and warm for 3–4 minutes. Pour over the rum and set aside.

2 Sift the flour and salt into a large bowl. Stir in the sugar and spices.

5 ▲ Mix the ground almonds and sugars for the filling. Add the lemon juice and enough egg to make a smooth paste. Shape into a 8 in (20 cm) sausage, cover and set aside.

6 Turn out the dough on to a lightly floured surface and knock back.

7 Pat out the dough into a rectangle about 1 in (2.5 cm) thick and sprinkle over the sultanas, currants, peel and almonds. Fold and knead to incorporate the fruit and nuts.

8 ▲ Roll out the dough into an oval about 12 × 9 in (30 × 23 cm). Roll the centre slightly thinner than the edges. Place the almond paste filling along the centre and fold over the dough to enclose it, making sure that the top of the dough doesn't completely cover the base. The top edge should be slightly in from the bottom edge. Press down to seal.

9 Place the loaf on the prepared baking sheet, cover with lightly oiled clear film and leave to rise, in a warm place, for 45–60 minutes, or until doubled in size.

10 Meanwhile, preheat the oven to 200°C/400°F/Gas 6. Bake the loaf for about 30 minutes, or until it sounds hollow when tapped on the base. Brush the top with melted butter and transfer to a wire rack to cool. Dust with icing sugar just before serving.

~ COOK'S TIP ~
You can dust the cooled stollen with icing sugar and cinnamon, or drizzle over a thin glacé icing.

German Pumpernickel

MAKES 2 LOAVES

1 lb (450 g) rye flour
8 oz (225 g) wholemeal flour
4 oz (115 g) bulgur wheat
2 teaspoons (10 ml) salt
2 tablespoons (30 ml) molasses
1½ pints (850 ml) warm water
1 tablespoon (15 ml) vegetable oil

~ COOK'S TIP ~

This bread improves on keeping for at least 24 hours, double-wrapped.

1 Lightly grease two 7 × 3½ in (18 × 9 cm) loaf tins. Mix the rye flour, wholemeal flour, bulgur wheat and salt together in a large bowl.

This famous German bread is extremely dense and dark, with an intense flavour. It is baked very slowly and although cooked in the oven, it is more like a steamed bread than a baked one.

2 Mix the molasses with the warm water and add to the flours with the oil. Mix to form a dense mass.

3 ▲ Place in the prepared tins, pressing well into the corners. Cover with lightly oiled clear film and leave in a warm place for 18–24 hours.

4 Preheat the oven to 110°C/225°F/Gas ¼. Cover the tins tightly with foil. Fill a roasting tin with boiling water and place a rack on top.

5 Place the tins on top of the rack and transfer very carefully to the oven. Bake the loaves for 4 hours. Increase the oven temperature to 160°C/325°F/Gas 3. Top up the water in the roasting tin if necessary, uncover the loaves and bake for a further 30–45 minutes, or until the loaves feel firm and the tops are crusty.

6 Leave to cool in the tins for 5 minutes, then turn out on to a wire rack. Serve cold, very thinly sliced.

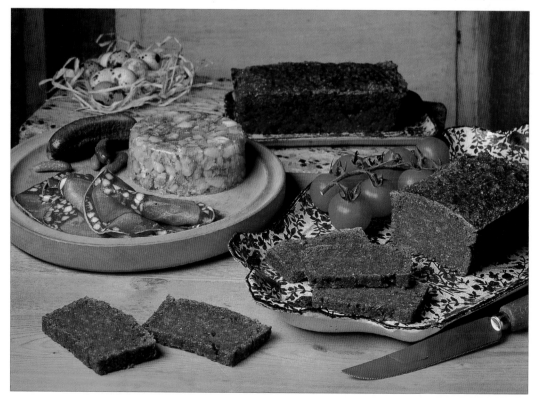

Swedish Vört Limpa

This festive Swedish bread is flavoured with warm spices and fresh orange. The beer and port work nicely to soften the rye taste. The added sugars also give the yeast a little extra to feed on and so help aerate and lighten the bread. It is traditionally served with cheese.

MAKES 1 LOAF

12 oz (350 g) rye flour
12 oz (350 g) unbleached white bread flour
½ teaspoon (2.5 ml) salt
1 oz (25 g) caster sugar
1 teaspoon (5 ml) grated nutmeg
1 teaspoon (5 ml) ground cloves
1 teaspoon (5 ml) ground ginger
1½ oz (40 g) fresh yeast
½ pint (300 ml) light ale
4 fl oz (120 ml) port
1 tablespoon (15 ml) molasses
1 oz (25 g) butter, melted
1 tablespoon (15 ml) grated orange rind
3 oz (75 g) raisins
1 tablespoon (15 ml) malt extract, for glazing

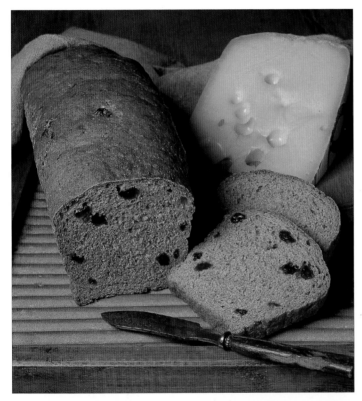

1 Lightly grease a 12 × 4 in (30 × 10 cm) loaf tin. Mix together the rye and white flours, salt, sugar, nutmeg, cloves and ginger in a large bowl.

2 In another large bowl, using a wooden spoon, blend the yeast into the ale until dissolved, then stir in the port, molasses and melted butter.

3 Gradually add the flour mixture to the yeast liquid, beating to make a smooth batter. Continue adding the flour a little at a time and mixing until the mixture forms a soft dough.

4 ▲ Turn out on to a floured surface and knead for 8–10 minutes until smooth and elastic. Place in an oiled bowl, cover with oiled clear film and leave to rise, in a warm place, for 1 hour, or until doubled in size.

5 Turn out the dough on to a floured surface and knock back. Gently knead in the orange rind and raisins. Roll into a 12 in (30 cm) square.

6 ▲ Fold the bottom third of the dough up and the top third down, sealing the edges. Place in the loaf tin, cover with oiled clear film and leave to rise, in a warm place, for 1 hour, or until it reaches the top of the tin.

7 Meanwhile, preheat the oven to 190°C/375°F/Gas 5. Bake for 35–40 minutes, or until browned. Turn out on to a wire rack, brush with malt extract and leave to cool.

Swedish Knackerbröd

Makes 8 crispbreads

1 lb (450 g) rye flour
1 teaspoon (5 ml) salt
2 oz (50 g) butter
¾ oz (20 g) fresh yeast
9 fl oz (275 ml) lukewarm water
3 oz (75 g) wheat bran

A very traditional Swedish crispbread with a lovely rye flavour.

1 ▲ Lightly grease 2 baking sheets. Preheat the oven to 230°C/450°F/ Gas 8. Mix the rye flour and salt in a large bowl. Rub in the butter, then make a well in the centre.

2 Cream the yeast with a little water, then stir in the remainder. Pour into the centre of the flour, mix to a dough, then mix in the bran. Knead on a lightly floured surface for 5 minutes until smooth and elastic.

3 Divide the dough into 8 pieces and roll each one out on a floured surface, to a 8 in (20 cm) round.

4 ▲ Place 2 rounds on the prepared baking sheets and prick all over with a fork. Cut a hole in the centre of each round, using a 1½ in (4 cm) cutter.

5 Bake for 15–20 minutes, or until golden and crisp. Transfer to a wire rack to cool. Repeat with the remaining crispbreads.

~ COOK'S TIP ~

The hole in the centre of these crispbreads is a reminder of the days when breads were strung on a pole, which was hung across the rafters to dry. Make smaller crispbreads, if you like, and tie them together with bright red ribbon for an unusual Christmas gift.

Finnish Barley Bread

Makes 1 Loaf

8 oz (225 g) barley flour
1 teaspoon (5 ml) salt
2 tablespoons (10 ml) baking powder
1 oz (25 g) butter, melted
4 fl oz (120 ml) single cream
4 tablespoons (60 ml) milk

In Northern Europe breads are often made using cereals such as barley and rye, which produce very satisfying, tasty breads. This quick-to-prepare flat bread is best served warm with lashings of butter.

1 ▲ Grease a baking sheet. Preheat the oven to 200°C/400°F/Gas 6. Sift the dry ingredients into a bowl. Add the wet ingredients. Mix to a dough.

2 Turn out the dough on to a lightly floured surface and shape into a flat round about ½ in (1 cm) thick.

3 ▲ Transfer to the prepared baking sheet and, using a sharp knife, lightly mark the top into 6 sections.

4 Prick the surface of the round evenly with a fork. Bake for about 15–18 minutes, or until pale golden. Cut into wedges and serve warm.

~ COOK'S TIPS ~

• This flat bread tastes very good with cottage cheese, especially cottage cheese with chives.
• For a citrusy tang, add 2–3 teaspoons (10–15 ml) finely grated lemon, lime or orange rind to the flour mixture in step 1.

Swedish Lusse Bröd

MAKES 12 BUNS

4 fl oz (120 ml) milk
pinch of saffron threads
14 oz (400 g) unbleached white bread flour
2 oz (50 g) ground almonds
½ teaspoon (2.5 ml) salt
3 oz (75 g) caster sugar
1 oz (25 g) fresh yeast
4 fl oz (120 ml) lukewarm water
few drops of almond essence
2 oz (50 g) butter, softened
FOR THE GLAZE
1 egg, beaten with 1 tablespoon (15 ml) water

Saint Lucia Day, the 12th of December, marks the beginning of Christmas in Sweden. As part of the celebrations, young girls dressed in white robes wear headbands topped with lighted candles and walk through the village streets offering saffron buns to the townspeople.

1 ▲ Lightly grease 2 baking sheets. Place the milk in a small saucepan and bring to the boil. Add the saffron, remove from the heat and leave to infuse for about 15 minutes. Meanwhile, mix the flour, ground almonds, salt and sugar in a bowl.

2 Cream the yeast with the water. Add the saffron liquid, yeast mixture and almond essence to the flour mixture and mix to a dough. Gradually beat in the softened butter.

3 Turn out on to a lightly floured surface and knead for 5 minutes until smooth and elastic. Place in an oiled bowl, cover with oiled clear film and leave to rise, in a warm place, for about 1 hour, or until doubled in bulk.

4 ▲ Turn out on to a lightly floured surface and knock back. Divide into 12 equal pieces and make into different shapes: roll into a long rope and shape into an "S" shape; to make a star, cut a dough piece in half and roll into two ropes, cross one over the other and coil the ends; make an upturned "U" shape and coil the ends to represent curled hair; divide a dough piece in half, roll into two thin ropes and twist together.

5 Place on the baking sheets, spaced well apart, cover with oiled clear film and leave to rise, in a warm place, for about 30 minutes.

6 Preheat the oven to 200°C/400°F/ Gas 6. Brush the glaze over the rolls. Bake for 15 minutes, or until golden. Transfer to a wire rack to cool. Serve warm or cold.

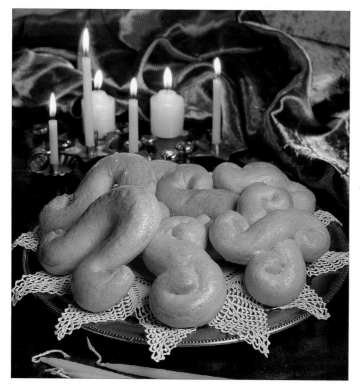

Savoury Danish Crown

Filled with golden onions and cheese, this butter-rich bread ring is quite irresistible and needs no accompaniment.

1 Lightly grease a baking sheet. Sift the flour and salt together into a large bowl. Rub in 1½ oz (40 g) of the butter. Mix the yeast with the milk and water. Add to the flour with the egg and mix to a soft dough.

2 Turn out on to a floured surface and knead for 10 minutes until smooth and elastic. Place in an oiled bowl, cover with oiled clear film or slide into an oiled polythene bag and leave to rise, in a warm place, for about 1 hour, or until doubled in bulk.

3 Knock back and turn out on to a lightly floured surface. Roll out into an oblong about ½ in (1 cm) thick.

4 ▲ Dot half the remaining butter over the top two-thirds of the dough. Fold the bottom third up and the top third down and seal the edges. Turn by 90 degrees and repeat with the remaining butter. Fold and seal as before. Cover with oiled clear film and leave to rest for 15 minutes.

5 Turn by a further 90 degrees. Roll and fold again without any butter. Repeat once more. Wrap in lightly oiled clear film and leave to rest in the fridge for 30 minutes.

6 Meanwhile, heat the oil for the filling. Add the onions and cook for 10 minutes until golden. Remove from the heat and add the breadcrumbs, almonds, Parmesan and seasoning.

7 Mix half the beaten egg into the breadcrumb mixture.

8 Roll out the dough on a floured surface into a rectangle 22 × 9 in (56 × 23 cm). Spread with the filling to within ¾ in (2 cm) of the edges, then roll up like a Swiss roll from one long side. Cut in half lengthways. Plait together with the cut sides up and shape into a ring. Place on the baking sheet, cover with oiled clear film and leave to rise, in a warm place, for 30 minutes.

9 Meanwhile, preheat the oven to 200°C/400°F/Gas 6. Brush the remaining beaten egg over the dough. Sprinkle with sesame seeds and Parmesan cheese and bake for 40–50 minutes, or until golden. Transfer to a wire rack to cool. Serve warm or cold, cut into slices.

MAKES 1 LOAF

12 oz (350 g) unbleached white bread flour
1 teaspoon (5 ml) salt
6½ oz (185 g) butter, softened
¾ oz (20 g) fresh yeast
7 fl oz (200 ml) mixed lukewarm milk and water
1 egg, lightly beaten
FOR THE FILLING
2 tablespoons (30 ml) sunflower oil
2 onions, finely chopped
1½ oz (40 g) fresh breadcrumbs
1 oz (25 g) ground almonds
2 oz (50 g) freshly grated Parmesan cheese
1 egg, lightly beaten
salt and freshly ground black pepper
FOR THE TOPPING
1 tablespoon (15 ml) sesame seeds
1 tablespoon (15 ml) freshly grated Parmesan cheese

Danish Julekage

MAKES 1 LOAF

1 oz (25 g) fresh yeast
5 tablespoons (75 ml) lukewarm milk
1 lb (450 g) unbleached white bread flour
2 teaspoons (10 ml) salt
3 oz (75 g) butter
15 cardamom pods
½ teaspoon (2.5 ml) vanilla essence
2 oz (50 g) light brown soft sugar
grated rind of ½ lemon
2 eggs, lightly beaten
2 oz (50 g) ready-to-eat dried apricots, chopped
2 oz (50 g) glacé pineapple pieces, chopped
2 oz (50 g) red and green glacé cherries, chopped
1 oz (25 g) dried dates, chopped
1 oz (25 g) crystallized stem ginger, chopped

FOR THE GLAZE

1 egg white
2 teaspoons (10 ml) water

FOR THE DECORATION

1 tablespoon (15 ml) caster sugar
½ teaspoon (2.5 ml) ground cinnamon
8 pecan nuts or whole blanched almonds

~ VARIATIONS ~

• You can vary the fruits for this loaf. Try glacé peaches, yellow glacé cherries, sultanas, raisins, candied angelica, dried mango or dried pears and use in place of some or all of the fruits in the recipe. Use a mixture of colours and make sure that the total weight is the same as above.

• Use walnuts in place of the pecan nuts or almonds.

In Scandinavia special slightly sweet holiday breads containing fragrant cardamom seeds are common. This exotic bread, enriched with butter and a selection of glacé and dried fruits or "jewels", is traditionally served over the Christmas period with hot spiced punch.

1 Lightly grease a 9 × 5 in (23 × 13 cm) loaf tin. In a measuring jug, cream the yeast with the milk.

2 ▲ Sift the flour and salt together into a large bowl. Add the butter and rub in. Make a well in the centre. Add the yeast mixture to the centre of the flour and butter mixture and stir in sufficient flour to form a thick batter. Sprinkle over a little of the remaining flour and set aside in a warm place for 15 minutes.

3 Remove the seeds from the cardamom pods. Put them in a mortar and crush with a pestle. Add the crushed seeds to the flour with the vanilla essence, sugar, lemon rind and eggs, then mix to a soft dough.

4 ▲ Turn out on to a floured surface and knead for 8–10 minutes until smooth and elastic. Place in an oiled bowl, cover with oiled clear film and leave to rise, in a warm place, for 1–1½ hours, or until doubled in bulk.

5 Knock back the dough and turn it out on to a lightly floured surface. Flatten into a rectangle and sprinkle over half of the apricots, pineapple, cherries, dates and ginger. Fold the sides into the centre and then fold in half to contain the fruit. Flatten into a rectangle again and sprinkle over the remaining fruit. Fold and knead gently to distribute the fruit. Cover the fruited dough with lightly oiled clear film and leave to rest for 10 minutes.

6 Roll the fruited dough into a rectangle 15 × 10 in (38 × 25 cm). With a short side facing you, fold the bottom third up lengthways and the top third down, tucking in the sides, to form a 9 × 5 in (23 × 13 cm) loaf. Place in the prepared tin, seam side down. Cover with lightly oiled clear film and leave to rise, in a warm place, for 1 hour, or until the dough has reached the top of the tin.

7 Meanwhile, preheat the oven to 180°C/350°F/Gas 4. Using a sharp knife, slash the top of the loaf lengthways and then make diagonal slits on either side.

8 Mix together the egg white and water for the glaze, and brush over the top. Mix the sugar and cinnamon in a bowl, then sprinkle over the top. Decorate with pecan nuts or almonds. Bake for 45–50 minutes, or until risen and browned. Transfer to a wire rack to cool.

~ COOK'S TIP ~

If the top of the loaf starts to brown too quickly during cooking, cover loosely with foil.

Scandinavian Sunshine Loaf

MAKES 1 LARGE LOAF

FOR THE STARTER

4 tablespoons (60 ml) lukewarm milk

4 tablespoons (60 ml) lukewarm water

¼ oz (7 g) fresh yeast

3¾ oz (100 g) unbleached white bread flour

FOR THE DOUGH

½ oz (15 g) fresh yeast

17 fl oz (500 ml) lukewarm water

1 lb (450 g) rye flour

8 oz (225 g) unbleached white bread flour

1 tablespoon (15 ml) salt

milk, for glazing

caraway seeds, for sprinkling

Scandinavia, Land of the Midnight Sun, has numerous breads based on rye. This splendid table centrepiece is made with a blend of rye and white flours, the latter helping to lighten the bread.

1 ▲ Combine the milk and water for the starter in a bowl. Mix in the yeast until dissolved. Gradually stir the flour with a metal spoon.

2 Cover the bowl with clear film and leave the mixture in a warm place for 3–4 hours, or until well risen, bubbly and starting to collapse.

3 Mix the yeast for the dough with 4 tablespoons (60 ml) of the water until creamy, then stir in the remaining water. Gradually mix into the starter to dilute it. Gradually mix in the rye flour to form a smooth batter. Cover with lightly oiled clear film and leave in a warm place, for 3–4 hours, or until well risen.

4 Stir the bread flour and salt into the batter to form a dough. Turn on to a floured surface and knead for 5 minutes until smooth and elastic. Place in an oiled bowl, cover with oiled clear film and leave to rise, in a warm place, for 1 hour, until doubled in bulk.

5 ▲ Knock back on a floured surface. Cut the dough into 5 pieces. Roll one piece into a 20 in (50 cm) "sausage" and roll up into a spiral shape.

6 Cut the remaining pieces in half and shape each one into a 8 in (20 cm) rope. Place in a circle on a baking sheet, spaced equally apart, like rays of the sun, and curl the ends round, leaving a small gap in the centre. Place the spiral shape on top. Cover with oiled clear film and leave to rise, in a warm place, for 30 minutes.

7 Preheat the oven to 230°C/450°F/ Gas 8. Brush the bread with milk, sprinkle with caraway seeds and bake for 30 minutes, or until lightly browned. Cool on a wire rack.

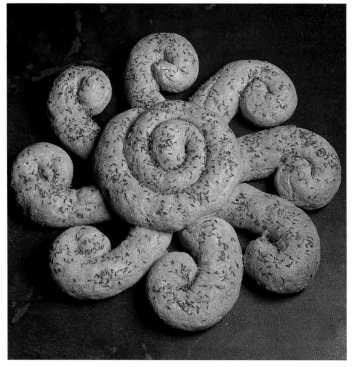

Spanish Pan de Cebada

This Spanish country bread has a close, heavy texture and is quite satisfying. It is richly flavoured, incorporating barley and maize flours.

MAKES 1 LOAF

FOR THE SOURDOUGH STARTER
6 oz (175 g) maize meal
scant 1 pint (560 ml) water
8 oz (225 g) wholemeal bread flour
3 oz (75 g) barley flour
FOR THE DOUGH
¾ oz (20 g) fresh yeast
3 tablespoons (45 ml) lukewarm water
8 oz (225 g) wholemeal bread flour
1 tablespoon (15 ml) salt
maize meal, for dusting

1 ▲ In a saucepan, mix the maize meal for the sourdough starter with half the water, then blend in the remainder. Cook over a gentle heat, stirring until thickened. Transfer to a large bowl and set aside to cool.

2 Mix in the wholemeal flour and barley flour. Turn out on to a floured surface and knead for 5 minutes. Return to the bowl, cover with oiled clear film and leave the starter in a warm place for 36 hours.

3 ▲ Dust a baking sheet with maize meal. In a small bowl, cream the yeast with the water for the dough. Mix the yeast mixture into the starter with the wholemeal flour and salt and work to a dough. Turn out on to a lightly floured surface and knead for 4–5 minutes until smooth and elastic.

4 Transfer the dough to a lightly oiled bowl, cover with oiled clear film or an oiled polythene bag and leave, in a warm place, for 1½–2 hours to rise, or until nearly doubled in bulk.

5 ▲ Knock back the dough and turn out on to a lightly floured surface. Shape into a plump round. Sprinkle with a little maize meal.

6 Place the shaped bread on the baking sheet. Cover with an upturned bowl. Leave to rise, in a warm place, for about 1 hour, or until nearly doubled in bulk. Place a roasting tin in the bottom of the oven. Preheat the oven to 220°C/425°F/Gas 7.

7 Pour ½ pint (300 ml) cold water into the roasting tin. Remove the bowl and immediately place the risen loaf in the oven. Bake the bread for 10 minutes. Remove the tin of water, reduce the oven temperature to 190°C/375°F/Gas 5 and bake for about 20 minutes. Cool on a wire rack.

Spanish Twelfth Night Bread

MAKES 1 LOAF

1 lb (450 g) unbleached white bread flour
½ teaspoon (2.5 ml) salt
1 oz (25 g) yeast
scant ¼ pint (140 ml) mixed lukewarm milk and water
3 oz (75 g) butter
3 oz (75 g) caster sugar
2 teaspoons (10 ml) finely grated lemon rind
2 teaspoons (10 ml) finely grated orange rind
2 eggs
1 tablespoon (15 ml) brandy
1 tablespoon (15 ml) orange flower water
silver coin or dried bean (optional)
1 egg white, lightly beaten, for glazing
FOR THE DECORATION
a mixture of candied and glacé fruit slices
flaked almonds

January 6th, Epiphany or the Day of the Three Kings, is celebrated in Spain as a time to exchange Christmas presents. Historically this date was when the Three Wise Men arrived bearing gifts. An ornamental bread ring is specially baked for the occasion. The traditional version contains a silver coin, china figure or dried bean hidden inside – the lucky recipient is declared King of the festival!

2 In a bowl, mix the yeast with the milk and water until the yeast has dissolved. Pour the yeast mixture into the centre of the flour and stir in enough of the flour from around the sides of the bowl to make a thick batter.

3 Sprinkle a little of the remaining flour over the top of the batter and leave to "sponge", in a warm place, for about 15 minutes or until frothy.

4 Using an electric whisk or a wooden spoon, beat the butter and sugar together in a bowl until soft and creamy, then set aside.

5 Add the citrus rinds, eggs, brandy and orange flower water to the flour mixture and mix to a sticky dough.

~ COOK'S TIP ~

If you like, this bread can be baked in a 9½ in (24 cm) ring-shaped cake tin.

1 ▲ Lightly grease a large baking sheet. Sift the flour and salt together into a large bowl. Make a well in the centre.

6 ▲ Using one hand, beat the mixture until it forms a smooth dough. Gradually beat in the reserved butter mixture and beat for a few minutes until the dough is smooth and elastic. Cover with oiled clear film and leave to rise, in a warm place, for 1½ hours, or until doubled in bulk.

7 Knock back the dough and turn out on to a floured surface. Gently knead for 2 or 3 minutes, incorporating the lucky coin or bean, if using.

8 Using a rolling pin, roll out the dough into a long strip measuring about 26 × 5 in (65 × 13 cm).

9 ▲ Roll up the dough from one long side like a Swiss roll to make a long sausage shape. Place seam side down on the baking sheet and seal the ends. Cover with oiled clear film and leave to rise, in a warm place, for 1–1½ hours, or until doubled in size.

10 ▲ Meanwhile, preheat the oven to 180°C/350°F/Gas 4. Brush the dough ring with lightly beaten egg white and decorate with candied and glacé fruit slices, pushing slightly into the dough. Sprinkle with almond flakes and bake for 30–35 minutes, or until risen and golden. Turn out on to a wire rack to cool.

Pan Gallego

12 oz (350 g) unbleached white bread flour
4 oz (115 g) wholemeal bread flour
2 teaspoons (10 ml) salt
¾ oz (20 g) fresh yeast
9 fl oz (275 ml) lukewarm water
2 tablespoons (30 ml) olive oil or melted lard
2 tablespoons (30 ml) pumpkin seeds
2 tablespoons (30 ml) sunflower seeds
1 tablespoon (15 ml) millet
maize meal, for dusting

This is a typical round bread with a twisted top from Galicia. The olive oil gives a soft crumb and the millet, pumpkin and sunflower seeds scattered through the loaf provide an interesting mix of textures.

2 ▲ In a bowl, mix the yeast with the water. Add to the centre of the flours with the olive oil or melted lard and mix to a firm dough. Turn out on to a lightly floured surface and knead for about 10 minutes until smooth and elastic. Place in an oiled bowl, cover with oiled clear film and leave to rise, in a warm place, for 1½–2 hours, or until doubled in bulk.

3 ▲ Knock back the dough and turn out on to a lightly floured surface. Gently knead in the pumpkin seeds, sunflower seeds and millet. Re-cover and leave to rest for 5 minutes.

1 Sprinkle a baking sheet with maize meal. Mix the flours and salt together in a large bowl.

4 ▲ Shape into a ball; twist the centre to make a cap. Transfer to the baking sheet and dust with maize meal. Cover with an upturned bowl and leave to rise, in a warm place, for 45 minutes, or until doubled in bulk.

5 Place a roasting tin in the bottom of the oven. Preheat the oven to 220°C/425°F/Gas 7. Pour about ½ pint (300 ml) cold water into the roasting tin. Remove the bowl and place the risen loaf in the oven, above the roasting tin. Bake the bread for 10 minutes.

6 Remove the tin of water and bake the bread for a further 25–30 minutes, or until well browned and sounding hollow when tapped on the base. Transfer to a wire rack to cool.

Portuguese Corn Bread

While the Spanish make a corn bread with barley flour, the Portuguese use white bread flour and maize meal. This tempting version has a hard crust with a moist, mouthwatering crumb. It slices beautifully and tastes wonderful served simply with butter or olive oil, or with cheese.

MAKES 1 LOAF

¾ oz (20 g) fresh yeast
8 fl oz (250 ml) lukewarm water
8 oz (225 g) maize meal
1 lb (450 g) unbleached white bread flour
¼ pint (150 ml) lukewarm milk
2 tablespoons (30 ml) olive oil
1½ teaspoons (7.5 ml) salt
polenta, for dusting

1 ▲ Dust a baking sheet with a little maize meal. Put the yeast in a bowl and gradually mix in the water until smooth. Stir in half the maize meal and 2 oz (50 g) of the flour and mix to a batter, with a wooden spoon.

2 ▲ Cover the bowl with lightly oiled clear film and leave the batter undisturbed in a warm place for about 30 minutes, or until bubbles start to appear on the surface. Remove the clear film.

3 Stir the milk into the batter, then stir in the olive oil. Gradually mix in the remaining maize meal, flour and salt to form a pliable dough.

4 Turn out the dough on to a lightly floured surface and knead for about 10 minutes until smooth and elastic. Place in a lightly oiled bowl, cover with lightly oiled clear film and leave to rise for 1½–2 hours, or until doubled in bulk.

5 ▲ Turn out the dough on to a floured surface and knock back. Shape into a ball, flatten slightly and place on the prepared baking sheet. Dust with polenta, cover with a large upturned bowl and leave to rise, in a warm place, for 1 hour, or until doubled in size. Preheat the oven to 230°C/450°F/Gas 8.

6 Bake for 10 minutes, spraying the inside of the oven with water 2–3 times. Reduce the oven temperature to 190°C/375°F/Gas 5 and bake for a further 20–25 minutes, or until golden and hollow sounding when tapped. Cool on a wire rack.

Mallorcan Ensaimadas

MAKES 16 ROLLS

8 oz (225 g) unbleached white bread flour
½ teaspoon (2.5 ml) salt
2 oz (50 g) caster sugar
½ oz (15 g) fresh yeast
5 tablespoons (75 ml) lukewarm milk
1 egg
2 tablespoons (30 ml) sunflower oil
2 oz (50 g) butter, melted
icing sugar, for dusting

These spiral- or snail-shaped rolls are a popular Spanish breakfast treat. Traditionally, lard or *saim* was used to brush over the strips of sweetened dough, but nowadays mainly butter is used to add a delicious richness.

1 Grease 2 baking sheets. Sift the flour and salt into a bowl. Stir in the sugar and make a well in the centre.

2 Cream the yeast with the milk, pour into the centre of the flour mixture, then sprinkle a little of the flour mixture evenly over the top of the liquid. Leave in a warm place for about 15 minutes, or until frothy.

3 In a small bowl, beat the egg with the oil. Add to the flour mixture and mix to a smooth dough.

4 Turn out on to a floured surface and knead for 8–10 minutes until smooth and elastic. Place in an oiled bowl, cover with oiled clear film and leave to rise, in a warm place, for 1 hour, or until doubled in bulk.

5 ▲ Turn out the dough on to a lightly floured surface. Knock back and divide the dough into 16 equal pieces. Shape each piece into a thin rope about 15 in (38 cm) long. Pour the melted butter on to a plate and dip the ropes into the butter to coat.

6 ▲ On the baking sheets, curl each rope into a loose spiral, spacing well apart. Tuck the ends under to seal. Cover with oiled clear film and leave to rise, in a warm place, for about 45 minutes, or until doubled in size.

7 Preheat the oven to 190°C/375°F/ Gas 5. Brush the rolls with water and dust with icing sugar. Bake for 10 minutes, or until light golden brown. Cool on a wire rack. Dust again with icing sugar and serve warm.

Italian Olive Bread

Black and green olives and good-quality fruity olive oil combine to make this strongly flavoured and irresistible Italian bread.

1 Lightly grease a baking sheet. Mix the flours, yeast and salt in a large bowl and make a well in the centre.

2 ▲ Add the water and oil to the centre of the flour and mix to a soft dough. Knead the dough on a lightly floured surface for 8–10 minutes until smooth and elastic. Place in a lightly oiled bowl, cover with oiled clear film and leave to rise, in a warm place, for 1 hour, or until doubled in bulk.

3 Turn out on to a floured surface and knock back. Flatten out and sprinkle over the olives. Knead to distribute the olives. Leave to rest for 5 minutes, then shape into an oval loaf. Place on the baking sheet.

4 ▲ Make 6 deep cuts in the top, and gently push the sections over. Cover with oiled clear film and leave to rise, in a warm place, for 30–45 minutes, or until doubled in size.

MAKES 1 LOAF

10 oz (275 g) unbleached white bread flour
2 oz (50 g) wholemeal bread flour
¼ oz (10 g) sachet easy-blend dried yeast
½ teaspoon (2.5 ml) salt
7½ fl oz (210 ml) lukewarm water
1 tablespoon (15 ml) extra virgin olive oil, plus extra, for brushing
4 oz (115 g) pitted black and green olives, coarsely chopped

> **~ VARIATION ~**
> For a nutty flavour, add some hazelnuts or pine nuts.

5 Meanwhile, preheat the oven to 200°C/400°F/Gas 6. Brush the bread with olive oil and bake for 35 minutes. Transfer to a wire rack to cool.

Italian Polenta Bread

MAKES 1 LOAF

2 oz (50 g) polenta
½ pint (300 ml) lukewarm water
½ oz (15 g) fresh yeast
½ teaspoon (2.5 ml) clear honey
8 oz (225 g) unbleached white bread flour
1 oz (25 g) butter
3 tablespoons (45 ml) pine nuts
1½ teaspoons (7.5 ml) salt
FOR THE TOPPING
1 egg yolk
1 tablespoon (15 ml) water
pine nuts, for sprinkling

Polenta is widely used in Italian cooking. Here it is combined with pine nuts to make a truly Italian bread with a fantastic flavour.

1 ▲ Lightly grease a baking sheet. Mix the polenta and 8 fl oz (250 ml) of the water together in a saucepan and slowly bring to the boil, stirring continuously with a large wooden spoon. Reduce the heat and simmer for 2–3 minutes, stirring occasionally. Set aside to cool for 10 minutes, or until just warm.

2 In a small bowl, mix the yeast with the remaining water and honey until creamy. Sift 4 oz (115 g) of the flour into a large bowl. Gradually beat in the yeast mixture, then gradually stir in the polenta mixture to combine. Turn out on to a lightly floured surface and knead for 5 minutes until smooth and elastic.

3 Cover the bowl with lightly oiled clear film. Leave the dough to rise, in a warm place, for about 2 hours, or until it has doubled in bulk.

4 ▲ Meanwhile, melt the butter in a small pan, add the pine nuts and cook over a medium heat, stirring, until pale golden. Set aside to cool.

5 Add the remaining flour and the salt to the polenta dough and mix to a soft dough. Knead in the pine nuts. Turn out on to a lightly floured surface and knead for 5 minutes until smooth and elastic.

6 Place in an oiled bowl, cover with clear film and leave to rise, in a warm place, for 1 hour, until doubled in bulk.

7 ▲ Knock back the dough and turn it out on to a floured surface. Cut the dough into 2 equal pieces and roll each piece into a fat sausage about 15 in (38 cm) long. Plait together and place on the baking sheet. Cover with lightly oiled clear film and leave to rise, in a warm place, for 45 minutes. Preheat the oven to 200°C/400°F/Gas 6.

8 Mix the egg yolk and water and brush over the loaf. Sprinkle with pine nuts and bake for 30 minutes, or until golden and sounding hollow when tapped. Cool on a wire rack.

Italian Prosciutto Loaf

This savoury Italian bread from Parma is spiked with the local dried ham. Just a small amount fills the loaf with marvellous flavour.

1 Grease a baking sheet. Sift the flour and salt into a bowl and make a well in the centre. Cream the yeast with 2 tablespoons (30 ml) of the water, then gradually mix in the rest. Pour into the centre of the flour.

3 Turn out on to a lightly floured surface and knead for 5 minutes until smooth and elastic. Place in an oiled bowl, cover with lightly oiled clear film and leave to rise, in a warm place, for 1½ hours, or until doubled in bulk.

MAKES 1 LOAF
12 oz (350 g) unbleached white bread flour
1½ teaspoons (7.5 ml) salt
½ oz (15 g) fresh yeast
8 fl oz (250 ml) lukewarm water
1½ oz (40 g) prosciutto, torn into small pieces
1 teaspoon (5 ml) freshly ground black pepper

> ### ~ VARIATION ~
> To make pesto bread, spread 3 tablespoons (45 ml) pesto over the flattened dough in step 4.

2 ▲ Gradually beat in most of the flour with a wooden spoon to make a batter. Beat gently to begin with and then more vigorously as the batter thickens. When most of the flour is incorporated, mix in the rest with your hand to form a moist dough.

4 ▲ Turn out the dough on to a floured surface, knock back and knead for 1 minute. Flatten to a round, then sprinkle with half the prosciutto and pepper. Fold in half and repeat with the remaining ham and pepper. Roll up, tucking in the sides.

5 Place on the baking sheet, cover with oiled clear film and leave to rise, in a warm place, for about 30 minutes. On a floured surface, roll into an oval, fold in half and seal the edges. Flatten and fold again. Seal and fold again to make a long loaf.

6 Roll into a stubby long loaf. Draw out the edges by rolling the dough under the palms of your hands. Place on the baking sheet, cover with oiled clear film and leave to rise, in a warm place, for 45 minutes, or until the loaf has doubled in size. Preheat the oven to 200°C/400°F/Gas 6.

7 ▲ Slash the top of the loaf diagonally three or four times, using a sharp knife, and bake for 30 minutes, or until golden. Cool on a wire rack.

Italian Focaccia

MAKES 2 LOAVES

¾ oz (20 g) fresh yeast

11–12 fl oz (315–350 ml) lukewarm water

3 tablespoons (45 ml) extra virgin olive oil

1¼ lb (500 g) unbleached white bread flour

2 teaspoons (10 ml) salt

1 tablespoon (15 ml) chopped fresh sage

FOR THE TOPPING

4 tablespoons (60 ml) extra virgin olive oil

4 garlic cloves, chopped

12 fresh sage leaves

This simple dimple-topped Italian flat bread is punctuated with olive oil and the aromatic flavours of sage and garlic to produce a truly succulent loaf.

4 ▲ Knock back the dough and turn out on to a floured surface. Gently knead in the chopped sage. Divide the dough into 2 equal pieces. Shape each into a ball, roll out into 10 in (25 cm) circles and place in the tins.

1 ▲ Lightly oil 2 10 in (25 cm) shallow round cake tins or pizza pans. Cream the yeast with 4 tablespoons (60 ml) of the water, then stir in the remaining water. Stir in the oil.

2 Sift the flour and salt together into a large bowl and make a well in the centre. Pour the yeast mixture into the well and incorporate the flour to make a soft dough.

3 Turn out the dough on to a lightly floured surface and knead for 8–10 minutes until smooth and elastic. Place in a lightly oiled bowl, cover with lightly oiled clear film, and leave to rise, in a warm place, for about 1–1½ hours, or until the dough has doubled in bulk.

5 ▲ Cover with lightly oiled clear film and leave to rise in a warm place for about 30 minutes. Uncover, and using your fingertips, poke the dough to make deep dimples over the entire surface. Replace the clear film cover and leave to rise until doubled in bulk.

6 Meanwhile, preheat the oven to 200°C/400°F/Gas 6. Sprinkle the loaves with olive oil and garlic for the topping and dot with sage leaves. Bake for 25–30 minutes, or until both loaves are golden. Immediately remove the focaccia from the tins and transfer them to a wire rack to cool slightly. These loaves are best served warm.

Italian Panini all'Olio

Makes 16 rolls

1 lb (450 g) unbleached white bread flour
2 teaspoons (10 ml) salt
½ oz (15 g) fresh yeast
8 fl oz (250 ml) lukewarm water
4 tablespoons (60 ml) extra virgin olive oil, plus extra for brushing

The Italians adore interesting and elaborately shaped rolls. This distinctively flavoured bread dough, enriched with olive oil, can be used for making rolls or shaped as one large loaf.

1 Lightly oil 3 baking sheets. Sift the flour and salt together in a large bowl and make a well in the centre.

2 In a jug, cream the yeast with half of the water, then stir in the remainder. Add to the centre of the flour with the oil and mix to a dough.

3 Turn the dough out on to a lightly floured surface and knead for 8–10 minutes until smooth and elastic. Place in an oiled bowl, cover with oiled clear film and leave to rise, in a warm place, for 1 hour, or until the dough has nearly doubled in bulk.

4 Turn on to a lightly floured surface and knock back. Divide into 12 equal pieces of dough and shape into rolls as described in steps 5, 6 and 7.

5 ▲ For *tavalli* (twisted spiral rolls): roll each piece of dough into a strip about 12 in (30 cm) long and 1½ in (4 cm) wide. Twist into a loose spiral and join the ends together to make a circle. Place on the baking sheets, well spaced. Brush the *tavalli* with olive oil, cover with oiled clear film and leave to rise, in a warm place, for 20–30 minutes.

6 ▲ For *filoncini* (finger-shaped rolls): flatten each piece of dough into an oval and roll to about 9 in (23 cm) in length without changing the basic shape. Make it 2 in (5 cm) wide at one end and 4 in (10 cm) wide at the other. Roll up, starting from the wider end. Gently stretch the roll to 8–9 in (20–23 cm) long. Cut in half. Place on the baking sheets, well spaced. Brush with olive oil, cover with oiled clear film and leave to rise, in a warm place, for 20–30 minutes.

7 ▲ For *carciofi* (artichoke-shaped rolls): shape each piece of dough into a ball and space well apart on the baking sheets. Brush with olive oil, cover with oiled clear film and leave to rise, in a warm place, for about 20–30 minutes. Preheat the oven to 200°C/400°F/Gas 6. Using scissors, snip 4–5 ¼ in (5 mm) deep cuts in a circle on the top of each *carciofi*, then make 5 larger horizontal cuts around the sides. Bake for 15 minutes. Transfer to a wire rack to cool.

Italian Ciabatta

This irregular-shaped Italian bread is so called because it looks like an old shoe or slipper. It is made with a very wet dough flavoured with olive oil; cooking produces a bread with holes and a wonderfully chewy crust.

MAKES 3 LOAVES

FOR THE BIGA STARTER
¼ oz (10 g) fresh yeast
6–7 fl oz (175–200 ml) lukewarm water
12 oz (350 g) unbleached plain flour, plus extra for dusting
FOR THE DOUGH
½ oz (15 g) fresh yeast
14 fl oz (400 ml) lukewarm water
4 tablespoons (60 ml) lukewarm milk
1¼ lb (500 g) unbleached white bread flour
2 teaspoons (10 ml) salt
3 tablespoons (45 ml) extra virgin olive oil

1 Cream the yeast for the *biga* starter with a little of the water. Sift the flour into a bowl. Gradually mix in the yeast mixture and enough of the remaining water to form a firm dough.

2 Turn out the *biga* starter dough on to a lightly floured surface and knead for about 5 minutes until smooth and elastic. Return the dough to the bowl, cover with lightly oiled clear film and leave in a warm place for 12–15 hours, or until the dough has risen and is starting to collapse.

3 Sprinkle 3 baking sheets with flour. Mix the yeast for the dough with a little of the water until creamy, then mix in the remainder. Add the yeast mixture to the *biga* and mix in.

4 Mix in the milk, beating thoroughly with a wooden spoon. Using your hand, gradually mix in the flour, lifting the dough as you mix. Mixing the dough will take 15 minutes or more and form a very wet mix, impossible to knead on a work surface.

5 Beat in the salt and olive oil. Cover with lightly oiled clear film and leave to rise, in a warm place, for 1½–2 hours, or until doubled in bulk.

6 ▲ Using a spoon, tip one-third of the dough at a time on to the baking sheets, trying to avoid knocking back the dough in the process.

7 ▲ Using floured hands, shape into oblong loaf shapes, about 1 in (2.5 cm) thick. Flatten slightly. Sprinkle with flour and leave to rise in a warm place for 30 minutes.

8 Meanwhile, preheat the oven to 220°C/425°F/Gas 7. Bake for 25–30 minutes, or until golden brown and sounding hollow when tapped on the base. Transfer to a wire rack to cool.

~ VARIATION ~

Add 4 oz (115 g) chopped, drained sun-dried tomatoes in olive oil in step 5.

Italian Panettone

MAKES 1 LOAF

14 oz (400 g) unbleached white bread flour
½ teaspoon (2.5 ml) salt
½ oz (15 g) fresh yeast
4 fl oz (120 ml) lukewarm milk
2 eggs
2 egg yolks
3 oz (75 g) caster sugar
5 oz (150 g) butter, softened
4 oz (115 g) mixed chopped peel
3 oz (75 g) raisins
melted butter, for brushing

This classic Italian bread can be found throughout Italy around Christmas. It is a surprisingly light bread even though it is rich with butter and dried fruit.

2 Sift the flour and salt into a bowl. Cream the yeast with 4 tablespoons (60 ml) of the milk, then mix in the remainder.

3 ▲ Pour the yeast mixture into the centre of the flour, add the whole eggs and mix in sufficient flour to make a thick batter. Sprinkle a little flour over the top and leave to "sponge", in a warm place, for 30 minutes.

1 Using a double layer of greaseproof paper, line and butter a 6 in (15 cm) deep cake tin. Finish the paper 3 in (7.5 cm) above the top of the tin.

4 Add the egg yolks and sugar and mix to a soft dough. Work in the softened butter, then turn out on to a lightly floured surface and knead for 5 minutes until smooth and elastic. Place in a lightly oiled bowl, cover with lightly oiled clear film and leave to rise, in a slightly warm place, for 1½–2 hours, or until doubled in bulk.

5 ▲ Knock back the dough and turn out on to a floured surface. Gently knead in the peel and raisins. Shape into a ball and place in the tin. Cover with oiled clear film and leave to rise, in a slightly warm place, for about 1 hour, or until doubled.

6 ▲ Meanwhile, preheat the oven to 190°C/375°F/Gas 5. Brush the loaf with melted butter and cut a cross in the top. Bake for 20 minutes, then reduce the oven temperature to 180°C/350°F/Gas 4. Brush the top with butter again and bake for 25–30 minutes more, or until golden. Cool in the tin for 5–10 minutes, then turn out on to a wire rack to cool.

Italian Pane al Cioccolato

This slightly sweet chocolate bread from Italy is often served with creamy mascarpone cheese as a dessert or snack. The dark chocolate pieces add texture to this light loaf.

MAKES 1 LOAF

12 oz (350 g) unbleached white bread flour
1½ tablespoons (25 ml) cocoa powder
½ teaspoon (2.5 ml) salt
1 oz (25 g) caster sugar
½ oz (15 g) fresh yeast
8 fl oz (250 ml) lukewarm water
1 oz (25 g) butter, softened
3 oz (75 g) plain continental chocolate, coarsely chopped
melted butter, for brushing

1 ▲ Lightly grease a 6 in (15 cm) round deep cake tin. Sift the flour, cocoa powder and salt together into a large bowl. Stir in the sugar. Make a well in the centre.

2 Cream the yeast with 4 tablespoons (60 ml) of the water, then stir in the rest. Add to the centre of the flour mixture and gradually mix to a dough.

3 Knead in the butter, then knead on a surface until smooth and elastic. Place in an oiled bowl, cover with clear film and leave to rise, in a warm place, for 1 hour, or until doubled.

4 ▲ Turn out on to a floured surface and knock back. Knead in the chocolate, then cover with oiled clear film; leave to rest for 5 minutes.

5 Shape the dough into a round and place in the tin. Cover with lightly oiled clear film and leave to rise, in a warm place, for 45 minutes, or until doubled.

6 ▲ Preheat the oven to 220°C/ 425°F/Gas 7. Bake for 10 minutes, then reduce the temperature to 190°C/ 375°F/Gas 5 and bake for 25–30 minutes more. Brush with melted butter and cool on a wire rack.

> ~ VARIATION ~
>
> You can also bake this bread in one large or two small rounds on a baking sheet.

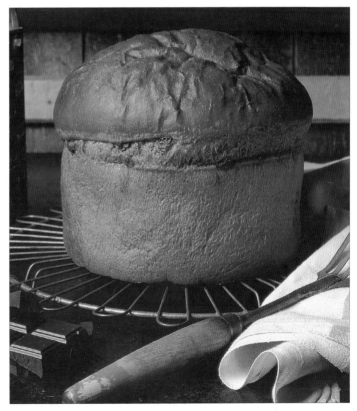

Sicilian Scroll

MAKES 1 LOAF

1 lb (450 g) finely ground semolina
4 oz (115 g) unbleached white bread flour
2 teaspoons (10 ml) salt
¾ oz (20 g) fresh yeast
12½ fl oz (360 ml) lukewarm water
2 tablespoons (30 ml) extra virgin olive oil
sesame seeds, for sprinkling

A wonderful pale yellow, crusty-topped loaf, enhanced with a nutty flavour from the sesame seeds. It's perfect for serving with cheese.

4 ▲ Turn out on to a floured surface and knock back. Knead, then shape into a fat roll about 20 in (50 cm) long. Form into an "S" shape.

5 Transfer to the baking sheet, cover with oiled clear film and leave to rise, in a warm place, for 30–45 minutes, or until doubled in size.

6 Meanwhile, preheat the oven to 220°C/425°F/Gas 7. Brush the top of the scroll with water and sprinkle with sesame seeds. Bake for 10 minutes. Spray the inside of the oven with water twice during this time. Reduce the oven temperature to 200°C/400°F/Gas 6 and bake for a further 25–30 minutes, or until golden. Cool on a wire rack.

1 ▲ Lightly grease a baking sheet. Mix the semolina, white bread flour and salt together in a large bowl and make a well in the centre.

2 In a jug, cream the yeast with half the water, then stir in the remainder. Add the creamed yeast to the centre of the semolina mixture with the olive oil and gradually incorporate the semolina and flour to form a firm dough.

3 Turn out the dough on to a lightly floured surface and knead for 8–10 minutes until smooth and elastic. Place in a lightly oiled bowl, cover with lightly oiled clear film and leave to rise, in a warm place, for 1–1½ hours, or until doubled in bulk.

> ### ~ VARIATION ~
> Although sesame seeds are the traditional topping on this delectable Italian bread, poppy seeds, or even crystals of sea salt, could be used instead.

Pane Toscano

This bread from Tuscany is made without salt and probably originates from the days when salt was heavily taxed. To compensate for the lack of salt, this bread is usually served with salty foods, such as anchovies and olives.

MAKES 1 LOAF

1¼ lb (500 g) unbleached white bread flour
12 fl oz (350 ml) boiling water
½ oz (15 g) fresh yeast
4 tablespoons (60 ml) lukewarm water

6 ▲ Fold the sides of the round into the centre and seal. Place seam side up on the baking sheet. Cover with oiled clear film and leave to rise, in a warm place, for 30–45 minutes, or until doubled in size.

7 ▲ Flatten the loaf to about half its risen height and flip over. Cover with a large upturned bowl and leave to rise, in a warm place, for 30 minutes.

8 Meanwhile, preheat the oven to 220°C/425°F/Gas 7. Slash the top of the loaf, using a sharp knife, if wished. Bake for 30–35 minutes, or until golden. Cool on a wire rack.

1 ▲ First make the starter. Sift 6 oz (175 g) of the flour into a large bowl. Pour over the boiling water, leave for a couple of minutes, then mix well. Cover the bowl with a damp dish towel and leave for 10 hours.

2 Lightly flour a baking sheet. Cream the yeast with the lukewarm water. Stir into the starter.

3 Gradually add the remaining flour and mix to form a dough. Turn out on to a floured surface and knead for 5–8 minutes until smooth and elastic.

4 Place in a lightly oiled bowl, cover with lightly oiled clear film and leave to rise, in a warm place, for 1–1½ hours, or until doubled in bulk.

5 Turn out the dough on to a lightly floured surface, knock back, and shape into a round.

Tuscan Schiacciata

MAKES 1 LOAF

12 oz (350 g) unbleached white
  bread flour

½ teaspoon (2.5 ml) salt

½ oz (15 g) fresh yeast

7 fl oz (200 ml) lukewarm water

4 tablespoons (60 ml) extra virgin
  olive oil

FOR THE TOPPING

2 tablespoons (30 ml) extra virgin
  olive oil, for brushing

2 tablespoons (30 ml) fresh
  rosemary leaves

coarse sea salt, for sprinkling

1 Oil a baking sheet. Sift the
flour and salt into a bowl and make a
well in the centre. Cream the yeast
with half the water. Add to the flour
with the remaining water and olive
oil and mix to a soft dough. Turn out
on to a floured surface and knead for
10 minutes until smooth and elastic.

This Tuscan version of Italian pizza-style flat bread can be rolled to varying
thicknesses to give either a crisp or soft, bread-like finish.

2 Place in a lightly oiled bowl, cover
with lightly oiled clear film and leave
to rise, in a warm place, for about
1 hour, or until doubled in bulk.

3 ▲ Knock back the dough, turn out
on to a lightly floured surface and
knead gently. Roll to a 12 × 8 in (30
× 20 cm) rectangle and place on the
prepared baking sheet. Brush with
some of the olive oil for the topping
and cover with lightly oiled clear film.

4 ▲ Leave to rise, in a warm place,
for about 20 minutes, then brush with
the remaining oil, prick all over with
a fork and sprinkle with rosemary and
sea salt. Leave to rise again in a warm
place for 15 minutes.

5 Preheat the oven to 200°C/400°F/
Gas 6. Bake for 30 minutes, or until
light golden. Cool slightly on a wire
rack. Serve warm.

Moroccan Holiday Bread

The addition of maize meal and a cornucopia of seeds gives this superb loaf an interesting flavour and texture.

MAKES 1 LOAF
10 oz (275 g) white bread flour
2 oz (50 g) maize meal
1 teaspoon (5 ml) salt
¾ oz (20 g) fresh yeast
4 fl oz (120 ml) lukewarm water
4 fl oz (120 ml) lukewarm milk
1 tablespoon (15 ml) pumpkin seeds
1 tablespoon (15 ml) sesame seeds
2 tablespoons (30 ml) sunflower seeds

5 ▲ Turn out the dough on to a lightly floured surface and knock back. Gently knead the pumpkin and sesame seeds into the dough. Shape into a round ball and flatten slightly.

6 Place on the prepared baking sheet and cover with lightly oiled clear film. Leave to rise, in a warm place, for about 45 minutes, or until doubled in bulk.

1 Lightly grease a baking sheet. Sift the flours and salt into a large bowl.

2 ▲ Cream the yeast with a little of the water in a jug. Stir in the remainder of the water and the milk. Pour into the centre of the flour and mix to a fairly soft dough.

3 Turn out the dough on to a lightly floured surface and knead for about 5 minutes until smooth and elastic.

4 Place in a lightly oiled bowl, cover with lightly oiled clear film and leave to rise, in a warm place, for about 1 hour, or until doubled in bulk.

~ VARIATION ~

For a plainer loaf, incorporate all the seeds in the dough in step 5 and leave the top of the loaf seedless.

7 ▲ Meanwhile, preheat the oven to 200°C/400°F/Gas 6. Brush the top of the loaf with water and sprinkle with the sunflower seeds. Bake the loaf for 30–35 minutes, or until it is golden and sounds hollow when tapped. Transfer the loaf to a wire rack to cool.

Greek Christopsomo

MAKES 1 LOAF

½ oz (15 g) fresh yeast

scant ¼ pint (140 ml) lukewarm milk

1 lb (450 g) unbleached white
    bread flour

2 eggs

3 oz (75 g) caster sugar

½ teaspoon (2.5 ml) salt

3 oz (75 g) butter, softened

grated rind of ½ orange

1 teaspoon (5 ml) ground cinnamon

¼ teaspoon (1.5 ml) ground cloves

pinch of crushed aniseed

8 walnut halves

beaten egg white, for glazing

A Byzantine cross flavoured with aniseed tops this Greek Christmas bread, which is also decorated with walnuts for good fortune. The fluffy, light, butter-enriched bread contains orange rind, cinnamon and cloves – all the lovely warm tastes associated with Christmas.

1 ▲ Grease a large baking sheet. In a bowl, mix the yeast with the milk until the yeast is dissolved, then stir in 4 oz (115 g) of the flour to make a thin batter. Cover with oiled clear film and leave to "sponge" in a warm place for 30 minutes.

2 Beat the eggs and sugar until light and fluffy. Beat into the yeast mixture. Gradually mix in the remaining flour and salt. Beat in the butter and knead to a soft but not sticky dough. Knead on a floured surface for 8–10 minutes until smooth and elastic. Place in an oiled bowl, cover with oiled clear film and leave to rise, in a warm place, for 1½ hours, or until doubled in bulk.

3 Turn out on to a floured surface and gently knock back. Cut off 2 oz (50 g) of dough; cover and set aside. Gently knead the orange rind, cinnamon and cloves into the large piece of dough and shape into a round loaf. Place on the baking sheet.

4 Knead the aniseed into the remaining dough. Cut in half and shape each piece into a 12 in (30 cm) rope. Cut through each rope at either end by one-third of its length. Place the two ropes in a cross on top of the loaf, then curl each cut end into a circle, in opposite directions.

5 ▲ Place a walnut half inside each circle. Cover the loaf with clear film and leave to rise for 45 minutes, or until doubled in size. Preheat the oven to 190°C/375°F/Gas 5. Brush the bread with the egg white and bake for 40–45 minutes, or until golden. Cool on a wire rack.

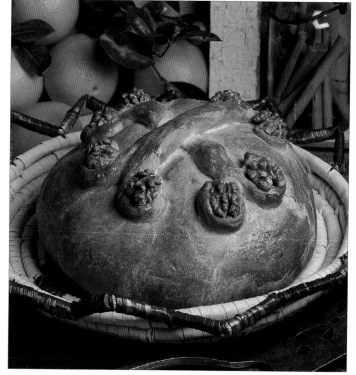

Greek Tsoureki

Topped with brightly coloured eggs, this plaited bread is an important part of the Greek Easter celebrations.

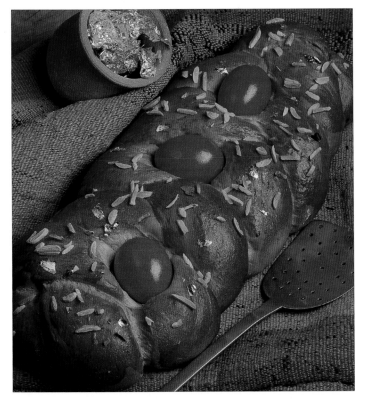

MAKES 1 LOAF

FOR THE EGGS
3 eggs
¼ teaspoon (1.5 ml) bright red food colouring paste
1 tablespoon (15 ml) white wine vinegar
1 teaspoon (5 ml) water
1 teaspoon (5 ml) olive oil
FOR THE DOUGH
1 lb (450 g) unbleached white bread flour
½ teaspoon (2.5 ml) salt
1 teaspoon (5 ml) ground allspice
½ teaspoon (2.5 ml) ground cinnamon
½ teaspoon (2.5 ml) caraway seeds
¾ oz (20 g) fresh yeast
6 fl oz (175 ml) lukewarm milk
2 oz (50 g) butter
1½ oz (40 g) caster sugar
2 eggs
FOR THE GLAZE
1 egg yolk
1 teaspoon (5 ml) clear honey
1 teaspoon (5 ml) water
FOR THE DECORATION
2 oz (50 g) split almonds, slivered

1 Grease a baking sheet. Place the eggs in a pan of water and bring to the boil. Boil gently for 10 minutes. Meanwhile, mix the red food colouring, vinegar and water in a shallow bowl. Remove the eggs from the boiling water, place on a wire rack for a few seconds to dry then roll in the colouring mixture. Return to the rack to cool and dry.

2 When cold, drizzle the olive oil on to absorbent kitchen paper, lift up each egg in turn and rub all over with the oiled paper.

3 To make the dough, sift the flour, salt, allspice and cinnamon into a large bowl. Stir in the caraway seeds.

4 In a jug, mix the yeast with the milk. In a bowl, cream the butter and sugar together, then beat in the eggs. Add the creamed mixture to the flour with the yeast mixture and gradually mix to a dough. Turn out the dough on to a lightly floured surface and knead until smooth and elastic.

5 Place in a lightly oiled bowl, cover with lightly oiled clear film and leave to rise, in a warm place, for about 2 hours, or until doubled in bulk.

6 Knock back the dough and knead for 2–3 minutes. Return to the bowl, re-cover and leave to rise again, in a warm place, for about 1 hour, or until doubled in bulk.

7 Knock back and turn out on to a lightly floured surface. Divide the dough into 3 equal pieces and roll each into a 15–20 in (38–50 cm) long rope. Plait these together from the centre to the ends.

8 Place on the prepared baking sheet and push the dyed eggs into the loaf. Cover and leave to rise, in a warm place, for about 1 hour.

9 Preheat the oven to 190°C/375°F/ Gas 5. Mix the egg yolk, honey and water for the glaze, and brush over the loaf. Sprinkle with almonds. Bake for 40–45 minutes, or until golden and sounding hollow when tapped. Cool on a wire rack.

Greek Olive Bread

MAKES 2 LOAVES

1½ lb (675 g) unbleached white bread flour, plus extra for dusting
2 teaspoons (10 ml) salt
1 oz (25 g) fresh yeast
12 fl oz (350 ml) lukewarm water
5 tablespoons (75 ml) olive oil
6 oz (175 g) pitted black olives, roughly chopped
1 red onion, finely chopped
2 tablespoons (30 ml) chopped fresh coriander or mint

+--+
| ~ VARIATION ~ |
| Make one large loaf and bake |
| for 15 minutes longer. |
+--+

1 Lightly grease 2 baking sheets. Sift the flour and salt together into a large bowl and make a well in the centre.

2 ▲ In a jug, blend the yeast with half of the water. Add to the centre of the flour with the remaining water and the olive oil; mix to a soft dough.

3 Turn out the dough on to a lightly floured surface and knead for 8–10 minutes until smooth. Place in a lightly oiled bowl, cover with lightly oiled clear film and leave to rise, in a warm place, for 1 hour, or until doubled in bulk.

4 Turn out on to a lightly floured surface and knock back. Cut off a quarter of the dough, cover with lightly oiled clear film and set aside.

The flavours of the Mediterranean simply ooze from this decorative bread, speckled with black olives, red onions and herbs.

5 ▲ Roll out the large piece of dough to a round. Sprinkle with the olives, onion and herbs, then bring up the sides of the circle and gently knead together. Cut the dough in half and shape each piece into a plump oval loaf, about 8 in (20 cm) long. Place on the baking sheets.

6 Divide the reserved dough into 4 equal pieces and roll each to a long strand 24 in (60 cm) long. Twist together and cut in half. Brush the centre of each loaf with water and place two pieces of twisted dough on top of each, tucking the ends underneath the loaves.

7 Cover with lightly oiled clear film and leave to rise, in a warm place, for about 45 minutes, or until the loaves are plump and nearly doubled in size.

8 Preheat the oven to 220°C/425°F/ Gas 7. Dust the loaves with flour and bake for 35–40 minutes, or until golden and sounding hollow when tapped. Cool on a wire rack.

Turkish Pitta Bread

These Turkish breads are a firm favourite in both the eastern Mediterranean and the Middle East, and have crossed to England and the USA. This versatile soft, flat bread forms a pocket as it cooks, which is perfect for filling with vegetables, salads or meats.

MAKES 6 PITTA BREADS

8 oz (225 g) unbleached white bread flour
1 teaspoon (5 ml) salt
½ oz (15 g) fresh yeast
scant ¼ pint (150 ml) lukewarm water
2 teaspoons (10 ml) extra virgin olive oil

~ VARIATION ~
Replace half the white bread flour with wholemeal bread flour.

5 ▲ Roll out each ball of dough to an oval ¼ in (5 mm) thick and 6 in (15 cm) long. Place on a floured dish towel and cover with oiled clear film. Leave to rise at room temperature for about 20–30 minutes. Meanwhile, preheat the oven to 230°C/450°F/Gas 8. Place 3 baking sheets in the oven to heat.

6 Place two pitta breads on each baking sheet and bake for 4–6 minutes, or until puffed up; they do not need to brown. If preferred, cook in batches. It is important that the oven has reached the recommended temperature before the breads are baked, to ensure that they puff up.

1 Sift the flour and salt together into a bowl. Mix the yeast with the water until dissolved, then stir in the olive oil and pour into a large bowl.

2 Gradually beat the flour into the yeast mixture, then knead the mixture to make a soft dough.

3 Turn out on to a floured surface and knead for 5 minutes until smooth and elastic. Place in a clean bowl, cover with oiled clear film and leave to rise, in a warm place, for 1 hour, or until doubled in bulk.

4 ▲ Knock back the dough. On a floured surface, divide it into 6 pieces and shape into balls. Cover with oiled clear film; leave for 5 minutes.

7 Transfer the pittas to a wire rack to cool until warm, then cover with a dish towel to keep them soft.

Polish Poppy Seed Roll

MAKES 1 LOAF

12 oz (350 g) unbleached white bread flour

½ teaspoon (2.5 ml) salt

1 oz (25 g) caster sugar

¾ oz (20 g) fresh yeast

4 fl oz (120 ml) lukewarm milk

1 egg, lightly beaten

2 oz (50 g) butter, melted

1 tablespoon (15 ml) toasted flaked almonds

FOR THE FILLING

4 oz (115 g) poppy seeds

2 oz (50 g) mixed chopped peel

2 oz (50 g) butter

3 oz (75 g) caster sugar

3 oz (75 g) raisins

2 oz (50 g) ground almonds

½ teaspoon (2.5 ml) cinnamon

FOR THE ICING

4 oz (115 g) icing sugar

1 tablespoon (15 ml) lemon juice

2–3 teaspoons (10–15 ml) water

A favourite sweet yeast bread in both Poland and Hungary, this has an unusual filling of poppy seeds, almonds, raisins and citrus peel spiralling through the dough.

1 Grease a baking sheet. Sift the flour and salt into a bowl. Stir in the sugar. Cream the yeast with the milk. Add to the flour with the egg and melted butter and mix to a dough.

2 Turn out on to a floured surface and knead for 8–10 minutes until smooth and elastic. Place in an oiled bowl, cover with oiled clear film and leave to rise, in a warm place, for 1–1½ hours, or until doubled in size.

3 Pour boiling water over the poppy seeds for the filling, then leave to cool. Drain in a fine sieve. Finely chop the peel. Melt the butter in a pan, add the poppy seeds and cook, stirring, for 1–2 minutes. Remove from the heat and stir in the sugar, raisins, ground almonds, peel and cinnamon. Set aside to cool.

4 Turn the dough out on to a lightly floured surface, knock back and knead lightly. Roll out into a rectangle 14 × 10 in (35 × 25 cm). Spread the filling to within ¾ in (2 cm) of the edges.

5 ▲ Roll up the dough, starting from one long edge, like a Swiss roll, tucking in the edges to seal. Place seam side down on the baking sheet. Cover with oiled clear film and leave to rise, in a warm place, for 30 minutes, or until doubled in size.

6 Preheat the oven to 190°C/ 375°F/ Gas 5. Bake for 30 minutes, or until golden brown. Transfer to a wire rack to cool until just warm.

7 ▲ Mix the icing sugar, lemon juice and sufficient water together in a small saucepan to make an icing stiff enough to coat the back of a spoon. Heat gently, stirring, until warm. Drizzle the icing over the loaf and sprinkle the flaked almonds over the top. Leave to cool completely, then serve sliced.

Polish Rye Bread

This rye bread is made with half white flour which gives it a lighter, more open texture than a traditional rye loaf. Served thinly sliced, it is the perfect accompaniment for cold meats and fish.

MAKES 1 LOAF
8 oz (225 g) rye flour
8 oz (225 g) unbleached white bread flour
2 teaspoons (10 ml) caraway seeds
2 teaspoons (10 ml) salt
¼ oz (20 g) fresh yeast
scant ¼ pint (140 ml) lukewarm milk
1 teaspoon (5 ml) clear honey
scant ¼ pint (150 ml) lukewarm water
wholemeal flour, for dusting

1 ▲ Grease a baking sheet. Mix the flours, caraway seeds and salt in a bowl and make a well in the centre.

2 In a bowl or measuring jug, cream the yeast with the milk and honey. Pour into the centre of the flour, add the water and gradually incorporate the surrounding flour and caraway mixture until a dough forms.

3 Turn out the dough on to a floured surface and knead for 8–10 minutes until smooth, elastic and firm. Place in an oiled bowl, cover with oiled clear film and leave to rise, in a warm place, for about 3 hours, or until doubled in bulk.

4 ▲ Turn out the dough on to a lightly floured surface and knock back. Shape into an oval loaf and place on the prepared baking sheet.

5 Dust with wholemeal flour, cover with oiled clear film and leave to rise, in a warm place, for 1–1½ hours, or until doubled in size. Preheat the oven to 220°C/425°F/Gas 7.

6 ▲ Using a sharp knife, slash the loaf with two long cuts about 1 in (2.5 cm) apart. Bake for 30–35 minutes, or until the loaf sounds hollow when tapped on the base. Transfer to a wire rack to cool.

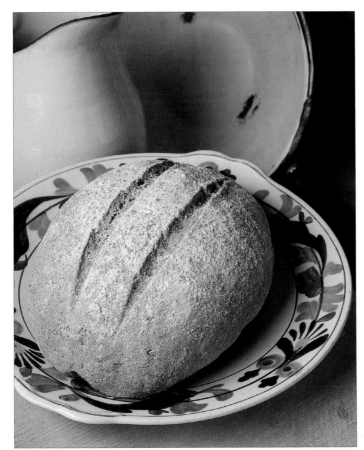

Hungarian Split Farmhouse Loaf

MAKES 1 LOAF

1 lb (450 g) unbleached white bread flour
2 teaspoons (10 ml) salt
½ teaspoon (2.5 ml) fennel seeds, crushed
1 tablespoon (15 ml) caster sugar
¾ oz (20 g) fresh yeast
9 fl oz (275 ml) lukewarm water
1 oz (25 g) butter, melted
1 egg white
2 teaspoons (10 ml) fennel seeds, for sprinkling

1 Lightly grease a baking sheet. Sift the white bread flour and salt together into a large bowl and stir in the crushed fennel seeds and caster sugar. Make a well in the centre.

A golden, fennel-seed-encrusted loaf with a moist white crumb. It is equally delicious made into rolls – just reduce the baking time to 15–20 minutes.

2 ▲ Cream the yeast with a little water, stir in the rest, then pour into the flour. Stir in enough flour to make a runny batter. Sprinkle more of the flour on top, cover and leave in a warm place for 30 minutes, until the "sponge" starts to bubble and rise.

3 ▲ Add the melted butter and gradually mix in with the remaining flour to form a dough. Turn out on to a floured surface and knead for 8–10 minutes until smooth and elastic. Place in an oiled bowl, cover with oiled clear film and leave to rise, in a warm place, for 45–60 minutes, or until doubled in bulk.

4 ▲ Turn out on to a floured surface and knock back. Shape into an oval and place on the baking sheet. Cover with oiled clear film and leave to rise, in a warm place, for 30–40 minutes, or until doubled in size.

5 Meanwhile, preheat the oven to 220°C/425°F/Gas 7. Mix the egg white with a pinch of salt and brush over the loaf. Sprinkle with fennel seeds and then, using a sharp knife, slash along its length. Bake for 20 minutes, then reduce the oven temperature to 180°C/350°F/Gas 4 and bake for 10 minutes more, or until sounding hollow when tapped. Transfer to a wire rack to cool.

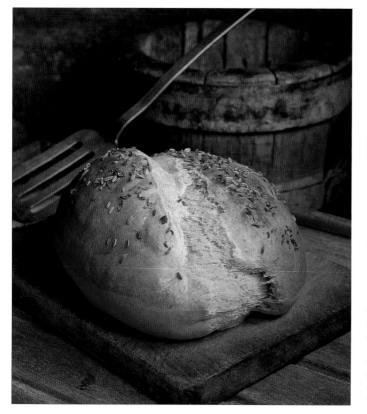

Russian Potato Bread

In Russia, potatoes are often used to replace some of the flour in bread recipes. They endow the bread with excellent keeping qualities.

1 ▲ Lightly grease a baking sheet. Add the potatoes to a saucepan of boiling water and cook until tender. Drain and reserve ¼ pint (150 ml) of the cooking water. Mash and sieve the potatoes and leave to cool.

2 Mix the yeast, bread flours, caraway seeds and salt together in a large bowl. Add the butter and rub in. Mix the reserved potato water and sieved potatoes together. Gradually work this mixture into the flour mixture to form a soft dough.

3 Turn out on to a floured surface and knead for 8–10 minutes until smooth and elastic. Place in an oiled bowl, cover with oiled clear film and leave to rise, in a warm place, for 1 hour, or until doubled in bulk.

4 ▲ Turn out on to a lightly floured surface, knock back and knead gently. Shape into a plump oval loaf, about 7 in (18 cm) long. Place on the prepared baking sheet and sprinkle with a little wholemeal bread flour.

5 Cover the dough with lightly oiled clear film and leave to rise, in a warm place, for 30 minutes, or until doubled in size. Meanwhile, preheat the oven to 200°C/400°F/Gas 6.

6 ▲ Using a sharp knife, slash the top with 3–4 diagonal cuts to make a criss-cross effect. Bake for 30–35 minutes, or until golden and sounding hollow when tapped on the base. Transfer to a wire rack to cool.

MAKES 1 LOAF

8 oz (225 g) potatoes, peeled and diced
¼ oz (10 g) easy-blend dried yeast
12 oz (350 g) unbleached white bread flour
4 oz (115 g) wholemeal bread flour, plus extra for sprinkling
½ teaspoon (2.5 ml) caraway seeds, crushed
2 teaspoons (10 ml) salt
1 oz (25 g) butter

~ VARIATION ~

To make a cheese-flavoured potato bread, omit the caraway seeds and knead 4 oz (115 g) grated Cheddar, Red Leicester or crumbled Stilton into the dough before shaping.

Jewish Challah

Makes 1 loaf

1¼ lb (500 g) unbleached white bread flour
2 teaspoons (10 ml) salt
¾ oz (20 g) fresh yeast
7 fl oz (200 ml) lukewarm water
2 tablespoons (30 ml) caster sugar
2 eggs
3 oz (75 g) butter or margarine, melted
For the glaze
1 egg yolk
1 tablespoon (15 ml) water
2 teaspoons (10 ml) poppy seeds, for sprinkling

~ COOK'S TIP ~

If wished, divide the dough in half and make two small challah, keeping the plaits quite simple. Reduce the baking time by about 10 minutes.

Challah is an egg-rich, light-textured bread baked for the Jewish Sabbath and to celebrate religious holidays. It is usually plaited with 3 or 4 strands of dough, but 8 strands or more may be used to create especially festive loaves.

3 Knock back, re-cover and leave to rise again in a warm place for about 1 hour. Knock back, turn out on to a floured surface and knead gently. Divide into quarters. Roll each piece into a rope 18 in (45 cm) long. Line up next to each other. Pinch the ends together at one end.

4 ▲ Starting from the right, lift the first rope over the second and the third rope over the fourth. Take the fourth rope and place it between the first and second ropes. Repeat, continuing until plaited.

5 Tuck the ends under and place the loaf on the baking sheet. Cover with oiled clear film and leave to rise in a warm place, for about 30–45 minutes, or until doubled in size. Meanwhile, preheat the oven to 200°C/400°F/ Gas 6. Beat together the egg yolk and water for the glaze.

6 ▲ Brush the egg glaze gently over the loaf. Sprinkle evenly with the poppy seeds and bake for 35–40 minutes, or until the challah is a deep golden brown. Transfer to a wire rack and leave to cool.

1 ▲ Lightly grease a baking sheet. Sift the flour and salt together into a large bowl and make a well in the centre. Mix the yeast with the water and sugar, add to the centre of the flour with the eggs and melted butter or margarine and gradually mix in the surrounding flour to form a soft dough.

2 Turn out on to a floured surface and knead for 10 minutes until smooth and elastic. Place in an oiled bowl, cover with oiled clear film and leave to rise, in a warm place, for 1 hour, or until doubled in bulk.

American Pumpkin and Walnut Bread

Pumpkin, nutmeg and walnuts combine to make a moist, tangy and slightly sweet bread with an indescribably good flavour. Serve partnered with meats or cheese, or simply lightly buttered.

MAKES 1 LOAF

1¼ lb (500 g) pumpkin, peeled, seeded and cut into chunks
3 oz (75 g) caster sugar
1 teaspoon (5 ml) grated nutmeg
2 oz (50 g) butter, melted
3 eggs, lightly beaten
12 oz (350 g) unbleached white bread flour
2 teaspoons (10 ml) baking powder
½ teaspoon (2.5 ml) salt
3 oz (75 g) walnuts, chopped

1 Grease and base line a loaf tin 8½ x 4½ in (21 x 12 cm). Preheat the oven to 180°C/350°F/Gas 4.

2 ▲ Place the pumpkin in a saucepan, add water to cover by about 2 in (5 cm), then bring to the boil. Cover, lower the heat and simmer for 20 minutes, or until the pumpkin is very tender. Drain, then purée in a food processor or blender. Leave to cool.

3 ▲ Place 10 oz (275 g) of the purée in a large bowl. Add the sugar, nutmeg, melted butter and eggs to the purée and mix together. Sift the flour, baking powder and salt into a large bowl and make a well in the centre.

4 Add the pumpkin mixture to the centre of the flour and stir until smooth. Mix in the walnuts.

~ COOK'S TIP ~
Use any leftover pumpkin purée in soup.

5 Transfer to the prepared tin and bake for 1 hour, or until golden and starting to shrink from the sides of the tin. Cool on a wire rack.

San Francisco Sourdough Bread

MAKES 2 LOAVES

FOR THE STARTER

2 oz (50 g) wholemeal flour

pinch of ground cumin

1 tablespoon (15 ml) milk

1–2 tablespoons (15–30 ml) water

1ST REFRESHMENT

2 tablespoons (30 ml) water

4 oz (115 g) wholemeal flour

2ND REFRESHMENT

4 tablespoons (60 ml) water

4 oz (115 g) white bread flour

FOR THE BREAD

1ST REFRESHMENT

5 tablespoons (75 ml) very warm water

3 oz (75 g) unbleached plain flour

2ND REFRESHMENT

6 fl oz (175 ml) lukewarm water

7–8 oz (200–225 g) unbleached
    plain flour

FOR THE SOURDOUGH

9 fl oz (275 ml) warm water

1¼ lb (500 g) unbleached white
    bread flour

1 tablespoon (15 ml) salt

ice cubes, for baking

1 ▲ Sift the flour and cumin for the starter into a bowl. Add the milk and sufficient water to make a firm but moist dough. Knead for 6–8 minutes to form a firm dough. Return to the bowl, cover with a damp dish towel and leave at 24–26°C/75–80°F for about 2 days. When it is ready the starter will appear moist and wrinkled and will have a crust.

In San Francisco this bread is leavened using a flour and water paste, which is left to ferment with the aid of airborne yeast. The finished loaves have a moist crumb and crispy crust, and will keep for several days.

2 Pull off the crust and discard. Scoop out the moist centre (about the size of a hazelnut), which will be aerated and sweet smelling, and place in a clean bowl. Mix in the water for the 1st refreshment. Add the wholemeal flour and mix to a dough.

3 Cover with clear film and return to a warm place for 1–2 days. Discard the crust and gradually mix in the water for the 2nd refreshment to the starter, which by now will have a slightly sharper smell. Gradually mix in the white flour, cover and leave in a warm place for 8–10 hours.

4 ▲ For the bread, mix the sourdough starter with the water for the 1st refreshment. Mix in the flour to form a firm dough. Knead for 6–8 minutes until firm. Cover with a damp dish towel and leave in a warm place for 8–12 hours, until doubled in bulk.

5 Gradually mix in the water for the 2nd refreshment, then mix in enough flour to form a soft, smooth elastic dough. Re-cover and leave in a warm place for 8–12 hours. Gradually stir in the water for the sourdough, then work in the flour and salt. This will take 10–15 minutes. Turn out on to a floured surface and knead until smooth and very elastic. Place in an oiled bowl, cover with oiled clear film and leave to rise, in a warm place, for 8–12 hours.

6 Divide the dough in half and shape into 2 round loaves by folding the sides over to the centre and sealing.

7 ▲ Place seam side up in flour-dusted *couronnes*, bowls or baskets lined with flour-dusted dish towels. Re-cover and leave to rise in a warm place for 4 hours.

8 Preheat the oven to 220°C/425°F/Gas 7. Place an empty roasting tin in the bottom of the oven. Dust 2 baking sheets with flour. Turn out the loaves seam side down on the prepared baking sheets. Using a sharp knife, cut a criss-cross pattern by slashing the top of the loaves 4–5 times in each direction.

9 Place the baking sheets in the oven and immediately drop the ice cubes into the hot roasting tin to create steam. Bake the bread for 25 minutes, then reduce the oven temperature to 200°C/400°F/Gas 6 and bake for a further 15–20 minutes, or until sounding hollow when tapped on the base. Transfer to wire racks to cool.

~ COOK'S TIP ~

If you make sourdough bread regularly, keep a small amount of the starter in the fridge. It will keep for several days. Use for the 2nd refreshment.

Boston Brown Bread

MAKES 1 OR 2 LOAVES

3½ oz (90 g) cornmeal
3½ oz (90 g) unbleached plain white flour or wholemeal flour
3½ oz (90 g) rye flour
½ teaspoon (2.5 ml) salt
1 teaspoon (5 ml) bicarbonate of soda
3½ oz (90 g) seedless raisins
4 fl oz (120 ml) milk
4 fl oz (120 ml) water
4 fl oz (120 ml) molasses or black treacle

Rich, moist and dark, this bread is flavoured with molasses and can include raisins. In Boston it is often served with savoury baked beans.

4 ▲ Fill the jug or tins with the dough; they should be about two-thirds full. Cover with foil or greased greaseproof paper and tie securely.

5 Bring water to a depth of 2 in (5 cm) to the boil in a deep, heavy-based saucepan large enough to accommodate the jug or tins. Place a trivet in the pan, stand the jug or tins on top, cover the pan and steam for 1½ hours, adding more boiling water to maintain the required level as necessary.

6 Cool the loaves for a few minutes in the jugs or tins, then turn them on their sides and the loaves should slip out. Serve warm, as a teabread or with savoury dishes.

> ### ~ COOK'S TIP ~
> If you do not have any of the containers listed below, use one or two heatproof bowls.

1 Line the base of one 2 pint (1.2 litre) cylindrical metal or glass container, such as a heatproof glass coffee jug, with greased greaseproof paper. Alternatively, remove the lids from two 1 lb (450 g) coffee tins, wash and dry the tins, then line with greased greaseproof paper.

2 Mix together the cornmeal, plain or wholemeal flour, rye flour, salt, bicarbonate of soda and raisins in a large bowl. Warm the milk and water in a small saucepan and stir in the molasses or black treacle.

3 ▲ Add the molasses mixture to the dry ingredients and mix together using a spoon until it just forms a moist dough. Do not overmix.

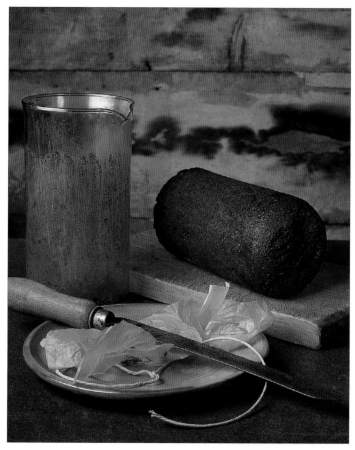

American Bagels

Bagels are eaten in many countries, especially where there is a Jewish community, and are very popular in the USA. They can be made from white, wholemeal or rye flour and finished with a variety of toppings, including caraway, poppy seeds, sesame seeds and onion.

MAKES 10 BAGELS
12 oz (350 g) unbleached white bread flour
2 teaspoons (10 ml) salt
¼ oz (6 g) easy-blend dried yeast
1 teaspoon (10 ml) malt extract
7½ fl oz (210 ml) lukewarm water
FOR POACHING
4 pints (2.5 litres) water
1 tablespoon (15 ml) malt extract
FOR THE TOPPING
1 egg white
2 teaspoons (10 ml) cold water
2 tablespoons (30 ml) poppy, sesame or caraway seeds

5 Preheat the oven to 220°C/425°F/ Gas 7. Place the water and malt extract for poaching in a large pan, bring to the boil, then reduce to a simmer. Place the bagels in the water a few at a time and poach for about 1 minute. They will sink and then rise again when first added to the pan. Using a fish slice or draining spoon, turn over and cook for 30 seconds. Remove and drain on a dish towel. Repeat with the remaining bagels.

1 ▲ Grease 2 baking sheets. Sift the flour and salt together into a large bowl. Stir in the dried yeast. Make a well in the centre. Mix the malt extract and water, add to the centre of the flour and mix to a dough. Knead on a floured surface until elastic.

2 Place in a lightly oiled bowl, cover with lightly oiled clear film and leave to rise, in a warm place, for about 1 hour, or until doubled in bulk.

3 Turn out on to a floured surface and knock back. Knead for 1 minute, then divide into 10 equal pieces. Shape into balls, cover with clear film and leave to rest for 5 minutes.

4 ▲ Gently flatten each ball and make a hole through the centre with your thumb. Enlarge the hole slightly by turning your thumb around. Place on a floured tray; re-cover and leave in a warm place, for 10–20 minutes, or until they begin to rise.

6 ▲ Place five bagels on each prepared baking sheet, spacing them well apart. Beat the egg white with the water for the topping, brush the mixture over the top of each bagel and sprinkle with poppy, sesame or caraway seeds. Bake for 20–25 minutes, or until golden brown. Transfer to a wire rack to cool.

American Monkey Bread

MAKES 1 LOAF

¼ oz (10 g) sachet easy-blend dried yeast
1 lb (450 g) unbleached white bread flour
½ teaspoon (2.5 ml) salt
1 tablespoon (15 ml) caster sugar
4 fl oz (120 ml) lukewarm milk
4 fl oz (120 ml) lukewarm water
1 egg, lightly beaten
FOR THE COATING
3 oz (75 g) sultanas
3 tablespoons (45 ml) rum or brandy
4 oz (115 g) walnuts, finely chopped
2 teaspoons (10 ml) ground cinnamon
4 oz (115 g) soft light brown sugar
2 oz (50 g) butter, melted

This American favourite is also called bubble bread – because of the "bubbles" of dough. The pieces of dough are tossed in a heavenly coating of butter, nuts, cinnamon and rum-soaked fruit.

1 Grease a 9 in (23 cm) spring-form ring cake tin. Mix the yeast, flour, salt and caster sugar in a large bowl and make a well in the centre.

2 Add the milk, water and egg to the centre of the flour and mix together to a soft dough. Turn out on to a floured surface and knead for about 10 minutes until smooth and elastic. Place in an oiled bowl, cover with oiled clear film and leave to rise, in a warm place, for 45–60 minutes, or until doubled in bulk.

3 ▲ Place the sultanas in a pan, pour over the rum or brandy and heat for 1–2 minutes, or until warm. Do not overheat. Remove from the heat and set aside. Mix the walnuts, cinnamon and sugar in a bowl.

4 ▲ Turn out the dough on to a lightly floured surface and knead gently. Divide into 30 equal pieces and shape into small balls. Dip the balls, one at a time into the melted butter, then roll them in the walnut mixture. Place half in the prepared tin, spaced slightly apart. Sprinkle over all the soaked sultanas.

5 ▲ Top with the remaining dough balls, dipping and coating as before. Sprinkle over any remaining walnut mixture and melted butter. Cover with lightly oiled clear film or slide the tin into a lightly oiled large polythene bag and leave to rise, in a warm place, for about 45 minutes, or until the dough reaches the top of the tin.

6 Meanwhile, preheat the oven to 190°C/375°F/Gas 5. Bake for 35–40 minutes, or until well risen and golden. Cool on a wire rack.

New England Fantans

These fantail rolls look stylish and are so versatile that they are equally suitable for a simple snack, or a gourmet dinner party!

1 Grease a muffin sheet with 9 3 in (7.5 cm) cups or foil cases. Mix the yeast with the buttermilk and sugar and leave to stand for 15 minutes.

2 ▲ In a pan, heat the milk with 1½ oz (40 g) of the butter until the butter has melted. Cool until lukewarm.

3 Sift the flour and salt into a bowl. Add the yeast mixture, milk mixture and egg and mix to a soft dough. Turn out on to a floured surface and knead for 5–8 minutes until smooth and elastic. Place in an oiled bowl, cover with oiled clear film and leave to rise, in a warm place, for 1 hour, until doubled in size.

4 ▲ Turn out on to a lightly floured surface, knock back and knead until smooth and elastic. Roll into an oblong measuring 18 x 12 in (45 x 30 cm) and about ¼ in (5 mm) thick. Melt the remaining butter, brush over the dough and cut it lengthways into 5 equal strips. Stack on top of each other and cut across into 9 equal 2 in (5 cm) strips.

5 ▲ Pinch one side of each layered strip together, then place pinched side down into a muffin cup or foil case. Cover with oiled clear film and leave to rise, in a warm place, for 30–40 minutes, or until the fantans have almost doubled in size. Preheat the oven to 200°C/400°F/Gas 6. Bake for 20 minutes, or until golden. Cool on a wire rack.

MAKES 9 ROLLS

½ oz (15 g) fresh yeast
5 tablespoons (75 ml) buttermilk, at room temperature
2 teaspoons (10 ml) caster sugar
5 tablespoons (75 ml) milk
2½ oz (65 g) butter
13 oz (375 g) unbleached white bread flour
1 teaspoon (5 ml) salt
1 egg, lightly beaten

~ VARIATION ~

Add 1 teaspoon (5 ml) ground cinnamon to the remaining butter in step 4 before brushing over the dough strips. Sprinkle the rolls with a little icing sugar as soon as they come out of the oven.

Mexican "Bread of the Dead"

MAKES 1 LOAF

3 star anise
6 tablespoons (90 ml) cold water
1½ lb (675 g) unbleached white bread flour
1 teaspoon (5 ml) salt
4 oz (115 g) caster sugar
1 oz (25 g) fresh yeast
6 fl oz (175 ml) lukewarm water
3 eggs
4 tablespoons (60 ml) orange liqueur
4 oz (115 g) butter, melted
grated rind of 1 orange
icing sugar, for dusting

~ VARIATION ~

Ice the bread with 2 oz (60 g)
icing sugar mixed with a little
orange liqueur.

A celebratory loaf made for All Souls' Day. Even though the name of this bread suggests otherwise, it is actually a very happy day when both Mexicans and Spanish people pay their respects to the souls of their dead. Traditionally, the bread is decorated with a dough skull, bones and tears.

1 ▲ Grease a 10½ in (27 cm) fluted round cake tin. Place the star anise in a saucepan with the water. Bring to the boil and boil for 3–4 minutes, until the liquid has reduced to 3 tablespoons (45 ml) Discard the star anise and leave the liquid to cool.

2 Sift the flour and salt together into a large bowl. Stir in the sugar and make a well in the centre.

3 In a jug, dissolve the yeast in the lukewarm water. Pour into the centre of the flour and mix in a little flour, using your fingers, until a smooth, thick batter forms. Sprinkle over a little of the remaining flour, cover with clear film and leave the batter in a warm place for 30 minutes, or until the mixture starts to bubble.

4 Beat the eggs, the reserved liquid flavoured with star anise, orange liqueur and melted butter together. Gradually incorporate into the flour mixture to form a smooth dough.

5 ▲ Turn out the dough on to a lightly floured surface and gently knead in the orange rind. Knead for 5–6 minutes until smooth and elastic. Shape into a 10½ in (27 cm) round and place in the prepared tin. Cover with lightly oiled clear film and leave to rise, in a warm place, for 2–3 hours, or until almost at the top of the tin and doubled in bulk.

6 Meanwhile, preheat the oven to 190°C/375°F/Gas 5. Bake the loaf for 45–50 minutes, or until golden. Turn out on to a wire rack to cool. Dust with icing sugar to serve.

Iranian Barbari

These small Iranian flat breads can be made in a variety of sizes. For a change, make two large breads and break off pieces to scoop up dips.

MAKES 6 BARBARI

8 oz (225 g) unbleached white bread flour
1 teaspoon (5 ml) salt
½ oz (15 g) fresh yeast
scant ¼ pint (140 ml) lukewarm water
oil, for brushing

1 Lightly dust 2 baking sheets with flour. Sift the flour and salt into a bowl and make a well in the centre.

2 ▲ Mix the yeast with the water. Pour into the centre of the flour, sprinkle a little flour over and leave in a warm place for 15 minutes. Mix to a dough, then turn out on to a lightly floured surface and knead for 8–10 minutes until smooth and elastic.

3 Place in a lightly oiled bowl, cover with oiled clear film and leave to rise for 45–60 minutes, or until doubled.

4 ▲ Knock back the dough and turn out on to a floured surface. Divide into 6 equal pieces and roll each one out to about 4 x 2 in (10 x 5 cm) and about ½ in (1 cm) thick. Space well apart on the baking sheets, and make four slashes in the tops.

> ~ VARIATION ~
> Sprinkle with sesame or caraway seeds before baking.

5 Cover the breads with lightly oiled clear film and leave to rise, in a warm place, for 20 minutes. Meanwhile, preheat the oven to 200°C/400°F/ Gas 6. Brush the breads with oil and bake for 12–15 minutes, or until pale golden. Serve warm.

Syrian Onion Bread

MAKES 8 BREADS

1 lb (450 g) unbleached white bread flour
1 teaspoon (5 ml) salt
¾ oz (20 g) fresh yeast
9 fl oz (275 ml) lukewarm water
FOR THE TOPPING
4 tablespoons (60 ml) finely chopped onion
1 teaspoon (5 ml) ground cumin
2 teaspoons (10 ml) ground coriander
2 teaspoons (10 ml) chopped fresh mint
2 tablespoons (30 ml) olive oil

The basic Arab breads of the Levant and Gulf have traditionally been made with a finely ground wholemeal flour similar to chapati flour, but now they are being made with white flour as well. This Syrian version has a tasty, aromatic onion and coriander topping.

~ COOK'S TIP ~

If you haven't any fresh mint to hand, then add 1 tablespoon (15 ml) dried mint. Use the freeze-dried variety if you can as it has much more flavour.

1 ▲ Lightly flour 2 baking sheets. Sift the flour and salt together into a large bowl and make a well in the centre. Cream the yeast with a little of the water, then mix in the remainder.

2 Add the yeast mixture to the centre of the flour and mix to a firm dough. Turn out on to a lightly floured surface and knead for 8–10 minutes until smooth and elastic.

3 Place in a lightly oiled bowl, cover with lightly oiled clear film and leave to rise, in a warm place, for about 1 hour, or until doubled in size.

4 ▲ Knock back the dough and turn out on to a floured surface. Divide into 8 equal pieces and roll into 5–6 in (13–15 cm) rounds. Make them slightly concave. Prick all over and space well apart on the baking sheets. Cover with oiled clear film and leave to rise for 15–20 minutes.

5 ▲ Meanwhile, preheat the oven to 200°C/400°F/Gas 6. Mix the chopped onion, ground cumin, ground coriander and chopped mint in a bowl. Brush the breads with the olive oil for the topping, sprinkle with the spicy onion mixture and bake for 15–20 minutes. Serve warm.

Indian Tandoori Rotis

There are numerous varieties of breads in India, most of them unleavened. This one, as its name suggests, would normally be baked in a tandoor – a clay oven which is heated with charcoal or wood. The oven becomes extremely hot, cooking the bread in minutes.

MAKES 6 ROTIS

12 oz (350 g) *atta* or fine wholemeal flour
1 teaspoon (5 ml) salt
8 fl oz (250 ml) water
2–3 tablespoons (30–45 ml) melted ghee or butter, for brushing

~ COOK'S TIP ~

The rotis are ready when light brown bubbles appear on the surface.

1 ▲ Sift the flour and salt into a large bowl. Add the water and mix to a soft dough. Knead on a floured surface for 3–4 minutes until smooth. Place in an oiled bowl, cover with oiled clear film; leave to rest for 1 hour.

2 ▲ Turn out on to a floured surface. Divide the dough into 6 pieces and shape each piece into a ball. Press out into a larger round with your hand, cover with oiled clear film and leave to rest for 10 minutes.

3 Preheat the oven to 230°C/ 450°F/ Gas 8. Place 3 baking sheets in the oven. Roll the rotis into 6 in (15 cm) rounds, place on the baking sheets and bake for 8–10 minutes. Brush with ghee or butter and serve warm.

Indian Naan

MAKES 3 NAAN

8 oz (225 g) unbleached white bread flour
½ teaspoon (2.5 ml) salt
½ oz (15 g) fresh yeast
4 tablespoons (60 ml) lukewarm milk
1 tablespoon (15 ml) vegetable oil
2 tablespoons (30 ml) natural yogurt
1 egg
2–3 tablespoons (30–45 ml) melted ghee or butter, for brushing

From the Caucasus through the Punjab region of northwest India and beyond, all serve these leavened breads. Traditionally cooked in a very hot clay oven known as a tandoor, naan are usually eaten with dry meat or vegetable dishes, such as tandoori.

1 ▲ Sift the flour and salt together into a large bowl. In a smaller bowl, cream the yeast with the milk. Set aside for 15 minutes.

2 ▲ Mix the yeast mixture, oil, yogurt and egg into the flour.

3 ▲ Mix to a soft dough and turn out on to a lightly floured surface. Knead for about 10 minutes until smooth and elastic. Place in a lightly oiled bowl, cover with lightly oiled clear film and leave to rise, in a warm place, for 45 minutes, or until doubled in bulk.

4 Preheat the oven to at least 230°C/450°F/Gas 8. Place 3 heavy baking sheets in the oven to heat.

5 Turn the dough out on to a floured surface and knock back. Divide into 3 and shape into balls.

6 ▲ Cover two of the balls of dough with oiled clear film and roll out the third into a teardrop shape about 10 in (25 cm) long, 5 in (13 cm) wide and with a thickness of about ¼–⅓ in (5–8 mm).

7 Preheat the grill to its highest setting. Meanwhile, place the naan on the hot baking sheets and bake for 3–4 minutes, or until puffed up.

8 Remove the naan from the oven and place under the hot grill for a few seconds, or until the top of the naan browns slightly. Wrap the cooked naan in a dish towel to keep warm while rolling out and cooking the remaining naan. Brush with melted ghee or butter and serve warm.

~ VARIATIONS ~

You can flavour naan in numerous different ways:
- To make spicy naan, add 1 teaspoon (5 ml) each ground coriander and ground cumin to the flour in step 1. If you would like the naan to be extra fiery, add ½–1 teaspoon (2.5–5 ml) hot chilli powder.
- To make cardamom-flavoured naan, lightly crush the seeds from 4–5 green cardamom pods and add to the flour in step 1.
- To make poppy seed naan, brush the rolled-out naan with a little ghee and sprinkle with poppy seeds. Press lightly to make sure that they stick.
- To make peppered naan, brush the rolled-out naan with a little ghee and dust generously with coarsely ground black pepper.
- To make onion-flavoured naan, add 4 oz (114 g) finely chopped onion to the dough in step 2. You may need to reduce the amount of egg if the onion is very moist to prevent making the dough too soft.
- To make wholemeal naan, substitute wholemeal bread flour for the white flour.

~ COOK'S TIP ~

To help the dough to puff up and brown, place the baking sheets in an oven preheated to the maximum temperature for at least 10 minutes before baking.

INDEX

Praise for John Hart and *The King of Lies*

"Treat yourself to something new and truly out of the ordinary."
—*Rocky Mountain News*

"This is a first novel that lunges off the page, just grabs the reader by the throat and won't let go. In the legal-thriller genre, which increasingly features protagonists transparently designed to be wildly individualistic, Work Pickens earns his individualism. And Hart is a fine stylist, turning phrases with a panache that recalls Raymond Chandler.... Readers will breathe in this fine novel like a breath of fresh air and, immediately after finishing it, wish for more." —*Booklist* (starred review)

"Hart's stunning debut, an exceptionally deep and complex mystery thriller, compares favorably to the best of Scott Turow.... Few readers will be able to resist devouring this tour de force in one or two sittings—or clamoring for more John Hart." —*Publishers Weekly* (starred review)

"This powerful debut literary thriller starts off slowly but builds momentum like a runaway train.... The writing is beautiful and the story is gripping, but it is the character study of a damaged Southern lawyer that puts this debut novel on the must-read list."
—*Library Journal* (starred review)

"A rare, remarkable book, a marvel from the first page to the last ... At times blunt and startling, at times full of grace and subtle wisdom, this novel is, without a doubt, one of the most compelling pieces of fiction I've ever read." —Martin Clark, author of *Plain Heathen Mischief*

"A top-notch debut ... Hart's prose is like Raymond Chandler's, angular and hard." —*Entertainment Weekly* (Grade: A)

"[An] ambitious debut thriller ... a gripping performance."
—*People* magazine

"A marriage of carefully crafted prose alongside have-to-keep-reading suspense."
—*The Denver Post*

"A masterful piece of writing."
—*The News & Observer* (Raleigh, North Carolina)

"A gripping mystery/thriller and a fully fleshed, thoughtful work of literature."
—*Winston-Salem Journal*

"*The King of Lies* moves and reads like a book on fire."
—Pat Conroy

"John Hart's debut . . . is that most engrossing of rarities, a well-plotted mystery novel that is written in a beautifully poetic style."
—Mark Childress, author of *Crazy in Alabama*

"Rookie of the Year."
—*BookPage*

"The best thing about reading *The King of Lies* is watching the character of Work Pickens evolve. . . . An ambitious debut from a promising new novelist."
—Sheri Reynolds, author of *The Rapture of Canaan*

"A stunning debut; absolutely relentless. I dare you to read the first chapter of *The King of Lies* and not be hooked."
—Steve Hamilton, Edgar Award winner and author of *Ice Run*

"A page-turner to the end!"
—Sally Brewster, president of the Southern Independent Booksellers Alliance

"If you want entertainment that will ensnare you, deprive you of sleep, and have you button-holing your friends about its greatness, you won't be disappointed in unknown author John Hart's first book. Take note: When Hart is famous, you'll brag about reading *The King of Lies* before anyone had heard of him."
—Peter Mergendahl, *Rockymountainnews.com*

"There hasn't been a thriller as showily literate as *The King of Lies* . . . since Scott Turow came along."
—Janet Maslin, *The New York Times*

Praise for John Hart and *The Last Child*

"With his best novel yet, the Edgar Award–winning Hart (*Down River*) firmly cements his place alongside the greats of the genre."
—*Library Journal* (starred review)

"Hart spins an impressively layered tale of broken families and secrets that can kill."
—*Publishers Weekly*

"In his third novel, Edgar winner Hart confronts murder, depravity, betrayal, and the like, while still finding room for tenderness."
—*Kirkus Reviews* (starred review)

"Hart once again produces a novel that is elegant, haunting, and memorable. His characters are given an emotional depth that genre characters seldom have, and the graceful, evocative prose lifts his stories right out of their genre and into the realm of capital-*L* literature. A must-read for every variety of fiction reader."
—*Booklist* (starred review)

"John Hart's *The Last Child* is a rare accomplishment—a compelling, fast-paced thriller written with a masterful, literary touch. You'll feel this story as much in your heart as in your gut. And this reader is keeping his fingers crossed that we'll see much, much more of Detective Hunt in the near future."
—Jeffery Deaver, author of
The Bodies Left Behind

"*The Last Child* is a beautifully written, gripping story that will have you staying up late, torn between a desire to know what happens and a reluctance to get to the book's end and break the spell. But don't worry: The characters will stay vividly alive in your imagination long after you've raced through the pages."
—*Winston-Salem Journal*

"Hart . . . is brilliant in the art of misdirection. . . . But his attention to language and tempo, his descriptions of settings and people, and his development of characters and their personal relationships all add a wonderful richness to his work. It is a richness that should make *The Last Child* a pleasure for any reader."

—*News & Observer* (Raleigh, North Carolina)

"What begins as a thrilling mystery soon evolves into an astute character drama where the preservation of family is critical. . . . Hart artfully employs the pattern of a whodunit to lead the reader down a twisted, thrilling path. What lies at the end, though, is wholly unexpected. . . . With the deft characterization of any good work of literary fiction and the subtle, satisfying plotting of a favorite mystery, *The Last Child* brings readers deep into the pathos of a small North Carolina community. This page-turner will stay in your mind long after you've read the final page."

—*The Atlanta Journal-Constitution*

"The missing-child story has been done so often that it takes something extraordinary to make it rise above the commonplace. And that is what John Hart has accomplished in his third novel, *The Last Child*. In the end, this is a novel about blood—the blood of life and death, the blood of kin, the blood of the past. And Hart has again brought forth a mystery/thriller that surpasses the humdrum and rises to serious literature."

—*Richmond Times-Dispatch*

"Hart's third novel, *The Last Child*, surpasses its superb predecessors. *The Last Child*'s atmospheric, hard-boiled story allows Hart to delve into a town's sinister secrets with a complex tale of broken families, despair, and hope."

—*South Florida Sun-Sentinel*

"John Hart is already much praised, but his third and most complex psychological thriller is a risk which has paid off with that same unshakable sense of discovery. The risk lies in the rarely attempted feat of writing a convincing child hero for adults. His success injects extra poignancy into an already compelling blend of Southern gothic mock-epic, outright horror, and dues-paying whodunnit. This one stays with you."

—*The Daily Telegraph* (UK)

"Be warned: The young hero of this compelling read will break your heart. *The Last Child* is one of those books that stays with readers long after the last page is turned." —*Calgary Herald* (Canada)

"The young boy at the story's center is a magnificent creation, Huck Finn channeled through *Lord of the Flies*. . . . Hart is still far too young for *The Last Child* to be called a crowning achievement, but the novel's ambition, emotional breadth, and maturity make it an early masterpiece in a career that continues to promise great things."

—*The Washington Post*

"Many books strive to build complex mythologies into their tales. Hart, instead, ambitiously sets out to debunk the greatest mythology of all: childhood itself. A study in reverse literary engineering, his is a brilliant vision beautifully realized." —*Providence Journal-Bulletin*

"If you haven't read John Hart, whose latest novel is *The Last Child*, you ought to." —Mike Lupica, New York *Daily News*

"Johnny's heartbreaking quest is described with great energy and sympathy." —*People* magazine

"Some of the most accomplished writing and page-turning reading this side of James Lee Burke. Add a cast of characters that would make Flannery O'Connor proud, and the result is remarkable."

—*Delta Magazine*

"With hints of Salinger in the rebellious boy, and of Dickens in the cast of misfits and wounded men and women, it's a novel suffused with grief and poignancy. There may be echoes of Grisham, but this is more deeply felt than the master has managed for years. It grips you by the throat and never lets go." —Geoffrey Wansell, *Daily Mail* (UK)

"John Hart established himself as a major literary talent with his first two novels: the critically acclaimed debut *The King of Lies* and the award-winning *Down River*. If he had never written another published word, he would be remembered for these. But his latest work is of such power that it threatens to eclipse the majesty of its older brothers. Hart writes as if he is channeling William Faulkner, or perhaps collaborating with the Cormac McCarthy of the *Blood Meridian* era. . . . On the one hand, you're afraid to turn the page; on the other, *The Last Child* is one of those rare books that you wish would go on forever, such is the power and the majesty of Hart's storytelling."

—Joe Hartlaub, *Book Reporter*

"Few novels succeed at blending genre with literary writing. Good mysteries aren't necessarily well written; good writing doesn't always translate into acclaim. John Hart occupies a short list of authors capable of blending style and genre with riveting prose. This is an engrossing mystery/thriller set in the South, the prose being compared to luminaries such as Harper Lee and William Faulkner, but with today's urgent voices, vices, and victories."   —Mary McReynolds, *The Oklahoman*

"Edgar winner Hart succinctly pulls together a terrifying, emotionally heartbreaking story that lays bare the extent of human emotions. Hart is an extraordinary storyteller, and his third novel, *The Last Child*, surpasses his superb first two."   —*The Sun* (Baltimore)

"*The Last Child* is John Hart's third novel and one that will earn his place in the ranks of America's truly great authors along with Mark Twain, Harper Lee, and Tennessee Williams."

—Ginger Stratton, *Reviewing the Evidence*

"Edgar winner John Hart is an extraordinary storyteller. Each of his three novels has depicted keen appraisals of human foibles with an emphasis on North Carolina history and a respect for the traditions of the Southern novel. But Hart has made each novel distinct, following no formula or similar style except for the superior quality of his prose."

—Olive Cogdill, *Detroit Free Press*

"Hart knows how sensitive boys feel and think behind those tough, smirking masks and with what ferocity they cling to their causes. Johnny is innocence and experience in perfect balance."

—Edward Morris, *BookPage*

"Hart twists in surprises at every turn, taking the reader through a maze of woodland and swamp that hold centuries-old secrets. Young Johnny Merrimon is a tour de force, refusing to fall when cut to the core. *The Last Child* rides a bumpy road to redemption. The harsh truth in the final few pages will leave the reader breathless (it brought unexpected tears to my eyes). I haven't read a crime thriller this memorable since Grisham's *A Time to Kill*. . . . Hart's keen sense of place and camouflaged emotions will break your heart."   —J. C. Patterson, *Book It*

Praise for John Hart and *Down River*

"This book should settle once and for all the question of whether thrillers and mysteries can also be literature."
                              —*Publishers Weekly* (starred review)

"As in his Edgar-nominated debut, *The King of Lies,* Hart takes his time, snaring the reader with evocative storytelling and lush prose."
                              —*The Boston Globe*

"*Down River* falls squarely in the league of the best of Southern novels."
                              —*South Florida Sun-Sentinel*

"A sensitive rumination on the emotional force of family dynamics."
                              —*The Washington Post*

"There are few books published that can legitimately be called a 'must-read,' but this is one of them."   —*Chicago Sun-Times*

"An engrossing, bittersweet reading experience that expertly evokes William Faulkner, John Grisham, and John Berendt."   —*Mystery Scene*

"If you value Harper Lee, James Lee Burke, Truman Capote, and Michael Malone . . . it's time to add John Hart to your bookshelves."
                              —Otto Penzler, *The New York Sun*

"*Down River* is a beautifully constructed story of personal redemption, family secrets, and murder—a small-town epic. . . . A truly splendid novel with a deep emotional core." —*Booklist* (starred review)

"Hart's sophomore effort surpasses his debut. . . . This work is reminiscent of Raymond Chandler's novels. . . . The writing is simply superb." —*Library Journal* (starred review)

"Sometimes, early success can be a curse for a writer. . . . That's definitely not the case with North Carolina's John Hart. . . . With *Down River* . . . he's only gotten better." —*Winston-Salem Journal*

"Hart's work invokes the spirit of the best of Southern literature. *Down River* puts readers in the mind of topics explored by Thomas Wolfe, Tennessee Williams, and William Faulkner, with a contemporary vision and edge that is memorable and haunting. Hart is a deep and strong talent whose future offerings will be greatly anticipated and welcomed." —*Book Reporter*

THE
KING OF LIES

ALSO BY JOHN HART

Down River
The Last Child
Iron House

THE
KING OF LIES

John Hart

Thomas Dunne Books
St. Martin's Griffin
New York

THE KING OF LIES. Copyright © 2006 by John Hart. All rights reserved. Printed in the United States of America. For information, address St. Martin's Press, 175 Fifth Avenue, New York, N.Y. 10010.

www.thomasdunnebooks.com
www.minotaurbooks.com

THE LIBRARY OF CONGRESS HAS CATALOGED THE HARDCOVER EDITION AS FOLLOWS:

Hart, John.
    The king of lies / John Hart.—1st ed.
        p. cm.
    ISBN 978-0-312-34161-9
    1. Murder victims' families—Fiction.   2. Fathers—Death—Fiction.   3. Fathers
and sons—Fiction.   4. North Carolina—Fiction.   5. Mystery fiction—Fiction.
6. Legal stories—Fiction.   I. Title.
    PS3608.A78575 E37 2006
    813'.6—dc22

2005049774

ISBN 978-1-250-02440-4 (trade paperback)

Second Minotaur Books Paperback Edition: May 2012

10   9   8   7   6   5   4   3   2   1

For Katie

ACKNOWLEDGMENTS

Nothing happens in a vacuum, and bringing a novel to publication is no exception. It takes time and faith, and the road can be long. To those who walked it with me, I would like to express my sincerest gratitude.

First and foremost, I would like to thank my wife, Katie, a source of constant support and invaluable advice—and the finest eye for fiction that a writer could ask to have looking over his shoulder. I love you, baby. To my agent and good friend, Mickey Choate, who wasn't scared to take a chance on a new guy—thanks for the faith and for the lessons. And along those lines, many thanks to my editor, Pete Wolverton, the most irreverent man I've ever met and the most capable. Let it never be said that you don't step to the plate. To Katie Gilligan, who is as sharp as a tack—thanks for putting up with me; you're the best. And a comprehensive and sincere thank-you to everyone at St.

ACKNOWLEDGMENTS

Martin's Press, St. Martin's Minotaur, and Thomas Dunne Books who worked so diligently to make this book possible.

To everyone who read the manuscript at its worst and still calls me a friend, my most profound gratitude. And to the following people, whose goodwill was so evident: Nancy and Bill Stanback, Kay and Norde Wilson, John and Annie Hart, Mary Hart, Charlotte and Doug Scudder, Sterling Hart, Ken Peck, Annie P. Hart, John and Megan Stanback, Anne Stanback, Charlotte Kinlock, Mark Stanback, Nancy Popkin, Joy Hart, John Betts, Boyd Miller, Stan and Ashley Dunham, Sanders Cockman, Sean Scapelatto, George Guise, Linda Parker, Darby Henley, Debbie Bernhardt Gray and Allison Wilson, and David and Jennifer Wilson. Special thanks to Clint and Jody Robins, who were always there, and to Mark Witte, a friend of the written word, who had a very fine idea. Thanks as well to James Randolph, attorney and friend, who took the time to make sure I'd not forgotten too much about the law, and to Erick Ellsweig, who knows why. If I have failed to mention anyone, the fault is purely mine. Rest assured that I know who you are and that you have my thanks as well.

There are others whom I have encountered along the way—people whose paths I never imagined I would cross—who have helped to make the whole experience more than I ever hoped it could be. My warmest gratitude to Mark Bozek and Russell Nuce, who bought the movie rights, and to the wonderful authors who have been kind enough to read this book and share their thoughts on it: Pat Conroy, Martin Clark, Steve Hamilton, Thomas Perry, Mark Childress, and Sheri Reynolds. What a privilege this has been for me.

Finally, an extra-special thanks to Saylor and Sophie, my daughters, for hanging the moon.

THE
KING OF LIES

CHAPTER

1

I've heard it said that jail stinks of despair. What a load. If jail stinks of any emotion, it's fear: fear of the guards, fear of being beaten or gang-raped, fear of being forgotten by those who once loved you and may or may not anymore. But mostly, I think, it's fear of time and of those dark things that dwell in the unexplored corners of the mind. Doing time, they call it—what a joke. I've been around long enough to know the reality: It's the time that does you.

For some time, I'd been bathed in that jailhouse perfume, sitting knee-to-knee with a client who'd just gotten life without parole. The trial had damned him, as I'd told him it would. The state's evidence was overwhelming, and the jury had zero sympathy for a three-time loser who had shot his brother during an argument about who'd get control of the remote. Twelve of his supposed peers, and not one cared that he'd been drinking, that he was cracked to the gills, or that

1

he didn't mean to do it. No one cared that his brother was an ass and a felon in his own right, not the jury and least of all me. All I wanted was to explain his appeal rights, answer any legal questions, and get the hell out. My fee application to the state of North Carolina would wait until the morning.

On most days I was ambivalent, at best, about my chosen profession, but on days like this I hated being a lawyer; that hatred ran so deep that I feared something must be wrong with me. I hid it as others would a perversion. And this day was worse than most. Maybe it was the case or the client or the emotional aftermath of one more needless tragedy. I'd been in that room a hundred times, but for some reason it felt different this time. The walls seemed to shift and I felt a momentary disorientation. I tried to shake it off, cleared my throat, and stood. We'd had bad facts, but the decision to go to trial had not been mine to make. When he'd stumbled from the trailer, bloody and weeping, he'd had the gun in one hand, the remote control in the other. It was broad daylight and he was out-of-his-head drunk. The neighbor looked out the window when my client started screaming. He saw the blood, the gun, and called the cops. No lawyer could have won the trial—I'd told him as much. I could have had him out in ten, but he refused to take the plea arrangement I'd negotiated. He wouldn't even talk about it.

The guilt may have been too much, or perhaps some part of him needed the punishment. Whatever the case, it was over now.

He finally tore his gaze from the jail-issue flip-flops that had known a thousand feet before his and forced his eyes to mine. Wet nostrils shone in the hard light, and his red eyes jittered, terrified of whatever they saw in that jigsaw mind of his. He'd pulled the trigger, and that brutal truth had finally taken root. The trail had wound its way across his face as we'd talked for the past few hours. His denials had sputtered to a halt, and I'd watched, untouchable, as hope shriveled and died. I'd seen it all before.

A sopping wet cough, his right forearm smearing mucus across his cheek. "So that's it, then?" he asked.

I didn't bother to answer. He was already nodding to himself, and I could see his thoughts as if written in the dank air that hung between us: life without parole and him not yet twenty-three. It generally took days for this brutal truth to bore through the bullshit tough-guy act that every dumb-ass killer carried into this place like some kind of sick birthright. Maybe this joker was smarter than I'd given him credit for. In the brief time since the judge handed down his sentence, he'd grown the lifer stare. Fifty, maybe sixty years behind the same redbrick walls. No chance of parole. Not twenty years, not thirty or even forty, but life, in caps. It would kill me, and that is God's own truth.

A glance at my watch told me I'd been in there for almost two hours, which was my limit. I knew from experience that the smell had by now permeated my clothes, and I could see the dampness where his hands had pawed at my jacket. He saw the watch come up and he lowered his eyes. His words evaporated in the still air, leaving a vacuum that my body settled into as I stood. I didn't reach to shake his hand and he didn't reach for mine, but I noticed a new palsy in his fingers.

He was old before his time, all but broken at twenty-three, and what might have been sympathy wormed into a heart I'd thought forever beyond such things. He started to cry, and his tears fell to the filthy floor. He was a killer, no question, but he was going to hell on earth first thing the next morning. Almost against my will, I reached out and put a hand on his shoulder. He didn't look up, but he said that he was sorry, and I knew that this time he truly was. I was his last touch with the real world, the one with trees. All else had been pared away by the razor-sharp reality of his sentence. His shoulders began to heave beneath my hand, and I felt a nothingness so great, it almost had physical weight. That's where I was when they came to tell me that my father's body had finally been found. The irony was not lost on me.

The bailiff who escorted me out of the Rowan County Jail and to the office of the district attorney was a tall, wide-boned man with gray bristles where most of us have hair. He didn't bother to make small talk as we wound through the halls packed with courthouse penitents, and I didn't push it. I'd never been much of a talker.

The district attorney was a short, disarmingly round man who could turn off his eye's natural twinkle at will; it was an amazing thing to watch. To some, he was a politician, open and warm. To others, he was the cold, lifeless instrument of his office. For a few of us behind the curtain, he was a regular guy; we knew him and liked him. He'd taken two bullets for his country, yet he never looked down on people like myself, what my father had often called "the soft underbelly of a warless generation." He respected my father, but he liked me as a person, and I'd never been sure why. Maybe because I didn't shout the innocence of my guilty clients the way most defense lawyers did. Or maybe because of my sister, but that was a whole different story.

"Work," he said as I entered the room, not bothering to get up. "I'm damn sorry about this. Ezra was a great lawyer."

The only son of Ezra Pickens, I was known to a few as Jackson Workman Pickens. Everybody else liked to call me "Work," which was humorous I guess.

"Douglas." I nodded, turning at the sound of the office door closing behind me as the bailiff left. "Where'd you find him?" I asked.

Douglas tucked a pen into his shirt pocket and took the twinkle from his eye. "This is unusual, Work, so don't look for any special treatment. You're here because I thought you should hear it from me before the story breaks." He paused, looked out the window. "I thought maybe you could tell Jean."

"What does my sister have to do with this?" I asked, aware that my voice sounded loud in the cramped, cluttered space. His eyes swiveled onto me and for a moment we were strangers.

"I don't want her to read about it in the papers. Do you?" His voice had chilled; the moment had not played well. "This is a courtesy call, Work. I can't go beyond the fact that we've found his body."

"It's been eighteen months since he disappeared, Douglas, a long damn time with nothing but questions, whispers, and the looks that people give when they think you can't tell. Do you have any idea how hard this has been?"

"I'm not unsympathetic, Work, but it doesn't change anything. We haven't even finished working the crime scene. I can't discuss the case with a member of the defense bar. You know how bad that would look."

"Come on, Douglas. This is my father, not some nameless drug dealer." He was clearly unmoved. "For God's sake, you've known me my whole life."

It was true—he had known me since I was a kid—but if there was any cause for sentiment, it failed to reach the surface of his lightless eyes. I sat down and rubbed a palm across my face, smelling the jailhouse stink that lingered there and wondering if he smelled it, too.

"We can do the rounds," I continued in a softer tone, "but you know that telling me is the right thing."

"We're calling it murder, Work, and it's going to be the biggest story to hit this county in a decade. That puts me in a tough spot. It'll be a media frenzy."

"I need to know, Douglas. This has hit Jean the hardest. She's not been the same since that night—you've seen it. If I'm going to tell her about our father's death, I'll need to give her some details; she'll want them. Hell, she'll need them. But most of all, I need to know how bad it is. I'll need to prepare her. Like you said, she shouldn't read it in the paper." I paused, took in a breath, and focused. I needed to visit the crime scene, and for that I needed his agreement. "Jean needs to be handled just right."

He steepled his fingers under his chin, as I'd seen him do a thousand times, but Jean was my trump, and he knew it. My sister had shared a special friendship with the DA's daughter. They'd grown up together, best friends, and Jean was in the same car when a drunk driver crossed the centerline and hit them head-on. Jean suffered a mild concussion; his daughter was nearly decapitated. It was one of those things, they said, and it could just as easily have been the other way around. Jean sang at her funeral, and the sight of her could pull tears from Douglas's eyes even now. She'd grown up under his roof and, apart from myself, I doubted that any one person felt her pain the way Douglas did.

The silence stretched out, and I knew that my arrow had slipped through this one small chink in his armor. I pressed on before he could think too much.

"It's been a long time. Are you sure it's him?"

"It's Ezra. The coroner is on-scene now and he'll make the official call, but I've spoken with Detective Mills and she assures me that it's him."

"I want to see where it happened."

That stopped him, caught him with his mouth open. I watched as he closed it.

"Once the scene is cleared—"

"Now, Douglas. Please."

Maybe it was something in my face, or maybe it was a lifetime of knowing me and ten years of liking me. Maybe it was Jean after all. Whatever the reason, I beat the odds.

"Five minutes," he said. "And you don't leave Detective Mills's side."

Mills met me in the parking lot of the abandoned mall where the body had been found, and she was not pleased. She radiated pissed-off from the bottom of her expensive shoes to the top of her mannish haircut. She had a pointed face, which emphasized her look of natural suspicion; because of this, it was impossible for anyone to find her beautiful, but she had a good figure. She was in her mid-thirties—about my age—yet lived alone and always had. Contrary to speculation around the lawyer's lounge, she wasn't gay. She just hated lawyers, which made her okay in my book.

"You must have kissed the DA's ass to get this, Work. I can't even believe I've agreed to it." Mills stood only five five or so but seemed taller. What she lacked in physical strength, she made up for in smarts. I'd seen her shred more than one of my colleagues who had presumed to challenge her on cross.

6

"I told him I won't leave your side, and I won't. I just need to see. That's all."

She studied me in the gray afternoon light and her animosity seemed to drain away. The sight of a softening expression in a face rigorously trained against such things was vaguely repellant, yet I appreciated it nonetheless.

"Stay behind me and touch nothing. I mean it, Work. Not one damn thing."

She began a purposeful stride across the cracked, weed-filled parking lot, and for a moment I was unable to follow. My eyes moved over the mall, the parking lot, and then found the creek. It was a dirty creek, choked with litter and red clay; it flowed into a concrete tunnel that ran underneath the parking lot. I could still remember the stink of it, the chemical reek of gasoline and mud. For an instant, I forgot why I'd come.

It could have happened yesterday, I thought.

I heard Mills call my name and I tore my eyes away from that dark place and the childhood it had come to represent. I was thirty-five now and here for a very different reason. I walked away from it, walked to Mills, and together we approached what had once been the Towne Mall. Even in its prime, it had been ugly, a prefab strip mall sandwiched between the interstate and a power-transfer station that chewed at the sky with towers and high-tension lines. Built in the late sixties, it had struggled for years with imminent closure. Only a third of the stores had had tenants as of a year ago, and the last one had fled with winter. Now the place crawled with bulldozers, wrecking balls, and itinerant workers, one of whom, according to Mills, had located the body in a storage closet at the back of one of the stores.

I wanted the details and she gave them to me in short, bitten sentences that the warm spring breeze could not soften.

"At first all he saw were ribs, and he thought they were dog bones." She threw me a glance. "Not bones that a dog would eat, but a dog skeleton."

I nodded foolishly, as if we weren't talking about my father. To my right, a hydraulic jackhammer gnawed concrete. To my left, the land rose to the heart of downtown Salisbury; the buildings there seemed to gleam, as if made of gold, and in a sense they were. Salisbury was a rich town, with a lot of old money and a fair amount of new. But in places, the beauty was thin as paint and could barely hide the cracks; for there was poverty here, too, although many pretended there was not.

Mills lifted the yellow crime-scene tape and ushered me underneath. We entered the mall through what used to be a double door, now a ragged mouth with crushed cinder-block teeth. We moved past boarded-up storefronts to the last in the row. The door was open beneath a sign that read NATURE'S OWN: PETS AND EXOTICA. Nothing more exotic than rats had been behind those plywood sheets for years—rats and the decaying corpse of Ezra Pickens, my father.

The power was off, but the crime-scene unit had set up portable spotlights. I recognized the coroner, whose pinched face I would forever remember from the night my mother died. He refused to meet my eyes, which was unsurprising. There had been many difficult questions that night. From the rest, I got a few polite nods, but most of the cops, I could tell, weren't happy to see me. Nevertheless, they moved aside as Mills guided me through the dusty store to the closet at the back. My gut told me that they moved out of respect for Mills and my father more than they did for any grief they might imagine me to feel.

And just like that, there he was, ribs gleaming palely through a long rip in a shirt that I had forgotten but now remembered quite well. He looked something like a broken crucifix, with one arm outflung and his legs folded together. Most of his face lay hidden beneath what looked to be a candy striper's shirt still on its hanger, but I saw a porcelain stretch of jawbone and remembered whiskers there, pale and wet under a streetlamp on the last night I saw him alive.

I felt eyes upon me, and they pulled me away. I looked at the gathering of eager cops; some were merely curious, while others, I knew, sought their own secret satisfaction. They all wanted to see it, my face, a defense attorney's face, here in this musty place where murder was more than a case file, where the victim was flesh and blood, the smell that of family gone to dust.

I felt their eyes. I knew what they wanted, and so I turned to look again upon the almost empty clothes, the flash of bone so pale and curving. But I would give them nothing, and my body did not betray me, for which I was grateful. For what I felt was the return of a long-quiescent rage, and the certain conviction that this was the most human my father had ever appeared to me.

CHAPTER

2

I stared at my father's corpse, doubting that I could forget the sight and wondering if I should even try. I bent, as if to touch him, and felt Mills shift behind me. She dropped a hand onto my shoulder, pulled me back. "Enough," she said, and her eyes were hard as she herded me away from the scene and back into my expensive but aging car. I watched her walk back to the gaping door, and twice she turned back to look at me. I gave her a nod as she turned for the last time and disappeared inside. Then I tried to call Jean from my cell phone. Her housemate, a rough-edged woman named Alex, picked up on the first ring. She was tight-lipped and physical. We didn't get along, and my list of questions was longer than her supply of answers. Her relationship with my sister had long ago poisoned the family well, and she made no bones of how she felt about me. I was a threat.

"May I speak to Jean?" I asked.

"No."

"Why not?"

"She's not here."

"Where can I find her?" There was silence on the other end, then the sound of a cigarette lighter. "It's important," I insisted.

I heard her inhale, as if she was thinking about it, but I knew better. Alex never gave willingly, not to me.

"At work," she finally said, making me wonder when was the last time my voice had been welcome in that home.

"Thanks," I said, but she had already hung up.

Confronting Jean was the last thing I wanted to do, especially at her work, where the stink of decline must have ground deepest into her skin. Yet it was the smell of pepperoni and mushroom that struck me first as I stepped into the old Pizza Hut on West Innes Street. It was a stale smell, one that churned up memories of junior high dates and fumbled kisses. We used to laugh at people like my sister, and the memory of that pulled my shoulders even lower as I walked to the counter.

I knew the manager by sight only, and was again informed that Jean was not available. "On a delivery," he told me. "Welcome to wait."

I took a seat in a red vinyl booth and ordered a beer to keep me company. It was cold and tasteless, which on this day was exactly what I needed. I sipped it as I watched the door. Eventually, my eyes wandered, exploring the people who clustered around their tables. There was an attractive black couple being served by a skinny white girl with studs in her tongue and a silver crucifix jammed through her eyebrow. They smiled at her as if they had something in common. Nearest to the buffet, two women challenged chair legs that looked spindly yet weren't, and I watched them urge their children to eat yet more, since it was all-you-can-eat Thursday.

Three young men sat at the table next to mine, probably from the local college and in for an early afternoon beer buzz. They were loud and coarse, but having fun. I felt the rhythms of their chatter and tried to remember what that age had been like. I envied their illusions.

The door opened to a spill of weak sunlight and I turned to see my sister move into the restaurant. My melancholy ripened as I watched. She carried her decline as I carried a briefcase, businesslike, and the red pizza box seemed at home under her arm. But her pale skin and haunted eyes would never fit my memories of her—no more so than the grubby running shoes or tattered jeans. I studied her face in profile as she stopped by the counter. It used to be soft but had grown angular, with a new tightness at the eyes and mouth. And her expression was hard to pin down. I couldn't read her anymore.

She was a year over thirty, still attractive, at least physically. But she'd not been right for some time, not the same. There was something off about her. It was clear to me, who knew her best, but others picked up on it. It was as if she'd ceased trying.

She stopped at the counter, put down the hot box, and stared at the dirty pizza ovens as if waiting for someone to cross her field of vision. She did not move once. Not even a twitch. I could feel the misery coming off of her in waves.

A sudden silence at the table of young men pulled my eyes away, and I saw them staring at my sister, who stood, oblivious, there in the gloom of the front counter.

"Hey," one of them said to her. Then again, a little louder: "Hey."

His friends watched him with open grins. He leaned half out of his seat, toward my sister. "How about I take some of that *ass* home in a box?"

One of his friends whistled lowly. They were all staring at her now.

I almost rose—it was a reflex—but when she turned to the table of young drunks and stared them down, I froze. Something twisted behind her face. She could have been anybody.

Or nobody.

She raised both hands and flipped them off, holding it for a few good long seconds.

Then the manager materialized from the back of the kitchen. He hitched at his belt, put the belly that covered it against the counter, and said something to Jean that I could not hear. She nodded as he spoke, and her back rounded as she seemed to sink under his words. He gestured minutely at the table, said a few more words, and then pointed in my direction. She turned and her eyes focused on me. At first, I thought she didn't recognize me; her mouth seemed to tighten with distaste, but then she came over, passing the table of drunks and giving them the finger one more time, her hand tucked against her chest, where the manager could not see it.

The boys laughed and went back to their drinking. She slipped into the booth opposite me.

"What are you doing here?" she asked without preamble or smile. Her eyes were empty above skin smudged purple.

I studied her more closely, trying to find the reason that she seemed so disjointed to me. She had the same clear skin, so pale that it was almost translucent; large, tilted eyes; a delicate chin; and dark hair that spilled across her forehead and down to her shoulders in an un-kempt wave. Up close, she was steady. Study her one piece at a time and she looked fine; nevertheless, it was wrong.

Something in the eyes, maybe.

"What did he say to you?" I asked, nodding toward the manager. She didn't bother to follow the gesture. Her gaze remained fixed on me; there was no warmth in it.

"Does it matter?" she asked.

"I guess not."

She lifted her eyebrows, turned her palms up. "So?"

I didn't know how to get to the place I needed to go. I spread my fingers on the slick red-checked material that covered the table.

"You never come here," she said. "Not even to eat."

I had barely seen my sister in the past year, so I didn't blame her. Wrong as it was, avoiding her had become something of a religion for me. Most times, I could never admit that, but those bruised eyes pained me. There was too much of our mother in them, and they'd not worked for her, either.

Indecision twisted my lips.

"They found Ezra's body," she stated. It wasn't a question, and for

13

an instant I felt pressure behind my eyes. "I'm guessing that's why you're here." There was no forgiveness in her face, just a sudden intensity, and in the place of surprise or remorse, it unsettled me.

"Yes," I said.

"Where?"

I told her.

"How?"

'They're calling it murder." I studied her face. Not a flicker. "But nobody knows much more than that."

"Did Douglas tell you?" she asked.

"He did."

She leaned closer. "Do they know who did it?" she asked.

"No," I responded. Unexpectedly, her hands settled around my own and I felt the warm sweat on her palms, which surprised me. It was as if I'd come to believe that no blood flowed in her—that's how cold she'd appeared to me. She squeezed my hands as her eyes moved over my face and picked me apart. Then she pushed back against the cracked and yielding vinyl.

"So," she said. "How are you taking all this?"

"I saw the body," I replied, appalled by my own words. In spite of what I'd said to Douglas, I'd not planned to tell her this.

"And . . ."

"He was dead," I said, ushering in a silence that lasted over a minute.

"The king is dead," she finally said, her eyes immobile on mine. "I hope he's rotting in hell."

"That's pretty harsh," I told her.

"Yes," she replied flatly, and I waited for something more.

"You don't seem surprised," I finally said.

Jean shrugged. "I knew he was dead," she said, and I stared at her.

"Why?" I asked, feeling something hard and sharp coalesce in my stomach.

"Ezra would never detach himself from his money or his prestige for so long. Nothing else would keep him away."

"But he was murdered," I said.

She looked away, down at the decomposing carpet. "Our father made a lot of enemies."

I sipped my beer to buy a few seconds. I tried to make sense of her attitude.

"Are you okay?" I finally asked.

She laughed, a lost sound that had no connection to her eyes. "No," she said. "I'm not. But it's got nothing to do with his death. He died for me on the same night as Mom, if not before. If you don't get that, then we've got nothing to say to each other."

"I don't know what you're talking about."

"You do," she said, an edge in her voice that I'd never heard before. "As far as I'm concerned, he died that night, the second Mom went down those stairs. If you don't see it that way, it's your problem, not mine."

I'd expected tears and found anger, but it was directed at me as much as at Ezra, and that troubled me. How far down separate paths had we traveled in so short a time?

"Look, Jean. Mom fell down those stairs and died. I feel that pain as much as you do."

She barked another laugh, but this one was ugly. "'Fell,'" she echoed. "That's rich, Work. Just fucking rich." She swiped a hand across her face and sniffed loudly. "Mom . . ." she began, then faltered. Sudden honeysuckle tears appeared at the corners of her eyes, and it occurred to me that until now I had seen no emotion in her, not since we'd buried our mother. She pulled herself together, raised unapologetic eyes.

"He's dead, Work, and you're still his monkey boy." Her voice strengthened. "His truth is dead, too." She blew her nose, crumpled the napkin, and dropped it on the table. I stared at it. "The sooner you come to terms with the only truth that matters, the better off you'll be."

"I'm sorry, Jean, if I've upset you."

She turned her gaze away and directed it out the window, where two starlings squabbled in the parking lot. The momentary tears had gone; without the sudden color in her face, you would never have known she'd been upset.

I smelled garlic and suddenly two pizza boxes appeared on the table. I looked up to see the manager, who ignored me and spoke to Jean.

"It's your favorite," he said. "Sorry." Then he turned and walked back to the kitchen, taking most of the garlic smell with him.

"I've got to go," Jean said flatly. "Delivery." She pulled herself out of the booth, jiggling the table and sloshing my beer. Her eyes didn't meet mine, and I knew that my silence would send her away without another word. But before I could think of something to say, she had scooped up the boxes and turned away.

I fumbled for my wallet, threw a couple of singles on the table, and caught her at the door. When she ignored me, I followed her into the sun and to her time-ravaged car. I still didn't know what I wanted to say, however. How dare you judge me? . . . Where have you found such strength? . . . You're all I have and I love you. Something like that.

"What did he mean?" I asked, my hand upon her arm, her body wedged into the open car door.

"Who?" she responded.

"Your manager. When he said 'It's your favorite,' what did he mean?"

"Nothing," she said, her face looking as if she'd swallowed something bitter. "It's just work."

For whatever reason, I didn't want her to go, but my imagination failed me.

"Well," I finally managed. "Can we do dinner sometime? Alex, too, of course."

"Sure," she said in the same voice I'd heard so many times. "I'll talk to Alex and call you."

And that, I knew, was that. Alex would make damn sure the dinner never happened.

"Give her my best," I said as she rocked into the tiny car and started the tired engine. I thumped the roof as she pulled off, thinking that the sight of her face in the window of that shitty car with the Pizza Hut sign strapped on top was the most pitiful thing I would ever see.

I almost got in my car then, and I wish now that I had. Instead, I went to the manager and asked what he'd meant and where Jean had gone. His answer revealed the cruel pull-the-wings-off-flies kind of torment I'd not seen since high school, and it was part of my sister's daily life. I was in my car and out of the lot before the restaurant door had closed behind me.

I used to look at homeless people and try to imagine what they had once looked like. It's not easy. Beneath the grime and degradation is a face once adored by someone. It's a truth that tricks the eye; our glances slide away. But something happened to ruin that life, to strip it bare; and it wasn't something big like war or famine or plague. It was something small, something that but for the grace of God could take us, too. It was an ugly truth, one my sister knew too well. She wasn't homeless, but fate and the callousness of others had conspired to take from her a life I knew her to love very much. It was a good life—many would say great—and were I to close my eyes, I could see it even now. She had been trusting then, aglow with the promise of years that stretched out like silver rails.

But fate can be a wayward bitch.

So can people.

My hands steered the car along a route I knew by heart, and I looked around as I drove. I passed the massive house we'd known since childhood, empty but for my father's dusty belongings and the tracks I'd left on those rare occasions when I stopped by to check on things. Two blocks more and my own house swam into view. It crowned a small hill and looked down its nose at passing traffic and the park that lay beyond. It was a beautiful old home, with good bones, as my wife often said; but still it needed paint, and the roof was green with moss.

Beyond my house was the country club, with its Donald Ross golf course, clay tennis courts, clubhouse, and swimming pool lined with idle tanned bodies. My wife was up there somewhere, pretending we were rich, happy, or both.

On the other side of the golf course, if you knew how, you could find a beautiful development full of Salisbury's finest new homes. It was chock-full of doctors and lawyers and other assorted rich people, including Dr. Bert Werster and his wife, Glena, the queen bitch herself. Glena and Jean used to run together, back when Jean, too, was married to a surgeon and had tanned tennis-player legs and a diamond charm bracelet. There had been a group of them, in fact, six or seven women who alternated bridge and tennis with margaritas and long husbandless weekends to Figure Eight Island.

Jean's nameless manager had told me the women still played bridge every Thursday, and they liked to order pizza.

This was my sister's life.

I pulled to the curb a block down from Dr. Werster's house, a tower of stone and ivy. I watched as Jean heaved herself up steps that to anyone else might have seemed welcoming, and imagined that pizza had never weighed quite so much.

I wanted to carry her burden. I wanted to take Glena Werster out with a long rifle shot.

Instead, I backed slowly away, worried that sight of me would only compound the load on her troubled and fragile shoulders.

I drove home, past the club, and did not see the bright clothes that flashed in the sun. At the top of my driveway, I killed the engine and sat under tall walls whose peeling paint mocked me. I checked to see that I was unobserved, rolled up my windows, and wept for my sister.

CHAPTER

3

It took twenty minutes to pull myself together; then I went in for a beer. Mail littered the kitchen counter and the answering machine blinked five new messages at me. I couldn't have cared less. I went straight for the fridge and wrapped my fingers around two bottle necks. They clanked, and I sipped from the first as I dropped my coat on the kitchen chair and moved through the empty, childless house to the front door, which opened to the world below. I sat on the top step, closed my eyes to the warm sun, and pulled hard on the bottle.

I'd bought the house several years ago, when Ezra's presence imbued the law practice with a patina of respectability and desperate souls paid dearly to touch the hem of his robe. He'd been the best lawyer in the county, which had made my job easy. We'd shared an office and a name. That meant I could cherry-pick my cases, and six weeks after a local grocery truck backed over an eight-year-old kid in the parking lot, I plunked down a $100,000 down payment.

I took another sip and sudden panic struck me as I realized that I couldn't remember the name of that poor kid. For a long minute, I agonized over just how soulless this made me, and then, like a breath, his name flooded my mind.

Leon William McRae. I pictured his mother's face on the day of the funeral, the way tears had channeled down dark grief-cut furrows to drip on the white lace collar of her best dress. I remembered her strangled words, her shame over her little boy's pine casket and his plot in the poor man's cemetery that lay in the shadow of the water tower; how she worried that he'd never feel the afternoon sun there.

I wondered now what she'd done with the money his death had brought, and hoped she'd made better use of it than I. Truth be told, I disliked the house; it was too big, too visible. I rattled in it like a quarter in a tin can. But I always liked to sit there at the end of the day. It was warm in the sun. I could see the park, and the oak trees made music of the wind. I would try not to think about choices or the past. It was a place for emptiness, for absolution, and rarely was it mine alone. Usually, Barbara fucked it up.

I finished my second beer and decided on a third. I dusted myself off and went inside. As I passed through the kitchen, I saw that the answering machine now had seven messages on it, and I wondered vaguely if one might be from my wife. Back outside, I reclaimed my seat in time to see one of my favorite park-walking regulars round the corner.

There was a certain magnificence to his ugliness. He wore a fur-lined hunting cap regardless of the weather and liked the earflaps down. Threadbare khaki pants flapped around legs walked scrawny, and his arms were as skinny as those of a starved child. Heavy glasses pulled at his nose, and his mouth, always whiskered, turned up as if in pain. He kept no schedule whatsoever, and walked compulsively: midnight in the pouring rain, stalking the tracks on the east side of town, or steaming in the morning sun as he marched through the historic district.

No one knew much about him, although he'd been around for years. I'd picked up his name once at a party—Maxwell Creason. There'd been talk about him that night. He was a regular fixture in town, and everyone saw him out walking, but, apparently, no one had ever spoken to him. No one knew how he supported himself and everyone assumed that he was homeless, one of the regulars at the town's few shelters, maybe a patient at the local VA hospital; but the speculation was never very profound. Mostly, there was laughter—about how he looked, why he walked so obsessively. None of the comments were pleasant.

I never saw him like that. For me, he was a question mark, and in some ways the most fascinating person in Rowan County. I would daydream of falling into stride so that I might ask him, What do you see, in these places that you go?

I did not hear the door open, but suddenly Barbara was behind me, and her voice made me jump.

"Honestly, Work," she began. "How often do I have to ask you to drink your beer on the back patio? You look like white trash squatting out here for the world to see."

"Evening, Barbara," I said, not turning around, eyes still on my mysterious walker.

As if realizing how harsh her words had been, she softened her tone.

"Of course, honey. I'm sorry. Good evening." I could feel her as she stepped closer, a mixture of perfume and disdain that fell around me like ashes. "What are you doing?" she asked.

I couldn't bring myself to answer. What could I say? "Isn't he magnificent?" I said instead, gesturing.

"Who? Him?" she asked, pointing as if with a gun.

"Yes."

"Oh for heaven's sake, Work. Sometimes I don't understand you. Really, I don't."

I turned finally, looked up at her, and found her beautiful. "Come sit with me," I said. "Like we used to."

She laughed in a way that made her suddenly ugly, and I knew that hope would change nothing.

"I used to wear blue jeans, too. But now I need to make dinner."

"Please, Barbara. Just for a minute or two." There must have been something in my voice, for she stopped in midturn and came to my side. Her lips flirted with a smile, and although the flirtation was brief, it made me think of smiles that were neither so bland nor so insincere, of times not so far back when her smile could blind me. I'd loved her then, or believed I did, and never doubted the choices that I had made. Back then, she was so confident in the rightness of us, and spoke of our future with a passion that felt prophetic. She said that we would be the perfect couple, that we would have the perfect life; and I believed her. She made me her disciple, showed me the future through her eyes, and it was dazzling and bright.

That was a long time ago, but even now I could close my eyes and see a yellowed shadow of that vision. It had seemed so easy.

I brushed the resin of a southern spring from the step and patted the broken tile. She bent slowly, and when she sat, forearms on her knees, I thought I saw the old love flutter in her eyes.

"Are you okay?" she asked, and looking at her, I thought she meant it. For an instant, my throat closed, and I felt that if I let the words out, the tears might follow. Instead, I gestured once more at the dwindling figure of my park walker and said again, "Isn't he magnificent?"

"Oh Jesus, Work," she said, getting back to her feet. "He's a horrible old man, and I wish he'd stop walking past our house." She stared at me as if at a stranger, and I had no words for her. "Damn it. Why do you have to make it so hard? Just take your beer and sit out back. Will you do that for me, please?"

As she stalked into the house, I rubbed at my face. Until then, it had never occurred to me that the man was old, and I wondered why my wife had picked up on the fact while I had not. I watched as he moved down a grassy bank to the shore of the small city lake that was the heart of the park, then faded into the playground, which seemed to grow smaller each passing year.

Inside, the house was cold. I called to Barbara, got no answer, and so moved into the kitchen for a beer that I knew better than to drink yet planned to anyway. I saw Barbara through the door to the living room, hunched over the paper, a glass of white wine untouched beside her. Rarely had I seen her so still.

"Anything in the paper?" I asked, my voice sounding small even to my own ears.

I carried my beer into the well of her silence and sat in my favorite chair. Her head was bowed; her skin shone pale as Ezra's bones and a still darkness filled the hollows of her cheeks. When she looked up, her eyes were red and getting redder. Her lips seemed to have thinned, and for a moment she looked scared, but then her eyes softened.

"Oh, Work," she said, tears leaking out to slide like oil down the high planes of her face. "I am so sorry."

I saw the headline then, and felt it odd that she could cry while I could not.

That night, as I lay in bed waiting for Barbara to finish in the bathroom, I thought of the newspaper article and the things it had said and left unsaid. It portrayed my father as some kind of saint, a defender of the people and pillar of the community. This brought my mind again to truth as a concept, and the naked subjectivity of something that should be pure essence. My father would have found the article a fitting epitaph; it made me want to vomit.

I stared through the window at a night made beautiful by a waxing moon, turning away only at the sound of Barbara's self-conscious cough. She stood transfixed, pinned between the moon and a soft spill of light from the bathroom closet. She wore something filmy that I had never seen, and her body was a ghost beneath it. She shifted under my scrutiny and her breasts moved in unison. Her legs were as long as always, yet they seemed more so tonight, and the darkness of their joining pulled my eyes down.

We'd not had sex for weeks, and I knew that she offered herself thus from a sense of duty. Strangely, that moved me, and I responded with a hard, almost painful need. I didn't want a wife just then. No communication. No feeling. I wanted to wall myself in soft flesh and pound the reality of this day from my bones.

She took my proffered hand and slid beneath the sheets, saying nothing, as if for her, too, this remained impersonal. I kissed her hard, tasting the salt of barely dried tears. My hands moved on her and in her, and somewhere along the way, her nightclothes vanished. She trailed her hair across my chest and offered her breasts to my mouth. I bit down, heard her stifled cry, and then was lost in the rush of blood and the *slap slap* of wet, happy flesh.

CHAPTER

4

I'd discovered in recent years that there was often a special silence in my wife's absence. It was as if the house itself had finally exhaled. And when I woke the next morning, I knew before opening swollen eyes that I was alone. As I lay there, five seconds into the first day of the rest of my life, I came to know that my wife no longer loved me. I didn't know why the realization struck, but I couldn't dispute it. It was fact, like my bones are fact.

I glanced at the bedside table, seeing nothing but the lamp and a water glass with smeared lipstick on its silvered edge. She used to leave little notes: "At the bookstore"; "Coffee with the girls"; "Love you." But that was before the money got tight. I wondered where she'd gone, and guessed the gym, there to sweat out what remained of me from the night before. She'd study her figure in the mirror, carve a smile onto careworn cheeks, and pretend she hadn't prostituted her life for a lukewarm marriage and a handful of shiny nickels.

I swung my feet from beneath the covers and stood. A glance at the clock showed it was almost seven. I felt the day loom and knew it would be a big one. By now, word of Ezra's death would have spread across the county and I expected to leave a wake in the day wherever I went. I carried this thought to the bathroom, where I showered, shaved, and brushed teeth in desperate need of it. A single clean suit remained in the closet and I pulled it on without pleasure, thinking of blue jeans and flip-flops. In the kitchen, I found a half-filled pot of coffee, poured a cup, and added milk. I took my coffee outside, under a diffuse and lowering sky.

It was early for the office and court didn't open until nine, so I went for a drive. I told myself it would be aimless, but I knew better. Roads lead somewhere; it's just a question of choice. This road carried me out of town and across Grant's Creek. I passed the Johnson place and saw a hand-lettered sign offering free puppies to a good home. My foot came off the gas and I slowed. For an instant, I considered it, but then I pictured Barbara's reaction and knew that I would never stop. Yet my speed trailed away, and I kept one eye on the rearview mirror until the sign dwindled to a whitish speck and then was gone. Around the bend, the speed limit climbed to fifty-five and I goosed it, rolling down the windows and missing my own dog, now two years in the ground. I tried to put him out of my mind, but it was hard; he'd been a damn good dog. So I concentrated on driving. I followed the yellow line past small brick houses and developments with trendy names like Plantation Ridge and Saint John's Wood.

"Country come to town," my wife would say, forgetting that my father was raised white trash.

Ten miles out, I came to the faded, shot-up road sign for Stolen Farm Road. I slowed and turned, liking the feel of tires on gravel, the steering wheel that hummed under my hand. The road passed through a wall of trees and entered a place untouched.

Stolen Farm was old, like the county was old, generations in the same family, with cedars grown tall along fence lines established before the Civil War. The farm had once been huge, but things change. Time had whittled it down to ninety acres, and I knew it teetered at the brink of bankruptcy and had for years. Only Vanessa Stolen remained of the family, and she'd been considered white trash since childhood.

What right did I have to bring my troubles to this place? I knew the answer, as I always did. None whatsoever. But I was tempted. Dew was on the grass, and she'd be up with coffee on the back porch. There'd be worry on her face as she stared out over fields that could make anyone else feel young again, but she'd be naked under that old cotton shirt she wore. I wanted to go to her, because I knew that she would take me as she always had; knew that she would put my hands on her warm belly, kiss my eyes, and tell me everything would be all right. And I'd want to believe her as I so often had, but this time she'd be wrong, so very fucking wrong.

I stopped at a bend in the drive and nosed forward until I could see the house. It sagged in on itself, and I ached to see more boards on the windows of the top floor, where in the past I'd stood at night to watch the distant river. A year and half had passed since I'd last been to Stolen Farm, but I remembered her arms and how they wrapped around my naked chest.

"What are you thinking?" she'd asked, her face above my shoulder, a ghost in the window.

"About how we met," I'd told her.

"Don't think about such nasty things," she'd replied. "Come to bed."

That was the last time I'd seen her; but a light still burned on the front porch, and I knew that it did so for me.

I put the car in reverse, yet remained for a moment longer. I'd always felt Vanessa's connection to the place. She'd never leave, I knew, and would one day be buried in the small cemetery tucked away in her woods. I thought then that it must be nice to know where you will spend eternity, and wondered if such knowledge brought peace. I thought that it might.

I turned and left, leaving, as I always did, some small piece of me behind.

Back on black pavement, the world lost its soft edge, and the drive to the office seemed harsh and full of noise. For nine years, I'd worked from a narrow shotgun office on what the locals called "lawyers' row." It was around the corner from the courthouse and across the street from the old Episcopal church. Other than a couple of secretaries next door, the church was the only attractive thing on the block; I knew every piece of stained glass by heart.

I parked the car and locked it. The sky above was growing darker, and I guessed the weatherman out of Charlotte might be right about a late-morning rain; it felt somehow appropriate. At the threshold of my office, I stopped and looked back at the red clay that rimmed my tires like lipstick, then went inside.

My secretary, the only one left, met me at the door with coffee and a hug that devolved into helpless sobs. For whatever reasons, she'd loved my father, and liked to imagine him on a beach somewhere, recharging just a little before storming back into her life. She told me that there had been numerous phone calls, mostly from other attorneys, sending their respects, but some from the local newspapers and even one reporter calling all the way from Raleigh. Murdered lawyers, it would appear, still had some print value. She gave me the stack of files I needed for court, mostly traffic matters and one juvenile offender, and promised that she would guard the fort.

I left the office a few minutes before nine, planning to enter court after it started and thus avoid any unnecessary encounters with well-wishers or the idle curious. So I entered the building through the magistrate's office. The tiny waiting room, even at this time of day, was crowded with the usual reprobates and deadbeats. Two men were cuffed to the bench, their arresting officers sharing a paper and looking bored. There was a couple swearing out an assault complaint against their teenage son, as well as two men in their sixties who were bloody and torn but too tired or sober to be mad at each other anymore. I recognized at least half of them from district criminal court. They were what we in the trade called "clients for life"—in and out of the system every couple months on one minor charge or another: trespass, assault, simple possession, whatever. One of them recognized me and asked for a card. I patted empty pockets and moved on.

Out of the mag's office, I headed into the new part of the building, where district court would be held. I passed the concession stand run by a half-blind woman named Alice, then slipped into an unobtrusive door with a small plaque that read LAWYERS ONLY. Beyond that door was another, this one with a security keypad.

I entered court from the rear and got my first nod from one of the bailiffs. It was like a signal, and suddenly every lawyer in the room was looking at me. I saw so many genuinely concerned faces that I froze momentarily. When your life is shit, it's easy to forget just how many good people are in the world. Even the judge, an attractive older woman, stopped calendar call and invited me to the bench, where she expressed her sorrow in a quiet and remarkably tender tone. I saw for the first time that her eyes were very blue. She pressed my hand lightly with her own and I looked down in momentary embarrassment, noticing the childish doodle she'd made on her judge's pad. She offered to continue my cases, but I declined. She patted my hand again, told me Ezra had been a great lawyer, and then asked me to take my seat.

Over the next two hours, I acted sad and negotiated pleas for clients I might never meet; then I went next door to juvenile court. My client was ten years old, charged with felony arson for burning down an abandoned trailer where older kids went to smoke pot and screw. The kid had done it, of course, but swore it was an accident. I didn't believe him.

The assistant district attorney running court was a cocky little twerp, two years out of law school. He swaggered, and was disliked by prosecutors and the defense bar alike—an idiot who'd never figured out that juvenile court is about helping kids more than it is about conviction rates. We tried the case before an ex-prosecutor turned judge, who found the child delinquent; but, like the rest of us with half a brain, the judge believed that the kid had probably done a public service and so let him off with juvie probation, a punishment designed to straighten out the parents as much as the kid. For me, it was standard fare. The kid needed help.

The assistant DA smirked. He walked to the defense table, pulled his lips back from too-large teeth, and told me he'd heard about my father. He flicked at those teeth with a purple-bottomed tongue and observed that Ezra's death raised as many questions as my mother's had.

I almost decked him, but I realized just in time that he would love it. Instead, I gave him the finger. Then I saw Detective Mills; she stood in the shadows near the exit, and I realized, once I saw her, that she'd been there for some time. If I hadn't been numb, that might have freaked me out; she was the kind of person you liked to keep track of. When I packed up my briefcase and walked to meet her, she gestured curtly.

"Outside," she said, and I followed her.

The hall was packed with warm bodies, and the lawyers stopped and stared. Detective Mills was lead investigator. I was the son of a murdered colleague. I didn't blame them.

"What's up?" I asked her.

"Not here," she said, seizing my arm and turning me against the flow of people, toward the stairs. We walked in silence until we turned down the corridor leading to the DA's office.

"Douglas wants you," she said, as if I'd asked another question.

"I guessed as much," I responded. "Do you have any leads?"

Her face was all sharp angles, making me guess that the previous day still bothered her; but I knew the drill. If anything went wrong, Mills would catch the heat, and I guessed word was already out about my visit to the scene. It broke all the taboos. Cops did not allow defense lawyers to walk through the crime scene and possibly contaminate evidence. Mills, bright as she was and no stranger to cover-your-ass politics, had probably papered the file with testimonials from other cops as to exactly what I had and had not touched. Douglas, too, would be prominently mentioned.

Her silence was thus not surprising.

Douglas looked like he had not slept at all.

"I don't know how the damn papers got hold of this so fast," he said as soon as I stepped through his door, coming half out of his seat. "But you damn well better not be involved, Work."

I just stared at him.

"Well come in," he continued, dropping back into his chair. "Mills, close that door."

Detective Mills closed the door and moved to stand behind Douglas's right shoulder. She jammed her hands into the pockets of her jeans, pulling back her jacket to show the butt of her pistol in its shoulder holster. She leaned against the wall and stared at me as if I were a suspect.

It was an old trick, probably done out of habit, but standing there she looked every inch the bulldog she was. I watched Douglas settle back in his chair, deflating as if shot with a dart. He was good people and knew that I was, too.

"Do you have any leads?" I asked.

"Nothing solid."

"How about suspects?" I pressed.

"Every fucking body," he replied. "Your father had a lot of enemies. Unhappy clients, businessmen on the wrong end of the stick, who knows what else. Ezra did many things, but walking lightly was not one of them."

An understatement.

"Anybody in particular?" I asked.

"No," he said, tugging at an eyebrow.

Mills cleared her throat and Douglas let go of his eyebrow. It was obvious that she was unhappy, and I guessed that she and the DA had exchanged words on how much to tell me.

"What else?" I asked.

"We believe that he died on the same night he disappeared."

Mills rolled her eyes and began to pace the office like a man ten years in the same cell.

"How do you know that?" I asked. No way could the medical examiner have been that specific. Not after a year and a half.

"Your father's watch," Douglas said, too long in this business to gloat over his own cleverness. "It was self-winding. The jeweler tells me it will run for thirty-six hours after the person wearing it stops moving. We counted backward."

I thought back to my father's watch, trying to remember if it had a date function.

"Was he shot?" I asked.

"In the head," the DA told me. "Twice."

I remembered the candy striper shirt over my father's head, the pale curve of exposed jawbone. Someone had covered his face after killing him, an unusual act for a murderer.

Mills stopped in front of the wide windows that looked across Main Street at the local bank. A light rain fell and thin gray clouds covered the sky like lint, but the sun still shone through, and I remembered my mother and how she always told me that rain and sun together meant that the devil was beating his wife.

Mills planted herself on the windowsill, arms crossed, the sky behind her darkening as the clouds thickened. The last sunlight disappeared, and I guessed that the devil's wife was down and bleeding.

"We'll need to examine Ezra's house," Douglas continued, and I nodded, suddenly tired. Douglas paused, then went on. "We'll also need to check his office. Go through his files and find out who might have reason to hold a grudge."

This brought my head up, and suddenly it all made sense. Ezra was dead. The practice was mine, which meant that Douglas and the cops needed me. Letting law enforcement paw through a defense attorney's client files was . . . well, it was like letting a defense attorney enter the crime scene. If I refused, they'd need a warrant. There would be a hearing and I would probably win. Judges were loath to undermine the attorney-client privilege.

I realized then that the DA had figured this out before calling me to his office the day before, and that made me ineffably sad. Quid pro quo is an ugly thing between friends.

"Let me think on that for awhile," I said, and Douglas nodded, tossing an enigmatic look at Detective Mills.

"We found the slugs," he said. "Both of them in the closet. One in the wall, one in the floor."

I knew what that meant, and doubted that Ezra had entered the closet voluntarily. He'd been ordered there at gunpoint. The first shot had caught him standing, passed through his skull, and embedded itself in the wall. The second shot had taken him lying down. The killer had wanted to make sure.

"And?" I said.

Douglas looked again at Mills and started tugging on his right eyebrow.

"We don't have full forensics yet, but they came from a three-fifty-seven," Douglas said, leaning forward in his chair, looking as if the movement hurt his ass. "We checked the records. Your father had a three-fifty-seven revolver, a stainless Smith & Wesson." I said nothing. "We need that gun, Work. Do you know where it is?"

His right hand came up again, working at the eyebrow. I thought very carefully before I spoke.

"I have no idea where that gun is."

He leaned back and put his hands in his lap.

"Look for it, will you? Let us know if you find it."

"I will," I said. "Is that it?"

"Yeah," Douglas said. "That's it. Just get back to me on those files. We'll need to get access, and I'd rather not bother the judge."

"I understand," I said, and did. I stood up.

"Just a second," Mills said. "I need to talk to you about the night your father disappeared. There are a lot of unanswered questions. There may be something of value."

The night Ezra disappeared was the same night my mother died. It was not an easy subject for me. "Later," I said. "Okay?"

She looked at the district attorney, who said nothing.

"Later today," she responded.

"Fine." I nodded. "Today."

Douglas kept his seat as Mills opened the door.

"Stay in touch," Douglas said, and lifted his hand as Detective Mills closed the door in my face. In the hall outside, with eyes like fingers upon me, I felt very alone.

I slipped down the back stairs and passed again through the magistrate's office. It was all but empty and I nodded at the woman behind the wire-mesh window. She popped gum at me and looked silently away. Outside, the sun still hid itself, but the rain had dwindled to mist, when what I wanted most was pounding rain. I wanted the grayness, the steady hiss and crackle of water straight from the void; I wanted purity on my face and the heaviness of a three-season suit ruined beyond repair. Without decision or action, I wanted to fade away, to be taken from view and put, for a whisper of time, in a place where no one knew me. Instead, I got the passing stare of two young boys; instead, I got damp.

It was not yet noon when I entered the office, and my secretary looked unsettled when I told her to go home. She packed her bag with uneaten lunch, a stack of legal pads, and a thesaurus, then left with a wounded step. I wanted to go upstairs and search Ezra's personal office, but his ghost stopped me on the stairs. I'd not been up there for six months and was too depressed to face the dusty splendor of a straw empire improvidently made mine. I decided instead to find an innocuous lunch and the courage to face again my childhood home and the memories of broken bones that lay like stained carpet on the formal staircase.

For twenty minutes, I drove, searching for a lunch spot that offered a chance of anonymity. Eventually, I just gave up and hit the drive-through at Burger King. I ate two cheeseburgers as I drove twice past my father's house. It challenged me with its thick columns, blank dull-eyed windows, and perfect alabaster paint. More castle than house, it hunkered behind hedgerows and box bushes that reminded me of pillboxes I'd once seen when Ezra took the family to the beaches of Normandy. My father, I knew, had willed the beast to me so that I could carry on his war against the old-money snobbery of this town that for years had dulled the lacquer of his magnificent achievement. But I knew now, as I always had, that that would never happen. Waging war took conviction, and while I understood the forces that drove my father, I could not relate to them. There are many kinds of poison, and I was not a fucking idiot.

I turned into the driveway, passed beneath the crossed arms of sentinel trees, and so stepped back in time, my childhood around me like broken glass. Keys jingled and I sat in the silence that followed. I saw many things that no longer were: my first bike and toys, long gone to ruin; a father flushed with early triumph; and my mother, alive, still happy, gazing at Jean's questioning smile. I saw it all, unyellowed by time; then I blinked and it was gone, ashes in a sudden wind.

The police were not there yet and the door was heavy with disuse as I stepped inside. I disengaged the alarm system and flipped on lights as I moved through the house. Dust lay thick on the floor and on the sheets that draped my father's furniture. Old tracks were visible as I walked slowly through the downstairs, passing the two dining rooms, the den, the billiards room, and the door to my father's wine cellar. Stainless steel gleamed dully in the kitchen, making me think of knives with ebony handles and my mother's pale, narrow hands.

I checked his study first, thinking to find the pistol in the top drawer with his silver letter opener and the leather journal that Jean had given him in place of a grandson. It was not there. I sat in his chair for a few seconds and stared at the only framed photograph, a faded black-and-white shot of a tumbledown shack and the unsmiling family that lived in it. Ezra was the youngest, a thick, dirty-legged boy in denim shorts, his feet bare. I peered into the black spots of his eyes and wondered at his thoughts on that day. I picked up the journal and riffed the pages, knowing that my father would never have trusted his secret self to paper, yet feeling some hope in spite of myself. It was empty, so I replaced it as I'd found it. My eyes wandered as I tried to find some sense of this man I had once presumed to know, but the room meant nothing to me. It was resplendent in old maps, leather furniture, and the mementos of a lifetime, and yet it rang so empty. The room itself was a trophy, I realized, and I could see him sitting there, and knew that he could smile at this room while his wife lay weeping in the big bed upstairs.

Sitting in his chair felt vaguely incestuous and I didn't stay long. As I left his study, I noticed that my tracks on the dusty floor were not alone. There were other tracks, smaller ones, and I knew that Jean had been here. The tracks led from the study back to the hall and then to the wide staircase. The prints disappeared into the carpet runner that climbed the stairs, then reappeared on the hardwood of the hall that led to my parents' room. I'd not been upstairs in over a year and the prints were obvious. They vanished on the Persian carpet that covered the bedroom floor, but by the bed, and the table where I'd hoped to find the gun, I found a half print in the dust. I looked at the bed and saw a circular indentation in the covers, as if some animal had curled there to nest.

I checked for the gun, found nothing, then sat on the bed and rubbed the impression away. After a thoughtful moment, I got up, and as I left the house, I shuffled my feet to make mute the dusty floor where once two children had played.

Outside, I leaned against the locked door, half-expecting Detective Mills to roll up the drive with a dozen squad cars in her wake. I tried to slow breathing that sounded very loud in a world of unusual quiet. From somewhere came a smell of new-mown grass.

I remembered my father's gun from the night I saw it shoved into my mother's face. When he saw me, there in the bedroom door, he tried to play it off as a joke, but my mother's terror was real. I saw it in her tear-stained eyes, in her posture, and in the way her hands pulled at the belt of her robe when she told me to go back to bed. I went because she asked me to, but I now remembered the still house and the creak of bedsprings as she made peace the only way she knew how. I came to hate my father that night, but it took a long time for me to realize the magnitude of that emotion.

I never learned what they'd been fighting about, but the image never scabbed over; and as I turned away from that place, I thought of my own wife's tears and her limp submission the night before—the bleak satisfaction I took from her smallness as I used her shamelessly. She'd cried out, and remembering the taste of salted tears, I thought, for that instant, that I knew how the devil felt. Sex and tears, like sun and rain, were never meant to share a moment; but for a fallen soul, an act of wrong could, at times, feel very right, and that scared the hell out of me.

I descended into my car and started the engine, and as I passed again beneath the trees that guarded this place and turned toward the park and home, my thoughts were dark with the dust of places the mind should never go.

CHAPTER

5

All I wanted was to peel off my suit, fall into bed, and find something better across the black, sandy gulf; but the moment I turned onto my block, I saw that it wasn't going to happen. The curving slope of driveway that should welcome a man at times like this glittered instead with shiny black and silver cars. The sharks had gathered. The friends of my wife had come, bearing their honeyed hams, their casseroles, and their eager questions. How did he die? How's Work holding up? Then, sotto voce, when Barbara couldn't hear: What was he mixed up in? Two bullets in the head, so I heard. Then lower still: *Probably deserved it.* Sooner or later, one of them would say what so many thought. White trash, they'd say, and eyes would glint above lips chapped by one too many tight smiles. Poor Barbara. She really should have known better.

On principle, I declined to be chased from my own home, but my car refused to make the turn into the driveway. Instead, I bought beer and cigarettes at the convenience store next to the high school. I wanted to carry the bag into the football stadium, mount the bleachers, and get slowly drunk above that rectangle of brown grass. But the gate was locked, and the chain was loud when I yanked on it. So I drove back to my father's house and drank in his driveway. I killed most of the six-pack before I managed to go home.

As I turned onto my block, I saw that the number of cars had grown, giving my house an unfortunate festive air. I parked on the street two houses down and walked. Inside, I found the crowd I suspected: our neighbors, several acquaintances from out of town, doctors and their wives, business owners, and half of the local bar, including Clarence Hambly, who, in many ways, had been my father's greatest rival. He immediately drew my gaze, for he stood tall and disdainful even in this monied gathering. He had his back to the wall, one elbow on the mantel, and a drink in his hand. He was the first to notice me, but looked away when our eyes met. I dismissed him, a minor irritation, and scanned the crowd for my wife, finding her across the room. Looking at her, I could say, without pause or reflection, that she was a beautiful woman. She had flawless skin, high cheekbones, and eyes that flashed. That night, she had salon-perfect hair and looked stunning in last season's most expensive dress. She was cloistered with her most regular companions, women whose hands were cold with jewels and thin blood. When she saw me, she stopped talking, and her friends turned as one. Their eyes dissected me, settling on the beer bottle I'd carried in; and when Barbara left their circle, they said nothing, yet I imagined sharp tongues poised to flay my naked back. I lit another cigarette and thought of the funeral yet to plan. Then Barbara materialized, and for a moment we were alone together.

"Nice party," I said, and then smiled so that my words would not sound so cruel.

She pressed hard lips against my cheek.

"You're drunk," she said. "Don't embarrass me."

That would have been the low point, had Glena Werster not chosen that moment to sweep through the front door. She flashed a smile that made her teeth look oiled, and her black dress was short and tight. The sight of her in my home made me ill. I thought of Jean and the weight of her tread as she'd mounted the steps to Glena Werster's pillared mansion.

"What's she doing here?" I asked.

Barbara watched over her wineglass as Glena nestled into the bosom of her little clique in the corner, and I saw worry in my wife's eyes. When she turned to me, her whisper was fierce.

"You be nice, Work. She's very important in this town."

By "important," I knew my wife meant that Glena Werster sat on the board of the country club, was filthy rich, and mean enough to ruin reputations for the joy of it.

"I don't want her here," I said, and gestured vaguely at the group of women huddled under the portrait of Barbara's father. "I don't want any of them here." I leaned closer and she pulled back so quickly that it stank of pure instinct. I spoke anyway. "We need to talk, Barbara."

"You've sweated through your shirt," she said, flicking three fingers across the buttons beneath my collar. "Why don't you go change." She started to turn away, but then she turned back. She reached for my face and I leaned forward. "Shave, too, would you?" Then she was gone, back to her circle of tight-lipped friends.

So I stood alone, lost in my own home as people uttered kind words, and I nodded as if I agreed with everything they said; yet I existed in an eerie kind of silence, and the warm words broke over me like surf on a half-deaf man. A few were sincere, but none understood the first thing about my father—what made him so inexplicable, so extraordinary, and so evil.

In a pilgrimage of fumbled words, I made it to the kitchen, where I'd hoped to find a cold beer. Instead, I saw that a full bar had been arranged, and I marveled darkly at my wife, who, in the cold wake of death, could make of the impromptu an occasion. I ordered bourbon on the rocks, then felt a hand on my shoulder and a voice like crushed ice asking the bartender to make it two. I turned to see Dr. Stokes, my neighbor, whose boot-leather features and white beard made him look very much like Mark Twain.

"Thank you," he said to the bartender. Then he steered me away from the bar with his firm doctor's hand and said, "Let's take a little walk." He led me through the kitchen and out into the garage, where graying sunlight stretched dusty rectangles on the floor. He released me into the emptiness, then sat on the steps with a grunt and a flourish. He sipped his drink, then smacked his lips. "Now that's a good friend."

"Yes," I said. "It can be."

I watched him watch me as he put down his drink and lit a cigar.

"I've been watching you," he finally said. "You don't look good."

"It's been a bad day."

"I'm not talking about today. I've been worried about you for years. Just not my place to say, if you follow."

"What makes today different?" I asked.

He looked at me and puffed blue smoke. "I've been married fifty-four years," he said. "You think I've never had that look, like your best friend just kicked you in the balls. It doesn't take a genius; my wife saw it, too." He flicked imaginary lint from his pant leg and studied his cigar as he continued. "Now, I can't do anything about your wife—a marriage is a man's own business—but there are some things you ought to hear, and I know damn well that no one else in there will tell you."

Unsure what to say, I balanced my drink on an overturned wheelbarrow and lit a cigarette. The silence stretched out as I fumbled the pack back into my shirt pocket. When I looked up, I saw that shadows filled the doctor's eyes, which made me strangely sad. He had warm eyes; always had.

"Your father was the biggest asshole I ever met," he said, then pulled on his cigar as if he'd commented on the weather. I said noth-ing, and after a few seconds the old man continued. "He was a self-centered bastard who wanted to own the whole damn world, but you know that."

"Yes," I said, and cleared my throat. "I know that."

"An easy man to hate, your father, but he would look you in the eyes as he slipped the knife in, if you know what I mean."

"No."

"He was honest about his avarice. Other honest men could see that."

"So?" I asked.

"Am I finished yet?" he asked, and I said nothing. "Then let me talk. There was also Jean. I never liked the way he raised your sister. Seemed like a waste of a perfectly good mind. But we can't choose our parents, and that's her bad luck. I've watched her, too, and now that Ezra's dead, I think she'll be all right."

A harsh laugh escaped me. "How closely have you watched her?" I asked, thinking that Jean was so far from being all right.

He leaned forward, a sharp glint in his eyes. "Closer than you, I bet," he said, and the truth of it stung. "I'm not worried about her. It's you that troubles me."

"Me?"

"Yes, now shut up. This is what I came out here to tell you. So pay attention. Your father was a big man, with big visions and big dreams. But you, Work, are a better man."

I felt tears sting my eyes and wished fervently that this man had been my father. There was blunt honesty in his face and in the way he moved his thickened hands, and for a moment I believed him.

"You're better because you don't want big things for small reasons. You're better because you care—about your friends and family, things that are right; you favor your mother that way." He paused for an instant and nodded. "Don't choke on Ezra's burdens, Work. I'm eighty-three years old, old enough to know a thing or two, and the most important is this: Life is goddamn short. Figure out what *you* want. Be your own man and you'll be better for it."

He stood slowly and I heard his joints pop. Ice rattled on glass as he drained his drink.

"Bury your old man, Work, and when you're ready, we'd love to have you over for dinner. I knew your mother well, God rest her soul, and I'd love to tell you about her happy times. And one last thing—don't lose any sleep over Barbara. She's a bitch by nature, not by choice. So don't be hard on yourself."

He winked at me and smiled around his cigar. I thanked him for coming, because I didn't know what else to say; then I closed the door behind him and sat where he had, on wood still warm from his narrow haunches. I sipped ice-watered bourbon, thought about my life, and wished the old man were right about all the things he'd said.

Eventually, my glass ran dry, but this I could fix. My watch showed it was almost five, and as I stood, I thought briefly of Detective Mills. I'd not called her and at the moment didn't care; all I wanted was that drink. I was in and out of the kitchen without a word, and if that offended people, then too bad. I'd had enough. So I returned to my dank cell to watch the shadows crawl and to drink my bourbon warm.

I stayed in that awful place long enough for the light to dim and the walls to tilt. I was not an angry drunk; I didn't get weepy and I didn't figure out a damn thing. My jacket went into a box filled with lawn clippings I'd never emptied and my tie ended up twisted around a nail in the wall, but I kept the rest of my clothes on, which was hard. I wanted to shake things up, break the complacency bowl, and for one crazy moment I pictured myself running naked through the house. I'd chat with my wife's friends and dare them to pretend, at the next inane social gathering, that it had never happened. And they would—that's what kept my clothes on. Every last one of them could look me in the eye over drinks or dinner the next week, ask in all earnestness how the practice was doing, and then tell me what a fine funeral it had been.

I wanted to laugh and I wanted to kill somebody.

But I did neither. I went back inside; I mingled and I talked. I kept my clothes on, and if I made an ass of myself, no one said a word to me about it. Eventually, I left, and as I sat in my car, windows down and purple light on me like a second skin, I thanked God for one thing: that, drunk as hell and drowning in faces and words without meaning, I had not uttered the one irretrievable thought that had haunted me. And searching my ruined eyes in the mirror, I acknowledged, to myself at least, that I thought I knew who had killed my father.

Motive. Means. Opportunity.

It was all there if you knew where to look.

But I did not want to look. I never had. So I twisted the mirror up and away. Then I closed my eyes and thought of my sister, and of times that were no less hard for their simplicity.

"Are you okay?" I asked Jean.

She nodded, tears dripping off her tiny pointed chin to soak into her white jeans like rain into sand. Her shoulders hunched lower with each sob, until she looked bent and broken, her hair hanging just low enough to cover the top of her face. I pulled my eyes off the little gray teardrop circles, trying not to look at the blood that spread from between her legs. Red and wet, it soaked the new pants she was so proud of, the ones our mother had given her on that morning of her twelfth birthday.

"I called Dad and he said he'd come get us. Soon. I promise. He said so."

She didn't say anything and I watched the red stain darken. Without a word, I took off my jacket and spread it across her lap. She looked at me then in a way that made me proud to be her big brother, like I made a difference. I slipped an arm around her shoulders and pretended that I was not half-scared to death.

"I'm sorry," she said tearfully.

"Everything's okay," I told her. "Don't worry about it."

We were downtown, at the ice cream parlor. Mom had dropped us off on her way to Charlotte for the afternoon. We had four dollars for ice cream and plans to walk home afterward. I barely knew what a girl's period was. When I first saw the blood, I thought she might be hurt, and only then did I realize that her eyes had been filling with slow tears for awhile. "Don't look," she'd said, and bowed her head to the tears.

Dad never came, and after an hour we walked home, my jacket around her waist. It was almost three miles.

At home, Jean locked herself in the bathroom until Mom got back. I sat on the front porch, looking for the courage to tell my father what a bastard he was—for not caring about Jean, for making a liar of me— but in the end I said nothing.

How I hated myself.

I woke in near darkness. There was a face in my window and I blinked at the thick glasses and heavy whiskers. I pulled back instinctively, not just because the man was so ugly.

"Good," he grunted. "I thought maybe you were dead."

His voice was guttural, with a heavy southern accent.

"What . . ." I said.

"Shouldn't sleep in your car. It's dangerous." He looked me up and down, glanced in the backseat. "Smart boy like you should know better."

The face withdrew and, like that, he was gone, leaving me half-asleep and still drunk. *What the hell was that?* I opened the door and clambered out, stiff and sore. I peered down the street and saw him pass from light to dark, long coat flapping around his ankles, earflaps loose on his ears. It was my park walker, and after years of silent passings, we'd finally spoken. This was my chance. I could put feet to pavement, catch him in the dark, and ask my question; yet I didn't move.

I let him go, the opportunity lost to the paralysis of indecision. I got back into my car, mouth like glue, and I looked for gum or a mint but found neither. I lit a cigarette instead, but it tasted horrible, so I tossed it. My watch showed it was ten o'clock; I'd slept for two, maybe three hours. I peered down the street at my house. The cars were gone, but lights still burned, and I guessed Barbara was up. My head was pounding and I knew that she was more than I could bear right then. What I really wanted was another beer and an empty bed. But what I needed was something entirely different, and as I sat there, I realized that I'd been putting off the inevitable. I needed to go up to Ezra's office, to make peace with his ghost and to look for his gun.

I turned the ignition, thought of all the stupid drunks I'd defended on DWI charges, then drove to the office. It was that kind of day.

I parked in back, where I always did, and let myself into the narrow hallway that ran past the tiny break room, the copy room, and the supply closet. When I got to the main office area, I flipped on a lamp and tossed my keys onto the table.

I heard something upstairs, a scrape followed by a low thump, and I froze.

Silence.

I stood and listened, but the sound didn't come again. I thought of Ezra's ghost, found the thought not funny, and wondered if I'd imagined it. Moving slowly, I walked to the front of the office and turned on every light. The stairwell to Ezra's upstairs domain gaped at me, all darkness and slick, shiny walls. My heart was up and running and I felt that unhealthy bourbon sweat. I smelled myself in the stillness and wondered if I was a coward after all. I reached for some kind of calm and told myself that old buildings settle and drunken men imagine things all the time. I reminded myself that Ezra was dead.

I flashed a glance around the place, but everything looked as it always had: desks, chairs, and filing cabinets—all in order. I looked back up the narrow stairwell and started to climb. I moved slowly, one hand on the rail. Five steps up, I stopped, thinking that I saw movement. I took one more hesitant step, heard something, and stopped. Then something huge, dark, and very fast descended upon me. It crashed into my chest and I was falling. I felt a moment of blinding pain; then all was blackness.

CHAPTER

6

I saw light. It flickered and died, then flickered again. It hurt. I didn't want it.

"He's coming around," a voice said.

"Well, that's something at least." I recognized the voice. Detective Mills.

I opened my eyes to bright, fuzzy light. I blinked, but the pain in my head didn't go away.

"Where am I?"

"Hospital," Mills said, and leaned over me. She didn't smile, but I smelled her perfume; it was ripe, like a peach too long in the bag.

"What happened?"

Mills leaned closer. "You tell me," she said.

"I don't remember."

"Your secretary found you this morning at the foot of the stairs. You're lucky you didn't break your neck."

I sat up against the pillows and looked around. Green curtains surrounded my bed. A large nurse stood at my feet, a bucolic smile on her face. I heard hospital voices and smelled hospital smells. I looked for Barbara. She wasn't there.

"Somebody threw a chair at me," I said.

"I beg your pardon," Mills said.

"Ezra's chair, I think. I was walking up the stairs and somebody pushed the chair down on top of me."

Mills said nothing for a long moment. She tapped a pen against her teeth and looked at me.

"I talked to your wife," she said. "According to her, you were drunk last night."

"So?"

"Very drunk."

I stared in dumb amazement at the detective. "Are you suggesting that I fell down the stairs?" Mills said nothing and I felt the first stir of anger. "My wife wouldn't know very drunk if it bit her on the ass."

"I corroborated her story with several people who were at your house last night," Mills said.

"Who?"

"That's hardly relevant."

"Relevant! Christ. You sound like a lawyer." Now I was mad. Mainly because I was being treated as if I were stupid. "Have you been to my office, Detective Mills?"

"No," she replied.

"Then go," I said. "See if the chair is there or not."

She studied me, and I could all but see the debate. Was this guy for real or just being an ass? If she'd ever considered me a friend, I saw right then that she did no longer. Her eyes were intolerant, and I guessed that the pressure was getting to her. There had been many stories in the paper—retrospectives on Ezra's life, thinly worded speculation about the manner of his death, vague details about the investigation—and Mills had been mentioned many times. I understood that this case would make or break her, but for some reason I'd imagined that our personal relationship would remain apart.

"What's your secretary's name?" she asked. I told her and she turned to the nurse, who looked uncomfortable. "Where's your phone?" The nurse told her to use the one in the triage nurse's office. Down the hall. Second door. Mills looked back to me. "Don't go anywhere," she said, and I almost smiled before I realized she wasn't making a funny.

She flapped her way through the curtains and disappeared. I heard her heels on the tile and then I was alone with the nurse. She fluffed my pillow.

"Is this the emergency room?" I asked.

"Yes, but Saturday morning is slow. Shootin' and stabbin' isn't done until tonight." She smiled and suddenly became a real person.

"What's wrong with me?"

"Oh, nothing but some bruises and such. Your headache might last longer than it would have otherwise." Another smile and I knew I wasn't the first Saturday-morning hangover she'd seen. "You'll be discharged shortly."

I laid my fingers on the warm dough of her forearm. "Has my wife been to see me? Five five. Short black hair. Pretty." She looked blank. "Hard eyes," I added, only half-joking. "Attitude."

"I'm sorry. No."

I looked away from the pity in her face. "Are you married?" I asked.

"Twenty-two years," she said.

"Would you leave your husband alone in the emergency room?" She didn't answer, and I thought, No, of course not; differences end at the hospital door.

"That would depend," she finally said. She smoothed my blankets, her hands moving sure and quick, and I thought she didn't want to finish the sentence.

"On?" I asked.

She looked at me and her hands grew suddenly still. "On whether or not he deserved it."

And there it is, I thought, the difference between her and me. Because I would be there regardless. No matter what. Suddenly, this nurse was not an unexpected friend, and with that bleak realization the warmth in the tiny curtained place evaporated. And even though she remained and tried to make further conversation, I found myself alone with my headache and the disjointed images of the previous night.

I *had* heard a sound. Wheels on wood flooring. Ezra's big leather chair being rolled to the top of the stairs. I knew I was right about that. I'd felt the weight, damn it.

I hadn't been that drunk.

When Mills appeared, she looked pissed. "I spoke to your secretary," she said. "There's no chair at the bottom of the stairs. There was no chair when she found you this morning. Furthermore, nothing is out of place. No windows are broken. No sign of a forced entry."

"But Ezra's chair . . ."

"Is at his desk upstairs," Mills said. "Where it has always been."

I thought back to the day before. I'd sent my secretary home early.

"Maybe I forgot to lock the door," I ventured. "Look, I'm not making this up. I know what happened." Both Mills and the nurse stared at me, wordlessly. "Goddamn it, somebody threw a chair down those stairs!"

"Listen, Pickens. You're not high on my list of favorites right now. I wasted an hour yesterday trying to track you down, and I'm not going to waste more time because you decided to tie one on. Do I make myself clear?"

I didn't know what infuriated me more, that Mills refused to accept what I'd told her or that my wife lacked the decency to come to the hospital. My head was about to split, my body felt like the loser at a Tyson fight, and I thought I might puke hospital green.

"Fine. Whatever."

Mills looked at me as if she'd expected more fight and was disappointed. The nurse said she had some papers for me to sign, then disappeared to fetch them. Mills stared at me and I stared at the ceiling, determined to keep my mouth shut. This day could go two ways. It could get better or it could get worse. After what felt like a long time pretending to be interested in white acoustic tile, Mills finally spoke.

"We still need to discuss the night Ezra disappeared." Her tone was softer, as if it had occurred to her that this information might be *relevant* and that I controlled it. I said nothing, and her temper finally exploded. "Damn it Work, he was your father!"

I looked at her then. "You don't know the first thing about it," I said, and immediately regretted the words. There had been venom in my voice, and I saw the surprise in the detective's eyes. "Listen. I need a shower. I need to talk to my wife. Can we do it this afternoon?" She started to speak and I cut her off. "Your office. Three o'clock. I'll be there."

"Don't make me regret this," she said.

"I'll be there. Three o'clock."

The ripe-peach smell lingered after Mills left. Would I make the meeting? Maybe. The night in question had been a bad one and I'd not talked about it. Ever. Some secrets you keep, and I'd shared this one with my sister alone. It was Ezra's last gift, a lie wrapped in guilt and mortified to pure shame. I'd lost sleep to that lie, and maybe my soul, too. What did Jean call it? *Ezra's truth.* Well, Ezra's truth was my truth; it had to be, and if Jean thought differently, she was kidding herself.

I lifted the sheet. Somebody had put me in a tie-up dress. Perfect.

The nurse let me dangle for almost an hour. When she finally appeared with my paperwork, I still had no clothes, and she left me for another twenty minutes while she collected them for me. The day was getting worse and the feel of dirty clothes against my skin only made it more so.

I limped out of the emergency room and into a day made dull by low scudding clouds. Sweat came instantly in the prickly damp heat. I felt for my keys, couldn't find them, and remembered I had no car, either. So I walked home, and if anyone saw me, they didn't offer a ride. At home, I closed the door as if against a pursuing wind. "I'm home," I called.

The house was empty, as I knew it would be. Barbara's car was gone. The message light blinked its red eye at me, and on the kitchen island I saw a note—a beige rectangle of expensive stationery, with Barbara's tight writing beneath a pen laid across it in a perfect diagonal. I walked over without real interest.

"Dear Work," it began, which surprised me. I expected something different. "I've gone shopping in Charlotte. Figured you could use the space. I'm sorry that last night was so hard for you. Maybe I could have been more supportive. And I agree . . . we do need to talk. How about dinner tonight? Just the two of us. Barbara."

I left the note where it lay and went for a shower. The bed was made, which reminded me that I had no clean suit for Monday. I looked at the clock; the cleaners closed in twenty minutes. I tossed the filthy remnant of my suit into the closet and took a shower.

When I got out, I dressed and went to the office. Inside, I pocketed my keys and looked around. Mills was right about some things. Everything looked normal. But somebody had almost killed me, and I wanted to know why. If there was an answer here, I expected to find it upstairs.

Ezra's office ran the length of the building. The walls were raw brick and looked warm above the twenty-thousand-dollar Persian rug. There were exposed beams, leather furniture, and Tiffany lamps. Ezra had had no taste of his own and had to pay for it. I tried to remember the decorator's name and failed. She'd liked oil paintings and low-cut tops. I saw her breasts once when she bent over to spread some fabric samples. Ezra had caught me looking and winked. It had made my skin crawl, but in sharing the pleasure of those full pale breasts, he'd treated me like an equal for the first and last time. How fucked-up was that?

Ezra's paintings spoke of money—the old kind. Looking at them, you heard the bugle and smelled the dogs. The people in these paintings had gamekeepers, gun bearers, and beaters. They hunted in fine clothes and returned to a silver table service and servants. They hunted hart and stag instead of deer, pheasant rather than quail. Their homes had names.

This was the beast that had ridden my father's back. Old money had humbled him, but more than that it had angered him. Because no matter how good he was, how successful, or how rich, he had always lacked that casual arrogance. Poverty had been his goad; it had driven him, but he'd never understood how strong it made him. Standing on his expensive rug, I wished now that I'd told him. I thought of the photograph of his family that he'd kept on his desk at home. He'd often stared into those tired faces and nodded as if in conversation. He'd fought to escape their world more than to provide for us, and that hurt in ways I'd never explored. Those people were long dead, too cold and rotten to be impressed, but those had been his priorities.

"Shadowboxing the past," Jean had once called it, stunning me with her perception.

I walked to his massive desk and examined the chair. There were scuff marks on the leather, but they could have been old. I rolled it off the carpet and listened to its wheels on the wood floor. It was the same noise I'd heard the night before. I replaced the chair and checked the walls of the stairwell. They were scuffed, too, but that could have been from anything. Back at the desk, I ran my hands over the leather and nodded, satisfied that I'd not imagined anything.

The previous night, I'd caught this chair in the chest. Mills could kiss my ass.

I looked around the office. Someone had come here for a reason.

I sat in Ezra's chair, now mine, and tossed my feet up on the desk. I looked for a sign. What was so important?

After Ezra disappeared, most of our clients followed suit. Ezra had courted them. Ezra had held their hands. He'd gotten the press, and they'd had no idea that most of the underlying work was mine. "Just business," they'd said, before taking their files to the first big city firm they could find. Ezra's death had made plenty of Charlotte lawyers rich, a fact that would kill him if somebody hadn't already done the job. He hated Charlotte lawyers.

And I was left on the court-appointed list, bottom-feeding.

So I doubted anybody was up here for his files. Truth be told, I didn't care if Mills got the files. There was nothing there. I'd combed through them months earlier, looking for crumbs. I just didn't want to make it easy.

Then I remembered why I'd come the night before. I searched Ezra's desk, his filing cabinets, and even the end tables adjacent to the long leather couch that sat against the wall. Nothing. No pistol. I opened the chest under the window and got down on my knees to peer underneath his desk. I went back downstairs and searched every conceivable place where a gun might be hidden. After half an hour, I had no doubt that my office was gun-free.

I climbed the stairs again, turned at the top, and walked out onto Ezra's expensive Persian rug. Immediately, I saw that something was different. It was a small thing, but it leaped out at me. I stopped. I stared at it.

Across the room, near the foot of Ezra's long couch, the corner of the rug was folded under. It lay directly in my line of sight: the corner, along with a foot or more of fringe, tucked under. I quickly scanned the rest of the office, but saw nothing else that seemed out of place. I walked across the room toward the folded corner. Seven long strides, then I felt something yield beneath my foot. I heard the low groan of flexing wood. I stepped back, saw a slight rise beneath the carpet. I stepped on it again. Another creak.

I flipped back the rug and found a section of loose flooring—two wide boards that rose minutely at one end, warped, as if by time or water damage. They were only a quarter inch higher than the rest of the floorboards, but the cut lines did not line up with the rest of the boards. It appeared that the ends had been sawed at some point; they were rough and still pale. The other boards were almost black with age, the cracks between them packed solid.

I dug my nails into the white, rough meat of the cut ends and lifted. The boards rose easily. Beneath them, I found a safe. I should not have been surprised—my father was a secretive man—and yet I stared at it for a long time.

It was long and narrow, set between the floor joists. Its front was brushed metal, with a numeric keypad on the right side. I settled onto my knees, considering this new problem. Should I tell Mills? Not yet, I decided. Not without knowing its secrets.

So I tried to open it. I guessed at the combination. I tried every birthday in the family and every Social Security number, too. I tried the date Ezra passed the bar and the date he married my mother. I tried phone numbers, then I ran everything backward. I wasted half an hour staring at the safe and punching buttons; then I beat on it with my fists. I hit hard. I tore skin. It was that much like my father— hidden, silent, and unbreakable.

Eventually, I rocked away from the hard metal. I wedged the boards back into place and straightened the rug. I studied the scene critically. The lump under the rug remained, small but visible. I stepped on it. The creak was audible.

I went downstairs to the supply closet. On the top shelf I found the claw hammer and nails we used to hang pictures and diplomas. The nails were too small to be of use, but on the back of the shelf I found a half box of ten-penny nails—big, heavy brutes, like you'd use to nail a coffin shut. I grabbed a handful. Upstairs, I drove four of them into the loose boards, two in each one. The hammer was loud, and I swung it a few times too many, scarring the boards when I missed. Two of the nails went in straight and two bent as I drove them; I pounded them flat. When I replaced the rug there was no discernible lump. I stepped on the boards. Silence.

I put the hammer and extra nails on top of Ezra's bookshelf and dropped wearily to the couch. It was deep. "Sleeps one, screws two," Ezra once said, and I'd found that joke funny. Now it was just hard and cold, so I climbed wearily to my feet. Back in my car, I swiped at my face with a shirtsleeve. I was spent and shaky, and blamed it on the hangover; but deep down I wondered if I was coming apart. I turned on the air conditioner and laid my forehead against the hardness of the steering wheel. I breathed in and I breathed out, and after awhile I straightened. I needed to do something, needed to move; so I put the car in drive and pulled into thin traffic.

It was time to see Jean.

You could always hear the trains coming at her house. She lived in the poor part of town, next to the tracks, in a house that time had not spared. It was small, white, and dirty, with a covered front porch and green metal rockers like the blacks used to have when we were kids. A rusty oil tank leaned against the clapboards, and once-bright curtains stirred in the fitful breeze that passed by her open windows. I used to be welcome there. We'd drink beer in the shade of the porch and imagine what it must be like to grow up poor. It wasn't hard; kudzu grew over the fence and there was a crack house a block away.

The trains came by about five times a day, so close that you felt the vibrations in your chest, deep and out of tune with your heart; and the whistle, when it blew, was so loud, you couldn't hear a scream if it came from your own throat. The train gave the air a physical presence, so that if you spread your arms wide enough, it might push you down.

I got out of the car and looked back up the street. Tiny houses settled in silence, and a dog on a chain walked small circles in the dirt of the nearest yard. It's a mean street, I thought, and crossed to my sister's house. The steps sagged under me and there was dirt on the porch. A musty smell wafted from the open window, and I saw shadowed humps beyond. I knocked at the screen door, sensed movement, and heard a woman's voice. "Yeah, yeah. Coming."

The door opened and Alex Shiften blew smoke at me. She leaned against the jamb and looked beyond me. "It's you," she said.

Alex was the most purely physical person I'd ever met. She wore cutoffs and a tank top with no bra. She was long and lean, with wide shoulders and well-defined arms. She was intense, focused, and I thought she could probably kick my ass. I knew she'd like to try.

"Hello, Alex," I said.

"What do you want?" she responded, finally meeting my eyes, cigarette dangling from her lips. Her hair was blond and cropped above broad cheekbones and narrow, tired-looking eyes. She had five rings in her right ear and wore thick black frames with no glass in them. Beyond naked antagonism, her eyes held nothing for me.

"I'm looking for Jean."

"Yeah, no shit. But Jean's gone." She started to edge back inside, her hand eager on the door.

"Wait a minute," I said. "Where is she?"

"I don't know," Alex answered. "Sometimes she just drives."

"Where?"

She moved back onto the porch, crowding me backward. "I'm not her keeper. She comes and goes. When we want to be together, we are; otherwise, I don't hassle her. That's free advice."

"Her car's here," I stated.

"She took mine."

Looking at her, I wanted a cigarette, so I asked for one. "I'm all out," she said, and my eyes fell to the pack wedged into her front pocket. Her eyes challenged me.

"You don't much care for me, do you?" I asked.

Her voice didn't change. "Nothing personal."

"What, then?" Alex had been around for almost two years; I'd seen her maybe five times. Jean would not talk about her, not where she came from, not what she'd done with her twenty-odd years. All I knew was where they'd met, and that raised some serious questions.

She studied me and flicked her cigarette into the bare dirt yard. "You're bad for Jean," she said. "I won't have it."

Her words stunned me. "I'm bad for Jean?"

"That's right." She inched closer. "You remind Jean of bad times. With you around, she can't let go. You drag her down."

"That's not true," I said, and gestured around me, taking in everything, including Alex. "I remind her of happy times. Before all this. Jean needs me. I'm her past. Her family, damn it."

"Jean doesn't look at you and see happiness. She sees weakness.

That's what you bring to the table. She sees you and remembers all the crap that went down in the pile of bricks you grew up in. The years she spent choking on your father's bullshit." Alex stepped closer. She smelled of sweat and cigarettes. I backed away again, hating myself for it. She lowered her voice. "Women are worthless. Women are weak."

I knew what she was doing and felt my throat tighten. It was Ezra's voice. His words.

"Fucking and sucking," she continued. "Isn't that what he would say? Huh? Beyond housekeeping, women are good for two things. How do you think that made Jean feel? She was ten the first time she heard him say that. Ten years old, Work. A child."

I couldn't respond. He'd said that only once, to my knowledge, but once was enough. They are not words a child easily forgets.

"Do you agree with him, Work? Are you your daddy's boy?" She paused and leaned into me. "Your father was a misogynistic bastard. You remind Jean of that, and of your mother; of how she took it and acted like Jean should, too."

"Jean loved our mother," I shot back, holding my ground. "Don't try and twist that around." It was a weak statement and I knew it. I could not defend my father and did not understand why I felt compelled to do so.

Alex continued, firing words at me like spit. "You're a stone around her neck, Work. Plain and simple."

"That's you talking," I said.

"Nope." Her speech was as flat as her gaze, devoid of doubt or question. I looked around the squalid porch but found no help, just dead plants and a porch swing, where, I imagined, Alex filled my sister with lies and hate.

"What have you been telling her?" I demanded.

"You see. There's the problem. I don't need to tell her. She's smart enough to figure it out."

"I know she's smart," I said.

"You don't act like it. You pity her. You condescend."

"I do not."

"I won't have it," she spat out, as if I'd interrupted her. "I've taken her beyond all that. I've made her strong, given her something, and I won't have you fucking it up."

"I do not condescend to my sister," I almost shouted. "I care for her. She needs me."

"Denial won't change fact, and she needs you like a hole in the head. You're arrogant, like your father; she sees that. You presume to know what she needs, as if you could ever understand, but here's the truth of it: You don't know the first thing about who and what your sister is."

"And you do, is that it? You know who my sister is? What she needs?" My voice was up. Anger moved in me and it felt good. Here was the enemy. Something I could see and touch.

"Yeah. That's right," she said. "I absolutely do.

"What?" I asked.

"Not what you want. Not empty dreams and illusions. Not a husband, a station wagon, and a weekly bridge club. Not the goddamn American dream. That package already sucked her dry."

I stared at her glittering eyes and wanted to jam my fingers in them; they saw too clearly how much I was like my father. I'd never trusted Jean to find her own way, a brutal truth, and the fact of that, thrown so bluntly in my face by this woman I barely knew, drained me.

"Are you sleeping with my sister?" I asked.

"You know something, Work, fuck you. I don't need to explain myself. Jean and I are together now. We know what we want, and you're not part of the equation."

"Who are you?" I demanded. "Why are you here?"

"Q and A is over, asshole. I want you out of here."

"What do you want with my sister?" I shot back. She clenched her fists at her sides and I saw the bunch and play of muscles under her skin. Blood suffused her neck. She twisted her lower jaw.

"You need to leave," she said.

"Jean owns this house."

"And I live in it! Now get the hell off my porch."

"Not until I talk to Jean," I said, and crossed my arms. "I'll wait." Alex stiffened, but I refused to back down. I'd been pushed around too much in the past twenty-four hours. I wanted my sister, needed to know that she was all right. I needed her to understand that I was there for her, that I always would be. Indecision fluttered on Alex's face. Then there was movement behind her, and the screen door swung open. Jean stepped onto the porch. I stared dumbly.

Her face was pale and puffy under tousled hair. Red rimmed her eyes and I saw that they were swollen.

"Just leave, Work," she said. "Just go home."

Then she turned and was gone, swallowed by the musty house. Alex grinned in bright triumph, then slammed the door in my face. I put my hands to the wood, then let them fall to my sides, where they twitched. I saw Jean's face; it hung in the air like smoke. There was grief there, and pity, a dread finality.

In numb disbelief, I returned to my car, where I swayed, an emotional cripple. I stared at the house and its dirt yard and heard the whistle of an approaching train. I held my breath to keep from screaming; then all was wind and thunder.

CHAPTER

7

I'd always heard about the last laugh, mostly from Ezra. I never knew that the last laugh could be something real, a thing you could remember and miss.

I could still hear my sister's laugh. It had always been a good one, even when she didn't quite get the joke. Usually soft, it had a peculiar hiccup in the middle. Her lips signaled it with a twitch; then her small white teeth appeared briefly, as if she were nervous; but sometimes it boomed and she snorted through her nose. Those laughs were rare. I loved them, mainly because she could never stop once she started, and tears would track silver down her face. Once, when we were kids, she laughed so hard, she blew a snot bubble with her nose, and we both laughed until we thought we might die for lack of air. It was the single best laugh of my life. That was twenty-five years ago.

I was there when Jean laughed her last laugh. I'd told a really bad joke, something about three lawyers and a dead body. She gave me her small laugh, the one with the hiccup. Then her husband came in and said that he was going to run the baby-sitter home. None of us knew they were sleeping together. So she kissed him on the cheek and told him to drive safely. He honked on his way down the driveway, and she smiled when she told me he always did that.

The accident happened at the rest stop two miles up the interstate. The car was parked. They were naked in the backseat, and he must have been on top, because the impact sent him through the windshield but left her in the car. He suffered a broken jaw, a concussion, and lacerations to his face, chest, and genitals, which seemed about right. The girl never regained consciousness, which was an absolute tragedy.

The state trooper told me that a drunk driver took the exit too fast, lost control, and slammed into their parked car. Just one of those things, he'd said. One of those crazy things.

Jean stood by her man for two months, until the paper announced that the comatose seventeen-year-old girl was pregnant; then she crumbled. I found her the first time she tried to kill herself. There was bloody water running under the bathroom door, and I dislocated my shoulder breaking it down. She'd kept her clothes on, and I later learned that she did that because she knew I'd find her and didn't want to embarrass me. The thought of that broke my heart beyond repair.

Ezra refused to commit her. I begged, I argued, and I yelled, but he was resolute; it would look bad for the family. So Jean stayed with him and with Mother, the three of them alone in that big house.

When her husband left, he took their only child. Too depressed to care, she let him. He presented her with custody papers and she signed them. Had it been a son instead of a daughter, I suspect that Ezra would have fought him over it. But it was a girl, and so he didn't.

That night, she tried again; this time it was pills. She wore her wedding dress and stretched out to die on our parents' bed. After that, she was institutionalized for eight months—Alex Shiften was her roommate. When Jean went home, Alex went, too. We never learned a thing about her. The two shared a conspiracy of silence. Our questions, which began politely, were politely ignored. The questions grew more pointed, as did their reactions to them. When Alex told Ezra to fuck off, I thought the bottom would drop out. We stopped asking. None of us knew how to handle them, and in our discomfort we pretended everything was all right. What a ship of fools.

As I drove away from that ragged dead-end street, I thought about laughter and how it was like breath; you never knew which would be your last. And it saddened me that Jean's last laugh had been such a small one. I wished I'd told a better joke.

I tried to remember my last laugh, but all I could think of was Jean and that snot bubble. That had been grand. But memory can be like a floodgate, once opened hard to close, and as I drove, images and feelings marched upon me like waves. I saw my mother, broken on the floor, then Ezra's safe, his cold smirk, and Alex Shiften's triumphant smile. I saw Jean as a child, and then grown, floating in a bathtub, her diluted blood a translucent shroud that shimmered across the floor and spilled down the stairwell. My wife's hands, cold upon me, and, inevitably, images of Vanessa Stolen—the sweat on her face and on her thighs, her high breasts, which barely moved as she arched her back off the damp flannel sheets. I felt her eyes, heard the stutter in her throat as she gasped my name, and thought of the secret that for so many years had kept me from giving myself to her. And of how profoundly I failed her in that deep dark place where both our lives changed forever.

But some things are stronger than doubt or self-recrimination. Need, for instance. To be accepted. Loved without judgment. Even when I couldn't reciprocate. Time and again, I had returned to the one place, the one person who had never failed me. I'd done this knowing the pain that lingered in my wake. I'd taken all and given nothing. As for something in return, she'd neither asked nor demanded, though hers would have been the right. And I'd tried to stay away; I'd tried and failed. I knew also that I would fail again now. My need was too great, an animal inside me.

So I turned off the road, turned off the world, and drove slowly down the cratered track that was Stolen Farm Road. It felt like a switch had been flicked in my head. Pressures fell away, concerns, too. I could breathe, and so I did, like I'd been long underwater. I passed through the shade of tall oaks and narrow, feathered cedars, and gravel crunched beneath my tires. I saw a shrike with a fence lizard in its claws and felt elemental, as if I, too, belonged here. It was a good feeling, though false, and there were no whispers beyond the wind.

I rounded the last bend and saw Vanessa's house. She stood on the front porch, shading her eyes, and for a moment I believed that she'd felt my approach. My chest tightened and I felt a stirring of body and soul. Even more than this place, this woman did things for me. She was farmwork-lean, with flaxen hair and eyes that shone like sun on water. Her hands were rough, but I loved them for the things they could do. I liked to watch her plant things, those hands in dark earth. It reminded me of what I knew as a child, that dirt is good and the earth forgives. Her breasts were small above a flat stomach, and her eyes were soft where tragedy would have made others hard or indifferent. Small lines cut the corners of her eyes and mouth but were inconsequential.

Looking at her, I felt my weakness. I knew this was wrong, knew that I could never give her what she so richly deserved. I knew it and for an instant I cared, but only for that instant. Then I was out of the car and in her arms, my mouth on hers, my hands no longer mine to control. I didn't know if I was on the porch or still in the drive. I didn't remember moving, yet all was motion. She rose into me and I was lost. No fear or confusion, just this woman and the world that spun around us like colored mist.

I heard distant sound and recognized my name; it burned in my ear. Then I felt her tongue cool it. Her lips moved over me—my eyes, my neck, my face. Her hands found the back of my head and they pulled my lips back to hers. I tasted plums, kissed her harder, and she weakened against me. I picked her up, felt legs around me. Then more motion and we were inside, up the stairs and onto the bed that knew so well the force of our passion. Clothes evaporated, as if burned away by flesh too hot to bear them. My mouth found her breasts, the hard, ready nipples, and the soft plane of her stomach. I tasted all of her. The dew of her sweat, the deep cleft of her, her legs like velvet bands across my ears. Her fingers clawed at my hair, tangled, and she pulled me up, said words I couldn't possibly understand. She took me in her roughened palm and led me into her. My head rocked back. She was heat, fire; she cried my name again, but I was beyond response, lost and desperate never to be found.

CHAPTER

8

I drifted for what felt like hours. Neither of us spoke; we knew better. Peace like this came rarely and was as fragile as a child's smile. She nestled against me, on her side, one leg thrown across my own. Her hand trailed lazily across my chest, down my stomach. Occasionally, her lips brushed my neck, and they felt like feathers.

I had my arm around her, my hand pressed against the smooth curve of her lower back. I watched the ceiling fan spin, brown blades against her creamy white ceiling. A breeze passed through the window, stroked us like a penitent breath. But I knew it couldn't last, as did she; it never had. We would talk, and as the words came, so, too, would the steady push of reality. I knew the pattern. It always started small, a vague itch in the mind, as if I'd left something undone. Then the face of my wife would make its silent, swift invasion, and the guilt would follow on tiny feet. But it was not the guilt of the adulterer; that had passed years ago, soon after Barbara's smile.

This was a different guilt, born of darkness and fear in that stinking creek so many years ago—the day we met, the day I fell in love and the day I failed her. That guilt was a cancer, and under its assault the cocoon would crumble and I would leave, hating myself for again using the only person in this world who loved me, wishing that I could undo the past and make myself worthy. But it was the one thing that I could never do, for if this guilt was a cancer, then the truth was a bullet in the head. She would hate me if she knew. So in time I would leave, as I always did, and already I was dreading the hurt in her eyes when I told her I'd call, and how she'd nod and smile as if she believed me.

I closed my eyes, let myself sink beneath the blanket of this momentary joy, but inside I was hollow, and cold was a fist around my heart.

"Penny for your thoughts," she said.

It had begun, but that was okay. I'd missed the sound of her voice.

"You wouldn't like them," I said. She rose up on an elbow and smiled down at me. I smiled back. "They're dark, horrible thoughts." I kept my voice light.

"Give them to me anyway. A present."

"Kiss me," I told her, and she did. I would give her my thoughts, those that she could bear. "I missed you," I said. "I always miss you."

"Liar." She cupped my chin in one hand. "Filthy rotten liar." She kissed me again. "Do you know how long it's been?"

I did—seventeen months and just under two weeks, each day an agony and an exercise in longing. "No," I told her. "How long?"

"Never mind," she said. "Let's not dwell on it." I saw the pain in her eyes. The last time I'd been with her was the night my mother died. I could still see the reflection of her face suspended in the windowpane as I stared into the night. I was searching then, looking for the strength to give her the truth. But her words had stopped me. "Don't think about such nasty things," she'd said. So I had not.

68

"Ezra's dead," I told her. "They found his body two days ago."

"I know. I'm sorry. I truly am."

She would never have raised the subject. Just one more way that she was unlike every other. But she'd always been like that. She didn't push or pry, didn't care for details. Vanessa lived in the moment; I'd always envied that about her. It was strength.

"How's Jean taking it?"

She was the first person to ask me that. Not what happened. Not how I was handling it. Her thoughts were of Jean because she knew that would be my biggest concern. I shuddered at the depth of her understanding.

"I'm scared for Jean," I said. "She's gone far away, and I don't know if I can get her back." I told her about my run-in with Alex. About Jean on the porch. "She's left me, Vanessa. I don't know her anymore. I think she's in trouble, but she won't let me help her."

"It's never too late. For anything. All you have to do is reach out."

"I have," I told her.

"Maybe you just think you have."

"I told you, I have."

I felt the force of my words as they passed my lips, and I didn't know where the anger came from. Were we talking about Jean or Vanessa? She sat up in the bed, cross-legged, and stared at me.

"Take it easy, Jackson," she said. "We're just talking."

Vanessa had never called me Work. She used my given name and always had. I'd asked her once why that was, and she'd told me I would never be work for her. I'd told her it was clever, and about the nicest thing I'd ever heard. I could still remember the way she'd looked. Sunlight flooded the open window and I'd noticed for the first time that she was not the young girl I'd once known; time and hard work had left their marks. But I didn't care.

"You're right, just talking. So how have you been?" I asked.

Her face softened. "I'm growing organics now," she told me. "Moving more and more of my production in that direction. Strawberries, blueberries, whatever. People are into that these days. It pays."

"So you're doing okay, then?" I asked.

She laughed. "Hell no. The bank's still after me every month, but I'm ahead of the curve on this organics thing. It will make a difference. This farm will never leave my hands. That, I promise you." She talked more about organic farming, about her aging tractor and the truck that needed a new transmission. She talked about her plans and I listened. At one point, she got up and brought two beers from the kitchen.

To me, Vanessa was a breath of fresh air. She moved to the seasons, touched the living earth every single day. I knew when it was raining, but not until I got wet.

"You know, time's a crazy damn thing," she said, handing me a beer. She slipped back onto the bed and put a pillow in her lap. A strand of hair hung over her left eye. I asked her what she meant. "I was thinking of our families," she told me. "The rise and fall of family fortunes."

I sipped at my beer. "What about them?"

"It's just crazy is all. I mean, think about it. Where was your family at the end of the Civil War?"

She knew exactly where my family had been; we'd talked about it many times. Five generations ago, my ancestor was a foot soldier from Pennsylvania who had the misfortune to get most of his foot shot off. He was captured and delivered to the Confederate prison in Salisbury, where he lingered several weeks before dying of dysentery and infection. He was buried in one of the four trench graves that eventually came to hold over eleven thousand Union soldiers. That was at the end of the war. His wife learned of his death and, pregnant with his unborn child, traveled to Salisbury. But he had no marker; his bones were lost among the thousands of other nameless souls. Word is, it broke her heart. She gave her last dollar to the physician who delivered my great-great-grandfather and died two weeks later. I've often thought of that ancestor, and wondered if her death drained the last true passion from my family.

She died of a broken heart. My God. What a thing.

Her son was passed around the county and spent most of his life shoveling manure on another man's plantation. My great-grandfather delivered ice in the summer and stoked rich men's furnaces in the winter. His son was a worthless drunk who beat my father for the fun of it. The Pickens were poor as dirt and treated like shit in this county until Ezra came along. He changed everything.

The Stolen family was just the opposite. Two hundred years back, this farm had been over a thousand acres, and the Stolens ran things in Rowan County.

"Lot of history in this bed," I said.

"Yep." She nodded. "Lot of love, too." I said nothing, and the silence spoke volumes, an old tale. She loved me and on good days understood that I loved her, too. Why I could not admit that was the problem. She didn't understand and I was too ashamed to explain it to her. So we existed in this horrible undefined state, with nothing to cling to when the nights were cold and endlessly successive. "Why are you here, Jackson?" she asked me.

"Do I need a reason?" I replied, feeling cheap.

"No," she said with feeling. "Never."

I took her grasping hand. "I'm here to see you, Vanessa."

"But not to stay."

I remained silent.

"Never to stay," she continued, and I saw tears in her eyes.

"Vanessa . . ."

"Don't say it, Jackson. Don't. We've been here before. I know you're married. I don't know what came over me. Just ignore me."

"It's not that," I said.

"Then what?" she asked, and I saw such anguish in her face that I lost my voice. I was wrong to have come. So very, very wrong.

She tried to laugh, but it died halfway. "Come on, Jackson. What?" But I couldn't tell her. She stared into my eyes for a long second and I watched as the fire burned out of her face and the resignation settled in. She kissed me, but it was a dead kiss.

"I'm jumping in the shower," she told me. "Don't you dare leave."

I watched her as she padded barefoot and naked from the room. Normally, we'd be in the shower together, her body alive under my soapy hands.

I drained my beer and lay weakly, listening to the birds outside. I heard the shower run in the bathroom and pictured Vanessa's face upturned to water straight from the well. It would taste fresh on her skin. I wanted to wash her hair, but instead I got up and went downstairs. There was more beer in the refrigerator and I carried one to the front porch. The sun felt good on my naked skin and it dried my sweat. Farmland stretched to the distant tree line and I guessed I was looking at strawberries. I leaned against the post and closed my eyes to the breeze. I didn't hear Vanessa come downstairs.

"Oh, my God. What happened to your back?" She moved quickly onto the porch. "It looks like somebody beat you with a bat." She put light hands on me, tracing lines of my bruises.

"I fell down some stairs," I told her.

"Were you drunk?"

I laughed. "A little, I guess."

"Jackson, you need to be careful. You could have killed yourself."

I wasn't sure why I lied to her. I just didn't want to tell her the whole truth. She had enough problems. "I'll be all right."

She took the beer from my hand and sipped. She was in a towel, her hair still wet. I wanted to wrap her into me and promise that I'd never let go. I wanted to tell her that I loved her, that I would spend the rest of my life just like this. Instead, I put one inadequate arm around her shoulder, and even that felt like a stranger's arm. "I love this place," I told her, and she accepted my words without comment. It was the closest I could come to sharing the truth of my feelings for her, and in some small way she knew this. Reality, however, had never been so simple.

"Are you hungry?" she asked, and I nodded. "Let's go to the kitchen." We went into the kitchen and she pulled a robe from the laundry room on the way. "Go put your pants on," she told me. "You can do anything you want naked except sit at my table." She popped me on the rear as I passed by.

She had a trestle table that dated back to the 1800s. It was dented and scarred. Sitting at it, we ate ham and cheese and spoke of little things. I drank another beer. I told her about Ezra's safe and the missing gun. She hesitated for a minute and then asked me how he died. Two bullets to the head, I told her, and she looked out the window.

"Do you feel any different?" she finally asked.

"I don't understand."

She looked at me then. "Does your life feel any different now that Ezra is dead and gone?" I didn't know what she meant and told her so. She didn't speak for awhile, and I realized she was debating whether or not to continue. "Are you happy?" she finally asked.

I shrugged. "Maybe. I don't know. I haven't thought about it in awhile." There was something in her eyes. "What are you getting at, Vanessa?"

She sighed. "I don't think you're living your life, Jackson, not for a long time now."

I grew still and tense. "Whose, then?"

"You know whose." Her voice was soft and she shied away as if afraid I might hit her.

"No, Vanessa, I don't." I was getting angry and didn't know why—didn't want to know why. Denial was a weapon; it killed truth, numbed the mind, and I was a junkie. Part of me recognized this, the same part that knew where she was going, but I ignored that part. That part hurt.

"Damn it, Jackson. I'm trying to help."

"Are you?" I demanded. "Who are you trying to help? Me or you?"

"That is not fair," she said. I knew she was right, but I didn't care. She was taking me places I didn't want to go. "It's you I'm worried about. It's always you!"

"Goddamn it, Vanessa. That's too much pressure. I've never asked for things to be the way they are. They just are."

"*That* is your problem."

I stared at her.

"Things never just are. We make choices, actively or not. You can affect the world, Jackson. Ezra's dead. Don't you feel that?"

"So we're back to Ezra," I said.

"We never left him. And that's the problem. You've never left him. You've been living his life for more than twenty years, and you've never seen it."

I didn't know what she was talking about, and in that instant her face seemed to transform. She was like the rest after all. "No," I said. "Not true."

"Yes." She tried to take my hand, but I pulled it back just in time.

"That is not fucking true!" I yelled.

"Why did you marry Barbara?" she demanded, and there was a stoic calm in her voice.

"What?"

"Why Barbara? Why not me?"

"You don't know what you're talking about."

"I do know. And always have."

"You're not making sense." I watched as she came out of her seat, hands on the table that had fed her family for generations. She leaned closer, and I noticed that her nostrils were flared.

"You listen to me, Jackson, and you listen well, because I swear to God that I will never say this again. But I need it to be said. Ten years ago, you told me you loved me. You damn well meant it, too. Then you married Barbara. Now I want you to tell me why."

I rocked back in my chair, felt my defensiveness, but couldn't do anything about it. My arms crossed over my chest as if to protect my heart. My head rang, and I rubbed at my temples, but the sudden pain refused to die.

"You married Barbara because Ezra told you to." She slapped her palm down on the table and I thought it sounded like a bone break- ing. "Admit it. One time, Jackson, and I'll never mention it again. You live Ezra's life, his choices. Barbara's family has a name; she went to the right schools, had the right friends. It's true. Admit it. Damn it, Jackson, be a man."

"No!" I shouted, suddenly on my feet. "I won't admit it because it's not true." I spun from the table and pounded upstairs to get the rest of my clothes and my keys. She was wrong and I refused to take any more. Her voice followed me.

"What about children?" she shouted. "You always wanted children!"

"Shut up, Vanessa!" My voice broke as I said it. I knew that she did not deserve it, but I could not yell loudly enough.

"Whose idea was that? Huh? Whose idea, Jackson? You used to talk about it all the time. Lots of kids! That's what you always planned—a houseful of them, a family to raise right, so you could be the father you wanted Ezra to be. Damn it, Jackson. Don't run away from this. It's too important!"

I ignored her. My shirt was on the floor and I found my keys under the bed. I pulled my shoes on without socks. The house was hot, stifling; I had to get out. I shouldn't have come at all.

She was waiting for me at the bottom of the stairs.

"Don't leave," she said. "Not like this."

Her voice and eyes were both soft, but it wasn't going to work. "Let me by," I told her. She stepped onto the first step, crowding me. Looking down, I saw the part in her hair, the light freckles on the bridge of her nose, eyes that looked too wide to be innocent.

"Please," she said. "Please, Jackson. I'm sorry. I take it back. Please don't go."

"Step aside, Vanessa." The pain in her face cut me, but I couldn't stop. This was her fight, not mine.

"Jackson, please. It's been so long. I can't lose you again. Stay. Have another beer." She reached for my hand.

The stairs were tilting; I couldn't catch my breath, and I didn't know what was wrong with me. I needed air, needed to get out. I shook my hand free and pushed past her.

"I shouldn't have come," I said, hitting the screen door so hard, it slammed against the house.

I felt her behind me, heard her steps on the porch and then on the gravel. Her breath was loud, and I knew that if I turned, I would see tears. So I didn't turn; I marched on, and she caught me at the car.

"Don't go," she said.

I didn't turn around. She put one hand on my shoulder, the other on the side of my neck, where heat still burned. She laid her face upon my back, and I hesitated. I wanted no one thing in my life more than to stay, but she wanted too much. Truth was not my friend.

"Please don't make me beg," she said, and I knew how much the words cost her. But I didn't turn around; I couldn't—one look at her and I would stay. And I wanted to; that's what killed me. If possible, I would never leave, but I needed my anger. I couldn't give it up.

"I'm sorry, Vanessa. I shouldn't have come at all."

She didn't try to stop me as I got into the car. I backed away without looking at her. I drove too fast, wheels loose in the gravel. I kept my eyes down and didn't look up until I was almost to the bend in the road. Then I saw her in the mirror, on her knees in the dust, face buried in her rough farm-girl hands. She looked small. She looked crushed.

My anger drained away and left me shaken to the core. She was the only woman I'd ever loved, and this was all she had of me, a palm-ful of dusty tears.

Sweet Lord, I thought. *What have I done?*

CHAPTER

9

I stopped at the paved road, as sick as if I'd just stepped on a baby bird. I couldn't bear to think about what had just happened, but it was in me now, inescapable. I felt her tears, her fingers, so light on my neck, and the plane of her cheek against my back. I reached for something solid: the wheel, the dash, the clock that read just after four. I took a deep breath and put the car back into gear. Then I remembered Detective Mills and our three o'clock meeting. Somewhere between cheating on my wife and destroying the woman I loved, I'd forgotten about it.

I stepped on the gas. The road ran black beneath me. I recognized a song on the radio and wondered when I'd turned it on. I punched at the button as hills rolled past on greased tracks and farmland fell away. Trailer parks and strip malls sprang up to follow me as I drove back into town, the smell of sex on me like a scarlet letter. I called the house to see if Barbara was there and hung up when she answered. Her voice was like syrup, and I considered speaking, just to see if it would sour; but if so, it would sour with questions I was not prepared to answer. I needed to calm down, get a grip. Chill the fuck out.

At the office, I used Ezra's shower to rinse sin from my flesh and wondered how many times he'd used it for the same purpose. Never, I thought. Ezra knew women but never knew guilt. Did I envy that in him? No. I nourished my guilt for the soul that it implied, and as I left, I gave Ezra's safe the finger. Fuck everybody. I needed some Work time. Maybe I'd get a dog after all.

Outside, I made it to my car before I saw movement from the corner of my eye. I spun around.

"I saw your car." It was Douglas, the district attorney. He looked tired, his eyes puffy above a nose the color of old wine. He looked at me strangely and I wondered if he'd been drinking. "You didn't answer my knock, so I waited."

I said nothing. For some reason, my heart refused to slow down. He walked across the ten feet that separated us, stopping just before he got too close. His eyes moved over me, taking in my wet hair and disheveled clothes. I felt heat in my cheeks but couldn't stop the flush. Douglas was a hard man to lie to. "Everything okay?" he asked, shoving a piece of gum into his mouth.

"Yes," I said, finding my voice. "Yes." I knew I was repeating myself.

"I ask because I just got off the phone with Detective Mills. She says you'd better be dead already. It's the only excuse that she'll accept." His eyes glittered more than twinkled and I realized they were his black eyes, his courtroom eyes. "Are you dead?" he asked.

"Close," I said, and tried a smile that died on the vine. "Look, I'm sorry about not meeting Mills. I had my reasons."

"Care to share them?" Douglas asked, crowding me without taking a step.

"I do not." He was unimpressed by the anger in my voice. He shoved his hands into his pockets and studied me. I tried to give him my poker face, my lawyer face, but there in the shadow of my dead father's building, it was hard. I had no idea what he saw, but I knew it wasn't the calm, collected face I'd once practiced in the mirror.

"I'm going to tell you something, Work, and I want you to listen well." I didn't even blink. "This is the last thing I can tell you as a friend. It's good advice, so you should take it." He paused, as if waiting for me to thank him, and sighed when I didn't. "Don't fuck around with Mills," he told me. "I mean it. She's pissed-off and frustrated. That makes her the most dangerous person in your world."

I felt a horrible chill move over me. "What are you saying, Douglas?"

"I'm not *saying* anything. This conversation isn't happening."

"Am I a suspect?" I asked.

"I told you the other day that everybody is a suspect."

"That's no answer," I replied.

Douglas rolled his shoulders and looked around the empty lot, up at the roofline, then put his eyes back on mine. He pursed his lips. "Ezra was a rich man," he said, as if that explained it all.

"So?" I didn't get it.

"Jesus, Work." Exasperation was in his voice, and he sucked in a deep breath as if to cool his temper. "Mills is looking for a motive and going through the usual suspects. I assume Ezra had a will."

"Oh shit," I said. "Are you kidding me?"

"Barbara has expensive tastes, and the practice . . ." He paused and shrugged.

"Come on, Douglas."

"I'm just stating the obvious, okay? You're a brilliant tactician, Work. You have one of the sharpest legal minds I've ever known. Hell, you're even decent in the courtroom. But you're no rainmaker. You won't take personal injury cases anymore and you won't kiss ass to get big clients. That's what built the practice and made Ezra rich. But a law practice is a business. Even Mills knows that, and she's been around enough to know that yours is barely solvent.

"Look. I know you didn't kill your father. Just don't give Mills a reason to look your way. Cooperate, for Christ's sake. Don't be a god-damn idiot. Give her what she wants and get on with your life. It's not complicated math."

"It's bullshit math!"

"One plus one is two. Add six or seven zeros and the math gets even more compelling."

I was stunned by his words, and his face had a sharp edge, as if he could cut me open and tell the future in my guts.

"Ezra had a lot of zeros," he concluded.

My insides twisted as if already between his thick, meaty fingers. "Has Mills discussed this with you?" I asked, needing to know.

"Not in so many words," the DA admitted. "But it doesn't take a genius, Work. I know where her mind is going with this. So do your-self a favor. Bend over, take it like a man, and move on with your life."

"Did Mills tell you that someone tried to kill me last night?" I asked.

He frowned at the interruption. "She may have mentioned some-thing about it."

"And?"

Douglas shrugged, his eyes far from mine. "She doesn't believe you."

"And you don't, either." I finished his unspoken thought.

"She's the detective," he said flatly.

"You think I made it up?"

"I don't know what to believe." A simple statement.

"Somebody pushed that chair down the stairs, Douglas. If they didn't mean to kill me, they sure as hell meant to do bodily harm."

"And you're saying it's connected to your father's death?"

I thought about the safe and the missing gun. "Maybe. It's possible."

"You should know that Mills doesn't buy it. She thinks you're gen-erating confusion, clouding the issues. If I thought you did it, and I'm just saying if, playing devil's advocate, then I'd be inclined to agree with Mills. It's Occam's Razor, Work. The simplest explanation is usually right."

"That's crap, Douglas. Somebody tried to kill me."

"Just give Mills your alibi, Work, and whatever else she wants. Let her check it out and be done with it."

I thought about what Douglas was asking me to talk about. I could hear the sound of a neck breaking under terrible force. "You know what happened that night, Douglas." It was a statement, a novel writ large.

"I know your mother died in a tragic fall, but that's all I know." His voice was unapologetic.

"It's enough," I said.

"No, Work, it's not. Because it's also the night your father disappeared and for all Mills knows, you and Jean were the last ones to see him alive. It's important, and no one's going to dance around your tender sensibilities. Your father was murdered. This is a murder investigation. Talk to her."

I thought that if he said *murder* one more time, I'd murder him. I didn't need a reminder. I saw my father's fleshless jawbone every time I closed my eyes, and even now I fought the image of his remains under the knives and saws of the medical examiner in Chapel Hill.

Douglas loomed. The silence behind his last words demanded a response, but I didn't look up. He wanted me to cough up the memory of that night like a bloody tumor so that Mills could paw through it, spread it out like finger paint, and discuss it with other cops over coffee and cigarettes. Cops I fought every day in court. I knew how it worked, the twisted voyeurism of people who had seen it all yet never got enough. I knew how they speculated about rape victims in the halls behind the courtrooms, pawed through photographs, and dissected a person's humanity in the quest to be the funniest cop of the day. I'd heard them joke about how people had been killed: Did it hurt? Do you think she begged? Was she alive when they fucked her? Conscious when the knife first touched her pale skin? Did he see it coming? I heard he wet himself.

It was a dark farce, a tragedy played out in the pain of victims in every town in the country. But this time it was my pain. My family. My secrets.

I saw Mother at the bottom of the stairs, her open eyes and blood-flecked mouth, her neck bent like a cruel joke. I saw it all: the red dress she wore, the position of her hands, the Cinderella slipper that lay upon the stairs where it had fallen. The memory was cruel and it cut, but if I looked up, I might see Ezra, and that would be worse. I wasn't ready for that. I couldn't do it. Not again. For if I looked beyond Ezra, I would see Jean. I would see what that night did to her, all of it, frozen on her face in that horrible tableau that still chased through my dreams. There was horror in her face, and rage, an animal force that transformed her. In that face I saw a stranger, someone who could kill, and that terrified me now more than ever. What had that night made of my sister? And was she now forever lost?

If I talked to Mills, it would all come back. She would poke and pry, try with her cop mind to ferret it out. She might see things, and I couldn't have that.

"No problem," I told the district attorney. "I'll talk to her."

"Be sure that you do," he replied.

"Don't worry." I unlocked my car, desperate to escape. "Thanks for worrying about me," I said, but my sarcasm was wasted effort. I climbed into my car, but he stopped me with a hand on my door.

"By the way," he said. "What *were* you doing the night Ezra disappeared?"

I tried to meet his eyes. "Are you asking for my alibi?" I asked, as if he was joking. He said nothing, and I laughed, but it sounded hollow. "As a friend or as the district attorney?"

"Maybe a little of both," he said.

"You're a funny man," I told him.

"Humor me," he said.

I wanted to get out of there, away from his questions and his flat eyes. So I did what any man would have done under the circumstances: I lied.

"I was home," I told him. "In bed. With Barbara."

He smiled a thin smile. "That wasn't so hard, was it?" he asked me. "No," I told him, surprised. "That wasn't hard at all."

He smiled a wider smile and I saw that food was stuck in his teeth, something brown. "Good boy," he said, trying to be friendly but sounding condescending. I tried to return his smile but couldn't. A nod was the best I could do, and even that hurt. He wasn't sure about me. I saw it in his eyes. Could I have killed Ezra? It was a question for him, and he would check my alibi. I also knew that he'd discussed this with Detective Mills. This was his county and a media case; he'd never sit on the sidelines. So he'd lied to me as I'd lied to him, and that meant one thing. Our friendship was dead, whether Douglas wanted it that way or not. He could hang someone for my father's death tomorrow, but I could never go back. That bridge was smoking ash.

He left then, and I watched his wide back as he shuffled across the lot to his tired Chevrolet sedan. He got in and drove away. He never looked back, and I realized that he knew it, too. Ezra's death was like a match dropped into damp tinder; it was a slow burn now, but only a matter of time until it flashed. I wondered what else would end a smoking ruin.

I started my own car and left the windows down. I drove my hair dry and smoked a couple of cigarettes to take away the smell of fresh soap. I thought of Vanessa's face in the afternoon light. That's what I would hold on to. How it started, not how it ended. Not what I would say to her the next time I caved to my weakness and sought redemption in her tender mercies.

I said her name once, then tucked it away.

It was almost six o'clock by the time I got home. I knew that something was off the minute I walked in. Candles perfumed the air and soft music played on the stereo. Barbara called from the kitchen and I answered her, dropping my jacket onto a chair back and moving slowly her way. She met me at the kitchen door with a glass of chilled white wine, a chardonnay that probably cost a fortune. She was wearing a smile and a very small black dress.

"Welcome home, baby," she said, and kissed me. Her lips parted and I felt the tip of her tongue. I couldn't remember the last time she'd called me baby, and the last time she kissed me that way, she'd been dead drunk. She pressed against me and, looking down, I saw her breasts swell from the top of her dress with the pressure. She wrapped her arms around my waist.

"Are you drunk?" I asked without thinking.

She didn't flinch. "Not yet," she said. "But two more glasses and you might get lucky." She ground against me, making me vaguely uncomfortable. I felt out of my depth. I looked over the top of her head, saw the pot and pans simmering on the stove.

"Are you cooking?" I asked, surprised. Barbara rarely cooked.

"Beef Wellington," she replied.

"What's the occasion?"

She stepped back, put her wine on the counter. "An apology," she said. "For the way I treated you last night. It was a bad time for you, a horrible time, and I could have been more supportive." She cast her eyes down, but I didn't believe her. "I should have been, Work. I should have been there for you."

Barbara had not apologized to me in years, not for anything. I was struck dumb.

She took my hands and peered at me with what had to be mock concern. "Are you okay?" she asked, referring to my fall, I guessed. "I should have come to the hospital, I know, but I was still mad at you." She made a pout of her lips and I knew that in her mind, that made everything okay. She turned away before I could respond and snatched up her wineglass. Her calm seemed less natural when half of the glass disappeared in one swallow. She turned again to face me and leaned against the sink, her eyes shiny. "So," she began again, her voice too loud. "How was your day?"

I almost laughed. I almost slapped her, just to see what expression would appear on her perfectly prepared face. Somebody tried to kill me last night and you didn't come to the hospital. I made love to a fragile and lonely woman, then ground her spirit into the dirt for reasons I'm too chickenshit to explore. My father is dead with a couple of bullets in his head, and the district attorney wants to know where I was on the night in question. I'd really like to choke the fake smile off your face, which, I think, means my marriage is in trouble. And my sister, whom I have failed in every possible way, hates me. And worst of all, this sister, whom I love—I'm pretty sure that she murdered our father.

"Fine," I told her. "My day was fine. How was yours?"

"The same," she said. "Go sit. The paper is on the table. Dinner will be ready in half an hour."

"I'll go change," I said, and walked from the room on wooden feet. I felt things as I moved: the wall, the banister. What was real? What mattered? If I walked back into the kitchen with shit in my mouth, would she kiss me and tell me I tasted like chocolate?

I splashed water on my face and put on khakis and a cotton rollneck sweater that Barbara had given me for Christmas several years back. I studied my face in the mirror, amazed at how complete it appeared, how calm and intact. Then I smiled and the illusion collapsed. I thought of the things Vanessa had said.

Barbara still stood at the stove when I walked back into the kitchen. Her glass was full again. She smiled as I poured more for myself. Wordlessly, we clinked glasses and drank. "Ten more minutes," she said. "I'll call you when it's ready."

"Do you want me to set the table?" I asked.

"I've got it. Go and relax."

I turned for the living room and the deep, soft couch. Ten minutes sounded good.

"Douglas stopped by," my wife announced. I stopped and turned.
"What?"

"Yeah, a routine visit, he said. Just to talk about the night Ezra disappeared."

"Routine," I repeated.

"To fill in the blanks, he said. For his forms."

"His forms."

She looked quizzically at me. "Why are you repeating what I say?" she asked.

"Am I?"

"Yes. Almost every word."

"I'm sorry. I didn't know I was."

"Honestly, Work." She laughed. "Sometimes." She turned back to the stove, her hand on a wooden spoon. I stood rooted, dimly aware that numbness was becoming my normal state of existence.

"What did you tell him?" I finally asked.

"The truth," she said. "What else?"

"Of course the truth, Barbara, but what specifically?"

"Don't snap at me, Work," she said. "I'm trying . . ." She trailed off, gesturing with the spoon at the cluttered kitchen. Drops of something yellow landed on the counter and I stared at them because I couldn't meet her eyes. When I did look up, I saw that she had her hand over her mouth and tears shimmered in eyes turned to the floor. Another man would have gone to her and put his arms around her, but my soul was already black with lies.

I gave her an awkward minute and she pulled herself together. "What did you tell him?" I asked again, more gently this time.

"Just what little I know. You've never told me much." Her voice was small. "I told him that after going to the hospital with"—she paused, barely able to finish the sentence; she'd almost said my mother's corpse— "with your mother, you went to your father's house. Then you came here. I told him how upset you were, you and Jean." She looked down again. "About how you two argued."

I stopped her. "I told you about that?"

"Not what you argued about. Not the words. Just that you fought about something. You were very upset."

"What else?"

"Jesus, Work. What is all this?"

"Just tell me, please."

"Nothing else to tell. He wanted to know where you were that night and I told him you were here. He thanked me and left. That's it."

Thank God. But I had to test her. I had to be sure.

I made my voice casual. "Could you swear that I was here all night? Could you testify to that?"

"You're scaring me, Work."

"No reason to be scared," I assured her. "It's just the lawyer in me. I know how some people might think, and it's best if we're clear on this."

She stepped closer, stopping in the kitchen door. She still held the spoon. Her eyes were very steady, and she lowered her voice, as if to give her words a special emphasis. "I would know if you'd left," she stated simply, and something in her face made me wonder if she knew the truth. That I *had* left. That I'd spent long hours weeping on Vanessa's shoulder before creeping back into our bed an hour before dawn, scared weak that she would wake up.

"You were here," she said. "With me. There can be no question about that."

I smiled, praying this time that my face would remain intact. "Good. Then we're settled. Thank you, Barbara." I rubbed my hands together. "Dinner smells great," I added lamely, turning away as quickly as might seem reasonable. I almost made it to the couch, when a thought stopped me. "What time did Douglas come by?"

"Four o'clock," she told me, and I sat down on the couch. Four o'clock. An hour before I spoke to him in the parking lot. I was wrong, then. Our friendship didn't die when he questioned me; the corpse was already cold and starting to stink. The fat bastard was testing me.

Dinner would have been great if I could have tasted it. We had caramelized Brie with slivered almonds, Caesar salad, beef Wellington, and fresh bread. The chardonnay turned out to be Australian. My wife was beautiful in the candlelight and at times I thought that maybe I'd misjudged her. She made clever remarks at the expense of no one, spoke of current events and a book we'd both read. Occasionally, her hand touched mine. I grew mellow with wine and hope. By half past nine, I thought maybe we had a chance after all. It didn't last long.

The plates had been cleared away, stacked in the sink for the people we'd be the next day. The remnants of dessert littered the table and we were halfway through a coffee and Baileys. A quiet contentment filled me, and I looked forward to loving her for the first time in forever. Her hand was on my leg.

"So tell me," she said, leaning closer, seeming to offer herself. "When do you think we'll move?" The question caught me by surprise. I didn't understand, but her eyes had a new glitter and I felt myself sobering, almost against my will. She sipped her wine, her eyes dark above the pale half-moon of the glass's edge. She waited in silence, as if only for me to pluck a date from the air.

"Move where?" I asked, because I had no choice. I dreaded her answer, mainly because I knew what it would be.

She laughed, but there was no humor in it. "Don't joke," she said.

The last of my pleasure vanished, devoured by the cruel hunger in her voice. "I'm not," I said. "Are you?"

I watched as her face softened but saw that it was forced. The muscles still clenched in her once-lovely jawline.

"Into Ezra's house. Into our new house."

"What in the world makes you think that we're moving into that house?"

"I just thought . . . I mean . . ."

"Damn it, Barbara, we can barely afford this house, and it's not even half the size of my father's."

"It's such a lovely home," she said. "I just assumed . . ."

"You assumed we'd move into an eight-thousand-square-foot house we can't afford to heat?"

"But the will—"

"I don't even know what's in the will!" I exclaimed. "I don't have a clue!"

"But Glena said—"

I exploded. "Glena! I should have known. Is that what you two were talking about last night?" I thought of the miserable hours I'd spent in the garage while my wife and her detestable friend planned Barbara's rise to eminence. "You had it all planned out."

A change came over Barbara as I watched. Suddenly, she was cool dispassion.

"It makes sense if we're going to start a family," she said, then sipped her wine and watched me with a hunter's patience. It was not fair. Barbara knew how much I wanted children. I sighed deeply and poured straight Baileys into my cup.

"Are you blackmailing me?" I asked. "Children for Ezra's house?"

"Of course not," she said. "I'm merely suggesting that children would be a logical next step for us, and we could use the extra space."

I tried to calm myself. Exhaustion descended upon me like wet cement, but I decided nonetheless that it might be time to face some ugly truths. Vanessa's tear-streaked face came unbidden to my mind. I thought of the things she'd said, the truths she'd thrust under my nose, truths so abhorrent to me that I'd crushed her rather than face them.

"How come we never had children, Barbara?" I asked.

"You said you needed to concentrate on your career." Her response was immediate and unrehearsed, and I realized that she believed it. An appalling silence filled my head, an arctic calm.

"I never said that," I assured her. The very thought of it was absurd. I had sacrificed more than enough to the hollow idol of my law career. I would never give up the idea of children.

"You most certainly did," Barbara said. "I remember it clearly. You wanted to concentrate on the practice."

"Every time I brought up children, Barbara, you told me that you weren't ready yet. You changed the subject. If it had been up to me, we'd have five by now."

Strange awareness moved across her face, a shadow of understanding. "Maybe it was Ezra," she said, then jerked, as if stunned that she had actually said the words.

" 'Maybe it was Ezra'?" I repeated.

"That's not what I meant," she said, but it was too late. I knew what she meant, and suddenly my ears roared, a cacophony that threatened to knock me from my chair.

Maybe it was Ezra.

Maybe . . . it . . . was . . . Ezra.

I gaped at my wife as if from a distance and I understood. Ezra wanted me to carry on his tradition of greatness. She wanted me to make more money. *Children would distract me.* Her features rippled into something that terrified me. Wife and father had conspired to rob me of my children and I'd let them do it, as plodding and dumb as any farm animal. The clarity overwhelmed me. I stumbled from my chair, her voice a distant buzz. Somehow, I found the bottle of scotch and poured a full tumbler. Barbara was looking at me. Her lips moved, and then she walked to the kitchen on a stranger's legs. Time stood still as she rinsed plates, loaded the dishwasher, and wiped down the counter. She looked at me as she worked, as if worried that I might disappear. But I could not move; there was no one to lead me. I think I laughed at that.

When she finally came for me, I was drunk beyond words, lost in depths I never believed could exist. Stolen! The children I'd always wanted, the family I'd looked forward to since college. By those I should trust the most, my life had been stolen from me. And I'd let it happen. Call it blind trust. Call it cowardice. Call it the complicity of inaction. I shared the guilt, and the enormity of that fact overwhelmed me.

As if through fog, my wife's hand reached for me. She led me to the bedroom, put me down, and stood before me. Her lips moved and the words followed sometime later. "Don't worry, darling. We'll figure it all out. I'm sure Ezra provided." Her words made little sense.

She undressed, hanging her top carefully before turning back to present her breasts to me like manna from some other man's heaven. She slipped off her skirt, revealing legs of carved bronze. She was a statue brought to life, a trophy for good behavior. Her fingers found the fasteners of the clothes that should have armored me but didn't; she took my pants with a victor's smile, told me to relax, and knelt before me. I knew this was wrong but hid behind closed eyes as she spoke in tongues and wove spells of terrible power; so I surrendered myself, and in surrender knew the damnation of the utterly corrupt.

CHAPTER

10

Sunday morning, early, I cracked my eyes to cold gray light. It stole under the blinds to touch the bed but left most of the room dark. Barbara slept beside me, her leg sweaty against my own. I edged to the far side of the bed and held myself still. I felt fragile. Glue bound my eyelids, and the tongue that filled my mouth tasted like something long dead. I thought of the brutal truths so often borne on predawn light. I'd had a few in my time, and they'd all led to this. I was a stranger to myself. I'd gone to law school for my father, married for my father; and for that same man, and for the vile woman who shared my bed, I'd surrendered my dreams of family—my very soul. Now he was dead and all I had was this truth: My life was not my own. It belonged to an empty shell that wore my face. Yet I refused to pity myself.

I lifted my head to peer at Barbara: sleep-matted hair, creased skin, open mouth that glistened on the inside. My face twisted at the sight, but still, even on this dawn of revelation, I had to acknowledge her beauty. But I hadn't married her for her looks; I could tell myself that and believe it. I'd married her for her intensity, her energy. The tail wind of her convictions had swept me into her wake: She would make the perfect wife and only a fool would let her go. Somehow I'd come to believe that, and I thought that now I knew the ugly reasons why. Vanessa had said it: I married her for Ezra. Jesus.

My feet found the floor and I groped my way out of the room. In the laundry room, I found a pair of dirty jeans and some flip-flops. I collected the telephone and a pack of cigarettes and sat on the front porch. Mist was over the park and it was cold. I shivered as I lit up and blew smoke at the world. Nothing moved, and in the stillness I felt very much alive. I dialed Vanessa's number. Her machine answered and I knew that she was already out of bed, barefoot in the wet grass. As I waited for the beep, I decided to tell her the truth: that she was right and that I was sorry. Not that I loved her. Not yet. That had to be face-to-face, and I wasn't ready. There were other issues there, stuff that had nothing to do with truth or with the fact that my life was a mess. But I did want her to know that I understood. That she was right and I was wrong. So I let it all out. The words were just words, a pale start all in all, but they had to count for something. As I turned the phone off, I felt good. I had no idea what the future held, but I didn't care.

So I sat and I smoked, and something moved inside me that I recognized from a long, long time ago. The sun rose and put its warm red fingers upon me, and for a moment I was at peace. Then I felt Barbara's presence and she stepped through the door.

"What are you doing out here?"

"Smoking," I said, and didn't bother to turn around.

"It's six-forty-five in the morning."

"Is it?"

"Look at me, Work."

I turned around. She stood in the open door, wrapped in a fleece robe. Her hair was a mess, eyes puffy above a miserly mouth. I knew that her thoughts, like mine, were on last night. "What are you thinking?" she asked.

I gave Barbara my eyes as a warning, but I knew that she could not decipher even that pale message. She'd have to know me to get it, and we were strangers. So I gave her my thoughts, spelled them out in flat black letters that any moron could read. "I'm thinking that my life has been hijacked, held for ransom that I could never pay. I'm looking at a world that I've never seen before and wondering how the hell I got here."

"Now you're being silly," she said, and smiled like she could play this off.

"I don't know you, Barbara, and I wonder if I ever did."

"Come back to bed," she commanded.

"I don't think so."

"It's freezing out here."

"It's colder inside."

Her frown deepened. "That hurts, Work."

"I've figured out that truth often does," I said, and turned my back to her. In the distance, a man was walking toward us along the street. He wore a long trench coat and a hunting cap.

"Are you coming or not?" she insisted.

"I think I'll go for a walk," I told her.

"You're half-naked," she said.

I turned and smiled at her. "Yes," I said. "Isn't that a hoot?"

"You're frightening me," she said.

I turned back to watch my park walker and felt her step out onto the porch. For a long minute, she stared down at me, and I could only imagine what she might be thinking. Suddenly, her hands were on my shoulders, her fingers kneading me. "Come to bed," she said in her voice of oiled silk and bedroom pleasures.

"I'm awake now," I told her, meaning it in so many ways. "You go." I felt her hands withdraw, and she stood silently—angry, puzzled, or both. She'd spread her angel's wings, offered to lift me up, and I'd shot her down. Where would she go now? What lever could she trust to move me when the last resort of ready flesh had failed her in the end? I knew only that quiet retreat was not an option for her.

"Who've you been talking to?" she asked, a new edge in her voice. I glanced at the phone at my side, thought of Vanessa Stolen, and marveled coldly at my perspicacity.

"Nobody."

"May I have the phone?"

I took another drag.

"The phone," she insisted.

When I looked at her, I saw what I expected to see, thin lips in a face gone pale. "Do you really want to do this?" I asked.

In one movement, she stooped and snatched up the phone. I didn't try to stop her. She pushed the redial button and I turned away, to the strange man in his long coat. He drew nearer, his eyes downcast, his face all but hidden. I wondered if Vanessa would answer and hoped not; beyond that, I felt nothing, not anger or fear, not even regret. I heard Barbara disconnect, and her voice, when she spoke, was tight with anger. "I thought you were done with her."

"I thought so, too."

"How long?" she demanded.

"I don't want to talk about this, Barbara. Not now." I climbed slowly to my feet, hoping as I turned that I would see tears in my wife's eyes, anything to show that she felt more than wounded pride. "I'm tired. I'm hungover."

"Whose fault is that?" she snapped.

I pushed out a deep breath. "I'm going for that walk," I told her. "We can talk later if you still want to."

"Don't walk away from me!"

"Walking won't put any more distance between us."

"Oh. So now your adultery is my fault."

"I'm not talking about this now," I told her.

"I may not be here when you get back," she threatened. I stopped halfway down the steps.

"Do what you have to do, Barbara. Nobody can blame you for that, me least of all." I turned away from her heavy breathing and started down the sidewalk, heading toward the street and the park, which shimmered with cold dew.

"She's a dirty little whore. I've never understood your obsession with her," Barbara said to my back, her voice climbing. "Never!" The last word was a shout.

"Careful, Barbara," I said without turning to face her. "The neighbors will hear." I heard the door slam and imagined that she'd locked it, too. I didn't care. My life dropped away as I stepped off the property and onto the sidewalk. I was a man, like any other. I had taken action, stood my ground. I felt real and it felt good.

At the bottom of the yard, I waited for this man I'd seen a thousand times yet never really met. I got a better look at him as he approached. He was magnificently unattractive, with melted features and a grimace that pulled his lip over brown teeth, which showed only on the right side of his face. He wore grimy glasses with thick black frames and his hair hung limply from beneath the hunting cap.

"Mind if I walk with you?" I asked as he came level with me. He stopped and tilted his head at me. Green irises swam in a yellow sea and his voice, when he spoke, was a smoker's voice. I heard the same heavy accent.

"Why?"

There was distrust there.

"Just because," I said. "Just to talk."

"Still a free country." He resumed his walking and I fell into step with him.

"Thanks."

I felt his eyes on my naked chest. "I'm not gay," he said.

"Me neither."

He grunted, said nothing.

"You're not my type anyway."

He barked a laugh that ended with a snort of approval. "A smart-ass, huh? Who'd have thought?"

We walked down the sidewalk, past the big houses and the length of the park. A few cars were on the streets and some kids were feeding the ducks. The morning mist was slowly burning off the lake.

"I've seen you," he finally said to me. "Seen you for years—sittin' up there on your porch. Must be one heck of a view."

I didn't know what to say to that. "It's a good place to watch the world pass by, I guess."

"Hmph. Better you should pass through the world."

I stopped walking.

"What?" he asked.

"A blinding flash of the obvious," I told him.

"Meaning what?"

"Meaning I think you are a very smart man."

"Yes," he said. "I think you are right." He laughed at my expression. "Come on. We'll walk and you can compliment me. It's a good plan."

"I know your name," I said as we left the park behind and moved toward Main Street and the poor neighborhoods that lined the tracks beyond.

"That right?"

"I just heard it around. Maxwell Creason, right?"

"Just Max."

I held out my hand and he stopped, forcing me to stop alongside him. He held my eyes for an instant, then lifted up his hands to hold in front of my face. The fingers were broken and bent, twisted into claws, and I saw with horror that most of the nails had been ripped off.

"Jesus," I said.

"You know my name," he said. "And I don't mean any offense when I say this, but let's just leave it at that."

"What happened?" I asked.

"Look, I'm glad to talk to you—God knows, it's been long enough—but I don't reckon I know you well enough to talk about that."

I stared down at his hands. They hung like deadwood at the ends of his arms.

"But . . ." I started.

"Why do you care?" he asked sharply.

"You interest me."

"Why?"

"I don't know," I told him. "Because you're different." I shrugged again, feeling the inadequacy of my words. "Because I believe you've never asked a person what he does for a living."

"And that's important to you?"

I thought about it. "I guess so."

He began to shake his head.

"I want to know because you're real."

"What's that supposed to mean?"

I looked away from his face because there was a sudden nakedness there. "I've seen you, too, you know, here and there, walking. But I've never seen you with anybody else. I think there must be honesty in being that alone."

"And you value that?"

I looked back at him. "I envy it."

"Why are you telling me all this?"

"Because you don't know me, I guess. Because for once I'd like to be honest, too—tell somebody that I'd just as soon shoot my wife as look at her again, and that I'd gladly run over her friends on the street just to hear the thump." I shrugged again. "Because I don't think you'd judge me."

Max Creason was not looking at me; he had turned away. "Ain't no priest," he told me.

"Sometimes things just need to be said."

He shrugged. "So do something different."

"That's it? That's your advice? Do something different?"

"Yes," the park walker said. "Stop being a pussy."

The word hung there between us, and on the other side was his face, his very serious face; and in the echo of that blunt honesty, I laughed. I laughed so hard, I almost split myself open; and long before I finished, Max Creason joined me.

Three hours later, I walked up my driveway wearing a blue T-shirt with black letters that read DIG MY ROOT and holding the leash of a nine-week-old yellow Lab I'd decided to call Bone. The Johnsons told me he was the pick of the litter, and I believed them. He was very much like my old dog.

I walked Bone to the backyard and saw my wife through the bathroom window. She wore Sunday church clothes and was practicing smiles in the mirror. I watched for a minute, then gave Bone some water and went inside. It was 9:45.

I found Barbara in the bedroom, clipping on her earrings as she bustled about, looking at the ground as if to find her shoes or the patience to deal with me. She didn't look up, but her voice was chipper.

"I'm going to church. Are you coming?"

This was an old trick. Barbara rarely went to church, and when she did, it was because she knew I'd never go. It was a guilt trip.

"Nope. I've got plans."

"What plans?" She finally looked at me. No other questions. No reference to our fight or to my infidelity.

"Guy stuff," I told her.

"That's nice, Work." She started from the room, then stopped. "That's just perfect." She stormed out.

I followed her through the house and watched her grab her pocketbook and her keys and slam the door behind her. I poured a cup of coffee and waited. It took about five seconds.

The door flew open and Barbara scrambled inside, locking the door behind her and turning, horrified, to me. I leaned against the sink and sipped my coffee.

"There's a bum in our garage!" she said.

"No," I replied in exaggerated disbelief.

She peered through the window blind. "He's just sitting there now, but I think he made a grab for me."

I straightened to my full height. "I'll take care of it. Don't worry." I strode across the kitchen and pulled Barbara away from the door. I stepped outside, my wife crowding behind me with the telephone in her hand. "Hey!" I said. The bum looked up from the old newspaper he'd pulled from our recycling bin. His squint pulled his lips over the dark, rotten teeth. "Come on in," I told him. Max stood. "The bathroom's down the hall."

"Okay," he said, and came inside. It took us five minutes to stop laughing after Barbara burned rubber out of the driveway.

CHAPTER

11

An hour later, I was showered, changed, and clear in my head for the first time in what felt like years. It may have been years. What I knew was this: All you have in life is family. If you are lucky, that includes the kind you married. I was not so fortunate, but I had Jean. I'd take the fall for her if I had to.

I made two phone calls, the first to Clarence Hambly; after my father, he was considered the finest attorney in the county. He drew up Ezra's will. He'd just returned from church but reluctantly agreed to meet me later in the day. Next, I called Hank Robins, a private investigator in Charlotte whom I'd used on most of my murder cases. His machine picked up: "I can't take your call right now, probably because I'm out spying on somebody. Leave your number so I don't have to trace it." Hank was an irreverent bastard. He was thirty now, looked forty on a rough day, and was the most fearless man I'd ever met. Plus, I liked him. I told him to call me on my cell phone.

I left Barbara a note saying I might not be home that night and put Bone in the car. We went shopping. I bought him a new collar, leash, and dog bowls. I also picked up a thirty-pound bag of puppy food and a box of jerky treats. By the time I got back to the car, he'd chewed the leather off one of the headrests, which gave me an idea. I drove a BMW that Barbara had insisted would draw clients, which, in retrospect, was hilarious. I still owed a few grand on it and resented every payment. I took it to a shade-tree lot off Highway 150 and traded it for a five-year-old pickup. It smelled bad, but Bone seemed to like the taste of it.

We were having lunch in the park when Hank finally called. "Work, my man! Been reading about you in the papers. How's my favorite suit holding up?"

"I have to admit that I've been better."

"Yeah. Figured as much."

"How's your schedule these days, Hank?"

"Always busy. I even work sometimes. What've you got for me? Another Rowan County tragedy of love and deception? Rival dope dealers? Not another remote-control killer, I hope."

"It's complicated."

"The best ones always are."

"Are you alone?" I asked.

"I'm still in bed, if that answers your question."

"We need to talk in person."

"Salisbury, Charlotte, or in between. Just tell me when and where."

That was a no-brainer. I'd take any excuse to get out of town and get some breathing room. "How about six tonight at the Dunhill?" The Dunhill Hotel was on Tryon Street in downtown Charlotte. It had a great bar, full of deep and shadowed booths, and would be almost empty on a Sunday night.

"Should I bring you a date?" Hank asked, and I heard a giggle from his end of the phone, a woman.

"Six o'clock, Hank. And that crack will cost you the first round." I hung up, feeling better. Hank was a good man to have on your side.

Ezra's attorney had made it plain that I should not arrive before two. I had half an hour. I put the dog bowls and trash into the truck and whistled for Bone. He was wet from the lake, but I let him ride up front. Halfway there and he was in my lap, head out the window. So, stinking of wet dog and used truck, I walked up the wide steps of the Hambly mansion on its sprawling acres just outside of town. The house was huge, with marble fountains, twelve-foot doors, and a four-room guest house. A plaque beside the door announced that Hambly House had been built circa 1788. I thought maybe I should genuflect.

Judging from Clarence Hambly's face, I did not measure up to the learned colleague he'd expected to appear on this day of holy worship. Hambly was old, lined, and straitlaced, but he stood tall in a dark suit and paisley tie. He had thick white hair and matching eyebrows, which probably added an extra fifty dollars to his hourly rate.

He was genteel, whereas my father had been aggressive, as mannered as Ezra had been bullish, but he was still full of it; I'd seen him in court enough times to know that his Holy Roller attitude never interfered with his shameless quest for high-dollar jury awards. His witnesses were well prepped and slick. The Ten Commandments did not hang on his office wall.

He was old Salisbury money, and I know that my father had hated that about him, but he was good, and my father had insisted on the best, especially where money was concerned.

"I would prefer to do this tomorrow," he said without preamble, his eyes moving up from my scuffed hiking boots to my grass-stained blue jeans and the frayed collar of the shirt I refused to let die.

"It's important, Clarence. I need to do this now. I'm sorry."

He nodded. "Consider it a professional courtesy, then," he said, and ushered me inside. I stepped into his marble foyer, hoping that there was no dog shit on my shoes. "Let's go into my study."

I followed him down a long hall, catching a glimpse through large French doors of the pool outside and the manicured gardens beyond. The place smelled of cigars, oiled leather, and old people; I was willing to bet that his maids wore uniforms.

His study was narrow but deep, with tall windows, more French doors, and floor-to-ceiling bookcases. Apparently, he was into antique guns, fresh-cut flowers, and the color blue. An eight-foot gold-filigree mirror hung behind his desk; in it I looked rumpled and small, which was probably intentional.

"I'm putting your father's estate into probate tomorrow," he told me as he closed double doors and pointed to a leather chair. I sat. He moved behind his desk but remained standing. He looked down at me from this position of assumed authority, reminding me of how much I hated lawyer bullshit. "So there's no reason we can't discuss the details now. For the record, however, I was going to call you this week to schedule a meeting."

"Thank you for that," I said, because I was expected to. Never mind the enormous fee he would collect as executor of Ezra's estate. I steepled my fingers and concentrated on looking deferential, when what I wanted to do was put my feet on his desk.

"Also for the record, accept my condolences on your loss. I know that Barbara must be a great comfort. She comes from a fine family. A beautiful woman."

For the record, I wished there was shit on my shoes. "Thank you," I said.

"Although your father and I were often on opposite sides of the table, I had tremendous respect for his accomplishments. He was a fine attorney." He eyed me from his great height. "Something to aspire to," he concluded meaningfully.

"I don't want to take any more of your time than necessary," I reminded him.

"Yes, of course. To business, then. Your father's estate was sizable."

"How sizable?" I interrupted. Ezra had been secretive about his finances. I knew very little about it.

"Sizable," Hambly reiterated. I looked blank and waited. Once wills are put into probate, they become public record. There was no reason for reticence.

Hambly grudgingly conceded. "Roughly forty million dollars," he said.

I almost fell out of my chair—literally. I would have guessed six or seven million at the most.

"In addition to his skills as a lawyer," Hambly continued, "he was an adept investor. Other than the house and the building on lawyers' row, it's all in liquid securities."

"Forty million dollars," I said.

"A little over, actually." Hambly met my eyes and, to his credit, kept his face neutral. He'd been born rich, yet would never see forty million dollars. It had to gall him, and I suddenly realized that this was another reason my father had gone to Clarence Hambly. I almost smiled, but then I thought of Jean and the miserable house she lived in. I smelled stale pizza and pictured her face in the window of her beaten-down car, the way she'd heaved herself up the steps of Glena Werster's stone monument to greed and ego. At least that will change, I thought.

"And?" I asked.

"The house and the building go to you outright. Ten million dollars will fund the Ezra Pickens Charitable Foundation. You will have a seat on the board. Fifteen million dollars goes into trust for you. Taxes take the rest."

I was stunned. "What about Jean?" I asked.

"Jean gets nothing," Hambly stated, then sniffed loudly.

I came out of my chair. "Nothing?" I repeated.

"Sit down, please."

I complied because I lacked the strength to stand.

"You know how your father felt. Women have no business dealing with money or finances. It might be imprudent to tell you this, but your father changed the will after Alex Shiften came on the scene. Originally, he planned for two million to go into trust for Jean, to be managed by this firm or by her husband, should she marry. But with Alex in the picture . . . You know how your father felt."

"Did he know that they were sleeping together?" I asked.

"He suspected."

"And so he cut her out of the will."

"Basically."

"Was Jean aware of this?"

Hambly shrugged but didn't answer the question. "People do funny things with their money, Work. They use it for their own reasons."

I felt an electric tingle as I realized Hambly wasn't talking about Jean anymore. "There's more, isn't there?"

"The trust for you," Hambly began, finally taking his seat.

"What about it?"

"You will have full, unfettered use of the income it generates until age sixty. Conservatively invested, it should provide at least a million dollars a year. At sixty, you get it all."

"But?" I sensed a catch.

"There are certain requirements."

"Such as?"

"You are required to be actively engaged in the practice of law until such time."

"What?"

"This point is exquisitely clear, Work. Your father felt it important that you carry on the practice, that you maintain your place in society and in the profession. He was concerned that if he just left you the money, you might do something imprudent."

"Like be happy?"

Hambly ignored my sarcasm and the raw, naked emotion that must have been in my voice. Even from the grave, my father was trying to dictate the terms of my life, to manipulate me. "He was not specific in that regard," Hambly said. "But he was very specific in others. This firm will act as trustee. It will be up to us"—he gave me a thin smile—"up to me, actually, to determine whether or not you are actively engaged in the practice of law. One of the criteria, for instance, is that you bill at least twenty thousand dollars a month, adjusted for inflation, of course."

"I don't bill half that now and you know it."

"Yes." Another smile. "Your father thought this might prove to motivate you."

"Unfucking believable," I said, anger finally finding a voice.

Hambly rose to his full height and leaned forward, hands splayed on his desk. "Let me make one thing clear, Mr. Pickens. I will not tolerate profanity in this house. Is that understood?"

"Yes," I said through clenched teeth. "I understand. What else?"

"Any year that you do not satisfy the requirements of the trust document, the income from the trust will go to the Ezra Pickens Foundation. If in two of any five years you fail to meet the requirements of the trust document, the trust will terminate and the full corpus of the trust will transfer irrevocably to the foundation. However, when you reach age sixty, should you comply fully, the entire balance becomes yours to do with as you please. I will provide you with copies of all documents, of course."

"Is that it?" I asked, my sarcasm so thick, no one could miss it. I should have known better.

"In essence," he said. "But there is one last, small thing. Should it ever be shown that you have given any money whatsoever to your sister, Jean Pickens, either directly or indirectly, the trust will terminate and all funds will transfer to the foundation."

"This is too much," I said, on my feet and pacing.

"It's your father's last will and testament," Hambly said, correcting me. "His dying wish. Few would complain after hearing that fifteen million would be theirs to play with. Try to look at it from that perspective."

"There's only one perspective here, Clarence, my father's, and it's twisted as hell." The older lawyer started to speak, but I cut him off, watching his face redden as my voice rose and my respect for the rules of his house vanished. "Ezra Pickens was a twisted, manipulating bastard who never gave two shits for his own daughter and cared just a shade more than a rat's ass for me. Right now, he's laughing in his fucking grave." I leaned over Hambly's desk. I felt spit fly off my lips and didn't care. "He was a first-class asshole and you can keep his money. You hear me? Keep it!"

I subsided backward as the last words left me. I'd never felt such rage, and it left me spent. For an instant, there was silence, broken only by the slight tremble in the old lawyer's clenched fists. His voice, when he spoke, was tightly caged.

"I understand that you are under severe stress, so I'll try to forget your blasphemy, but don't ever come to this house again." His eyes hinted at the strength that made him such a good lawyer. "Ever," he reiterated. "Now, as your father's attorney and the executor of his estate, I'll tell you this: The will is valid. It goes into probate tomorrow. You may find that your position on this matter changes as your temper cools. If so, call me—at the office. As a final matter, I'll tell you something else. I hadn't planned to, but your behavior has changed my mind. Detective Mills has been to see me. She wanted to see your father's will."

If Hambly was watching for a reaction, he wasn't disappointed. My anger fled, replaced by something less honorable, something cold and slick that coiled in my stomach like a snake. It was fear, and with it in me, I felt naked.

"At first, I denied her, but she returned with a court order." Hambly leaned closer and spread his hands; he didn't smile, although I could feel it in him. "I was forced to comply," he said. "She was intrigued. You might wish to explain to *her* how fifteen million dollars does not interest you." He straightened and his fingers snapped shut. "Now, my courtesy has come to an end, as has my patience. Anytime you wish to offer your apology for desecrating my Sunday rest, I will consider it." He gestured at the door. "Now, good day to you."

My mind was awash, but one question had to be asked. "Does Mills know that Ezra cut Jean out of the will?" I asked.

"That question," he replied, seeming to relax into himself, "is best presented to Detective Mills. Now go away."

"I need to know, Clarence." I held my hands out, palm up. "Please."

"I'll not interfere with her investigation. Take it up with her or leave it alone."

"When did he cut her out? What date?"

"My obligation to you does not extend beyond that of executor and primary beneficiary to this will and the trust it establishes. Given the circumstances surrounding your father's death and the police interest in the matter, it would be unwise, for either of us, to take this matter further. I intended no other impression. Once the will is in probate, you may contact me at any time during business hours to discuss any relevant matters. Beyond that, we have nothing to talk about."

"What date was this will executed?" I demanded. A reasonable question, one within my rights.

"November fifteenth," Hambly said. "Year before last."

One week before my father disappeared.

I left, too angry to be scared. But I knew how it would play to the cops. If Jean knew that Ezra was going to cut her out of two million because of her relationship with Alex, it would be one more reason to kill him. That's how Detective Mills would see it. Did Jean know? When did she know? When did Ezra cut her out? I could hear Mills asking those exact questions. But had she?

Damn Clarence Hambly and his petty vindictiveness!

Back in the truck, Bone scrambled into my lap and licked my face. I rubbed his back, glad for the company. I realized that for the past days, while addled by alcohol, grief, and anger, the world had moved on. Mills had not been idle; she'd targeted me. I was a suspect. The concept was too much. I couldn't get my head around it. In the past day, I'd come to understand so many things, none of them pleasant. Now this. I had fifteen million dollars, but only if I surrendered what little remained of myself.

I sat in that driveway, under windows that looked like mirrored eyes, and dark thoughts twisted my mouth into a bitter smile as I thought of Ezra's will and his last effort to manipulate me. My life was still a mess, but in this regard I knew something that Ezra didn't, something that he could never imagine. Black humor moved where the fear snake had been; it bubbled like hot oil and it released me. I pictured Ezra's face, the horror if he only knew, the utter disbelief. I didn't want his money. The price was too high. The thought made me laugh, so that's what I did as I drove away from Hambly House, circa 1788. I laughed like an idiot. I fucking howled.

Yet by the time I got home, the hysteria was gone and I was empty. I felt lacerated inside, as if I were full of glass; but I thought of Max Creason, who'd had his fingers broken and his nails ripped out, yet who still has the strength and humor to tell a total stranger to stop being a pussy. It helped.

I put Bone in the backyard with food, water, and a belly rub, and then I went inside. My note to Barbara was where I'd left it. I picked up the pen and added this: "Don't be surprised to find a dog in the backyard—he's mine. He can come inside if you want." But I knew it wouldn't happen; Barbara didn't like dogs. The one I'd brought to the marriage, another yellow Lab, had never gotten to come inside. We'd been together for three years when I married Barbara; then he went from constant companion to barely tolerated nuisance, another casualty to poor choices. I vowed that would never happen again. As I watched Bone from the kitchen window, I felt the great hollowness of the house around me, its emptiness, and I thought of my mother.

Like my father, she was raised dirt-poor, but, unlike Ezra, she'd been content in her own skin. She'd never wanted the big house, the cars, and the prestige, none of it. Ezra, however, had been ravenous, and as he *bettered* himself, he came to resent her for the constant reminder she was. Ezra had hated his past, been ashamed of it, and history had shared his bed.

This was my theory, for how else could two people rise from abject poverty, bear two children, yet end up worse than strangers?

Years of this resentment had made my mother as hollow as this house, the well into which Ezra had dumped his anger, his frustration, and his hatred. She'd taken it all, borne it, until she was a shadow, and all she had for her children was her fierce embrace and the admonition to be silent. She'd never stood up for us, not until the night she died. It was that brief strength, that incandescent flash of will that had killed her, and I'd let it happen.

The argument had been about Alex.

When I closed my eyes, I could see the ruby red carpet.

We were at the top of the stairs, on the broad landing. I looked at my watch because I had to look away from Jean and from my father. She was defying him, and the explosion was building. It was four minutes after nine, dark out, and I barely recognized my sister. She was not the broken-down wreck that the psychiatric hospital had sent back to us. Not even close.

Mother stood, stunned, hand to her mouth. Ezra was shouting, Jean shouting back, jabbing a finger into his chest. It could not end well, and I stared as if at a train wreck; and I watched my mother reach out, as if she could stop the train with her ten small fingers.

And I did nothing.

"That is enough!" my father yelled. "That is how it's going to be."

"No," Jean said. "Not this time. It's my life!"

Father stepped closer, towered over her. I expected Jean to melt away, but she did not.

"It stopped being your life when you tried to kill yourself," he said. "Then it became mine again. You're barely out of the hospital. You can't possibly think right about anything. We've been patient, we've been nice, but now it's time for her to go."

"Alex is none of your business. You have no right to ask that."

"Let's get one thing clear right now, young lady. I'm not asking. That woman is trouble and I'll not have her messing up your head. She's just using you."

"For what? I'm not rich. I'm not famous."

"You know what."

"You can't even say it, can you? For sex, Dad. Yeah. For sex. We're fucking all the time. What're you going to do about it?"

Father went suddenly still. "You're an embarrassment to this family. It's disgraceful the way you two carry on."

"So there it is," Jean said. "It's got nothing to do with me. It's all about you! It's always been about you! Well, I've had it."

Jean turned to walk away. She didn't look at me, didn't look at Mother; she just turned and took a single step. Then Ezra grabbed her. He jerked her so hard that she fell to her knees.

"Don't you walk away from me! Not ever!"

Jean pulled herself to her feet and twisted her arm free. "That's the last time you'll ever put your hands on me," she told him.

The moment seemed to freeze, Jean's words hanging between them. I saw my mother's face, pure despair, and again her eyes beseeched me. Yet the shadow of my father held me, and Mother must have sensed this.

"Ezra," she said.

"You stay out of this," he commanded, eyes on Jean like a promise of violence.

"Ezra," she repeated, taking a monumental step toward him. "Just let her be. She's grown now, and she's right."

"And I told you to shut it!" His eyes never left Jean, and when she tried again to turn away, he snatched her up and shook her, an angry boy with a boneless doll; but Jean had bones, and I feared they might break. "I said don't you ever walk away from me!" Then he was grunting, incoherent, and Jean's head was loose on her neck. I watched as my mother took hell into her hands.

"Leave her alone, Ezra." She pulled at his massive arm. Jean had gone completely limp, but he continued to shake her. "Damn it, Ezra," she shouted. "Leave my daughter alone!" She began to beat on his shoulders with her narrow fists, and tears shone in the seams of her face. I tried to move, to speak, but I was paralyzed. Then he struck out, a

backhand that traveled forever; and then she was falling. Time seemed
to stand still but didn't; then she was crumpled at the foot of the stairs,
another boneless doll in the house my father made.

Jean collapsed when my father released her. He stared at his hand
and then at me.

"It was an accident, boy. You see that, don't you, son?"

I looked into his eyes, saw for the first time that he needed me, and
felt myself nod; it was an irrevocable step.

"Good boy," he said. Then the ground fell away and I tumbled into
the deep well of self-loathing.

I have yet to find its bottom.

If they'd found Ezra with only one bullet in his head, I'd have called
it suicide. How else to deal with the truth of his actions? And yet the
greatest sin can be one of omission; such was my burden, the cost of
which was my mother's life and my immortal soul. Protecting Jean
was my responsibility. I knew my mother's weakness as I knew my father's rage. Without words, she'd begged me to intervene, pleaded as
only the weak can plead. I don't know why I didn't act, but I fear that
my soul is flawed by some tragic weakness born under my father. For
it was not love for him that stayed my hand, never love. Then what?
I've never known, and that question haunts me still. So I've lived with
my failure, and slept with the memory of a cartwheel dance down
ruby-covered stairs.

Jean was barely conscious when it happened; she never knew for
certain, but she guessed, and in my eyes she saw the lie that had become Ezra's truth. When asked, I said that Mother had slipped. She
had tried to intervene in an argument and she'd slipped. It was just
one of those things.

Why did I cover for my father? Because he asked me to, I guess.
Because, for the first time, he needed me. Because her death *was* an
accident, and because I believed him when he said that nothing good

could come of the truth. Because he was my father and because I was his son. Maybe because I blamed myself. Who the hell knows?

So the police asked their questions and I spoke the horrible words; thus Ezra's truth became my own. But the rift between Jean and me was irreparable; it grew into a chasm and she retreated into her life on the other side. I saw her at the funeral, where the last shovel of dirt went onto our relationship as much as it did onto mother's casket. She had Alex, and for her that was enough.

By midnight on the night of my mother's death, the police had gone. We followed the darkened ambulance because we didn't know what else to do. At the back door of the hospital, she left us, carried by strangers into that pale, still building, taken to some cold room where the dead wait in silence. We stood in a light November rain, we three, speechless under a streetlamp and the weight of our own private thoughts. The truth of her death lay upon us, and our eyes refused to meet. But I studied my father when I could, caught the play of water down his face, the clench of muscles under whiskers that gleamed white under the light. And when the words finally came, they came from Ezra, as I knew they must. "Let's go home," he said, and we understood. There was nothing else to say.

At the house, the lights were on, and we sat in the living room while Ezra poured drinks. Jean refused to touch hers, but mine disappeared like magic and Ezra poured another. Jean's hands clenched and unclenched, wrestled on her lap, and I saw bright half-moons where nails bit into her palms. She rocked minutely, wound tight, and at times I heard her keen. I reached for her, but she jerked away. I wanted to tell her that I was not Ezra, not that it would have mattered. I see that now.

No one spoke and the minutes drew out, the only sound that of ice on glass and the heavy tread of Ezra's pacing.

We all jumped when the phone rang. Ezra answered it; he listened, hung up, and looked at us, his children. Then he left the house without a word. We were stunned, floored, and Jean left right behind him, a look on her face that I've never forgotten. At the door, she turned, her words like razors in my soul. "I know he killed her. And damn you for protecting him."

It was the last time I saw Ezra alive. For ten long minutes, I stayed in that house of horrors, that house of broken dolls; then I, too, left. I drove to Jean's, but her car was gone and no one answered when I knocked. The door was locked. I waited for an hour, but she didn't return. I went home and, in the best voice I could manage, informed my wife of the night's events. Then I had another drink. Eventually, I put her to bed, then sneaked out. I spent the rest of the night at Stolen Farm, weeping on Vanessa's shoulder like a goddamn child. At dawn, I crept into bed, where I put my back to my wife and watched gray light swell from beneath the blinds. I kept myself utterly still and held on to Ezra's truth as if for my very life. At the time, I thought it was worth something, but time can be a murderous bitch.

I felt pain and looked down at my hands, clenched so tightly on the kitchen sink that they were bloodless. I released them and they burned, but the pain was relative. I forced the images of that night back into the past, where I'd tried so hard to keep them. I was home. Bone was in the backyard. Ezra was dead.

I heard an engine outside and walked to the laundry-room window. A car was moving slowly up the driveway, and recognizing it, I thought of fate and of inevitability.

My life had become a Greek tragedy, but I'd done what I thought I had to do—to keep the family whole, to save what was left. I could not have known that Ezra would be killed, that Jean would despise me; but there is an undeniable sharpness to fact. Mother was dead. So was Ezra. Nothing would change that, not my own guilt, not a lifetime of pain. Done is done, end of fucking story. So I asked myself, as I had so many times, What price redemption, and where to find it?

I had no answer to that, and I feared that when the time came, I would lack the strength to pay the price. So standing there in that hollow house, I promised myself one thing, that when all this was past and I stood looking back, I would not face the same regret.

I prayed for strength.

Then I walked outside, where I found Detective Mills waiting in the driveway.

CHAPTER

12

Y ou'd better not have car keys in your hands," Mills said as I stepped onto hard concrete and squinted at the light reflected off her windshield. I held my hands out, palms up, to show they were empty.

"Relax," I told her. "I'm not going anywhere." She was wearing loose brown pants, low-heeled boots, and sunglasses. As always, the butt of her pistol showed from beneath her jacket. It was an automatic. The grip was checkered wood; I'd never noticed that before. I tried to remember if Mills had ever shot anyone. Regardless, I had no doubt that she could pull the trigger.

"As God is my witness, I don't know what to do with you, Work. If it weren't for Douglas, we'd be doing this at the station house. I have zero patience for your wounded-bird act. It's bullshit. You're going to tell me what you know and you're going to do it now. Do I make myself clear?"

Strain and fatigue were painted on her face thicker than the makeup she tried to conceal it with. I shook out a cigarette and leaned against her car. I didn't know what she was making of all this, but I had an idea. "You know why defense lawyers lose cases?" I asked her.

"Because they're on the wrong side."

"Because they have stupid clients. I see it all the time. They say things to the police that they can't take back, things that might be misconstrued, especially when there's pressure to break the case." I lit the cigarette, looked down the hill at a passing ambulance, its lights off. "It has always amazed me. It's as if they think that their cooperation will convince the cops to look at somebody else. It's naïve."

"But it keeps people like you in business."

"There is that."

"Are you going to talk to me or not?" Mills demanded.

"I'm talking to you now."

"Don't be a smart-ass. Not today. I don't have the patience for it."

"I've read the papers and I've been in this business a long time. I know the pressure you're under." Mills looked away, as if to deny what I was saying. "If I were smart, I would keep my mouth shut."

"You don't want to be on my bad side, Work. I can promise you that."

"That's what Douglas told me."

Emotion tugged at the corner of Mills's mouth. "Douglas was out of line."

"He just told me to cooperate." Mills crossed her arms. "Are we going to be straight with each other?" I asked. "No crap?"

"No problem," she said.

"I'll be as honest with you as you are with me. Fair?" She nodded. "Am I a suspect?" I asked her.

"No." She didn't hesitate, and I knew she was lying. I almost laughed, she was so transparent, but it would have been an ugly laugh, an "I can't believe this shit is happening" laugh.

"Do you have any suspects?"

"Yes."

"Anybody I know?"

"Everybody," she said, parroting the district attorney. I thought of Jean and prayed that she had not gotten that far in her interview with Clarence Hambly.

"Have you looked into his business dealings? Ex-clients?"

"I can't talk about the investigation."

"I know you talked to Hambly," I told her, watching closely for a reaction, getting none, just the same unbending mouth and eyes I couldn't see. "I know that you know about the will. Seems to me there are fifteen million reasons why you should be looking at me for the murder."

"That Hambly. He's a pompous windbag. He should learn to keep his mouth shut." Watching her, I finally understood why she hated lawyers so much. She couldn't intimidate them, and it killed her.

"So," I prodded. "I'm not a suspect?"

"Douglas says to lay off you. He says there's no way you killed your father, not for money. I can't find any other motive."

"But you've looked."

"I've looked."

"And you're going along with that?"

"As long as you're straight with me, I'll give Douglas his say. For now. But in the end, it's my investigation. Jerk me off and I'll come down on you so hard, your friends will bleed. Is that clear?"

"Crystal," I told her. "What else did you learn from Hambly?" I tried not to show how desperate I was for this information.

Mills shrugged again. "That your father was stinking rich and that if you didn't kill him, you're one lucky bastard."

"It's just money," I said.

"That's good," she told me. "Just money."

"Are we going to do this?" I asked.

"Yeah. Fine. About time."

"Then let's drive," I said. "Barbara will probably be home soon and I don't need her involved in this."

"Oh, I'll talk to Barbara," Mills said pointedly, making it clear that she was still the cop.

"But later, okay? Come on. You drive."

She took off her jacket and tossed it in the backseat. Her car smelled of the same overripe peach perfume I remembered from the hospital. She had the usual cop radios and a shotgun locked to the dash. Voices chattered on the radio and she turned it down as she backed down my driveway. I studied her from the corner of my eye, took in the cuffs, mace, and spare clip on her belt, the way her shirt gapped open, showing a pale lace bra that didn't go with the rest of her. Muscles stood out in her jaw, and I suspected that she would much rather have me in custody than squiring me around town on the city's nickel. I thought about what a good cop she was, reminded myself to be careful of what I said. She was looking for an excuse.

Once on the street, she turned right, past the park. We drove to Main Street in silence; then she pointed the car out of town, toward the long, impossibly narrow roads so typical of the county. "So talk," she said. "And don't leave anything out. I want to know everything that happened on the night your father disappeared. Don't edit. Don't choose. Give me everything."

So we drove, and I tried to speak with great care.

"Why were you there, at his house?"

"My mother's idea. Dinner. Trying to make peace, I guess."

Mills turned fractionally, cut her eyes away from the road. "Peace between . . . ?"

"Jean and my father."

"What were they fighting about?" she asked.

"*Fighting* is too strong a word. There was just a distance there. One of those father-daughter things."

"Specifically what?"

I wanted to lie, to protect Jean completely, but I feared that Mills would find the truth elsewhere. A lie now would only make it seem more important. That was the problem with talking to cops. You never knew what they knew. In the end, that's how they nailed you.

"I think it was about Alex."

"Your sister's girlfriend?"

"Yes."

"Your father didn't approve?"

"No, but it was an old argument. We'd been there before."

"Your sister was not mentioned in your father's will."

"She was never in the will," I said, lying. "My father had old-fashioned views about women."

"And why did your mother intervene?"

"She just got worried. It was a loud argument."

Mills kept her eyes on the road. "Did your father beat Jean?" she asked.

"No."

She looked at me. "Did he beat your mother?"

"No."

"Who was it again that called?"

"I don't know."

"But you were there when the call came in."

"I didn't answer it."

"Tell me exactly what your father said."

I thought back. "'I'll be there in ten minutes.' That's what he said. He answered the phone. He listened. Then he said he'd be there in ten minutes."

"He didn't say where?"

"No."

"He didn't tell you where he was going?"

"No."

"Who had called?"

"No. Nothing. He just left."

"How long was he on the phone?"

I thought about it. "Thirty seconds."

"Thirty seconds is a long time."

"It can be," I said.

"So someone had a lot to say."

"What about phone records?" I asked. "Lugs, pin numbers, anything like that?"

JOHN HART

"No luck," Mills said before she caught herself discussing the case and quickly changed the subject. "There had to be something else. Did he take anything with him? Say anything? How did his face look? Was he angry, sad, thoughtful? What direction did he drive?"

I thought about it, really thought about it. That was something I'd never done. How *had* he looked? What was in his face? Something. Resolution, perhaps. Determination. Yes. And anger. But something else, too. Smugness, I thought. The bastard looked smug.

"He looked sad," I told Mills. "His wife had just died and he looked sad."

"What else?" Mills pushed. "Did he take anything? Did he stop between the phone and the door going out? Think."

"He stopped for his keys," I said. "Just for his keys." And then I thought, *My God—his keys.* Ezra kept his keys on a hook board by the kitchen door. One set for his car, one set for his office. I saw it happen like it had been this morning. He moved past me, into the kitchen, his hand reached out—and he took both sets of keys. I saw it. He was planning to go to the office! But why? And had he made it before he was killed?

"There were no keys on his body," Mills said.

"Any sign of his car yet?" I asked, eager to distract her. I didn't want to talk about the keys. Not until I knew what it all meant. Why would Ezra go to the office? I thought about his missing gun, and I thought about his safe. It had to be opened.

"I can't talk about that. Did you ever hear from him again?"

"No."

"Phone calls? Letters?"

"Nothing."

"Why didn't you report him missing?" she asked.

"I did."

"Six weeks later," Mills reminded me. "A long time. That troubles me."

"We assumed he was in mourning somewhere, getting away from it all. He's a grown man."

122

"*Was* a grown man."

"What's your point?"

"My point is that he didn't even show up for the funeral, and still you didn't report him missing. That's just suspicious. No other word for it."

How to explain that? My father was not at the funeral because he killed her. He knocked her down the stairs and broke her neck! I'd figured that the guilt was destroying him. That he knew better than to face Jean and me with empty words and crocodile tears. Because not even Ezra could eulogize about what a fine person he'd killed. I'd guessed he was dead drunk or at the bottom of a high bridge. To me, that made sense. A lot of sense.

"Grief makes people do funny things," I said.

Mills gave me a very pointed look. "That's what I keep telling myself," she said. "If you know what I mean."

I didn't know what she meant, but her expression helped me guess. She still liked me for the crime. That was good for Jean, which made it good for me. But I couldn't do prison. I'd die before I did life in a box. But it wouldn't come to that; that's what I told myself. There had to be a way.

"I guess that brings us to the big question," Mills said. We were at the park. She turned onto the side street that ran past the lake and stopped the car. I could see my house and I got her message. You're not home yet. That's what she was telling me. Not by a long shot.

The engine ticked as it cooled. I felt her eyes on me. She wanted to look at me now, to focus. The car began to warm in the sun; the air grew stale, and I wanted a cigarette. I met her eyes as steadily as I could. "Where was I on the night in question?" I said.

"Convince me," she replied.

Decision time. I had an alibi. Vanessa would back me up, no matter what. The truth of that coursed through me like cool water. Measured against trial, conviction, and prison, it was the most valuable thing in the world. It's what every cornered criminal would kill to have. But did I want it? The answer was yes. I wanted it so badly, I could taste it. I wanted to turn Mills's withering stare away from me. I wanted to sleep in my own bed and know that I would never be some convict's bitch. I wanted to give her my alibi like a gift. Wrap it in pretty paper with a big bow.

But I couldn't. Not until Jean was in the clear. Should I be absolved, they would look to her. Dig deeply enough and they'd find a reason to like her for the crime, be it our mother's death, Ezra's will, or a lifetime of overpowering abuse. For all I knew, she'd kill for Alex. And thinking back to that night, as I had so many times, I knew that she could have done it. It was all in her face, the rage at her mother's death and the dismay of such utter betrayal. Ezra had left and she'd left right behind him. She could have followed him easily enough. And, like all of us, she'd known where he kept the gun. Motive, means, and opportunity—the holy trinity of criminal prosecution. Douglas would eat her alive if he knew. So I had to know she was safe before playing the alibi card. Yet I felt the weakness in me, fluttering deep and low. Strangely, the knowledge of it made me strong. I looked at Mills, whose face was all hard edges and sharp lines. In her glasses I saw my own features, distorted and unreal. It was too close to what I felt on the inside, so I grasped at that strength, and told one more lie.

"It's like I told Douglas. Dad left. I went home. I was in bed with Barbara all night."

Something moved on her face, a predatory glint, and she nodded as if she'd heard what she expected to hear. Or what she hoped to hear. She gave me a smile that made me nervous without knowing why.

"That's it, then?" she asked. "Think hard."

"That's it."

"Okay." She started the car and drove me the rest of the way home. "Don't leave town," she told me as I stepped out of her car.

"Ha-ha." I said. "That's funny."

"Who's joking?" she asked, flashing that same troubling smile. Then she backed down the driveway and was gone. I lit a cigarette and watched the empty spot in the road where her car had been. Then it occurred to me—why her smile troubled me. I'd seen it before, in court, right before she pulled the rug out from under whichever defense lawyer had the misfortune of underestimating her.

CHAPTER

13

I had a client early on, my first murder case. I was young, still idealistic, and even though he was guilty, I felt for him. He'd killed his neighbor in a drunken fight over a shared driveway. He didn't think the gun was loaded. He just wanted to scare the guy, a common enough story, until a bloody hole appeared in the man's chest.

The trial took eight days. I beat the murder charge, but the jury came back with manslaughter. My client bought seven and a half years, not bad in the big picture. Two hours after the verdict, I got a call to come to the infirmary at the county jail. My client had chugged half a gallon of cleaning fluid in an unsuccessful suicide attempt. The guards were laughing about it at central processing. The jail, they explained between smiles, used nontoxic supplies. My client would shit green for a week, then be okay. Happens all the time. Wink, wink, ha-ha.

I found my client in the infirmary. He was fetal and weeping, oblivious to me and to the guard stuck with suicide watch. It took him five minutes to meet my eyes and another five to respond.

"Don't you get it?" he pleaded.

I was speechless, clueless, I didn't get it.

"Look at me."

I shook my head to show I needed something more.

Then he screamed, veins like cords in his neck. "Look at me!"

I turned to my eyes to the impassive guard, who shrugged. "He's a bitch," the guard said. "Just look at him." My client was small and well formed, with fair skin and straight white teeth. He was attractive, maybe even beautiful.

Suddenly, in a sickening, visceral way, I got it.

"I can't go back to prison," he finally told me. "I'll die first. I'll fucking kill myself." He swore it to me. "One way or another."

Eventually, the story came out. He'd done time before, which I knew. Here's what I didn't know. There was a group of them. Sometimes only three or four. Sometimes seven. They'd tape a centerfold to his naked back and take turns—a screwdriver in his ear to keep him docile. He showed me the scar from the one time he'd fought back. He was still deaf in that ear.

He described it between choking, gut-wrenching sobs. That's what he was going back to. Sometimes for hours at a time.

"I can't do it, man. I just can't."

The next day, he was transported to Central Prison in Raleigh. Two weeks later, he finally managed to kill himself. He was twenty-seven years old, same as I was at the time. I've never forgotten him, for his was the most horrible display of utter despair that I've ever witnessed. Since then, I've skirted the prison system with something like morbid fascination, safe behind my briefcase, yet close enough never to forget what I saw in that young man's eyes.

So, yes. Mills scared me. Terrified me, in fact. I was playing a dangerous game, the stakes brutally real. But Ezra was dead, his shadow as tattered as his flesh, and I was finally learning a few things about myself.

I gave Mills two minutes to disappear, then threw myself into the truck. I had to talk to Jean, to warn her about Mills. Tell her to keep her mouth shut. And if she wouldn't listen, I'd make her. *One way or another.*

Powerful words.

I raced up Main Street but was stopped by an approaching train. So I cut right to Ellis Street and shot across the bridge, the train beneath me a black snake of chattering coal. I didn't know if Mills had talked to Jean or not. She could be en route, even stopped by this very train. So I drove with one eye on the road and dialed Jean's house on the cell phone. I got a busy signal, waited, and hit redial. Twice more I got a busy signal and then it was ringing. I was halfway there, doing fifty in a thirty-five, and the phone kept ringing. I counted fifteen rings, but no one answered. I slammed the phone down, tried to calm myself, but failed. I was near panic. Suddenly, the tension and fear were upon me, hot on my face, like sweat. I pictured Jean in prison and knew that she couldn't make it; it would kill her, sure as the bullets in Ezra's head.

Traffic began to fall away as I moved off the heavily traveled streets and onto the narrow ones where the houses dwindled onto small lots. Children played on the pavement, and I had to slow down for fear of killing one. I passed more and more dirt driveways as the tracks again drew near. Cars littered yards like derelicts and rust streaked the tin roofs of mill houses in their second century. The curbs fell into crumbled ruin and then I was on Jean's street. A tiny boy dangled from the tire-swing in the yard opposite her house, and he watched blank-eyed, his feet trailing in the dust. A face appeared at the window behind him, two eyes and a hint of mouth, then vanished behind mustard yellow curtains that flicked closed as I turned my head away.

I parked in front of Jean's house and turned off the truck. Alex Shiften sat on the front porch, tipped back in a rocking chair, feet on the rail. A cigarette hung from her mouth and she watched me from behind her glassless frames. The corners of her mouth dipped as I got out. I heard the train in the distance, and wind moved the treetops, but I couldn't feel it. The kudzu was still on the banks of the track.

I pulled myself taller and walked into the yard, twigs snapping under my feet. Alex never took her eyes off me. When I got closer, I saw that she had a knife in her hand, calmly shaving down a piece of wood. Her hair was uncombed, sticking up in spiky tufts, and the hard muscles of her arms moved as she whittled. She stood before I got to the steps, barefoot and wearing tight faded jeans.

"What do you want?" she demanded.

"Why didn't you answer your phone?" I shot back.

"Caller ID," she said, and smiled coldly.

I put one foot on the stairs and stopped. Her smile grew into a smirk as she folded the blade away and put the knife into her pocket, as if to say that she didn't need it to deal with me. She leaned against the pillar, and I felt an overwhelming sense of déjà vu. "I need to talk to Jean," I said.

"You always need to talk to Jean."

"Is she here? It's important."

"Gone," Alex replied.

"To work?"

Alex shrugged and looked away, smoke exploring the air around her head.

"Damn it, Alex! Is she at work?"

She stared down at me and slowly gave me the finger. An unrecognizable sound escaped my throat and I pushed past her, into the house. She didn't follow, which surprised me. I'd expected a fight.

The screen slammed behind me and I was in shadow, breathing musty air that smelled of cabbage. Alex's voice followed me. "Look all you want. It won't change anything. Jean's not here and she's got no use for you. So take one last look and then get the hell out."

The rooms were small, with low ceilings, the furniture old and shabby. I moved across the sagging floor in light that fingered through dusty windows to play upon my feet and the thin green rug. I passed the television, saw a framed photo of my mother there, and continued into the kitchen, knowing better than to look for one of me or of Ezra. Pots were stacked in the rack to dry, two places set at the narrow table under the window facing the backyard and the tracks that ran straight into the distance. An African violet was on the windowsill, its purple blossom a bright splash of lonely color.

I called Jean's name but knew already that Alex was right; I knew too well the feel of an empty house. I looked into the bedroom with no real hope and saw the single neatly made bed. I noticed the neat stack of catalogs on the table next to it, the facedown novel, and the water glass on its coaster. I remembered how I used to sit by Jean's bed at night and talk of childish things. Even then she used a coaster. She'd said that wood, like people, needed protection. I understood now that she'd been talking more about herself than about the table. I didn't get it—not then.

Suddenly, I missed her. Not the idea of her, but the intimacy we'd once shared, back when the world was smaller and sharing secrets was an easier thing to do. I put my fingers on the table, looked around the room, and wondered if they shared laughter here, if there was joy in their lives. I hoped so, but I doubted it. Alex was all about control. And Jean, she wanted direction, needed it desperately, and she'd take her cue from anybody.

I searched for some sign of our shared past, anything to indicate that she thought of those days or missed them at all, but there was nothing. My eyes traveled over the bare walls, the bookshelves, and then back to the bed. I turned to leave as the train passed so close, it shook the house; it screamed its mournful scream and was past, fading like memories of childhood.

I was almost to the door when it registered. I stopped and turned, walked back to the tall, narrow bookshelf in the corner, and stooped, my knees popping like an old man's. Wedged into the corner of the bottom shelf, almost as if hidden, was a tattered copy of *The Hobbit*, my gift to Jean on her ninth birthday. The cover was creased, the spine broken and fragile under my fingers. I'd put an inscription on the second page. I still remembered it: "For Jean—because little people can have adventures, too." I opened the book, but the second page was gone. Torn out or fallen out, I didn't know.

I put the book carefully back on the shelf.

Outside, I found Alex in her chair. "Satisfied?" she asked.

I fought to keep my temper down. Angering Alex wouldn't get me what I wanted.

"Do you know when to expect her?" I asked.

"No."

I removed a business card from my wallet and extended it to Alex. She looked at it but didn't take it. I placed it on the porch rail. "Will you ask Jean to call me when you see her? My cell-phone number is on the bottom."

"She won't call you, but I'll tell her."

"It's important, Alex."

"You already said that."

"Please. Just tell her." Alex hitched her hands behind her head. "If she calls me, I won't need to come back and bother you," I said. "Think about it."

"What's it about?" she asked.

"That's for me and Jean," I told her.

"I'll find out anyway."

"That's fine, but not from me." I stepped off the porch, turned, and gestured at my card on the rail. "It's the number on the bottom."

"Yeah, yeah."

I moved into the yard, anxious to be away from Alex and her quiet smugness; then I heard the knife blade click open and the sound of a small laugh. "I know what it's about anyway," Alex said. I kept walking, tired of her bullshit. I was almost to the truck. "'You have the right to remain silent. . . .'" she said, and I froze.

"What did you say?" I asked, stepping away from the truck, keys dangling in my hand. Her smile spread like a cancer.

"'Anything you say may be used against you in a court of law.'" She was on her feet, hands on the rail, hips thrust against the wood, leaning out, taunting. I walked toward her and she leaned farther out over the rail, her mouth open beneath shiny eyes; she was enjoying herself.

"'If you cannot afford a lawyer, one will be appointed for you.'" Then she laughed, either at my expression or at her own cleverness. Both perhaps.

"What the hell are you talking about?" I asked.

She looked down at me and I up at her. The moment drew out. "We met a very pretty lady," she finally said. "Me and Jean."

"What?"

"A very pretty lady. A very curious lady." She waited, as if for me to speak, but I couldn't. "A very well-armed lady."

"Mills." The name tunneled past my lips.

"She had lots of fun questions," Alex said.

I knew that Alex was toying with me, twisting this in my guts for her own amusement. I shrank beneath a terrible sense of failure, of impending doom. I should have spoken to Jean immediately after I learned of Ezra's body. I should have warned her, used my law degree for something good for a change. But at first, I'd been scared, that day at Pizza Hut, scared that she would walk away, leave me forever. Scared that I would see the truth in her eyes, that she *had* killed him. Scared that my suspicions would be made irrevocable fact. Scared of how I'd handle that. Then, for days, I'd been drunk and full of self-pity. I'd said nothing, and opened the door to ruin. What had Jean told her? How far down the road had she traveled while I wallowed in the trough of my fetid marriage and wasted life? I tasted despair like bile. Mills was no fool. Of course she would investigate Jean.

"Questions about you," Alex continued.

I felt the return of a certain calm. "Why do you hate me so much?" I asked.

"I don't hate you at all," she said. "You're just in my way."

"You're not going to tell me what I want to know, are you? About Mills?"

"Like you said . . . that's for you and Jean."

I saw in her face that she was done. She'd had the last word and was content. She settled back into her chair and picked up the piece of whittled wood, gestured to my truck with it. "Go on," she told me. "I'll tell Jean you stopped by."

I walked away and didn't look back until I was in the truck with the engine on. She didn't know it, but she'd given me something. More than what she'd intended. I was in her way, she'd said. That meant that Jean still cared for me, one way or another, and that was better than nothing.

I called Pizza Hut as I drove away and was told that Jean was not working today. For the next hour, I drove around town, looking for her car. I checked the mall, the movie theaters, and doughnut shops. She was nowhere. Finally, in quiet desperation, I called her house again. No one answered.

At five o'clock, I left for Charlotte to meet Hank Robins. Traffic was unusually light on I-85, so I made good time. By six, I was ensconced in a deep leather booth at the back of the bar. The place was dimly lighted, and there was soft music that sounded vaguely Celtic. I found a half-empty pack of Gitanes cigarettes next to the glass ashtray and shook one out. I tore off a match, lit up, and dropped the pack onto the lacquered wood table as the waitress weaved through the room. She reminded me of Jean, something in the way she walked. The smile she offered was tired. I wanted a Manhattan, something strong, but I ordered a beer instead, a Beck's.

For all intents and purposes, I had the place to myself, so I sipped my beer and blew smoke rings through the dim shaft of light that speared my table from above.

"Nice," a voice said, and Hank Robins slid into the booth opposite me. He pointed at the ragged remains of the smoke ring. "Good form."

"You're late," I told him.

"Sue me," he said.

He took my hand and pumped it a couple of times, smiling through the smoke. "How are you, Work?" he asked, then went on without a pause. "I'm real sorry about all this. I know it's got to suck."

"You don't know the half of it."

"That bad?"

I shrugged.

"What's a guy got to do to get a drink around here?" he asked, then raised his voice. "Waitress. Two more."

Hank was an anachronism. He stood five eight, weighed about 140, yet was the most fearless man I'd ever met. I'd never seen it myself, but word was that he'd take on guys twice his size and come out on top. He had thick black hair, merry green eyes, and a chipped front tooth. Women loved him.

We'd worked a dozen cases together and I knew he was good. We got along, because neither one of us labored with illusion; we were realists, although he managed to do it without giving a damn. To him, the world would never make sense, so he just went with it. Nothing surprised him, yet he found humor everywhere he looked. I admired that about him. The world I saw was ragged.

Our waitress appeared with drinks and the same tired smile. She kept her eyes on Hank, so I studied her. Midforties, I guessed, with heavy features and bitten nails. "Thanks, doll face," he said, and gave her his dazzling chipped-tooth smile. She looked embarrassed, but she swept away with a livelier step.

"Do you ever piss them off?" I asked.

"Only the smart ones."

I shook my head.

"Hey," he said. "Everybody likes a compliment. It's a cheap way to make the world a better place." He sipped his beer. "So what's up with you? You look like shit."

"Where's my compliment?" I asked.

"That was your compliment."

"Thanks."

"Seriously, man. How are you?"

Suddenly, my eyes felt heavy. I couldn't pull them up from the bottle they stared at so intently. There was no answer for his question. Because no one wanted to hear the truth of how I was.

"Hanging in there," I finally said.

"I bet you're tired of giving that answer," he said, letting me know that I wasn't putting one over on him. Then he smiled to show that he was okay with that. "If you change your mind . . ."

"Thanks, Hank. I appreciate that."

"So," he said. "Let's talk business. I assume you want me to help figure out who killed your father."

My surprise must have shown on my face. But of course that was what he'd think; I should have seen it coming. I had to be careful. Hank and I were colleagues and occasional drinking buddies, but I had no idea how far his loyalty would extend. He was clearly puzzled.

"I never liked him much," I said. "The cops can handle that one."

"Okay," Hank said slowly, obviously at a loss but not wanting to push. He drummed his fingers twice on the table. "So . . ." He waited for me to fill in the blanks. So I did. Somewhat. It took a while. Then I told him what I wanted.

"Jesus," he said. "I didn't know you had such a high opinion of me."

"Can you do it?" I asked.

"I wish I could say yes, but I can't. You want to find out who tossed that chair down the stairs, and I don't blame you. But I'm not a fingerprint technician and I don't have access to AFIS or any other fingerprint database. What you need is a cop and a full crime-scene work-up. That's out of my league."

"The cops won't go there," I told him. "They don't believe me, and I'm not sure I want to push it."

"Then you're screwed, man. I'm sorry."

I shrugged. His answer didn't really surprise me. But I wanted to know who was responsible. It had happened, and it had happened for a reason. Maybe it had something to do with Ezra's death and maybe it didn't; either way, it was important. "What about the safe?" I asked.

"For that, you need a locksmith or a criminal. I'm neither."

"I thought that maybe . . ."

"What? That maybe I'd know someone?" I nodded. "As it turns out," he said. "I do. But he's in lockup. Ten to twelve. Why don't you just use a locksmith?"

"Because I don't know what's in there, and I don't want some stranger knowing, either. Not when the cops are so interested."

"You hoping to find the gun?"

I nodded. If the gun was in the safe, then maybe Jean hadn't killed him after all. And if she hadn't . . . then I'd get rid of the evidence. Besides, who knew what other secrets Ezra had tucked away in that safe?

"I'm sorry, Work. I feel like I'm letting you down. All I can tell you is this: People are predictable. When they set combination locks, they usually use numbers that are important to them. You should think about that."

"I already tried. Birthdays, Social Security numbers, phone numbers."

Hank shook his head sadly, but the twinkle in his eyes was not unkind. "I said predictable, Work, not stupid. Think about your father. Figure out what was important to him. Maybe you'll get lucky."

"Maybe," I echoed, unconvinced.

"Look, man. I'm sorry you wasted your time. I wish I could help."

"Well, there is one other thing," I told him. "It's personal."

"I can do personal." He pulled on the beer, waiting.

"It has to do with Jean."

"Your sister."

"Right." Then I told him what I wanted.

He took out a piece of paper and a pen. "Okay," he said. "Tell me everything you know about this Alex Shiften."

So I told him what I knew. It didn't take long.

He tucked the paper away in his shirt pocket just as two women seated themselves at the bar. They were both in their midtwenties, both beautiful. They looked at us, and one of them waved minutely. Hank played it off, but I wasn't fooled. "Did you set this up?" I asked, gesturing at the women.

His grin gave him away even before he spoke. "I thought you could use the cheering up."

"Well thanks, but I've got enough women in my life right now.

One more is the last thing I need." I started out of the booth. He stopped me with a hand on my arm.

"This one doesn't have to be in your life, Work. Just your pants. Trust me."

"Thanks anyway," I said. "Maybe next time."

Hank shrugged. "Have it your way. But listen, before you go." His voice was low and serious. "Take care, all right? This case is getting big press, even here in Charlotte. Whoever's working it won't care about stepping on toes. So watch your ass."

For a moment, I thought I'd been indiscreet, that I'd opened myself too much. That he'd guessed at the larger truth. But there was nothing in his eyes beyond simple goodwill.

"I'll do it," I told him, and put a twenty on the table.

"Hey, man. My treat."

"Buy your friends a round on me. We'll talk later."

Outside, the day died a slow, purple death, its breath a sigh of wind on the near-empty streets. A narrow blade of orange scarred the darkening clouds, then faded as I watched. I felt the heat of the day trapped in the concrete beneath my feet; it made me think of hell, yet cooled even as I walked.

If I was to save Jean, then I wanted to save her all the way, and that meant dealing with Alex. To do that, I needed information. That's where Hank came in. I wanted him to ferret out whatever truth made Alex tick. Jean loved Alex. Fine. But what did Alex want? Hard as I tried, I couldn't find the capacity for love in her. Yet she found something in my sister. I just wanted to make sure it was nothing bad.

CHAPTER
14

Back on the interstate, I drove as fast as the pickup could handle, and forty minutes later I turned onto her street. The streetlamps were burned out or broken, but I saw a glimmer of light behind her windows. I stepped out of the truck to the sound of a distant bark and the call of crickets in the brush along the track. Somewhere a television played. I climbed the shallow steps to her porch and glanced through the narrow crack of the curtains. The room beyond was dark, but I saw them in the kitchen, at the table. Jean had her back to me; Alex's face was a dim blur above her shoulder. There were candles on the table, a warm flicker, and I heard Jean laugh. Who was I to judge Alex? I'd not made my sister laugh since that long-ago night when her husband left with the baby-sitter and her world evaporated at a rest stop on I-85.

I almost left, but still there was a corpse, and the certainty that Mills would not rest. I knocked and heard the laughter die, the scrape of chairs. Then there was Jean, her eyes heavy as she said my name in surprise. Alex, behind her, frowned in annoyance and slipped an arm across Jean's throat, cupping her shoulder with long, tapered fingers.

"Hi, Jean," I said. "Sorry to bother you."

"What are you doing here?"

Her face was warmer than the last time I'd been here, and I flicked a glance to the flinty black points that Alex called eyes. "Didn't Alex tell you I came by earlier, looking for you?" Jean shifted and I saw Alex tighten her grip.

"No," Jean said uncertainly, her head turning a fraction before squaring back on me. "She didn't mention it."

I looked between the two, from Jean's pale face to the brittle lines of her lover's. Jean's eyes were moist, and I thought I smelled wine. "May I come in?" I asked.

"No," Alex said before Jean could reply. "It's late."

Jean put her hand on Alex's arm and gave it a squeeze. "No," she said. "It's all right. He can come in." She gave me a half smile, and I felt a wash of gratitude.

"Thanks." I entered her house, smelling the perfume Alex wore as I pushed past her. Jean turned on lights, and I saw that she was wearing a dress and pale pink lipstick. I noticed that Alex, too, was well dressed. The house still smelled of food. "Is this a bad time?" I asked. Jean hesitated, but Alex filled the void.

"We're celebrating an anniversary." She paused, as if she wanted me to ask. "Two years together." She moved her hand to the back of Jean's neck. Her point was plain, so I addressed myself to Jean.

"I need to talk to you. It's important." I saw Alex sneer, thought of her taunting words on my last visit. "I know this is a bad time, but it won't take long." Alex released my sister and flung herself onto the couch, her hands again behind her head, a look of wide-eyed expectancy on her face. "I'd like to speak to you alone," I said.

Jean's glance moved between us, confusion making her vulnerable, and I remembered how when we were kids, she would go anywhere with me.

"You should talk here," Alex said to Jean.

"We should talk here," Jean parroted, and I watched her sit next to Alex, the way she settled against her. "What do you want to talk about?"

"Yes, Work," Alex said. "What *do* you want to talk about?" Her eyes were laughing. *You have the right to remain silent.*

I tried to come up with the best approach, the best way to raise such a delicate subject, but all the rehearsed lines, all the clever ideas that had come to me during the drive to and from Charlotte dried up and blew away like dust.

"You don't have to talk to the police," I said. She tensed, alarmed, and turned to Alex. "In fact, it would be best if you didn't."

"I don't know what you mean," she said, her mouth working as if to find other words. "The police? What are you talking about?" She seemed frightened, nervous, suddenly alive on the couch. Alex laid a hand on her leg and she calmed visibly. Then, as if accepting the inevitable, she said, "Oh, you mean Detective Mills?"

"That's right." I nodded. "She's the lead detective on Father's murder investigation. We should have talked about this sooner. . . . I just want you to understand how this works. What your rights are—"

Jean cut me off, her eyes wild. "I don't want to talk about this. I can't talk about this." She struggled off the low couch.

"I don't—"

"Detective Mills said not to talk about this with anybody. She said I had to keep quiet."

Her behavior puzzled and concerned me. "Jean," I began.

"I didn't tell her anything about you, Work. Honestly. She asked a whole bunch of questions, but I didn't say anything about you."

Alex spoke into the silence of my dismay. "Just tell him, Jean. It's the only reason he's here."

"What are you talking about?" I demanded, and Jean stared at me as if I were a stranger. Her mouth opened; her lips silvered with saliva from her tongue.

"Mills thinks you did it," Alex said. "That's what she wanted to talk to us about. She thinks you killed Ezra."

"That's what she said?"

"Not in so many words."

"What did you tell her?" I asked, my eyes on Alex but the question meant for Jean. Alex didn't say a word, and Jean seemed to be slipping further away. She nodded several times.

"I can't talk about this," she said. "I can't. Just can't."

I saw that tears had gathered in her eyes. She looked panicked, pacing from side to side like a caged animal.

"It's okay, Jean," I told her. "Everything's okay."

"No!" she shouted. "No, it's not."

"Just take it easy."

"Daddy's dead, Work. He's dead. Killed. He killed Mom and somebody killed him. Somebody, somebody." Her voice trailed away with her eyes, which moved aimlessly across the floor. She stopped pacing and began to rock, her fingers twisted white against each other.

Looking at Jean, at her waxen face, I finally accepted the truth of my worst fear. She had killed Ezra. She'd pulled the trigger and the truth of that was unhinging her. Her mind was adrift, rudderless behind eyes that saw some unspeakable horror. How long had she been like this? And was she already too far gone?

I found myself on my feet, reaching to offer what comfort I could. I touched her shoulder and her eyes snapped up, wide and white. "Don't touch me!" she said. "Don't anybody touch me."

She backed away, hands outstretched. She found the bedroom door with her back and pushed it open. "You should just go home, Work. I can't talk to you."

"Jean," I implored her.

Her eyes were still wet, glazed under the dim bulbs. She backed farther into the bedroom, her hand on the door, ready to close it. "Daddy always said that done is done, and that's where we are. I said my piece, Work. I told that woman nothing about you. Now you go home. Done is done." A strange gurgling noise escaped her, half sob, half laugh. "Daddy's dead . . . and done is done." Her eyes moved from me to Alex. "Right, Alex?" she said. "That's right, huh?" Then, eyes still wild, she closed the door.

I felt light-headed. Jean's words filled my mind. Her words and her face, an expression I could never forget. I started when I felt Alex's hand on my shoulder. The front door was open and she pointed at it.

"Don't come back," she told me. "I mean it."

I gestured helplessly at the door that hid my sister. "What have you done to her?" I asked, knowing that, for once, Alex was not to blame. Knowing and not caring. My arm dropped to my side. "She needs help, Alex."

"Not from you."

"There's nothing you can say or do that will make me abandon her." I stepped closer. "Either you get her some help or I will. Do I make myself clear?"

Alex didn't back down, and I felt her finger, hard on my chest. "You stay away from Jean! From us and from this house!" She jabbed at me, her eyes fierce. "You," she said, jabbing again, "are the problem. You!"

We stood there. The line had been drawn, but in her eyes I saw a glimmer of terrible truth. I *was* the problem. Not entirely, but in part. I could taste the guilt.

"This isn't over," I told her.

"Get the fuck out," she said.

For once, I didn't argue; I just walked dumbly into the sweet night air. The door closed with a click and I heard the bolt drop.

I was outside the gates, and I was utterly alone.

I retreated into the womblike silence of the truck and, eyes on the darkened house, I relived the moments of Jean's deterioration. How long, I wondered, until she tried to kill herself yet once again? The signs were there, and some dark part of my mind spoke nightmare words.

The third time's the charm.

And I feared that it was only a matter of time.

I started the truck and the engine put a vibration inside of me. I felt the stutter in my heart as the truth of what I'd learned began to squeeze it. There could no longer be any question. Jean had killed him. My baby sister. She'd put two bullets in his head and left him to rot. Her words rang in my head—*done is done*—and I knew, more now than ever, that it would fall to me to save her. She could never do prison. It would kill her.

But what course to take? How to keep Mills from putting two and two together? It was not easy math, and I could only come up with one answer. Keep her eyes on me. I'd take the fall for Jean if I had to, but that was the last resort.

There had to be a way.

When I got to the park in front of my house, I realized that I couldn't remember the drive that had gotten me there. I'd been at Jean's and now I was at the park. Blink. Gone. Scary stuff.

I turned onto the side street that ran beside the lake, toward home, and saw a pickup truck parked at the curb, facing the lights of my house. As I drew closer, I recognized it. I slowed down, way down. It was Vanessa's.

I pulled up next to it and stopped. I turned off the engine. I saw her through the window, hands gripping the top of the steering wheel, her head on her hands, as if asleep or in prayer. If she knew I was there, she didn't show it, and for long seconds I watched her, aware of my breath in the silence. Slowly, reluctantly, she lifted her head and turned to face me. In the darkness, I could see little of her, just the outline of features I knew so well. I rolled down my window.

"What are you doing here?" I asked her.

"You scared me," she said stiffly.

"I didn't mean to." She sniffed and I realized that she'd been crying, watching my house and crying.

"I got your message," she said. "I thought I wanted to see you. But . . ." She gestured at the house, and I noticed for the first time that there were strange cars in the driveway and that all the lights were on. She wiped at her cheeks and I knew that I'd embarrassed her.

"You thought . . ." I began.

For a long minute, she said nothing. A car turned onto the road, and in its headlights she was drawn and beautiful. "You hurt me, Jackson." A pause. "I don't think I can let you hurt me like that again. But then you left that message. . . ." She broke then, and a tiny sob escaped before she clamped down again.

"I meant it. All of it."

"I've got to go," she suddenly declared. Her hand found the ignition.

"Wait," I said. "Let me go home with you. Back to the farm." I would tell her everything—about Jean, about Ezra, but mostly about my feelings for her, and about the shame I'd hidden from her all those years. "There's so much to say."

"No." Her voice was sharp and loud. Then softer: "I can't go there. Not again."

"Yes, you can."

"No, I can't. If I did, I fear you would destroy me, and I've decided that nothing is worth that." She put her truck into gear. "Not even you."

"Vanessa, wait."

"Don't follow me, Jackson."

Then she was gone, and I stared at her taillights; they grew smaller, turned, and disappeared. I closed my eyes but could still see red. Eventually, I went home, parked between a Mercedes and a BMW, and entered the kitchen through the garage. There was laughter in the dining room beyond; it rolled across me as I walked into the room.

"Oh, there you are," my wife said. "Just in time for the second course."

Then she was up and sweeping toward me, a smile creasing her face beneath eyes I could not read. There were two other couples there, the Wersters and a pair I couldn't name. They were smiling, amused, and suddenly Barbara was at my side, smelling of perfume and wine. She brushed at my shirt. Up close, I saw that she was worried. No, I thought. She looked terrified. She leaned into me, hugged me, and said very quietly, "Please don't make a scene." Then she leaned back. "We've been worried about you."

I looked beyond her; everybody was nodding and smiling, perfectly groomed above a linen cloth and polished silver. Red wine in cut crystal held the light of a dozen candles, and I thought of Jean and the melted wax on her wobbly kitchen table. I saw her in orange prison fatigues, in line for lunch as something brown and lukewarm was slapped from a spoon onto a molded metal tray. The image cut so deeply, I had to close my eyes. And when I opened them, Bert Werster still sat in my chair. "I'll go change," I said, then turned and walked out. I passed through the kitchen, picked up a bottle of bourbon, and walked straight out the back door.

As it closed behind me, I heard another burst of laughter. Outside, in the night air, I looked at the sky and tried to bleed away the tension. Then I heard more laughter, like the sound of passing traffic, and knew that it would not be that easy. How long, I wondered, until they realized I wasn't coming back? What excuse would Barbara offer for the imperfection of her marriage?

I walked around back, where I found Bone scrabbling to get under the fence. I put him in the truck, and I drove us away from that place without a backward glance. I couldn't save Jean, not tonight. But Vanessa was in pain, and I decided that it was time to deal with this shit once and for all. So as I watched the road, bright in the headlights, I thought of what I would say to Vanessa. I thought of the day we'd met. The day we'd jumped for Jimmy. I was twelve years old, and they said I was a hero. They said I was brave, but I wouldn't know about that. What I remember was being scared, and then being ashamed.

His name was Jimmy Waycaster. Everybody called him "Jimmy-One-T." There was a reason for that.

CHAPTER

15

Jimmy had only one testicle, a fact that followed him when he transferred in from some place out of county. His parents had no other children, which didn't stop Coach from putting him at shortstop the next spring. First game of the season, and Jimmy took one on the second pitch. When Jimmy dropped, there was stunned and absolute silence. Until he started screaming.

As it turned out, Jimmy's family was poor. And the surgery to save his last testicle was expensive. One of the other parents organized it, and two weeks later we jumped for Jimmy. It happened at the Towne Mall, back when it was open and fresh, before bodies were turning up in boarded-up stores. The plan was simple. Kids would collect pledges and jump rope in teams of four. So much for every hour the team jumped. It was supposed to last an entire day. There were twenty teams. Eighty kids.

Vanessa was one of them. So was I.

She was beautiful.

I guessed she was around fifteen, a freshman or a sophomore, which was pretty cool. Not many of the older kids turned out to jump for Jimmy's nut. I noticed her purple dress the minute I walked in. She was down the long corridor, across from Sky City. She caught me staring once or twice but didn't seem to mind. She even smiled, but it was a nice smile, not slutty or anything.

After that, I thought mostly about her smile, and what it would be like to kiss it. I thought about it a lot. It was that kind of smile.

There were a lot of parents, but none of them paid much attention. It was just a bunch of kids jumping rope. Every ten minutes, we'd switch, so you'd have thirty minutes before your next shift. Time to go to the arcade, hang with your friends, and watch the girl in the purple dress. Then it was your turn and you'd jump. It was an all-day thing. Parents appeared and disappeared, shopped and went for coffee.

Two hours into the day and I couldn't stop thinking about her. She had blond hair and wide blue eyes. Her legs were long beneath hips that flared just a little. She laughed a lot and was nice to the younger kids. I thought she was about the finest thing I'd ever seen, and with our eyes we seemed to find each other.

"Don't waste your time," a voice said. I recognized it without looking—Delia Walton, snotty bitch daughter of somebody or other. She and a couple of other girls pretty much ran the school. They were the popular ones, with flawless skin and gold beads that gleamed at their throats.

"What's her name?" I asked.

"Vanessa Stolen," Delia informed me. "She's old. In high school."

I just nodded, eyes still on Vanessa Stolen. Delia didn't like it. She knew what I was seeing.

"She's white trash," Delia insisted.

"Isn't it your turn to jump?" I asked.

"Yes," she said, and waved dismissively.

"Then go jump," I told her, and walked away.

Lunch came and went and the kids kept jumping. I heard an adult say that we'd probably raise over eight thousand dollars, which seemed like a lot for a nut.

It was about three o'clock when I saw the girl in the purple dress go outside. It didn't surprise me when I followed her, just scared me a little. But the day wouldn't last forever.

Outside, a hot wind blew; it carried the smell of exhaust into the parking lot. Cars flew by on the interstate. Birds watched from the power lines. Then I saw her, down by the creek, near where it flowed under the parking lot. She was watching her feet, kicking at tiny stones. She looked serious and I wondered what she was thinking and what I should say to her when I finally got the nerve.

She passed the last of the cars. We were far from the mall. No one else was around. No kids. No parents. Just us. She was almost at the creek, the tunnel dark along the steep overgrown bank. Clouds passed over the sun and it grew dark. The wind stilled itself and for a moment I looked up.

Then I saw Vanessa start, her hands flying up as if to catch something, but she didn't make a sound. She took a single step backward. Then a man, long-armed and bent, surged up and out of the creekbed. He had nasty clothes, red eyes, and a ragged beard. He snatched her up, hand over her mouth, and was gone, back into the creek and the tunnel that ran beneath the parking lot.

I looked for help but saw only empty cars and the mall, which seemed so far away. I stood paralyzed, but then I heard a muffled scream. Before I knew what I was doing, I was down the bank, so scared that I could barely breathe; then I heard her again, more a whimper than a scream, and the blackness swallowed me. I thought of the purple dress, and the smiles she'd given me. I took another step, into the black hole, and then it was just the three of us. But I thought of her face, her blue eyes wide above grimy fingers; I saw the flash of her pale legs as he *dragged her down, how they kicked in terror—and I stumbled on, like in a dream. . . .*

I rolled down the windows, wanting the wind. The images had not been this strong in years, and this time it was different, like someone wanted to hurt me. I thought of blue daisies that looked like open eyes, and then I was back in time, back in the dark, like it was happening now and not twenty-three years ago.

. . . Black water moved like tar in the darkness. I felt it in my sneakers and licking at my shins. I heard them ahead, a single high squeal and then only the creek—its murmur, a few faint splashes. I stopped and looked back at the square of light that was already so far away.

I wanted to go back, but that's what cowards did, sissies. So I moved on and it got darker. I put my hands out like a blind man; rocks tripped me and the dark tried to pull me down, but in my head I could still see the girl. Then there was pale light far ahead, and I thought I saw them.

I tripped, went down hard. My hands sunk into muck and I felt slimy water splash onto my face. Something moved against my arm and I almost screamed. But I got up instead. Be strong, I told myself, then I put my hands out again and walked toward the distant light.

It was like being blind, but worse. So much worse . . .

A blind man would not have done what I did, and I said it under my breath as I pulled up at Vanessa's house and turned off the truck.

"A blind man would not have done it."

I ducked my head and peered through the windshield. Light burned in her house; it shone through the windows and cut into the dark like blades. Except for the windows that had been boarded up, I thought. They were dark and sightless.

Gouged out.

Blind.

. . . *The girl screamed, a long, drawn out NO that was choked off; then I heard a man's voice, low and urgent.*

"Shut up, you dirty little slut. Shut up or . . ."

The rest was lost. A rough mumble.

Then I saw them, definitely saw them, dark figures pinned against a spill of weak light. Her legs scrabbled, kicked up water, and he was shaking her as he dragged her. Her head looked twisted under his arm. Her arms beat against his, but they were small arms. She screamed again and he hit her. One, two, three times, and she didn't move again, just hung from his arms. She was helpless, and I knew then that there was no one else. Just me.

Suddenly, I tripped again, landed hard, facedown in water that tasted like gasoline and mud. When I looked up, half-blinded by the water in my eyes, I could tell that he had heard. He was still . . . looking back. I huddled down, blood loud in my ears. I didn't know how long he stood like that, but it felt like forever.

He would come back. He would find me and he would kill me.

But he didn't. Eventually, he turned and kept walking. I almost went back then, but I held on to her smile and prayed to God like I never had in church. I didn't know if he heard or not, but I went forward instead of back. I could still hear the sound of his fist against her face. One, two, three . . .

Don't let her be dead.

I heard his steps very clearly, dragging through the water as if he was running, and the light grew from pitch-black to dark gray, until I could see my hands. The light was still far away, but I could see it. There was a storm drain, and I knew we must be far under the parking lot by now. I reached for the wall and found it, slimy concrete, like snot, under my fingers.

They stopped beneath the drain, overlit by that half-dead light. A concrete shelf rose above the creek like an altar, and he threw her down.

He looked in my direction, but I knew he couldn't see me. Yet he stared, as if he sensed me after all. Close to panic, I looked back the way I had come; the tunnel behind me stretched away, a throat.

Then his gaze was gone, torn away by his impatience. He was talking again, mumbling to himself, and it was in his voice, the eagerness.

"Yes, yes, yes. Oh yes . . ."

His fingers moved on her. I heard fabric tear and walked closer. His voice swelled up as her purple dress was ripped away. It spread beneath her, torn wings, and above it, in the light, her body shone like cold marble. His voice rose and fell, a chant, a crazy man's ditty.

"Thank you, Lord. Thank you. Yes. So long, so long, so long. Oh, my sweet, sweet Lord . . ."

He moved between us, his back to me, so that I saw her face and the bottoms of her legs. Again fabric tore and I heard his voice.

"Ohhh . . ."

It was a moan. Her panties floated past me on silent water. I looked down and watched them, blue daisies on a field of black—eyes staring in the dark. They drifted against my leg, spun away, and were gone, down the wet throat behind me.

I tore my eyes up, realizing how close I'd come, no more than twenty feet away, the light touching me. Her eyes were open and staring. Her mouth, too, gaped and I saw where he'd beaten her. Her lips twitched and a low gurgle escaped. Her fingers fluttered in my direction; then he struck her again, and her lips didn't move after that. Her eyes were still open but showed mostly white. I felt anger and I nursed it, needing it. It made me strong.

My foot touched something beneath the water and I knew what it was.

I reached down, my fingers closing on a rock the size of a baby's skull. . . .

I stared at the light that spilled from Vanessa's house, but it didn't drive the images away; so I closed my eyes, rubbed at them, fearing that I might start to tear at them instead.

. . . I raised the rock over my head and took another step, expecting him to turn and see me, to come for me, too. But he didn't. All he saw was the girl.

Another step, and the fear rose alongside the anger; and it was stronger. He would kill us both. I saw that. I should have gone for my father. This man was huge and he was crazy and he would kill us. He would kill us sure as shit. I was about to turn and run. Already I was beginning to accept it. Beginning to turn away.

Then he moved. And I saw her, a marble statue on a concrete pedestal . . . .

She was perfect.

I couldn't tear my eyes away. I'd never seen a naked girl before, not like that. Not a real one. I felt funny looking at her, ashamed and dirty, but I couldn't stop. And I noticed that my feet weren't moving. The rock felt loose in my hand, my head light on my shoulders. My breathing went funny, and she seemed to rush at me, until she filled my eyes. I looked at her breasts and then down to the soft blond hair that filled the space between her legs. I'd forgotten the man, my danger, everything but her, spread on that altar. It was only a few seconds but felt longer, and all I did was stare.

Then he moved, dirty fingers on her stomach, moving down, like snakes into a nest; then he was on her, grunting like an animal, baked-bean teeth dark on her pale and helpless breasts.

I couldn't move.

Then I saw her eyes, and I saw that there was nothing in them; and in that emptiness, I found myself again. My hand tightened; the rock came up.

I walked into the light. I took two steps before I saw his face, and his crazy eyes. They were on me. Right on me! And his lips were pulled back over those pudding teeth, and he was smiling, his body still pumping, like a separate animal. And his words, when he spoke, they penetrated me.

"You like what you see, don't you, boy?"

I froze.

"I seen you watchin'."

*Red filled his eyes, making him less than human. But his body contin-
ued to move. Up and down. Up and down. Grunt. Grunt. Grunt. Eyes
like grease on my face. And again that terrible smile. He knew.*

"Well, get a good look boy . . . 'cause you're next."

*And then he was off her, laughing, coming at me, his arm out, as if
to put it around my shoulder.*

"Lord, sweet Lord."

*His mouth a dark, stinking hole. Fingers twitching. A wave of odor,
like a dead dog I'd once found by the roadside.*

*"Adam and Eve!" he shouted. "Eve and now Adam." He leaned for-
ward, bent low until he looked like a huge rat. "Let us pray."*

*He repeated the same words, over and over. "Let us pray. Let us
pray. . . ." Until they bled into one high-pitched cackle that ended when
he was mere feet away. Then with curled lips, he changed the words,
and spoke them slowly. "Let us play. . . . Let us play."*

Then his fingers were on me, and I began to scream.

*But even as I screamed, I swung the rock, hit him somewhere, but he
just laughed harder. I tried to hit him again, but he pulled the rock
from my hand and tossed it down. I heard it splash, as if down a very
deep well. Then my face hit the wall and I tasted blood. Again and
again, until I could no longer scream. I felt his hands on me, all over
me, but I couldn't move. I was barely there, just barely, but still . . . I felt
his hands. The slickness of his tongue on my cheek.*

. . . And I was sobbing.

*But then there was flashing light, and distant shouting voices. I saw
him squint, lips pulled back, tongue out like meat gone bad. Then he
looked back down, caressed my face with one hand.*

*"You a lucky little boy," he said. "Yes, Lord." Then he dropped me in
the water. My head cracked the wall again, and I saw stars. When they
cleared, he was still there, crouched over me, eyes glowing but scared,
his hand on my crotch, squeezing. "But I'll remember you. Adam on a
cross . . . oh yes. You'll always be my little Adam."*

Then he was gone, shambling down the tunnel, away from the light and the voices, which seemed so far away, but coming closer. I thought of the girl, naked and helpless, but this time it was different. I crawled through the mud and pulled myself up. I gathered the shreds of her dress and closed them about her. I placed her hands on her stomach, closed her bloodied legs.

That's when I saw that she was looking at me, the blue gleam of one eye just visible through the swollen flesh.

"Thank you," she said, and I could barely hear her.

"He's gone," I told her. "Everything's gonna be okay."

But I didn't believe it, and I didn't think she did, either.

I thought I was done, thought that it was safe, but another memory, like a predator, followed fast on the heels of the last.

It was something my father had said. I was in bed; it was late, but I couldn't sleep. I hadn't really slept in the two weeks since they'd pulled us out of that hole and into the wide-eyed crowd that pointed like we couldn't see them. The girl, broken, held together by the jacket they'd wrapped around her. Me, bloody teeth chattering, trying not to cry.

My parents were arguing in the hall, not far from my door. I didn't know what started the argument. I heard my mother first.

"Why do you have to be so hard on him, Ezra? He's just a boy, and a very brave one at that."

I crept to the door, cracked it, and peered out. My father had a drink in his hand. His tie was loose and he made my mother look very small in the dim light.

"He's no fucking hero," my father had said. "No matter what the papers say."

He knocked back the drink and put a hand on the wall above my mother's head. Somehow he knew my shame, the burning in my mind that kept me up at night. I didn't know how he knew, but he did, and I felt hot tears slide down my cheeks.

"He's having a tough time, Ezra. He needs to know that you're proud of him."

"Proud! Ha! He's just a dumb-ass kid who should have known better. It's sick the way you coddle him. . . ."

I didn't hear the rest. I closed the door and climbed back into bed. He didn't know.

Nobody did. Just me. *And him.*

I seen you watchin'. . . .

I opened my eyes, done because I could do no more. Now I had to tell Vanessa how I'd failed her. She was raped at the age of fifteen and I'd watched it happen, allowed it to happen.

I should have done more.

I looked up at her house and felt a sudden twist of nausea. A man was standing on her porch, staring down at me. I'd not seen him come out. Had no idea how long he'd stood there. Who he was or why he was there. He came slowly down the steps. I climbed from the truck and met him at the front of it. He was younger than I, probably thirty, with thick brown hair and close-set eyes. He was tall, with big shoulders and large, heavy hands that hung like iron from the sleeves of a denim shirt.

"Ms. Stolen doesn't want to see you," he said without preamble, one hand out, fingers spread. "She wants you to leave."

"Who are you?" I asked.

"That's none of your business." He stepped closer, his hand mere inches from my chest. "Why don't you just get back in your truck and go home."

I looked past him and saw Vanessa's face, formless in the kitchen window. *I seen you watchin'. . . .*

"No," I said, angry. "*This* is none of your business." I gestured sharply, meaning the farm, myself, Vanessa. . . . I had things to say, and I meant them to be said. "I want to talk to Vanessa." I took a step forward and his hand settled like a weight onto my chest.

"I don't think so."

Suddenly, I was filled with rage, bursting with it. All the frustrations of my life seemed to boil up within a matter of seconds, and this nameless man represented all of it.

"Get out of my way." Low, cold, and dangerous, even to my ears.

"Not gonna happen," he said.

Anger. Rage. I was alive with it, like I might explode. His face was hard and heavy, and the pressure was building inside of me. The murder. The investigation. The searing need to talk to Vanessa. In a flash that smelled of prophecy, I saw Detective Mills cuffing Jean, and the way my baby sister sat in a darkened cell and sawed at her wrists with a piece of dull jagged metal. Everything was coming apart, and all I had was this moment and the fury that defined it with such perfect clarity. So that when he pushed me, I decked him, unloaded on him. And the shock of impact that traveled up my arm was a goddamn gift. He dropped to the ground, and I stood over him, hoping that he would get up and give me an excuse. But when he rolled off his back, sitting on the dirt, he looked surprised and hurt. "Jeez, mister. Why did you do that?" Suddenly, he looked much younger. More like twenty.

My anger bled away and left me old.

Then Vanessa was leaping off the porch, standing before me, hands on her hips. "What the fuck is wrong with you, Jackson? What is your fucking problem?"

I felt confused, drunk.

"How dare you come here and behave like that? I want you to leave. Right now. Go home. Get out of here."

She was helping him to his feet, her hand tiny in his. I saw them sleeping together, and felt new pain.

"I wanted to talk to you," I said, and it sounded lame even to me. I was lost, hands out.

"I told you not to follow me."

"This time is different."

But she walked away from me, until she was on the porch, holding the door for the man to move inside. Then she turned and looked down on me as if from a great height, and the porch light held her in its insubstantial grasp.

"Get off my property, Jackson. I mean it!"

I stood dumbly, awed by the pain that welled up to consume me; but it was not until she was gone, the door between us like a rip in the universe, that I realized she'd been wearing a purple dress.

Through the window I saw her at the kitchen table. She was crying, convulsing beneath the hand he'd placed on her shoulder.

I left, heavy with the words she refused to let me say. And it was only as I turned off the farm and onto the black pavement that I realized I had no bed to go to. So I went to the office, to Ezra's space, and with one lamp burning, tossing its warm light on the ceiling, I stretched out on the leather couch and pulled Bone onto my chest. He closed his eyes and was soon asleep. I stared at the ceiling until well after midnight, but my eyes kept wandering to the long, antique rug. I reached out my hand to touch it.

I thought of the safe and of the secrets my father had kept.

Eventually, sleep found me, but not before I realized that it was Monday and I had to be in court. That did not seem real.

CHAPTER

16

I woke in the dark; I didn't know where I was and I didn't care. I held on to the dream: two hands entwined, passing over green fields, the sounds of a dog and of laughter; a flash of blue skies that refused to end, and blond hair, like silk, against my face.

The dream had been of Vanessa, and of things that would never be.

There had been a child, too, with golden skin and her mother's cornflower eyes. She was four or five. She was radiant.

Tell me the story, Daddy. . . . Skipping through tall grass.

What story?

She laughed. *You know what story, Daddy. My favorite . . .*

But I didn't know. There was no story, no favorite; nor would there be. The dream was gone. I'd thought Vanessa would always be there. I'd thought that I had time. For some reason, I'd believed that things would simply work out.

What a fucking idiot.

Tell me the story, Daddy. . . .

I sat up and swung my legs off the couch, rubbed my hands across my face. It's never too late, I told myself; but in the dark the words felt lame, and I thought of the boy I'd once been. Then I said it again, out loud, stronger. "It's never too late."

I looked at my watch. Five-fifteen. Monday. Three days ago, I'd stood above my father's corpse. Now Ezra was gone, and so, too, the comfort of illusion; Vanessa had been so right about that. He'd been the structure and the definition, and I wondered where such power had come from. Was it a gift I'd made to him or something that he'd stolen? In the end, it didn't matter. My life was a house of cards, and the wind of Ezra's passing had knocked it flat.

I pulled on my shoes, thinking that the day already felt very much like Monday.

I found Bone on the overstuffed chair and guessed I'd been snoring. He was warm and loose as I carried him to the truck. At home, I put on a pot of coffee to perk while I showered and dressed. When I got out, Barbara was waiting. She sat on the counter, wrapped in the same fleece robe she'd worn the day before. She looked like hell.

"Good morning," I said noncommittally. She watched me as I toweled off, and I wondered what she saw.

"Hardly," she replied. "I didn't really sleep." I wrapped the towel around my waist, and she stated the obvious. "You didn't come home."

"No." I felt the need to say more but decided not to.

"Were you . . ." She hesitated. "Were you at her place?"

She did not need to elaborate. "No," I said.

"Then . . ."

"At the office."

She nodded and then watched silently as I rummaged in the closet. I'd forgotten that I had no clean suit, so I pulled on khakis and a rumpled cotton button-down that I usually wore around the house. I could feel her eyes on me but didn't know what to say, so I dressed in a silence made more awkward by our ten years of marriage.

"Work," she finally said. "I don't want to go on like this." I heard the forced calm in her voice, so I matched it with my own. I looked at her as I spoke; it was required.

"Do you want a divorce?" I asked.

She came off the counter, startled. Her voice rose. "Good God. No! Why on earth would you think a thing like that?"

I tried to hide my disappointment, realizing only then how desperately I wanted to be rid of this marriage.

"Then what . . . ?"

Barbara came to me and put her hands on my chest. She tried to smile, but it was pitiful to watch. Her breath explored my face, and I wanted to turn away. I'd been so sure. She took my hands and placed them around her waist, leaned into me.

"I want it to be like it was, Work. I want to fix things." She squeezed me, trying to appear playful, and failing. "I want to make you happy. I want *us* to be happy."

"Do you think that's possible?" I asked.

"Of course it is."

"We're not the same people we were, Barbara. We've changed." I removed my arms from around her waist and stepped back. Her voice, when she spoke, had an all too familiar edge. It was sharp and quick.

"People don't change, Work, only circumstances."

"Now, you see, that's where we're different." I pulled on my coat. "I have to go," I said. "I've got court this morning."

She followed me through the house. "Don't walk away from me, Work," she shouted, and I saw my father's face. I snatched my keys from the kitchen counter, ignoring the coffee, which suddenly smelled of bile. At the door, her hands found my arm and she pulled me to a stop. "Please. Wait just a minute." I relented and leaned against the wall. "There's still hope for this marriage, Work."

"Why do you say that, Barbara?"

"Because there has to be."

"That's no answer."

"Marriages have been made of less." She put her hand to my face. "We can make this work."

"Do you still love me, Barbara?"

"Yes," she said immediately. "I still love you." But I saw the lie in her eyes, and she knew it.

"We'll talk later," I said.

"I'll make dinner tonight," she said, suddenly smiling. "You'll see. Everything will be fine." Then she kissed my cheek and sent me off to work, like she had in the early days of our marriage. The smile was the same, as was the feel of her lips on my face, just like a thousand other times. I didn't know what that meant, but it couldn't be good.

I went out for breakfast and coffee. I had a bacon, egg, and cheese sandwich, which would have tasted great had I not found a copy of Sunday's paper. The story of Ezra's death and the ongoing investigation was still on page one, but there was not much else to say. For some reason, they showed a picture of his house. My house now. I scanned the article and was relieved to find my name absent. Another first.

I paid for the meal and walked outside. The day was crisp, with pewter skies and gusting winds. I shoved my hands into my pockets and watched the traffic pass. Somehow I was not surprised to see Detective Mills's car turn into the parking lot. It was one of those things that just felt right, like it had been preordained. I leaned into her window when she rolled it down.

"Are you following me?" I asked her. She didn't smile.

"Coincidence," she said.

"Is it?"

She gestured at the restaurant behind me. "I eat here twice a week," she said. "Wednesdays and Fridays."

I studied her: She had on a tight brown sweater and jeans. Her weapon was on the seat next to her. I couldn't smell her perfume. "Today is Monday," I told her.

"It's like I said. Coincidence."

"Really?"

"No," she said. "I stopped by your house. Your wife said she thought you might have come here."

I felt a foreboding chill, and I didn't know if it was because Detective Mills had been looking for me or because she and my wife had been breathing the same air.

"What do you want?"

"Douglas and I still want to get together with you about your father's files. Have you had a chance to go through them?"

"I'm working on it." A lie.

"Will you be in the office today?" Mills asked.

"I have court this morning. Then I'm going to the jail for an hour to see some clients. I'll be in the office by noon."

Mills nodded. "We'll be in touch." Then she drove away, and I stood watching after her. Eventually, I got into the truck and drove to the office. It was early still, and my secretary had not yet arrived, for which I was thankful. I could not bear her mournful eyes and the disappointment that seemed to shine from them whenever she looked at me. I ignored the stairs to the big office and settled into the chair in my own small office at the back corner of the building. The voice-mail light blinked at me until, with a small sigh, I pushed the button. It took ten minutes to get through all the messages, most of which were from various reporters. They all assured the utmost discretion . . . if I could just spare a moment to make a few comments about my deceased father. One, however, stood out. The call had come in that morning, about an hour before.

The reporter's name was Tara Reynolds; I knew her well. She worked for the *Charlotte Observer,* had the criminal beat for North Mecklenburg and the counties that bordered Charlotte to the north . . . Cabarrus, Iredell, and Rowan. Our paths crossed from time to time. She never misquoted me or abused the initial trust I'd given her. Murder cases were often tried in the press, and I was not above using her when circumstances called for it. She operated the same way; and yet there was an invisible line that neither of us ever crossed. Call it mutual respect. Maybe even liking.

Tara was in her midfifties, heavyset, with brilliant green eyes and a smoker's voice. She was beyond jaded, expected the worst of everyone, and believed that her job was the most important one in the world. She may have been right. She answered on the second ring.

"I want you to know that I never do this."

That was the first thing she said to me.

"What?" I asked.

"Just listen. I'm going to tell you some things and then we'll never mention this again."

She had my attention, yet she seemed suddenly hesitant. "What is it, Tara?"

"Just a sec. . . ." I could tell that her hand covered the mouthpiece. Muffled voices filtered through and then there was silence. "Sorry about that," she said. "I'm going to make this quick. You know that I've got sources?"

"I know that." Tara usually knew more about the murder cases in this county than everybody but the cops and the DA's office. I never learned how she did it, but she did.

"The word from inside Salisbury PD is that your name's coming up . . . a lot."

"What?"

"There's a lot of talk, Work. They're looking at you pretty hard for the murder." Her voice was low and urgent, as if she thought I'd not believe her.

"Somehow I'm not surprised."

"Just listen. There are a few things you might not know. First, they've identified the ammunition that killed your father. The bullets were Black Talons—fairly rare, illegal for awhile now. In and of itself, no big deal, but they checked the local gun-store records. Your father bought three boxes of Black Talons just before they were taken off the market."

"So . . ."

"So, it ups the odds that his gun was used. They think you had access to that gun." A pause. "Has it turned up yet?"

She was testing me, probing for information. "I don't know."

"Well, it hasn't, and until it does, that looks suspicious."

"What else?" I asked, knowing there had to be more. I could hear her breathing on the other end, the click of a lighter and the sharp inhale as she lit up.

"They're saying your alibi won't hold up." Another drag. "They're saying that you lied about your whereabouts."

There it was.

"Why do they believe that?" I asked, amazed that my voice sounded as calm as it did.

"I don't know, but it's firm. Add the money factor into it and it looks solid."

"You're talking about . . ."

"Yeah, yeah. The fifteen million."

"Word spreads fast," I said.

"You don't know the half of it."

"Are there other suspects?" I asked.

"You know, I'd have been worried if you'd not asked that question."

"Are there?" I pressed.

"Yeah. There are. There were several business deals where the other guy got the short end. Forgive me for saying this, but your father was a real ass. He was sharp but not exactly scrupulous. He screwed over a lot of people."

"Anybody in particular?"

"A few. But nobody else with such an obvious incentive. Some criminal defendants who got out around the time he was killed. They're being checked out. The DA was pulling out all the stops until some question came up about your alibi. Now Mills has forced his hand. He's not backing you anymore."

I was not surprised. Mills must have been all over Douglas about my going to the crime scene. She'd let me be there because he'd asked her to. Nobody would care about that if the case was shot because of it. In the end, it was her call. She'd swing if the wind blew the wrong way on this one. Normally, I'd have felt badly for Douglas, because our friendship had caused this problem, but not now. Now I couldn't have cared less.

Douglas would prosecute the case, whoever they arrested. Jean or me. That meant that Douglas was coming after the family, and the past was irrelevant. I remembered him from the parking lot, the way his face had hung so slackly around his ripe-plum nose. I was meat to him now; he'd swallow me or spit me out, just like anybody else.

"Who says my alibi is no good?" I asked, knowing she couldn't help me.

"Don't know. But it's somebody with a reason to know different. The cops believe it. Mills says she liked you from the get-go. She's all but accused you of hampering her investigation. But the pressure's on her. Everybody knows she let you onto the crime scene. Now she sees cracks in your story, and word is, she's like a kid in a candy store."

"Mills is a bitch."

"I try not to go there, but I can't disagree. I know she hates lawyers, but I can't blame her for that, either." She said it jokingly, but it fell flat. "Sorry," she said. "Just trying to cheer you up."

"My wife can swear that I was with her all night." I just wanted to try the alibi on, see what she would make of it.

"Biased testimony, Work. Any prosecutor worth a lick could shoot holes in it before breakfast."

She was right. Barbara's testimony was better than nothing, but not by much, especially in light of Ezra's will. A jury could well imagine a wife would lie for her husband. Throw in fifteen million dollars and it was a given.

"There's a bright side to all this," Tara told me. "Want to hear it?" She went on before I could answer. "Do you know this lawyer, Clarence Hambly?"

"Yes."

"He's saying that you knew nothing about the will. That your father gave explicit instructions that you not know of it under any circumstances. That's taken some of the wind out of Mills's sails. Hambly is very credible."

I pictured the old man staring down at me from his lofty height, a twist of distaste on his patrician mouth. But just because Hambly believed it didn't make it so. That's what Douglas would argue to the jury. I could hear him: I would never doubt the word of this upstanding gentleman. He would beam at the jury and place a hand on the old man's shoulder to show that they were on the same side. I am quite certain that he never discussed the will with this defendant. He'd stop and point his meaty finger, damning me. But there are other ways, ladies and gentlemen. And the defendant is a smart man, an educated man. Here he'd raise his voice. A lawyer! Who for ten years shared an office with the decedent. Who for thirty-five years had access to the poor man's home. . . . His own father!

That's how he'd play it. It's how I would. He'd need a motive.

Fifteen million dollars, ladies and gentlemen. A lot of money . . .

"And don't forget the obvious," the reporter said. "They still don't have a murder weapon. It's a big hole."

Not as big as the one in my father's head, I thought, amazed at my own callousness. If anything, my dislike for the man had grown since his death. "Is there anything else?" I asked.

"One more thing," she told me. "It's important."

"What?"

"I don't think you did it. That's why we're talking. Don't make me regret it."

I understood what she meant. If word escaped that she'd told me these things, her sources would dry up. She could face criminal charges.

"I understand," I told her.

"Listen, Work. I like you. You're like a little boy playing dress-up. Don't get caught with your pants down. It wouldn't be the same without you. I mean that."

Unsure what to say, I thanked her.

"And when the time is right," she said, "you talk to me and me only. If there's a story, I want an exclusive."

"Whatever you want, Tara."

I heard her light another cigarette. She muttered something under her breath. Then her voice firmed.

"This last bit's going to hurt, Work, and I apologize. But it's out of my hands."

A horrible pit opened in my stomach, and I felt my heart drop through it. I knew what she was going to say before she said it. "Don't, Tara," I said. "Don't do it."

"It's my editor's call, Work. The story's going to run. It won't be specific, if that helps. Sources close to the investigation say . . . that sort of thing. It won't say you're a suspect, just that you're being questioned in connection with the murder."

"But you'll use my name?"

"I can buy you a day, Work, maybe two, but don't count on it. It's going to run and it will be front page."

I couldn't keep the bitterness out of my voice. "Thanks for nothing."

After a long silence, Tara said, "I didn't have to tell you at all."

"I know. It doesn't make it any easier."

"I gotta go, Work. Take care." She hung up.

I sat in silence for a long time, thinking of what she'd said. I tried to picture it, the train wreck that was now bearing down on me, but I couldn't. The next day, or the day after that. It was too huge, too intense. I thought of the other things she'd said—because I had to. I absolutely had to.

Black Talons. They were hard to come by. That Ezra's own gun had been used against him now seemed a certainty. I thought of my last visit to his house, of the bed upstairs and the place where someone had curled up to rest or to weep. Jean had been there, looking for some kind of peace, I guessed. It was where it had started, on the night that now seemed so long ago. She would have gone there for the gun; we all knew that's where he kept it. How many times, I wondered, had she returned to that place, and what did she think while there? Would she undo the past if she could?

Then there was the fifteen million. No one would believe I had no use for it. It would appear to be an obvious and self-serving lie.

And the cops knew that I'd not been home with Barbara. That presented a huge question. Where had that information come from? Suddenly, I thought of Jean, how her mouth had worked wetly beneath those kaleidoscope eyes. . . . *Done is done.* . . . *Daddy's dead and done is done.*

But I couldn't keep my mind off Tara. Why was she helping me? What was it she'd said? That I was like "a little boy playing dress-up." That's how she saw me, a little boy in his father's suit. She was right, I realized, but for the wrong reasons. It looked like dress-up because my father's suit would never fit. The problem, however, was not the size of the man, but the choice of suit, a truth I was gradually coming to accept. The vultures were circling, looking for a carcass, a body to feed the clanking machine that was justice. And I knew for fact that my father could never have put himself in the sights. He could never have made that sacrifice. I prayed that I would be strong enough to do what had to be done. I pictured my sister, and found that it helped. But the panic was still there, waiting, and I pushed the thoughts away, pounded them down with something like hatred.

Jean was right. The old man was dead, and done is done. Only one thing mattered now.

I leaned back in the chair I'd used for so many years and studied the walls, where diplomas and my law license hung; I saw the office as if for the first time. There were no personal touches, no paintings or photographs, not even of my wife. It was as if a part of me had never accepted my life, and saw this all as merely temporary. Yet if that were true, it was a small part of me indeed. Until that moment, it had all seemed normal enough. Yet I knew I could move out of that office in five minutes, and it would be as if the past ten years had never been. The room would show little change. Like a prison cell, I thought. The building wouldn't miss me, and part of me wanted to torch the place. For what could it matter now? One cell was much the same as another.

There should be pictures on the walls, I thought, then placed a call to Stolen Farm. I told myself I was calling to apologize, to try one more time to set the past to rights, but that was not the whole truth. I needed to hear her voice. I wanted to hear her say that she loved me, just one more time.

No one answered.

By the time I left for court, the day had closed in on itself; the sky was shuttered with heavy clouds that threatened rain. I seemed to bow under the pressure of that sky, and I was bent by the time I walked into court. I'd expected to be treated differently, like everyone knew, but that didn't happen. I'd imagined the worst, a public shunning, but in the end it was just another day in court. So I sat through calendar call in near silence, addressing the court when my cases were called off the docket: one for plea, one for trial. Then I went to meet my clients in the crowded hallway.

They were petty cases, misdemeanors; I had to glance at the files to remember what my clients were charged with. It was typical Monday bullshit, except I had one guy who I thought might be innocent. I'd take his case to trial.

We stood in the burned tobacco smell by the outside door, a trash can for my desk. I dealt with the plea first. He was forty-three years old, overweight, and divorced. He nodded compulsively as I spoke, his lower lip loose over tobacco-stained teeth, his shirt already soaked through with sickly sweet perspiration. The "fear sweats" we called them. I saw it all the time. For most, criminal court was a foreign place, something that would never really happen. Then suddenly, it became real, and you heard your name called out in that room full of criminals, armed bailiffs, and the stiff-faced judge who sat above it all. By noon, the hall would be ripe, the courtroom even worse. There were 540 cases on the docket that day, a microcosm of greed, anger, jealousy, and lust. Just pick an emotion, and you'd find the crime to embody it. And they moved around us, an endless sea, each looking for his lawyer, his witness, or his lover. Some just looking for a smoke to kill the hours until their case was called. Many had been through the system so often, it was old hat. Others, like my guy, had the sweats.

He'd been charged with assault on a female, a class-A1 misdemeanor, just shy of a felony. He lived across the street from a very attractive young woman who'd been having marital problems with her pastor husband. How had my client known this? For several months, he'd used a scanner to intercept their cordless phone calls. During this time, he'd convinced himself that the cause of their problems was her infatuation with him, an assertion that anyone with working eyes could tell was absurd. And yet he believed it. He believed it now, just as he had six weeks ago, when he'd forced his way into her trailer, pinned her against the kitchen counter, and rubbed his crotch all over her. There'd been no rape, no penetration; the clothes had stayed on. He was reticent about why he finally left. I suspected premature ejaculation.

At our first meeting, he'd wanted to go to trial. Why? Because she'd wanted him to do what he did. He should not be punished for that. Should he? "It ain't right, I tell you. She loves me. She wanted it," he'd said.

I hated the sweaters. They'd listen to you, but they always wanted to get too close, as if you could truly save them. Three weeks before, we'd met in my office, and he'd told me his side of the story. The victim's side of it was unsurprising. She barely knew his name, found him physically repulsive, and had not slept through the night since the day it happened. I found her entirely credible. One look at her and the judge would drop the hammer on my guy. No question about it.

Eventually, I convinced my client that a plea of simple assault would be in his best interest. It was a lesser charge, and I'd worked a deal with the DA. He'd do community service. No time.

In the hallway, he licked his lips, and I saw dried spit at the corners of his mouth. I wanted to explain what was expected and how to address the court. All he wanted to talk about was her. What did she say about him? How did she look? What was she wearing?

He had all the makings of a client for life. The next time, it might be worse.

I warned him that the judge would order him to stay away from the victim, that going near her would be a violation of the terms of the plea. He didn't get it, or if he did, he didn't care; but I'd done my job, as disgusting as it was, and he could go back to his little hole and his dark fantasies of the preacher's wife.

The second client was a young black man, charged with resisting arrest. The cop said he'd hampered an arrest, that he'd incited a watching crowd by yelling at the cops to fuck off. My client had a different story. It had taken four white cops to catch the lone black man who had been arrested. When the charging officer had walked past my client, he'd been smoking a cigarette, at which point my client had said, "That's why you can't catch nobody, 'cause you smoking." The cop had stopped, said, "You want to go to jail?" My client had laughed. "You can't arrest me for that," he'd told him.

The cop had cuffed him and tossed him in the patrol car. And here we were.

This client, I believed, mainly because I knew the cop. He was fat, mean, and a chain-smoker. The judge knew it, too. I thought we had a good chance at acquittal.

The trial took less than an hour. My client walked. Sometimes reasonable doubt is easy to find. Sometimes it's not. As I was shaking his hand, moving away from the defense table, I looked over his shoulder and saw Douglas standing in the shadowed alcove at the back of the courtroom. He never came to district court, not without reason. I lifted my hand out of habit, but his arms remained crossed over his fat man's chest. I looked away from his hooded eyes to say good-bye to my beaming client, and when I looked back, Douglas was gone.

Like that, the last of my delusions fell away, leaving me naked before the truths I'd denied all morning. The room tilted and sudden dampness warmed my face and palms—the fear sweats, this time from the inside. I stumbled from court on weak legs, passed other lawyers without hearing or seeing them. I plowed through packed humanity in the hall, groping my way like a blind man. I almost fell through the bathroom door, and didn't take time to close the stall. Files slipped unheeded to the floor as my knees struck the damp, urine-stained tile. Then, in one unending clench, I vomited into the stinking toilet.

CHAPTER

17

Eventually, I got to my feet. I walked outside and found the wind; it gusted against my face as if to scrub it clean. Behind me, the courthouse rose up, pale against the monolithic sky. The light was silver and wan, a cold light, and people streamed past on the sidewalk below me. Normal people doing normal things, yet they seemed to bow beneath the pressure of the sky, leaning into the sidewalk as they forged uphill toward the restaurants and shops. None of them looked at the courthouse as they passed. They probably never gave it a thought, and in a way I hated them, but it was more like envy.

My eyes traveled up the street to the faded door of the local downtown bar. I needed lunch but wanted a drink. I wanted it so badly, I could actually taste it. Standing there, fantasizing about a cold beer, I realized just how much I'd been drinking the past few years. It didn't bother me. It was the least of my problems, a small revelation among the ugly multitude. But I decided against it. Instead, I turned for the office, moving down the broad courthouse steps.

I stepped onto the sidewalk and turned toward lawyers' row. I watched my feet, so it took several moments before I noticed the strange looks, but eventually I felt them. As I walked, people stopped and stared, people I knew: a couple of lawyers, a lady from the clerk's office, two patrolmen walking to court for trial. They all stopped to watch me pass, and it felt unreal, like they were frozen in time. I saw every expression with great clarity: disbelief, curiosity, disgust. There were whispers, too, as lawyers I'd known for ten years refused to meet my eyes and spoke behind raised hands. My steps faltered and slowed as I moved through this strange scene, and for a moment I thought that I'd been mumbling to myself or that my fly was open. Yet as I turned the corner onto lawyers' row, I saw the unbearable truth, and thus came to understand.

The police had come to my office, descended upon it. Patrol cars strobed at my front door. Unmarked vehicles leaned drunkenly, two wheels on the sidewalk, two on the street. Officers moved in and out of my office, carrying boxes. Bystanders stood in loose groups, and I recognized almost every one of them. They were the lawyers who worked all around me. Their secretaries. Their interns and paralegals. In one instance, a wife, her hand to her throat, as if I might steal her jewelry. I froze, yet somehow I clung to my dignity. Only one lawyer met my eyes, and it was as I'd imagined it would be. Douglas was distant, massive in a long gray coat that hung on him like a sack. He stood at the door and our eyes met in silent accord. Then he shook his head, and parted the crowd to walk toward me. It took an effort of will, but I moved forward to meet him on even terms.

He raised his hands, palms up, but I spoke first. People kept their distance and watched in silence.

"I assume you have a search warrant," I demanded.

Douglas took in my appearance and I knew that he saw what he expected to see. Red-eyed, haunted. I looked guilty. When he spoke, there was no sadness in his eyes. "I'm sorry it had to come to this, Work, but you left me no choice."

Police officers continued in and out of my office, and, looking over Douglas's shoulder, I saw my secretary for the first time; she looked small and beaten.

"There's always a choice," I said.

"Not this time."

"I'd like to see the warrant."

"Of course." Douglas produced the warrant and I looked at it without seeing it. Something was wrong with this picture and I needed time to figure out what it was. When it hit me, it hit me hard.

"Where's Mills?" I looked around. Her car was nowhere to be seen.

Douglas hesitated, and in that hesitation I saw the truth of it.

"She's at my house. Isn't she? She's searching my goddamn house!"

"Now, take it easy, Work. Just settle down. Let's do this by the book. We both know how it works."

I stepped closer, noticing for the first time that I was taller than Douglas. "Yeah. I know how it works. You get frustrated and I get screwed. Do you think people are going to forget this?" I gestured. "Look around. There's no going back."

Douglas was immovable and unmoved. He stared at my chin, so close that he could have stretched out his lips and kissed it. "Don't make this any harder than it has to be. Okay? None of us wants to be here."

I couldn't keep the sarcasm out of my voice. "You're forgetting about Mills."

Douglas sighed, the first sign of emotion. "I told you not to piss her off. I warned you." He hesitated, as if debating. "You shouldn't have lied to her."

"What lie?" I demanded, my voice rising higher than I'd planned. "Who says I lied?"

In shock, I saw his face shift. It seemed to soften. He took my arm and turned me away from the watching crowd. Together, we walked down the sidewalk until we were out of earshot. Seen from a distance, it would have looked like any normal day on lawyers' row, two attorneys consulting over a case or sharing a tasteless joke. But this was no normal day.

"I'm telling you this because it's on the affidavit supporting the warrant, and you'd have gotten around to it eventually. We couldn't get the warrant without probable cause. . . ."

"Don't lecture me on the law of search and seizure, Douglas. Just get to the point."

"It's Alex Shiften, Work. She contradicts your alibi. You told Mills that on the night your mother died, you, Jean, and Ezra left the hospital and returned to Ezra's house. You also told her that after you left Ezra's house, you went straight home and were there all night with Barbara. Alex says that's not true; she swears to it, in fact."

"True or not, how the hell would Alex know that?"

Douglas sighed again, and I realized that this was the part that pained him. "Jean told her. Jean went to your house later that night. She wanted to talk to you, she says. She got there in time to see you leave. This would have been late, sometime after midnight. She watched you drive off and then she went home and told Alex. Alex told Mills, and here we are." He paused and leaned in toward me. "You lied to us, Work. You left us no choice."

I lowered my eyes and closed them. The events of that night were becoming clear to me. Jean followed Ezra to the mall and killed him. Then she went to my house in time to see me leave for Stolen Farm. She knew that I'd left. She'd told Alex as much. But they did not know where I'd gone or what I'd done. What I wondered was why. Why had Jean gone to my house? And did she still have Ezra's gun when she got there?

When I looked up, I saw that Douglas had settled into a posture of patient complacency. I gave him a cold smile. "Your warrant's grounded on hearsay, Douglas."

"I don't need a lecture, either, Work. Alex came forward first; then we talked to Jean. She was reluctant—you should know that—but she corroborated Ms. Shiften's story."

I felt ill all over again as cold sweat explored my neck and rolled down my spine. I saw Jean's face, the wild abandon in her eyes as she'd sobbed. "Daddy's dead . . . and done is done. . . . Right, Alex? . . . That's right, huh?" What crushed me, however, was the knowledge that she'd told the police about it. Douglas knew that; it was in his eyes.

I felt Douglas's fingers around my arm. "You're not going to tell me that Jean lied, now are you, Work? Jean wouldn't lie. Not about something like that."

I looked past Douglas, watching the crowd of people who had been colleagues at worst, friends at best. Who now were what? Lost to me. Gone, as if I were already in prison. The fear snake uncurled in my belly, but I ignored it as I answered the district attorney as best I could.

"I can't imagine that she would make that up, Douglas. Not Jean."

It was true. I had left in the middle of the night, and apparently Jean had seen me. But what did she believe? Had she convinced herself that I'd killed our father? Was she that far gone? Or was she setting me up? If death was sufficient punishment for the man who killed her mother, what was appropriate justice for me? I'd made Ezra's truth my own. How badly did she hate me for that?

"Barbara supports my alibi, Douglas. I was with her all night and she'll testify to that fact. Just ask her."

"We have," Douglas said.

"When?" I asked, stunned.

"This morning."

Now I saw it. "Mills," I said. "She spoke to Barbara this morning." I pictured Mills at the restaurant. She'd known then that the warrants would be served. That's why she'd wanted to know my schedule. "Are you taking me into custody?" I asked.

Douglas pursed his lips and looked away, as if the question embarrassed him. "That would be premature," he finally said, which meant that he lacked sufficient evidence for an arrest. Then I understood. If Barbara had said anything different, Douglas would have served an arrest warrant, as well. That's why they'd waited so late to talk to her. They'd known what she'd say, and an alibi might have prejudiced their application for a search warrant. A judge might have hesitated. So get the warrant first, they'd figured. And if Barbara had told them anything other than what she had, then Douglas and I would have been having a different conversation altogether.

I nodded, studying the street scene one last time, as if to memorize all the little things I'd always taken for granted. "Fine. Then I'll get out of your way." I started to turn, when Douglas spoke.

"If you want to make a statement, Work, now would be a good time."

I turned back, leaned forward. "Fuck you, Douglas. There's your statement."

Douglas didn't bat an eye. "You're not helping yourself, Work."

"Do you want that statement in writing?" I asked.

Douglas frowned and glanced back at my office. "Don't talk to Jean about this," he said. "She's got enough on her plate without you adding to her troubles. I don't want you confusing the issues for her. She's given a sworn statement and that's all that matters."

"You don't have that authority, Douglas. You can't order me to stay away from my sister."

"Then call it another warning. Interfere with any phase of this investigation and I'll come down on you so hard, you won't believe it."

"Is there anything else?" I asked.

"Yeah. There is. Hambly probated your father's will today. Congratulations."

I watched him walk away. To my office. To my life. Such as it was.

He disappeared inside, and the crowd milled around my office door. In that instant, I was too furious to be scared, disturbed only by the ease with which the security blanket of my life had been ripped to shreds. Again the eyes were upon me, but they were not curious ones. And that, most of all, angered me to the point of disgust. These were people I knew, people who knew me. Yet there it was, plain in every glance. I was more than a suspect. I stood condemned, alone in a hostile country. So I left. I walked around the block and returned to the parking lot in back of the building. I got in my truck and I drove away, destination unknown.

Eventually, I arrived at the park, my house before me like a stranger's. It glowed in the eerie light, and loomed taller than normal against the gunmetal sky. The cops were there, too, at least a dozen of them; and my neighbors, like my colleagues, had gathered for the feast. Word would be all over town within the hour. In my head I saw the expressions of shocked disbelief, but the undercurrent of true emotion would be there as well, the dark thrill of another's utter collapse. Tongues would wag, and Ezra would emerge as the martyred hero, the hardworking, brilliant attorney who'd dragged his family from poverty, only to face this final reward. I saw it now. I'd killed him for the money.

I pictured the police in my house. Specifically, I pictured Mills, pawing through my things, my drawers, my desk. Looking in my closet, under my bed, and in my attic. Nothing would be sacred. Mills would see to that. My life would be stripped bare, tagged and bagged. I knew these people, damn it! And they now knew things about me that were nobody's business but my own. What I ate. What I drank. What kind of toothpaste I used. My wife's underwear. Our preferred method of birth control. The whole thing pissed me off, so instead of leaving, I drove to the house. Barbara was there, pacing the driveway in panic and despair.

"Thank God," she said. "Oh, thank God. I tried to call you. I tried . . ."

I put my arms around her out of long habit, feeling her bewilderment but nothing else. "I'm sorry. I've been in court. My cell phone was off."

She began to sob, her voice muffled by my chest. "They've been here for hours, Work. They're going through everything. And they're taking things! But they won't tell me what." She pulled back, her eyes wild. "Do something! You're a lawyer, for God's sake. Do something!"

"Did they show you a warrant?" I asked.

"Yes. They showed me something or other. I think that's what it was."

"Then there's nothing I can do. I'm sorry. I hate this as much as you." I tried to put my arms around her again, to offer what I could, but she pushed away, her hands hard on my chest.

"Goddamn it, Work! You are worthless! I swear to God. Ezra would never have let this happen. He'd have been so on top of this, the cops wouldn't have dared to cross him!" She turned away, hugging herself.

"I'm not my father," I said, meaning it in so many ways.

"You're damn right about that!" Barbara spat out. Then she gestured at the gathering crowd. "They're going to have a field day with this. That much I can tell you."

"Screw them," I said.

"No, screw you, Work. This is our life. My life. Do you have any idea what this means? Do you?"

"I think I know better than you what this means." But she didn't hear me. I tried again. "Listen, Barbara. They're going to do this with or without us. There's no reason to stay here. Let me take you somewhere. I'll go inside and try to get some of your things. Okay? You don't need to see this. Then we'll go to a hotel."

She was already shaking her head. "No. I'm going to Glena's house."

The momentary charity I'd felt toward my wife evaporated, leaving me chilled. "Glena's house," I said. "Of course."

When she turned to me, her face was bleak. "Tomorrow, Work. Tomorrow we'll talk, but right now I need to get away. I'm sorry." She turned away. As if on cue, a horn sounded, and I saw Glena Werster's black Mercedes at the curb below the house. When my wife turned back to me, I thought she'd changed her mind.

"You make this go away, Work." There was winter in her voice. "You make this go away. I can't take it." She began to turn.

"Barbara . . ." I stepped toward her.

"I'll find you tomorrow. Until then, please leave me alone."

I watched her all the way down the driveway, until she climbed into the sleek sedan. She embraced Glena and then they were gone, around the corner, toward the country club and the fortress of Glena's home. As I stared across the park, a horrible thought occurred to me. Barbara had never asked me if I'd done it. It'd never even come up.

Suddenly, I felt a presence behind me, and I knew it was Mills before I turned. She had on blue pants and a matching jacket; I didn't see her pistol. Her face was calm, which surprised me. I expected antagonism. I expected triumph. I should have known better. Mills was a professional; she wouldn't gloat until she had a conviction. After that, all bets were off. I'd probably get Christmas cards in prison.

"Where's your car?" she asked.

"What?" Her question took me off guard.

"Your BMW? Where is it?"

"I don't understand."

"Don't be an ass, Work. It's included in the warrant. I want it."

Of course she'd want the car. Who knew what a thorough forensic analysis might reveal? Ezra's hair in the carpet. Bloodstains in the trunk. Even as I spoke, I realized how my words would sound.

"I sold it."

She studied my face as if she could read something there.

"That's convenient," she said.

"Coincidence," I told her.

"When did you sell it?"

"Yesterday."

"Yesterday," she repeated. "You've had that car for years. You sold it days after Ezra's body was found, the day before I execute a search warrant, and you want me to believe that it's coincidence?" I shrugged. "Why did you sell the car? For the record." Her threat was more than implied.

I gave her a reckless smile. "Because someone told me to stop being a pussy."

"You're playing a dangerous game, Work. I'm warning you."

"You're in my house! You're in my office! Warn me all you want. For the record, I sold the car because I felt like it, because it didn't fit anymore; something you'd never understand. But if you want to waste your time, you can find it on that car lot west of town, the one on Highway One-fifty. Help yourself."

She was pissed. With the car out of my control, its evidentiary value would plummet. I knew that it didn't matter—the car had nothing to do with Ezra's death—but she didn't know that, and for an instant I enjoyed her loss of composure. As victories went, it was cheap, but I'd take it.

"I want the truck, too," Mills said, gesturing at the old truck, which looked shrunken beneath the towering house. At the moment, it was all I had left.

"Is it in the warrant?"

Hesitation. "No," she finally said.

I gave an ugly laugh. "Are you asking for my consent?"

Mills eyed me. "You're burning up any goodwill that might be left. You know that."

"Oh. We've crossed that bridge. You want my truck, you get another warrant."

"I will."

"Fine. Until then, no way."

Our eyes locked, she swelled with bottled emotion, and I knew that this went way beyond professional. She hated me. She wanted me locked up, and I wondered if it was like this in every case. Or was there something about me or about this case? Something personal?

"Are you almost done in there?" I asked her, gesturing at the house.

She showed her teeth. They were small and white, except for one in the front, which was slightly yellow. "Not even close," she said, and I realized that she was enjoying herself. "You're welcome to come in and watch. It's your right."

My control slipped. "What is your problem with me, Detective Mills?"

"It's nothing personal," she said. "I've got a dead man, a missing gun, and a man with fifteen million reasons to lie to me about where he was the night in question. It's enough for me and it was enough for the warrant. If I had more, I'd arrest you. That's how sure I am. If that means I've got a problem with you, then yeah, I do. So come inside, stay out here, whatever. I'm just getting warmed up." She turned away and just as quickly turned back, her finger up like an erection. "But know this. I'm getting that car. And if it turns out that you lied to me about its location, then I'm going to have another problem with you."

I stepped closer, my voice rising to match hers. "Fine. Do your job. But I've made a career out of shredding search warrants. Not just how they're drawn but how they're executed. Be careful how you use it. Your case already has one big hole in it."

I was referring to my presence at the crime scene, and I saw my comment hit the mark. I knew what she was thinking. Any physical evidence linking me to the crime scene could have been carried in the day they found the body, not the day Ezra was killed. Any defense attorney worth his law license could use that to hang a jury. Mills had reason to worry. We'd squared off in court many times, and she knew that I could work the angles. If she screwed up with this warrant, the judge could throw the case out before it got to trial. Hell, she might not even get an indictment. Watching her mouth work, I felt some small satisfaction. Yes, I had to protect Jean, but nothing said I had to make this easy for Mills, Douglas, or anybody else. It was a thin line.

"I'm going in back to get my dog," I told her. "Unless you want to search him, too." She said nothing, just tightened her jaw. "And when this is said and done, I'll expect your apology." It was a bluff—no way would this end well for me.

"We'll see," she said, then turned and stalked away.

"Lock up when you're done," I called after her, but it was an empty gesture. I'd landed a couple of punches, but she'd won the fight, and she knew it. At the door, she turned and looked back. She gave me the same cold yellow-toothed smile, and then she went inside.

CHAPTER

18

I escaped into my truck and drove. I passed cars, stopped at signs, and turned from one street to another, but there was nowhere to go; all choices led back to the same life. It was a bad time, one of ugly questions and despicable truths. So I returned to the park, full of children, old men, and scattered windblown litter. Mills was still at my house. I parked at the curb and watched the police move in and out, tracking suspicion and indifference. It angered me, but it was a toothless rage. In this, I was helpless, and my fingers tightened on the wheel as if it were Mills's neck. When my cell phone rang, the noise jarred me; it took time to find the phone and bring myself to answer it.

"Hello."

"Hey, Work. How you doin'?"

It took a second to place the voice. "Hank?"

"Who else?" He sounded strained. Was it just the day before that

I'd met him in Charlotte? It felt like a week. I tried to focus. "Sorry. What's up?"

"Are you okay?" he asked.

"Yeah." I paused, knowing that I was being short with him. Knowing also that I sounded far from okay. "Talk to me." I rubbed at my eyes.

"I called your office," he said. "A cop answered. He asked for my name." He hesitated, offering me the chance to say something, but I remained silent. What could I say? I almost laughed. "Then I called your house. Guess what?"

"I know. I'm in my car right now, watching the cops run in and out like it's on the parade of homes."

"I don't know what to say about this."

"Don't say anything, then."

"It's awkward, Work. It puts me in a bad position." He paused. "I take it they have a warrant?"

"I think they're hoping to find the murder weapon," I said. "Or anything else to incriminate me." I knew what he was thinking. They'd have needed probable cause to get the warrant. That meant they had something on me.

"Any real chance of an indictment?" he asked.

"Very likely," I said.

Hank went silent. Considering the news, I didn't blame him. We were acquaintances and drinking buddies, but not friends in any real sense. I could almost see the math. He relied on defense lawyers for most of his work, but no one in his position could afford to alienate the police. "That serious?" he finally asked. I knew the last thing he wanted was to get involved.

"Could be. The lead investigator's got it in for me. You'll probably read about it in tomorrow's paper."

"Mills?" he asked, not needing a response. I guessed he was playing for time, trying to decide how he felt about all this. "Is there anything I can do for you?"

His hesitation was clear. Getting involved in this could do him nothing but harm. It was to his credit that he'd even asked, but I knew what answer he wanted.

"Not now, Hank. But I appreciate it."

"Hey. Your dad was an ass, but I don't believe you murdered him."

"Well, thanks for that. It means something, Hank. Not many people are saying it right now."

His tone warmed. "Don't let them rattle you, Work. You've seen all this before. You know how it works."

You know how it works. Douglas had used the same words.

I decided to change the subject. "So what's up, man? Any chance of good news?"

Hank was no fool. He understood. I needed to move this conversation forward, onto neutral ground. "I went to Charter Hills this morning," he said. "I spent a couple hours poking around."

Charter Hills was a mental-health facility in Charlotte, one of the best in the state. It was where Ezra had finally committed Jean after her second suicide attempt. Even now, I saw it in stark clarity. Warm colors and fresh flowers did nothing to hide the pain of those condemned behind its tall brick walls; and condemned they were, whether their presence was voluntary or not. I'd visited Jean there many times; she'd never spoken to me, and her physician had told me that was normal. I hadn't believed him. How could I? She was my sister.

She'd been long months in that place. It was where she'd met Alex Shiften.

"Look, Hank . . ." I began.

"They have no record of a patient named Alex Shiften," he said, cutting me off.

"What?"

"No record at all."

"That's not possible," I said. "It's where they met."

"I don't think so, not unless she was there under a different name."

I tried to concentrate, but it was hard. "What are you saying?"

Hank sighed. "I don't know what I'm saying. That's the trouble. It

doesn't add up and I don't have enough information to even speculate; but something stinks. I can smell it."

My mind was still so full of Mills that I had trouble focusing, but
none of this would matter if Jean survived the investigation only to be
left alone with Alex. She was trouble. Somehow I knew that, and I
needed to handle this one detail. Before it was too late. Unfortunately,
I was at a loss.

"What do you suggest?" I asked.

"I need a picture of Alex," he said without hesitation.

"What are you going to do?"

"I'm going back to Charter Hills. Then we'll see."

I felt a wave of gratitude. Hank would not cross the police, fine;
but he'd go through with this, for me and for Jean. That made him a
stand-up guy in a world that suffered from a lack of them. Somehow
I'd make it up to him.

"Thank you, Hank." I paused because I had to.

"Forget about it. It's a little thing."

"Do you want me to mail you the picture?" I managed to ask.

"Too slow. Put it in your mailbox once the cops leave. I'll drive up
to Salisbury sometime tonight. It could be late. If you're home, you'll
see me. If not, I'll take it and go. Either way, I'll call you if I learn
anything."

"That's awesome, Hank. I'll take care of it."

On the other end, Hank started to say something, then stopped.
For a long second, I heard his breathing. "You understand? Don't
you, Work?" He wasn't talking about Alex or Jean.

"Hey. Life's a bitch. I appreciate what you're doing."

"Okay. I'll call you."

Then he was gone, and I hung up the phone. I looked at Bone, but
he was asleep on the seat next to me. How could so much happen at
once? How could the world be normal one day and a smoking pit the
next? I closed my eyes and pictured grass that bent in a wind from
some faraway place. When I looked up, there was a man at my window, staring through the glass. I was too drained to be startled. It was

Max Creason—same hunting cap, same sublime ugliness. He wore a bright red poncho, as if he, too, expected rain. I rolled down the window.

"Hey, Max," I said. "How are you?"

He studied me intently, his eyes bright behind his thick, filthy glasses. Then he gestured at my house. "There're cops at your house." His tone was more questioning than definitive, but I didn't take the bait. It seemed to anger him, for his lips pulled up over his stained teeth, and he made a strange sound deep in his throat. He leaned closer. "When I met you, I didn't know who you were. Didn't know you were the son of this murdered lawyer that's in the paper every day." It sounded like an accusation. He looked at the house and then back at me. "And now the police are in your house. They think you did it? You're a suspect?"

"I don't want to talk about it, Max. It's complicated."

"Talk is good."

"No. Talk is painful. It's good to see you again, but this is a bad time."

He ignored me. "Come on," he said, stepping back from the truck. "Let's walk."

"Thanks, but no."

It was as if he didn't hear me. He opened the truck door. "No, this'll be good. Just let the dog lie. You come on and walk with me." He gestured for me to get out of the truck, and I gave in. I had nowhere to go anyway.

So I left Bone to sleep in the truck and fell in beside Max. He led me down the hill to a narrow dirt footpath that ran beside the lake, away from my house. I didn't look back. He took long strides, and his poncho flapped around his legs. We walked for nine or ten minutes, past the lake, the public tennis courts, and across a gravel parking area. Neither of us spoke until the park was lost behind a small hill. We were on a narrow side street, lined with modest homes. Children's toys littered some of the yards. Others were immaculate. It was a transitional neighborhood. Newlyweds and nearly deads. But what did any of that matter?

"I'm gonna tell you a story," Max finally said. He rolled his eyes at me. "It's an important one, so listen up. I'm gonna tell you about my hands." He lifted them from his sides and then let them drop; they were dirty but pale against the red poncho, and his fingers were long.

"You remember. You asked me before. Now I'll tell you."

"Why?"

"I've got my reasons. Now shut up. No one in this town has heard this story and it's not easy for me to talk about."

"Okay."

"I got these in Vietnam," he said, and I knew he meant his hands. "I was just a guy, no different from anybody else, halfway through my second tour. We got caught, out on patrol, and we lost just about everybody. A few got away. Not me, though. I took a round through the leg and ended up in an NVA prison camp. There was a colonel running the place who thought I knew more than I did."

I saw his hands twitch.

"Either that or he was just plain mean. In the end, I guess it don't really matter. He worked on me for a few weeks, messed my hands up pretty good, then tossed me in a hole for five years. I almost died in that place." His voice seemed to trail off. "Five damn years," he said again, then fell silent. I could tell his mind was far away.

"Five years in jail," I said into the emptiness, trying to imagine it. His voice, when he replied, was bitter.

"Wasn't no jail, damn it. It was a dirt-floor cage eight feet wide. Five years, man. They let me out twice a month. Rest of the time, all I could do was sleep, shit, or pace. Mostly, I paced. Four steps and turn. Four and turn." He looked at me. "I can't handle closed spaces, Work. That's why I walk. When the walls close in, I just get out. You know, because I never could before." He gestured with his whittled-down hands—at the trees, the sky, everything. "You'll never know what this means." He closed his eyes. "This space."

I nodded, but I thought I might damn well find out one day.

"But why are you telling me this?" I asked him.

He opened his eyes and I saw that he was not crazy. Tortured and tormented, but not crazy.

"I have a problem with authority," he said. "You understand? I can't stand the sight of a uniform. And the cops round here have done nothing to make me feel any different. They don't exactly treat me with love and respect." A grin split his lumpen face. "I can't talk to the cops. I won't. You see?"

I understood, but I didn't get it. What did any of this have to do with me? I asked him. He didn't answer right away. Instead, he turned and walked. I hurried after him.

"You see how I walk," he said. "All the time. Anytime. Day or night. Don't matter. The walls close in and I walk 'cause I have to."

We turned right, onto a neat street, where the houses all had an individual charm. Max stopped in front of one, a small cottage with green grass and a hedgerow that separated it from its neighbors on both sides. The house was yellow, with blue shutters and a pair of rocking chairs on the front porch. Roses snaked up a trellis that bordered a stone chimney. I looked up at Max, suddenly realizing how tall he was.

"I'm talking to you because I won't go to the cops." My frustration must have shown, because he took off his hat and scratched at the matted hair beneath. "He was killed the night after Thanksgiving, right? It was raining."

I nodded, a strange sensation in my stomach.

"And they found his body in the Towne Mall, the empty one down by the interstate? Where the creek goes under the parking lot?"

"What . . ." I began, but he didn't respond to me. It was as if he were talking to himself, but with his eyes so hot on me, I could feel them.

"I'm tellin' you this story so you understand. It's important."

"What's important?" I asked.

"I'm tellin' you because I don't think you killed that man."

The sensation in my stomach expanded, heat rushing out into my limbs, my fingers tingling. "What are you saying?"

"I walk all the time," he said. "Sometimes by the tracks. Sometimes the park." A pause. "Sometimes by the interstate." I realized that I had seized his forearm. It was hard and scrawny beneath the slick plastic. He didn't even notice. "I remember that night because of the rain and because it was right after Thanksgiving. It was late, after midnight. And I saw the cars, near the mall. There are never cars there at night. It's a dark place with maybe a bum or two, maybe some junkies, but that's about it. Once I saw a fight there, a long time ago, but never cars. Not that late."

My heart was thudding, my lips dry. What was he saying? I peered through those thick, filthy lenses, looking for something. For some sense of what he was about to say. For some reason not to be afraid.

"You heard something?" I said. "Saw something? What?" I realized that I was squeezing his arm so hard that my hand hurt, but he showed no sign of discomfort. I forced my hand to relax.

"Maybe it's important. Maybe not. I don't know. But I think that maybe the cops should know. Someone should tell them."

"Tell them what?" It was almost a shout.

"I saw somebody come out from the mall that night—quick, but not running. This person moved past the cars and tossed something into the storm drain, then got in one of the cars and bailed."

The enormity of Max's revelation spilled over me. "Last year," I said. "Night after Thanksgiving. You saw a person exit the Towne Mall, throw something into the storm drain, and then leave in a car?"

Max shrugged. "Like I said."

"Did you see what this person looked like?" I asked.

"No."

Relief surged through me. He could not identify Jean.

"It was dark, raining, and this person was far away, wearing a coat and a hat. All dark. But I don't think it was you."

I released his arm, but he paid no attention. "Why not me?"

"This person was shorter, I think. Medium. You are too tall."

"Was it a man or a woman?"

"Who can say? Could have been either."

"But you are certain it wasn't me."

Max shrugged again. "For years I've seen you. You never do anything. You sit on your porch and drink beer. I've known a lot of killers, seen a lot of dead men; I don't reckon you could kill a man. But that's just me, my opinion."

I should have been offended, but I wasn't. He was right. In spite of going to law school, getting married, and running a practice, I never *did* anything. I coasted.

"What was this person wearing?" I asked.

"Dark clothes. A hat. That's all I can say."

"How about the cars? Can you tell me anything about them?"

"One big. One not so big. Not black, I think. But dark."

I thought for a minute. "Which car did this person leave in?"

"The smaller one. I'm sorry I can't tell you more. They were a ways off and I wasn't really paying attention."

"What happened to the bigger one?"

"It was still there when I left. I was just walking by. I didn't stay. Two days later, I walked by the same place, but the car was not there."

"What did this person throw into the sewer, Max? Did you see it?"

"Nope, but I have a theory, same as you."

"Tell me," I said. But I knew.

"When a person throws something into a hole in the ground, it's gonna be something they don't want to be found. The papers say the cops are looking for the gun that killed your father. I think maybe you look in the storm drain and you'll find it. But that's just me talking, and I'm just a guy."

I saw it through his eyes. Like I'd been there. Of course it was the gun. And if the cops found it? Game over. But the irony was like a fork in my guts. When they found Ezra in the Towne Mall, it was bad enough, but the memories of that awful day so long ago were just that, memories. But this was the tunnel, the throat, and I had to go there, to get the gun before the cops did. Before Max decided that he should tell someone else. Lord help me.

"You were right to tell me, Max. Thank you."

"You gonna tell the cops?"

I couldn't lie to his face, so I gave him the best truth I could. "I'll do what has to be done. Thanks."

"I had to tell you," Max said, and there was something in his voice, something unsaid. I turned back to him just as a car passed us. His eyes were on that car, and he watched it until it was gone; then he looked down upon me. "I've been in this town for nineteen years, Work, almost twenty. I probably walked ten thousand miles in that time. You're the only person who ever asked to walk with me . . . the only one who ever wanted to talk. That may not seem like much to you, but it means something to me." He put one of his shattered hands on my shoulder; his eyes were steady on mine. "Now that's not easy for me to say, but it had to be said, too."

I was moved by his sincerity, and realized that we'd traveled our own painful roads in this town. They were different, our roads, but maybe just as lonely.

"You're a good man, Max; I'm glad that we met." I held out my hand, and this time he shook it, best as he could. "So come on," I said. "Let's walk." I started to turn, but he didn't follow me.

"This is where I stop," he said.

I looked around at the empty street. "Why?"

He gestured at the yellow cottage. "This is my house."

"But I thought . . ." Fortunately, I stopped myself. "It's a lovely home, Max."

He studied the house as if looking for some imperfection, and then, finding none, he looked back at me. "My mother left it to me when she died. I've been here ever since. Come on inside. We'll grab a couple beers and sit on the porch."

I stood loose and still, embarrassed by all the years I'd seen him walk past my house, and by all the assumptions I'd made. In some ways, I was as bad as Barbara, and that fact humbled me.

"Max?"

"Yeah." His face twisted in a smile that no longer looked so gruesome to me.

"May I ask a favor? It's important."

"Ask away. I might even say yes." Another smile.

"If anything should happen to me, I'd like you to take my dog. Look after him. Take him walking with you."

It would be a good life, I thought.

Max studied me before he spoke. "If something happens to you," he said with great solemnity, "I'll take care of your dog. We're friends, right?"

"Yes," I said, meaning it.

"Then good. But nothing's gonna happen. You'll tell the cops about the gun, and take care of the dog yourself. Now come on. I bought beer just for you."

So we sat on his front porch, looked across his tidy lawn, and sipped beer from the bottle. We spoke, but not of important things; and for that brief time, I was not lonely, and neither, I thought, was he.

CHAPTER

19

I found Bone asleep in the truck, curled in the sun. One look up the hill and I could tell the house was empty, but I couldn't face it; that body was still warm. So I went to the office. It still felt like Ezra's building and I thought it would be easier to start there.

It was a little after four and the street was empty, sidewalks, too. I wanted to be angry, but walked like a victim. I went in through the back door and saw my office first. Drawers were pulled out, filing cabinets stripped bare. Case files, personal documents, all of it. My financial information, medical records, photographs. Even a journal I wrote in once in a blue moon. My whole life! I slammed the drawers shut, the sounds like breaking fingers in the quiet building. I glanced in the break room and saw that they'd helped themselves to drinks from my refrigerator. Cans and candy wrappers still littered the small scratched table, and the room stank of cigarettes. I scooped up trash and stuffed it violently into a plastic bag. I cleared half the mess, then flung the bag to the floor. There was no point.

I went upstairs to Ezra's office. It, too, was in shambles, but I ignored the mess and went straight to the corner of rug that hid the dead man's safe. I took a handful of fringe and pulled the rug back. Everything looked the same: two dented boards held fast by four nails—two of them cleanly driven, two bent and hammered into the wood.

The cops had not found it, which made me savagely content. If anyone had the right to tear down the old man's last secret, I did.

The hammer was where I'd left it, and I used the clawed end to pry at the nails. The bent ones came out, but the other two refused. The claw barely fit into the crack between the boards, but a hard yank brought them up with an animal squeal. I tossed them down and bent over the safe. Hank had said to think about what was important to Ezra if I wanted to open it without a locksmith. So I tried to think clearly of the dead man whom fate had made my father.

What was important to him? A simple question. Power. Standing. Prominence. Yet it all came down to money.

In the heart of my father's million-dollar house was his study, and on the desk there was a single framed photograph. It had been there forever, a reminder and a goad. How many times had I caught him staring at it? It was who and what he was: what he'd strived to bury yet couldn't bear to forget. In his heart, and in spite of his overwhelming accomplishments, my father had always been the same grubby boy with scabby knees. The dark eyes had never changed.

I'd been born into comfort, and both of us had known all along that I lacked his hunger. That hunger had made him strong, but it'd made him hard, as well. Ruthlessness was a virtue, and the lack of it in me was, to him, the surest proof that he had fathered a weakling. So where I searched for meaning, he'd sought power. His life had been a determined climb to the top, and it all came down to money; it was the foundation. Money had bought his house in the best neighborhood. Money had bought cars, paid for parties, and financed political campaigns. It was a tool, a lever, and he'd used it to shift the world around him, the people, too. I thought of my career, and knew I'd chosen the easy route. He'd bought me off. I could face that now. Maybe he'd bought us all, except for Jean. For her, the cost was too heavy, and, unable or unwilling to bend, she'd snapped under the weight of it. So in the end, Ezra had paid the price. The whole thing reeked of karma.

I studied the safe. I'd discovered it by accident and could have gone the rest of my life without knowledge of its existence, yet it weighed upon me.

Money and power.

I remembered my father's first million-dollar jury award. I was ten, and he took the family to Charlotte to celebrate. I could still see him, teeth clamped on a cigar, proudly ordering the best bottle of wine in the restaurant, and how he'd turned to Mother. "Nothing can stop me now," he'd said. And I remembered Mother's face, too, her uncertainty.

Not us. *Me.*

She'd put her arm around Jean, and at the time I didn't recognize it, but looking back, I knew she'd been scared.

That verdict was the beginning. It was the largest jury award in the history of Rowan County, and the press made my father famous. After that, people came looking for Ezra Pickens.

And he was right. Nothing could stop him. He was a celebrity, an icon, and his ego grew with his fame and with his fortune. Everything changed for him after that.

For us, too.

I still remembered the date of the verdict. It was the day Jean turned six.

I typed the date into the keypad. Nothing. I replaced the boards and hammered in four new nails. I took my time, and they sank into the wood, straight and clean. I spread the rug with a sigh and turned away.

It would have been too easy.

I moved around the office, closing drawers, turning off lights, and was about to leave, when the phone rang. I almost didn't answer it.

"Damn all generosity!" It was Tara Reynolds, calling from her office at the *Charlotte Observer*. "My editor is about to stroke out."

"What are you talking about, Tara?"

"Have you seen the *Salisbury Post*?" Unlike the *Observer*, it ran in the afternoons. It would have hit the stands less than an hour ago.

"No."

"Well, you should pick up a copy. You're page-one news, Work, and it's a freakin' injustice, that's what it is. I bust my ass on this story, I'm all set to break it, and some idiot from the *Post* gets a call that the cops are at your office and just walks on over and takes your damn picture."

My voice was cold. "I'm sorry to inconvenience you."

"'Police search home, office of slain lawyer's son.' That's the headline. There's a picture of you standing with the district attorney in front of your office."

"That was four hours ago," I said.

"Hey, good news travels fast. The article's short. Do you want me to read it to you?"

So, the story was now official. Fifty thousand people subscribed to the *Post*. In twenty-four hours, it would be in the *Observer*, which had close to a million readers. Strangely, I felt more calm than not. Once you lose your reputation, your worries become more concrete: life or death—freedom or prison. Everything else pales.

"No," I said. "I do not want you to read it to me. Other than making my day even worse, is there some reason you called?"

"Yeah. I want you to appreciate me. Because right now, I'm the only one doing any favors."

"Appreciate what?" I asked bitterly.

"News," she said. "With the same proviso as last time. You tell no one where you heard it, and I get the exclusive when this is said and done."

I didn't speak right away. I had a sudden splitting headache. None of this would go away. Not on its own.

"Do you have someplace else you need to be?" Tara demanded sarcastically. "If so, just tell me and I'm gone. I don't have to play games."

"No games, Tara. I just needed a second. It's been a long day."

She must have heard the despair in my voice. "Hey, I understand. I get caught up in things, the curse of the type A personality. I'm sorry."

She didn't sound particularly sorry, and my words, when they came, were short and bitten off. "It's okay," I said. "You use me. I use you. No reason to take it personally. Right?"

"That's exactly right," she said, oblivious. "So here's my news. The police have figured out why your father was in that old mall."

"What?"

"Actually, it would be more accurate to say that they've figured out how he was in that mall."

"What do you mean?"

"The property was going into foreclosure. Your father was retained to represent the bank. He would have had keys to the property."

This surprised me. While I didn't know everything about my father's practice, I should have been aware of the case, if only peripherally.

"Who owned the property?" I asked.

"I'm checking on that. All I know now is that it was a group of investors, some local, some not. They bought the mall several years ago, when it was about to fold. They pumped millions into renovations, but the tenants never materialized. They were hemorrhaging money when the bank finally dropped the ax."

"Is there any chance of a connection?" I asked. "Are the police looking into it?"

"I don't think so."

"Are you serious?" I demanded. "Ezra was foreclosing on a multimillion-dollar operation, was killed on the property, and the cops don't see a connection?"

I heard Tara light up a cigarette, pausing before she spoke. "Why would they, Work? They've got their man." She exhaled, and I pictured her wrinkled lips and the bright pink lipstick that bled into the cracks.

"No, they don't," I said. "Not yet."

"Well, that brings me to my second piece of news."

I knew trouble when I heard it. "What?"

"I don't have specifics, you understand? But word is that they found something in your house that incriminates you."

"That's not possible," I said.

"I'm just telling you what I heard."

"But . . . you must know more than that."

"Not really, Work. Only that Mills about had an orgasm. And that's a direct quote from my source."

I thought of all the people who had been in my house since Ezra disappeared, all the parties, dinners, and casual visits. Jean had been there once or twice, Alex, too. Even the district attorney. Christ, half the town had passed through those doors at some point in the past eighteen months. What in the hell was Tara talking about?

"You're not holding out on me, are you?" I asked. "This one is important."

"I've told you all I know. That's the deal." Another long exhale, and I knew she had something else to add. "Have you told me everything?" she finally asked.

"What do you want to know?"

"It all comes back to the gun, Work. They want the murder weapon. Have you had any more thoughts on that?"

I saw Max's face, and felt the dampness of that hole. I smelled mud mixed with gasoline, and suddenly couldn't breathe. For a moment, I'd forgotten.

"Still no sign," I finally told her.

"Would you like to make a statement? I'd be glad to put forth your side of the story."

I thought of Douglas. "That would be premature," I finally said.

"Call me if you change your mind."

"You'll be the first."

"You mean the only."

"Right."

She paused and I could almost smell the smoke; she liked menthols. "Listen," she said. "I'm not really such a cold bitch. It's just that thirty years of this has taught me a thing or two, like never get emotionally involved in the stories I cover. It's nothing personal. I just have to keep my distance. It's a matter of professionalism."

"Rest assured, you're very professional," I told her.

"That was uncalled for."

"Maybe. But I seem to be surrounded by professionals today."

"Things will work out," she said, but we both knew the truth. Innocent people went to jail all the time, and good guys bled as red as the rest.

"Take care," she said, and for an instant she sounded like she meant it.

"Yeah. You, too."

The line went dead and I settled the receiver back on its cradle. Suddenly, things weren't so clear. Why, on that night, did Ezra go to that nearly abandoned mall? His wife had just died. His family was coming apart at the seams. Who called him, and what was said in that hushed conversation? It was after midnight, for Christ's sake. Did he go first to the office, and if so, why? My father had driven a black Lincoln Town Car, so Max's big dark car had to have been Ezra's, but who owned the other one? Jean had a dark car, but so did a thousand other people in town. Was I wrong? Could there be some other reason for my father's death? I turned to an ugly reality, one that I'd shied away from because I simply could not face it. The old mall was less than a mile from where I sat. Its destruction was almost complete, but the parking lot was untouched, as was the low dank tunnel that ran beneath it. If Max was right and the killer had ditched the gun in the storm sewer, then it would be there still, lying in that grim place like the memories that had defiled my dreams, if not my very life. I would have to return, to claim the legacy of my father's last breath, and I didn't know if I could do it. But there was no choice. If the gun was Ezra's, I'd know it. Then I could dispose of it, so that Mills could never use it against Jean. And if it wasn't his gun? If by some miracle I was wrong, and it was not my sister that pulled the trigger?

I thought of Vanessa, pictured her face the last time I'd seen her. She'd kicked me out, spilled her tears on the hands of another man. Would she step forward if I asked? Would she utter the words to set me free?

I had to believe that she would. Whatever harm I'd done to her, she was a good woman.

My watch showed it was almost five. I glanced around the ruined office and, for a moment, considered cleaning it up, but this was not my life, so I locked up and left the place untouched. Outside, the clouds had pulled apart and a careworn light filtered through. People were leaving the surrounding offices, packing up and going home to the same dreams that used to mean so much to me. No one spoke to me. No one raised a hand. I drove home and parked beneath high walls of peeling paint and windows as colorless as sanded lead. And when I finally went inside, it was like walking into an open wound. Our bed was pulled apart, my desk riffled, and clothing littered the floor. Every room was the same, yet each was worse than the last. I closed my eyes and saw Mills and her smug smile as she'd left me in the driveway to resume this slow and visceral penetration.

I wandered through the house, touched once personal and private things, then shuffled into the kitchen and took down a bottle of bourbon and a glass. It slopped as I poured it, but I didn't care. I sat at the breakfast table and downed half the glass before I realized what I was seeing, right there on the table before me. I slammed the glass down so hard that the remaining bourbon exploded out of its mouth and settled in a wide wet arc onto the face of the newspaper that Mills had so carefully placed there for me to find.

It was the *Salisbury Post*, and there I was on the front page. It was not the headline that enraged me, but the fact that Mills had put the paper there for me to find. And that act, so simple, had been calculated to inflict pain. She'd caught me at home, defenses down, and slit me open me with a fifty-cent newspaper.

My glass shattered on the wall. Then I was on my feet.

The writer didn't have many facts, but the implication was more than between the lines. The son of a wealthy dead lawyer was being investigated. He was one of the last to see the victim alive and had somehow managed to compromise the crime scene. And there was a will, with fifteen million dollars at stake.

Not much, I thought, but more than enough for a public crucifixion. And soon there would be more, along with any unflattering information they could ferret out of my neighbors or colleagues.

I looked again at the paper and future headlines flashed through my mind.

LOCAL LAWYER GOES TO TRIAL . . . PROSECUTION RESTS . . . JURY SAYS GUILTY IN PICKENS MURDER TRIAL . . . SENTENCING TODAY . . .

The phone rang. I snatched it up.

"What!" Brutal and short.

At first there was silence, and I thought no one was there. But then I heard a wet snuffling noise and what was clearly a choked-off sob.

"Hello," I said.

Crying. Sobbing. A susurration of wet helplessness that dwindled to a keen so high, I could have been imagining it. I heard a dull and rhythmic thumping, and I knew it was Jean, striking her head on the wall or rocking so hard in her chair that it sounded in protest. My own problems dwindled into some distant place.

"Jean," I said. "It's okay. Calm down."

I heard a mighty intake of breath, as if her lungs were nearly starved yet had found the courage for one last, great effort. The air rushed in, and when it came out, it carried my name, but weakly, so that I almost missed it.

"Yes. It's me. Are you okay?" I tried to stay calm, but Jean had never sounded this bad, and I saw her blood on a sagging floor or spurting into hot pink water. "Talk to me, Jean. What is it? What's happening?"

More wet, stifled breathing.

"Where are you?" I asked. "Are you at home?"

She said my name again. A curse. A benediction. A plea. Maybe all three. Then I heard another voice, Alex's, but it was distant.

"What are you doing, Jean?" Footsteps boomed on wooden floors, accelerated, grew louder. "Who are you talking to?" Jean said nothing. Even her breathing stopped. "It's Work, isn't it?" Alex demanded, her voice louder, as hard as the receiver clenched like an ax in my hand. "Give me the phone. Give it."

Then it was Alex on the phone, and I wanted to reach through the line and beat her.

"Work?"

"Put Jean back on the phone! Right now, goddamn it!"

"I knew it was you," she said, and her voice was unruffled.

"Alex, I am so serious, you would not believe it. I want to talk to my sister and I want to talk to her now!"

"It's the last thing she needs right now."

"That is not for you to decide."

"Jean's too upset to know what she's doing."

"That still doesn't make it your decision."

"Whose, then? Yours?"

I said nothing, and for that instant I could hear Jean crying in the background. I felt a terrible helplessness.

"You know what she's been through, Alex. You know her history. For God's sake, she needs help."

"Yes, she does, but not from you." I tried to speak, but Alex cut me off. "Let me make one thing perfectly clear. Jean is upset because she saw your picture in the paper, you dumb shit. Black print implicating you in her father's murder. Is it any wonder she's upset?"

Then I got it. I understood. The article had compounded Jean's guilt. She'd killed her father, and her brother was taking the blame for it. No wonder she was falling to pieces. The possibility might have occurred to her—that day she spoke to Detective Mills—but the reality was different, and it was pulling her apart. The revelation staggered me. I was out of my depth, and knew I could do more harm than good. Poor Jean. What more must she endure?

"If anything happens to her, Alex, I'll hold you responsible."

"I'm hanging up now. Don't come over here."

"Tell her that I love her," I said, but Alex was already gone. I put the phone down and sat at the breakfast table, there in the back corner of my kitchen. I stared at the wall and then dropped my head into the cradle of my hands. Everything seemed to collapse—the room, my insides—and I wondered what further grief the day could possibly bring.

When I looked up, I saw the bottle of bourbon. I reached for it and pulled straight from the bottle. Hot liquor shot out and I drank too much, choking. I closed my eyes on the burn, wiped away something that felt like tears, and heard a gentle knock on the glass window of the garage door. I looked up, startled, and saw Dr. Stokes's face on the other side. I stared for a moment, and he cracked the door. He wore a seersucker jacket, a white shirt, and jeans. His white hair was neatly combed.

"I won't ask if this is a bad time," he said. "Mind if I come in?"

His was a welcome face, lined, warm, and sincere, and I nodded. He entered with economical movements, passing through a narrow space that closed quietly behind him. He put his back to the door and clasped his hands in front of his belt. His eyes moved over the kitchen, but it was a brief journey. He spent a little more time on me.

"Where do you keep the glasses?" he asked. He was stately and elegant, perfectly composed. I pointed at the cabinet, still uncertain of my own voice. He moved farther into the kitchen and stopped next to me. I thought he would offer his hand or pat me on the back. Instead, he reached for the newspaper and folded it closed; then he was past. He stepped over the shards of my broken glass and filled two fresh glasses with ice. "You don't have ginger ale, by any chance?" he asked.

"Under the wet bar," I replied, climbing to my feet.

"Sit down, Work. You look whipped." He returned to the table and poured bourbon over ice. "You like ginger ale with bourbon?" he asked.

"Sure. Yes." I remained standing. He was so matter-of-fact that nothing felt quite real. He studied me again as he finished making the drinks.

"Gonna burn your insides out, drinking it straight from the bottle like that." He handed me a glass. "Why don't we try the study?"

We walked through the long foyer and into the study, a small room with dark wood trim, green walls, and twin leather chairs flanking the cold fireplace. I turned on several lamps so that it would not appear so gloomy. Dr. Stokes sat opposite me and sipped his bourbon and ginger.

"I wouldn't have come over had Barbara been here," he said. He turned one palm up. "But . . ."

"She's gone," I said.

"So it would seem."

We drank in silence for a moment or two.

"How's your wife?" I asked, knowing how absurd it sounded under the circumstances.

"She's fine," he answered. "She's playing bridge down the street."

I looked down into the depths of the cold brown liquid that filled my glass. "Was she home when the police were here?"

"Oh yes. She saw the whole thing. Hard to miss, actually. There being so many of them and here for so long." He sipped. "I saw you in your truck, down by the lake. My heart went out to you, boy. I feel bad that I didn't come down, but at the time it seemed like the wrong thing to do."

I smiled at the old gentleman and at his understatement. "I would have been bad company, yes."

"I'm sorry that this is happening, Work. For what it's worth, I don't believe that you did it, not for a second. And I want you to know that if we can do anything to help, all you have to do is ask."

"Thank you, sir."

"We're your friends. We will always be your friends."

I nodded, thankful for the words, and we were silent for a moment.

"Have you ever met my son, William?" Dr. Stokes asked unexpectedly.

"He's a cardiologist in Charlotte. I've met him. But it's been four or five years since I saw him last."

Dr. Stokes looked at me and then down to his own glass. "I love that boy, Work, more than life itself. He is, quite literally, my pride and joy."

"Okay."

"Bear with me, now. I haven't gone senile just yet. There's a story coming, and there's a message in it."

"Okay," I said again, no less puzzled.

"When Marion and I first moved to Salisbury, I was right out of residency at Johns Hopkins, younger than you are now. In many ways, I was a damn idiot, not that I knew it at the time. But I loved medicine. I loved everything about it. And I was eager, you understand, ready to build a practice. All Marion wanted was to start a family. She'd been patient through my residency, but she was as eager for that as I was for my career, and eventually we had our son."

"William," I stated into a sudden silence.

"No," Dr. Stokes finally said. "Not William." He took another sip, draining the glass down to a pale liquid, more melted ice than anything else. "Michael was born on a Friday, at four in the morning." He looked at me. "You never knew Michael. He was way before you were born. We loved that boy. He was a beautiful child." He laughed a bitter laugh. "Of course, I only saw Michael in small increments of time. Dinner a few times a week. An occasional bedtime story. Saturday afternoons in the park down there." He gestured with his head, through the wall, down the hill, to the park we both knew so well. "I was working hard, putting in the hours. I loved him, you know, but I was busy. I had a thriving surgery practice. Responsibilities."

"I understand that," I said, but he may not have heard me. He continued as if he'd not.

"Marion wanted other children, of course, but I said no. I was still paying off med-school debt and barely had time enough for one child as it was. I was just too busy. That's a hard thing for me to say, but there it is. She didn't like it, mind you. But she accepted it."

I watched shadows move on one side of the old man's face as he looked back down, and the way he tilted the glass in his seamed and heavy fingers. How he watched light move through the shifting ice.

"Michael was three and a half years old when he died. It took the cancer seven months to kill him." He looked up at me then, and I saw that his eyes were dry. That didn't prevent the pain from showing through. "You don't need the details of those months, Work. Suffice it to say, they were about as bad as a man could imagine. No one should live through times like that." He shook his head and paused. When he spoke again his voice had waned. "But if Michael had not died, we never would have had William. That's another hard thing to say, and most times I can't look at it straight on, not like it was a trade. Michael is a memory now, an unfulfilled promise; but William is real and he's been that way for almost fifty years. I can't picture what my life would have been. Maybe it would have been better. I'll never know. What I do know is the son I have, and I can't separate that out."

"I don't understand why you're telling me this, Dr. Stokes."

"Don't you?"

"I'm sorry. I'm not thinking very clearly right now."

He leaned forward and placed a hand on my shoulder. I felt the heat of it, and the pull of his weathered, knowing eyes.

"Hell is not eternal, Work. Nor is it devoid of all hope. That's what his death taught me, that you never know what's waiting on the other side. For me, it was William. There'll be something for you, too. All you need is faith."

I considered his words. "I haven't been to church in a long time," I said, and felt the firm grip of his practiced hand as he climbed to his feet and leaned on my shoulder. The light was full on his face when he spoke.

"It doesn't have to be that kind of faith, son."

I walked behind him as we moved back through the house, and I stopped him at the door. "What kind of faith, then?" I asked.

He turned and patted me on the chest, above the heart. "Whatever gets you through," he said.

CHAPTER

20

It was four in the morning, cold and damp. I stared at the hole, a rip in the earth, and a blacker black I'd never seen. Around it the world paled to gray, and I felt naked in that pallid light. I was squatting in weeds at the edge of the parking lot. A steep bracken-covered bank led down to the glint of water, and I heard it gurgle thickly around the storm-swept litter that had collected at the tunnel's mouth. What remained of the mall was a hundred yards away. Like everything, it felt alien in the skeletal light, a crumbled fortress surrounded by dozers and trucks, hard-edged and immovable. I heard distant noise, but here it was hushed. Only the water spoke, and it did so in the tongue of twelve-year-old boys. It said, Come, enter, be afraid.

I'd parked behind the tire store that bordered the mall property. It was closed, of course, but other vehicles were parked there and the truck would arouse no suspicion. I'd dressed for the job, in dark clothes and rubber boots. I carried a bat, and if I'd owned a gun, I'd have been carrying that, too. I also had a heavy flashlight, but the batteries weren't great. I hadn't checked them until I'd gotten there, and I knew that if I left now for new ones, I might not return. Ever.

From my position, the creek ran diagonally under the parking lot. It passed within a hundred feet of the mall before angling away to Innes Street. The first storm drain was the one I wanted. It was opposite the entrance where Ezra had been found. It was where the gun had been tossed. I knew what was beneath that drain: a concrete shelf that rose like an altar, and a red-eyed memory waiting to unman me.

"Fuck it," I said. "That was a long time ago."

I blundered through the brush, my feet loose and dangerous beneath me. I fell once but was quickly back on my feet, and then I hit the water with a splash that sounded too loud. My face was scratched from the brambles, but I still had the flashlight, still had the bat.

I was committed. I had to move soon. Slim chance or not, a cop could come by at any second. If I was found there, it would be over. Too many questions and not enough answers. So this time the blackness and the tunnel were my friends, a sanctuary, but my breath was loud in the windless space between the high banks.

I'd sworn I'd never go back.

I turned on the light and stooped into the low entrance. It was smaller than I remembered, lower, more narrow. The water came to midshin, and the bottom felt the same, a mixture of rock and deep muck. I shone the light down the length of the tunnel; it stretched away, square and wet, then faded to gloom. There was a lot of old trash and dead branches, and in places I saw narrow tracks of mud that rose from the water like alligator backs. I ran my fingers along the wall. The concrete was slick and wet. I remembered it vividly, and thought of blood, tears, and screams. I tapped the bat against the wall and walked on.

After two dozen steps, the tunnel mouth was a dull metal square, like a quarter I'd put on the tracks as a kid and pulled from the gravel after the train had passed. Twenty more and even that was gone. I was deep in the throat, but my breathing sounded steady and my heart rate was normal. I felt strong, and realized that I should have done this years ago. It was free therapy, and part of me wanted to find the bastard that had damn near ruined me. But he was gone. He had to be.

I pushed on, and each step took me further from those childhood terrors. But when I reached the shelf beneath the drain, it was bare. No gun. For a moment, I didn't care. In the cone of weak yellow light, the shelf was stained, as if by blood, and I stared, seeing a past that rose like an apparition, sudden, vicious, and so real, I could touch it. And I lived it again—the fear, the pain, all of it. But this time it wasn't about me. It was about her, and that's what I saw—the sticky blood that had looked black on her thighs, her battered eyes, and the brief blue glimmer as she'd thanked me.

Dear God. Thanked me.

I grew dizzy, and then my hands were on the concrete, my fingers clawing as if to gouge out the past. But it was just concrete, and my fingers merely flesh. I thought of a child on a playground, yelling for a do-over. But this wasn't childhood, and there were no do-overs. So I put it behind me, shoved it. Done is done.

I set the flashlight on the shelf and wiped at my mouth with the back of my sleeve. I plunged my hands into the water and felt along the bottom, my search becoming increasingly frantic. I found lots of mud and plenty of rocks, but no gun. The light flickered. I saw movement in the line where light met dark, a rat. Two of them, one crouched against the wall, one swimming against the current.

I dropped to my knees and widened the search. It had to be there! If it had entered the water, it shouldn't have gone far. There wasn't much current. But I thought about storms, and the heavy runoff that carried trash and dead branches so far into the tunnel. Could it carry a gun, too? Sweep it away?

I rocked back on my heels, shone the light down the tunnel; it ran for half a mile before exiting on the other side of the lot. A long way.

I looked for the rats. One was gone. The other seemed to watch me with something like contempt.

Maybe Max was wrong. Maybe this wasn't the right storm drain. Maybe the gun wasn't here at all. Someone might have found it. If I were looking for a place to smoke crack, this would be as good as any. People must find their way into this place from time to time.

I shone the light into the water, searched all around the concrete slab.

Nothing.

I sat on the slab, beaten, breathing hard, and the light flickered again. I didn't care. Let it go out. Leave me blind. The tunnel held no terror for me now. My demons were in the past and needed no substance to harm me. I leaned against the cold wet wall and splayed my fingers where Vanessa had lain. Did this place remember?

I shone the light on the walls around me, doubting it. It was just a place and had no need for memory. Then I looked up. It took a second for it to register, but when it did, I felt new hope. The storm drain did not empty straight into the tunnel; there was another ledge, three feet wide and half again as high, near the roof of the tunnel. It looked deep.

I clambered onto the slab, dirty, dripping, bent almost double. It was more than a ledge. It was another small tunnel. It ran back from the wall for three or four feet. I saw light from the storm drain at the end of it. The space was choked with debris: twigs, dried vegetation, litter. I reached in and began to pull it out; it rained around my legs, onto the slab and into the creek. I pulled out more and more. Faster. Frantically. I could not quite reach the very back. I strained harder, my face crushed into the concrete, tendons stretched. My mouth opened as I pushed. Then I felt something hard. My fingers scraped it, drew it closer. They seized it, knew it for what it was and ripped it out. It was a gun. Max was right.

I hunkered down onto the slab, a primitive man. I put the light onto the gun, knew right away that it was *the* gun, Ezra's gun. He'd never allowed me to handle it, not even to touch it, but I'd known it since childhood. Having seen it shoved into my mother's face, how could I ever forget it? It was a stainless-steel Smith & Wesson, with a custom pearl grip. Set into the pearl was a silver medallion, my father's initials carved into the metal. He'd been very proud of it, a rich man's gun, and it confirmed what I'd known for so long.

Jean had known where he kept the gun.

I cracked the cylinder: six shells, two of them spent. I saw the tiny divots made by the firing pin. Such small marks, I thought, touching them, to make such an enormous hole in my universe. I turned the pistol over. It was heavy, dull, and dirty. I didn't doubt that it would fire if I pulled the trigger. For a moment, I held the image in my mind, unable to deny the simple elegance of such an act, of my suicide, here of all places.

I snapped the cylinder closed, and for an instant the reality of my discovery overwhelmed me. This was the instrument of my father's death, the last thing he'd seen on earth. My fingers ached around the hard metal as I tried to picture my father's eyes. Had they begged? Held contempt? Or had they finally shown some kind of love? What had he made of the fate that brought his daughter to use his own gun against him? Had he accepted responsibility, or had he been dismissive even at the very end? I ran my fingers over the cylinder. I knew the answer and it pained me. Jean lived with his contempt; it was all he'd ever had for her—her birthright and her dark inheritance.

What a shame. What a horrible, fucking shame.

Suddenly, I needed to get the hell out, away from the rats, the smells, and the memories. I had to get rid of the gun and figure out my next step. But first I used a bandanna to wipe the gun down. I opened it up again and wiped down the inner workings. I extracted every shell and wiped them down, too. I'd known people to fry for failing to do that. Then I reloaded it and wrapped it in the bandanna.

If the cops found me with the gun, Jean would be clear. In that, at least, I'd achieved something, but it wasn't enough, not yet.

I took one last look around that dismal place, then turned my back on it. I expected to feel something as I left, but there was nothing, just the echo of footsteps that carried me back to fresh air and to the moon, which made the world seem more than what it was. And in that silver place, between high banks that felt like walls, I wanted to kneel and give some kind of thanks, but did not. Instead, I climbed up, through the thorns, until I stood on top of the tunnel, above it, and the water's voice was a whisper I could barely hear.

CHAPTER

21

So it had come to this. I had the murder weapon in my hand, an accomplice after the fact. I was dirty, wet, and bloody, scared that the cops would find me before I did what I had to do. It was a bad place to be. I wasn't a wanted man yet, but I felt the noose and knew that it was only a matter of time. Five days had passed since they'd found my father's body, a lifetime in which I'd learned a few things about living, stuff the old man should have taught me. He used to say that everybody's got snakes to kill, and I thought I knew what he meant. But a man can't kill his snakes without opening his eyes to see them, a truth he forgot to mention.

I was alone on the bridge, five miles outside of town. The sun was almost up, and I could hear the river. It sounded resolute, and I leaned over the guardrail as if I could draw upon its strength. My fingers explored the pistol, and I thought of Jean, of what it must have been like for her to pull the trigger, to walk away, to try to go on. I finally understood her suicide attempts, and I wished I could tell her that. For in my own way, I'd traveled the same sad road. What before had seemed insane now made perfect sense. Oblivion. Release. I got it, the seduction and tender mercy embodied in those words. After all, what did I have to lose? A career I cared about? Family? The love of a woman I loved in return? Only the unbearable nearness of Vanessa, and the belief that it could have been something great.

If I had anything, it was Jean. She was the last of my family, and in this alone could I do something good for her. If I killed myself, here with this gun, they would blame me for Ezra's death. Case closed. Maybe then she could find some kind of peace; leave Salisbury and go to a place where the ghosts of loved ones lost haunted others but not her. Would that I could do the same with Vanessa.

But that would never happen. She had moved on, and rightly so. So to hell with it. One moment of courage.

I cocked the pistol, and there was finality in the sound of it.

Did I come here to do this thing? No. I'd come to ditch the gun, make sure that it was never found and used against Jean. But it felt right, the thought of an ending. A single moment, a flash of pain perhaps, and Jean would be free of everything. Mills would have her pound of flesh, and my life, at the end, would serve some kind of purpose.

I stared over the river, watched new light touch the fog on the water and give it depth. A golden rim of sun appeared above the trees, my last, and I stared as it seemed to leap skyward. The world sprung into stark clarity, and I saw so very much of it: the green fields, the dark trees, and the muddy snake of river that steamed as if it, too, was being consumed.

I put the barrel under my chin, pressed it there, and sought the strength to pull the trigger, sought it in a wave of faces. Saw my mother as the floor fell away beneath her. Jean, crushed, and how she'd damned me for making Ezra's truth my own. I saw her face at the funeral, the disgust when I'd tried to take her hand. Then Vanessa—beaten senseless and fucked like an animal in the stinking mud. And shame so absolute that even now it poisoned me. It had driven Vanessa away, and I'd allowed it. That was the worst, and in a burst of resolute self-loathing, I found the strength I sought. The trigger moved under a finger that seemed to burn, and I pushed the gun so hard against my chin that it forced my head up. I opened my eyes to look again at the sky. It curved above me like the hand of God, and held therein a single hawk, wings spread and motionless. It seemed to hover, but it cared nothing for me. It circled, and I watched it. Then it cried once and flew off, and I knew that I could not pull the trigger.

The gun spun away; it hung from my finger, and in the silence the tears finally came. They burned down my cheeks, fell into the pool of my lap, and I did not look up as I dropped the gun into the river below. I knelt as my shoulders shook and I put my forehead on the cold metal rail. At first, I cried for the memories and for the failures, for all that should have been yet was not, but as the seconds slipped around me, they brought a great and terrible truth. I was alive, and I wept for that life. It was all that I had left, and so the tears came for it. Not for joy's sake, but for existence, for this breath that even now burned my lungs, and for the many times that I would look at the sky and remember.

And so I left the river. I felt new strength, a determination—something that felt like hope. I realized as I drove what had happened. I'd hit bottom again, and this time I'd bounced. I was not alive from a lack of courage, but from the sudden discovery of it. I could have pulled the trigger but did not. Why? Because life was not perfect and never would be. Max was right about that.

So I went home. I stopped at the bottom of the driveway and checked the mailbox. The picture of Alex that I'd left for Hank was gone, so he must have come at some point. In a way, I was glad to have missed him; I'd heard the mistrust in his voice and could not bear to see it in his eyes. Later, maybe, but now I was used up.

Exhaustion settled on me as I entered the kitchen. I could barely pull off my boots, and I could tell that the house was empty, not that I'd expected anything different. I wanted food and needed coffee, but the chair felt too good. So I sat at the small desk where Barbara spent so much of her day, writing small notes and talking to her friends on the telephone. I could almost feel her there, her smell and her practiced laugh of quiet amusement. I put my feet on the desk. My pants were damp and muddy, and they smeared her stationery. I sat like that for a long time, staring at the blinking red eye of the answering machine. Eventually, I pushed the button, and the machine's mechanical voice informed me that I had seventeen messages.

Thirteen were from reporters. I erased them. One was from Hank, confirming that he'd picked up the photo, and three were from Barbara. In the first, she was pleasant. In the second, she was polite. But in her last message, she was angry. She didn't shout, but I recognized the controlled, clipped tones. Where was I? That was the question, and I knew what she imagined. I was at Vanessa's.

I erased hers, too, and looked at my watch. It was 6:30, a new day. Sleep was impossible, so I went to put on some coffee. I had the pot in my hand, under the faucet, when the phone rang. I let the machine get it. By the time Barbara's outgoing message had played, I'd shut off the water and turned for the coffee machine. I froze when I heard Jean's voice. It was weak and strained, worse than before.

"Work, are you there?" A broken voice. "Work, please . . ." She coughed.

I dropped the pot in the sink and it shattered. I snatched up the phone. "I'm here, Jean. Don't hang up."

"Good," she said, and I could barely hear her. "Good. I wanted . . ." She began to cough. "I wanted to tell you . . ."

"Jean. What? I can't hear you. Where are you?"

". . . tell you that it's okay. That I forgive you. Will you remember that?"

"Jean," I shouted, suddenly frantic. "Where are you? Are you okay?"

For a time, there was only my voice and the sound of her breath, and when I spoke again, I begged her, "Please. Tell me what's going on."

"Tell me that you'll remember. I need to hear it."

I answered, not knowing why, knowing only that she needed to hear it and that I needed to say it.

"I'll remember."

"I love you, Work," she said, and I could barely hear her. "Don't let Alex tell you different." Her voice trailed away, then came back, seemingly stronger. "We were always family. Even when I hated you."

I knew then what she had done and I couldn't bear it.

Then her voice again, the barest whisper. "It should have meant more. I should have . . ."

"Jean!" I shouted. "For God's sake!"

I thought she'd hung up, for after my explosion there was only silence, but then I heard her, a thin wheeze that became a faint laugh, like wind through grass.

"That's funny," she said. "God." Then she inhaled. "I'll tell him."

I heard the phone drop from her hand and hit the floor, and then her voice, as if from a distance. "For God's sake," she said, but she was no longer laughing.

"Jean!" I screamed. "Jean!" But she did not respond, and those horrible words chased again through my head: *Third time is the charm.*

I put the phone down but kept the line open. I called 911 with my cell phone, told the dispatcher what had happened, and gave her Jean's address. She assured me that she would send EMT immediately, and I hung up. Then I dialed Jean's house, but the line was busy. That's where she was.

I pulled on the same muddy boots, grabbed my keys, and flew out the door. The truck was not built for the way I drove it, but there was no traffic yet and I beat the ambulance to her house. Loose boards vibrated beneath my feet as I crossed her porch at a run. I pounded on the door, shouting for Alex, but nothing happened. A dog barked at me from across the street. I aimed for the spot between the handle and the frame and I kicked the door. Wood splintered and I was inside, in the dark and the must, calling for Jean, shouting her name. Suddenly, Alex was there, framed in the bedroom door. She wore boxer shorts and a T-shirt, and her hair stood up in spikes. I could tell she'd just awakened.

"Where's Jean?" I demanded.

"What the fuck are you doing?" she yelled back. "Did you just break in my door?"

I crossed the room in three strides, grabbed Alex by the shoulders, and shook her so hard, I heard her teeth click.

"Where's Jean, Alex? Where is she?"

Alex tore away from me, stepped back to the bedroom door, and reappeared with a gun in her hand. She cocked the hammer, pointed it at me.

"Get the fuck out of my house, Work, before I put a hole in you."

I ignored it. For me the gun was inconsequential, like I'd never seen one before. "Damn it, Alex. Something's wrong with Jean. She called me. She's hurt. Where is she?"

My words found their way through her rage and the gun wavered. "What are you talking about?"

"I think she's trying to kill herself."

Uncertainty showed on her face. Her eyes darted around the house. "I don't know," she said. "She's not in bed."

"What do you mean? Come on, Alex."

"I don't know. I was asleep. You woke me up. She's not in bed."

"Your phone is off the hook. She has to be here."

"We take it off the hook every night."

I glared around the small house. There was only the bedroom, the kitchen, the bathroom, and the room we were standing in. I checked all the rooms, but Jean was not in any of them.

"Her car," I said, running to the kitchen window and throwing back the dusty curtain. But there was only Alex's car, the roots that rose from the bare dirt, and the oily stain where Jean's car should have been.

"Damn! It's not here." I went back to Alex, saw that her gun was on top of the television. "Where would she be? Think, Alex."

But she was at a loss, and stood uncertainly, shaking her head and muttering to herself. "She wouldn't do that. She wouldn't leave me." Alex reached out for my arm, and her eyes were fierce. Her voice steadied. "Not Jean. Not without me."

"Well here's a news flash. She did. Now where would she go?"

Alex started to shake her head, when suddenly it hit me, and I knew with absolute clarity where my sister had gone.

"Does Jean have a cell phone?" I asked.

"Yes."

"Oh my God. She's at Ezra's house."

"How do you know?"

"I just do." I turned for the door, my mind racing. "Do you know Ezra's address?"

"Yes."

"Call 911, give it to them."

"Then what?"

"Stay here, in case the ambulance shows up. If they do, then lead them to Ezra's."

"No," Alex said. "She needs me. I should be there."

"Not this time."

"You can't stop me, Work."

I turned at the door. "She called me, Alex. Not you."

Alex shrank under the words, but I took no satisfaction from the pain they caused her. Nevertheless, I had one more thing to say.

"I warned you, Alex. I told you she needed help, and I'm holding you responsible."

Then I was out the door and sprinting for the truck. My father's house was only a couple of miles away, but the roads were filling with cars. I passed three on a solid yellow line, going eighty in a thirty-five. I caught air over the tracks, then went the wrong way down a one-way street but shaved two blocks off the trip. I fishtailed into the driveway, clipped one of the box bushes, and stopped behind Jean's car. I hit the back door at a run and bounced off it. It was locked. Damn! I fumbled for my keys, realized I'd left them in the truck, and had to run back for them. But then I had the key in the door and it moved under my weight. I was inside, shouting, turning on lights. Her name echoed off marble floors, ran down paneled halls, and returned as if to haunt me; otherwise, the house wept with silence.

I moved as fast as I could: the kitchen, the study, the billiards room. It was a big house, and it had never seemed more so. She could be anywhere, I realized, and I thought of the bed upstairs; but then I knew, and I ran for the foyer. I rounded the corner and saw her at the foot of the stairs. She was unmoving, ashen, the rug beneath her sopping with blood.

I hit the floor beside her, my knees squelching in her blood. Her wrists had been opened with long vertical cuts, and I saw the razor blade, bright and red on the carpet.

Blood still pulsed weakly from the cuts, and I called her name. No response. I ripped off her shoes, pulled out the laces, and tied them around her arms, jerking them tight just above the cuts. The blood flow ceased, and I checked her pulse, feeling for the big vein beneath her jaw. I couldn't find it. I pushed harder, touched it. The pulse was hesitant, feeble, but it existed, and I thanked God under my breath. But I didn't know what else to do; I had no training. So I crossed her arms on her chest, tried to elevate them, then put her head in my lap and held her as best I could.

I studied her face, looking for a reason to hope, but it was blood-less and as pale as bone china. Blue veins showed through the skin of her closed eyelids, and they looked bruised. Her mouth hung loosely and I saw where she'd bitten down, bright red moons on her cracked lips. Her face was slack and her features sagged, but she was the same Jean, my sister. We used to laugh, damn it, and I swore then that I would make it better if she lived. Somehow I would do that, because it couldn't end like this. Not for her.

I stroked the hair from her face and talked to her. My words had no meaning beyond apology; they blurred, ran into the minutes that stretched away like hours, and later I could never recall them, although I might have begged her to please not leave me alone.

Then there was noise around me, the clatter of a gurney and calm, efficient voices. Hands were upon me and I did not know them, but they led me away and steadied me so that I could see. Jean was surrounded by men in white, and they moved over her, binding her wrists, slipping a needle into her arm, and covering her so that the last of her warmth should not escape. Someone asked me if the tourniquets were mine and I nodded. "Probably saved her life," the man told me. "A close thing."

I covered my face with my hands and dared to trust that she would live. When I looked up, Alex was there. She met my eyes over the stillness of her lover, and her old pride was back, her anger and her strength, but in that moment we shared the same thought: If Jean lived, it would be because of me, and Alex acknowledged that fact with her eyes and with fingers that fluttered before her mouth, as if to stop words that she could not take back. But I nodded nonetheless and she nodded back.

Then Jean was on the gurney and it took her from this place she'd chosen. For a moment, I was alone with Alex, and she came to where I sat slumped against the wall. Her jaw moved beneath sealed lips and her hands were fists, beating the tops of her thighs as she sought for words.

"Will you go to the hospital?" she finally asked.

"Yes. You?"

"Of course."

I nodded, looked down, and noticed that her feet were bare. She shifted her weight from one foot to the other.

"Do you think she'll be okay?" she asked.

I thought about the question. "I think she'll live," I said. "The paramedics think so." I paused, studied her face, saw that she'd been crying. "Do you think she'll be okay? I mean . . . well, you know what I mean."

"She's strong," Alex said. "Strong enough, I thought. But now I don't know. I feel like I don't know anything. I always thought . . . We always said . . ."

Her voice trailed away and she wiped at her nose. I thought of something she'd said back at Jean's house, and I understood, but the understanding left me chilled.

"You always said you'd go together? Is that it?"

Alex stepped back as if struck, and I saw that she'd left a bloody footprint on the hardwood floor, a perfect little foot. I could even see the lines.

I told her what was on my mind. "'Not without me.' That's what you said."

"What?" Her voice was loud, and I knew that I was right.

"'She wouldn't do that. . . . Not without me.' Those were your words. I want to know what they mean."

I climbed to my feet, growing angry. "Did you talk about this? Doing it together? Is that what you meant?"

"No." Another step back.

"Is that the kind of help you've been giving her? Is it?" A shout. "Then it's a miracle she's alive at all, and no damn wonder that she called me instead of you."

Alex stopped moving, and there was a sudden resoluteness in the way she stood and in the tone of her voice. She was no longer defensive, but upset herself, pissed-off—the Alex I knew so well.

"It wasn't like that," she said.

"It was a call for help, Alex, and she called me. Why did she do that? Why not you?"

"You couldn't possibly know how it was, and you could never understand. Don't flatter yourself. You're all the same."

"Who?" I demanded. "Men? Heterosexuals?"

"Pickens men," Alex replied. "All men. Take your pick. But mostly you and your damn father."

"Try me," I said. "Explain it to me."

"You have no right to judge us."

My voice rose and I let it. I was furious. I was scared. And I could not bear the comparison she'd made. I pointed at the empty door, toward the hall through which they'd rolled my sister to the ambulance.

"I do have the right," I shouted. "Goddamn you, Alex. I do. She just gave it to me, and you can't change that. If Jean lives—and you should pray that she does—then we'll see who has the right. Because if so, I'm going to have her committed, so that she can get the help she needs."

"If you're around," Alex said, and her eyes glittered with insect intensity.

"Are you threatening me?" I asked.

Alex shrugged, and her features dropped. "I'm just saying it seems like you've got other worries, other things to occupy your mind."

"What are you implying?"

"I'm not implying anything. I'm stating the obvious. Now, if you're finished with your tirade, I'm going to the hospital to be with Jean. But remember this." She stepped closer. "You have never had power over me, never, and as long as I'm around, you'll never have power over Jean, either."

I looked at Alex, at her bottled rage, and felt my own fall away. How had we come to this?

"She said that she loves me, Alex. In spite of everything, she still loves her big brother. So, you see, I don't need power over her. I don't want it. She called me and I saved her life. Just like I did before she met you. Think on that. Then let's figure out what we can do to help this person we both love so much."

If I'd expected Alex to back down, I should have known better.

"That's not what I meant, Work, and you know it. Stop being such a fucking lawyer."

She turned and left, her bare feet soundless as she fled the truth. I heard the door slam, the muffled sound of her car, and then I was truly alone in the great house I'd known for so long. I looked at the rug spread beneath the stairs, the lake of blood that filled the space with its own peculiar scent. Footprints led away from it, and tracks from the gurney, growing lighter, transparent, and then disappearing altogether. I saw Jean's cell phone and picked it up. I held it, studied the dried blood on it, and then placed it on the small table by the door.

I told myself I should go to the hospital, but I knew from bitter experience that Jean would live or die whether I was there or not; and I was so tired, so unable to deal with Alex again. I thought of the big bed upstairs, pictured myself on its snowy sheets; I wanted to roll into them, touch their cleanness, and pretend that I was a child again and had no worries. But I could not; I was not that person anymore, not a child and not a deceiver. So I lay down on the carpet, next to the drying wasteland of my sister's life.

CHAPTER

22

At the hospital, they told me that she would live. If I'd been a minute later, she would not have. That's how thin the margin was, around seventy heartbeats. They would allow only one visitor at a time, so I had the nurse ask Alex for five minutes. We passed each other in the hall outside Jean's room and both of us tried to be nice. It was awkward, and we looked like victims in the bright, clean light.

"How is she?" I asked.

"They say she'll make it."

"Brain damage?"

Alex shook her head, pushed her hands farther into the pockets of her grubby jeans. I saw where Jean's blood had dried between her toes. "They don't think so, but they won't swear to it."

"They sound like lawyers," I said, but Alex did not smile.

"Yeah."

"Has she regained consciousness?"

"No."

"Listen, Alex. When Jean wakes up, she'll need to see people who care about her, not people who hate each other. I'd like to give her that."

"You mean fake it."

"Yes."

"I'll do it for Jean, but the line's been drawn for us. Don't let my act fool you. You're bad for her, even if she doesn't see it that way."

"All I care about is getting her better, and I want her to know that people love her."

Alex looked down the hall, away from Jean and from me. "I'm going for coffee. I'll be ten minutes."

"Okay. Thanks."

She took two steps and turned. "I wouldn't have shot you," she said.

Her statement surprised me. Until then, I'd forgotten all about the gun in her hand and how steady it had seemed. "Thank you," I said.

"I just wanted you to know that."

Jean's hospital room was exactly like every other one in which she'd awakened after a failed suicide attempt. The bed was narrow and mean, with steel rails, stiff sheets, and a bright spread that somehow appeared colorless. Tubes snaked into her body, green in the light of her monitors, and the curtains were drawn. I walked around her bed and opened them. The morning light was warm, and in it Jean looked like a wax figure, pallid and incomplete. I wanted to mold her into something else, a survivor; but I lacked that qualification, and could still feel the barrel under my own chin. Only then did it occur to me how close we both had come, and standing above her, I tried to make sense of it all. I knew only that we lived, an immense but lonely truth. I sat and took her hand. When I looked at her face, I found her eyes open and watching me. Her lips moved, and I leaned closer.

"Am I alive?" she asked in a whisper.

"Yes," I answered in a cracked voice. "You are." I bit down on my lip. She was so weak. "It was a close thing."

She turned her head away from me, but not before I saw tears slip from beneath her tightly shut eyes. When Alex returned, she was asleep again, and I left without saying a word about it. Maybe I was selfish. I didn't care.

I leaned against the wall in the corridor for what felt like a long time. Before I left, I looked into the room, through the small window with wire in the glass. The curtains were pulled again, and Alex sat where I had, holding Jean's hand. Jean had not moved; she faced the wall, and I wondered if she was still asleep. Would she turn from Alex as she had from me? Or was Alex truly her life, whereas I was welcome only at the ending of it?

I almost left, but I saw Jean move; she turned, saw Alex, and covered her face with her hands. Alex said something and Jean began to tremble, the tubes dancing beneath her forearms. Then Alex was on her feet, leaning over her; she pressed her face to Jean's and they both grew still. So I left, an unwelcome member of our sad little family.

I had the elevator to myself, but when it opened into the lobby, I saw Detective Mills standing by the exit. She was looking out the window, but I knew she was waiting for me. I walked toward her and saw a marked patrol car idling at the curb. A uniformed officer leaned on the hood, his hand on the butt of his pistol. He was young and looked eager.

"Are you here for me?" I asked. Mills turned at the sound of my voice and studied me. I was bloodstained and filthy. Next to me, she looked every inch the instrument of justice; her shoes shone and I could still see the crease in her pants. When she spoke, I smelled her mouthwash.

"I am," she said.

"What about him?" I gestured at the young cop outside. Mills shrugged but did not respond.

"Cheap theatrics," I said. "There's no need."

Outside, the cop got into his cruiser and left. He did not look at Mills or at me. Mills watched him drive away before she turned back to me.

"A little jumpy, aren't you, Work?"

"Whatever."

She smiled. "I never said he was with me."

"How did you find me?" I asked.

"I heard about your sister," she said. "I figured you'd be here."

"Thanks for your consideration." I couldn't keep the bitterness from my voice.

"Your sarcasm isn't necessary."

"I'm not in the mood for you, Detective. Not this morning. Not in this hospital. So if you'll excuse me."

I stepped around her, walked through the exit and into the parking lot. The morning had warmed and the sky was clear and blue. Traffic was loud from the road beyond the manicured hedge, and people moved around me, but I felt Mills behind me. She wore heels, and her footsteps were loud and fast. I knew she wouldn't let me off the hook that easily, so I spun around to confront her.

"What do you want, Detective?"

She stopped a few feet away from me, a safe distance, and I saw the pistol butt hanging from beneath her jacket. She gave me the same cold smile.

"I hoped we might have a chance to talk. There are some things I need to discuss. Maybe there are some things you'd like to say. Either way, I've got nothing better to do right now."

"I do," I said, and turned.

"What happened to your face?" Mills asked.

"What?" I turned back.

"Your face. It's cut."

My fingers moved to my face as if guilty of some sin. "Scratches," I said. "Just scratches."

"How'd you get 'em?" Mills asked lightly.

"I went for a walk in the woods."

She looked away and nodded. "Is that where you got so muddy?" she asked.

"Is there some point to this?"

"Why were you in the woods?"

"I was burying bodies."

"More sarcasm," Mills noted disapprovingly.

This time, I shrugged.

"Maybe we should have this discussion at the station."

"The station," I repeated flatly.

Mills looked around the parking lot and up at the scrubbed blue sky as if she found it all slightly distasteful. When her eyes settled back on me, the expression remained.

"It might be more productive," she said.

"Do you have an arrest warrant?" I asked. Mills shook her head. "Then the answer is no."

"So you claim you've never seen your father's will?"

The sudden question threw me; it was unexpected, and a veil dropped over her face as she posed it. I sensed danger. "Why do you ask?"

Mills shrugged. "It's what you told me before. I just want to make sure that all my facts are straight. You said that you'd never seen the will, knew nothing of its contents. Is that about right?"

I knew what she wanted. Knowledge of the will meant motive, and alarm bells started ringing in the back of my head. Cops were like lawyers. The best questions were the ones to which they already knew the answer.

"I'm not prepared to discuss this. My sister just tried to kill herself. I'm still covered in her blood. Does this make sense to you?"

"I just want the truth, Work. Like everybody else."

"I know what you want, Detective."

She ignored my hostility. "Is that right?"

"If you want the truth, then why don't you look into the mall fore-closure? There were millions at stake there, too—angry investors, and my father in the middle of it. For Christ's sake, he was killed in the damn mall. Or is that not relevant to you?"

Mills frowned. "I didn't know that you were aware of that."

"There may be other things of which you're unaware. Are you looking into it or not? Do you even know who the investors are?"

"I'll run this investigation as I see fit."

"Obviously."

"Don't get smart with me, Work. It's not worth it."

"Then take your blinders off and do your job!"

Her voice dropped. "Your father was just the messenger. Killing him wouldn't stop the foreclosure. You're a lawyer. You know that."

"Murder is rarely cold-blooded; people kill in emotional states. Hate, anger, revenge, lust. If you don't know the players, how can you rule it out? There could be a thousand other reasons out there."

"You forgot one," Mills said.

"What?"

"Greed," Mills said.

"Are we done?" I demanded.

"Yeah. For now."

"Good," I said. "I need a bath." I turned away.

"Don't leave town," Mills called after me. I spun on my heels and stalked back to her.

"Don't play your little power games with me, Detective. I know the system, too. Arrest me or don't, but until you do, I'll come and go as I please."

Something glinted in her eyes, but she said nothing; so I walked to my truck and slammed the door against Mills and all she represented. The small space stank of mud, gasoline, and blood, yet the smell of her sickly sweet mouthwash overrode it all. I cranked the engine and drove out of the parking lot. I turned toward home, not realizing until I was almost there that Mills was behind me. I got her point: I could come and go as I pleased, but the last word was hers.

I parked at the top of my driveway and climbed out. Mills had stopped on the street, next to my mailbox. She honked twice and pulled away, but she didn't leave; she drove around the block and parked on the side street next to the lake. I saw her and she saw me, and that's how it was until I went inside.

In the kitchen, I gripped the counter until my arms shook, and anger made the room tremble. When I let go, the last of my strength had fled. In my body I was dead, yet my mind had resolved on a single purpose. Right or wrong, good or bad, I knew what I needed.

The phone was warm against my ear and for an instant I felt her beating heart, as if my head were on her chest. I sat on the floor and dialed her number. It rang, and I could hear it, as if I were there instead of in my own home—shrill in the kitchen, soft in the hall. I pictured her rushing to answer it, across the front porch, screen door banging, the smell of turned earth and the soap she used. I saw the curve of her lips as they crafted my name. But she never came, just her voice on the machine, and it was not the same. Not even close. I could not bring myself to leave a message.

So I replaced the phone on its cradle and climbed wearily up from the floor. I spent half an hour in the shower but could not get warm. When I ran out of hot water, I toweled off and climbed into bed. I thought I was too scared to sleep. I was wrong.

I dreamed in black and white, of shadows on the floor that stretched like bars across bare feet. My toes were dark with blood; I was running, in pain, and the shadows spun across me as if a giant fan stood between the sun and me. Light, then dark, faster and faster, and then there was only dark. I stopped running. I was blind. I was deaf. But still I felt it. Something approached.

"Hello, Barbara," I said without turning over.

"It's three o'clock," she said.

"I didn't sleep much last night," I told her.

"I know," Barbara said.

Reluctantly, I turned. She was wearing a pink Chanel suit with a pillbox hat. Her face was perfect, but the diagonal light cut tiny shadows at the corners of her mouth.

"How do you know?" I asked.

She put her purse on the dresser and began switching on lights. She moved as she spoke, as if she did not want me to see her face.

"When you didn't pick up the phone, I came over. At about four o'clock, I should say. I was worried. I felt bad that I was not here for you." She turned on the last light and stood uncertainly, smoothing her skirt as if it were wrinkled. She still could not look at me. "You can't imagine how surprised I was to find an empty house."

"Barbara," I began, not knowing what to say.

"I don't want to hear your excuses, Work. I couldn't bear the insult. I can accept that you went to her because I was not here for you; in that regard, I share some of the blame. But I don't want to talk about it, and I don't want you to lie to me about it. You're not that good a liar."

I propped myself against the headboard. "Sit down, Barbara." I patted the bed beside me.

"Just because I'm talking to you doesn't mean that I've forgiven you. I'm here to tell you how things are going to be, so that we can get through this as an intact family unit. First, I don't think you killed your father."

I interrupted. "Well, thank you for that."

"I wasn't being sarcastic. Please let me finish."

"Okay, Barbara. Go ahead."

"You will not see this Vanessa person again, and I will stay here and help you get through this. Whatever has to be faced, we will face together. I will swear with my dying breath that you were with me when they say Ezra was killed." She finally looked at me. A strange light burned in her eyes, and her voice, when she continued, was as brittle and hard as shale. "We will smile at our neighbors. We will not hide as if in shame. When people ask how we are, we shall tell them. Splendid. We are splendid. I will cook for you and eventually I will sleep with you. All this will pass, and when it does, we will still have to live in this town."

Her voice had not changed, an unshakable monotone, and I watched her in disbelief as she continued to outline the way it was going to be.

"We'll stay in for the most part, but occasionally we'll go out, for appearances' sake. Everything will be as it always was. Glena has made some calls. Things are bad, but they'll get better. Once this blows over, we'll be okay."

"Barbara," I said.

"No," she shouted. "You do not interrupt me. Not now. Not after this." She pulled herself together, looked down on me, and painted a smile onto her face. "I am offering you a chance, Work. Once this is over, we can go back."

"Back to what?" I asked.

"To normalcy."

She chose that moment to sit and place a hand upon my leg. I started to laugh, a shabby noise, devoid of even rudimentary joy. I sounded crazy, even to myself, and I watched as if from behind plate glass as Barbara recoiled in confusion.

"'Normalcy,'" I parroted. "Our old life. That's no gift, Barbara. Or are you too wired into the program to even see that?"

She stood. "What are you saying?"

I climbed slowly from the bed, naked and not quite myself. I looked at this woman, this wife of mine. I thought of our past, felt the emptiness of our shallow joys and trivial dreams. I put my hands on her shoulders.

"There are few things that I know right now, and one of them is this. I'll never go back to the way things were." I thought of the shadow bars from my dream. "It's just another kind of prison." I stepped back and my hands fell to my side. Barbara's mouth hung open, then snapped shut. I looked down at myself. "I'm going to find some clothes," I said, and walked past her. She followed me into the bathroom.

"It's her, isn't it?"

"Who?"

"That bitch has already turned you against me."

I turned and said coldly, "To which bitch are you referring?"

"Don't play games with me. I won't be made a laughingstock and I won't lose you to some inbred country slut."

"I don't know anybody that matches that description, and if I did, this would have nothing to do with her. This is about me! This is about us! About choices and priorities. It's about opening your fucking eyes and seeing the truth we're drowning in! Our life is a joke. We are a joke. Can't you see that? Can't you admit it, even to yourself? We're together out of habit, because we can't admit the mistake we made and because the truth is too damn hard."

"Truth!" she said. "You want truth? Well, here it is. You think you don't need me anymore. All this money's coming your way, so now you can go and run off with your little country whore."

"What money?"

"That's funny, Work. We live in poverty for ten years and now that the end is around the corner, I'm not good enough for you. I read the papers. I know about the fifteen million that Ezra left you."

I laughed at the absurdity of it. "First of all, only you could think that we've been living in poverty, and never mind that I've given you every dime I've ever made. As for Ezra's will, I'll never see any of that money."

"That's right, because I'm your alibi and you're pissing me off."

"I don't want an alibi. I don't need it. Go keep up your own fucking appearances. Leave me out of it."

A crystalline silence fell between us, and I dressed behind her turned back. I was pulling on socks when Barbara spoke again. "I think maybe we both got a little carried away. I don't want to fight and I know that you're very upset. I think maybe you're projecting that onto me, I don't know. Let's just step back a minute."

"Fine," I said. "Whatever." I stuffed my feet into scuffed leather shoes and cinched up my belt.

"Let's just get through this trouble and then we can look at our situation a little more calmly. We've been together a long time. There's got to be a reason for that. I think we're still in love. I feel it.

When this is behind us and our money worries are gone, everything will look different."

"There's not going to be any money, Barbara. I'd have to sell my soul for it, sacrifice what's left of my life, and I can't do that. I can't let him have the last laugh."

"What last laugh? Who are you talking about? For Christ's sake, Work. It's fifteen million dollars!"

"It could be a billion, for all I care." I pushed past her. "We can talk later, but I don't know what else there is to say."

"It's just the timing, Work. The situation." She followed me through the house. "Everything fades. You'll see. It'll get better."

I passed through the kitchen, grabbed my keys and my wallet. "I don't think so, Barbara. Not this time." Then I was in the driveway, and she filled the door behind me.

"You're my husband, Work. Don't walk away from me."

I started the engine.

"Goddamn it! You're my fucking husband!"

I drove away, knowing that in one thing my wife was right. Everything fades.

CHAPTER

23

I went to the office because I had to do something. If I didn't do something, I would drink, and if I drank, I would get drunk. The thought appalled me because it was so tempting. But booze was just more rank escapism, like denial and self-deception.

I sat at my desk, ignored the mess, and looked up the number for the medical examiner in Chapel Hill. He was an ex–football player, an ex-smoker, and an ex-husband. He was a good medical examiner and a decent witness on the stand. We'd consulted on several cases and we got along. He wasn't scared of a drink.

His secretary put me through.

"I don't know if I should be talking to you," he said without preamble. His tone surprised me.

"Why not?"

"We don't exist on some pedestal, you know. We do read the papers."

I knew where he was going. "So?" I asked.

"I can't discuss my findings with you."

"He's my father."

"For God's sake, Work. You're a suspect."

"Look, I know he was shot twice. I know the type of ammunition. I just want to know if there's anything else. Anything unusual."

"We go back a ways. I'll admit that. But you're putting me in a tough spot. There's nothing I can tell you, not until the lead detective or the district attorney clears it. Damn it, Work! You know better."

"You think I did it."

"What I think is irrelevant."

"You're the medical examiner. Nothing you think is irrelevant in a murder case."

"We're not having this discussion, Work. If this goes to trial, I'll not be sandbagged on the stand by allegations of impropriety. I'm hanging up now."

"Wait," I said.

A pause. "What?"

"I need to make funeral arrangements. When can you release the body?"

There was an even longer pause before he finally spoke. "I'll release the body when I get the paperwork from the DA's office. Same as always." He paused again, and I could tell that something bothered him.

"What is it?" I asked.

"I'd rather release it to your sister," he said slowly. "For the same reasons."

"She's in the hospital," I said. "She tried to kill herself this morning."

"I didn't know that."

"Well, now you do."

A silence stretched between us. He'd met Jean once or twice.

"I'll take it under advisement, Work. Until the paperwork comes. Then we'll see."

"Thanks for a whole lot of nothing," I said.

"I'll make a note of this conversation for the file, and someone from this office will contact you when the paperwork is finalized. Until this is cleared up, I don't want you calling here again."

"What is your problem?"

"Don't jerk me off, Work. Don't play me. I heard about your trip to the crime scene. You played Mills and now she's paying for it. It could cost her the case, maybe her job. I'll not be embarrassed like that and I'll not be manipulated. Not me and not this office. Now, good-bye."

He hung up, and I stared at the phone in my hand. Eventually, I put it down. What had he seen when he closed his eyes, held the phone to his ear, and heard my voice? Not a professional. Not a colleague and not a friend. He'd heard what he'd never heard, there in his rarified office, with the gleaming tables and the rows of silent dead. He'd heard the voice of the violator, the killer who filled his days with chemical smells and cold, unmoving blood. I'd known him for eight years and he thought I did it. I had been judged and found capable. Douglas, Mills, my wife. The whole damn town.

I closed my eyes and saw thin blue lips mouthing words I could not hear but recognized nonetheless. *White trash,* they said. They were a woman's lips, flanked by diamond earrings that sparkled like the sun itself. I saw the lips twist into a mirthless smile. *Poor Barbara. She really should have known better.*

Before I knew what I was doing, I was on my feet. I ripped the phone off the desk and threw it across the room. It struck the wall and cracked apart, leaving a hole the size of my forehead. I wanted to crawl into it and disappear. Instead I climbed to my feet and picked up the pieces of the shattered phone. I could not put them back together, so I dropped them on the floor. I touched the hole in the wall. Everything was coming apart.

I went to my secretary's desk because I couldn't bear the thought of my father's. I called the funeral home. If the mortician felt strange talking to me, it didn't show in his voice. It was liquid and measured, as if poured from one of the glass containers I always imagined filling the basement of his mortuary. Not to worry, he told me. All I needed to provide was a date for the service. Everything else was arranged.

"By whom?" I asked.

"Your father. He provided for everything."

"When?"

The mortician paused, as if speaking of the dead in anything but quiet respect required careful consideration.

"Some time ago," he said.

"What about the casket?"

"Chosen."

"The plot?"

"Chosen."

"The eulogy? The music? The headstone?"

"All provided for by your father," the mortician said. "He was, I assure you, quite thorough in his preparations." He paused. "In all respects, the perfect gentleman and the perfect client. He spared no expense."

"No. He wouldn't."

"Is there any other way in which I might be of assistance to you in this difficult time?"

He had asked that question so many times, I felt the insincerity of it even through the phone.

"No," I said. "No, thank you."

His voice deepened. "Then may I suggest that you call again? Once things have settled down. All I require is the date you wish for the service to be held."

"Fine," I said. "I'll do that." I almost hung up, but then I asked the question that had lurked in my mind for the past minute. "Who did my father choose to deliver the eulogy?"

The mortician seemed surprised. "Why, you, of course."

"Of course," I said. "He would."

"Will there be anything else?"

"No. Thank you."

I put the phone down and sat in silence. Could I deliver his eulogy?

Perhaps. But could I say what he would want me to say? When Ezra made his choice, I was a different man, his monkey boy and the repository of *his* truth. Through my words, he would live one more time, and do it so that all present would remember and be humbled. This is why he'd chosen me, because he had made me, and because he was sure of his craft. Yet my words were merely that, and memories dim with time. So he'd created the Ezra Pickens Foundation, through which his name would live in perpetuity. But still that was not enough, thus the fifteen-million-dollar bribe, to ensure that I would continue his grand tradition.

I wanted to throw my arms around him, tell him that in some small way I would always love him, and then beat him half to death. For what is the price of vanity, or the cost of immortality? A name is just a name, whether it's carved in flesh or in marble; it can be remembered in many ways, and not all are good. All we'd wanted was a father, someone who gave a damn.

I rested my head on the desk, on wood that was cool and hard. I turned my cheek to it and spread out my hands. It made me think of high school. I closed my eyes, smelled erasers, like singed rubber, and the room melted away. I was in the past.

It was our first time; I was fifteen, Vanessa was a senior. Rain stuttered on the tin roof, but the barn at Stolen Farm was dry, and her skin shone palely in the premature twilight. When lightning flashed, it illuminated the world outside and sealed us in our private place. We were explorers, and when the thunder roared, it did so for us, louder each time, keeping pace with our bodies. Below us, in stalls that smelled of straw, horses stamped their hooves as if they knew and approved. I could still smell her. I could hear her voice.

Do you love me?

You know I do.

Say it.

I love you.

Say it again. Keep saying it.

So I did—three syllables, a rhythm, like our bodies had a rhythm.

Then her voice was in my ear. It was soft. It said my name, Jackson, again and again, until it filled me, a spirit.

And then it was louder.

I opened my eyes and was back in my office. I looked up and she was there, flesh and blood, in the doorway. I was scared to blink for fear that she might simply vanish.

"Vanessa?"

She wrapped her arms around herself and stepped into the room. She seemed to solidify as she moved, as if she carried some new reality into the one I'd come to loathe. I wiped at my eyes, still fearing the emptiness of vision.

"I thought you might need a friendly face," she said, and her voice passed through me like the ghost of a loved one long dead. I thought of the things she needed to hear—of my wrongness, of my need, and of my sorrow.

But my voice betrayed me and rang harsh in the pregnant stillness. "Where's your new man?" I asked, and her face melted into that of a stranger.

"Don't lash out at me, Jackson. This is hard enough as it is. I almost didn't come."

I found my feet. "I don't know why I said that. I'm sorry. It's none of my business anyway." I paused, looked at her as if she might still disappear. "I'm an idiot, Vanessa. I barely know myself anymore." I reached out with empty hands and she stopped, safe on the other side of the room. I let my arms drop. "I feel transparent. I can't hold on to my thoughts." I pictured the shattered phone, the hole in the wall. "Everything's coming apart." I stopped speaking, but she finished my thought.

"It's been hard."

"Yes."

"It's been hard for me, too," she said, and I saw the truth of her words. The skin was stretched over the bones of her face, pulled tight by her own problems. Her eyes looked hollow and deep, and I saw new lines around her mouth.

"I tried to call you," I said. "No one answered."

She lifted her chin. "I didn't want to talk to you. But then this happened. I thought you might need somebody. I thought . . . maybe . . ."

"You thought right," I said.

"Let me finish. I'm not here to be your girlfriend or your mistress. I'm here to be your friend, because nobody should have to deal with this alone."

I dropped my eyes. "Everybody acts like I did it. People look away from me."

"What about Barbara?" Vanessa asked.

"She's using this against me. A weapon." I looked away. "It's over between us," I said. "I won't go back to her."

"Does she know?" Vanessa asked. She had reason for skepticism; I'd often spoken of leaving Barbara.

I lifted my head, found Vanessa's eyes, and tried to communicate directly through them. I wanted her to know the truth of what I said. "She hasn't accepted it. But she knows it."

"I suppose she blames me?"

"Yes, even though I told her different. She can't accept the truth."

"Ironic," Vanessa said.

"What?"

"Not long ago, I would have welcomed the blame. If it meant we could be together."

"But not now," I said.

"No. Not now."

I wanted to say something to make those words go away, but I was so close to losing her, and the thought of such utter aloneness paralyzed me.

Vanessa's face had paled and her lips made a thin line as she watched me search for words and fail.

"I'm thirty-eight years old," she said. "Almost forty." She walked across the room, confronted me over the desk. "I've only wanted three things in this life, Jackson, just three: the farm, children, and you."

She paled further, as if her blood had suddenly thinned. Her eyes looked enormous. I knew what this was costing her.

"I wanted you to be the father of my children. I wanted us to be a family." A tear escaped and she wiped it away before it could get very far. "I loved you more than I thought a woman could love a man. Since childhood, Jackson. My entire life. We had what few people ever do; it would have been so right. And then you left me, just like that, after almost ten years. And you married Barbara. That damn near killed me, but I dealt with it. I got over you. But then you started coming around—once a month, twice a month, but I didn't care. You were there, with me again, and that was all that mattered. I knew that you loved me, even when you used me. Then Ezra disappeared, and you came to me that night, the night your mother died. I gave you everything I had. I held you. I poured myself into you, made your pain my own. Do you remember?"

I could barely meet her eyes. "I remember."

"I thought that with Ezra gone you would find yourself again, the boy I fell in love with. I so wanted that. I wanted you to be strong and I thought that you would be, so I waited. But you didn't come. For a year and a half, I didn't hear a word from you, not a sign, and I had to deal with losing you all over again. A year and a half, Jackson! I almost made it, too. But then, you bastard, you came back again, last week, and in spite of everything, I let myself believe. And why not? I asked myself. You felt it. Eighteen months and we still had the same passion, like no time had passed. But it had. I had finally pulled myself together, moved on. I had a life. I was as happy as I'd ever hoped to be. It wasn't bliss, but I could face the day. Then you showed up, out of nowhere, and you tore me apart."

She looked at me and her eyes were dry. "I don't think I can forgive you for that. But it taught me something, an ugly, brutal lesson that I've taken to heart."

"Please don't," I said, but she continued ruthlessly, impaling me with her words.

"There's something untouchable in you, Jackson, some part of you that is a wall between us; it's tall and it's thick, and it hurts when I hit it. I've left blood on that wall. I can't beat against it anymore. I won't."

"What if you didn't have to?"

Vanessa looked surprised. "You admit there is a wall?"

"I know what it's made of," I said.

"What?" Her voice rang with doubt.

"Once I tell you, there's no taking it back. It's ugly and I'm ashamed of it, but I've tried to tell you."

"Why didn't you?" Vanessa asked.

I hesitated. "Because you won't love me anymore."

"It couldn't be that bad."

"It's worse. It's the reason for everything bad between us. It's why I can't open up to you. It's why I let Ezra talk me into marrying Barbara, because I couldn't tell you this thing. Even now it scares me." I looked into her eyes and knew that I had never been so naked. "You'll hate me for it."

"How can you say that?"

"Because I hate myself."

"Don't say that."

"But I do."

"For God's sake, Jackson. Why?"

"Because I failed you when you needed me most, and because the reason that you love me is a lie." I reached across the desk and seized her hand. "I'm not what you think I am, Vanessa. I never have been."

"You're wrong. Whatever you think this is, you're wrong, because I know exactly who and what you are."

"You don't."

"I do." She retrieved her hand. "You're not as complicated as you think you are," she said.

"So, you want to hear this?"

"I need to," she said, and I understood. There's a difference between need and want. In spite of her brave words, she did not want to hear this.

I walked around the desk, and she stiffened. I feared that she would turn away, yet an animal stillness held her. She dwindled into herself and a mirrored glaze moved across her eyes. Then I filled the space before her, a clumsy giant, and in the shadow of her open, naked soul, I recognized the remarkable strength that was required to love me for so long and with such conviction.

I sat on the desk, but she would not allow our eyes to meet. I wanted to put my arms around her, knew better, and took her hands instead. Some emotion made them limp—fear, I guessed—and I knew that she had withdrawn to someplace inside herself. I presumed to tilt her chin and seek her in the depths of those mirrored eyes.

"Vanessa," I said.

Our faces were inches apart, her breath a feathered touch, and as she opened herself to me, her hands closed slowly around my own. I wanted to apologize, to explain, and to beg forgiveness, but none of that came out.

"I have always loved you," I said. "From the very first time I saw you. And I have never stopped loving you, not even for an instant."

She began to tremble and the façade that she'd carved onto her face crumbled as if made of sand. Tears filled her eyes, and I knew that I could hold nothing back; but emotion closed my throat, and in silence her tremors grew, until she tilted forward and leaned into me. She shook, and I armored her with my body; then the dam of her resolve burst and she began to cry, so that when she spoke, there was a distance between her words, as if they traveled from a deep place and required all the fuel of her breath to make themselves heard. I almost missed what she said.

"I told myself," she began, and then had to start over. "I told myself that I would not cry."

I held her tighter. I could not think clearly, so I murmured to her as I would to a child. "It's okay," I told her. "Everything will be okay."

I wanted to believe the words, so I repeated them. I did so time and again, like that long-ago day in the barn at Stolen Farm, when words and body heat seared our souls into something resplendent. It could be like that again, and so I told her: "Everything will be okay."

I did not hear the door open. I neither saw my wife nor heard her, not until she spoke.

"Well," she said, and her voice sundered the paper home I'd built with my words. "Isn't this cozy."

It was not a question.

Vanessa pulled away, turned to the door and the voice that could not have sounded crueler. Barbara stood ten feet away, flowers in one hand, a bottle of wine in the other.

"I must say, Work, I'm a little surprised." She tossed the flowers in a wastebasket and placed the wine on a side table.

"What are you doing here, Barbara?" There was no mistaking the anger in my voice. Vanessa backed away, but Barbara went on as if she had not heard me.

"The way you talk about this little slut at home, I thought you'd used her up." Barbara's eyes moved over Vanessa as if they could focus heat and char flesh at will. "I guess you wanted one more fling for the road." I saw Vanessa wilt, and felt my heart break. "For old time's sake." Barbara stepped closer, her eyes still hot on Vanessa. "I guess I was wrong."

"That's not true," I said. "None of it." But already Vanessa was heading for the door. Her name passed my lips, but my feet were slow. She passed Barbara before I could reach her, and my wife's words slipped through the thin armor of her exposed back.

"Did you really think you could compete with me?"

Vanessa turned, caught my eye one time, then slammed the door shut behind her. Barbara yelled at the silent door.

"Stay away from my husband, you white trash whore!"

Suddenly, I did not know myself. Rage carried me to Barbara's side and tightened my hand on her arm. Rage spun her around. Rage lifted my hand. But I brought it down. I slapped her so hard, I knocked her to the floor. Then rage filled me again, threatened to kick her, to crush her into utter and silent submission. Rage wanted blood. Rage wanted payback. And the rage was strong.

I had to fight it down, crush it through sheer will. Otherwise, I might have killed her.

Barbara must have seen it burn in my eyes, for she did not say a word until the killing light dimmed. In its absence, she saw what she expected to see, the man she'd been married to for ten years. The empty man. The shell.

If she'd seen the truth, she would have never opened her mouth to me again.

"Are you finished?" she asked. "Finished acting like what you think a man should be?"

"Is that supposed to hurt?"

"Truth sometimes does."

"Listen, Barbara. I told you before. We're finished."

She smoothed the back of her hand against her cheek. "We're through when I say we're through. I'll not be made a laughingstock. Not by that woman and not by you."

"You are so like my father," I said, and put my hand on the door. She smiled, and I stared, amazed that I'd not seen it sooner. She *was* like my father. Same values. Same detachment.

"I'll take that as a compliment," she said, climbing to her feet, straightening her clothing with a contemptuous air.

"It wasn't meant as one."

She breathed deeply through her nose. Her face was flushed, her eyes as shiny and hard as new dimes. "One of us has to be strong," she said. "And we both know who that is."

I paused halfway out of the office. "Don't kid yourself. You can call a lunatic a genius, but at the end of the day he's still crazy."

"What's that supposed to mean?"

"It means that an obsession for control is not the same thing as strength; it's just obsession." I thought of Vanessa. "I know what strength looks like," I said.

I don't know what she saw on my face: disgust, maybe pity. And the truth was this: My wife has never been strong, just angry, and there's a huge difference. Deep down she knew this.

"You need me, Work. Whether you know it or not, you will always need me."

As I passed down the empty hall in pursuit of Vanessa, I heard

Barbara's final words. They rang with her confidence and I told myself that it was false. This time, she was wrong.

"You know where to find me," she screamed, and I walked faster. "You'll come back." I broke into a run. "You always do!"

I hit the exterior door with my shoulder. It flew open and the afternoon light blinded me. I squinted, shaded my eyes, and saw Vanessa behind the wheel of her truck. She reversed out of her parking spot and sped toward the exit. She slowed at the street but didn't stop, then turned right and accelerated, blue smoke spewing from the exhaust. I ran behind her, called her name. I smelled burned oil, heard my breath and my beating heart. People stared, but I didn't care. I sprinted down the yellow line and I called Vanessa's name.

She didn't stop.

But I wasn't going to let her go, not this time, so I ran back for my truck. I'd catch her on the road or at home. Somewhere. And we'd finish what we'd begun.

I was out of shape and breathing hard when I hit the grass strip that separated the parking lot from the road. I stumbled, caught myself before I went down, then fumbled for my keys. I found the right one, shoved it into the lock, and turned it. She couldn't be too far away, no more than a mile.

I looked up as I opened the door and saw Barbara standing by the rear entrance of the building. Her face was expressionless as she watched me. I, for one, had nothing to say. My eyes probably said it all.

Then I was inside the truck, the engine hot, my foot on the gas. I backed out of the spot, pointed the truck toward the exit. And just like that, my universe changed. Suddenly, there were cars everywhere, pouring into the parking lot. Flashing lights. Uniforms. I was blocked in, surrounded by vehicles.

Nobody drew weapons, but I saw the guns and my heart stuttered. I found it hard to breathe; I knew what was happening. Then Mills was at my door, and she knocked on my window, her face surprisingly empty.

I'd created this scene in my mind on countless occasions: lying awake at night, feeling the wheels turn, so grinding and relentless. Somehow I'd thought that it would never happen, but I'd pictured Mills, and always, without fail, I'd imagined a fierce glee. Somehow, this nothingness was worse.

I rolled down the window, not really feeling my arms.

"Would you turn off the engine and step out of the car, please." A stranger's voice.

I did what she asked, and the ground felt rubbery beneath my feet.

Mills closed the truck door behind me, and I was very conscious of the sound it made, a metal door slamming shut. Uniformed officers flanked me; I didn't recognize them, and I realized that Mills must have chosen them personally.

Mills continued, and as she spoke, I felt hands turn me, bend me over the hood of my own vehicle.

"Jackson Pickens, you are under arrest for the murder of Ezra Pickens. You have the right to remain silent. . . ."

The metal was hard, unforgiving. I saw rust I'd never seen before. I smelled my own breath. I heard a grunt and realized it was mine.

"Anything you say can and will be used against you in a court of law. . . ."

I looked up and saw Barbara. She was still against the building and I sought her face. It was almost as empty as Mills's had been, but something bent her features and it looked like anger.

I felt the cuffs cinched tight around my wrists. Somebody pulled me upright by the back of my shirt. People had collected on the sidewalk and they stared. I stared back as Mills finished reading me my Miranda rights from a card.

"You are entitled to an attorney." Here she looked up and met my eyes. "If you cannot afford one, one will be appointed to represent you."

I didn't want to look at her face, so I tilted my face to the sky, suddenly thinking of the hawk I'd seen from the bridge. But this sky was empty, and if redemption moved in it, it did so in a place that I could not see.

"Do you understand these rights as I have explained them to you?"

Finally, I looked at her. "Yes. I understand them." Another stranger's voice, this one from my own mouth.

"Search him," Mills said, and again the hands were upon me. They patted me down, ran up my legs, groped my crotch and my armpits. They took my wallet and my pocketknife. Under the public eye, they took my belt. I was not a person anymore. I was part of the system.

I knew how it worked.

I was escorted to one of the patrol cars and placed in the backseat. Again, my ears resonated with the metallic clang of a slammed door. The sound lasted a long time; when it was gone, I saw that the crowd had grown, and saw also that Barbara was gone. She would not want to be seen, but I imagined her in one of the windows, one eye on me and one on the crowd. She would need to know who had personally witnessed my public disgrace.

Outside, Mills spoke to several of the uniformed officers. My truck would be impounded and searched. I would be taken to the Rowan County Jail and processed. I knew the drill.

I would be stripped, subjected to a cavity search, and dressed in a loose orange jumpsuit. I would be given a blanket, a toothbrush, a roll of toilet paper, and a pair of used flip-flops. I would be given a number. Then I would be given a cell.

Sooner rather than later, I would be questioned, and I knew that I had to prepare for that.

But right now, it didn't matter. I couldn't see it. Instead, I saw Vanessa, and how she would hurt when I failed to come after her.

How long would she wait before she closed the door on me forever?

The answer was unavoidable.

Not long, I thought.

If at all.

I thought of Jean and tried to remain calm. Reasons, I told myself.

There are reasons for this. Good ones. If not me, then Jean. I focused on that, and it kept me grounded. This was just the first step. They were taking me to jail, not prison. No one had convicted me yet.

But I couldn't fool myself for long, and as we drove away, I waited for the fear sweats to find me.

CHAPTER

24

The room was square and had wire cages over the lightbulbs; it smelled of feet. Time-bent black linoleum tiles rippled across the floor and gave the room a warped feel, like giant hands had twisted it, and I wondered if it was bad construction or my state of mind. The room was at the back of the police station, and like similar rooms at the jail, this one had green walls, a metal table, and two chairs. It also had a mirror, and I knew that Mills was behind it. She knew that I knew she was behind it, and that just made it silly.

In spite of everything, I felt a strange smile cross my face. Maybe it was because I knew that I had an alibi. If I broke, I had an out, and that made everything surreal. Maybe I was closer to the edge than I realized. Whatever the case, the feeling persisted.

They'd brought me in the back, through the parking garage, then down a concrete hall to this place that smelled like feet. They'd removed my cuffs and left. I'd been sitting there for an hour but had not touched the water pitcher on the table. I'd heard cops joke about the technique. Suspects with full bladders often spoke too freely, just to get it over with and get to the john. The wait was also common. They liked for the reality to settle in; they liked the fear sweats.

So I sat still and tried to prepare myself, but what I really wanted was a cigarette. I thought of all the clients who had been in this room before me.

When Mills came in, she brought the ripe-peach smell with her. Another detective followed her in, and I knew his face but not his name. Mills sat opposite me and he leaned against the wall, next to the mirror. He had big hands and a small head; he hooked his thumbs in his pockets and watched me without blinking.

Mills put the usual things on the table—pad, pen, tape recorder, manila file folder. Then she put a piece of paper in front of me and I recognized the Miranda waiver form. She turned on the tape recorder and announced the date and the time. She identified everyone present, and then she met my eyes.

"Mr. Pickens, you have previously been advised of your Miranda rights. Is that correct?"

"May I have a cigarette?" I asked.

Mills glanced at Detective Small Head and he produced a pack of Marlboro Lights. I took one from his hand, slipped it between my lips. He leaned across the table, lit it with a cheap pink lighter, and retreated to his place against the wall.

Mills repeated the question. "Have you previously been advised of your Miranda rights?"

"Yes."

"Do you understand those rights?"

"I do."

"Before you is the standard North Carolina Miranda waiver form. It explains your rights. Will you please read the form out loud?"

I picked up the paper and read it for the benefit of the tape recorder and any judge who might be asked to scrutinize the legality of this interrogation.

"Do you understand these rights?" Mills was taking no chances.

"I do."

"If you are willing to speak to us at this point, I'd ask you to indicate your willingness on the waiver form, then date and sign it."

All such waiver forms have a box you can check if you're willing to proceed with the interrogation. Under the law, once a suspect is in custody and requests the presence of counsel, the police are required to suspend the interrogation immediately. Anything said after that time is inadmissible in court; in theory, so is any evidence the cops find based on such statement.

I told all my clients the same thing: "Don't ever sign that damn waiver. Ask for a lawyer and keep your mouth shut. Nothing you say will help you."

I ignored my own advice, signed the waiver, and passed it over. If Mills was surprised, she hid it well. She slipped the signed form into her manila folder, as if afraid I might change my mind and tear it up. For a moment, she appeared uncertain, and it occurred to me that she'd never anticipated that I'd cooperate. But I needed information, and I wouldn't get it without playing along. They'd found something. I wanted to know what it was. It was a dangerous game.

I took the initiative. "Have I been indicted?"

"This is my interrogation." Her demeanor remained calm; she was still the detached professional, but it wouldn't last long.

"I can always retract my waiver," I said.

Few people realize this. You can sign a waiver in blood, answer questions all day, and then still change your mind. They then have to stop the interrogation, a thing that no cop wants to do until he's ready. I saw a muscle twitch in Mills's jaw. The deck is stacked in the cops' favor, and they often benefit from people's ignorance of the system.

"No. There's no indictment."

"But you have an arrest warrant?"

She hesitated again, but then answered. "Yes."

"What time did you get it?"

Her mouth constricted into a narrow pucker, and I saw Detective Small Head straighten against the wall.

"That's not important."

I could see the struggle on her face. Her answer would piss me off, but so would her silence. And I knew Mills; she wanted me to talk, wanted it so badly, she could taste it. If I talked, she could trip me up, score an early victory. If I exercised my right to remain silent, she would be denied that pleasure. But she wanted the early hit. She wanted blood, and had faith in her ability to get it.

"One o'clock," she finally said.

"Yet you waited until after five to arrest me."

Mills looked down at her pad, embarrassed to have this conversation as part of the official interrogation tape. Cops have rules, too. Don't let suspects take control of an interrogation.

"I just want to make sure we understand each other," I continued. "I know why you waited." And I did. By arresting me after five, I had no chance to go before a judge on a bail motion, not that day. That meant at least one night in jail, and that was personal, like the newspaper she'd left on my kitchen table. She wanted me to feel the noose, plain and simple.

"Are you finished?" she asked.

"Just so we understand each other."

"Then let's get on with this." She began systematically, and I had to admit that she was good. She established my identity, my relationship to the deceased, and my occupation with minimum dialogue. She wanted a clean, crisp transcript. She questioned me about the night my father died, and she was thorough. She wanted every moment accounted for, and I gave her the same story I'd given before. Mother's accident. The hospital. Ezra's house. The phone call. His sudden departure. I played down the severity of his argument with Jean, and I confirmed once again that after I'd left Ezra's house, I was at home for the rest of night. "No," I told her. "I never saw my father again."

"What about his gun?" she asked.

"What about it?"

"Did you know where he kept it?"

"Lots of people did."

"That doesn't answer my question."

"I knew where he kept it."

"Do you know how to fire a gun?"

"You point and you pull the trigger. It's not rocket science."

"Do you know where it is now?"

"No," I told her. "I have no idea."

So she went back to the beginning. She went over every detail again and yet again. She approached my story from different angles, searching for inconsistencies, the tiny lies that every guilty person tells. "What time did you go to bed? How about your wife? What did you talk about? Tell me about the argument. Tell me what happened at the hospital. What else did your father say before he left? How about the phone call? Let's go over that again."

On and on, for hours. "How did you get along with your father? What was your financial arrangement in regards to the practice? Were you partners or were you an employee? Did you have a key to his house? Did he lock his office at night? How about his desk?"

I asked for water and Mills poured a glass from the pitcher. I took a small sip.

"When did you first learn about the will?"

"I knew he was leaving me the house, but I knew nothing else about it until I met with Hambly."

"Your father never discussed it?"

"He was a secretive man, especially about money."

"Hambly tells me you were angry about the terms of the will. He says you cursed your father's name."

"Jean was not included."

"And that bothered you."

"I think it's cruel."

"Let's talk about your mother," Mills said. I stiffened.

"What about her?"

"Did you love her?"

"What kind of question is that?"

"Answer the question, please."

"Of course I loved her."

"What about your father?"

"He loved her, too."

"That's not what I meant."

"He was my father."

"That doesn't answer the question," she said.

"I think it does."

She leaned back in her chair, enjoying this power she had over me. "Were you friends?"

I thought about it, and almost lied. I wasn't sure why the truth came out, but it did. "He was my father and my business partner. We were not friends."

"Why not?"

"He was a hard man. I don't think he had many friends."

Mills flipped the pages of her pad, looking back over some previous notes. "The night your mother died."

"That was an accident," I said, a little too loudly.

Mills looked up, the pages still held between her fingers. "So you've said. But questions were asked. There was an inquest."

"Haven't you read the report?" I asked.

"I've read it. It raised some questions."

I shrugged as if this wasn't killing me. "People die. Questions are asked. That's how it's done."

"Where was Alex Shiften?" she asked.

The question took me off guard. "Alex?"

"Yes. During the argument. After the argument. Where was she?"

"I don't know," I told her truthfully.

Mills made a note on her pad and then changed tack seamlessly. "You've never seen your father's will. Is that right?"

She'd asked this before. "I've never seen his will," I told her. "I never knew any details. Until I spoke with Clarence Hambly, I had no idea that his estate was so large." I sensed movement and looked at Detective Small Head. He hadn't actually moved, but the razor's edge of his mouth had turned up at one corner, and suddenly I felt the true danger of the game I was playing. I couldn't see Mills's trap, but I sensed it. My next words were spoken slowly. "I certainly didn't know that he'd left me fifteen million dollars."

I put my eyes back on Detective Mills and saw the first gleam of triumph. Whatever she had up her sleeve, I was about to find out. She opened the manila folder and removed what looked like a document sealed in a clear plastic evidence bag. She read the evidence number into the record, took the document out, and then laid it before me. I knew what it was before it hit the table. A glance confirmed my suspicions. "The Last Will and Testament of Ezra Pickens," it read.

"You've never seen this document?" she asked.

"No," I said, a hollow place opening in my stomach. "I've never seen it."

"But according to the title of this document, it is your father's will. Is that a fair statement?"

"It purports to be the last will and testament of my father, yes. You'd need Clarence Hambly to confirm it."

"He has," Mills said, making her less-than-subtle point. Everything would be confirmed. Every word I said. "And you've never seen it before?"

"No."

"No, you've not seen it?"

"That's correct."

Mills picked up the document.

"I am turning to page five," Mills said. "There is a sentence here that has been marked with a yellow Hi-Liter. The last three words of that sentence have been underlined three times in red ink. I'm going to show this to you and ask you if you have ever seen this."

She presented the document, placing it faceup on the table. The feeling of surreal calm that had enveloped me started to crumble.

"I have never seen this before," I said.

"Will you please read the highlighted portion."

I felt Detective Small Head detach himself from the wall. He crossed the room and stood behind Mills. In a shallow voice I read my father's words; it was a voice from the grave, and it damned me.

"To my son, Jackson Workman Pickens, I leave, in trust, the sum of fifteen million dollars." Red ink underscored the dollar figure. Whoever did it had pressed down hard, as if in anger or expectation. I could not bring myself to look up. I knew what the next question would be. It came from Mills.

"Will you explain for us how this document, which you have never seen, came to be in your house?"

I could not answer them. I could barely breathe. My father's will had been found in my house.

They had their motive.

Suddenly, a hand crashed down on the table before my eyes. I jumped in my chair, looked up at Mills. "Damn it, Pickens! Answer the question. What was this doing in your house?"

Mills continued, pounding me with words as she'd pounded the table with her open palm.

"You knew about the will," she said. "You needed the money, and you killed him!"

"No," I finally said. "None of that is true."

"Hambly told us that your father planned to change the will. He was cutting you out, Pickens. Fifteen million dollars was about to fly out the window, and you freaked. So you put two in his head and you waited for the body to be found. That's how it happened, isn't it? Admit it!"

I was stunned. He was going to cut me out? Hambly had never mentioned that. I filed the issue away, concentrated on the present. This was a hard blow, a strategic nightmare, but I'd faced worse. I had to think. I had to be calm. I took a slow, deep breath, told myself to think about the transcript of this interview, think about a future jury. This was a deposition, I told myself. Nothing more.

I almost believed it.

"Are you through?" I asked, leaning against the back of my seat. My voice was quiet, and I knew that the sound of it made Mills's histrionics seem extreme. She was on her feet, leaning over the table. She studied my face and straightened. "May I pick this up?" I asked, indicating my father's will.

Mills nodded, took a step back, and sat down. Much of the color had faded from her face. "As long as you're still planning to talk to me," she said.

I declined to answer. I lifted the document from the table and slowly flipped through the pages. I needed something. Anything.

I found what I was looking for on the signature page.

"This is a copy," I said, laying the document back down and squaring the edges.

"So?" I saw brief concern tighten her eyes. It showed in her voice, too.

"So there are only a few originals of any will. Usually the client keeps one, as does the drafting attorney. Two originals, then. Maybe three. But copies, by their very nature, can be limitless in their number."

"That's irrelevant. All that matters is that you knew the terms of the will."

Arguing with me was her first real mistake. She'd opened the door, given me license to speculate, and it was my turn to lean forward. I wanted my next words on the transcript; I spoke clearly.

"You acquired a copy of the will from Clarence Hambly. You did so prior to the search of my home. That's one person that we know of who had a copy—you. I can also assume that you gave a copy to the district attorney. That's two. Clarence Hambly, of course, had one of the originals, so he could also have made a copy. That makes three people with copies of the will who have also been inside my home within the past few days." I counted on my fingers, bending each one back as I spoke. "Hambly was at Ezra's wake the night after his body was discovered. That's one. The district attorney stopped by the other day to speak with my wife. He made a special trip to visit her at the house. Nowhere else. The house. That's two. And you were there during the search. That makes three. Any one of you could have planted that copy."

"Are you challenging my integrity?" Mills demanded. "Or that of the district attorney?" I saw that the color was back in her cheeks. My words had hit the mark. She was getting angry.

"You're challenging mine. So why not? Three people, all of whom had a copy of the will, all of whom have been in my house within the past several days. That's a compelling problem for you, Detective Mills. People love a good conspiracy theory. And let's not forget Hambly's office staff. He has fifteen support people working there, plus another five lawyers. Any one of them could have copied that document. Have you checked them out? I bet a hundred bucks could buy a copy of a dead man's will, if you found the right person. What's the harm in that, right? Barbara and I have had countless people in our house over the past year and a half. One of them buys a copy of the will and plants it in our house. That's a simple picture. You should check them out as well."

Mills was furious, which was how I wanted her. Her voice rose as she spoke. "You can twist this all you want, but no jury will buy it. Juries trust cops, trust the district attorney. The will was in your house. You knew about the fifteen million."

"I wouldn't be so quick to insult the juries of this county. They're smarter than you think. They may surprise you."

Mills saw the danger of letting me take control just as I smiled. I was calm. She was not. She had called the jury stupid. I had paid them a sincere compliment. It was on the record.

"This line of questioning is over," Mills said. Her eyes burned with conviction, and I saw real hatred there.

I wasn't ready to let it go. Not yet. I wanted one more theory on the record. "Then there's the person that broke into Ezra's office," I said. "The one who tried to kill me with the chair. I wonder what he was after. Maybe he stole a copy of the will."

"That is enough." Mills was back on her feet, her hands clamped on the table's edge. I would get nothing further from her; that was plain.

So I said the only thing left to say.

"Very well. I withdraw my Miranda waiver and assert my right to remain silent. This interview is over."

Mills swelled as blood suffused her face. She had tasted the kill and liked it; but then I'd shut her down, blown massive holes in her theory. It would not be enough by itself—I knew that—but it made her look bad, cast some small shadow of doubt. She'd not fully considered the significance of the will being a copy. An original would have been much more damning. But it was all smoke and mirrors in the end. She had what she wanted. I was on record. I'd never seen the will, yet it was found in my house.

And fifteen million dollars—that would sway most juries.

Yet as Mills stormed out and left me alone with these thoughts, I had to deal with two more questions that, in their own way, were even more troubling: Why did my father want to cut me out of the will, and why hadn't Hambly told me about it?

I rubbed my hands across a face that felt as if it belonged to another man. Razor stubble, deep lines—I ground my palms into raw eyes, opened them when I heard Detective Small Head approach the table. He dropped a telephone onto the surface.

"One phone call, counselor. Better make it a good one."

"How about some privacy?" I asked.

"No chance," he replied, and moved back to lean against the wall.

Already the interview was moving behind me. I looked at the telephone and remembered Vanessa's face as she'd fled the sound of Barbara's voice. I had one phone call, so I thought of all the lawyers I knew, then dialed the only number that made any sense whatsoever. I heard the phone ring at Stolen Farm and squeezed the receiver so tightly that my hand ached. Was I looking for my alibi? Maybe, for a moment, but most of all I wanted her to know that I'd not abandoned her. Please, I begged silently. Please pick up. But she didn't, just her voice, indifferent, asking that the caller leave a message. But I couldn't. What could I say? So I lowered the phone back to its cradle, dimly aware of the detective's curious stare, and the fact that, far from here, an unfeeling machine carried the sound of my anguished breath.

CHAPTER

25

In my imagination, the cells were always cold, but the cell they took me to was hot. That's the first thing I noticed; after that, it was the size. Narrow and mean, eight by six, with a small window where I'd always pictured bars. But the glass had wires in it. I noticed this as I pressed my face against the window, trying to see more of this place to which Mills had sent me. I'd not seen her after she stormed off, but she didn't leave me alone for long. Detective Small Head and two uniformed officers had cuffed me again and led me through a warren of hallways to the heavy steel door that guarded the entrance to the police station's parking garage. Then into a cruiser for the short ride to the county jail, where I was processed.

That part was worse than I'd ever imagined. They took my name, took my clothes, and with a flashlight and a rubber glove, they took the last pitiful rag of my dignity. Detective Small Head watched, and lit a cigarette when they spread my cheeks.

Eventually, someone tossed me an orange jumpsuit and I put it on, ashamed of my eagerness. The legs were too short, and the crotch drooped almost to my knees. My heels hung off the back of the flip-flops, but I stood as straight as I could. Detective Small Head smiled as he said, "Sleep well, counselor." Then he was gone, and I was alone with the guards, who contrived to act as if they'd never seen me before, instead of two or three times a week for the past ten years.

I stood there for another ten minutes while the senior guard finished his paperwork and the younger one ignored me. No one else entered and no one else left. Ten minutes, the three of us, and not a word spoken. The pen rasped across paper in triplicate, and his meaty forearm left a damp spot on the desk as he moved down the form. Even the top of his head looked bored. I wanted to sit, but the only other chairs had leather straps and I couldn't go there. They were thick, stained with sweat and blood, and one had teeth marks in it. I stepped away from it.

"Going somewhere?" the older guard asked wryly. I shook my head. "Just relax, counselor. Time is the one thing you've got plenty of." Then he went back to work, and the younger one sat on the edge of the desk, picking at his fingernails.

I studied the walls, the floor, and tried not to look at the door that led to the interview rooms. I'd walked through it a thousand times, but that was not my destination. This time, they would take me through another door, into the general population; and as I stood there, I felt the truth of the guard's words. Time was the one thing I had, and in that time I felt it—the reality. Not the concept or the possibility, but the bones of it, the flesh and hair of it. I was in jail, accused, and in that blink of time the fear sweats descended upon me. They warped the room, soured my stomach, and I fought a sudden surge of nausea.

I was in jail. I would go to trial.

Finally, the older guard finished his paperwork and looked up. His eyes flicked over me and I saw the recognition in them, but he ignored my obvious distress. He'd seen it all before. More times than he could probably count. "Pod four," he said, indicating to the younger man where he was to take me.

I followed the guard out of central processing and into a world where nothing felt real. They'd taken my watch, but I felt the lateness. We passed blank doors, and I saw the flickering reflection of my face in the tiny black windows with the guillotine wire.

I lost track of the turns, aware, in any real sense, of only the sounds and the smells: the guard's polished shoes cracking on the concrete floor, the whisper of flip-flops worn as thin as skin. Sounds of a distant argument abruptly ended. Metal on metal. The smell of antiseptic, packed humanity, and the faintest whiff of vomit that was not my own.

We moved deeper into the institution, down an elevator, down another hall, away from the last hint of fresh air. I followed his back, and it led me deeper. Once he looked at me and mouthed a question, but I had nothing to say; my thoughts bled together, shattered, and were lost. I felt hunted, and I shied away from blind corners and dark recesses. I smelled my fear, and envied the guard his casual arrogance. In that long walk, he became a god, and I came to dread the moment he would cast me loose in this place.

And so I followed him as far as he would lead me, into the hard-cornered space that was pod four, an octagonal area with doors on its perimeter. There were eight of them, and I saw more than one face pressed against the small glass panes. One door stood open, and the guard gestured toward it. At the door, he turned, and I saw that he was not a god after all. He looked uncertain. He seemed to shuffle his feet without actually doing so. Finally, he met my eyes.

"I'm sorry about this, Mr. Pickens," he said. "You were always very polite to me."

Then he gestured me inside, closed the door, and left me alone. I heard the door to the pod slam shut, and thought about the guard. I could not recall ever having seen him before, but I must have; and his kind words, in this unkind place—they almost broke me.

So, like those other nameless charges of the great state of North Carolina, I now pressed my face against the glass as if by sight alone I could expand the black hole that had become my world. Looking across the pod, I found another face, a pair of dark eyes that seemed to hang above a glass-flattened nose and the black slash of a mouth. For a long moment, our eyes locked; then he pulled back from the glass and kissed it with thin whiskered lips. I recoiled from the sight but couldn't look away, not until his eyes were back, and I saw that he was taunting me. So I flipped him off and dropped onto the narrow, rigid mattress of my bunk. My heart hammered, my hurried breath a fog around me. I lay for a minute, then a harsh buzzer resounded through the tight metal confines of my new world. The sound had barely faded when the lights went out, leaving me in a darkness so profound, it could only originate from the soul itself. The world constricted around me, and in that horrible second I was again a boy, crippled beneath the earth. Those hands were upon me, that voice in my ear, and the smell of breath like rotting meat.

But this was different. The guard had called me by name, Mr. Pickens, and that childhood was lost behind me. So I forced myself to my feet, gripped the steel sink until my breathing slowed, and then I paced in the blackness, feeling my way like a blind man. And suddenly I thought of Max Creason. Four paces and turn, for five years—four and turn. He gave me strength, and I made the cell my own, and the darkness with it. I walked it, and while I knew that I could survive this interlude, I knew as well that I could never do life behind bars. Better I'd pulled the trigger on the bridge. So I paced and I thought, and as the night wore on, one thing became very clear. If I managed to get out of this, I would never take freedom of choice for granted. I'd spent most of my life in a prison of my own making, trapped behind bars of fear, expectations and the opinions of others; and none of that mattered, not a whit. That it took the murder of my father and my own arrest to see this almost made me laugh, but this was not a laughing place and never would be. So I searched for a way out. The next day I would be taken to court for my first appearance. With any luck,

I would be arraigned and given an expedited bail hearing. Some-how I would make that bail. Then there would be some time before I went to trial. I would figure something out or I would go back to the bridge.

One way or another.

The night wore away, until it too was as thin as skin, and as it did, I paced and I thought; I thought about a great many things.

CHAPTER

26

The courtroom was crowded with lawyers, reporters, and other defendants. There were families, friends, and witnesses, the usual mix, but mostly I saw the other lawyers; they filled the space before the bar, motionless, as if in my absence they'd claimed the right of judgment. I searched their faces as I entered the room, flanked by guards, steel on my wrists. What did I search for? A friendly smile. A nod. Anything from the life I used to have. But I got nothing. The eyes turned away, or they glazed, as if looking at a stranger. So I was led past them, beyond them, to the defense table where I'd sat a thousand times as one of their number; and there was Douglas, who used to be my friend, and with him was Detective Mills. They watched me from the prosecution table, and like the others, they'd found veils for their eyes.

I'd prepared myself for this moment, in the small predawn hours, and so was able to keep my back straight as I assumed a position behind the chair reserved for the accused. The manacles clanked as I placed my hands on the back of that chair, and the bailiffs stepped back. A quiet descended on the room, remarkable only in its completeness. Normally, there was a background hum, as lawyers muttered behind raised hands, bailiffs maintained order, and defendants practiced lines they hoped would sway the judge. I'd heard people pray and I'd heard people weep. Some screamed obscenities and were manhandled from the court. I'd heard it all, a daily cacophony that every lawyer learned to tune out, but I'd never encountered a silence as expectant as this.

The judge was the same older woman who'd given such heartfelt condolences to me on the day after my father's body had been discovered. Even now her eyes were not unkind. I looked from her to Douglas, who seemed uncertain for a moment. But then he turned my way, and he straightened to a more predatory stance when he saw me watching. There would be no help there; he was committed, and would fight me every step of the way.

The judge spoke, and even though she spoke softly, her words were an avalanche in the silence. "Bailiff," she commanded. "Remove Mr. Pickens's handcuffs, please."

A murmur ran through the double row of attorneys seated before the bar. Douglas leaned into the prosecution table.

"I object, Your Honor. The defendant is accused of murder."

The judge cut him off. "Are you suggesting that attorney Pickens presents some physical threat to this court?" Her mockery was thinly masked, and I saw a faint blush creep into the district attorney's neck.

"The defendant is in custody. The defendant is accused of murdering his own father."

"The defendant is a member of this bar! He will be treated as such until such time as he is proven guilty. Do I make myself clear?"

I felt a lump in my throat and an overwhelming gratitude for her words.

"Yes, Your Honor," the DA said. "Perfectly clear."

"Good. Bailiff, remove the cuffs." The bailiff stepped forward and I held out my hands. The cuffs fell away. I wanted to thank her but could only nod.

The judge looked at me more closely. "Will counsel approach the bench," she said. I hesitated, unsure if I was included in her summons. "That means you, too, Mr. Pickens," she said. I rounded the table, nearly brushing shoulders with the DA, and together we approached the bench. We had barely arrived when Douglas addressed the judge in a harsh whisper.

"I protest again, Your Honor. This man is here as a defendant, not as a lawyer. This display is undermining my position in this courtroom and in this case."

The judge leaned forward. "And I have made my position very clear on this, as well. Unlike you, Mr. DA, I will await the evidence before I convict this man, in my mind or in any other manner. He has served as an officer of this court for ten years, and I am not willing to pretend otherwise."

"I want my objection on the record."

"Fine. On the record. But this is my courtroom, and I will run it as I see fit. Mr. Pickens will not be treated like a common street thug."

"Justice is supposed to be blind, Your Honor."

"Blind but not stupid," the judge responded. Then she looked directly at me. "And not without some feeling."

"Thank you, Your Honor," I managed to say.

She studied my face for long seconds before speaking. "How did you come by that black eye, Mr. Pickens?"

My fingers moved of their own accord, touching the swollen purple flesh beneath my left eye. "Nothing serious, Your Honor. A disagreement with another inmate. Earlier this morning."

"Bailiff?" She turned her eyes on the bailiff.

He cleared his throat. "One of the prisoners was trying to intimidate him, Your Honor. But just verbally. Mr. Pickens started it."

"That's not the entire story, Your Honor."

She looked back down at me. "Would you like to elaborate?"

"It's not important." I thought of the inmate across the pod. Although I'd never represented him, I'd seen him in and around court for years. He was a drug addict and a wife beater. He'd come straight for me as soon as the cell doors opened and we lined up for breakfast.

The judge, however, continued to hold my eyes, and it was clear that she wanted an answer, so I shrugged. "He wanted my orange juice, Your Honor."

She turned her hawkish eyes on the district attorney. "You assured me this man would be kept out of the general population," she said, and looking at her intent features, I realized something. She had signed the arrest warrant. She felt responsible.

"I did, Your Honor. I cannot control events inside the jail."

Again her eyes found mine; they moved over my face, and in them I saw a profound sadness.

"Very well," she said. "That will do."

We returned to our respective places and the proceeding continued. The judge advised me of the charges against me, first-degree murder, and informed me of my right to an attorney.

"Do you wish to have an attorney to represent you, Mr. Pickens?"

"No, Your Honor." At my words, a ripple moved through the lawyers assembled behind me, and I had another revelation. They wanted the case, each one of them; it would be a high-profile one, with lots of press. Television interviews, newspaper, radio—even a loss would make a reputation for the attorney who represented me. A victory and the attorney might succeed Ezra himself. "I intend to represent myself," I said. The last thing I wanted was another person prying for a truth better left uncovered.

"Sign the waiver," I was told. A bailiff handed me the form wherein I waived my right to court-appointed counsel. This was a mere formality. Only the indigent qualified for state-sponsored lawyers. I signed the form and the bailiff passed it up.

Now we came to the crux of the matter. Normally, this would have concluded a defendant's first appearance. Later, he would face a probable-cause hearing, wherein the state carried the burden of convincing a judge that sufficient probable cause existed to bind the defendant over to superior court, there to stand trial for whatever felony charge he faced. Once past probable cause, a person could request bail, but all of this took time. And there was one significant problem, and I knew of only one way around it.

"Your Honor," I said. "I move for an expedited bail hearing."

Douglas surged to his feet. "I object, Your Honor. I most strenuously object."

"Sit down," the judge said, exasperation clear on her withered features. "Of course you object." She turned her attention to me, laced her fingers, and leaned into her words. "This *is* very unusual, Mr. Pickens. You know that as well as I. There are procedures to be followed. Steps. We'll need to have the probable-cause hearing. Your case will have to be bound over to superior court." She paused, as if embarrassed by her lecture. Clearly she was puzzled.

"I waive probable cause," I said, and my words generated a windstorm of conversation among the lawyers seated behind me. The judge leaned back, as surprised as the rest. No defense attorney going to trial waives probable cause. The state has to show its case at the probable-cause hearing. Not all of it, necessarily, but the broad strokes. It's a perfect opportunity to probe for strengths and weaknesses. Beyond that, there is also the possibility that the judge will find insufficient probable cause and dismiss the charges. I knew this, of course, but I knew something else, as well. Douglas would object to any local judge hearing the matter. Too much bias, he'd claim. The judge would have to recuse. Another judge would be brought in, someone from out of county. And that would take time, time in jail, time behind bars. It could be days.

Gradually, the buzz of conversation faded and the courtroom settled again into near-perfect silence.

"Are you aware of the ramifications of your request?" the judge asked, rustling beneath her robes. "The probable-cause hearing is one of the cornerstones of procedural due process. I am loath to proceed at this point, Mr. Pickens. I fear that your judgment maybe clouded."

I focused on a point beyond the judge and looked neither right nor left as I spoke. "Shall I renew my motion, Your Honor?"

She sighed, and her words descended into the courtroom as if weighted down with regret. "Very well, Mr. Pickens. Let the record show that the defendant has waived his right to a hearing on probable cause and moves this Court for an expedited bail hearing." She raised her voice as Douglas came to his feet. "A motion that this Court is inclined to grant."

"I object," Douglas almost shouted.

The judge settled back into her chair and waved a narrow hand. "Approach," she commanded. "Both of you." At the bench, she looked down on us with the stern disapproval of a schoolmistress and used the same parchment hand to cover the microphone. Douglas opened his mouth to speak, but she rode him down with iron-shod words. "What is the problem here, Douglas? You've arrested him, charged him, and brought him before this Court. Do you honestly think that he's a flight risk? . . . No? Neither do I. Now, I've seen your evidence, and between us, it's got holes in it. But that's your bailiwick, not mine. What's mine is this decision." She looked pointedly at my face, and I felt her eyes linger on the injuries. "You intend to rebut these charges, do you not, Mr. Pickens?"

"I do."

"And you intend to do so in court. Is that not also true?"

"Yes."

"So you'll be here."

"I wouldn't miss it," I said.

"There, Douglas," the judge said. "He wouldn't miss it." I thought I heard teeth grind. "Now, we are off the record and speaking in private, and since I will not preside over the trial, I am going to say what I must." She directed her next words at me. "I signed the warrant because I had no choice. On paper, probable cause to arrest did exist, and if I'd not signed it, some other judge would have." She turned to the district attorney. "I don't think he did it, Mr. DA, and if you quote me on that, I'll deny it. But I've known this man for ten years, and I cannot believe he killed his father. I won't. So you can stand up in this court and argue against bail. You can rant and rave. Your choice. But I'll not have this man put back into the general population. That's *my* discretion. *My* prerogative."

I looked at Douglas, whose calcified features barely moved as he spoke. "It will stink of favoritism, Your Honor."

"I'm sixty-nine years old, and have no plans to run for reelection. Do you think I give a damn? Now, step back. Both of you."

My feet carried me back to the defense table, where I sat down. I risked a glance at Douglas, who was red-faced and studiously ignoring Detective Mills.

"Mr. Pickens," the judge said. I came to my feet. "Do you have anything further you wish to offer the Court in support of your motion?"

"No, Your Honor." I sat down, grateful to the judge for many things. Standing before this crowd to argue the reasons why I should be trusted outside of lockup would have been unpleasant at best. She had spared me that humiliation.

"Anything from the state?" she asked. If Douglas wanted to raise hell, he could. He could argue a great many points, many of which would make sense. He could make the judge look bad, and I hoped he would not do that. Slowly, he stood, his eyes on the tabletop, stretching the moment until it almost burst.

"The state requests only that bail be reasonable, Your Honor."

Again, an excited stir ran through the packed courtroom, an energy wave that broke against my back before receding into yet another hushed expectancy.

"Bail is set at two hundred and fifty thousand dollars," the judge said. "The defendant is bound over to superior court and remanded into custody until such time that bail is satisfied. This court will stand in recess for fifteen minutes." Then she banged her gavel once and rose to her feet, looking small and withered inside the black robe of her office.

"All rise," the bailiff thundered, and so I did, then watched in stillness as she slipped through the door behind her bench and the court-room erupted into unabashed speculation.

I looked at Douglas, who had not moved. Muscles worked in his jaw as he stared at the door through which the judge had exited. Then his head swiveled, as if he felt me. He gestured to the bailiffs, and within seconds the cuffs were back on. Our eyes locked. Mills mouthed near-silent words into his ear, but he continued to ignore her. There was something in his eyes, and it was something unexpected. I knew this even though I could not recognize what it was. I knew only that it was not the normal look I'd seen him give other defendants. Then he surprised me by smiling. He stepped to my side, and his voice was like warm oil.

"I'd say that went rather well for you, Work." Mills remained at the table, her face inscrutable. Behind us, several lawyers turned to watch, but none approached. We existed in a pocket of silence that seemed to belong to us alone. Even the bailiffs felt momentarily insubstantial. "You should be back on the street within a couple hours."

I tried to pin him with my eyes, but in the orange coveralls and steel bracelets, I'd lost that power. His smile blossomed, as if he, too, had arrived at the same conclusion. "Why are you talking to me?" I asked.

"Because I can," he replied.

"You're a real ass, Douglas. I wonder how I've missed it all these years."

His smile vanished. "You missed it because you wanted to miss it, like all defense lawyers. You want the deal. You want to be my buddy, so I'll make your job easier. It's a game and always has been. You know it as well as I do." His eyes flicked left and right and he raised his voice ever so slightly. "But the game's over, and I don't have to play it anymore. So enjoy your little victory. The next judge won't be so easy on you, and you can rest assured that I won't be."

Again, something felt odd, something in his eyes, maybe, something in what he said or how he said it. I tried to figure it out, when suddenly it became clear. Douglas was playing to the audience.

Lawyers were watching, and Douglas was playing to them. I'd never seen him grandstand before. Looking at his face, sorting this out, a question occurred to me. I'd thought about it the night before, yet I had almost forgotten it. Before I'd considered my words, they were out, and their effect was immediate.

"Why did you let me go to the crime scene?" I asked.

Douglas looked uncomfortable. His eyes darted at the surrounding lawyers, then settled back on me. His voice dropped.

"What are you talking about?" he asked.

"The day they found his body, when I asked for permission to go to the crime scene. I didn't think you'd agree; no reasonable district attorney would have. But you did. You almost ordered Mills to show me the body. Why did you do that?"

"You know why I let you go," he said.

"For Jean."

"For Jean. That's right."

A silence stretched in the wake of his words. For both of us, Jean had that power, which was probably the only thing that remained common to us both.

"It won't help you as much as you think," he said, referring to my presence at the crime scene. "I won't allow it to."

"Maybe it already has."

"What's that supposed to mean?"

"It means that a man has a lot of time to think in jail, Douglas. A whole lot of time."

I was taunting him, and he finally realized it. But I'd scored a point; I'd made him doubt, if just for an instant. His face closed down like a carnival ride. The power just drained away, leaving everything still. For an instant, we had an eye thing going, the kind of unspoken communication I'd only had once or twice in my life. It was not so much a message as a feeling, one of cold, the kind I'd expected to find in jail yet, strangely, had not. But like that cell, his eyes were empty, dark, and timeless. Then some unfathomable emotion twisted his mouth into a cruel smile, and with a nod to the bailiffs, he sent me away.

The next hours dragged, as I waited, perhaps in vain, for someone to bail me out. They'd given me a phone again, and I'd called the only person I could. But Barbara was not there, or she chose not to answer. So I left a message for my wife and waited to see if she would leave me to rot.

They put me in a padded detox cell down the hall from central processing. The judge's doing, I guessed. At some time, the walls may have been white. Now they were a mixture of browns, like burled wood. At times, I wanted to throw myself at them, scream as if I were indeed strung out. I'd never lived a longer day. The room seemed to shrink with each passing hour, and I came to wonder just how much my wife had come to loathe me. Would she leave me in jail out of spite? I honestly couldn't say.

Eventually, they came for me, processed me in reverse. I tipped the stained manila envelope onto the counter. My watch spilled out, followed by my wallet, which contained money, credit cards, identification. All present and accounted for; I signed the little piece of paper that said so. They gave me back my clothes—wrinkled, my belt, my shoes. And as I put them on, I felt the change come upon me. I became a human being again, and again I passed through the jailhouse doors, this time walking into the musty lobby, where normal people waited for people like me. What did I expect? Barbara? A faceless bail bondsman? Truthfully, I had not thought about it, not since I'd first felt underwear against my skin. In the mounting excitement of my rebirth into the human race, I expected to walk beneath blue skies, breathe fresh air, and eat a decent meal. My future was so uncertain, that was all I could expect. I did not expect Hank Robins. I did not expect what he would eventually tell me.

"What are you doing here?" I asked him.

He gave me a crooked smile, one that showed his chipped front tooth. "I should ask you."

"Yeah. I guess so."

There were two other people in the room. One was a washed-out woman who could have been thirty or could have been fifty. She sat on the hard plastic chair, head tilted against the wall, mouth open; she reeked of tobacco and hard living, all wrinkle and no laugh line. Her sunburned thighs hung loosely under cutoffs too short for a teenager. She clutched her purse like a talisman, and I wondered how long she'd been waiting, and for whom. The other person was a uniformed cop. I watched him sign in at the bulletproof window, then check his weapon into one of the steel lockboxes mounted on the wall. He never turned his back on us, not completely, and Hank watched him with ill-concealed distress. I knew that Hank did not wish to be associated with me under my current circumstances, and I wondered what could have brought him to see me.

"Come on," I said. "Let's talk outside. I've had enough of this place."

Hank nodded around another smile. "You don't have to tell me twice. Place gives me the screamin' willies."

Outside, the air was a tonic, and we leaned against the chest-high concrete wall and watched the traffic crawl along Main Street. It was late afternoon, the sun low and golden in the sky. Two of the district criminal courts were still in session and there were a few defendants lingering about, waiting for their cases to be disposed of. I'd seen two attorneys in the hall as we left, but there were none outside, a fact for which I was grateful.

"You don't have a cigarette, do you?" I asked.

"No, sorry. But hang on a sec." Before I could tell him not to worry about it, Hank had approached one of the few people scattered along the wall. When he returned, he had a crumpled pack of Marlboros and a book of matches. He handed them to me.

"Guy over there," he said and gestured with his thumb, "he was in court today, same as you. He said, 'Give 'em hell.'"

I lit a cigarette and wondered briefly what the guy's crime had been. I tucked the pack in my shirt pocket.

"Don't take this the wrong way, Hank. But you're not the person I expected to see."

He leaned against the wall, back to the passing traffic, and crossed his arms. He didn't look at me right away.

"I was in court this morning, too," he finally said. "Came up to talk to you and caught your performance. I figured somebody ought to call your wife, seeing as how she wasn't there. Thought somebody should tell her to arrange for bail."

"I tried to call her."

Hank nodded, looked at me with something like pity. "Me, too. No answer. But I wasn't in stir, so I went to see her." Hank looked up at the roofline of the jail, where it connected to the courthouse. "She didn't answer when I rang the doorbell, so I went around back. I found her on the patio, sipping iced tea and reading *Cosmo*."

A silence fell between us, and I knew that telling me this made Hank uncomfortable. "Maybe she didn't know," I said, meaning my court appearance.

"She knew," Hank said. "She looked guilty as hell when she saw me."

"She knew, and she wasn't going to bail me out?"

"Not as bad as all that. She'd made some calls, she said, and was waiting for the money to be put together."

"What calls?" I asked. Hank shrugged.

"Didn't ask. Don't know. But she asked me if I would meet you."

"That's it?" I asked.

Hank twitched and then patted his pocket. "I almost forgot. She asked me to give you this." He handed me a note, folded twice. I recognized her stationery. She used to spray perfume on it. Because she loved me, she said. I opened the note and read it. It was brief and unscented.

"She wants me to know that she still loves me, very much, and that some dirty bum stole my dog."

"I know," Hank said. "I read it."

I refolded the note and put it in my pocket.

"I'm sorry, man," Hank said. "Life's a bitch."

I nodded.

"So is your wife."

"Why are you here, Hank?" I asked again.

"Maybe to save your ass," he said, and I looked up from my shoes, searching his face for the punch line. "I'm serious," he said. "Look. I had my doubts, okay. I mean, who wouldn't? Fifteen million dollars is a lot of jack. So, sure, I thought you might have popped him. But I told you I'd check up on Alex, and I did."

Had I been walking, I would have stumbled. Driving, I would have wrecked. "What does Alex have to do with any of this?"

"Maybe nothing. Maybe something. That's what we're going to find out."

"Let's back this up, Hank. What the hell are you talking about?"

Hank took my arm, turned me toward the wide, shallow stairs that led off the concrete platform. "Not here, okay. In the car."

"Are we going somewhere?"

"Raleigh," he said.

"Raleigh," I repeated.

"To ask a few questions."

"Of whom?" I asked. We reached the top of the stairs. Beneath us, the sidewalk beckoned. I hesitated, wanting answers. Hank's hand settled on my shoulder, seeming to urge me down the stairs.

"Just keep walking," he said, and something in his voice made me turn. He was looking back over his shoulder, and I followed his gaze to the courthouse door. Sunlight gilded the glass, and I did not understand. I almost missed it. Then a thin tissue of cloud blotted the sun's face, and I saw him there, behind the glass: Douglas, watching us, a frown of concentration on his heavy features.

"Forget about him," Hank told me. "He's tomorrow's problem."

I turned away, let the private investigator lead me down the stairs. "I'm parked over here," Hank told me. We walked down the hill, past three parked sheriff's cars, the secure judge's entrance, and a street crew that worked with loud, foul-smelling equipment that ripped at a small section of asphalt. Hank gestured down the narrow side street that ran along the unmarked cemetery where free blacks had been buried almost two hundred years earlier. We turned left, and the noise dwindled behind us. I started to feel like myself again, less like a punch-drunk fighter. We separated at his car, a dark green Buick sedan, and I stepped off the curb and walked to the passenger door. He unlocked the doors, but I caught his eye over the roof before I got in.

"Alex?" I asked, but he ignored me, and I felt his door slam shut. The car rocked, as if agitated; so I got in, and took my question with me.

"It's not her real name," Hank told me five seconds later. "That's why I couldn't find a record of her at the hospital in Charlotte. Jean was in the system, plain as day, but no Alex Shiften. To me, that stank of something, but I couldn't tell what. Not until I went back with that picture you gave me."

"So you got the picture?" I asked numbly, dealing with the little detail because I could not focus on the great big one that sat like an elephant on my lap.

"Early," Hank responded. "A little after five, and then I drove back to Charlotte in time for the shift change at the hospital. I flashed the photo, asked my questions, and eventually found the right guy, an orderly with a deep appreciation for Benjamin Franklin."

"What did he tell you?"

"He knew Alex all right, but not by that name. According to him, her name is Virginia Temple. She'd been at Charter Hills for three months before Jean showed up. Apparently, they hit it off pretty quick. For a couple months there, your sister spoke to no one but her."

"Virginia," I repeated. The name felt made up. Alex Shiften was too hard to be a Virginia, too sharp, like calling a razor blade a butter knife.

"It gets worse," Hank said. "She transferred in from Dorothea Dix."

"The hospital in Raleigh?"

"The state hospital in Raleigh. The place where they keep the criminally insane."

"Not everybody there is a criminal," I said. "Just some."

"That's right. Just some. But some of those eventually get out, and usually they're transferred to a place like Charter Hills. A stepping-stone to normal living, like a halfway house."

"And you think that may be the case with Alex?"

Hank shrugged.

"Well shit," I said.

"Exactly," Hank replied, and started the car. "That's exactly what I thought."

He dropped the transmission into drive.

"I'm not supposed to leave the county," I said. "It's part of the standard bail arrangement."

He put the car back into park and turned to face me. "Your call, Work. I can drive you home if you want and check it out myself. No sweat at all."

I didn't want the judge to regret her kindness, but this was too important to play by the rules; and rules, I had recently decided, weren't necessarily good. I'd played my whole life by the book, and that life wasn't looking very pretty right now. "Screw it. Let's go."

"That's my boy."

"But we have to make a couple stops on the way out of town."

"It's your life," Hank said, accelerating away from the curb. "I'm just driving."

CHAPTER

27

It was a short drive to Clarence Hambly's office. Like most lawyers in town, he worked close to the courthouse. Hank pulled into his parking lot, a crowded space, its brick accents designed to make the cracked concrete look less austere. The building itself was over two hundred years old, a four-over-four antebellum structure with a large addition in back, hidden from the street.

"So, what are we doing?" Hank asked.

"I have to ask some questions. It won't take long."

The lobby was crowded with criminal defendants whom Hambly would shuck off on some junior associate for a buck twenty-five an hour or a flat fee, based on the charge and the likelihood of their taking a plea. He had a rear entrance and private stairwell for his more august clients. They'd go straight up, to the personal assistant who guarded his office. I knew that I'd never get past her unannounced, so

287

I didn't even bother. Instead, I cut through the crowd in the main lobby and put my hands on the gleaming cherry-wood counter. One of Hambly's assistants, an older woman, asked if she could be of some assistance, then stepped back once she looked up and recognized me.

"I'd like to see Clarence," I said.

"That's not possible," she replied.

"I'd like to see him now. And I'm very willing to raise my voice. So please just let him know that I am here."

She looked me up and down, thinking about it. I knew for a fact that she'd handled hundreds of frustrated, angry clients, so she had to size me up. After a few seconds, she picked up the phone and told Hambly's assistant that I was there to see him. It took a good minute.

"You can go up," she said.

Hambly met me at his office door and stepped aside to let me in. The office was long and elegant, with views of the courthouse on the other side of Main Street. He did not ask me to sit, just studied me from above his paisley bow tie.

"Most people make an appointment," he said.

"This won't take long," I replied, closing the door. I took a step closer to him and planted my feet widely. "I want to know how a copy of my father's will came to be in my house."

"I didn't realize that one had."

"Who had a copy?"

"This conversation is highly inappropriate," Hambly said.

"It's a simple question."

"Very well. I gave two originals to your father and kept one here. If he made copies, that was his own business. I have no idea how one ended up in your house."

"You've seen the one that the police have in their custody?"

"I have, but I cannot say for certain that it is the one found in your house. They asked me to identify it and I did."

I pushed. "Yet, it is an accurate copy. You verified that for them."

"Yes," he conceded.

"Why didn't you tell me that Ezra was going to cut me out of his will?"

"Whatever gave you that idea?"

"Mills," I said.

Hambly smiled tightly, a gleam in his eyes. "If Mills told you that, she did so for her own reasons. Yes, your father contemplated some minor changes, but he never intended to remove you as a beneficiary. He was quite firm on that. I suspect that Mills was trying to trick you into some indiscretion."

"What changes?"

"Nothing significant and nothing that was ever put into place. Ergo, nothing that concerns you as the beneficiary of his estate."

"Is your copy of the original accounted for?" I asked.

"Filed with the probate court. I'm certain that they would show it to you, if you asked."

"Yet you made copies."

"Of course, I made copies. This is a law office. I represent the estate."

"Who else did you give copies to? Mills? Douglas? Who else?"

"Don't raise your voice to me, young man. I won't tolerate it."

"Try this on then, Clarence. If I am convicted of Ezra's murder, can I inherit under the laws of North Carolina?"

"You know that the state will not allow a killer to profit from his crime in that way."

"Then who retains control of Ezra's assets?"

"What are you implying?" Hambly demanded.

"Who?"

"All of your father's assets pass to the foundation."

"And who controls that foundation?"

"I do not appreciate your insinuation."

"You would have control of the entire forty million dollars. Isn't that correct?"

Hambly stared at me, his face tight with barely contained fury. "I find you and your petty machinations insufferable, Work. Get out of my office."

"You were in my house. For the first time ever since I bought it, you were in my house. Why?"

"I was there because Barbara invited me to be there. And because it was the respectful thing to do. I should not have to explain that to you. Now, get out," he said, and took me by the arm. Outside of his office, before the pretty young assistant who had come suddenly to her feet, I jerked my arm free.

"Somebody planted that document in my house, Clarence. It had to come from somewhere."

Hambly straightened to his full height and looked down the length of his nose. I saw color in his face, and the pulse of blood in the big veins that ran down his neck. "Earlier today, I held some pity for you, Work. But that's gone. I will look forward to your trial date." He pointed a thin arm toward the stairwell, and I saw that it trembled. "Now, please leave."

"Very well, Clarence. Thank you for your time." I walked down Hambly's private stairs and did not look back. I heard his office door slam.

I found Hank in the car, his arm out the open window.

"How'd it go?" he asked.

"I don't know," I said.

"Really?"

I looked at Hank. "Really."

"So where to now?"

"Highway Six-oh-one, toward Mocksville. I'll show you where to turn."

We rolled out of town, and as we drew closer to Stolen Farm, I felt the spring inside of me grow tighter. My head was heavy with densely packed emotions. It grew more so as we approached Vanessa's house and stopped in front of it.

"Wait here," I told Hank, getting out of the car, leaning in through the open window.

"Jesus, Work."

I held up my hands, palms out. "Last time," I told him.

Stolen Farm lay in the shadow of the neighboring woods. Thin fingers of light reached for the farmhouse but fell short, satisfied with the faded red wall of the old barn. We'd parked in the rutted drive, house to the left, barn to the right. I didn't see Vanessa's car, but her nameless man was there; he watched me from the gaping mote-filled cavern that bisected the barn. If I'd looked up, I would have seen the door to the loft, where Vanessa and I found what we'd thought would last forever. I didn't look up. I looked at her man. He'd been working on the tractor. Grease covered his hands and the heavy wrench he held. He leaned against the tall molded tire with a proprietary air and studied me as I crossed the dry dirt toward him. He looked bigger than I remembered; he was heavily muscled, and depressingly young, but definitely the same guy.

"That's far enough," he said. I stopped, still ten feet away, and held up my hands.

"I'm not looking for any trouble," I told him. "I just want to talk to Vanessa."

His mouth opened to an unasked question, and he put the wrench down on the engine cowling of the tractor. He moved toward me, wiping his hands on his pants. Worry creased his face.

"I thought she was with you," he said.

I dropped my hands, feeling foolish. I might have decked him the other night, but it was clear to me now that he was not intimidated.

"What are you talking about?"

He stopped, towering over me. He searched my face as if for something specific, then flicked his eyes at the house. I followed his glance, hoping to see Vanessa, but the old place was still and dark.

"She didn't come home last night."

"What?"

"And I haven't seen her all day."

A familiar pit opened in my stomach. Something moved in the young man's eyes, and I knew it for what it was. I stepped closer.

"Start at the beginning," I told him. "Tell me everything."

He nodded and swallowed hard. He wanted to tell me. The thing in his eyes made him need to tell me. It was fear; the young man was afraid, and suddenly I was, too.

CHAPTER
28

"So what was that all about?" We were on the interstate, ten minutes north of town. Hank had started to speak at least five times, but something in my face had stopped him. I didn't want to answer him. I didn't want to say the words, yet for some reason I did. Maybe I hoped they wouldn't sound so bad if spoken out loud.

"Someone important to me has gone missing."

"Someone important? Who do you—Oh, I get it. A girlfriend?"

"More than that," I said softly.

"Plenty of fish in the sea, Work. Trust me on that."

I rolled down the window because I needed the smell of something clean. Wind buffeted my face, and for a moment I could not breathe.

"You're wrong about that, Hank," I finally said.

"Then we're swimming in different bodies of water."

Not swimming, I thought, *drowning,* and for a moment I was.

"So who was the guy?" I didn't answer, and Hank looked his question at me a second time. "The guy?"

I settled back into my seat, the headrest soft and sweet-smelling on the heels of jail-issue bedding. "Just drive, Hank. Do you mind? I need to think."

His words came from far away. "Sure, man. Whatever. It's a long trip."

He was right. It was.

But we made it to the crowded parking lot of Dorothea Dix Hospital by late twilight. We didn't speak until he killed the engine. I peered up through the windshield. Of all the miserable places in this world, I thought, this one must hold the darkest secrets. I thought of Bedlam, and screams choked with vomit. "Talk about the screaming willies," I said.

"It's not as bad as you might think," Hank said.

"You've been here before?"

"Once or twice." He did not elaborate.

"And?"

"And I've never been on the secure floors. But the rest of it is just like any other hospital."

I studied the grounds again. "Except for the razor wire," I said.

"There is that."

"What now?" I asked.

"How much money do you have?"

I checked my wallet instinctively, forgetting that I'd already counted the money when it was returned to me. "Three hundred and seventy dollars."

"Give it to me." He separated out the three hundred-dollar bills and gave me back the rest. "This should do it." I watched him fold the bills together and tuck them into the front pocket of his jeans. "Ready?" he asked.

"As I'll ever be," I said, meaning it. He punched me lightly on the shoulder.

"Relax," he told me. "This will be fun."

When we got out of the car, he donned a windbreaker and checked something in the inside pocket. I couldn't tell what it was, but he grunted lightly, as if satisfied. I looked up at the hospital, black and sharp-edged against the dark purple sky. Light seemed to jump from the windows and die on the way down.

"Come on," Hank said. "Try to relax."

We started toward the main entrance to the hospital. "Hang on," Hank said. I watched him trot back to the car, unlock it, and reach inside. He came back with the picture of Alex that I'd left in the mailbox. "Might need this," he said. The picture flashed in the weak light, but I saw Alex's face perfectly. Like the building, it had sharp edges, and I wondered, not for the first time, what had brought her to this place. What had brought her here and what had she carried away? What had she taken home to my sister, and was it as evil as my troubled mind made it out to be?

I needed an answer, and looking at Hank, I thought we had a good shot at finding one.

We walked into the lobby. Halls shot off in multiple directions. An elevator bank faced us. The hospital smell was overwhelming.

Hank approached a row of newspaper machines and dug some change from his pockets. "Have you read the Charlotte paper today?"

I shook my head. "No."

He dropped his change into the machine that vended the *Charlotte Observer*. He retrieved a paper and handed it to me. "You'll need this," he said.

I didn't understand. "What for?" I asked, holding the paper as if I'd never seen one before.

"Are you serious?" he asked, and turned away.

"Oh." I tucked the paper under my arm. Hank looked up at the bewildering proliferation of signs and seemed to find what he wanted. I didn't have a clue what that was, but when he told me to follow him, I did. Soon we were lost in the maze, and the ever-present signs beckoned us deeper into the hospital. Hank kept his eyes down, like he knew exactly where he was going. He looked at no one and no one looked at him. I tried to follow suit. Eventually, we turned onto a hall that ended at a small waiting room. In the corner, on the wall, a television showed us its blank screen. A sticky note informed passersby that it was out of order.

A row of vinyl seats lined one wall. Two more halls ran away in opposite directions, their polished floors agleam with the reflection of fluorescent lighting from above. Voices echoed around us: passing nurses, medical students, a box on the wall paging doctors. Across from us was a blue swinging door beneath a sign that said EMPLOYEES ONLY.

"This is the place," Hank said. I looked around again, sure I must have missed something. Hank fished a plastic identification badge from his jacket pocket and clipped it onto his shirt. It had his picture on it, a name I'd never heard before, and the name of the hospital. It looked just like every other employee identification badge I'd seen since we entered.

"Where did you get that?" I whispered.

"It's forged," he replied curtly.

"But . . ."

He flashed his crooked grin. "I told you I'd been here before."

I nodded. "Okay. What do you want me to do?"

"Wait here," he said. I followed his gaze to the row of uncomfortable red vinyl seats. "Read the paper. This might take a while."

"I want to come," I said.

"I know you do, and I don't blame you, but people will talk to one person when they might not talk to two. One is a friendly chat. Two is an interrogation."

He read the emotion on my face, knew how important this was to me.

"Relax, Work. Read the paper. If there is an answer to be found here, I'll find it. Okay? This is what I do. Trust me."

"I don't like this."

"Don't think about it." Hank turned away, then just as quickly turned back. "Give me the sports section," he said. I fumbled it out of the paper and handed it to him. He rolled it up and saluted me with it. "Icebreaker," he said. "All-important in this business."

I sat stiffly on the hard chair and watched as Hank walked boldly through the door designated for employees only. He didn't look back, and when the door swung shut, it swallowed him whole.

I settled back. I opened the paper and stared blankly at words that swam. When people passed, I tried to look normal, as if I belonged, but it was hard, for in my racing mind I was a criminal.

I sat there for what my watch said was only fifty-five minutes. The watch lied. It was a lifetime.

Time and again, that blue door swung open. A black man came out the first time, then a white woman and a fat man who could never be mistaken for Hank Robins. Another woman. Two men. An endless stream, and they all wore the same badge of identification. Again and again the door swung wide, and each time it did, the spring of my body wound a little tighter. Hank had been found out. He wasn't coming.

Then I saw him, in the brief flash as the door swung shut behind an old man pushing a bucket. He was coming out, and the next time the door opened, it was for him. He did not smile, but in his eyes I saw a fierce satisfaction. He took me by the arm before I could say a word; then we were walking, our footsteps loud in the hard-tiled and resonant halls that were the arteries of this place.

"That wasn't so bad, was it?" he asked in a voice so normal, it surprised me. I'd expected a whisper.

"Did you get it?" I asked, meaning the answer to our question.

The fierceness moved from his eyes to his mouth, and he smiled. "Oh yes. I got it."

I wanted to shake it out of him. "And?"

"And it's something."

We walked in a silence that just about killed me, but eventually we made it to the car. Hank slipped behind the wheel, started the engine, and hit the door-lock button. He still had not said a word. He backed out of the parking spot and navigated us through the inland sea of parked vehicles. Finally, he looked at me. "Buckle up," he said.

"Are you fucking with me?" I asked. "Because this is not a good time." He did not respond, and his eyes remained steady on the road.

"I'm just getting my thoughts together, Work. There's a lot to say and I'm trying to figure out the best way to do it. I don't want to freak you out."

"You're freaking me out right now."

But he would not be rushed, and he kept his mouth shut until we were on Interstate 40, driving west at exactly nine miles over the speed limit.

"Have you ever heard of East Bend?" he finally asked.

"Maybe. I think so."

"It's a little place. Pretty, with horses. It's on the Yadkin River, not far from Winston-Salem."

Headlights flashed on Hank's face from across the grassy divide, unidentified cars driven by nameless people. In the dark intervals, Hank's face was a blurred profile. Then he turned to look at me.

"You should go there sometime. There's this little vineyard there, right on the river. . . ."

"Is there some reason you're stalling?"

He looked at me again, and headlights filled the space around us. "Alex is from there. It's where she grew up. For the first fourteen years anyway."

"And?"

"Look, Work . . . the details are sketchy. All I've got is what the nursing assistant told me, and bought information isn't always reliable. I haven't verified any of this."

"Fine. You're absolved of the consequences of any misinformation. Just tell me what you heard."

"She killed her father, Work. She cuffed him to the bed and set it on fire."

"What?"

"She was fourteen. Her mother was in the bed, too, but she survived. It was Daddy she was after." He paused. "And she got him, too. Cooked him right to the bed."

I felt Hank's eyes on me, gauging my reaction, but there was none; then Hank continued, his voice a flat line.

"She waited for him to stop screaming, and then she called 911 and walked out of the house; she watched it burn. When the fire truck arrived, she met them at the curb, said her mother might still be alive. They found her under the bedroom window, burned over seventy percent of her body. She was cut up pretty bad, too, from diving through the glass. When the police showed up, the girl told them what she'd done. She didn't lie about it, but she didn't gloat, either. Rumor is, she didn't shed a single tear. The nursing assistant didn't know if she went to trial or not, but the state sent her to psychiatric lockup. She spent four years at Dorothea Dix, but she was a minor when she did the job. So when she turned eighteen, they released her to Charter Hills, where she met Jean."

"That was only three years ago," I said.

"She's young."

"She doesn't look it."

"She's led a hard life, no mistake there. It'll age a person."

"Are you sympathizing with her?" I asked.

"Not at all," Hank said. "But they couldn't tell me what went down before she killed him. She must have had a reason, and it's not too hard to guess what it was." I sensed him shrug. "I have a soft spot for hard-luck cases." He left the rest unspoken. I didn't have the details, but I knew that Hank's childhood had been no picnic.

The silence drew out. Cars passed us.

"That's it?" asked. "That's all we know?"

"I tried to buy a copy of her file, but the guy wouldn't go there. He said gossip was one thing, stealing documents was another; but he was pretty sure of what he told me. Said it was common knowledge among the staff."

Hank checked his mirror and passed a pickup truck. One of its headlights was out, so it seemed to wink at us as we passed. I saw the sign for Interstate 85, and we remained silent until we'd left I-40 and pointed south, toward Jean and the woman who guarded so well the secrets of her violent past.

Hank reached into his pocket and handed me back two of the hundred-dollar bills. "It only took one," he said.

"So that's it?"

"Basically."

I sensed Hank's hesitation. "What does 'basically' mean?" I asked.

Hank shrugged again. "The guy was scared of her."

"Of Alex?"

"Alex. Virginia. He said everybody was pretty much scared of her."

"Except Jean," I said.

I felt his eyes again, measuring me in the dark. "Except Jean," he finally said. "Jean loved her."

I nodded silently, then looked again at Hank. There had been something in his voice.

"Is there something you're not telling me?"

He shook his head. "Not really. Just something I heard at Charter Hills."

"What?"

A shrug. "Something a guy said. Another floor worker, one of the guys I talked to the other day. I asked him about Jean and Alex, and something he said stuck with me. He said that Jean loved her like a preacher loves his God." Hank took his eyes off the road. "His words, not mine."

I pictured them together.

A *preacher and his God*. Obedience. Subservience.

"Could she really love her that much?"

"Who the hell knows? I've never had anything like it." He sounded wistful. I said nothing for a long time, and Hank, too, seemed content with his own thoughts.

"Do you think Alex could have killed my father?"

"Assuming you didn't do it?"

"Very funny." I wasn't laughing.

"Do you know where she was the night Ezra went and got himself shot?"

"No."

"Did she have a reason to want him dead?"

I thought of Ezra, and of his persistent disdain for Alex. I saw the fight between him and Jean, the night that everything went to shit. The fight had been about Alex. Ezra had tried to force them apart.

"She had a reason," I said.

"And seven years ago, she cooked her father to his bed."

I nodded to myself. "I guess it's possible."

"There you go."

CHAPTER

29

We rolled into Salisbury after midnight. The town was quiet, with few cars moving and fewer lights burning. I felt like a ghost as we whispered through the stillness. Even Hank was subdued, and I guessed that, like me, he could not shake the image of what Alex had done.

When Hank pulled into my driveway, I got out and walked around to his window. He rolled it down.

"Listen, Hank. I really appreciate what you've done; it means a lot."

"You'll get my bill," he replied.

"Better send it soon," I said.

"You're not going back to jail, Work. We both know how this is going to end. Alex is your man. Take what we learned to Mills and get her to check it out."

"Maybe. We'll see." I still had to talk to Jean. "Listen, about the bill . . ."

"It's going to be a big one."

"Bigger than you think," I said.

He eyed me. "What do you mean?"

I put my hands on the frame of his window, leaned against the car. "I need you to find somebody for me. It's important."

"Your girlfriend?"

"Her name is Vanessa Stolen. You know where she lives. I need to find her. I need to talk to her. I need . . ." My voice trailed away, then came back. "I just need her."

An overwhelming conviction came over me that she was dead. "She never leaves like this." That's the last thing the big farmhand told me, there by the tractor at Stolen Farm. "Not without making provision for her animals. She'd never leave them unattended."

"What about you?" I'd asked.

"*I just work here, mister. If she needs me to take care of things while she's gone, she always calls. I've got my own place to look after, too. She knows that.*"

In my mind I'd seen them together, her body alive under his heavy calloused hands. I'd thought she'd given herself to him, and that her gift had killed the last, best part of me.

"Just find her for me, Hank. There are things that need to be said."

"What else can you tell me about her? Anything that might help me find her. Family. Friends. Places she might go. That sort of thing."

"She has no family. She's the last. I don't know if she has any friends, and as far as I can tell, she rarely leaves the farm. The place is her life."

"When did you see her last?"

"Right before I was arrested."

"I hate to ask this," Hank said. "But is it possible that she doesn't want to be found? People get to that point, Work. Sometimes we just need to disappear for awhile." He looked away, as if he had to in order to finish his thought. "You're married. You were arrested for murder.

Maybe the fling wasn't worth it anymore. Maybe the cost was too high."

"It wasn't like that," I said. "Don't try to make it like that."

"Take it easy, man. I see it all the time. I had to ask."

"It wasn't like that."

Hank just nodded, still not looking at me, and an awkward silence formed around us. He looked at his watch. "It's late. I'm going home. But I'll look for your missing friend tomorrow. Okay? I'll find her."

"You're a good man, Hank. I appreciate it."

"I'll call you later."

He rolled up the window and drove away; and it was only then that I noticed that Barbara's car was gone. I walked into an empty house and found another one of her notes on the kitchen counter. She was staying at Glena's house for the night.

I was too keyed up to sleep. For it seemed increasingly possible that Alex was responsible for Ezra's death. She'd killed her own father. Why not mine? But there was more to the story, and I wanted to know it all. I had to. It felt like a piece was missing. Once I had it, and once Hank found Vanessa, then I would go to Mills. But not before.

I turned on my computer and did a White Pages search for East Bend, North Carolina. I found two Temples listed, a husband and wife and a Rhonda Temple. I wrote down her address. Then I realized that I had no vehicle. Mills had impounded the truck when she'd arrested me. I considered waiting until morning, but I could not face six hours awake in that depleted house. In the end, I called Dr. Stokes. He met me at his back door. He had on striped pajamas. His hair was in disarray.

"I'm sorry to wake you up, Dr. Stokes, but it's kind of important."

He waved away my words. "I said I'd help and I meant it. Plus, it's been a long time since someone called me with an emergency in the middle of the night. I kind of miss it." He stepped out of the house and we stood on the concrete driveway. He looked small under the porch light. "Which car do you want?" He gestured at the two cars parked there, a dark blue Lincoln and a wood-paneled minivan.

"Whichever. I don't care."

"Then you'd better take mine," he said. He walked back inside and came out with a set of keys. He handed them to me.

I looked at the Lincoln. It was large and polished. I knew that it would be fast. I gestured toward it as I spoke. "I'll take good care of it," I said.

Dr. Stokes chuckled. "That's Marion's car, Work." He continued to shake his head. "I drive that one." He pointed at the minivan. It had to be nine years old.

"Oh. Okay. I'll be back by midmorning."

"Take your time. I have no plans tomorrow."

I found the town of East Bend at 2:30 in the morning. It was a bump on Highway 67, thirty miles outside of Winston-Salem. There was not much there: a restaurant, a real estate office, a few convenience stores. I walked into the only store that was open, bought a cup of questionable coffee, and asked the clerk if they sold maps of East Bend. He was probably twenty, with long hair under a camouflage hunting cap. He laughed at my question.

"That's a good one," he said. "I'll have to remember that one."

"I'm looking for Trinity Lane," I said as I paid.

"You'll never find it."

"That's why I'm asking for directions."

"It's not a real road. That's why you won't find it. It's just a dirt road, the kind where they let you make up a name for it, but the sign is blue instead of green. That's how you can always tell if it's a real road or not. Green means real. There's an *e* in both of them—*green* and *real*. That's the best way to remember."

"There's an *e* in blue also."

"Shit. You're right."

"I'm looking for a woman named Rhonda Temple." He didn't answer me. He stood behind the counter, patted his belly, and stared back. "I don't mean her any harm, if that's what you're worried about."

He laughed again and showed his stained teeth. "You can kill her, for all I care. That woman is without doubt the meanest bitch I ever did meet. What do you want to talk to her for?"

"Was she in a fire seven or eight years ago?"

"That's her."

"That's what I want to talk to her about."

"Hell, everybody around here can tell you about that. That crazy kid of hers set the place on fire. Cuffed her old man to the bed and left him to burn."

"Alex."

"Naw. Not Alex."

"Virginia, I mean. The daughter's name is Virginia."

"That's her."

"Did you know her?"

"Not really. She was only a year or two older, but she was damaged goods. She was like fourteen when they sent her away."

I leaned on the counter. "Any idea why she did it?" I asked.

He lifted his cap and scratched his head. "Just mean, I guess. And crazy as a shithouse rat."

"So how do I find this woman's house?"

"Oh. Go on down that way and take a left at the blinking yellow. Look for the blue sign on the left, a dirt road. She's at the end of it."

I looked at him. "I thought you said I'd never find it."

"Well you wouldn't have if I hadn't told you. You going down there tonight?"

"Maybe," I said. "I haven't decided."

"Well, I wouldn't if I were you. Going down blue sign roads at three in the morning is liable to get you shot."

I thanked him and turned to leave. "Hey, mister."

"Yeah."

"Don't let her scare you." I waited for something more. "She's ugly as shit."

As much as I wanted to speak with Rhonda Temple, mother of Virginia Temple, aka Alex Shiften, I knew that the store clerk had a point. I sipped coffee in the parked car and thought about how I would handle it. I thought about Dr. Stokes and his feelings on faith, hell, and the chance of salvation. Eventually, I dozed.

I found Trinity Lane at a few minutes before seven, right where it was supposed to be, although I almost missed it. At some point, a car had hit the blue sign and now it leaned at an angle, twisted and almost hidden in the scrub growth that bordered the two-lane blacktop. Trinity Lane itself was a rutted dirt track, a gash in the wooded verge. It curved away before me, a dim alley in the weak morning light. I passed derelict single-wides as I moved deeper into the woods. Some were burned out, others simply worn down and abandoned. Fiberglass insulation hung from places where siding had been stripped away, and rusted appliances bled slowly into the weed-choked red clay. It was a dismal place.

The road ended five hundred yards in, at the rear bumper of a twenty-year-old Dodge Omni. It was parked in the bare dirt yard of the last trailer, a single-wide with a satellite dish beside it. I climbed warily from the car. There was a refuse pile behind the trailer, at the point where the land fell away to the river. A few lifeless items hung from a clothesline. A light burned behind one of the windows.

I knocked on the aluminum door.

The woman who opened the door was clearly the woman I sought. Her face and hands were severely scarred, not only from the fire but from the glass of the window she'd leapt through to escape the flames. The right side of her face, from the nose to the ear, was a textured nightmare, and long scars, puckered and white, crisscrossed her face. She had wild gray hair, thick glasses in pink frames, and a cigarette with a plastic filter on the end.

"Who the hell are you?" she asked. "And what the fuck are you doing at my house this early in the fucking morning?"

"Ma'am, my name is Work Pickens. I drove up from Salisbury. I'm sorry to bother you so early, but it's very important that I speak to you about your daughter."

"Why the hell should I talk to you?"

"I honestly don't have an answer for that. You don't know me and you don't owe me. I'm just asking."

"You want to talk about my daughter? Are you a cop or a reporter or something?" She looked me up and down.

"No. I'm none of those things."

"What are you, then?"

I ignored her question. "Virginia Temple. She's your daughter, right?"

She took a drag on the plastic filter, studied me with reptile eyes. "She came out of me, if that's what you mean. But she's no daughter of mine."

"I don't understand," I said.

"That girl was ruined by the time she was ten. She wasn't my baby no more, even then. But when she did this to me, when she set the fire and killed my Alex, well, I decided then and there that she weren't no child of mine. Not then and not ever again."

I couldn't help but look at the scars, and I thought of what it must have been like to wake up engulfed in flame. "I'm sorry about your husband."

"Are you stupid?" she asked. "I don't care about that worthless shit. He got what he deserved and I'm better off with him dead. I'm talking about my Alex." Her eyes misted and she swiped at one of them.

"Alex? I don't understand."

"Alex was the only thing good in my life."

I stood there, confused. "Ma'am . . ."

"Goddamn it. Alex was my other daughter, my baby. She was seven when it happened. That bitch Virginia killed her, too. Or didn't you know that?"

CHAPTER

30

Rhonda Temple pretty much shut down after her outburst. She wouldn't talk much at all, not about Virginia and not about why she'd done what she did. But she did tell me how Alex, her youngest daughter, had come to die. The story stayed with me on the drive back to Salisbury, and I knew that the time had come to confront Jean. I had to ask the question. I had to know.

I parked Dr. Stokes's car and walked to the entrance of the emergency room. I nodded at a doctor who stood smoking outside, then entered the brightly lit hospital. It was quiet, and for a moment it felt more like a mausoleum than a hospital. The triage nurse's desk was empty. No one sat on the long benches or chairs in the waiting room. I could hear the hum of fluorescent lighting and the pneumatic hiss of the door as it slid shut behind me. I saw movement behind a glass partition, a flash of white coat, but that was it. The place was dead.

So, feeling more like a ghost than ever, I passed through the reception area and into the long hall. It led me past vending machines, telephones, and the closed doors of the small hutchlike offices where low-grade administrators worked from nine to five. I found the bank of elevators and stepped inside. I pushed the button for the third floor.

The nurse's station on Jean's wing was empty and I walked quickly past it. As I reached my sister's room, a nurse turned the corner, moving toward me, but her head was down. She didn't see me, so I went inside and closed the door. The room was dark after the hallway, but not entirely without light. Some filtered in from outside, and the monitors cast their eerie glow. I half-expected to find Alex there, and honestly didn't know what I'd do if I did. Fortunately, she wasn't there. I needed Jean's attention, not another pissing contest.

When I took Jean's hand, it felt desiccated, as if she had bled out after all; but it was warm, and I looked down at her as I held it. Her eyes moved beneath her lids, and I wondered what she was dreaming about. Something bad. Her life was a nightmare. There would be no reprieve behind closed eyes. I wanted to wake her but did not. I sat in the chair by her side and held her fevered hand. Eventually, I put my head on the narrow margin of bed, and leaning forward, perched on that unyielding chair, I finally fell asleep.

At some point, I, too, must have dreamed. I felt her hand on my head and heard her voice. *How could you, Work? How could you do it?* Her hand fell away, along with her words, but in the clairvoyance of dreams, I knew that she was weeping.

When I woke, it was with a start. Jean's skin was washed charcoal, her eyes twin slits of darkness, but then she blinked, and I knew that she was awake and had been watching me.

"When did you get here?" Her voice was as arid as her hands. I rubbed my eyes.

"Do you want some water?" I asked her.

"Yes, please."

I poured some into the plastic cup on her bedside table. "There's no ice."

"It doesn't matter." She drank the water and I refilled her cup.

I looked at the saline bag suspended above her, followed the tube to where its needle entered her arm beneath a white X of tape. It was easy to recall the red sea of her blood on the floor of our parents' house. She'd probably be dehydrated for a week.

I looked at her face, saw the slackness around her mouth, and wondered what she was on. Antidepressants, maybe? Sedatives? She saw me looking and turned away.

I did not want to ask her the things that had to be asked. She was transparent, and I knew that I had never seen a more fragile person.

"How are you, Jean? Are you holding up okay?"

She blinked at me, and for an instant I thought she wouldn't answer. She drew up her knees, puddled into herself, and I thought she was going to turn away from me, as she'd done the last time.

"They say you saved my life." The statement was utterly devoid of emotional context.

They say your car is blue. Like that.

I almost lied. I didn't want her to hate me for doing what I'd done. "I might have," I said.

"Even Alex says it. She says you found me and put tourniquets on my arms. She says one minute later and I would have died."

I looked at my fingers, remembering the slipperiness of her blood; how hard I'd jammed those fingers into her neck, looking for a pulse. "You called me," I said. "I came."

"That's the third time," she continued. I felt her movement and looked up in time to see her turn her face away. "You must hate me," she said.

"No." I put my hand on her arm, turned her back so that I could see her face. "Never, Jean. Don't you ever think that. I could never hate you." I squeezed her shoulder and said the words that should have come easily but never had. "You're my sister. And I love you."

It was her turn to nod. She did so in fitful jerks as folds closed over her eyes like curtains and tears pooled on the shelf of her wasted cheeks before spilling down her face in two long, hot arcs. She swiped at the tears with one arm, scrubbing them away with the heavy bandage that covered her wrist. She opened her mouth to speak but then closed it, the words unsaid. Instead, she continued to nod. But I understood. The words were hard. That's how we were raised.

Do you need anything? I wanted to ask. More water? Another pillow? I meant to ask these things, but that's not what I said. There was a larger question, a dangerous one. But it couldn't wait any longer. I needed to know. I couldn't go to Mills until I heard it from Jean herself.

"Did you do it?" I asked.

Jean looked horrified.

"What?" Almost a moan, and the tears came faster, but I couldn't stop. Every action of the past week had been based around my assumptions that Jean had pulled the trigger. I'd gone to jail for those assumptions. I now faced life in prison for them.

"Did you kill him?" I asked again. "Did you kill Ezra?"

Jean's mouth gaped and then collapsed. "I thought *you* did it," she said. It was her child's voice, so vulnerable that I saw the truth of her words. She really believed that I'd done it.

"Is that what Alex told you, Jean? Is that why you think I did it? Because she told you I did it?"

Jean shook her head, hair moving over her eyes, coming to rest on her forehead. I saw that she'd pulled the sheet to her throat. Her eyes spilled confusion.

"You did it, Work. You had to have done it."

"I thought you did it," I said, and Jean rocked as if my words were bullets. Her eyes widened and she pushed deeper into the pillows that mounded behind her.

"No." She shook her head again. "It had to be you. It had to be."

"Why?" I asked, leaning closer. "Why me?"

"Because . . ." Her voice trailed off. She tried again. "Because . . ."

I finished her thought. "Because if you didn't do it, and I didn't do it, then Alex did. Is that what you were going to say?"

This time, she did roll away; she curled into a fetal ball, as if I might kick her, and for that moment I was at a loss. Jean hadn't done it. Had I not known the truth about Alex, I would not have accepted that fact.

I'd been so damned sure.

"There are some things about Alex, Jean. Some things you might not know." I had to jolt her out of her complacency, force her to accept the truth.

She spoke from across the chasm I'd opened between us. "I know everything there is to know about Alex, Work. There's nothing you can tell me."

"Do you know that's not her real name?"

"Don't do this, Work. Don't try to come between me and Alex."

"Did you know it?" I asked again.

Jean sighed. "Virginia Temple. That's her real name. She changed it when she was released."

"Do you know she killed her father?" I asked.

"I know," she said.

"You know about that?" I couldn't believe it. "Do you know how she killed him?" Jean was nodding, but I couldn't stop. The horror of it was still too fresh in my mind. Cooked meat. Charred lungs. Alex watching and her mother sliced to ribbons. "She handcuffed him to the bed and set it on fire. She burned him alive, Jean. For Christ's sake, she burned him alive!"

Suddenly, I was on my feet. Beneath me, Jean contracted even further. She was hugging her knees to her chest, cringing, and I saw that the line from her saline bag had a kink in it. The sight calmed me down, forced me to get a grip on my raging emotions. I knew that I was losing it. It was all too much. I took a deep breath, then leaned over to straighten the kink, but when my hand brushed against her arm, she flinched.

"I'm sorry, Jean. I'm really sorry." She declined to respond, and her body rose up as she sucked in a mighty breath. I found the chair again and fell into it. I buried my face in my palms, pressed against my eyes until I saw sparks. But for her wet breath, the room was silent. I took my hands away and looked at her. She was still clenched in a ball.

"It scares me, Jean. It scares me that she killed her father, and it scares me that she has this power over you." I paused, looking for better words. "It just scares me."

Jean did not respond, and for a long time I watched her in silence. After a few minutes of this, I felt the need to move, to do something. I got up and went to the window. I pulled back the curtain and stared across at the parking deck. A car pulled in and turned on its headlights.

When Jean spoke, I could barely hear her.

"She had a pool. Growing up, she had a pool."

I walked back to the bed. When she rolled her face off the pillow, I could see the wet spot of her tears. "A pool," I said, letting her know I was there and that I was ready to listen. I sat down. Her eyes were huge and raw; she showed them to me briefly, then turned back to the wall. I looked at her back and waited for her to go on. Finally, she did.

"It was one of those aboveground pools, like we used to make fun of when we were kids. A poor kid's pool. She didn't care that it was cheap or flimsy. She didn't care that it sat behind a single-wide or that it was visible from the road. She was a kid, you know. And it was a pool." Jean paused. "The best thing that ever happened to her."

I could see it as if I were there; yet I already sensed the truth of it. It was the way she said it. The pool was not the best thing that ever happened to her. Not by a long shot.

Jean continued. "When she turned seven, her father implemented the new policy. That's exactly how he said it. 'We're implementing a new pool policy.' He tried to make a joke out of it. She didn't care one way or another. But if she wanted to hang out around the pool, she had to be wearing high heels and makeup. That was the policy." She paused, and I heard her sharp intake of breath. "That's how it started."

I knew where this was going, and I felt my insides clench in disgust. Hank had been right.

"The policy didn't include her mother. Just her. She told me once that her mother stopped hanging out at the pool after that. She didn't do anything about it. She just didn't want to see it. Her father was out of work that year, so that's what they did. They hung out at the pool. In the summer, I guess, that was enough. Watching, I mean. But two weeks after they closed up the pool for the winter, it started."

I did not want to hear this. I wanted her to stop. But I had to hear it and she had to say it. We were trying to find the road.

"He didn't just fondle her, Work. He raped her. He sodomized her. When she fought back, he beat her. After that summer, she wasn't allowed to have pajamas. For God's sake, she had to sleep naked. Another policy. It didn't start slow and build up. It exploded into her life. One day she was seven. The next day she was getting it regular. His term. But in spite of that, it somehow got worse over time, like he got bored with her and had to find new ways to make it fun. She can't talk about some of the things he did, not even now. And she's the strongest person I know.

"It went on for years. He never did go back to work. He drank more and he gambled more. On three occasions, he loaned her out to cover his gambling debts. A hundred dollars here, two hundred there. She was eleven the first time. The guy was a shift foreman at the rubber plant in Winston-Salem. He weighed three hundred pounds. Alex weighed a little over seventy."

"Her mother . . ." I began.

"She tried to tell her mother once, but she didn't want to hear it. She accused her of lying and slapped her. But she knew."

Jean fell silent.

"She could have gone to the authorities," I said.

"She was a child! She didn't know any different. By the time she turned thirteen, it started to get a little better. He molested her less and beat her more." Jean rolled her eyes to me. "She was getting too old for him. She hit puberty and he started to lose interest."

"She was fourteen when she killed him," I said. "Well past puberty."

A sound escaped Jean's throat, part laugh and part strangled cry. She turned her entire body over, raised herself up on one elbow as if to meet me eye-to-eye. "You don't get it, Work."

"If he'd stopped abusing her—"

"She had a sister!" This time, she yelled. "That's why she did what she did. A seven-year-old sister named Alexandria."

Suddenly, I understood. I understood everything.

"On the day that Alex killed her father, her sister had just turned seven years old. Her party was the day before. Guess what her daddy gave her."

I knew the answer.

"High heels, Work. Her own high heels and a tube of lipstick. For daddy's little girl. And she loved it. She didn't know what it meant; she just wanted to dress up like her big sister. That's why Alex killed him."

I didn't want to speak. I didn't want to hurt my sister further, but knew that I probably would. Hank had told me that Jean loved Alex like a preacher loves his God. So be it. But this was no divine being, no benevolent soul. She was damaged, a killer, and Jean had to understand the truth of this. For her own good.

"What happened to her sister?" I asked. "Did Alex ever tell you that?"

Jean sniffed loudly, but her voice was calmer. "She doesn't talk about her sister. I guess they lost touch after Alex was locked up. Her sister probably didn't understand, not at that age."

I had to do it fast, before I froze. She had to know.

"Her sister died, Jean. She ran back into the house and she burned to death along with her father."

Jean's mouth formed into another silent, seemingly toothless black circle.

"Accident or not, she killed her sister. And for some reason, she took her name. Alexandria, Alex. It can't be a coincidence. She killed her father, she killed her sister, and, as far as I'm concerned, she killed Ezra, too."

Jean's body trembled. "She would have told me," she said, then looked suddenly suspicious. "Why are you doing this?" she demanded.

"I'm sorry, Jean. I know it hurts, but I had to tell you. You deserve the truth."

"I don't believe you."

"I swear it, Jean. On our mother's name, I swear it's the truth."

"Get out of here, Work. Get out and leave me alone."

"Jean . . ."

"You always took Dad's side. You've always hated her."

"She killed our father, and she wants me to fry for it."

Jean rose from the mattress, a gray and quaking shadow of herself; her sheets fell away and she swayed on the narrow bed. I feared she would tumble off and crack her skull on the hard floor. Her finger stabbed at me, and I saw the denial in her. I'd pushed it too hard, too fast.

I'd lost her.

"Get out!" she screamed, and burst into tears. "Get out! Get out of here, you fucking liar!"

CHAPTER

31

I fled the room because I had no choice. Jean was distraught; I'd pushed her to a dangerous place. She had two things in this world, Alex and me. But right now, Alex was all that mattered to her, and I'd tried to take that away.

But at least I had the truth, finally. Jean had not killed Ezra. She was not a murderer, and without that weight on her conscience, she might eventually pull out of the nosedive that had brought her to this hospital in the first place. Yet the alternatives could be equally devastating. Someone was going down for Ezra's murder, and the way it looked now, it would either be Alex or me. Could Jean recover from either of those eventualities? She would have to. It was just that simple.

For me, things had changed dramatically. I might have been willing to take the rap for Jean, but not for Alex. No way in hell.

I leaned against the wall. It was hard and cold under my back, and

I closed my eyes. I thought I heard her weeping, but then the sound was gone. Imagination, I told myself. Guilty conscience.

When I opened my eyes, a nurse was standing in front of me. She looked worried.

"Are you okay?" she asked. The question took me by surprise.

"Yes."

She studied me. "You're as pale as a sheet and look dead on your feet."

"I'm okay. Just tired."

"I'm not going to argue about it," she told me. "But if you're not a patient, you'll have to leave. Visiting hours aren't for another hour."

"Thanks," I said, and walked off. When I looked back, she was watching me, a puzzled look on her face. I could almost read her mind. Don't I know you from somewhere? She was thinking. Then she turned away.

As I followed the hall toward the elevators, I thought about Alex. I was no shrink, so I could only guess at the state of her mind, but it had to be a wreck. Why the name change? I could understand wanting to escape her childhood, but why take her dead sister's name? Because she'd died untouched and unspoiled, purified by her innocence and by the fire that killed her? Or was it guilt, and the desire that she live on in some small way? I would probably never know. But one thing was crystal clear, and that is what scared me. Alex Shiften was fiercely loyal, and she would take drastic measures to eradicate any perceived threat to herself, to Jean, or to their relationship. She killed her father to protect her sister. She killed Ezra to protect her relationship with Jean. Now I was the threat, and she was setting me up for the murder. She'd turned Jean against me. She'd undermined my alibi, somehow acquired a copy of the will, and planted it in my house.

Suddenly, I froze, paralyzed by a thought that came unbidden yet with horrifying clarity. Alex had undermined my alibi. She knew that I was not home with Barbara when Ezra was shot. Did she know where I was that night? Did she know about Vanessa? Dear God! Did she know that Vanessa could give me an alibi? Now Vanessa was missing.

She didn't come home last night.

I couldn't finish the thought. But I had to. There was no time left for fear or denial. So I asked the question. If Alex knew that Vanessa could ruin her plans, would she kill her?

The answer was unequivocal.

Absolutely.

The elevator opened. I pushed through the waiting crowd of green shirts and white coats and nearly sprinted for the exit. Outside, I realized that I had no plan. Nowhere to go. I looked at my watch. It was 10:30. I called Stolen Farm, knowing better than to hope, yet doing so with every fiber of my being. Just pick up. Please, pick up. The phone rang four times, and each unanswered ring was a nail in my heart. Alex had killed her. She was dead.

The grief almost overwhelmed me, yet through the pain, like a whispering traitor, came a single selfish thought. I had no alibi. I could go to jail for the rest of my life. The presence of that thought made me think that maybe I should. I squashed it and it did not resurrect itself, for which I was grateful.

Next, I called Hank. I had to talk to him, now more than ever. He didn't answer at home, so I tried his cell phone.

"I was about to call you," he said.

"Hank, thank God."

"Shut up for a minute. We've got big fucking problems." I heard his hand go over the mouthpiece, heard muffled voices. Almost a minute passed before he came back on the line. "Okay. I'm outside."

"Listen, Hank. I think I'm onto something about Vanessa."

"Work, I mean this in the most polite way, but we don't have time to deal with your missing girlfriend. I'm at the police station now."

"In Salisbury?"

"Yeah. I came here to check accident reports before I started looking for your friend. But it's a damn hornet's nest down here. We need to talk, but not on the phone. Where are you right now?"

"I'm at the hospital. I'm standing outside the emergency room exit."

"Stay there. Try to stay out of sight. I'll be there in a couple of minutes."

"Hank, wait." I caught him before he hung up. "What the hell is going on?"

"They found the gun, Work. The one you threw in the river."

"What?"

"Just sit tight. Two minutes." He hung up, and I stared at the dead cell phone in my hand for what may have been the longest two minutes of my life.

They'd found the gun. Could Alex have been responsible for that, too?

When Hank turned into the parking lot, I met him at the curb. I climbed into his sedan. He neither looked at me nor spoke. He turned left out of the parking lot, made several seemingly random turns, and then stopped at the curb. We were in a residential neighborhood. It was quiet, nobody in sight. Hank stared wordlessly through the windshield.

"I'm waiting for you to speak," he finally said, looking at me.

"What do you mean?"

His face was hard; so were his eyes. When he spoke, I found that his voice had chilled, as well. "What river? What gun? Those are the questions you should have asked. It concerns me that you did not ask those questions."

I didn't know what to say. He was right. An innocent man would have asked the questions.

"I didn't kill him, Hank."

"Tell me about the gun."

"There's nothing to tell." The lie came instinctively.

"You don't have many people in your corner, Work, and you're about to be all alone. I don't help people who lie to me; it's that simple. So you take a minute, and think about the next words that come out of your mouth."

I'd never seen Hank so tense, like he could punch me in the face or rip his own hair out. But it was more than anger. He felt betrayed, and I couldn't blame him.

If Jean hadn't pulled the trigger, then I had no reason to lie about the gun. In fact, I should want the police to have it, if that would help convict Alex. But I'd wiped it down and ditched it, a crime in and of itself. Yet all that mattered right now was finding Vanessa, and if Hank could help me do that, then I would tell him anything he wanted to know. I had one question first.

"How'd they find the gun?"

Hank looked like he was about to drive off and leave me, so I spoke again.

"Swear to god, Hank. Just tell me that and I'll answer your questions."

He seemed to mull it over. "Someone called in an anonymous tip, said that they'd seen someone toss a gun into the river. A diver from the sheriff's department went down this morning and found it right where the caller said it'd be. That was about an hour ago. They know it's Ezra's gun because it has his initials right there on it."

"Do they know who made the call?" I was thinking about Alex. She would have had to know that the gun was clean before she'd do something like that. She would not want it traced back to her.

"The guy didn't identify himself, but he described someone who looks a hell of a lot like you. Same build, same age, same hair, same car. They're trying to track him down to do a lineup. If they find him, you'll be the first to know. Mills will have you downtown so fast, your head will spin. And if he identifies you, that's it; you're as good as convicted."

"It was a guy?" I asked. "The caller?"

"Didn't you hear me? They're trying to link you to the gun."

"But the caller. It was a man?"

Not a woman?

"Look. That's what I heard, okay? It's not like I was on the phone. I heard it was a guy. Now tell me about the fucking gun. I don't want to ask again."

I scrutinized his features. He wanted me to be innocent; not because he liked me, although I thought that maybe he did, but because he did not want to be wrong, not about something like this. Hank Robins would never help a killer, and, like everybody, he hated to be played.

"You want to know why I ditched the gun if I didn't kill him." It was a statement, not a question.

"Now we're getting somewhere."

So I opened my mouth. I started talking and didn't stop until I'd explained it to him. He didn't say a word until I was through.

"So, you were going to take the heat for Jean."

I nodded.

"That's why you ditched the gun."

"Yes."

"Tell me again why you thought that Jean had pulled the trigger."

I'd been vague about this. No way could I discuss the night Mom died, not with Hank or anybody else. I didn't know if he'd accept my theory without understanding what could have driven my sister to murder, but that was the chance I'd have to take. That body was buried, and I meant for it to stay that way.

"Jean has not been well, mentally, for a long time now. She and Ezra had problems."

"Hmmm," Hank said, and I knew that I was losing him. "Problems."

"It's a family matter, Hank. I can't talk about it. You can believe me or not. Help me or not. But that's all I can say about it."

He was silent for a full minute. He didn't look away from my face, and I could almost see the wheels turning.

"There's a lot you're not telling me."

"Yes. But like I said, it's family stuff." I hesitated. I didn't want to beg but knew that I was close. "I didn't kill him, Hank. He was deceitful, arrogant, and a first-class bastard. All right. I admit that. But he was my old man. I could have beaten him bloody on any number of occasions, but I could never have killed him. You've got to believe me."

"And the fifteen million dollars?" Hank asked, doubt again clouding his features.

"I've never cared about making money," I said.

Hank raised an eyebrow at me. "Making money's not the same as having it. Your father was born poor. I bet he understood that."

"I don't want it," I reiterated. "Nobody gets that, but I don't. He left me the house and the building outright. That's probably one point two million. So I'll sell them, give half to Jean, and still be richer than I'd ever planned on being."

"Six hundred grand ain't fifteen million."

"It's enough," I said.

"For about one guy in a million." Hank paused. "You that guy, Work?"

"I guess I am."

Hank settled back in his seat. "I'd take the fifteen million," he said, and I knew then that he would help me.

He put the car in drive and eased away from the curb. We drove in silence for a few minutes.

"So what do you want me to do?" Hank asked. "The way I see it, we have a couple choices. We dig deeper on Alex or we go talk to Mills, let her check Alex out. Now I understand if you don't want to talk to Mills, so I'll be glad to handle that. That would probably be the best idea, the more I think about it. You'll have to come clean about the gun, but nobody says that has to be done quickly. Once Mills is convinced, once she's built a case against Alex, maybe then we'll tell her. Of course, if they find the anonymous caller, that point will be moot. It's not going to be pretty, no matter how we do it. Mills would chew your face off if she could get away with it. She won't be easy to convince. She wants you to be guilty. It's almost personal."

I was barely listening; my mind was elsewhere. "I think Alex will come looking for me," I said.

"What do you mean?"

"I told Jean about my suspicions. Alex won't sit still for that. She'll come looking for me."

Hank was already shaking his head. "If she's the killer, that's the last thing she'll do. She'll play dumb. She'll wait for the world to land on you. All the hard work's done. She can relax and watch her tax dollars at work."

"Maybe," I said, but was not dissuaded.

"So, do you want me to talk to Mills?"

"I want you to find Vanessa," I said. "That hasn't changed."

"Damn it! This is not the time to waste energy looking for some missing person. I don't care how you feel about her. As soon as Mills finds that caller, you'll be arrested, and as far as we know, they've already back-traced it. They could do a photo lineup easily enough. They could be coming for you already, and this time there won't be any bail. Not after attempting to destroy evidence. No judge alive would let you out. You'll rot in jail, Work. So get your priorities straight! Playtime is over."

"I want you to find her, Hank."

"For fuck's sake, Work. Why?"

I didn't want to say this, because it was not the most important reason, and I already felt bad enough. But Hank had to hear it.

"She's more than my girlfriend, okay? She's my alibi."

"What?" Hank's disbelief was plain on his face.

"I was with her when Ezra was shot. I was at Stolen Farm."

"Well, Jesus, Work. Why didn't you just tell me that?"

"For Jean's sake, Hank. But there's one other thing. And I hope I'm wrong about this."

"What?" Hank asked.

"I think Alex knew that Vanessa was my alibi. It's possible that she went after her; she may have already killed her."

Hank settled into my revelation; his features solidified into resigned determination. "I'll find her, Work." He did not smile. "Alive or dead. I'll find her."

"Find her alive, Hank," I said, but he didn't respond. He looked at me once, then put his eyes back on the road.

"Is your car at the hospital?" he asked.

"I have a car there."

When we arrived at the hospital, I directed him to Dr. Stokes's minivan. "I want you to go home," Hank told me.

"Why? There's nothing for me there."

"Actually," he said. "There is. Toothbrush, razor, clothes. I want you to pack all that crap up and find a motel room somewhere off the beaten track. Not too far away, just someplace you can lay low for a day or so. Get cleaned up. Get some sleep. Once I find Vanessa, we'll go to Mills. But I don't want to do that until we can walk in her front door with a sworn alibi."

I got out of the car, leaned in the open door. "What are you going to do?"

"My job, Work. If she can be found, I'll find her. Once you're set up, let me know where you are. Call me on my cell."

"I don't think I can just sit around." I tried to find the words to express what I felt. It was difficult. "I don't want to hide anymore."

"Twenty-four hours, Work. Thirty-six at the most."

"I don't like it." I started to close the door.

"Hey," Hank said. I turned back, and he said, "Don't waste any time at the house, okay? Get in and get out. Mills could be looking for you already."

"I understand," I said, and watched him drive away.

I got in the minivan and went home. I looked at the high walls where once-white paint had grayed and then peeled. Barbara had always said the house had good bones, and she was right about that; but it had no heart, not with us living inside it. In place of laughter, trust, and joy, there was a hollow emptiness, a kind of rot, and I marveled at my blindness. Was it the alcohol, I wondered, that had made it bearable? Or was it something else, some inner failing? Maybe it was neither. They say that if you drop a frog into boiling water, he'll hop right out. But put the same frog into cold water and slowly turn up the heat, and he'll sit quietly until his blood begins to boil. He'll let himself be cooked alive. Maybe that's how it was for me. Maybe I was like that frog.

I thought about that, and then I thought about what Hank had said. His heart was in the right place. His head, too, for that matter. But I couldn't go to a hotel. I couldn't hide and I couldn't pretend that this would just go away. If Mills came for me, she came. Alex, too, for that matter.

Done is done, I thought, and went inside.

I found Barbara in the kitchen, poised ten feet from the door, as if frozen or about to turn away. For a split second, her face seemed fluid, but then her mouth opened in a half smile and she ran to meet me. I stood there, straight-armed and stiff, as she threw her arms around me and squeezed.

"Oh, Work. Oh, honey. I'm so sorry I didn't meet you at the jail. I just couldn't." The words came fast from her overeager mouth, and the feel of them against my jail-grimed neck unsettled me. She pulled back, framed my face with her hands. Her words accelerated onto a slippery track. They ran over one another, tripped, and fell. They were soft and too sweet, like chocolate left in the sun. "People have been looking at me, you know," she said. "The way people look sometimes, and I know what they're thinking. And I know it's no excuse, not compared to what you've been through, of course, but still it hurts. And I couldn't go there, not to the jail, not to see you like that. I just knew that wouldn't be a good thing for us. Unhealthy, you know. So when your Mr. Robins showed up, I asked him if he would meet you. I hope that was okay. I thought it would be. But then you didn't come home, and you didn't call, and I didn't know what to think." She sucked in a breath. "There're just so many things I wanted to say to you, and not being able to, why, that was just about the worst."

She fell silent, and in the absence of my response, awkwardness blossomed between us. She took her hands from my face, slid them to my shoulders, and squeezed me twice before allowing them to fall away. Eventually, they clutched the front of her shirt and settled there, white-knuckled.

"What was it?" I asked. She looked startled, as if she did not expect me to speak after all. "What was it that you wanted to say to me?"

She laughed, but it was born small and died a second later. She unclenched a hand and rubbed my right shoulder. She did not look at my face.

"You know, honey. Mainly just that I love you. That I believe in you. Those sorts of things." She finally risked a glance at my face. "The kinds of things I hoped you'd want to hear, especially at a time like this."

"That was very considerate of you," I managed to say, for the sake of civility.

She actually blushed and smiled. She cast her eyes at the floor as if her carefully groomed eyelashes could still entice me. When she looked up, her uncertainties had vanished. Her voice firmed, as did her eyes and the renewed grip on my shoulders.

"Listen, Work. I know this is difficult. But we'll get through it, okay? You're innocent. I know that. There's no way you'll go back to jail. This will pass, and when it does, we'll be fine. We can be the perfect couple again, like we were in the old days. People will look at us, and that's what they'll say: What a perfect couple. We just have to hang on and get through this. Get through it together."

" 'Together,' "I parroted, thinking of the frog.

"It's just a glitch. Huge and unfortunate, but just a glitch. That's all. We can handle it."

I blinked, and this time I actually saw the frog. The water bubbled and his blood began to boil. I wanted to scream, to warn him, but did not; and as I watched, his eyes boiled away. Poof. Right out of their sockets.

"I need a shower," I said.

"Good idea," Barbara agreed. "You take a nice hot shower, and when you get out, we'll have a drink. We'll have a drink and everything will be okay." I started to turn away, but she spoke again, so softly that I almost missed it. "Just like old times," she whispered. I looked at her eyes, but they were impenetrable, and her lips curved into the same half smile. "I love you, honey," she said. I turned out of the kitchen, and she called after me, her voice already fading. "Welcome home."

I went to the bedroom, where I found the bed perfectly made and flowers in a vase. The shades had been opened and light flooded in. In the mirror above the dresser I looked old and stepped upon, but there was resolution there, too; and I watched my eyes as I emptied my pockets and shed my days-old clothing. They did not look so old or so stepped upon as the rest of me.

In the shower, I turned the water as hot as I could bear. I lifted my face to the nozzle, let the water beat upon me. I didn't hear the shower door open. I felt the draft, and then I felt her hands. They settled on my back like autumn leaves. I might have flinched.

"Shhh," Barbara said gently. "Be still." I started to turn. "Don't turn around," she said.

She reached around me and wet her hands in the shower. She ran the soap between them and replaced it on the soap dish. Then she put her hands on my chest, which grew slick beneath them. She must have felt my resistance, in my tense muscles, in my unyielding posture—perhaps in the rigidity of my silence. Yet she chose to ignore it, and her hands lathered a path from my chest to my stomach. She molded herself against my back and I felt the firm press of her flesh against my own. Water cascaded across my shoulders, forced its path down the joining of our bodies, and she opened herself to it, let it wet her. She slithered against me, insinuated her slender leg between my own. And her hands worked down to a place where in the past they had always been welcome.

"Barbara." My voice was an intruder. Her fingers worked harder, as if persistence alone could make me want the absolution she thought was in her power to offer.

"Just let me do this," she said.

I did not want to hurt her. I wanted nothing to do with her at all. "Barbara," I said again, more insistently this time. I reached for her fingers. She pulled me around to face her.

"I can do this, Work."

The front of her hair was wet, the back still dry, and her face was so serious that I almost laughed; yet there was desperation in her eyes, as if this was all she had left to offer and she knew it. For a moment, I did not know what to say, and in that moment she lowered herself to her knees.

"For God's sake, Barbara." I could not keep the disgust out of my voice, and I pushed roughly past her; I opened the door and grabbed my towel. Steam followed me out, along with a dread silence. The water stopped. I did not look back. When Barbara stepped out next to me, she didn't bother to cover herself. She ignored the water that ran into her eyes and pooled on the floor; and I ignored her until I knew she would not simply walk away. So I turned and faced her, my towel heavy with cooling damp, my heart just heavy.

"My life's falling apart, too," she said. But it wasn't sadness I saw in her eyes. It was anger.

CHAPTER

32

In my closet I found a row of empty hangers, which was fine. I would never wear a suit again; I was pretty sure of that. I pulled on a pair of jeans, an old button-down shirt, and running shoes that I'd worn out years ago. On the top shelf was a battered, disreputable baseball cap, and I put that on, too.

I found Barbara in the kitchen. She was making a pot of coffee; her robe was cinched tight.

"What can I do to make it right?" she asked. "I want it to be right with us, Work. So just tell me."

A week before, I would have wavered and broken. I'd have told her that I loved her and that everything would be all right. Part of me would have believed it, but the rest of me would have screamed its thin scream.

"I don't love you, Barbara. I don't think I ever did." She opened her mouth, but I continued before she could speak. "You don't love me, either. Maybe you think you do, but you don't. Let's not pretend anymore. It's over."

"Just like that," she said. "You say so and it's over." Her anger was obvious, but it may have been ego.

"We've been on a downward spiral for years."

"I'm not giving you a divorce. We've been through too much. You owe me."

"'Owe you'?"

"That's right."

"I don't need your agreement, Barbara; I don't even need cause. All it takes is a year's separation."

"You need me. You won't make it in this town without me."

I shook my head. "You might be surprised at how little I need." But she ignored me and moved across the kitchen floor on feet that were invisible beneath the hem of her robe.

"We have our problems, Work, but we're a team. We can deal with anything."

She reached for me.

"Don't touch me," I said.

She allowed her hands to drop, but they did so slowly. She looked up at me, and already she seemed to be retreating.

"Okay, Work. If that's what you want. I won't fight you. I'll even act civilized. That's what you want, isn't it, a dry, emotionless parting? A clean break. So that you can get on with your new life and I can try to figure what mine will be. Right?"

"My new life might well be prison, Barbara. This may be the biggest favor I've ever done for you."

"You won't go to prison," she said, but I merely shrugged.

"I'll do the best I can for you, moneywise; you won't have to fight me."

Barbara laughed, and I saw some of the old bitterness steal into her eyes. "You don't make enough money now, Work. You never have, not even when Ezra was alive, and nobody made money the way he did."

Her words rang in my head, and something clicked. "What did you just say?"

"You heard me." She turned away, picked up a pack of cigarettes, and lit one. I didn't know when she had started smoking again. She was in college the last time I saw a cigarette between her lips, but this one danced in her mouth as she spoke. "You could barely make it with Ezra looking out for you. As it is, I don't know a single lawyer in town who makes less money than you do." She blew smoke at the ceiling. "So keep your empty promises. I know what they're worth."

But that wasn't what struck me.

Making money's not the same as having it. Hank's words.

"Would you say that Ezra liked making money?" I asked. "Or did he like having it?"

"What are you talking about, Work? What does any of that matter? He's dead. Our marriage is dead."

But I was onto something. The pieces weren't in place, but something was there and I couldn't let go of it. "Money, Barbara. The achievement of it or the possession of it? Which was more important?"

She blew out more smoke and shrugged, as if nothing mattered anymore. "Having it," she said. "He didn't care about working for it. It was a tool."

She was right. He depended on it. He could use it, and suddenly I knew. Not the exact combination to his safe, but I knew where to find it. And just like that, opening the old man's safe became the most important thing in my world. It was something I had to do, and I knew how to do it.

I've got to go," I said. I put my hand on her arm and she did not flinch away. "I'm sorry, Barbara."

She nodded and looked at the floor, more smoke writhing from her lips.

"We'll talk more later," I said, and picked up the keys. I stopped at the garage door and looked back. I expected her to appear different somehow, but she didn't. She looked as she always had. My hand was on the door when her voice stopped me a final time.

"One question," she said.

"What?"

"What about your alibi?" she asked. "Aren't you worried about losing your alibi?"

For an instant, our eyes locked. She let her shutters drop, and I saw into the depths of her. That's when I knew that she knew. She'd known all along; so I said the words, and with their passing, a weight seemed to fall away, and in that instant even Barbara was untainted.

"You were never my alibi, Barbara. We both know that."

She nodded slightly, and this time the tears came.

"There was a time I would have killed for you," she said, and looked back up. "What was one little lie?"

The tears came faster, and her shoulders trembled as if finally exhausted by some invisible load. "Are you going to be okay?" I asked.

"We do what we need to do, right? That's what survival is all about."

"It's just a question of getting to the point where it has to be done. That's why we'll both be okay. Maybe we can part as friends."

She sniffed loudly, and laughed. She wiped at her eyes. "Wouldn't that be something?"

"It would," I agreed. "Listen, I'll be at the office. I won't be long. When I get back, we'll talk some more."

"What are you going to the office for?" she asked.

"Nothing, really. I just figured something out."

She gestured at the pain-filled space around us: the room, the house, maybe the entirety of our lives together. "More important than this?" she asked.

"No," I replied, lying. "Of course not."

"Then don't leave," she said.

"It's just life, Barbara, and it gets messy. Not everything works out the way you want."

"It does if you want it badly enough."

"Only sometimes," I said. Then I left, closing the door on the life behind me. I started the car and turned around. The children were still in the park, tiny flashes of color as they ran and screamed. I turned off the radio, put the car in drive, and then I saw Barbara in the garage. She watched me in utter stillness, and for an instant she did look different. But then she waved at me to wait and ran light-footed to the window.

"Don't go," she said. "I don't want it to end like this."

"I've got to."

"Damn it, Work. What's so important?"

"Nothing," I said. "Nothing that concerns you."

She wrapped her arms around herself and leaned over as if her stomach hurt. "It's going to end badly. I know it will." Her eyes grew distant. She looked down at the park, as if the sight of the children affected her, too. "Ten years of our lives, and it'll all be wasted. Just gone."

"People move on every day, Barbara. We're no different."

"That's why it never could have worked," she said, and I heard blame in her voice. She looked down at me. "You never wanted to be special, and there was nothing I could do to make you want that. You were so ready to be satisfied. You took the scraps from Ezra's table and thought you had a banquet."

"Ezra was chained to that table. He was no happier than I was."

"Yes, he was. He took what he wanted and took pleasure in taking it. He was a man that way."

"Are you trying to hurt me?" I asked. "Because this is unpleasant enough as it is."

Barbara smacked her hand on the top of the car. "And you think it's pleasant for me? It's not."

I looked away from her then, turned my eyes down the hill to the flashes of color that stained the dark green grass. Suddenly, I wanted to be away from this place, but something remained to be said. So I said it.

"Do you know what our problem is, Barbara? You never knew me. You saw what you wanted to see. A young lawyer from a rich family, with a near-famous father, and you assumed you knew me. Who I was. What I wanted. What I cared about. You married a stranger, and you tried to turn him into someone that you recognized. For ten years, you beat me down, and I let you do it; but I could never be what you wanted. So you grew frustrated and bitter, and I grew despondent. I hid from myself, as if it would all just go away, and that makes me as bad as you. We married for the wrong reasons, a common-enough mistake, and if I'd been man enough, I would have ended it years ago."

Barbara's lips twisted, "Your self-righteousness makes me ill," she said. "You're no better than me."

"I don't pretend to be."

"Just go," she said. "You're right. It's over. So just go."

"I'm sorry, Barbara."

"Save your fucking sympathy," she said, and walked back to the house.

I let her go, and for that moment I seemed to float; but the absence of pain can pass as pleasure for only so long, and I still had things to do. I pointed her car toward the office.

A psychiatrist could probably explain my obsession with opening Ezra's safe. In tearing down his last secret, I was replacing him, assuming his power. Or struggling to understand him. To outdo him. Truthfully, it was nothing that complicated. I'd worked in that building for ten years, thirteen if you counted the summer jobs during law school. During that time, my father had made no reference to the safe. We were family. We were partners. He shouldn't have kept secrets from me. Yes, I was curious, but more than that I was disturbed; and some part of me believed that tearing down this secret would make my father known to me once and for all. Our truest self is often the person we allow no one else to see—who we are when we are alone. In the real world, we edit. We compromise and prevaricate.

I wanted to see the man behind the curtain.

For what I'd realized was this, and I should have seen it sooner: Ezra cared about having money; it was the curse of growing up dirt-poor. Money bought food. Money fixed the roof. Having it meant survival. So the million-dollar jury award that made him famous and ultimately rich was not the most important thing after all. I'd been wrong about that. Because big-dollar jury verdicts are appealed, and even if they're not, nobody cuts a check the day of the verdict. Making money versus having money. In that equation, only one date matters: the day you deposit the check.

I didn't know what date that was, but there would be records. Somewhere in the office was a deposit record showing a cash infusion of $333,333.33, exactly one-third of one million dollars. By the time he died, a few hundred grand amounted to chump change, but that was the money that had made him. I should have seen it.

I parked in back and looked up at the tall, narrow building. Already I felt like a stranger there, and Barbara's words echoed in my mind: *ten years . . . wasted. Just gone.*

I got out of the car. No one was around, but in the distance I heard sirens, and I thought of Mills. She was looking at Ezra's gun, slapping her open palms against the hard muscles of her thighs. She would find the anonymous caller and I would be identified. I would be arrested, tried, and convicted. All I had was Hank, and the faded hope that Vanessa Stolen could save both body and soul.

Inside, the office was musty, as if weeks or months had passed since last I'd been there. Shadows stretched through slatted blinds, and dust hung in the alternating bars of light. The place was silent and unwelcoming, as if my thoughts had betrayed me. I did not belong. That was the message. The building knew.

I locked the door behind me, moved down the short hall and into the main reception area. Sound was muffled; I pushed through air that felt like water, and accepted that much of what I felt was formless dread. I tried to shake it off.

The cops had seized my computers, so I went down the narrow, creaking staircase to the basement, where boxes rose in jagged mounds and a single bare bulb dangled as if from a gibbet. The place was packed with old case files, tax records, and bank statements. I saw broken furniture, an exercise machine that dated to the seventies, and eight different golf bags. It was a mess, and the oldest stuff was in the very back. I waded through it, trying to figure out the system. The boxes were stacked haphazardly but were grouped together by dates. So the files from any given year would be found together, buried in a mass grave.

I located what I thought would be the right year and started tearing open boxes. There was no order to it at all, which surprised me. Ezra had always been meticulous in his affairs. Files numbered in the thousands, crushed into misshapen cardboard cartons. And inside the larger boxes I found smaller containers holding monthly calendars, receipts, message slips, dried-out pens, and paper clips. There were half-used legal pads and discarded Rolodex cards. It was as if Ezra had emptied his desk every year and then started fresh with new supplies. I opened his day planner for December, saw the small exclamation point he'd placed on December 31, and realized then why this was so different. It was a finished year, and like so much of his past, Ezra had boxed it away to be forgotten. Ezra had always cared about the future. Everything else was one step above refuse.

I found what I was looking for in the bottom of the seventh box, buried beneath a foot and a half of divorce pleadings. I recognized the well-creased spine of the thick black ledger book that Ezra had always preferred. It made a cracking sound when I opened it, and I fingered the green paper, now browned at the edges, and saw the rows of Ezra's precise figures. My first impression was of smallness. Small writing and small numbers—nothing like his stature or the billings he would soon come to achieve. I found the deposit entry on the thirty-third page. The deposit above it was for fifty-seven dollars, the one below for an even hundred. His handwriting was unvaried, so that one-third of a million dollars might well have been a daily deposit. Looking at it, I could only imagine the satisfaction that entry must have given him. Yet, it was as if he'd bottled up any symptoms of joy or pleasure. Maybe he'd been selfish with it; maybe he'd just been disciplined. But I could still remember the night he took us out to celebrate. "Nothing can stop me now," he'd said. And he'd been right, until Alex shot him in the head.

I left the basement and turned off the light. The smell of moldering cardboard followed me as I headed for Ezra's office. I paused at the foot of the stairs, remembering the sound of a heavy chair crashing down; but now there was only silence, and so I broke it, my feet heavy on the timeworn stairs. The rug looked different; maybe it was the light, but it seemed to ripple at the far corner. I pulled it back, wondered again if my mind was playing tricks on me. The wood was chipped at the edge, gouged around the nail heads. The marks were unfamiliar, small, as if made by a flathead screwdriver. I ran my fingertips over them, wondering if someone else had been here.

I dismissed the thought. Time was not on my side, and I had a number burning holes in my brain. I grabbed the hammer and went to work on the nails. I tried to slip the claw beneath the heads. I gouged more wood, scratched the nail heads shiny, but could not get them out. I rammed the claw into the crack at the boards' ends and leaned back on the handle. No give. I pulled harder, felt the tension in my back as I heaved. But the four big nails were too much.

I ran back to the basement, back into the weak light of that one dangling bulb, then around the cardboard junkyard to the tool corner, where I'd seen a snow shovel, a ladder, a busted rake, and an old car jack. I found the lug wrench that went with the jack; it was two feet long with a sharp, tapered end. Back upstairs, breathing hard, I pushed the narrow end between the boards, pounded the other end with the hammer. Steel slipped into the crack where that yellow-white wood seemed to smile at me. I jammed the hammer against the base of the wrench for leverage, held it there with my foot, and then I put one hundred and ninety pounds on that long wrench. I leaned into it, heard wood crack and then splinter. I shifted down the board. Pried up one ragged piece and then another, until the whole thing came loose. I ripped the boards out, felt splinters in my palm and ignored them. I threw the ruined boards aside.

The safe challenged me, and for a moment I was afraid; but I pictured my old man's ledger entry, knew it was the right number. I was ready to tear him down, ready to know, so I dropped again to my knees. I knelt above this last piece of him, said a silent prayer, and typed in the date that he'd made the largest deposit of his life.

The door swung up on silent hinges, opened to darkness; and then I blinked.

The first thing I saw was cash, lots of it, banded together in stacks of ten thousand. I removed all of it. The money was solid in my hand, a brick of currency that I could smell over the mustiness. At a glance, it looked like almost $200,000. I put it on the floor beside me, but it was difficult to look away. I'd never seen so much hard currency. But I wasn't here for money, so I returned to the gaping hole.

There were pictures of his family. Not his wife and children. Not that family. But the one that raised him, the impoverished one. There was a faded picture of Ezra and his father. Another of his father and his mother. One of several dirty, blank-eyed children who may have been siblings. I'd never seen these before, and I doubted that Jean had, either. The people looked used up, even the children, and in one group shot I saw what had made Ezra different. It was something in his eyes, like in the photo on his desk at home. There was strength in them, as if, even as a child, he could move worlds. His brothers and sisters may have sensed this, for in the photographs they seemed to hover around him.

But they were all strangers to me. I'd never met a single one of them. Not once.

I put the photos next to the money and returned to the safe. In a large velvet box I found some of my mother's jewelry—not what she was wearing when she died, but the really expensive stuff, which Ezra once referred to as "fuck you baubles," and only brought out when he wanted to impress a man or make the guy's wife look cheap. Mother hated to wear them, and she once told me that they made her feel like the devil's concubine. Not that they weren't beautiful; they were. But they, too, were tools, and never intended as anything else. I put the box aside, planning to give it to Jean. Maybe she could sell them.

The videotapes were on the bottom, three of them, unmarked. I held them as I would a snake, and wondered briefly if I'd been wrong—that maybe there were things about a father that a son should never know.

Why would he keep videotapes in a safe?

A VCR and a television sat in the corner. I picked a tape at random and put it in the player. I turned on the television and pushed the play button.

At first, there was static, then a sofa. Soft lights. Voices. I looked at the long leather couch behind me, then back at the screen. They were the same.

"I don't know, Ezra." A woman's voice, somehow familiar.

"Humor me." That was Ezra.

I heard the sound of a gentle smack, a burst of girlish laughter.

A woman's legs, long and tan. She ran past the camera, flung herself onto the couch. She was naked, laughing, and for an instant I saw a flash of white teeth, and equally pale breasts. Then Ezra heaved into view, filling the screen. He shrank as he moved to the couch, but I heard him mumble something. Then her voice: "Well, come on, then." Her arms above her head, face obscured. Her legs opened, the left finding the back of the curved leather couch, the right circling his waist, guiding him down.

He collapsed onto her, buried her under his massive body; but I saw her legs, and she had the strength to rise up beneath him. "Oh yeah," she said. "Like that. Fuck me like that." And he did, slamming her, driving her down and into the yielding leather. Narrow arms escaped from beneath him, found his back, and dragged claw marks into his skin.

Watching, I felt sick, but I could not look away. Because some part of me knew. It was the voice. The way her legs joined. That brief, horrible flash of teeth.

I knew, and in bleak disbelief I watched my father nail my wife to the couch.

CHAPTER

33

The images were hammer blows. He used her, manhandled her, and her eyes, when I saw them, glowed like an animal's. There was no office, no world; it was gone, obliterated, and I could not feel the floor that rushed up to meet my knees. My stomach clenched, and my mouth may have filled with bile, but if it did, I never tasted it. Every sense was overwhelmed by the one that I could forever do without. Sights no man should see swelled and burst like rotten fruit. My wife, on her back, then on her hands and knees. My father, hairy as any farm animal, grunting over her as if she, too, were mindless flesh, and not the wife of his only son.

How long? The thought found me. *How long had this gone on?* And then, quick on its heels: *How could I have missed it?*

And just when I could take no more, the screen went dead. I sagged into myself and waited for a collapse that never came. I was numb, staggered by what I'd seen and by what the sight implied. Her voice, when she spoke—it shocked the hell out of me.

"You nailed the boards down."

I turned and saw her. She stood by Ezra's desk. I hadn't heard her come up the stairs and so had no idea how long she'd been there. She lowered the remote control to the desk. I climbed to my feet. She looked calm, but her eyes were glazed and her lips were damp.

"Do you know how many times I've tried to open that damn safe?" She sat on the edge of the desk and looked at me; her face remained pale, and her voice was equally colorless. "Late at night, usually, while you slept. It was the best thing about being married to a drunk. You were always a heavy sleeper. I knew about the tapes, of course. I shouldn't have let him do that, but he insisted. I didn't know he kept them in the safe until it was too late."

Her eyes were lightless, and when she blinked, her body seemed to tilt. She looked drugged, and may well have been. I didn't know her. I never had.

"Too late for what?" I asked, but she ignored me. She pulled at her ear with one hand and kept the other hand behind her back. I knew then that I'd been wrong about a great many things.

"It was you that night," I said. "You pushed the chair down the stairs."

I looked around the office. There was only one way out.

"Yes," Barbara said. "I'm sorry about that. But I guess it was bound to happen, sooner or later. I've been up here so many times." She shrugged, and the gun appeared. It was in her left hand, and she acted as if it weren't there. I froze at the sight of it. It was small and silver, an automatic of some kind. She used the barrel to scratch at her cheek.

"What's the gun for, Barbara?" I tried to make my voice as non-threatening as possible. She shrugged again and looked at the gun. She tilted it this way and that, as if fascinated by the play of light along its glittering edge. Her face was slack. She was clearly not herself, and I thought she had to be stoned or mentally adrift.

"Something I've had for awhile," she said. "This town is getting so dangerous these days, especially for a woman alone at night."

I knew that I was in danger, but I didn't care.

"Why did you kill him, Barbara?"

Suddenly, she was on her feet, jabbing the gun in my direction, and the vacuous calm of her eyes disappeared, replaced by something entirely different. I flinched, expecting the bullet.

"I did that for you!" she screamed. "For you! How dare you question me? I did it all for you, you ungrateful bastard."

I held up my hands. "I'm sorry. Try to calm down."

"You calm down!" She took three uneven steps toward me, holding the gun as if she meant to use it. When she stopped, she didn't lower the gun. "That son of a bitch was going to change the will. I fucked him for six months before he agreed to do it right in the first place." She laughed, the sound like fingers on a chalkboard. "That's what it took, but I did it, and I did it for us. I made that happen. But he was going to undo all of that, put it back the way it was. I couldn't allow that. So don't you pretend that I never did anything for you."

"That's why you slept with my father? For money?"

"Not for money. Money is a thousand dollars or ten thousand. He'd never trust you with fifteen million dollars. He was going to leave you three." She laughed bitterly. "Just three. Can you believe it? Rich as he was. But I convinced him. He changed it to fifteen. I did that for you."

"You didn't do it for me, Barbara."

The gun began to shake in her hand, and I saw her fingers whiten where she gripped it. "You don't know me. Don't pretend that you know me. Or what I've been through. Knowing that the tapes were here. Knowing what it would mean if somebody else found them."

"Can you put the gun down, Barbara? It's not necessary."

She didn't respond, but the barrel drifted lower, until it pointed at the floor. Barbara's eyes followed it and she seemed to slump. For an instant, I dared to breathe, but when her face came up, her eyes sparkled.

"But then you started seeing that country whore again."

"Vanessa didn't have anything to do with us," I said.

The gun came up, and Barbara screamed, "That bitch was trying to steal my money!"

I had a horrible revelation. "What did you do to her?"

"You were going to leave me. You said so yourself."

"But that had nothing to do with her, Barbara. That was about us."

"She was the problem with us."

"Where is she, Barbara?"

"She's gone. That's all that matters."

Inside, I felt something tear. Vanessa was the only reason I had left for living. So I said what was on my mind.

"I've slept with you enough times to know when you're faking." This time, I stepped toward her. My life was over. I had nothing. This woman had taken everything and I let my anger build. I gestured at the blank screen, but in my mind I still saw her, and the way she screamed. "You loved it. You loved fucking him. Was he that good? Or did you just like the idea of hurting me?"

Barbara laughed, and the gun came up. "Oh. Now you're a man. Now you're a tough guy. Well, let me tell you. Yes, I loved it. Ezra knew what he wanted and knew how to get it. He had power. I don't mean strength. I mean power. Fucking him was the biggest rush I ever had." Her top lip curled. "Coming home to you was a joke."

I saw something in her face, and had another revelation. "He dumped you," I said. "He liked having sex with you because of the power he held. He controlled you, manipulated you; but then he realized that you liked it, and once that happened, he got bored. So he dumped you. That's why you shot him."

I was right. I knew that I was. I saw it in her eyes, and in the way her lips twitched. For a moment, I felt a fierce joy, but it didn't last.

I saw her pull the trigger.

CHAPTER

34

I dreamed again of contentment, of green fields, the laughter of a small girl, and Vanessa's cheek pressed softly against my own; but dreams are fickle deceivers, and they never last. I caught a final fleeting glimpse of cornflower eyes and heard a voice so faint, it must have crossed oceans; and then the pain hit with such ferocity that I knew I was in hell. Fingers peeled back my eyelids, and red light was everywhere, beating at the world. Hands ripped at my clothes, and I felt metal against my skin. I struggled, but bone-white fingers forced me down and bound me. Blank faces flickered in and out; they floated, spoke a language I couldn't understand, and then were gone, only to return again. And the pain was ever constant; it pulsed like blood, it channeled through me, and then there were more hands upon me and I tried to scream.

Then there was motion and a white metal sky that rocked as if I were at sea. I saw a face I'd come to loathe, but Mills did not torment me further. Her lips moved, but I couldn't answer; I didn't understand. Then she left, just as I understood, and so I called out. I had the answer. But bloody hands forced her back, until she pushed them away, found the place above me, and leaned into my words. I had to shout, because I was in a deep well and falling fast. So I did. I screamed, but her face fell forever into the white sky and I crashed into the powdered ink that filled the bottom of the well. And my last thought as darkness settled around me was to wonder at a white sky in hell.

But even in that blackness, time seemed to pass, and on occasion there was light. The pain rose and fell like the tides, and when it was weak, I imagined faces and voices. I heard Hank Robins arguing with Detective Mills, who, I sensed, wanted to ask more questions; but that didn't make sense. Then Dr. Stokes, looking old with worry. He held a clipboard and was talking to a strange man in a white coat. And once Jean was there, and she wept with such force that it killed me to see it. She told me she understood, that Hank had told her everything—about the jail and my willing sacrifice. She said that she loved me but knew that she could never spend life in prison for me. She said that made me better than her, but that didn't make sense, either. I was in hell, but it was hell of my own making. I tried to explain that to her, but my throat wouldn't open. So I watched in silence and waited for the well to pull me back in.

Once, I thought I saw Vanessa, but that was hell's cruelest joke, and I did not rise to it. I closed my eyes and wept for the loss of her, and when I looked up, she was gone. I was alone, cold in the dark. The cold seemed to last forever, but eventually the heat found me, so that I remembered. I was in hell. Hell was hot, not cold. And hell was pain, so that when I woke and found it all but gone, I thought the dream had returned. I opened my eyes, but there was no child, no field, and no Vanessa. Perhaps the torments of this place were more than purely physical.

When finally I woke, I blinked in the cool air and heard the rustle of movement; so that when a face appeared above me, I was prepared for it. It was blurry at first, but I blinked it into focus. It was Jean's.

"Relax," she said. "Everything's fine. You're going to be okay."

A stranger appeared beside her, the man in the white coat. He had dark features and a beard that glistened as if oiled. "My name is Dr. Yuseph," he said. "How do you feel?"

"Thirsty." A dry croak. "Weak." I could not lift my head.

The doctor turned to Jean. "He can have an ice chip, but only one. Then another in ten minutes or so."

I heard the clink of a spoon, and Jean leaned over me. She slipped an ice chip into my mouth. "Thanks," I whispered. She smiled, but there was pain in it.

"How long?" I asked.

"Four days," the doctor replied. "In and out. You're lucky to be alive."

Four days.

He patted me on the arm. "You'll recover; it'll hurt, but you'll get there. We'll put you on solid foods as soon as you feel up for it. Once your strength returns, you'll start physical therapy. It won't be long before you're out of here."

"Where am I?"

"Baptist Hospital. Winston-Salem."

"What about Barbara?" I asked.

"Your sister can tell you anything you want to know. Just take it easy. I'll be back in an hour." He turned to Jean. "Don't tire him. He'll be weak for some time yet."

Jean reappeared at the bedside. Her face was swollen, the flesh around her eyes as dark as wine. "You look tired," I said.

She smiled wanly. "So do you."

"It's been a tough year," I said, and she laughed, then turned away. When she looked back, she was crying.

"I'm so sorry, Work." Her words broke, and the edges seemed to cut her. Her face reddened and her eyes collapsed. The tears devolved into sobs.

"For what?"

"For everything," she said, and the words, I knew, were a plea for forgiveness. "For hating you." Her head bowed, and with terrible effort I reached for her. I found her hand and tried to squeeze it.

"I'm sorry, too," I whispered. I wanted to say more, but my throat closed again, and for a long time we shared a bittersweet silence. She held my hand with both of hers and I stared at the top of her head. We couldn't go back to the way it had been for us; that place was a garden overgrown. But looking at her, I felt as close to our childhood as I ever had. And she felt it, too, as if we'd reached back to a time when apologies mattered and do-overs were a simple word away. I saw it in her eyes when she looked up.

"Did you see all your flowers?" she asked with a timid, brittle smile.

I looked past Jean and saw the room for the first time. Flowers were everywhere, dozens of vases with cards.

"Here's a card from the local bar—every lawyer in the county signed it." She handed me an oversized card, but I didn't want it. I still saw the way they'd looked at me in court, the ready condemnation in their eyes.

"What about Barbara?" I asked, and Jean put the card, unopened and unread, back on the table. Her eyes moved over the room, and I was about to repeat the question.

"Are you sure you're ready to talk about this?" she asked.

"I have to," I said.

"She's been arrested."

I exhaled a mixture of relief and despair; part of me hoped that her betrayal had been the dream. "How?" I asked.

"Mills found you. You'd been shot twice, once in the chest and once in the head." Her eyes drifted upward, and I touched my head. It was bandaged. "The one in your chest went through a lung. The head shot just grazed you. At first, she thought you were dead. You almost were. She called the paramedics and they transported you to Rowan Regional. Eventually, you were brought here."

"But what about Barbara?"

"You were conscious in the ambulance. You managed to tell Mills who'd shot you. She arrested Barbara two hours later."

Jean's voice trailed off and she looked away.

"What?" I asked. I knew there was more.

"She was having a late lunch at the country club, as if nothing had happened." Her hand settled onto mine. "I'm sorry, Work."

"What else?" I had to move on. I could see her so clearly, sipping white wine, a fake smile plastered to her face. Lunch with the girls.

"They found the gun at your house, hidden in the basement, along with a lot of money and Mother's jewelry."

"I'm surprised Mills doesn't think I put them there and shot myself." I could not keep the bitterness from my voice.

"She feels terrible, Work. She's been here a lot, and she's not afraid to admit her mistake. She wanted me to tell you she was sorry."

"Mills said that?"

"And she left something for you." Jean got up and walked across the room. When she came back, she held a stack of newspapers. "Most are local. Some are from Charlotte. You look good in print. Mills even made a public apology." She picked the top copy off the stack. I saw a picture of Barbara being led from a police cruiser. She was cuffed, trying to hide her face from the cameras.

"Put it down," I said.

"Okay." She dropped the papers onto the floor by the bed and I closed my eyes. The picture of Barbara brought it all back, the pain and betrayal. For a moment, I could not speak. When I finally looked at Jean, her eyes were veiled, and I wondered what she was seeing.

"Do you know?" I asked.

"About Barbara and Daddy?"

I nodded.

"Yes, I know. And don't you dare apologize."

I closed my mouth; nothing I could say would make it go away. It was a part of us now, as much his legacy as the color of my hair.

"He was a horrible man, Jean."

"But now he's gone, so let that be an end to it."

I agreed, even though I knew there would never be an end to it. His presence among us lingered, like the smell of something dead but unburied.

"Would you like some more ice?" Jean asked.

"That would be nice."

She fed me the ice, and as she hovered there, I saw the fresh scars on her wrists. They were tight and pink, as if the skin had stretched too tightly over the veins. To better protect them, perhaps. I didn't know. With Jean, I never did; but I hoped, and I thought that maybe it was not too late to pray.

"I'm fine," she said, and I realized that I'd been staring.

"Are you really?"

She smiled and sat back down. "You keep saving my life," she said. "There must be some value in it."

"Don't joke, Jean. Not about this."

She sighed, leaned back, and for a moment I feared I had pushed too hard. The line between us had grown vague, and I didn't want to step over it. But when she spoke, there was no resentment, and I realized that she was taking her time and wanted me to understand.

"I feel like I've come through a long, dark tunnel," she said. "It doesn't hurt to stand straight anymore, like something's let go inside of me." She clenched her hands in front of her stomach and then opened them, a ten-petaled rose. "It's hard to explain," she said, but I thought I understood. Ezra was gone; maybe that brought closure. Maybe not. But it was not my place to fix Jean. That was a truth I'd come to understand. She had to do that herself, and looking at her smile, I thought she had it in her.

"And Alex?" I asked.

"We're leaving Salisbury," she said. "We need to find a place of our own."

"You didn't answer my question."

Jean's eyes were expressive and very real. "We have issues, like everybody, but we're dealing with them."

"I don't want to lose you," I said.

"I feel like we just found each other, Work. Alex understands that. It's one of the things we've been dealing with; and while she'll always have issues with men, she swears that she'll make an exception for you."

"Can she forgive me for dredging up her past?"

"She knows why you did it. She respects your reasons, but don't ever mention it to her."

"So we're okay?" I asked.

"Wherever we go, you'll always be welcome there."

"Thank you, Jean."

"Have some more ice."

"Okay."

She fed me the ice and I felt my eyes grow heavy. Suddenly, I was exhausted, and I closed my eyes as Jean moved around the room. I was almost gone when she spoke.

"There's one card you might like to read. It's more of a letter, actually." I cracked my eyes. Jean was holding an envelope. "It's from Vanessa," she said.

"*What?*"

"She was here for awhile, but said she couldn't stay. She wanted you to have this, though." She handed me the envelope, which was thin and light. "She thought you would understand."

"But, I thought . . ." I couldn't finish the sentence.

"Hank found her at the hospital in Davidson County. She'd gone to the feed store in Lexington and was crossing the street, when somebody hit her."

"Who?" I asked.

"Nobody knows. All she remembers is a black Mercedes that came out of nowhere."

"Is she okay?"

"Broken ribs and bruises all over, but she'll survive. They kept her at the hospital overnight. She was pretty doped up on painkillers."

"I thought she was dead."

"Well, she's not, and she was pretty broken up to see you like this."

Suddenly, I couldn't see. The letter in my hand was hope for the future, something I thought I'd lost. I wanted to read her words, to see the letters made by her hands. But my fingers were clumsy.

Jean took the envelope from my hands. "Let me," she said.

She tore it open, removed the folded page, and put it back in my hand. "I'll be outside if you need me," she said, and I heard the door close behind her. I blinked, and when my vision cleared, I looked at the note Vanessa had left for me. It was short.

Life is a torturous journey, Jackson, and I don't know if I can handle any more pain. But I'll never regret the day we met, and when you're ready to talk, I'm ready to listen. Maybe some good can come of all this. I hope so, but I know too well the cruelness of fate. No matter what happens, remember this—every day I thank God that you're alive.

I read it three times, and fell asleep with it on my chest.

When I opened my eyes again, I felt ten times better. It was late, dark outside, but someone had turned on the lamp in the corner. I saw Mills in the chair, and I managed to sit up in bed before she looked up from the book she was reading.

"Hey," she said, getting up. "I hope you don't mind, but Jean has been here around the clock and was exhausted. I told her I'd stick around." She stood, looking uncertain. "I thought you might have some questions."

"I guess I should say thanks," I said. "For saving my life."

If possible, Mills looked even more uncomfortable. "And I owe you an apology."

"Forget about it," I said, surprising myself. "The past is dead. I don't intend to think about it too much." I gestured at the chair next to the bed. "Sit down."

"Thanks." She sat and put her book on the table. I saw that it was a mystery, and for some reason that struck me as funny, her being a detective and all.

"I really don't know what I want to hear," I told her. "I haven't had much time to think about any of this."

"I have a couple questions," Mills said. "Then I'll start at the beginning and tell you anything you want to know."

"Okay."

"Where did you find your father's gun?" she asked, and I told her about the creek, about my nighttime search down the throat.

"I sent a team through that tunnel," she said, visibly upset. "They should have found it."

I explained how I'd found it wedged deep in the debris-choked crevice, but I refused to tell her how I knew to look there. She pushed, of course, but I wasn't going to give Max to her.

"Somebody tipped me off, Detective. That's all I can tell you."

When finally she let it go, she did so as a favor, her way of making up for the harm that she'd done to me. But moving the conversation forward was awkward; letting go was not easy for Mills.

"So you did what you did to protect Jean? Because you thought she might have been involved?"

"That's right."

"But why? Why would you think Jean killed him?"

I thought about her question. How much could I give her? How much did she really want? Most importantly, was I still the guardian of Ezra's truth? I had come to terms with what had happened, with how my mother passed from this place. But would the truth serve any good purpose? I had to ask myself: Would Jean sleep any better? Would my mother's soul?

"Jean was not at home after she left Ezra's. I went there looking for her."

Mills interrupted. "She went for a drive. She was upset and went for a drive. Then she went to your house to talk things over. She got there in time to see you leave."

I nodded. It was the simplest explanation, but it had never occurred to me. "Jean has not been right for awhile, Detective. She was angry, unstable. I couldn't take the chance."

I would keep Ezra's truth, but not for him. Some truths are best left alone; it was really that simple.

Mills was clearly frustrated. "There's a lot you're not telling me, Work."

I shrugged. "Not as much as you think, and nothing that will affect your case."

"Was Jean the real reason you wanted to visit the crime scene?" she finally asked, and in her eyes I saw that she already knew the answer. I'd gone to the crime scene for one reason only; and, in spite of what I'd told Douglas, giving Jean details was not it. And now, safe on the other side of everything, I allowed myself a very small smile.

"No."

Mills did not return the smile. She knew that I'd worked it out in advance and she knew why. My manipulations had caused her great embarrassment and could have cost her much more—the case, her reputation, her job. But I saw that she understood. I'd gone to the crime scene for one very specific reason—to hamper my eventual prosecution. I'd been willing to take the fall for Jean, but I hadn't wanted to go to prison unless I was forced to. I'd figured that if it went to trial, I could use my presence at the crime scene to confuse the issue— maybe hang the jury, maybe get an acquittal. While no guarantee, it had been something.

"I had to do it," I said to her. "When Ezra never came back, I eventually figured out that he had to be dead. I thought that Jean had done it. I couldn't let her go to jail." I paused, thinking about Ezra's long absence and the dark thoughts that haunted me during that time. "I had eighteen months to think about things."

"You had it planned out—from that first day when Douglas called you into his office. The day we found his body. That's why you pushed Douglas to let you onto the crime scene."

"*Plan* is too big a word. I just figured that it couldn't hurt."

"You know what I think?" she asked. "I think you're a better lawyer than Ezra ever gave you credit for."

"I'm no lawyer," I said, but Mills didn't seem to hear me.

"You're a good brother, too. I hope Jean knows what you were willing to do for her."

I looked away, embarrassed.

"Let's talk about how you saved my life," I said.

"All right. I'll start there, and if something occurs to you, then stop me."

"Okay."

She leaned forward and put her elbows on her knees. "I was coming to arrest you," she said.

"Because of the gun?" I asked. "Because you identified me?"

For a moment, she looked startled, and then angry. "Hank Robins told you. That little bastard. I knew he was sniffing around, but I thought I'd kept that information bottled up pretty tight."

"Don't hold it against him, Detective. Not everyone thought I was guilty."

Mills looked pained by the tone of my voice. "Point taken," she said. "But it's funny how things work out."

"How so?"

"If we hadn't identified you, I wouldn't have gone there to arrest you. You'd have bled to death on your office floor."

"A close thing," I said.

"They often are."

"Who identified me?"

"Just some guy out fishing. He was about a hundred feet upriver, sitting on an old bucket and waiting for something to bite. He didn't want to identify himself because he'd been drinking all night and didn't want his wife to know."

"A bad witness," I said, wondering if he had also witnessed my despair, seen the barrel pressed so hard under my chin. I tried to read Mills, to see if she knew, but she was inscrutable.

"A bad witness," she agreed, her eyes shifting away from my face. And I knew that she knew.

"And Barbara?" I tried to keep my face straight and my voice level, but it was hard. For good or bad, I'd spent ten years of my life with her; I couldn't pretend this wasn't killing me.

"We arrested her at the country club. She was poolside, having lunch with some of her friends."

"Glena Werster?" I asked.

"Yeah, she was there."

"Glena Werster has a black Mercedes."

"So?"

"Vanessa Stolen was run down by a black Mercedes."

Suddenly, Mills was a cop again. "Do you think Ms. Werster was responsible?"

"Do I think she would put herself at risk to help one of her friends? No. Their friendship was a parasitic thing; Barbara used Glena for her prestige and Glena used Barbara like a dishrag. What I do believe is that Barbara wanted Vanessa out of the way, and she was too smart to use her own car."

"Do you think Ms. Werster could have been aware of this?"

"I think it can't hurt to ask."

"I intend to," Mills said.

The thought of Glena Werster trying to deal with Detective Mills made me smile. "I wish I could be there," I said.

"You don't care for Ms. Werster?"

"No, I don't."

"Then I won't go easy on her," Mills said in total seriousness.

"Will you let me know?"

"I will."

"Then let's get back to Barbara," I said.

"At first, she acted tough, you know, angry. But by the time the cuffs went on, she was crying." Mills showed me her teeth, and I recognized her animal grin. "I enjoyed that part."

"You always do."

"Do you want me to apologize again?"

"No," I said. "Go on."

"I've spent a lot of time with your wife."

"Interrogating her?"

"Discussing things," Mills said.

"And?"

"And she refused to confess. She said I'd made a grave mistake. She threatened to sue. The same innocent act I've seen a hundred times. But then she learned that you were alive, and something in her seemed to break."

"She confessed?" I asked.

Mills shifted in her seat. "That's not exactly what I meant."

"What then?"

"I mean she broke. She's incoherent."

I tried to absorb this. "Is it an act?"

Mills shrugged. "We'll see, but I doubt it."

"Why?"

"She babbles. She lets things out, little pieces of information no sane person would tell the cops. We've pieced it together from what she's said. The will, her affair with Ezra. And we found the tapes, along with the money and the jewelry."

I hesitated, but had to ask. "Is that common knowledge?"

"Her and Ezra? I'm afraid so."

A silence stretched between us as I thought about what Mills had said. Eventually, she broke it. "Frankly, I'm surprised she didn't destroy the tapes. They were pretty damning."

"She loved him," I said. "In some sick, twisted way I'll never understand. But she did." In my mind I saw her face, and the way her eyes seemed to glow.

"It takes all kinds, I guess."

I thought back to the night this all started, the night my mother died. "So it was Barbara who called Ezra that night, after we left the hospital."

"Actually, it was Alex."

My jaw may have dropped, but Mills continued evenly.

"She knew about the fight between Jean and your father; she knew what it was about. She called Ezra. She offered to leave town for fifty thousand dollars. She said she would disappear, leave Jean alone. The mall is next to the interstate. She told him to meet her in the parking lot with the cash. She'd get on the road and leave Salisbury forever. I believe he went to the office for the cash, his gun, too, probably. Then he paid her off and she left. That was the last time anybody saw him alive, except for Barbara, of course."

"I can't believe Alex would do that." *Take his money. Leave Jean.* "None of that makes sense to me."

"She didn't spend the money. She didn't want it, not like any other person would. She just wanted to show Jean the kind of person her father was. She wanted to drive them apart. And it would have worked, too, I bet, but it wasn't necessary."

"Ezra disappeared and that was that. Alex had what she wanted. Namely, my sister."

"Free and clear," Mills said.

Except for me, I thought.

"So after Alex left, did he call Barbara or did she call him?"

"A lot of what I believe is just theory right now, but it seems to fit, based on things that Barbara has said and the information that I've collected throughout the investigation. Here's how I see it. The night your mother died, the three of you were at Ezra's house after you left the hospital. Ezra got the phone call, which we now know was from Alex; he left to get money from his office and to meet her near the interstate. Jean left right after he did, which is, in part, why you thought she might have been responsible. If he went to the mall, Jean could have followed him. You checked her house and found that her car was gone. It makes sense, assuming she had a motive." Mills looked hard at me. "It still troubles me that you won't explain what you think that motive might have been. . . ." I returned her measured gaze and said nothing. "But I guess I'll have to let that one go, as well.

"So, Ezra went to his office and collected fifty thousand in cash from his safe. Maybe he got the gun there. Maybe it was in his house or in his car. We'll never know. But he meets Alex at the mall and pays her off. Alex leaves, satisfied that her plan has worked. Now we have Ezra at the mall. This is about the time that you left home and went to Stolen Farm—let's say one in the morning, maybe a little later. I don't think Ezra would have called your house, knowing that you were probably there. That means that Barbara called him, shortly after you left, I would imagine. She wanted to talk to him about his wife's death or about the will. Maybe she just wanted a tumble. I don't know that part yet. But let's assume Ezra gets the call while he's at the mall. . . ."

"She loved him," I said.

"You said that before."

I rolled my shoulders. "Maybe she thought that he would take her if she left me. Maybe she saw a window of opportunity with my mother gone. Maybe she wanted to talk to him about that."

Mills studied me for long seconds as my words dwindled. "Are you okay to talk about this?" she asked.

"I'm okay," I said, but I wasn't.

"All right. For whatever reason, they meet at the mall. Ezra has just finished manipulating Alex out of his life. His wife is dead. My guess is that he wanted a clean slate and told your wife as much. I think that he called it off, told her that it was over and that he was going to change the will back to the way he wanted it. He's done with her, right? So your wife gets her hands on the gun somehow. He couldn't have seen that coming. She orders him into the closet and shoots him dead; puts a second one in his head to make sure. She closes the closet door, walks out of the empty building, and tosses the gun into the storm drain. Then she gets into her car and goes home, arriving there well before you do. By this time, Jean is at home with Alex, knowing that you left your house on some mysterious errand. There's no one there to see Barbara leave and then return; so that when Ezra goes missing and then turns up dead, Jean assumes you were involved. Or maybe she didn't assume that, at least not until his body turned up. But then you gave me a false alibi, one that Jean knew to be factually inaccurate. She thinks back to the night in question and draws a reasonable conclusion."

I was already nodding to myself. "It makes sense."

"It would have looked something like that. Exactly like that? Who knows? Only Barbara can tell us for certain. But she won't. I don't know if she even can. In time, maybe . . ."

"What about Ezra's car?"

"Stolen, probably. Barbara would have wanted the body discovered in due course so that the will could be put into probate. The car would have eventually drawn some kind of attention, so she left it there. She kept Ezra's office keys in order to enter your office at night to try to retrieve the tapes. The car keys were probably in the car, an invitation to whoever stole it." Mills showed her teeth in a brief smile. "It must have killed her—these past eighteen months—knowing that all that money was in reach if only someone would find the body."

"There's still one thing I don't understand."

"What's that?" Mills asked.

"If Barbara was in this for the money, why did she try to kill me? She can't inherit if I'm dead. So why didn't she take the money and jewelry from the safe and just leave? Why put herself at risk by sticking around if she had nothing to gain?"

For the first time, Mills looked genuinely pained, and she stared at her folded hands for a very long time.

"Detective?" I'd never seen her this hesitant. Finally, she looked up, and there were shadows in her eyes.

"It's true what you told me, isn't it? You never read your father's will."

"The only time I saw it was when you showed it to me."

She nodded and looked back down at her hands.

"What?" I asked.

"Barbara did convince Ezra to increase the amount of money left to you in trust. She was telling the truth when she told you that. Here's what she didn't tell you. There was an unusual clause in the will. It must have been Barbara's idea. According to Clarence Hambly, your father had it inserted into the will about six months before he died. This would have been after they started sleeping together, Ezra and Barbara. But Ezra changed his mind. Hambly says that he intended to have the clause removed. Maybe he understood what an incentive it could be."

"I don't understand."

"I think your father came to sense just how dangerous your wife could be. I don't know this, Work, but I feel it. I think at the end he understood. He saw that it put you at risk. Your father asked Hambly to draw up new documents; they had scheduled a meeting so that he could sign them. Barbara killed him before he could make the change official."

"What did it say, this clause?"

I heard Mills's breath, and when she looked up, she was the most human I'd ever seen her. Her voice was flat, but I saw that this hurt her. "In the event of your death, the fifteen million would go into trust for any offspring you had. Barbara would be the executor of that trust and would have almost unlimited discretion in how to use the money."

"I don't understand," I said, but then I did. "Barbara's pregnant," I said.

Mills could barely look at me. "She *was* pregnant, Work. She miscarried yesterday."

CHAPTER

35

Douglas stopped by once; he hung in the door until I saw him, then offered a smile that played more like a grimace. The skin was loose beneath his eyes and under his chin. He looked like hell. He tried to apologize, and explained that it was just his job, nothing personal; but he shied from my eyes, and, unlike Mills, he didn't mean a word he said. He'd sunk his teeth into me and liked the taste of it. I'd seen it in court, and in the way he smiled when the bailiffs put the cuffs back on me. Any regret was born of embarrassment, and the knowledge that another election was just around the corner. For even in Rowan County, no voter liked a fool, and the papers had crucified him. He told me that he wouldn't prosecute me for attempting to destroy evidence, then looked away and said that, nonetheless, it was his duty to report my behavior to the state bar. We both knew that such a report would result in my eventual disbarment. But the thought of that didn't bother me in the least, and he looked surprised when I told him not to worry about it. When he attempted another smile, I suggested he have a nice day, then told him to get the fuck out of my hospital room.

I had other visitors, too: lawyers, neighbors, even some old friends from school, all of whom were probably just curious. They all said the same things, and they all rang false with me. I knew who had believed in me, and a few flowery words would never make me forget those who had not. But I did what I had to do. I thanked them for the visit and wished them a happy life. Dr. Stokes was a different story. He stopped by several times, and we talked about small things. He told me stories of my mother, and of things I'd done as a child. He was good for me, and I felt a little stronger after each conversation. On his last visit, I held out my hand and told him that he had a friend for life. He gave me a smile, told me that he'd never doubted it, and insisted that the next drink was on him; then he shook my hand gently but solemnly, and there seemed to be a light upon him as he walked from the room.

Jean and Alex came by on the day before they released me. They were packed and ready to leave.

"Where?" I asked.

"Up north. Vermont, maybe."

I looked at Alex, who returned my gaze with the same unswerving strength as always. Yet this time there was no animosity, and I knew that Jean had not lied to me. When the time was right, I would be welcome.

"Take care of her," I said.

She put out her hand and I shook it. "I always will," she said.

I looked back to Jean. "Send me your address," I told her. "I'll have some money for you once I sell the house and building."

"I wish you would reconsider. We don't want anything of his."

"It won't be from him. It will be from me."

"Are you sure?"

"I want you to have it," I said. "Use it well. Build a life."

"It's a lot of money."

I shrugged. "I owe you more than money, Jean. This is the least I can do."

Jean looked at me then, looked so deeply that I could not hide the emptiness I felt, the reverberation of utter aloneness. Nor could I hide the guilt that rose within me every time I looked at her. Eventually, I had to turn away.

I heard her voice, and there was something new in it. Strength, maybe? A clarity of her own? "Will you give us a minute, Alex?"

"Sure," Alex said. "Take care, Work." And then we were alone behind the closed hospital door. Jean pulled up a chair and sat beside me.

"You don't owe me anything," she said.

"I do."

"For what?"

I marveled that she could even ask the question. "For everything, Jean. For not protecting you better. For not being a better brother." My words fell into the narrow place between us. My hands twitched beneath the thin sheet, and I tried again because I wanted her to understand. "For not having faith in you. For letting Ezra treat you the way he did."

Then she laughed, and the sound of it hurt me; those words had not come without cost. "Are you serious?" she asked.

"I'm serious."

The smile fell from her face. She settled back into her chair and studied me with overly moist eyes. But she wasn't on the verge of tears, far from it. "Let me ask you a question," she said.

"Okay."

"And I want you to think about it before you answer."

"All right."

"Why do you think he brought you into the practice?"

"What?"

"Why did he encourage you to go to law school? Why did he give you a job?"

I did like she'd asked. I thought about it before I answered. "I don't know," I finally said. "I've never thought about it before."

"Okay, another question. Was there a time when your relationship with him changed? And I'm talking about a long time ago."

"Do you mean like childhood?"

"I mean exactly like childhood."

"We used to be close."

"And that stopped when?"

"Look, Jean, what's the point of all this?"

"When did it change?"

"I don't know, all right? I don't know."

"Jesus, Work. You can be really dense sometimes. It changed overnight. It changed on the day we jumped for Jimmy. Before that, you were a chip off the old block, but then you went into that creek. After that, everything changed between you. I never understood why, not then. But I've thought about it, and I think I do now."

I didn't want to hear any more. The truth was too ugly; it never shut up, and this is what it said. It said that my father sensed something different about me after that day. He felt the change, and knew to be ashamed of me, even if he didn't know exactly why. It said that he could never respect me after that. He smelled my degradation like old garbage, and so he turned away. Even now I know that he died despising me.

I finally looked at my sister, expecting to see some small shadow of the same emotion.

"You know?" I asked.

"You started that day a boy, Work, Ezra's little boy—a reflection of him, perhaps, but no more than that. Something he could look down on with vague pride, point to, and say, That's my son; that's my boy. But you came out of that hole a man, a hero, a person everyone looked up to, and he couldn't handle that. You were the center of attention, not him, and he hated that, hated it enough to grind you down and keep you down, so that you would never surpass him like that again. That's when it changed for you and that's why it changed."

"I don't know, Jean."

"How many grown men do you think would have gone down that hole all alone? Not many, I can tell you that, and certainly not our father. I saw his face when they pulled you out and the crowd started cheering."

"They cheered?" I asked.

"Of course they did."

"I don't remember that," I said, and didn't. I remembered scornful eyes, ridicule, and pointing fingers. I remembered Ezra, drunk and telling my mother that I was just a dumb-ass kid. "He's no fucking hero." That's what he'd said.

"Vanessa Stolen would probably have died that day, raped and killed at fifteen. How many twelve-year-old boys have saved a life? How many grown men? It's a rare thing, and it took courage. Only our father could make you blind to that, but that's what he did, and he did it intentionally."

Her words were destroying me. I was no hero. He'd been right about that. But what she said next penetrated some of the fog that filled my mind.

"Ezra brought you into the practice to keep you beneath him."

"What?"

"You're not cut out to be a lawyer, Work. You're smart as hell, no question, but you're a dreamer. You have a big heart. Nobody knew that better than Ezra. He knew that you could never be cutthroat like he could, and you would never care about money like he did; that meant that you could never succeed like he had. Having you in the law kept Ezra safe. As long as you were there, you would never be the man that he was. Never as strong, never as confident." She paused and leaned toward me. "Never a threat."

"Do you really believe that?" I asked.

"Trust me."

"None of that lets me off the hook, though. I still owe you."

"You just don't get it, do you? He treated you worse than he ever treated me. For me, it was simple misogyny. I was female and therefore of little value. But for you, it was personal. He waged a campaign against you, Work. He went to war, and no one can do that like our father could. Good or bad, he was a force." She laughed again, a bitter and dismayed sound. "You talk about protecting me from him. Jesus, Work. You never had a chance."

"Maybe," I said. "I'll have to think about it."

"You do that," she said. "He's dead. Don't let him drag you down any further."

Suddenly, I was too tired to talk about Ezra anymore. It would probably take years to sort out the mess he'd made of my head, but the carnage seemed less absolute. And maybe Jean was right. Maybe I needed to give myself a break. I was only twelve when it happened, and that seemed terribly young to me now.

"I'm going to miss you, Jean."

She stood and put her hand on my shoulder. "You were going to go to prison for me, Work. That makes you a very good man. Better than anyone I've ever known. You remember that when things get you down."

"I love you, Jean."

"I love you, too," she replied. "And that's what family is supposed to be about." She crossed the room and stopped at the door. She opened it and looked back. "I'll call you when we get where we're going."

Then she stepped out of the room, and as the door swung shut, I saw Alex materialize beside her. She slipped her arm around my sister and turned her down the hall. I watched until the door closed between us, and saw, in that last second, that Jean was crying; but it was a good cry, a healthy cry, and I knew that when they found their place, she would call. I took great comfort in that.

I was packing my few belongings the next day when Max appeared in the door of my room. He looked exactly the same.

"You want your dog back?" he asked without preamble.

"Yes," I said.

"Damn!" he said, and walked off. I heard his raised voice from down the hall. "You come to me when you want him. Maybe I'll let him go, maybe not, but we'll have beer regardless."

I laughed for the first time.

An hour later, I went home to a house that rattled when I walked inside. I wouldn't miss it, I knew, but I took a beer onto the front porch and sat where I liked to sit. I watched the sun descend on the park across the street. It touched the treetops and I thought about another beer. But I didn't get up, and the sun went down as I watched. I sat there long into the night and listened to the sounds around me. They were comfortable sounds, city sounds, and I wondered if I would miss them.

The next day, they'd put Ezra in the ground, and once he was there, I planned to seek out Vanessa. I would say what I had to say, make whatever promises were necessary. I wanted her back, if she would have me, but only after the truth was told. If I had to beg, I would. That was the curse of clarity, and the price I would happily pay. For I saw things now like I never had before. I was ready to make my own path, but I wanted her to walk it with me; I wanted to make the life I should have had all along.

So when the sun came up the next day, I took my time in shaving. I brushed my teeth and I combed my hair. I put on my favorite jeans and a pair of sturdy boots. The funeral was at ten, but I had no plans to go. Jean said it best, really, when I asked her if she would attend.

"He died for me that night, Work. Like I've always said. They can't bury him any deeper."

I did drive past the church, however, and I saw the long black car that would carry him to the hole they'd dug. And when they came out, I was still there. Maybe I wasn't like Jean; maybe I needed to see. But whatever the reason, I followed the line of cars to the cemetery outside of town. When they turned in the main gate, I continued past. I found the feeder road that ran along the ridge and drove until I found a place where I could watch. There was a tall tree there, and I leaned against its dimpled trunk and looked down on the gray mourners as they departed their expensive cars. They puddled around the rectangular pit, which looked so small from where I stood, and I saw a man, probably the preacher. He held out his arms as if for silence, but his words were lost in a sudden wind, which was just as well. For what could he say to make it right for me?

I stayed until they shoveled in the dirt, and when all were gone, I walked down to look upon the settling mound. There was no headstone yet, but I knew what it would say. They'd come to me for the words, and I'd done the best I could.

Ezra Pickens, it would read. *His Truth Travels with Him.*

I stood there for a long time, but mostly I looked at the place where my mother lay. Would she thank me for putting him there? Or would she rather have been left alone? Again, I'd done the best I could. What I thought she would want. By his side, she had lived, uncomplaining; so be it in death. But in my heart I was angry, and knew that I would always question the wisdom of this choice. But what I'd told Barbara was true. Life gets messy, and death, it seemed, was no exception.

When I heard a distant engine, I paid it no attention. I probably should have known better, so that when Vanessa appeared beside me, I would have had a smile to greet her; but all I saw was fresh-turned earth and the hard edges of my mother's graven name, until she spoke and touched me on the shoulder. I faced her then, and she took my hand. I said her name and she took all of me. Her arms were slim and strong, and she smelled like the river. I leaned into her, and her hand moved on the back of my neck. When I pulled away, I did so for a reason. I wanted to see her eyes, to see if there was cause to hope. And there was, for there was clarity there, too; and I knew, before I even spoke, that we would be okay.

Yet the words had to be said, although not in the shadow of Ezra's mounded earth. So I took her farm-worn hand and led her slowly up the hill to the shady place I'd found. I told her first that I loved her, and she looked away, down to the rows of chiseled stone. When she looked back, she tried to speak, but I stopped her with a finger. I thought back to the day we met, the day we jumped for Jimmy. It's where it started, where everything changed, and where our future almost ended. If we were to have a chance together, she needed to hear about that day, as I needed to tell her; so I said what I had to say, and truer words have never been spoken.

EPILOGUE

Many months have passed, and the pain has lessened to an occasional throb. I still have trouble sleeping at night, but I don't mind; my thoughts are not unpleasant. I keep Vanessa's letter in the drawer of my bedside table, and I read it from time to time, usually at night. It reminds me of how close I came, and that life is not a given. It keeps me honest, and maintains what I've come to call "this precious clarity."

The clock reads just after five, and although my days start early now, there is no hurry; and the dream is still fresh upon me. So I swing my feet onto the cool floor and walk from the room. In the hallway, there is light from the moon, and I follow it to the window. I look down on still fields, then to my right and to the river. It winds into the distance, a silver thread, and I think of currents and of time, of things that have been swept away.

The courts ruled that the cash and jewels from my father's safe were part of his estate. They would go to the foundation. But the buildings sold quickly, and for a better price than I'd hoped. In the end, I sent over $800,000 to Jean, and she used it to purchase a cabin on the wooded shores of Lake Champlain. I've not visited yet. Still too soon, Jean told me, the world still too entirely theirs. But we are talking about Christmas.

Maybe.

As for my share of the money, I used it as best I could. I restored the aging farmhouse, bought a decent tractor, and acquired the adjacent two-hundred-acre parcel. It is good land, with rich soil and a bold stream. I also have my eye on eighty acres that borders to the south, but the sellers know my ambitions and their price is still too high. But I can be patient.

I hear the door swing open behind me and smile in spite of myself. She only wakes when I find my way to this window. It's as if she knows I'm here and rises to join me in looking down on this garden we've made. Her arms slip warm across my chest, and I see her face in the window—Vanessa, my wife.

"What are you thinking about?" she asks.

"I had the dream again."

"The same one?"

"Yes."

"Come back to bed," she says.

"In a minute."

She kisses me and returns to bed.

My hands find the windowsill and I feel the cold draft coming through. I think of what I've learned and of those things I have yet to discover. Farming is a tough life, replete with uncertainty, and much of it is new to me. Yet I've grown lean and welcome the long hours that have made my hands so hard. It suits me, this life. There is no rush, neither to judgment nor to action; and that, perhaps, has led to the greatest change of all, for I have yet to face a single regret.

Yet I remain my father's son, and it is not possible to escape fully the reprehensible choices he made. I know that I can never forgive him. But fate, which can be so wayward, is not without a sense of justice. Ezra played his games with Barbara, manipulated her for his own twisted ends. At her insistence, he changed his will, inserted a clause providing that any child of mine would inherit the fifteen million dollars in the event of my death. It was Barbara's idea, her safety valve, and I am quite certain that my father planned to change it once he was through with her. But she killed him before he could sign the new documents. Maybe that's why she shot him. I'll never know. But I realized, when I finally read through his will, that there was no time limit involved. So I did the research, and what I learned was this: When I die, whenever that might occur, my child will inherit a large part of Ezra's millions. I filed a caveat on the matter, seeking declaratory judgment. Hambly fought it, of course, and the loss still embitters him. But the will was specific, and the law favored my interpretation.

After awhile, I retrace my steps and slip under the covers. She's warm, on her side, and I flatten myself against her. The dream seems more real each time, and each time takes longer to leave me. We walk over green grass, the three of us.

Tell me the story, Daddy.

Which one?

My favorite.

I reach for Vanessa, my hand finding her belly. She sinks deeper under the covers and nestles back against me.

"I hope it's a girl," I whisper.

"It is," she says, and settles her hand upon my own.

I can't say if she knows this or simply feels it. For me, it is enough. I hear her voice from the dream—my little girl—and I contemplate the vast fortune that will one day be hers. I think for the last time of my father, and of his feelings about women and money. There is poetry in this, an irony that completes the circle, and I wonder if he is restless in that dark and forever grave.

I stay in bed for a few more minutes, but the day beckons and I am restless. I pull on jeans and a sweater, and Bone follows me downstairs. It is cold outside, and I stand on the porch in the predawn light. I take a breath that fills me up and look out across the silent fields. There is a low mist in the hollow places, and the hilltops rise to meet the coming sun.

Turn the page for a sneak peek at John Hart's new book

IRON HOUSE

Available Summer 2011

Trees thrashed in the storm, their trunks hard and black and rough as stone, their limbs bent beneath the weight of snow. It was dark out, night. Between the trunks, a boy ran and fell and ran again. Snow melted against the heat of his body, soaked his clothing, then froze solid. His world was black and white, except where it was red.

On his hands and under his nails.

Frozen to the blade of a knife no child should own.

For one instant the clouds tore, then darkness came complete and an iron trunk bloodied the boy's nose as he struck a tree and fell again. He pulled himself up and ran through snow that piled to his knees, his waist. Branches caught his hair, tore skin. Light speared out far behind, and the sound of pursuit welled like breath in the forest's throat.

Long howls on the bitter wind . . .

Dogs beyond the ridge . . .

CHAPTER

1

Michael woke reaching for the gun he no longer kept by the bed. His fingers slid over bare wood, and he sat, instantly awake, his skin slick with sweat and the memory of ice. There was no movement in the apartment, no sounds beyond those of the city. The woman beside him rustled in the stew of their sheets, and her hand found the hard curve of his shoulder. "You okay, sweetheart?"

Weak light filtered through the curtains, the open window, and he kept his body turned so she could not see the boy that lingered in his eyes, the stain of hurt so deep she had yet to find it. "Bad dream, baby." His fingers found the swell of her hip. "Go back to sleep."

"You sure?" The pillow muffled her voice.

"Of course."

"I love you," she said, and was gone.

Michael watched her fade and then put his feet on the floor. He touched old scars left by frostbite, the dead places on his palms and at the tips of three fingers. He rubbed his hands together and then tilted them in the light. The palms were broad, the fingers long and tapered.

A pianist's fingers, Elena often said.

Thick and scarred. He would shake his head.

The hands of an artist . . .

She liked to say things like that, the talk of an optimist and dreamer. Michael flexed his fingers and heard the sound of her words in his head, the lilt of her accent, and for that instant he felt ashamed. Many things had come through the use of his hands, but creation was not one of them. He stood and rolled his shoulders as New York solidified around him: Elena's apartment, the smell of recent rain on hot pavement. He pulled on jeans and glanced out the open window. Night was a dark hand on the city, its skin not yet veined with gray. He looked down on Elena's face and found it pale in the gloom, soft and creased with sleep. She lay unmoving in the bed they shared, her shoulder warm when he laid two fingers on it. Outside, the city grew as dark and still as it ever got, the quiet pause at the bottom of a breath. He moved hair from her face, and at her temple saw the thread of her life, steady and strong. He wanted to touch that pulse, to assure himself of its strength and endurance. An old man was dying, and when he was dead, they would come for Michael, and they would come for her, to make Michael hurt. Elena knew none of this, neither the things of which he was capable nor the danger he'd brought to her door, but Michael would go to hell to keep her safe.

Go to hell.

Come back burning.

That was truth. That was real.

He studied her face in the dim light, the smooth skin and full, parted lips, the black hair that ran in waves to her shoulder then broke like surf. She shifted in her sleep, and Michael felt a moment's bleakness stir, a familiar certainty that it would get worse before it got better. Since he was a boy, violence had trailed him like a scent. Now, it had found her, too. For an instant, he thought again that he should leave her, just take his problems and disappear. He'd tried before, of course, not one time but a hundred. Yet, with each failed attempt, the certainty had only grown stronger: he could not live without her; he could make it work. Michael dragged fingers through his hair, and wondered again how it had come to this place. How had things gone so sour so fast?

Moving to the window, he flicked the curtain enough to see down into the alley. The car was still there, black and low in the far shadows. Distant lamplight starred the windshield so that he could not see past the glass, but he knew at least one of the men who sat inside. His presence was a threat, and it angered Michael beyond words. He'd made his bargain with the old man, and expected the deal to be honored. Words still mattered to Michael.

Promises.

Rules of conduct.

He looked a last time at Elena, then eased two silenced thirty-eights from the place he kept them hidden. They were cool to the touch, familiar in his hands. He checked the loads and a frown bent his face as he turned from the woman he loved. He was supposed to be beyond this, supposed to be free. He thought once more of the man in the black car.

Eight days ago they'd been brothers.

Michael was at the door and almost out when Elena said his name. He paused for a moment, then lay the guns down and slipped back into the bedroom. She'd shifted onto her back and one arm was half raised. "Michael . . ."

The name was a smile on her lips, and he wondered if she was dreaming. She shifted and a warm-bed smell rose in the room. It carried the scent of her skin and of clean hair. It was the smell of home and the future, the promise of a different life. Michael hesitated, then took her hand as she said, "Come back to bed."

He looked into the kitchen, where he'd left the guns next to a can of yellow paint. Her voice had come as a whisper, and he knew that if he left, she would ride the slope back into sleep and not remember. He could slip outside and do the thing he did well. Killing them would likely escalate matters, and others would certainly take their place; but maybe the message would serve its purpose.

And maybe not.

His gaze traveled from Elena to the window. The night outside was just as black, its skin stretched tight. The car was still there, as it had been the night before and the night before that. They would not move against him until the old man died, but they wanted to rattle him. They wanted to push, and every part of Michael wanted to push back. He took a slow breath and thought of the man he desired to be. Elena was here, beside him, and violence had no place in the world they wished to make. But he was a realist first, so that when her fingers flexed on his, his thoughts were not just of hope, but of retribution and deterrence. An old poem rose in his mind.

Two roads diverged in a yellow wood . . .

Michael stood at a crossroad, and it all came down to choice. Go back to bed or pick up the guns. Elena or the alley. The future or the past.

Elena squeezed his hand again. "Love me, baby," she said, and that's what he chose.

Life over death.

The road less traveled.

The New York dawn came scorching hot. The guns were hidden and Elena still slept. Michael sat with his feet on the windowsill and stared down into the empty alleyway. They'd left around five, backed from the alley and sounded a single blow of their horn as the sightlines collapsed. If their goal had been to wake or scare him, they'd failed miserably. He'd been out of bed since three and felt great. Michael studied his fingertips, where flecks of yellow paint stained them.

"What are you smiling at, gorgeous?" Her voice surprised him and he turned. Elena sat up in bed, languorous, and pushed long, black hair from her face. The sheet fell to her waist and Michael put his feet on the floor, embarrassed to be caught in a moment of such open joy.

"Just thinking of something," he said.

"Of me?"

"Of course."

"Liar."

She was smiling, skin still creased. Her back arched as she stretched, her small hands fisted white. "You want coffee?" Michael asked.

She fell back against the pillows, made a contented sound, and said, "You are a magnificent creature."

"Give me a minute." In the kitchen, Michael poured warm milk into a mug, then coffee. Half and half, the way she liked it. Café au lait. Very French. When he came back, he found her in one of his shirts, sleeves rolled loosely on her narrow arms. He handed her the coffee. "Good dreams?"

She nodded and a glint sparked in her eyes. "One in particular seemed very real."

"Did it?"

She sank into the bed and made the same contented noise. "One of these days I'm actually going to wake up before you."

Michael sat on the edge of the bed and put a hand on the arch of her foot. "Sure you will, baby." Elena was a late sleeper, and Michael rarely managed more than five hours a night. Her climbing from bed before him was a near impossibility. He watched her sip coffee, and reminded himself to notice the small things about her: the clear polish she preferred on her nails, the length of her legs, the tiny scar on her cheek that was her skin's only imperfection. She had black eyebrows, eyes that were brown but could look like honey in a certain light. She was lithe and strong, a beautiful woman in every respect; but that's not what Michael admired most. Elena took joy in the most insignificant things: how it felt to slip between cool sheets or taste new foods, the moment's anticipation each time she opened the door to step outside. She had faith that each moment would be finer than the last. She believed that people were good, which made her a dash of color in a world blown white.

She sipped again, and Michael saw the exact moment she noticed the paint on his hands. A small crease appeared between her brows. The cup came away from her lips. "Did you paint it already?"

She tried to sound angry, but failed; and as he shrugged an answer to the question, he could not keep the smile from touching every part of his face. She'd envisioned them painting it together—laughter, spilled paint—but Michael couldn't help it. "Too excited," he said, and thought of the fresh yellow paint on the walls of the tiny room down the hall. They called it a second bedroom, but it was not much larger than a walk-in closet. A high, narrow window was paned with rippled glass. Afternoon light would make the yellow glow like gold.

She put the coffee down and pushed back against the bare wall behind her. Her knees tented the sheet and she said, "Come back to bed. I'll make you breakfast."

"Too late." Michael rose and went back into the kitchen. He had flowers in a small vase. The fruit was already cut, juice poured. He added fresh pastry and carried in the tray.

"Breakfast in bed?"

Michael hesitated, almost overwhelmed. "Happy Mother's Day," he finally managed.

"It's not . . ." She paused, and then got it.

Yesterday, she'd told him she was pregnant.

Seven weeks.

They stayed in bed for most of the morning—reading, talking—then Michael walked Elena to work in time to get ready for the lunch crowd. She wore a small black dress that accented her tan skin and dark eyes. In heels, she stood five-seven and moved like a dancer, so elegant that beside her Michael looked angular and rough, out of place in jeans, heavy boots, and a worn T-shirt. But this was how Elena knew him: rough and poor, an interrupted student still hoping for a way back to school.

That was the lie that started everything.

They'd met seven months ago on a corner near NYU. Dressed to blend in and carrying heavy, Michael was on a job and had no business talking to pretty women; but when the wind took her scarf, he caught it on instinct and gave it back with a flourish that surprised him. Even now, he had no idea where it came from, that sudden lightness, but she laughed at the moment, and when he asked, she gave him her name.

Carmen Elena Del Portal.

Call me Elena.

She'd said it with amusement on her lips and a fire in her eyes. He remembered dry fingers and frank appraisal in her glance, an accent that bordered on Spanish. She'd tucked an unruly strand of hair behind her right ear and waited with a reckless smile for Michael to offer his name in return. He almost left, but did not. It was the warmth in her, the utter lack of fear or doubt. So, at two fifteen on a Tuesday, against everything he'd ever been taught, Michael gave her his name.

His real one.

The scarf was silk, and very light to land with such force on two lives. It led to coffee, then more, until emotion came in its wildness, and the coming found him unprepared. Now here he was, in love with a woman who thought she knew him, but did not. Michael was trying to change, but killing was easy. And quitting was hard.

Halfway to work, she took his hand. "Boy or girl?"

"What?" It was the kind of thing normal people asked, and Michael was dumbfounded by the question. He stopped walking, so that people veered around them. She tilted her head.

"Do you hope it's a boy or a girl?"

Her eyes shone with the kind of contentment he'd only read about in books, and looking at her then was like looking at her on the first day they'd met, only more so. The air held the same blue charge, the same sense of light and purpose. When Michael spoke, the words came from the deepest part of him. "Will you marry me?"

She laughed. "Just like that?"

"Yes."

She put a palm on Michael's cheek, and the laughter dwindled. "No, Michael. I won't marry you."

"Because?"

"Because you're asking me for the wrong reasons. And because we have time." She kissed him. "Lots of time."

That's where she was wrong.

Elena worked as the hostess for an expensive restaurant call Chez Pascal. She was beautiful, spoke three languages, and at her request, the owner had hired Michael, eight days ago, to wash dishes. Michael told her that he'd lost his other job, that he needed to fill the days before he found a new one or the student loan finally came through; but there was no other job, no student loan, just two more lies in a sea of thousands. But Michael needed to be there, for while no one would dare touch him while the old man breathed, Elena was under no such protection. They'd kill her for the fun of it.

Two blocks from the restaurant, Michael said, "Have you told your family?"

"That I'm pregnant?"

"Yes."

"No." Emotion colored her voice, sadness and something dark. Michael knew that Elena had family in Spain, but she rarely spoke of them. She had no photographs, no letters. Someone had called once, but Elena hung up when Michael gave her the phone. The next day, she changed the number. Michael never pushed for answers, not about family or the past. They walked in silence for several minutes. A block later, she took his hand. "Kiss me," she said, and Michael did. When it was done, Elena said, "You're my family."

At the restaurant door, a blue awning offered narrow shade. Michael was slightly in front, so he saw the damage to the door in time to turn Elena before she saw it, too. But even with his back to the door, the image stayed in his mind: splintered wood, shards of white that rose from the mahogany stain. The grouping was head-high and tight, four bullet holes in a three inch circle, and Michael could see how it went down. A black car at the curb, gun silenced. From Elena's apartment, the drive was less than six minutes, so it probably happened just after five this morning. Empty streets. Nobody around. Small caliber, Michael guessed, something light and accurate. A twenty-two. Maybe a twenty-five. He leaned against the door and felt splinters through his shirt, a cold rage behind his eyes. He took Elena's hand and said, "If I asked you to move away from New York, would you do it?"

"My job is here. Our lives . . ."

"If I had to go," he tried again. "Would you come with me?"

"This is our home. This is where I want to raise our child . . ." She stopped, and understanding moved in her face. "Lots of people raise babies in the city . . ."

She knew of his distrust for the city, and he looked away because the weight of lies was becoming too much. He could stay here and risk the war that was coming, or he could share the truth and lose her. "Listen," he said. "I'm going to be late today. Tell Paul for me." Paul owned the restaurant. He parked in the alley, and had probably not seen the door.

"You're not coming in?"

"I can't right now."

"I got you this job, Michael." A spark of rare anger.

Michael showed the palm of his hand and said, "May I have your keys?"

Unhappy, she gave him the set Paul let her use. He opened the restaurant door and held it for her. "Where are you going?" she asked.

Her face was upturned and still angry. Michael wanted to touch her cheek and say that he would kill or die to keep her safe. That he would burn the city down. "I'll be back," he told her. "Just stay in the restaurant."

"How strange you're being."

"I have to do something," he replied. "For the baby."

"Really?"

He placed his hand on the plane of her stomach and pictured the many violent ways this day could end. "Really," he said.

And that was truth.

CHAPTER

2

There comes a time. Michael did not know how long the words had been there, but they ran through his head as he walked, a refrain timed to the sound of his shoes on concrete. He'd tried to do it right and respectfully. He'd tried to be nice.

But there comes a time.

Michael hailed a cab and gave the driver an address in Alphabet City. When they arrived, he pushed a fifty through the glass and told the man to wait.

Michael's apartment was a third-floor walk-up with two bedrooms, bars on the windows, and a reinforced steel door. Elena had never been there, and he planned to keep it that way. The second bedroom closet held rifles and handguns, body armor and stacks of cash. There was a long shelf of knives and various edged projectiles, neat coils of shiny wire. Things that might be difficult to explain.

Michael disengaged the alarm and crossed the large living room. Tall windows let in midday light, but he ignored the things it touched: the wall of books, the fine furnishings and original art. He made for the short hall at the back, walked past the room that held his gear and into the bedroom beyond. The bed was large but clean-lined and spartan, and on the dresser sat the only photograph he owned. Pressed between glass, faded and cracked, the picture was of two boys in a snowy field splotched with mud. Not sure that he would ever see the apartment again, Michael slipped the photograph from its frame and carried it with him to the closet. It was the only thing he owned that really mattered.

At the closet door, Michael stripped out of his clothes and left them in a heap. From a long cedar rack he selected a pair of hand-tooled English shoes, then a custom suit from a row of twenty. The suit was English, too, as were the shirts. He slipped into a cream-colored shirt and a tie dark enough to mirror the occasion of his visit. The old man appreciated a good suit. He considered it a matter of respect, and so did Michael. He put the photograph in the jacket's inside pocket, then returned to the cab, where he gave the driver another address. They rode north and east to where the river touched the upper Fifties. If you were rich and wanted privacy, Sutton Place was a good area to call home. Celebrities lived there, and politicians, and no one looked twice at long cars with mirrored glass. The old man owned the entire building in which he planned to die, and while the FBI undoubtedly knew who lived in the five-story town house with a view of the river, none of the neighbors had a clue, and that was the point. After a life in the press and in the courts, after three incarcerations, forty-seven years of persecution and public scorn, the old man wanted to die in peace.

Michael didn't blame him.

He had the cabbie drive by the residence and then stop a full block north, near the defunct Sixtieth Street heliport. The space was a dog run now, and when Michael stepped from the cab he saw well-dressed women chatting while small dogs played. One of the women saw him and said something to her friends, so that all three turned as Michael paid off the cab. Michael nodded once, then turned to walk twice past the house, once moving south, then coming back north. A portico drive led to private parking in the back. When he stopped before the door, he stood with his palms up, eyes moving between the security cameras mounted at the corners and above the main door. Someone moved behind a third-floor window. Curtains stirred at the ground level, too.

Eventually, Michael knocked, and after a long minute the door swung open to reveal four men. Two were low-level soldiers whose names Michael had never bothered to learn. In their twenties, they wore dark pants and shirts that shone like silk under their suit jackets. One chewed gum, and both stood with fingers inside their coats, as if Michael needed to be told they carried. Under slicked hair, their faces were lean and frightened. They'd heard stories of Michael, of the things he'd done. He was a fighter, and a killer, a prince of the street so widely feared he rarely had to kill anymore. His presence alone was sufficient. His name. The threat of his name.

The third man was a stranger, young and calm and lean, but the fourth, Michael knew well. He stood an inch taller than Michael, but weighed thirty pounds less, narrow-shouldered and thin to the point of desiccation. Dapper in bottle-green pants and a brushed velvet coat, he was forty-four years old, balding on top and vain enough to care. Michael knew from long acquaintance that his arms and chest carried more than a dozen scars. Knife wounds. Bites. Bullet holes. Eighteen years ago, he'd shown Michael things that would make a grown man faint. Michael was fifteen years old at the time, hard but not that hard.

In the years since, he'd taught Michael many things, and even now was the most dangerous man Michael knew. He moved back a pace and Michael stepped into the dim interior. The entry hall was massive, with white and black marble floors and a red-carpeted stairway that curved up both sides of the room before meeting on a landing twelve feet higher. A billiards room filled the space to Michael's right, and he could see through into the formal parlor, the small study beyond. He sensed movement deeper in the house, saw food on a long table, other men, other guns, and Michael knew then that they were marking time, waiting in stillness for the old man to die.

The man in the velvet coat held Michael's gaze for long seconds, and Michael saw a nick where he'd cut himself shaving. "Hello, Jimmy. I want to see him."

"He can't save you." The response was laconic, condescending.

"No one's asking."

Jimmy blinked once, then allowed Michael to come a few more feet into the house. He motioned for one of his boys to shut the door. Jimmy wasn't smiling, but there was no gun in his hand, either. His voice, when he spoke, was soft and free of accent, a difficult thing for the illiterate Jersey boy Michael knew him to be. But Jimmy was all about illusion. Money. Clothes. Expensive cars. Jimmy thought he was more than he was, which was one of the things that made the two men different. Michael *knew* he was going to hell.

"You've got some serious nerve, Michael. Showing up here like you're still welcome."

Michael saw how tired Jimmy looked, how stretched. His dark eyes pulled in light, and there was no sign of friendship there. "The old man released me, Jimmy. He gave standing orders that I was to be left alone. Are you saying I'm not welcome in his house?"

"I'm saying it's a good thing Vincent's not here."

Vincent was thirty-six years old, with degrees from Columbia and Harvard, not because he cared about the education, but because he craved respectability in a city that knew his name too well. He donated to visible causes, dated models and pale-faced society widows. Vincent himself was lean and handsome, a tall man with a narrow waist and dark eyes capable of exceptional deceit. Elegant and soft-spoken, he was smart and cold and vicious. The old man's only son, he and Michael had been friends once—brothers—but that bridge was burned to smoke and ruin. Eight days had passed since Michael quit the life. One week and a day. A world of change.

"How is Vincent?" Michael masked the rage with sarcasm. Vincent drove a black Audi, and Michael knew for fact that he kept a twenty-five in the glove compartment.

"He stepped out." Jimmy shrugged. "He'll be back."

"That doesn't answer my question."

Jimmy rolled his narrow shoulders, turned his lips down. "Vincent has offered to forgive you, Michael. How many times, now? Three times? Four? All you have to do is repent. Come back to us."

"Things have changed. I want out."

"Then you leave him no choice."

Michael pictured the bullet holes in the door of Chez Pascal. Two double-taps. Head height. "Nothing personal, right?"

"Exactly."

"And the wishes of his father? The man who built this from nothing? Who built you from nothing? What about him?"

"The son is not the father."

A moment's irony touched his eyes. At fifteen, the old man had made Michael Jimmy's student, and in that capacity he became a mirror to Jimmy's vanity, something Jimmy could point to and say, "Look at this instrument I've made." The old man's business had thrived with the two of them on the street, for as effective as Jimmy had been by himself, it was nothing compared to what they'd done together. They'd killed their way from one river to the other, north to south and over into Jersey. Russian mob. Serbians. Italians. It didn't matter. If somebody crossed the old man, they took him down. But after all these years, that's all Michael was to Jimmy, a weapon.

Disposable.

Michael looked from Jimmy to the man he'd never met. He stood three feet behind Jimmy's right shoulder, a spare man in linen pants and a golf shirt tight enough to show straps of lean, hard muscle. "Who's he?" Michael asked.

"Your replacement."

Michael felt a pang that was neither loss nor hurt, but one more broken strand. He looked the man over and noticed small things he'd missed. Fine white scars on both forearms, one finger that lacked a nail. The man stood six feet tall and looked vaguely Slavic, with wide-spaced eyes and broad planes of cheekbone. Michael shrugged once, and then dismissed him. "I'm no rat," he said to Jimmy.

"No? How long have you been with this woman of yours? Three months? A year?"

"What does it matter? It's personal."

"It matters because you only told us about her eight days ago. You kept her a secret, and keeping secrets from us is one step away from spilling ours. It's two sides of the same coin. Secrets. Lack of trust. Priorities."

"I said I'm no rat."

"Choice comes with consequence, Michael. It's the first rule of life. You made your choice."

"So did the old man. When he let me go."

"Maybe the old man's gone soft. Maybe there are consequences for that choice, too."

That was Michael's replacement—a crisp voice with a slight accent—and Michael could not believe the disrespect, here in the man's own house. He held the man's Slavic gaze, then stared hard at Jimmy and waited for him to meet his eyes. "I've seen you kill a man for less," Michael said.

Jimmy picked daintily at the nail of his smallest finger, then said, "Maybe I don't disagree."

"I want to see him." Michael's voice grated. Every man here owed his life to the old man. What they had. Who they were. Honor the old man and the old man honors you. That's the way it was done, old school and proper.

In some ways, Jimmy agreed. "Nobody walks away, Michael. That's how it's always been. The old man was wrong to tell you that you could."

"He's the boss."

"For now."

Michael's heart beat twice as he considered that. "You were in the car. Last night. Behind Elena's apartment. You were with Vincent."

"Pretty night for a drive . . ."

"You bastard."

Jimmy saw the anger and rolled onto the balls of his feet. It had long been a question between them, who could take whom. Michael watched the glint come into Jimmy's eyes, the cold and narrow smile. He wanted it, was eager, and Michael knew, then, that there would be no easy out, no graceful exit from a life he no longer desired. For too many people, the matter was personal.

Fingers tightened on holstered weapons and the moment stretched, but before it broke, there was movement on the stairs, a nurse on the landing. In her forties, she looked like a smaller version of Jimmy, but vaguely female. When Jimmy turned and lifted his chin, she said, "He wants to know who's here."

"I'll be right there," Jimmy told her, and cold touched his face when he looked back at Michael. "Stay here." He motioned to the young Slavic man. "Watch him."

"Where's Vincent?" Michael demanded.

Jimmy offered a second slit of smile, but otherwise ignored the question. He mounted the stairs on light feet, and when he came back down, he said, "He wants to see you." Michael moved for the stairs, but Jimmy stopped him. "Not yet." He twisted a finger like he was stirring tea, so Michael lifted his arms, and let Jimmy pat him down. He checked Michael's legs to the groin, his arms to the wrist. He smoothed fabric over Michael's chest and back, then fingered the collars of his jacket and shirt.

"None of this is necessary," Michael said.

Jimmy's gaze moved from low to high, and the gaze lingered. "I don't know you anymore."

"Maybe you never did."

A hand flapped on his narrow wrist. "Enough. Go. Up."

On the second floor Michael saw a nursing station filled with monitors tinted green. Cables snaked down the stairs and under the table that held the equipment. The nurse sat with her feet flat on the floor, eyes glued to the monitors. In a small room behind her, an iron-haired priest sat in a comfortable chair, eyes slightly closed, fingers crossed in his lap. He wore shined shoes and black clothing with a white collar at the throat. When the nurse looked up, Michael asked, "Are we that close?"

She glanced at Jimmy, who nodded in permission. "We've resuscitated him twice," she said.

"What?" The old man *wanted* to die. Resuscitating him was a cruelty. "Why?" Michael demanded. "Why would you put him through that?"

She glanced at Jimmy. "The son . . ."

"It's not up to the son! He made his wishes plain. He's ready."

The nurse raised her hands and looked horrified. "I can only—"

Michael cut her off. "How bad is the pain?"

"The morphine can barely touch it."

"Can you give him more?"

"More would kill him."

"Is he lucid?"

"In and out."

Michael stared at the priest, who stared back, terrified. "How long does he have?"

"Hours. Weeks. Father Jim has been here for five days."

"I want to see him." Without waiting for a response, Michael moved to the next landing, and stopped beside broad double doors. Jimmy leaned a shoulder against the frame and flicked a piece of lint from his velvet jacket. Michael said, "It's wrong, Jimmy. He wants to die."

"It's Vincent's choice. Let it go."

"And if I can't?"

Jimmy shrugged.

"I'm not your enemy, Jimmy. I just want out."

Jimmy examined his other sleeve. "There's only one way out, and you know it. When the old man dies, so do you. Either that or you convince us to trust you again."

"That's two ways."

Jimmy shook his head. "One is a way out, one is a way back in. Different animals."

"Convince you how?"

He blinked a lizard's blink. "Kill the woman."

"Elena's pregnant."

Jimmy used one hand to turn the knob. "Not my problem."

"I don't want to kill you, Jimmy."

"You think you can?"

He pushed the door wide, grinned.

And Michael went in to see the old man.

CHAPTER

3

Michael stepped in and Jimmy left him alone with the dying man who'd all but saved his life. A Persian rug stretched to far windows and a coffered ceiling rose ten feet above Michael's head. No lamps burned, and all the curtains but one were drawn so that pale light ghosted in to touch a chair, the bed, and the wasted man in it. The space was long, narrow, and the gloom made it feel hollow. Michael had spent countless hours in the room, long months as the old man failed, but eight days had passed since his last visit, and change lay like a pall. Airless and overly warm, the room smelled of an old man dying. It smelled of cancer and pain.

Michael crossed the room. A cross hung above a narrow bed with metal rails. Fluids ran into the old man's veins through needles slipped under his skin. The robe he wore was one Michael had given him eight years ago, and in it he looked reduced. Flesh had faded from his face, as had the last of his color. His head was death's head, bones too prominent, veins that showed like thread through wax. His eyes were clenched, lips drawn back from his teeth, and Michael wondered if the pain was insidious enough to find him even as he slept.

Michael sat in the chair and studied the cross on the wall. The old man did not have a religious bone in his body, but his son did. In spite of his sins, and there were many, Vincent attended Mass every week. He agonized over his father's lack of contrition, and it was for this reason, Michael suspected, that the old man had been resuscitated twice. Vincent feared that his father, unrepentant, would go to hell, and Michael wondered at the depth of such hypocrisy.

He lifted a framed photograph from the table near the old man's head. Taken a decade and a half earlier, it showed Michael with the old man. Michael was sixteen, broad-shouldered but skinny in a suit that could not hide that fact. He leaned against the hood of a car, laughing, the old man's arm around his neck. He was laughing, too. Michael put the photo where the old man could find it, then stood and walked to the wall of books on the north side. The shelves ran the length of the room and held a collection the man had been working on for over thirty years. They shared a love of the classics, and many of the books were first editions, including several by Hemingway, Faulkner, and Fitzgerald. Michael removed *The Old Man and the Sea*, then sat back down. He riffled the pages, but was too distracted to read. Through the window, he saw the river and then Queens. The old man had been born there to a prostitute with no interest beyond folding money and the next bottle it could buy. Shut up for years in a basement tenement, he'd been left alone for days at a time, unwashed and half-starved until he was orphaned at age seven. He told Michael once that he'd never known a childhood harder than his until their paths crossed. That fact made them family, he said. Because no one else could understand the loneliness they'd known, the fear. He said it gave them clarity, made them strong. And Vincent hated Michael for that, for having that bond with his father.

But Michael cherished it, not just because he was so otherwise alone in the world, but because the similarities *did* make a difference; because not even Vincent grasped the scope of depravation that defined his father's early days. He did not know that the scars on the old man's feet came 'from rat bites in the crib, or that his missing fingers came from frostbite in the days before his mother died. The old man spoke of those things only to Michael, because only Michael could understand. He was the only one who knew the full story, the only person aware that the old man had chosen this room for the view, so that his last earthly sight would be the place from which he'd dragged himself one brutal day at a time. Michael found an undeniable elegance in this. The tenement house that almost killed the man was a river's breadth away, and a lifetime apart.

The sun moved higher and light slipped from the old man's face. So sunken were his eyes that Michael missed the moment they opened. One instant they were hidden, and the next they were simply there, pinched and deep and shot with red.

"Vincent?"

"It's Michael."

The frail chest rose and fell in small, desperate pants and Michael saw pain bite deeper. Skin gathered at the corners of the old man's eyes and his brows compressed at the center. "Michael . . ." His mouth worked. Something glinted in the sun that still touched his neck, and Michael realized that he was crying. "Please . . ."

Michael turned his face away from the thing he was being asked to do. For months now, the old man had begged to die, so eager was the pain. But Vincent had refused. Vincent. His son. So the old man had suffered as Michael watched the illness take him down. Weeks stretched to months, and the old man had begged.

God, how he had begged.

Then, eight days ago, Michael had told him about Elena. He explained that life had become more than the job, that he wanted out, a normal life. And listening, his pain-filled eyes so very intent, the old man had nodded as hard as such a sick man could. He said he understood just how precious life should be. *Precious.* Fingers clawed into Michael's arm. *Short!* And with those words still in the air above his lips, he'd told Michael that he loved him.

Like a son.

His fingers had tightened as he pulled Michael closer.

You understand?

A coughing fit took him then, and when he could speak again, he released Michael to live life as he wished, then asked him to take his own life in return. There was no irony in his request, just hurt; and now he was asking again.

"I can't."

Michael's neck bent because the words were insufficient. He'd killed so many times that this should be the most simple of things. A gentle pressure. A few seconds. But he remembered the day the old man found him, cut a dozen times and fighting for his life under a bridge in Spanish Harlem. He said he'd heard of this wild boy who lived with the homeless, and had come to see for himself. He'd wondered if the stories were true.

A sound escaped the old man's lips but there were no words beyond anguish. Michael had come to assure Vincent that he was no threat. Failing that, he'd hoped to find enough strength in the old man to make certain that his orders were followed, even after death. But seeing the agony behind his hunted eyes, what Michael felt was ashamed. He was thinking of himself first, and the old man deserved more. Michael took his hand and looked at the photograph of them leaning on the hood of his car. His arm circled Michael's neck, head tipped back.

They were laughing.

Michael looked down on the old man's face. He saw how it had been, and how it was now: the life he'd had and the one he wanted to quit. Torment wracked his features, but through the pain and fear, Michael saw the old man's soul, and it was unchanged.

"Don't be afraid," the dying man whispered.

Michael could barely hear him, so he asked, "Are you sure?"

The old man nodded without words, and Michael's fingers tightened on his hand. "They'll come for me," Michael said. "Vincent. Jimmy. They'll try to kill me."

He needed the old man to know the repercussions of this thing he asked. If Vincent came, Michael would kill him. The truth of this filled the old man's eyes, but it was only when he said, "Make a good life," that

Michael truly believed he understood. There was such sadness in his eyes, and it had nothing to do with his own death. Whether the old man lived or died, Vincent would come.

And Michael would kill him.

"I knew . . ." His voice failed, and Michael leaned closer. "I knew when I released you . . ."

Michael forced despair from his face. He'd killed so many, and loved so few. "May I have this?" Michael lifted the photograph that sat by the bed. The old man did not answer, but his fingers moved on the sheet. Michael slipped the photo from its frame, and put it with the other in his pocket. "Elena's pregnant," he said, but it was unclear if the old man heard. Tears filled his eyes and he was nodding as if to hurry Michael on. Michael kissed him on the forehead, then placed one hand on his chest and the other across his mouth and nose. "Forgive me," he said. And as he shut off the old man's air, their eyes remained locked. Michael made a gentling noise, but the old man never fought, not even at the end. His heart stuttered, then beat a final time, and through his hands, Michael felt a rush of peace so immense it had to be his imagination. He straightened as monitors flatlined and alarms screamed on the landing below. He closed the dead man's eyes and heard loud voices, feet on the steps.

The old man was gone.

And they were coming.

Michael moved to the bookshelf, his eyes on the black rectangle that had until a few minutes ago held the old man's copy of Hemingway's classic novella. In the space behind, he found the two nine millimeters he'd put there three months ago. Each one had fifteen in the clip and one up the pipe.

Vision.

Foresight.

And Michael's replacement lacked both.

He came through the right-side door with his own gun low and his smile half-cocked. Michael gave him three steps and enough time to see what was going to happen.

Then he shot him in the heart.

By that time two more men were in the room, both armed. Michael recognized the grunts from the foyer. One yelled, "Whoa, whoa, whoa . . ." but both were bringing up guns, barrels going long to short. Michael took one step and shot them both in under a second. They dropped and he heard shouts from the stairs. Three men, maybe more. Fear in their voices. Michael said nothing, but crossed the room and stood four feet from the left-hand door, which remained closed. Fear was a cancer for those who were not used to this, so time was on his side, but not by much. He listened for steps on carpet, and when shoes showed through the gap beneath the door, he put two rounds through the wood, center mass.

A body hit the floor, and Michael rounded onto the landing, where he found three more men, two in full retreat down the stairs and another with a gun in his hand and pointed. But it takes more than a trigger finger to shoot a man. When someone is shooting back, it takes the kind of cool that rock stars can only fake. Michael had that cool, and so did Jimmy.

No one else in the house was even close.

Two bullets flew wide of Michael's shoulder, and he tapped the shooter once in the forehead, stepping past before he was even down. The other men pulled up short, one shooting wildly, the other hands up and empty. Michael shot the first and kept both guns trained on the second. He was in his late sixties, a street thug from the old days kept around for sentimental reasons. He was a gopher now: ran errands, cooked food. His hands were steady above his head, his face resigned. Michael stopped one step above him and put a barrel so close to his cheek he could feel heat from the metal. "Where's Jimmy?"

"Gone. Ran."

"How long?"

"Just this second."

Michael glanced down at the open door, the hint of city beyond. He pressed hot metal against the man's cheek. "If you're lying, I'll kill you slow."

"I'm not lying."

"What about the nurse? The priest?"

"Same thing."

"Are they on the payroll?"

The man nodded, which meant they would keep their mouths shut. Michael looked again at the open door. "You have car keys?"

The man pulled a ring from his pants pocket. "The Navigator," he said. "Out back."

"Anyone else in the house?"

He shook his head. The smell of burned powder was everywhere, a gray haze under the chandelier. Michael studied his face and remembered a few conversations they'd had. His name was Donovan. He had grandchildren.

"Tell Vincent I'm out." Donovan nodded, but Michael realized the lie even as he did. The old man was dead at Michael's hand. Blood ran down the walls, the stairs. He was nowhere close to out. Not after this. Michael gestured with the gun. "Beat it."

Donovan fled, and Michael went back upstairs. He stood by the bed and looked down on the husk of the man he'd killed. He'd been a hard man, but full of kindness for those he loved. Michael remembered a conversation they'd had on the morning of his fourteenth birthday. A year had passed since that day under the bridge, and the old man wanted to know why.

Why was I on the streets?

Yeah. The old man turned his lips, tilted his head. *Smart kid. Good looking. You could have gone to the authorities, anybody. Why take the hard road? Why the streets?*

I had my reasons.

That's all you're going to say?

Humor shone in the old man's eyes, a kind of pride.

Yes, sir.

Whatever you were running from, Michael, it can't touch you now. You know that, right? Not here. Not with me.

I know that.

And you still won't tell me?

I have reasons for that, too.

He'd ruffled the boy's hair and, laughing, said, *A man should have his reasons.*

And in all this time, Michael had never told him why he'd chosen the hard road. Because the old man was right. A man should have his reasons.

And his secrets.

Michael straightened the old man's arms. He closed the withered lids and smoothed the blanket across his chest. He kissed one still-warm cheek, then the other; and when he stood, tears burned hot in his eyes. He lifted Hemingway's novella from the bedside table, then stood for a long while, looking down. "You were good to me," he said, and when he left, he took the book.

He had reasons for that, too.

CHAPTER

4

There were people in the world who could kill better than Michael. A rifle shot from a thousand yards was beyond his skill, so were explosives and poisons and mass murder of any kind. He'd come into the business fighting for his life, and that was all about up close and personal. It was about food and shelter and keeping the blood in his veins. Those lessons came fast on the street, and Michael knew as a child that it was better to be vicious than soft, fast than slow. He learned to steal and scheme and wound, and that was his gift, an utter lack of mental weakness. Jimmy had simply taken that gift and magnified it. He'd honed a natural capacity for violence, then taught Michael an economy of movement that he still found satisfying.

Michael thought of Donovan. Old and gray. White stubble on his face. Jimmy would be appalled that Michael let him live, but Jimmy was not Michael's only teacher. There was also the old man, and it was his death that taught Michael how he wished to live. Not once during his slow decline did the old man dwell on money or power or reputation. He pined for women lost and the daughters he never had. A world too narrowly embraced.

Make a good life . . .

There had never been more than a small chance that Vincent would let Michael quit the life peacefully, either to honor the wishes of his father or to avoid the kind of grief that Michael could lay at his door. But small as the chance may have been, it was gone now. Michael had killed Vincent's father when he would not, and shot dead six of his men. As long as Michael lived, Vincent would look weak, and that made killing Michael good business. But it would be personal, too, and Michael wondered if the old man had really understood the confrontation his death would set in motion. There was an instant's doubt, but Michael shrugged it off

He knew.

The building's walls were thick, the windows armored, but gunplay is loud. So Michael moved fast. In the security room, he disabled the security cameras, front and back, then removed the zip drives and put them in a bag with the book and his photographs. Vincent would know who'd done this, but Michael had no plans to leave video proof.

He checked his appearance and saw red spattered on the legs of his pants, his shirt, the backs of his hands. Normally, Michael would never risk a public appearance in anything but spotless condition. He would change and bag the clothes, strip the guns and dispose of the pieces in any number of quick and efficient ways. Storm drains. Dumpsters. The East River. But the circumstances were not normal. There'd been no planning, no intent to kill the old man or wage war. The entire event had taken eighty seconds, and Michael was on autopilot, moving fast. Jimmy remained alive and Elena was on the street, unprotected.

Outside, Michael fired up the Navigator and blew south. He needed to get out of the city, and Elena had to come, too. Michael felt a moment's guilt as the lies he would tell spooled out like videotape, but truth would be the matter of another day.

This was about survival.

Halfway to Tribeca, he hit heavy traffic. He called the restaurant from his cell and asked for Elena. "Everything okay?" he asked.

"Paul's angry."

"Am I fired?"

"Do you care?"

"I care about you." Michael tried to make it light, but she did not respond to the silence that followed. She was angry, and Michael understood that. "Listen, I'll be there soon. Don't go anywhere."

"Where would I go?"

"Just don't leave the restaurant."

Michael hung up the phone and tried to bull through the dense stream of cars. He gunned one narrow gap after another, horns blaring, heavy car rocking. Twice, he rode tires onto the curb, and twice it made no difference. Traffic was a snake of impatient metal. When he got to Tribeca, more than an hour had passed. Sixty-two minutes since he'd killed the old man. Michael double-parked the big SUV across from the restaurant. He checked parked cars and windows on the narrow street. Pedestrians were thick on the sidewalk. Michael slipped one pistol into the glove compartment and tucked the other under his jacket. He figured two minutes to get Elena someplace quiet, another three to get her away from the restaurant. Michael had money. They would fade into the city, and then he would get her out. Someplace with mountains, he thought. Someplace green. He felt it, like it was already there, the future. But the future can be a tricky bitch. His cell phone rang as he killed the engine. He looked at the screen, and it rang four times before he answered.

He knew the number.

Vincent's number.

He opened it feeling unease and regret and pity. For all his faults, Vincent had loved his father. "Hello, Vincent."

For long seconds, Michael heard only breath, and he could picture Vincent on the other end of the line, his manicured nails and lean face. Vincent played strong, but deep down, he was weak enough to care about the trappings of power. He liked to see himself reflected in the faces of other men. Fear. Envy. But his father knew better, and preferred Michael's company for that reason. They were stripped down, both men free of illusion and false want. Power, for them, was a tool to secure food, shelter, safety. That's what childhood taught them.

Appearance means nothing.

Vincent never grasped the difference, never understood why Michael shined so brightly in his father's eyes; and when his voice came over the phone, Michael knew that years of jealousy and distrust had finally darkened to something more.

"He made you family, Michael. You had nothing. You were nobody."

"Your father was in pain."

"The choice was not yours to make."

"I loved him. He begged me."

"You think you're the only one he begged? He'd have asked the cleaning lady, a stranger, anybody."

"I only did what you should have done a month ago."

"He's burning in hell because of you."

"He died as he wished to die."

"You're dead, Michael. So is your girlfriend."

"Don't make me your enemy, brother. We can still walk away from this."

"Dead bitch. Dead motherfucker."

There was no going back, Michael saw. No peace to be made. "Goodbye, Vincent."

"Do you see the restaurant?"

The question was so pointed that Michael felt a blade of fear slip into his heart. He scanned the street again. "Where are you, Vincent?"

"Did you think we wouldn't plan for this? Did you think you could just walk away? Honestly, brother."

He stressed the last word, mocking.

"Vincent . . ."

"This was supposed to be for both of you, but I want you to see it happen."

"Don't . . ."

"I hear that she's pregnant . . ."

Michael flung down the phone and wrenched open the door. His feet touched city pavement and he managed seven steps in a dead run before the restaurant exploded. Flame blew through the windows and the force lifted him from his feet, flung him into the Navigator. Black smoke roiled in the aftershock, and for a moment there was no sound. The roof flew apart as a secondary explosion slammed outward, then Michael's ears opened and he heard screaming. Flames poured out in towers of heat and smoke. Cars collided on the street, while on the sidewalk, people were dead or dying. A man ran blindly, clothing aflame, then collapsed as Michael watched. And the flames roared higher. They licked at neighboring buildings, and Michael found himself on his feet.

Elena . . .

He walked closer, eyes blurred and one hand out to test the heat. It scorched his palm from fifty feet out, and a corner of his mind shut down. He could not bear to see her face, to picture it blistered and burned and ruined. He let the heat roll over him, sensed the crush of movement on the street, the frenzied motion and the quiet, still dead. Glass shattered in a car too close to the flames. A black Escalade glided around the corner and stopped. Michael catalogued people and faces, the shock and fear, the sound of distant sirens. And even with Elena's death fresh on his mind, he realized what was going down two seconds before it actually happened.

He turned back to the Escalade as the windows slid down. Vincent sat in the front, his face sharp as glass under brown hair sparsed with gray. He made a shooting motion with the finger and thumb of his right hand, and from the backseat, an automatic weapon opened fire. Michael dove and rolled as bullets ripped into a car behind him. People screamed and the crowd panicked. Bodies went down, shot and then trampled underfoot. More bullets slammed metal, but the shots flew wide and scattered. Michael rose from cover, pistol in hand. He fired nine rounds in three seconds. His shots pocked metal on the Escalade, shattered glass, and sudden fear blossomed on Vincent's face. He banged the dash, shouted something at the driver and rubber barked as the big vehicle cut hard to the right and jumped the curb. Michael sprinted behind it, away from the heat, the screams. He clambered over stalled cars, felt hard pavement slam through his shins. He ran in a dead sprint, and stayed close for a full block, then the road cleared and the big engine gunned. Michael pulled up and put his last rounds through the back windshield. He doubted they were fatal—too far, too much movement—but he liked the feel of it, the chance he might get lucky.

Either way, Vincent was dead.

Now or later.

Dead.

Michael watched the car disappear, then realized that he was standing on a city street with a drawn weapon in his hand. People were staring. Men in suits. Cabbies. A woman in a black dress.

Mouth open.

Staring.

Michael lowered the gun. "Elena?"

She stood in a loose jumble, shocked and confused. A paper bag dangled from her right hand. It was white, crumpled at the top. She looked from the gun to Michael's face. Her skin was pale, fine hair mussed in a sudden breeze. Around her, people began to push back. Several turned and ran. At least one was dialing a cell.

"Michael?"

Every part of him wanted to grab her up and never let go. He wanted to shield her from the aftershock of what had just happened. The fallout. The way he knew her life was about to change. But mostly he wanted to hold her, to pour out his feeling of relief and love. Instead, he grabbed her by the wrist, his fingers hard and unforgiving.

"We have to go," he said.

"You were shooting at that car . . ."

"We have to go now."

He began to pull her down the street, tucking the gun out of view as several bystanders found their courage and began to shout for help. A frail woman on the far sidewalk pointed and said, "Stop him. Stop that man."

"Michael, what the hell is going on?"

"We have to go."

"You said that." Elena pulled back on her arm, but Michael did not let go. He broke into a half-run, dragging her behind him. "You're hurting me," she said, but he ignored that, too. Sirens were close. Smoke roiled above the roofline ahead, and the streets teemed with terrified people. "Where are we going? Michael . . ." She trailed off as they rounded the corner. In front of them, the restaurant burned more fiercely than ever. "Is that . . . ?"

"It is."

People were down and bleeding, cut by shrapnel and flung glass. Burned. Shot. Many stood dumb and unmoving. Others scrambled in the wreckage, trying to help the wounded. Elena began to cry.

"But Paul . . ."

"He's dead."

"The others?"

"Dead."

"Oh, God." Elena stumbled when she saw the first charred body, its torso smoking where fabric still burned. They passed a woman whose lower leg had been shattered by a bullet. Michael pulled Elena through the rubble. She stumbled again and went halfway down before Michael caught her.

"What's happening?" She was in shock, grasping to make sense of what she saw. "Where did you get that suit?"

"Almost there."

A cop car screeched around the corner two blocks away. A fire tuck followed. Michael opened the Navigator's door and pushed Elena in.

"Don't touch me." Her eyes were open but glazed, so wide the firelight danced. Michael snapped the seat belt across her waist.

"It's me," he said. "You're okay."

"Don't touch me."

Michael rounded the vehicle and climbed behind the wheel. He cranked the engine and eased forward, tires crunching on glass and shattered brick. Beside him, Elena stared at the ruined street, the blank eyes and the walking wounded. Michael kept one eye on the approaching cop car. He crawled for half a block, then accelerated when the road finally cleared.

Chaos was everywhere.

No one looked at them twice.

He drove two blocks more and the scene fell away. Buildings

JOHN HART

obscured the flame and black smoke rose to mist. At Hudson Street, Michael turned south, then cut west on Chambers. Elena said nothing. She looked at everything but Michael. "Elena," he said.

"Not yet." She shook her head.

He worked the car south, past Ground Zero and the North Cove Yacht Harbor. At Battery Park City, he pulled to the curb and sat for a long moment. He said her name, but she ignored him. Michael checked traffic around them, then removed one gun from the glove compartment, and the other from his under jacket. Wordlessly, he stripped and wiped the guns; then he pulled two zip drives from the duffel bag and got out of the car. He felt Elena's eyes on his back as he walked to the water's edge and flung the pieces far into the river. Back in the car, he said, "Are you okay?"

"Did you just throw a gun into the river?"

"Two, actually."

"Two guns."

"Yes."

Elena nodded once, and her fingers crinkled the white paper bag in her lap. It was small, and when she smoothed the wrinkles, Michael saw that it came from a pharmacy two blocks from the restaurant. She lifted the bag, then let it settle. "I was nauseous," she said, and smoothed the bag again. "Morning sickness." She used two fingers to dash liquid from her eyes and Michael knew she was in shock. "I would have been inside the restaurant."

Trembling fingers brushed the plane of her stomach, and Michael could see her thoughts as if they hung in the air between them.

If not for the baby . . .

Her hands came up, and their emptiness was rich in meaning. The car. The fire. The guns. "What's happening, Michael?"

She needed the truth, he knew. For her safety, for so many reasons. But how could he tell her that the child she carried belonged to a liar? That her coworkers died in her place? That she remained a target? How could Michael tell the woman he loved that he'd killed seven people before lunch? She searched his face, frightened, and when he hesitated, her gaze fell to his shirt.

412

"Elena . . ."

She touched a dark splotch on the white cloth, traced it with a finger. "Is that . . ."

"Listen to me . . ."

"Is that blood?"

She looked at him then, really looked. She saw similar stains on his pants, on the backs of his hands. "I'm going to be sick." She folded at the waist, her skin the color of old bone. Michael reached out a hand, but she shied, one hand groping for the door. It swung open and she spilled out onto the street, the sunburned grass that stretched to the river. She managed a dozen steps, then sank to her knees. When Michael tried to approach, she said, "Stay away."

He watched her heave over brown grass, and was so distraught that when his phone rang, he barely heard it. He tore it from his pocket and felt the world slow when he saw the number. He almost didn't answer, but then he did. He turned his back on Elena, and, using every ounce of self-control he possessed, said, "You're a dead man, Vincent."

"Your brother's next."

Michael felt heat on his neck, smelled the river. He looked at Elena and the moment seemed to freeze. "I don't have a brother," he said.

"Yes, you do."

The phone went dead. Michael blinked and an image rose: his brother, like a ghost.

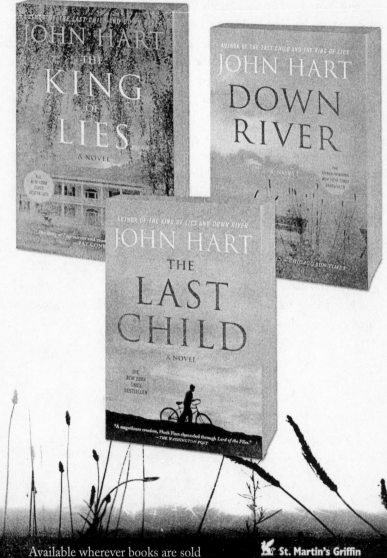